FABLES: THE DELUXE EDITION

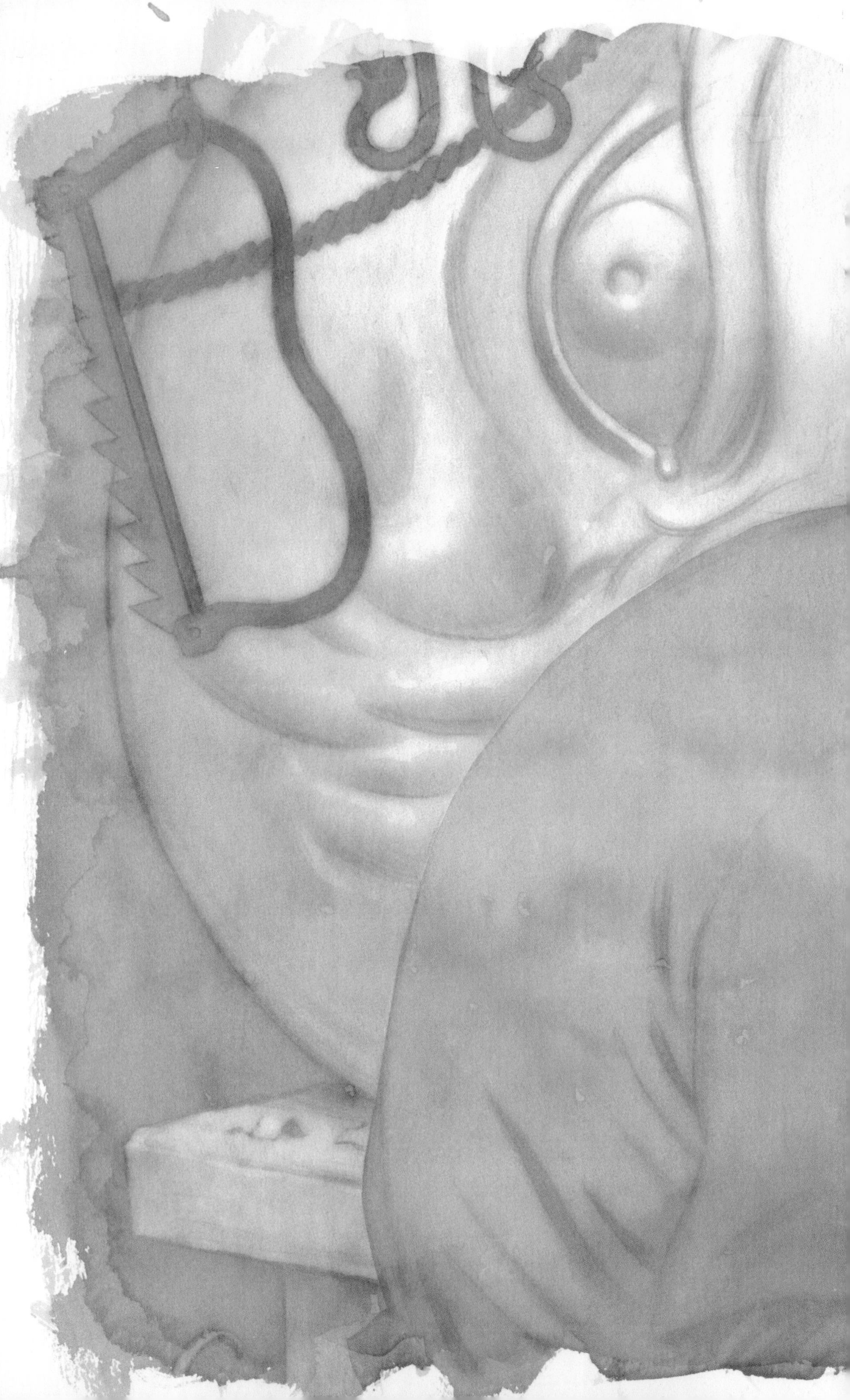

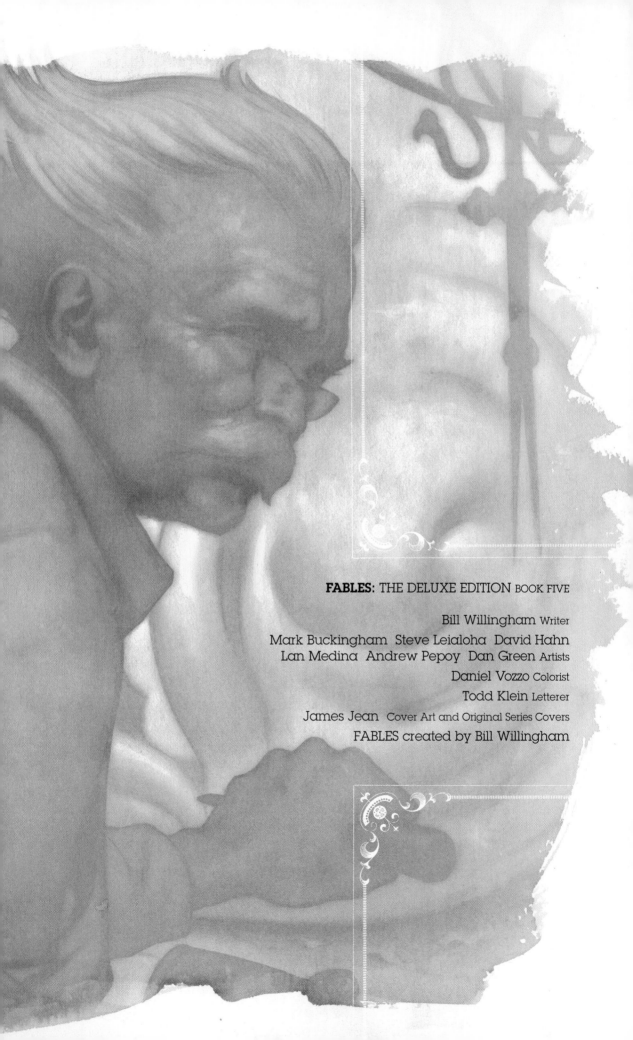

FABLES: THE DELUXE EDITION BOOK FIVE

Bill Willingham Writer

Mark Buckingham Steve Leialoha David Hahn
Lan Medina Andrew Pepoy Dan Green Artists

Daniel Vozzo Colorist

Todd Klein Letterer

James Jean Cover Art and Original Series Covers

FABLES created by Bill Willingham

This collection of intrigues and adventures
is dedicated with friendship and gratitude to
Jenette Kahn, who was the first to invite FABLES
into DC's halls, and later was the first to show me
the side of Hollywood never discussed (because
no one would believe it), filled with kind and
generous people of unimpeachable character.
Yes, I eventually learned the other side exists,
too — the arrogant, backstabbing, soul-crush-
ing side, which perhaps dominates, is lovingly
mocked in our first story here, and stands in
stark contrast to Jenette and her ilk (hello Adam,
hello Lisa), islands of respect and decency in an
otherwise monster-filled sea.
— Bill Willingham

This volume is dedicated to all my friends and
family in my own "Homelands" of the West of
England, and in particular to my oldest friend
Andrew Pring.
— Mark Buckingham

Shelly Bond Executive Editor – Vertigo
and Editor – Original Series
Mariah Huehner Angela Rufino
Assistant Editors – Original Series
Scott Nybakken Editor
Robbin Brosterman Design Director – Books
Louis Prandi Publication Design

Hank Kanalz Senior VP – Vertigo & Integrated
Publishing

Diane Nelson President
Dan DiDio and Jim Lee Co-Publishers
Geoff Johns Chief Creative Officer

Amit Desai Senior VP – Marketing & Franchise
Management
Amy Genkins Senior VP – Business & Legal Affairs
Nairi Gardiner Senior VP – Finance
Jeff Boison VP – Publishing Planning
Mark Chiarello VP – Art Direction & Design
John Cunningham VP – Marketing
Terri Cunningham VP – Editorial Administration
Larry Ganem VP – Talent Relations & Services
Alison Gill Senior VP – Manufacturing & Operations
Jay Kogan VP – Business & Legal Affairs, Publishing
Jack Mahan VP – Business Affairs, Talent
Nick Napolitano VP – Manufacturing
Administration
Sue Pohja VP – Book Sales
Fred Ruiz VP – Manufacturing Operations
Courtney Simmons Senior VP – Publicity
Bob Wayne Senior VP – Sales

Library of Congress Cataloging-in-Publication Data

Willingham, Bill.
  Fables : the deluxe edition, book five / Bill
Willingham, Mark Buckingham, Steve Leialoha,
David Hahn, Lan Medina.
     p. cm.
  "Originally published in single magazine form as
Fables 34-45."
  ISBN 978-1-4012-3496-6 (alk. paper)
  1. Fairy tales–Adaptations–Comic books, strips, etc.
2. Legends–Adaptations–Comic books, strips, etc. 3.
Graphic novels. I. Buckingham, Mark. II. Leialoha,
Steve. III. Hahn, David, 1967- IV. Medina, Lan. V.
Title. VI. Title: Fables. Book five.
  PN6727.W52F356 2012
  741.5'973–dc23

                                              2012025426

Logo design by Brainchild Studios/NYC

FABLES: THE DELUXE EDITION BOOK FIVE

DC Comics, 1700 Broadway
New York, NY 10019
A Warner Bros. Entertainment Company.
Printed in Canada. Fourth Printing.
ISBN: 978-1-4012-3496-6

SUSTAINABLE FORESTRY INITIATIVE
Certified Chain of Custody
Promoting Sustainable Forestry
www.sfiprogram.org
SFI-00507
This label only applies to the text section.

Table of Contents

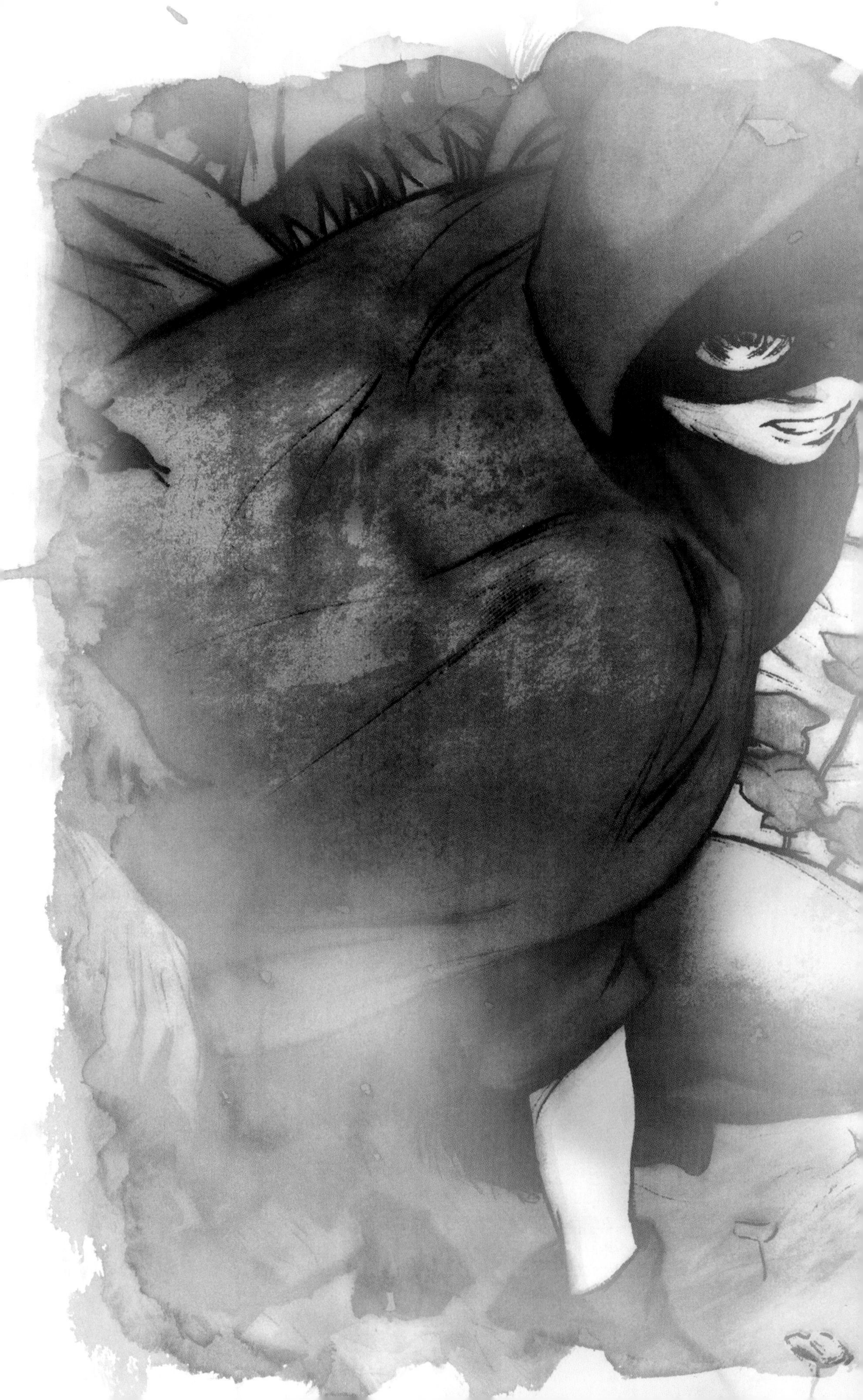

Introduction

When I was writing JACK OF FABLES with Bill Willingham, everyone always wanted to know what it was like to work with him. Was he difficult? A petty tyrant? Did he slough all the work off on to me and just sign his name to it? Sadly for the purposes of anecdote, none of those things is true. Bill was a prince the whole way through, and we only had one argument the entire time we were writing the book.

See, Bill wanted to have Babe the Blue Ox talk about wearing "cheaters." I argued that nobody knew what "cheaters" were, and it would ruin the joke. He alleged that *everyone* knew what "cheaters" were, because in Bill's mind everything Bill knows is something everyone ought to know. If you need to take a break to look up "cheaters" on the Internet, go ahead. I'll wait.

Anyway, the thing to know about Bill Willingham in order to understand his writing process, and why he's so good at it, is that he's constitutionally unable to stop asking "what if."

Most people find creativity tiring. It's hard work thinking up new ideas. Creatively speaking, most of us are the miller's daughter trying to spin straw into gold; it's very hard work and it doesn't often lead to much. Bill, on the other hand, is Rumplestiltskin. He spins the common straw of thought into the gold of brilliant ideas as effortlessly as he breathes. He never asked me for my firstborn, though. Which is lucky for him, because she can be a holy terror.

Watching Bill go off on one of his "what if" jags is a sight to see. I encountered it more than once on JACK OF FABLES, and again from time to time on ideas that we came up with that never saw the light of day. To get an inkling of what that's like, let's imagine a conversation between Bill and me as if it were a conversation between J.R.R. Tolkien and C.S. Lewis.

Bill: Here's an idea.

Me: Do tell.

Bill: Okay, so what if there was this world, call it... Middle Earth. And in that world there were all sorts of different creatures: call some "orcs," call some "hobbits." That kind of thing.

Me: Okay, that sounds pretty interesting.

Bill: Right, so what if one of those "hobbit" things gets a magic ring from a wizard and has to go on a quest? Maybe, I don't know, he has to destroy it in a volcano.

Me: Okay, great. Do that.

Bill: Oh, but wait! What if the ring was a ring of power created by a dark lord — for the sake of argument we'll call him Sauron — and there are undead wraiths whose job it is to retrieve the ring?

Me: Sounds like a fine idea to me.

Bill: Oh, and the ring makes you invisible!

Me: I think that's good enough.

Bill: Ooh — and what if there are also some wise elves who are about to leave the world forever, and one of them falls in love with a human and has to become mortal?

Me: Now you're just getting carried away.

Bill: Okay, but if we throw in some walking trees, then we'll really have something...

Now, the downside is that if Bill were actually Tolkien, there's a good chance that *The Lord of the Rings* would never have been written, because that would have been the sixth idea that Bill had come up with that week, and who has the time? And if TBS started showing a *Cheers* marathon? Forget it. If that happened, the output of what would encompass some writers' entire careers might be lost to the ages.

The truth is, having the ideas is the fun part. Then comes the arduous process of actually writing. As Peter DeVries put it, "I love being a writer; what I can't stand is the paperwork." Bill and I are writing-avoidance enablers. We know that we can call each other at any time and start a long, frivolous conversation that masquerades as something timely, for the sole purpose of finding a way to get out of writing. (The power went out while I was working on this introduction last night and I was thrilled.)

It seems strange, I realize, that what most people consider to be the sum total of our actual job is, to us, the scut work. But that's how it is. Bill likes to refer to an episode of *The Dick Van Dyke Show*, where Rob is lying on a couch, and when Laura asks him what he's doing, he answers, "Writing." That's our favorite kind of writing.

And that's the trick, right there. That's the key to what makes Bill such a damn good writer. He's *always* writing. He never stops. The reason that his stories are so rich and compelling is that he's been crafting them his entire life. In some cases, story elements come to his mind literally *years* before he uses them. In this collection, the title of chapter two of "Arabian Nights (and Days)" is "Djinn and Tonic, With a Twist." Clever title, right? Well, Bill came up with that title years earlier. He used it as the title to a short story, and then later scrapped the entire story and kept the title. How many writers do you know who would scrap an entire story just to scavenge the title from it?

That's Bill Willingham in a nutshell. One of the most important things I've learned from him (and I've learned a lot), is that there will always be other stories, other ideas. FABLES is rich, living proof of that. As of this writing, DC has published 114 issues of FABLES, 50 issues of JACK OF FABLES, and other series and spinoffs and special issues and a novel, and there's no end in sight. When people ask him if there's an end to the story, he now answers, "There *was* an end to the story, but I already used it, back in issue 75." Again, how many writers do you know who would toss off the big ending to the story they'd been planning for years, on the assumption that some more stories would probably come along?

Here's another example of Bill's approach. I was visiting him at his home several years ago and he had a big corkboard hung on one wall. Its purpose was clear: it was a FABLES storyboard of sorts. *Aha*, I thought. *This is how he does it. This is how he keeps it all straight. There's a complex process! I knew it!* The board had several cards pinned to it; not many. I plucked one down at random and read it. I was initially excited because it was a storyline for a character who had long since perished. I asked Bill, "Wow, are you bringing this character back?" He waved the card away. "Oh, no, that card's been there for years. I never use that stupid board." Another thing I learned from Bill: if

it's not worth keeping straight in your head, it's not worth keeping.

Understand that these are *advanced* writing tips; the beginner is well advised not to use Bill as a role model in terms of process. You don't start off juggling with flaming torches. You start with the writer's equivalent of scarves and beanbags: index cards, plot outlines, spreadsheets, whatever you need. But at some point you have to pick up the torches, set those bad boys on fire, and toss them up in the air, and that's what Bill has been doing for years.

One of my favorite memories of Bill happened a few years ago. We were driving from Los Angeles to Las Vegas. If you've ever made that drive, you know that it covers a lot of wide open space, and that there's not a lot to look at except for seemingly endless stretches of desert. Somewhere along the way we came up with an idea for a comic book series; I won't go into the details of it, but it was pretty clever. We discussed the idea at length, for about three hours, going through the ins and outs of the world, the characters, their abilities, the rules. The sun was setting over the desert and coloring the mesas gold and orange and purple, and there was this brilliant idea just pouring out of us. It was going to be great! I was elated.

Later, I asked Bill, "How come we never did anything with that idea we had on the drive to Las Vegas?" He just shrugged. I didn't understand then, but I understand now. There was no point in putting it down on paper; the story had already been written, already been told, and its only audience was the two of us and a desert sunset.

So I'm glad that Bill took the time to write down all of the stories in this book. He didn't *have* to. He probably didn't even *want* to. But he did.

Thanks, Bill.

— Matthew Sturges
February 2012
Austin, Texas

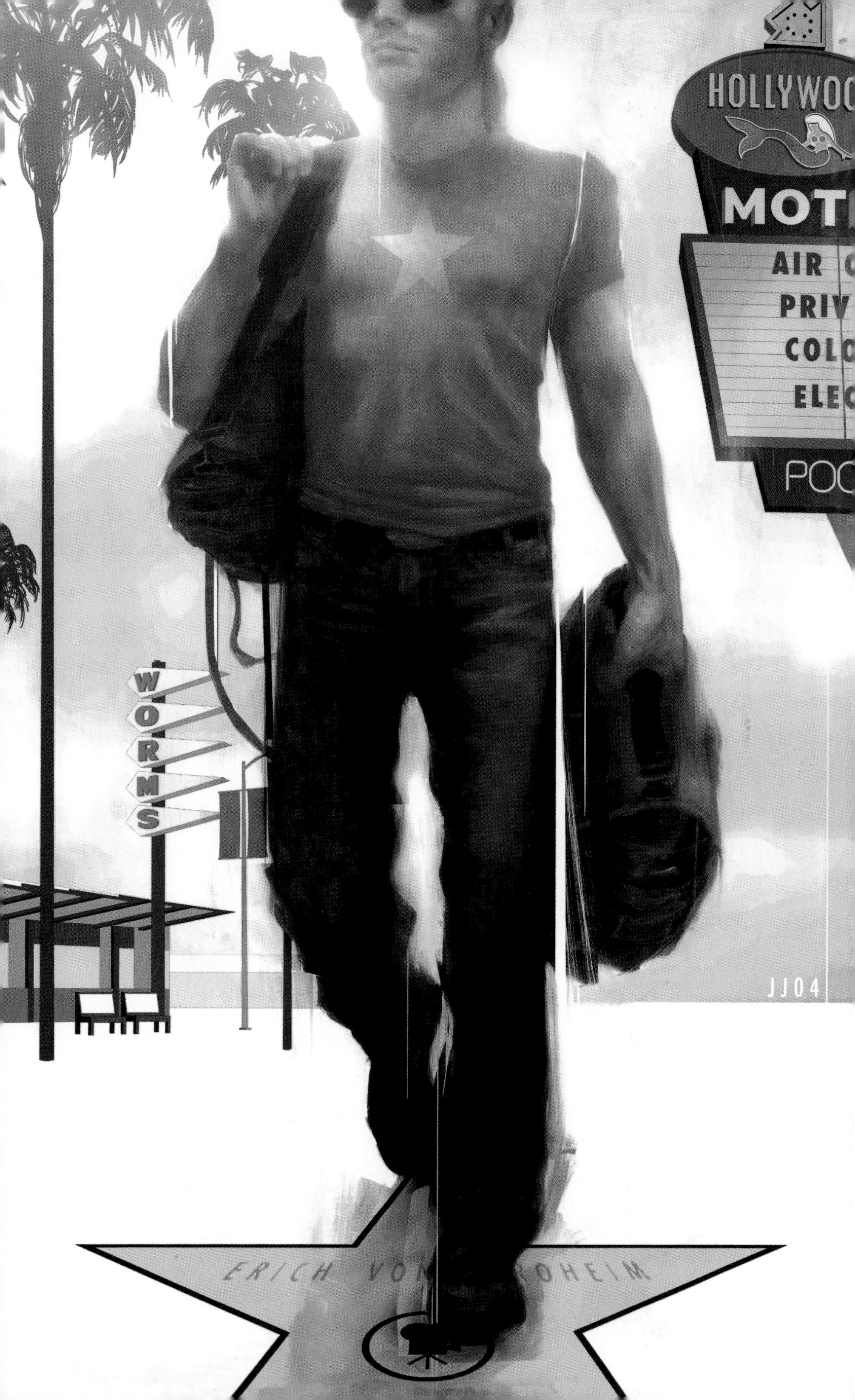

HOLLYWOO
MOT
AIR C
PRIV
COLO
ELEC
POO
WORMS
JJ04
ERICH VON ROHEIM

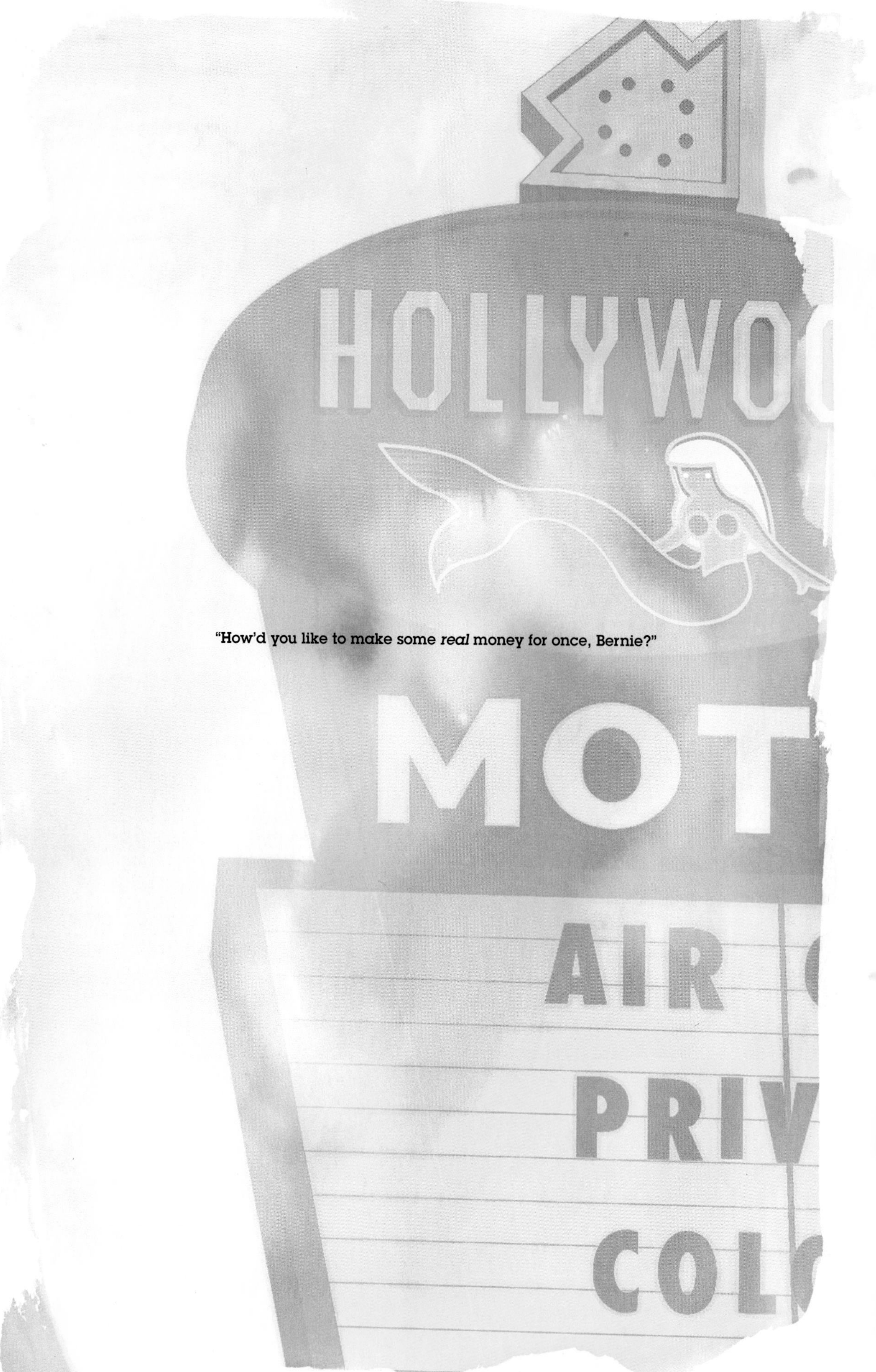
HOLLYWOO
MOT
AIR
PRIV
COL

"How'd you like to make some *real* money for once, Bernie?"

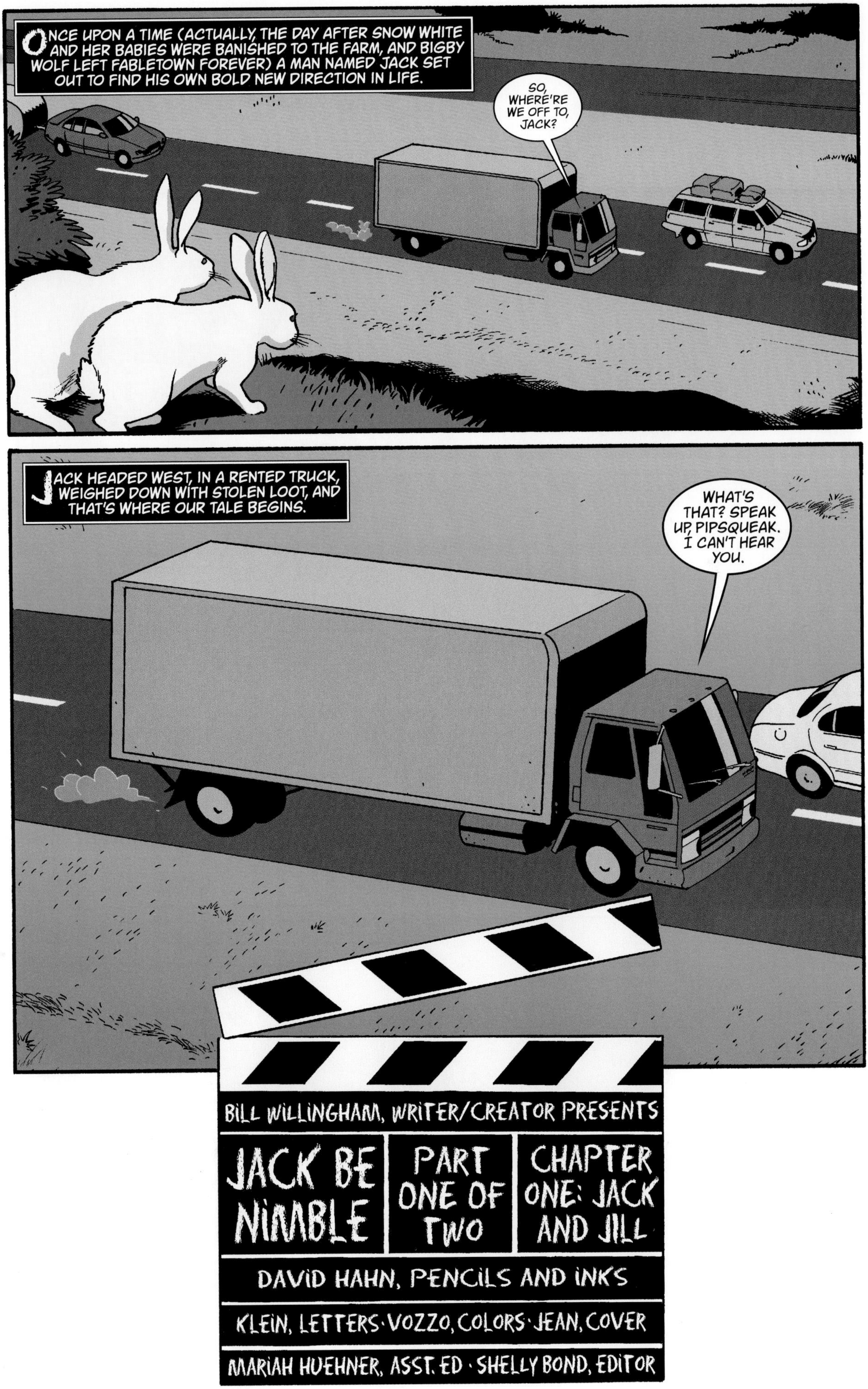
ONCE UPON A TIME (ACTUALLY, THE DAY AFTER SNOW WHITE AND HER BABIES WERE BANISHED TO THE FARM, AND BIGBY WOLF LEFT FABLETOWN FOREVER) A MAN NAMED JACK SET OUT TO FIND HIS OWN BOLD NEW DIRECTION IN LIFE.
SO, WHERE'RE WE OFF TO, JACK?
JACK HEADED WEST, IN A RENTED TRUCK, WEIGHED DOWN WITH STOLEN LOOT, AND THAT'S WHERE OUR TALE BEGINS.
WHAT'S THAT? SPEAK UP, PIPSQUEAK. I CAN'T HEAR YOU.
BILL WILLINGHAM, WRITER/CREATOR PRESENTS
JACK BE NIMBLE
PART ONE OF TWO
CHAPTER ONE: JACK AND JILL
DAVID HAHN, PENCILS AND INKS
KLEIN, LETTERS · VOZZO, COLORS · JEAN, COVER
MARIAH HUEHNER, ASST. ED · SHELLY BOND, EDITOR

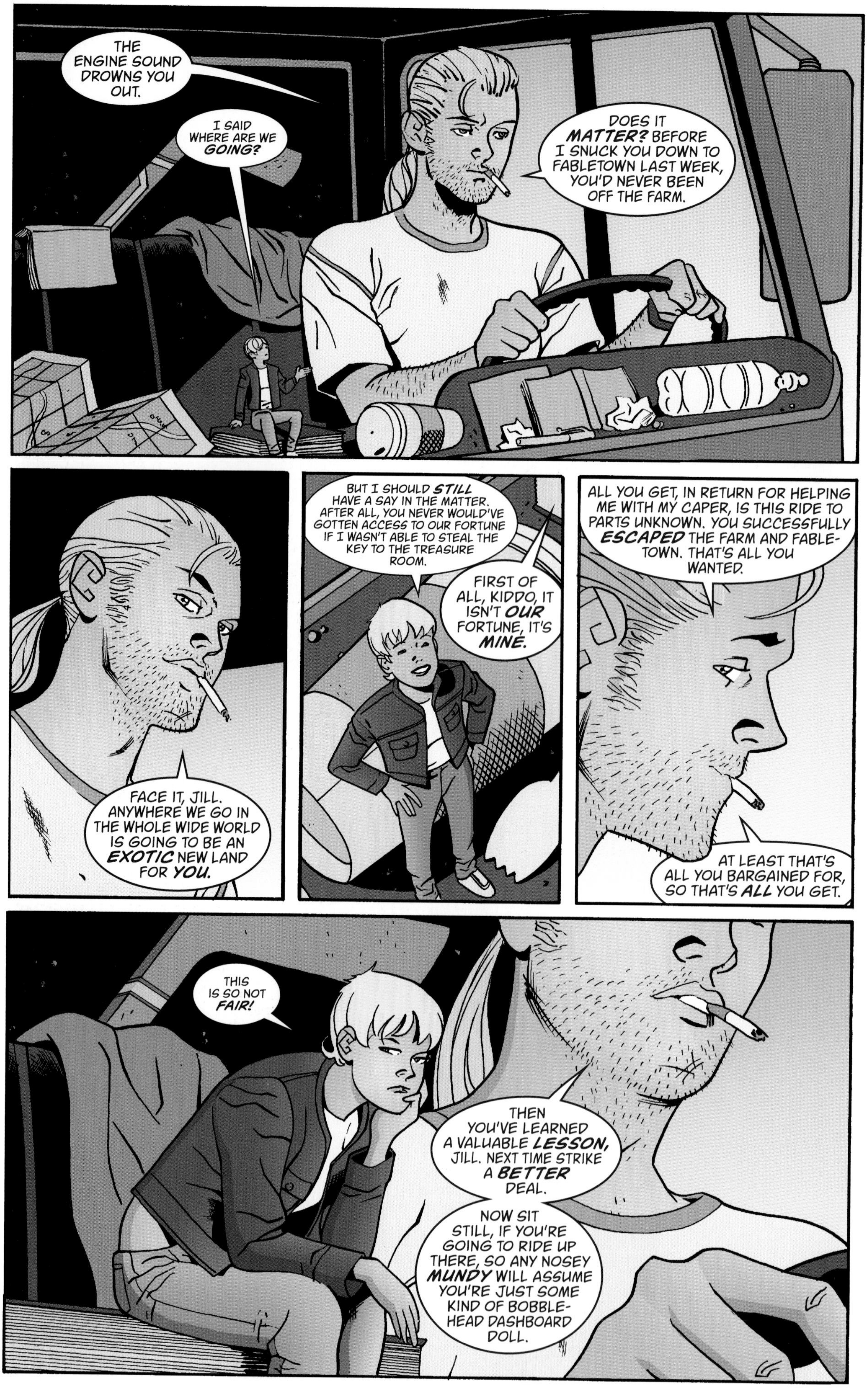
THE ENGINE SOUND DROWNS YOU OUT.
I SAID WHERE ARE WE GOING?
DOES IT MATTER? BEFORE I SNUCK YOU DOWN TO FABLETOWN LAST WEEK, YOU'D NEVER BEEN OFF THE FARM.
FACE IT, JILL. ANYWHERE WE GO IN THE WHOLE WIDE WORLD IS GOING TO BE AN EXOTIC NEW LAND FOR YOU.
BUT I SHOULD STILL HAVE A SAY IN THE MATTER. AFTER ALL, YOU NEVER WOULD'VE GOTTEN ACCESS TO OUR FORTUNE IF I WASN'T ABLE TO STEAL THE KEY TO THE TREASURE ROOM.
FIRST OF ALL, KIDDO, IT ISN'T OUR FORTUNE, IT'S MINE.
ALL YOU GET, IN RETURN FOR HELPING ME WITH MY CAPER, IS THIS RIDE TO PARTS UNKNOWN. YOU SUCCESSFULLY ESCAPED THE FARM AND FABLE-TOWN. THAT'S ALL YOU WANTED.
AT LEAST THAT'S ALL YOU BARGAINED FOR, SO THAT'S ALL YOU GET.
THIS IS SO NOT FAIR!
THEN YOU'VE LEARNED A VALUABLE LESSON, JILL. NEXT TIME STRIKE A BETTER DEAL.
NOW SIT STILL, IF YOU'RE GOING TO RIDE UP THERE, SO ANY NOSEY MUNDY WILL ASSUME YOU'RE JUST SOME KIND OF BOBBLE-HEAD DASHBOARD DOLL.

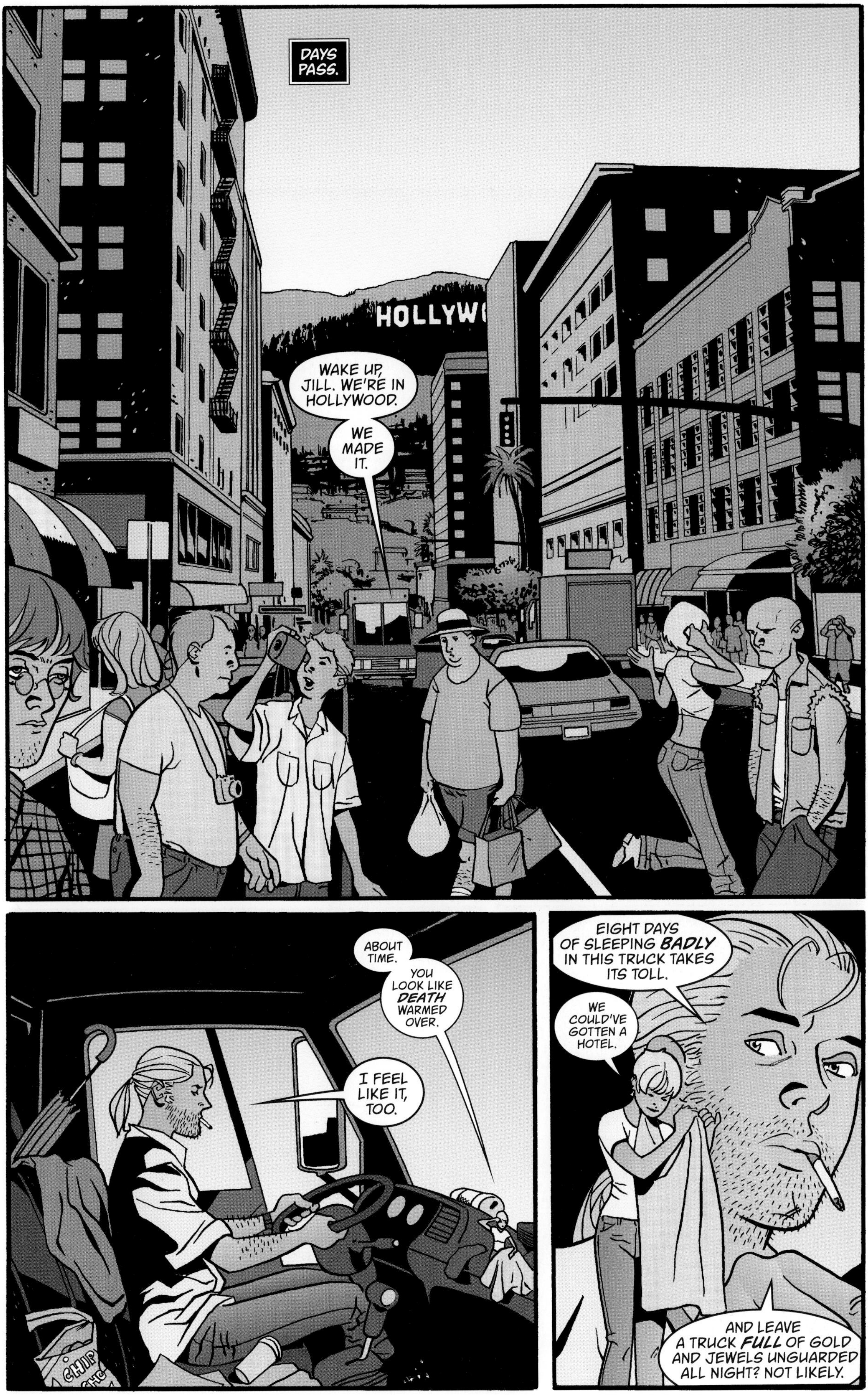
DAYS PASS.
WAKE UP, JILL. WE'RE IN HOLLYWOOD.
WE MADE IT.
ABOUT TIME.
YOU LOOK LIKE **DEATH** WARMED OVER.
I FEEL LIKE IT, TOO.
EIGHT DAYS OF SLEEPING **BADLY** IN THIS TRUCK TAKES ITS TOLL.
WE COULD'VE GOTTEN A HOTEL.
AND LEAVE A TRUCK **FULL** OF GOLD AND JEWELS UNGUARDED ALL NIGHT? NOT LIKELY.

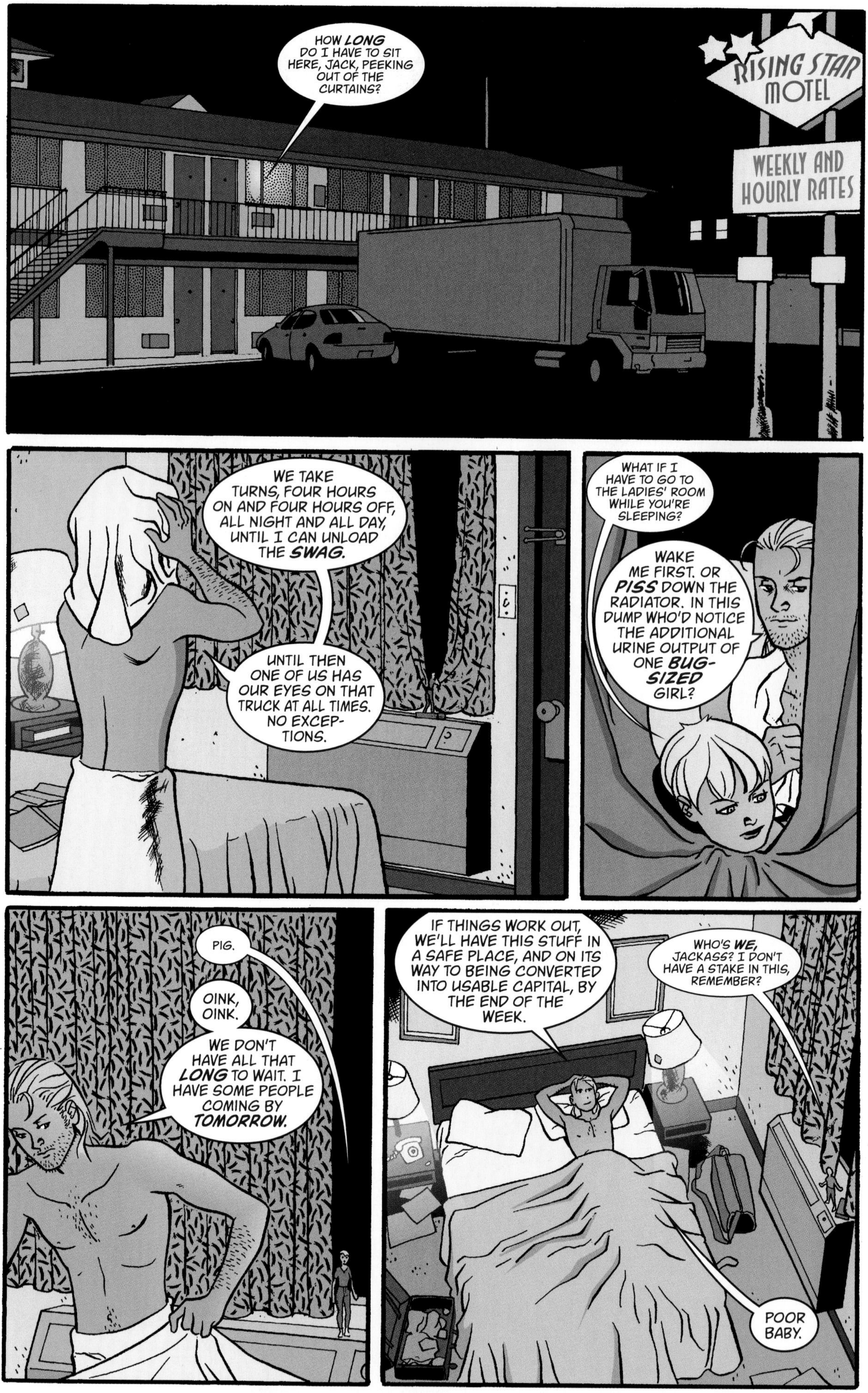
HOW LONG DO I HAVE TO SIT HERE, JACK, PEEKING OUT OF THE CURTAINS?
RISING STAR MOTEL
WEEKLY AND HOURLY RATES
WE TAKE TURNS, FOUR HOURS ON AND FOUR HOURS OFF, ALL NIGHT AND ALL DAY, UNTIL I CAN UNLOAD THE SWAG.
UNTIL THEN ONE OF US HAS OUR EYES ON THAT TRUCK AT ALL TIMES. NO EXCEPTIONS.
WHAT IF I HAVE TO GO TO THE LADIES' ROOM WHILE YOU'RE SLEEPING?
WAKE ME FIRST. OR PISS DOWN THE RADIATOR. IN THIS DUMP WHO'D NOTICE THE ADDITIONAL URINE OUTPUT OF ONE BUG-SIZED GIRL?
PIG.
OINK, OINK.
WE DON'T HAVE ALL THAT LONG TO WAIT. I HAVE SOME PEOPLE COMING BY TOMORROW.
IF THINGS WORK OUT, WE'LL HAVE THIS STUFF IN A SAFE PLACE, AND ON ITS WAY TO BEING CONVERTED INTO USABLE CAPITAL, BY THE END OF THE WEEK.
WHO'S WE, JACKASS? I DON'T HAVE A STAKE IN THIS, REMEMBER?
POOR BABY.

CHAPTER TWO: THE TESTIMONY OF BERNARD STEIN

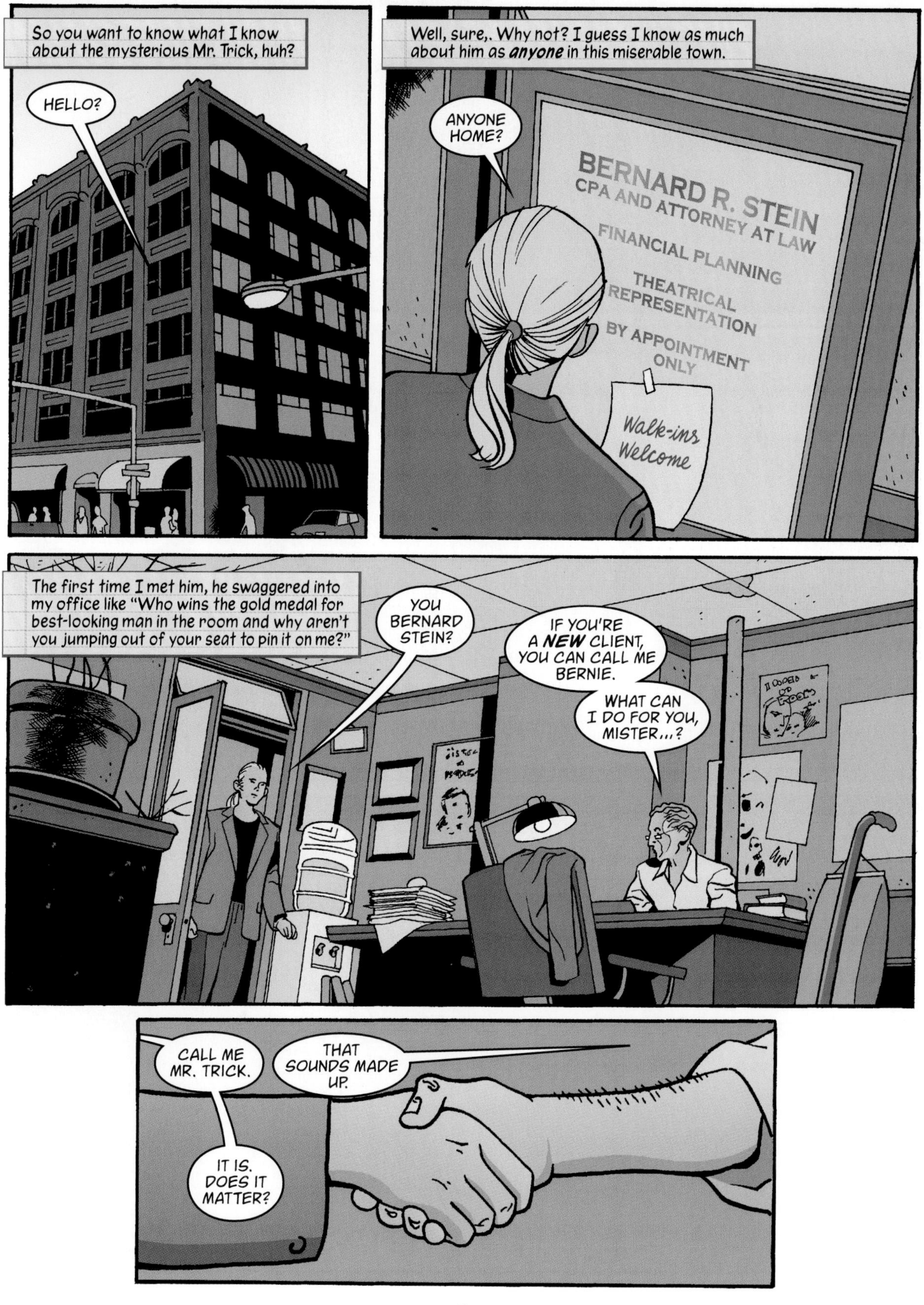

So you want to know what I know about the mysterious Mr. Trick, huh?
HELLO?
Well, sure,. Why not? I guess I know as much about him as ***anyone*** in this miserable town.
ANYONE HOME?
BERNARD R. STEIN
CPA AND ATTORNEY AT LAW
FINANCIAL PLANNING
THEATRICAL REPRESENTATION
BY APPOINTMENT ONLY
Walk-ins Welcome
The first time I met him, he swaggered into my office like "Who wins the gold medal for best-looking man in the room and why aren't you jumping out of your seat to pin it on me?"
YOU BERNARD STEIN?
IF YOU'RE A ***NEW*** CLIENT, YOU CAN CALL ME BERNIE.
WHAT CAN I DO FOR YOU, MISTER...?
CALL ME MR. TRICK.
THAT SOUNDS MADE UP.
IT IS. DOES IT MATTER?

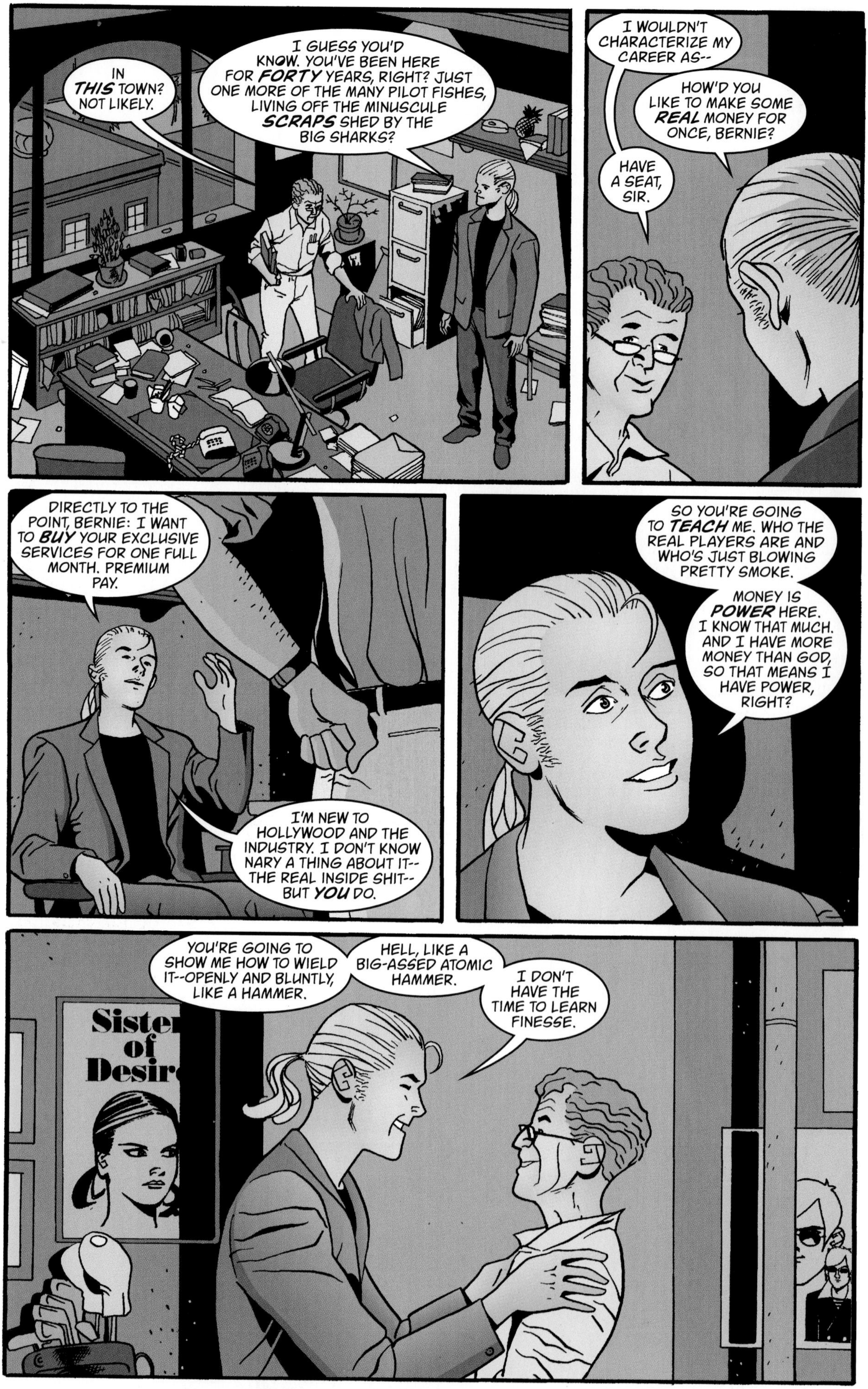
IN THIS TOWN? NOT LIKELY.
I GUESS YOU'D KNOW. YOU'VE BEEN HERE FOR FORTY YEARS, RIGHT? JUST ONE MORE OF THE MANY PILOT FISHES, LIVING OFF THE MINUSCULE SCRAPS SHED BY THE BIG SHARKS?
I WOULDN'T CHARACTERIZE MY CAREER AS--
HOW'D YOU LIKE TO MAKE SOME REAL MONEY FOR ONCE, BERNIE?
HAVE A SEAT, SIR.
DIRECTLY TO THE POINT, BERNIE: I WANT TO BUY YOUR EXCLUSIVE SERVICES FOR ONE FULL MONTH. PREMIUM PAY.
I'M NEW TO HOLLYWOOD AND THE INDUSTRY. I DON'T KNOW NARY A THING ABOUT IT--THE REAL INSIDE SHIT--BUT YOU DO.
SO YOU'RE GOING TO TEACH ME. WHO THE REAL PLAYERS ARE AND WHO'S JUST BLOWING PRETTY SMOKE.
MONEY IS POWER HERE. I KNOW THAT MUCH. AND I HAVE MORE MONEY THAN GOD, SO THAT MEANS I HAVE POWER, RIGHT?
YOU'RE GOING TO SHOW ME HOW TO WIELD IT--OPENLY AND BLUNTLY, LIKE A HAMMER.
HELL, LIKE A BIG-ASSED ATOMIC HAMMER.
I DON'T HAVE THE TIME TO LEARN FINESSE.
Sister
of
Desir

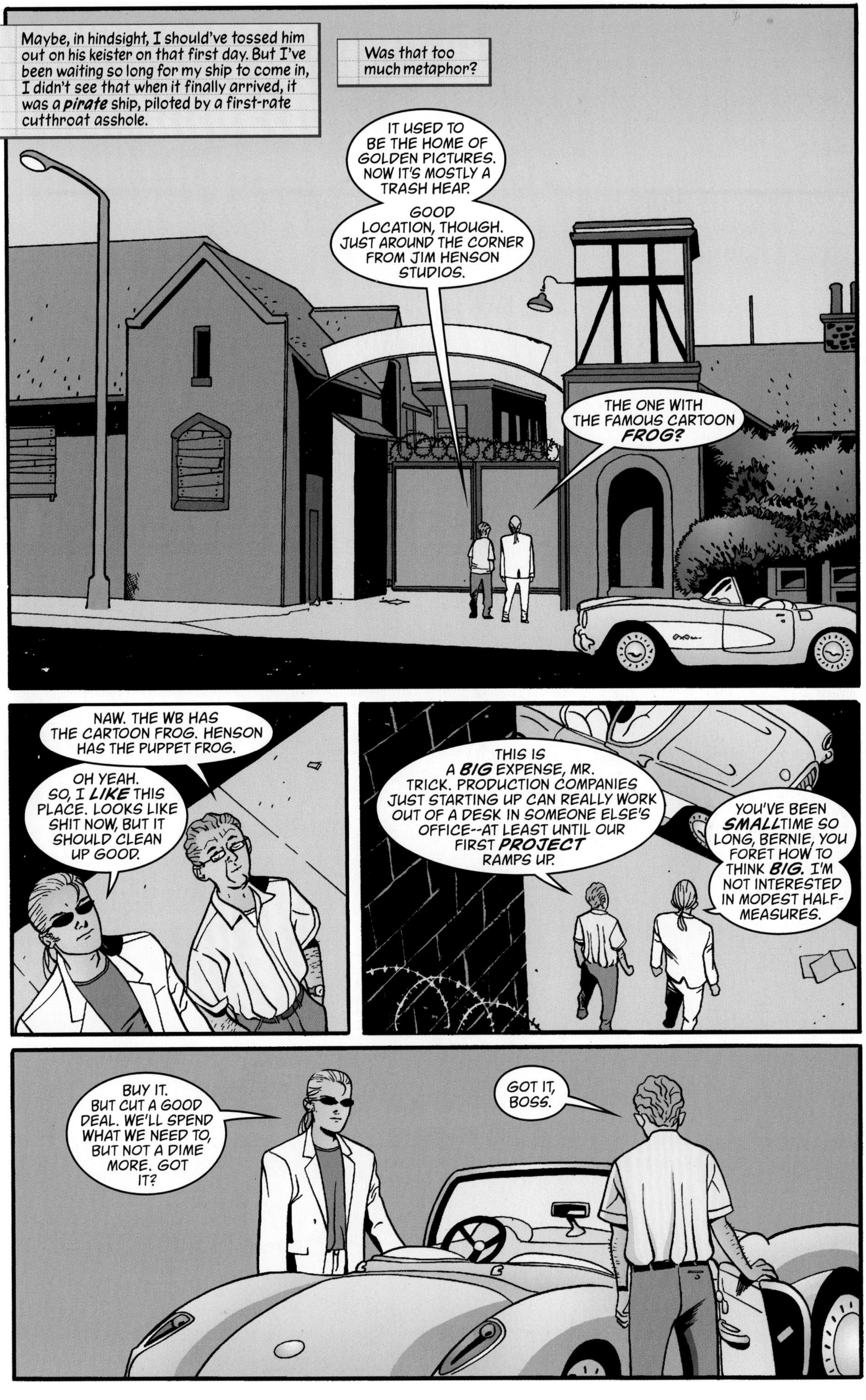

Maybe, in hindsight, I should've tossed him out on his keister on that first day. But I've been waiting so long for my ship to come in, I didn't see that when it finally arrived, it was a pirate ship, piloted by a first-rate cutthroat asshole.
Was that too much metaphor?
IT USED TO BE THE HOME OF GOLDEN PICTURES. NOW IT'S MOSTLY A TRASH HEAP.
GOOD LOCATION, THOUGH. JUST AROUND THE CORNER FROM JIM HENSON STUDIOS.
THE ONE WITH THE FAMOUS CARTOON FROG?
NAW. THE WB HAS THE CARTOON FROG. HENSON HAS THE PUPPET FROG.
OH YEAH. SO, I LIKE THIS PLACE. LOOKS LIKE SHIT NOW, BUT IT SHOULD CLEAN UP GOOD.
THIS IS A BIG EXPENSE, MR. TRICK. PRODUCTION COMPANIES JUST STARTING UP CAN REALLY WORK OUT OF A DESK IN SOMEONE ELSE'S OFFICE--AT LEAST UNTIL OUR FIRST PROJECT RAMPS UP.
YOU'VE BEEN SMALLTIME SO LONG, BERNIE, YOU FORET HOW TO THINK BIG. I'M NOT INTERESTED IN MODEST HALF-MEASURES.
BUY IT. BUT CUT A GOOD DEAL. WE'LL SPEND WHAT WE NEED TO, BUT NOT A DIME MORE. GOT IT?
GOT IT, BOSS.

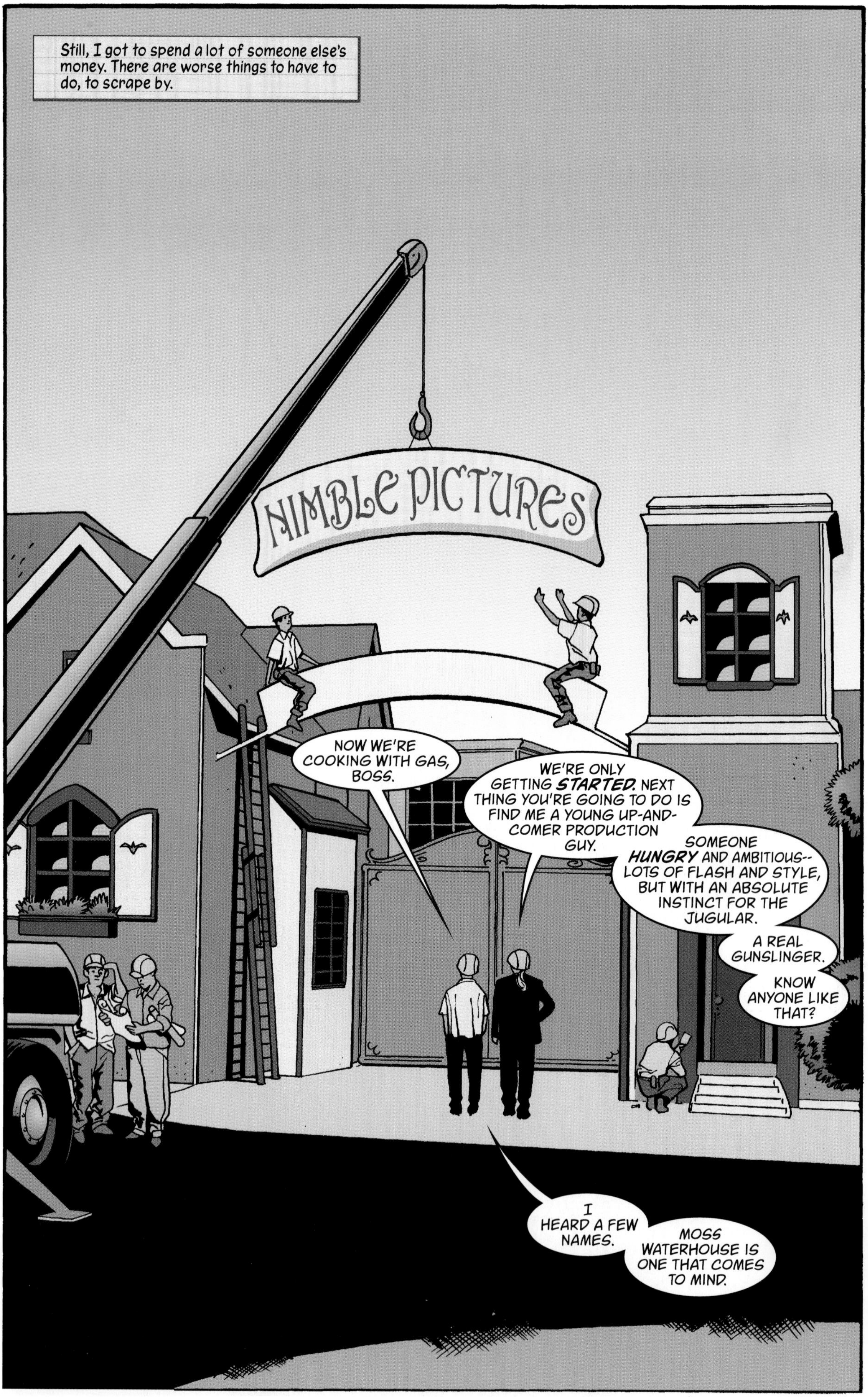
Still, I got to spend a lot of someone else's money. There are worse things to have to do, to scrape by.
NIMBLE PICTURES
NOW WE'RE COOKING WITH GAS, BOSS.
WE'RE ONLY GETTING STARTED. NEXT THING YOU'RE GOING TO DO IS FIND ME A YOUNG UP-AND-COMER PRODUCTION GUY.
SOMEONE HUNGRY AND AMBITIOUS-- LOTS OF FLASH AND STYLE, BUT WITH AN ABSOLUTE INSTINCT FOR THE JUGULAR.
A REAL GUNSLINGER.
KNOW ANYONE LIKE THAT?
I HEARD A FEW NAMES.
MOSS WATERHOUSE IS ONE THAT COMES TO MIND.

CHAPTER THREE: THE TESTIMONY OF MOSS WATERHOUSE

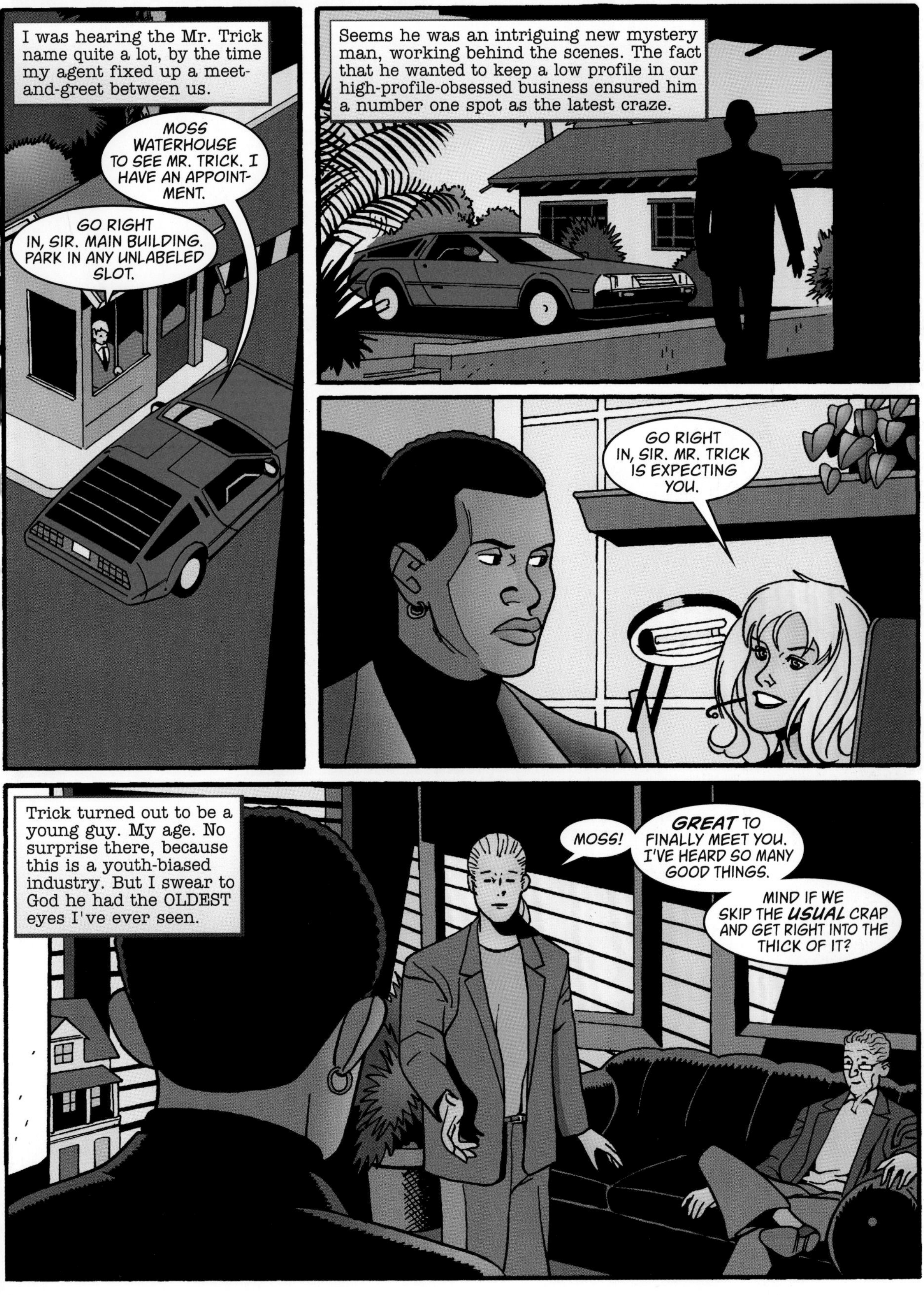

I was hearing the Mr. Trick name quite a lot, by the time my agent fixed up a meet-and-greet between us.
MOSS WATERHOUSE TO SEE MR. TRICK. I HAVE AN APPOINTMENT.
GO RIGHT IN, SIR. MAIN BUILDING. PARK IN ANY UNLABELED SLOT.
Seems he was an intriguing new mystery man, working behind the scenes. The fact that he wanted to keep a low profile in our high-profile-obsessed business ensured him a number one spot as the latest craze.
GO RIGHT IN, SIR. MR. TRICK IS EXPECTING YOU.
Trick turned out to be a young guy. My age. No surprise there, because this is a youth-biased industry. But I swear to God he had the OLDEST eyes I've ever seen.
MOSS!
GREAT TO FINALLY MEET YOU. I'VE HEARD SO MANY GOOD THINGS.
MIND IF WE SKIP THE USUAL CRAP AND GET RIGHT INTO THE THICK OF IT?

I'm SERIOUS. It was like looking at a THOUSAND-year-old man in a young guy's body.

I WANT YOU HERE, TO RUN OUR SHOP. BE THE PUBLIC *FACE* OF NIMBLE PICTURES.

THE JOB'S YOURS, IF YOU CAN CONVINCE ME YOU'RE THE MAN FOR IT.

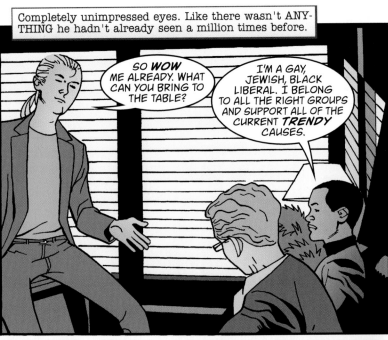

Completely unimpressed eyes. Like there wasn't ANY-THING he hadn't already seen a million times before.

SO *WOW* ME ALREADY. WHAT CAN YOU BRING TO THE TABLE?

I'M A GAY, JEWISH, BLACK LIBERAL. I BELONG TO ALL THE RIGHT GROUPS AND SUPPORT ALL OF THE CURRENT *TRENDY* CAUSES.

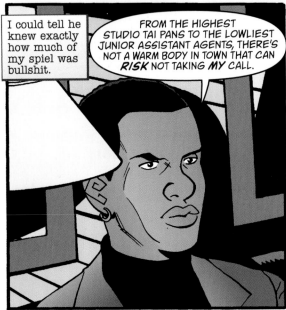

I could tell he knew exactly how much of my spiel was bullshit.

FROM THE HIGHEST STUDIO TAI PANS TO THE LOWLIEST JUNIOR ASSISTANT AGENTS, THERE'S NOT A WARM BODY IN TOWN THAT CAN *RISK* NOT TAKING *MY* CALL.

But I don't think he cared.

WANT TO *TEST* ME? NAME ANYONE AND I'LL HAVE HIM ON THE PHONE IN THE NEXT MINUTE.

NOT NECESSARY. YOU'RE *HIRED*. WANT TO HAGGLE OVER SALARY AND BONUSES NOW?

I'm embarrassed to admit I LIKED him right away.

NO, MY AGENT WILL HANDLE THAT PART. YOU'LL *LIKE* HIM. HE'S A COMPLETE FLESH-EATER.

GOOD ENOUGH. HANG ON FOR A MOMENT AND WE'LL GO TO LUNCH.

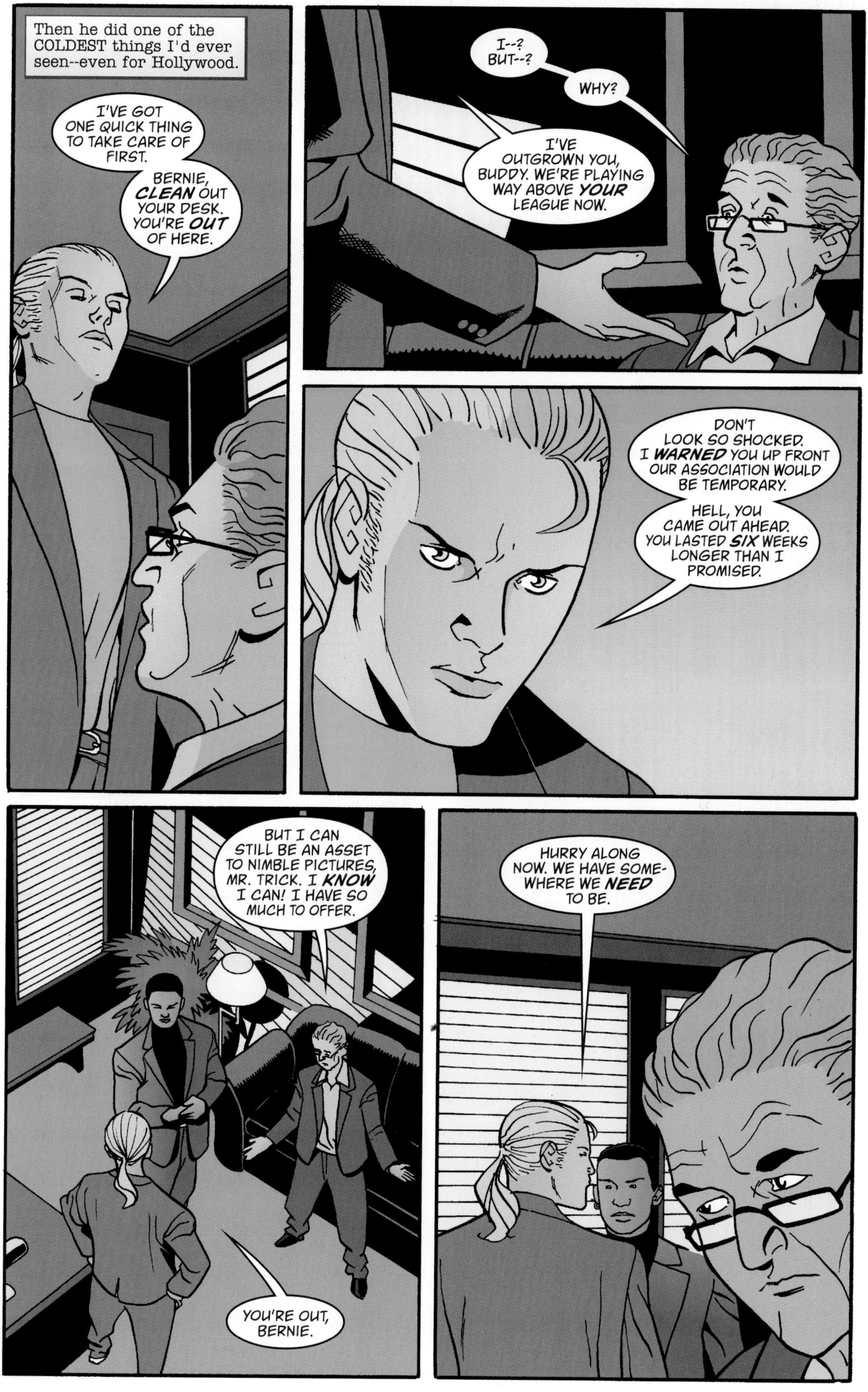
Then he did one of the COLDEST things I'd ever seen--even for Hollywood.
I'VE GOT ONE QUICK THING TO TAKE CARE OF FIRST.
BERNIE, CLEAN OUT YOUR DESK. YOU'RE OUT OF HERE.
I--? BUT--?
WHY?
I'VE OUTGROWN YOU, BUDDY. WE'RE PLAYING WAY ABOVE YOUR LEAGUE NOW.
DON'T LOOK SO SHOCKED. I WARNED YOU UP FRONT OUR ASSOCIATION WOULD BE TEMPORARY.
HELL, YOU CAME OUT AHEAD. YOU LASTED SIX WEEKS LONGER THAN I PROMISED.
BUT I CAN STILL BE AN ASSET TO NIMBLE PICTURES, MR. TRICK. I KNOW I CAN! I HAVE SO MUCH TO OFFER.
YOU'RE OUT, BERNIE.
HURRY ALONG NOW. WE HAVE SOME-WHERE WE NEED TO BE.

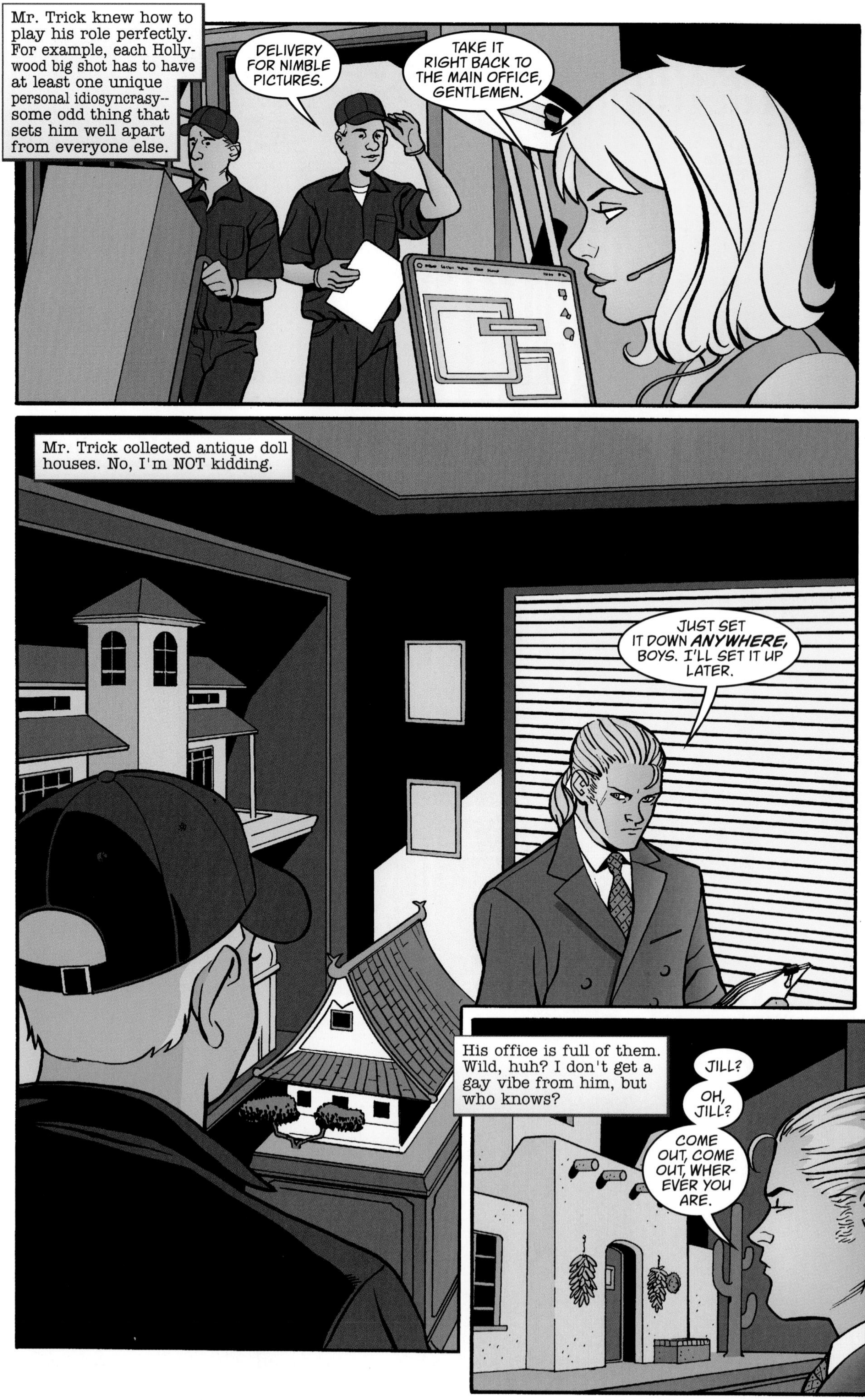
Mr. Trick knew how to play his role perfectly. For example, each Hollywood big shot has to have at least one unique personal idiosyncrasy-- some odd thing that sets him well apart from everyone else.
DELIVERY FOR NIMBLE PICTURES.
TAKE IT RIGHT BACK TO THE MAIN OFFICE, GENTLEMEN.
Mr. Trick collected antique doll houses. No, I'm NOT kidding.
JUST SET IT DOWN *ANYWHERE,* BOYS. I'LL SET IT UP LATER.
His office is full of them. Wild, huh? I don't get a gay vibe from him, but who knows?
JILL?
OH, JILL?
COME OUT, COME OUT, WHEREVER YOU ARE.

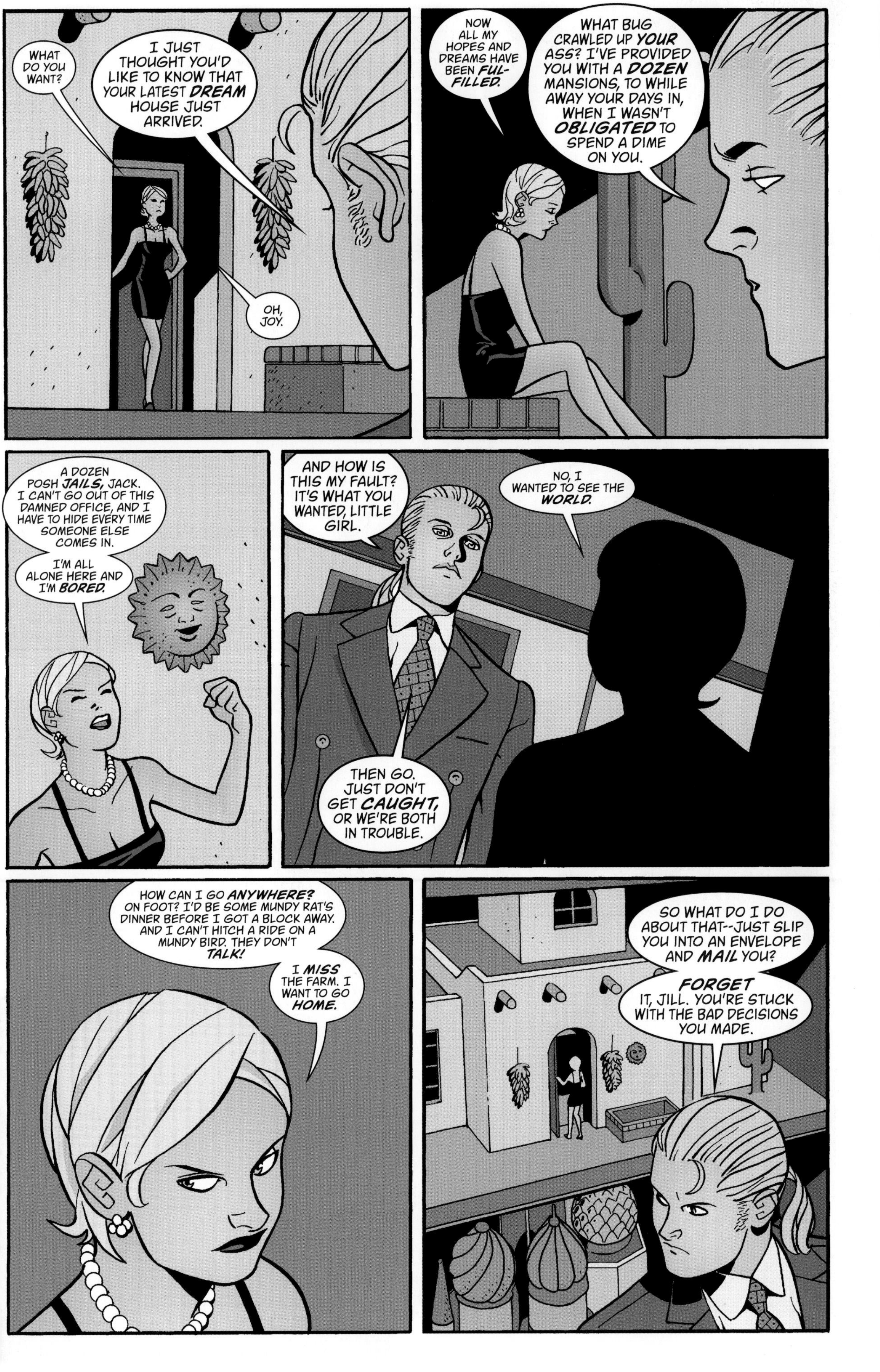
WHAT DO YOU WANT?
I JUST THOUGHT YOU'D LIKE TO KNOW THAT YOUR LATEST DREAM HOUSE JUST ARRIVED.
OH, JOY.
NOW ALL MY HOPES AND DREAMS HAVE BEEN FUL-FILLED.
WHAT BUG CRAWLED UP YOUR ASS? I'VE PROVIDED YOU WITH A DOZEN MANSIONS, TO WHILE AWAY YOUR DAYS IN, WHEN I WASN'T OBLIGATED TO SPEND A DIME ON YOU.
A DOZEN POSH JAILS, JACK. I CAN'T GO OUT OF THIS DAMNED OFFICE, AND I HAVE TO HIDE EVERY TIME SOMEONE ELSE COMES IN.
I'M ALL ALONE HERE AND I'M BORED.
AND HOW IS THIS MY FAULT? IT'S WHAT YOU WANTED, LITTLE GIRL.
NO, I WANTED TO SEE THE WORLD.
THEN GO. JUST DON'T GET CAUGHT, OR WE'RE BOTH IN TROUBLE.
HOW CAN I GO ANYWHERE? ON FOOT? I'D BE SOME MUNDY RAT'S DINNER BEFORE I GOT A BLOCK AWAY. AND I CAN'T HITCH A RIDE ON A MUNDY BIRD. THEY DON'T TALK!
I MISS THE FARM. I WANT TO GO HOME.
SO WHAT DO I DO ABOUT THAT--JUST SLIP YOU INTO AN ENVELOPE AND MAIL YOU?
FORGET IT, JILL. YOU'RE STUCK WITH THE BAD DECISIONS YOU MADE.

CHAPTER FOUR: THE TESTIMONY OF CHARLENE SPECK

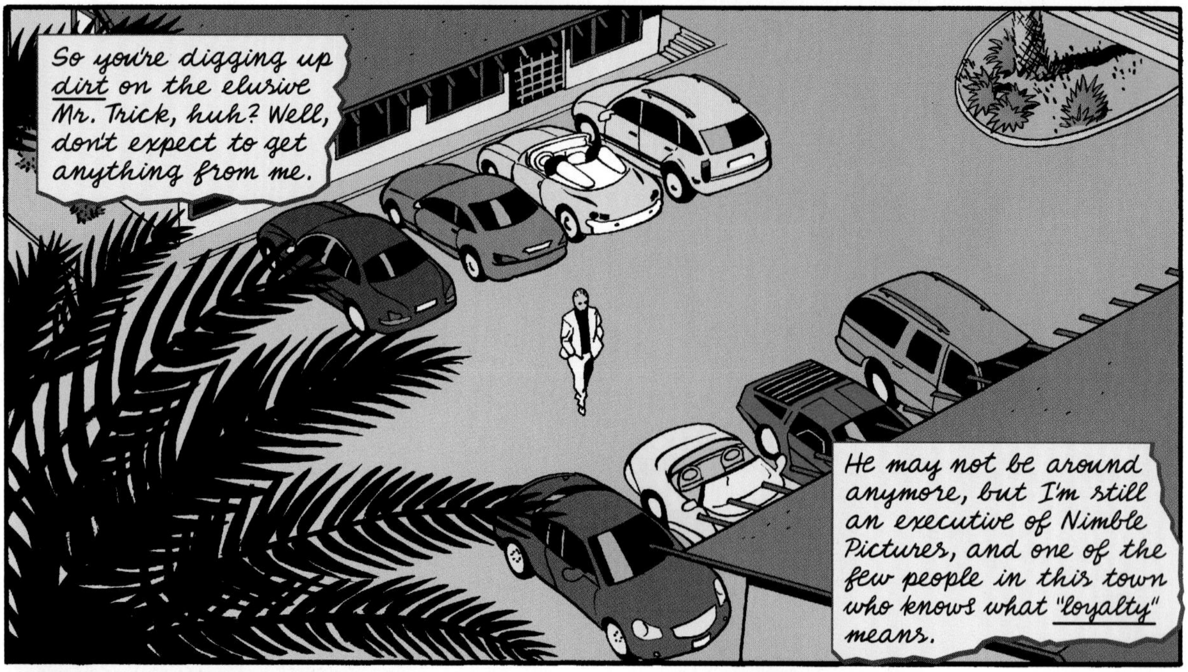

So you're digging up dirt on the elusive Mr. Trick, huh? Well, don't expect to get anything from me.
He may not be around anymore, but I'm still an executive of Nimble Pictures, and one of the few people in this town who knows what "loyalty" means.

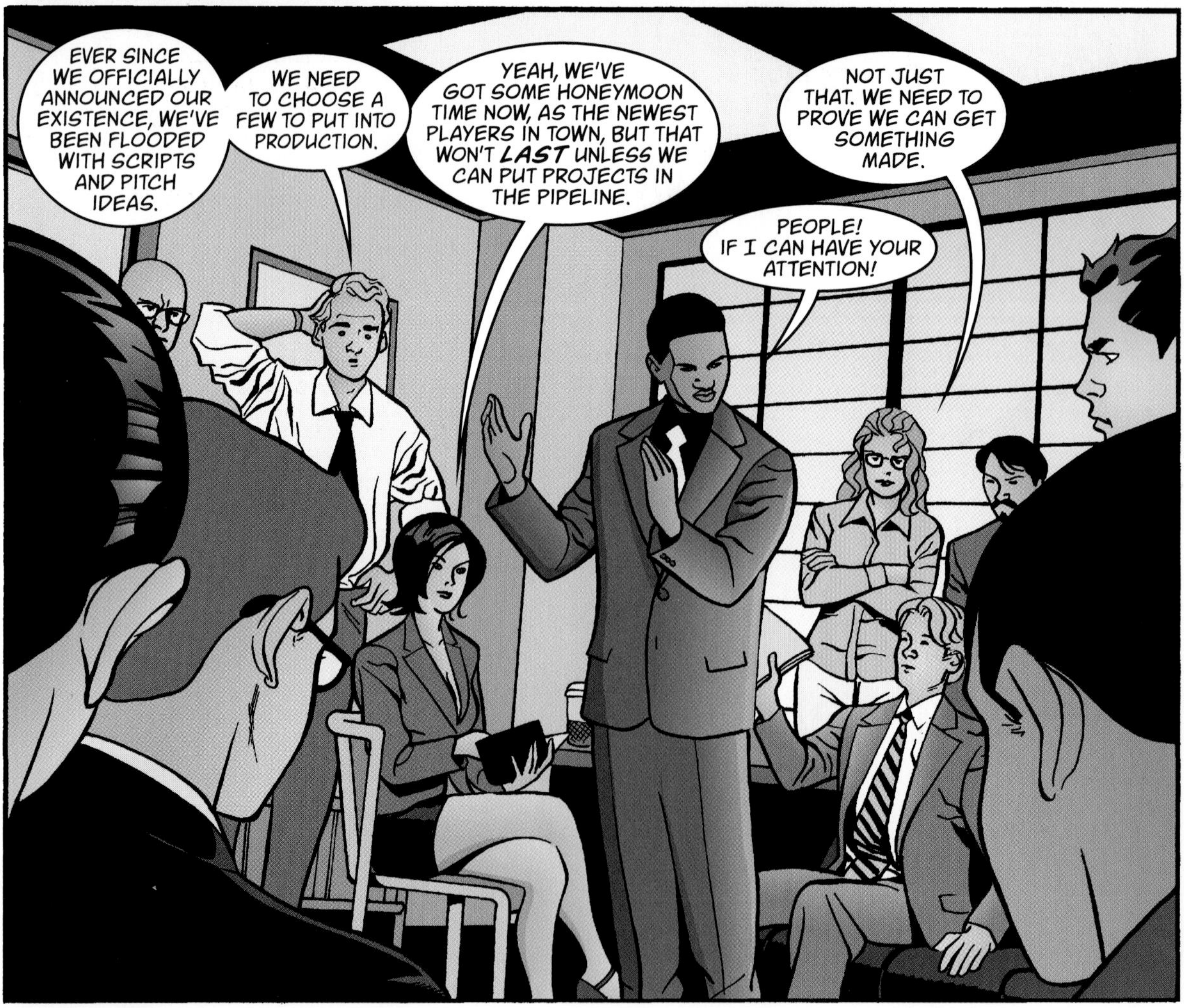

EVER SINCE WE OFFICIALLY ANNOUNCED OUR EXISTENCE, WE'VE BEEN FLOODED WITH SCRIPTS AND PITCH IDEAS.
WE NEED TO CHOOSE A FEW TO PUT INTO PRODUCTION.
YEAH, WE'VE GOT SOME HONEYMOON TIME NOW, AS THE NEWEST PLAYERS IN TOWN, BUT THAT WON'T LAST UNLESS WE CAN PUT PROJECTS IN THE PIPELINE.
NOT JUST THAT. WE NEED TO PROVE WE CAN GET SOMETHING MADE.
PEOPLE! IF I CAN HAVE YOUR ATTENTION!

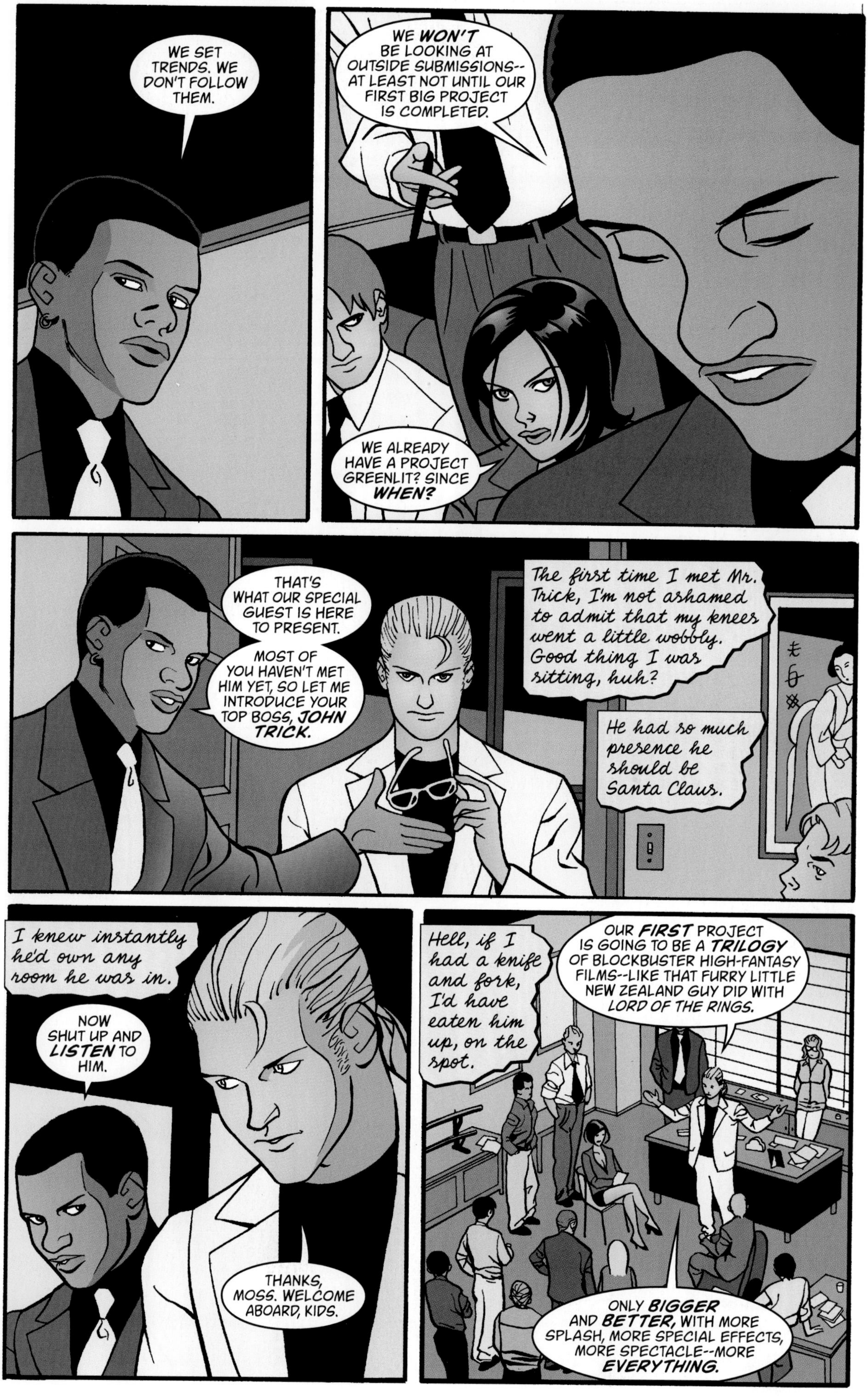
WE SET TRENDS. WE DON'T FOLLOW THEM.
WE WON'T BE LOOKING AT OUTSIDE SUBMISSIONS--AT LEAST NOT UNTIL OUR FIRST BIG PROJECT IS COMPLETED.
WE ALREADY HAVE A PROJECT GREENLIT? SINCE WHEN?
THAT'S WHAT OUR SPECIAL GUEST IS HERE TO PRESENT.
MOST OF YOU HAVEN'T MET HIM YET, SO LET ME INTRODUCE YOUR TOP BOSS, JOHN TRICK.
The first time I met Mr. Trick, I'm not ashamed to admit that my knees went a little wobbly. Good thing I was sitting, huh?
He had so much presence he should be Santa Claus.
I knew instantly he'd own any room he was in.
NOW SHUT UP AND LISTEN TO HIM.
THANKS, MOSS. WELCOME ABOARD, KIDS.
Hell, if I had a knife and fork, I'd have eaten him up, on the spot.
OUR FIRST PROJECT IS GOING TO BE A TRILOGY OF BLOCKBUSTER HIGH-FANTASY FILMS--LIKE THAT FURRY LITTLE NEW ZEALAND GUY DID WITH LORD OF THE RINGS.
ONLY BIGGER AND BETTER, WITH MORE SPLASH, MORE SPECIAL EFFECTS, MORE SPECTACLE--MORE EVERYTHING.

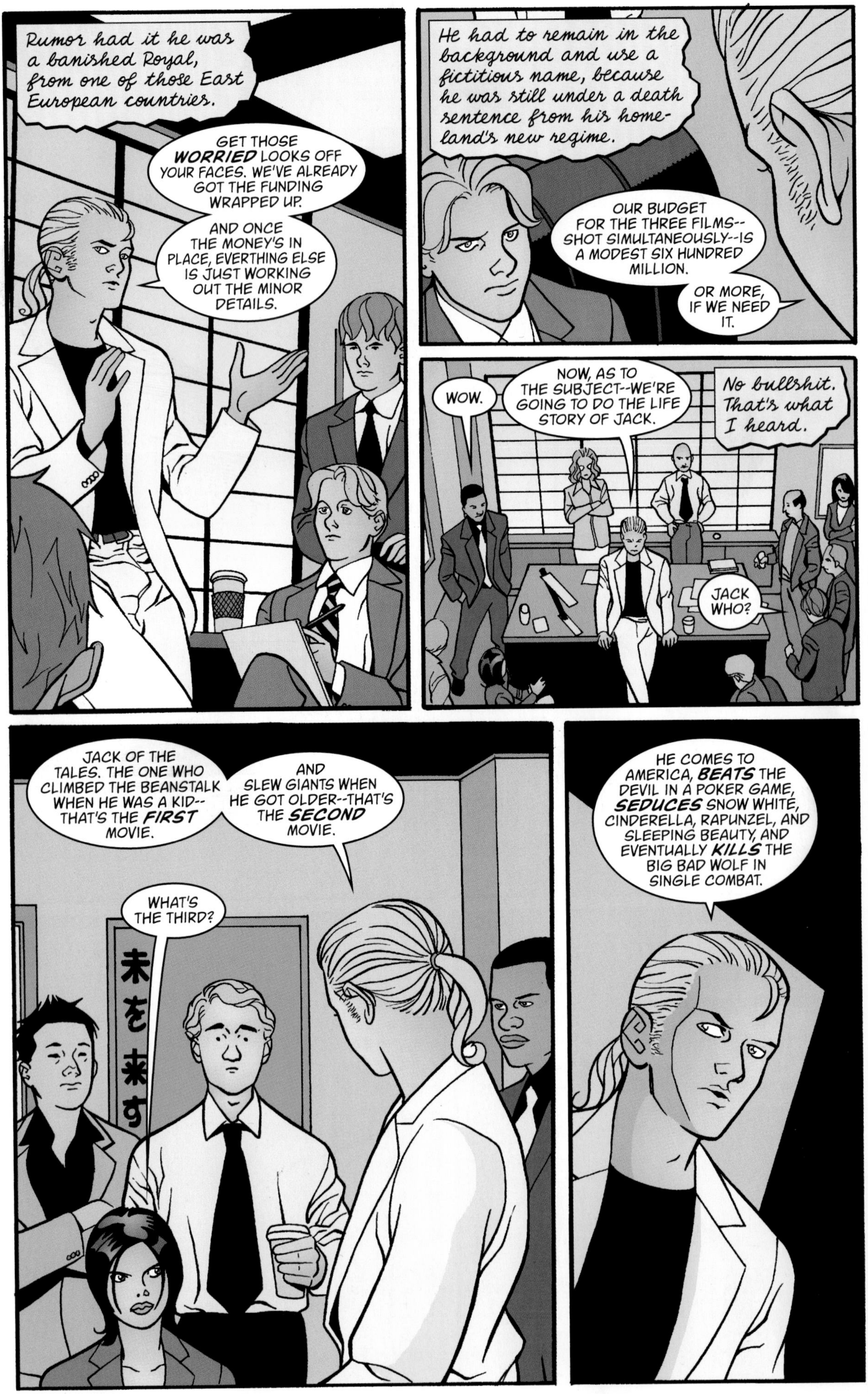
Rumor had it he was a banished Royal, from one of those East European countries.
GET THOSE WORRIED LOOKS OFF YOUR FACES. WE'VE ALREADY GOT THE FUNDING WRAPPED UP.
AND ONCE THE MONEY'S IN PLACE, EVERTHING ELSE IS JUST WORKING OUT THE MINOR DETAILS.
He had to remain in the background and use a fictitious name, because he was still under a death sentence from his homeland's new regime.
OUR BUDGET FOR THE THREE FILMS--SHOT SIMULTANEOUSLY--IS A MODEST SIX HUNDRED MILLION.
OR MORE, IF WE NEED IT.
WOW.
NOW, AS TO THE SUBJECT--WE'RE GOING TO DO THE LIFE STORY OF JACK.
No bullshit. That's what I heard.
JACK WHO?
JACK OF THE TALES. THE ONE WHO CLIMBED THE BEANSTALK WHEN HE WAS A KID--THAT'S THE FIRST MOVIE.
AND SLEW GIANTS WHEN HE GOT OLDER--THAT'S THE SECOND MOVIE.
WHAT'S THE THIRD?
HE COMES TO AMERICA, BEATS THE DEVIL IN A POKER GAME, SEDUCES SNOW WHITE, CINDERELLA, RAPUNZEL, AND SLEEPING BEAUTY, AND EVENTUALLY KILLS THE BIG BAD WOLF IN SINGLE COMBAT.

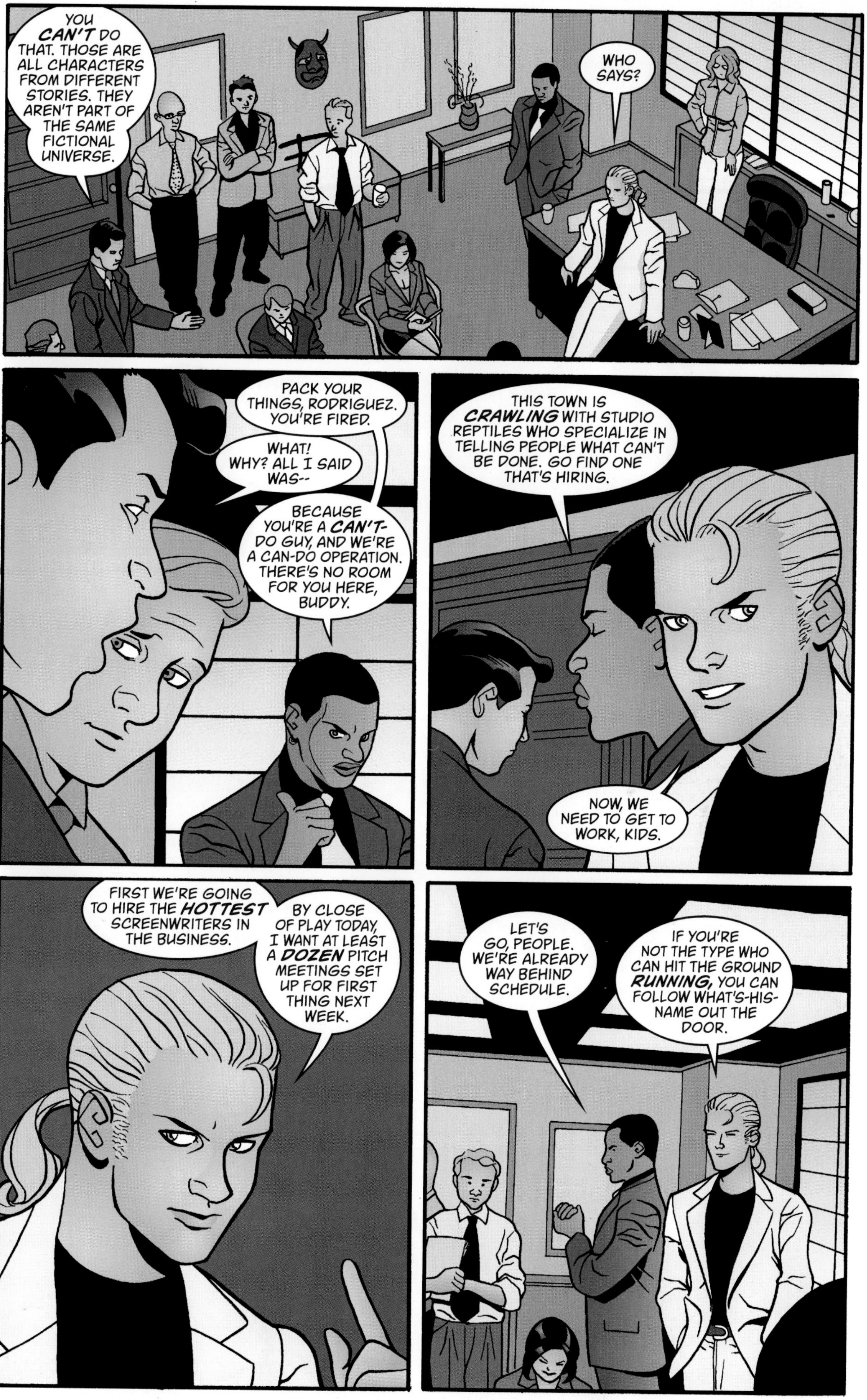
YOU CAN'T DO THAT. THOSE ARE ALL CHARACTERS FROM DIFFERENT STORIES. THEY AREN'T PART OF THE SAME FICTIONAL UNIVERSE.
WHO SAYS?
PACK YOUR THINGS, RODRIGUEZ. YOU'RE FIRED.
WHAT! WHY? ALL I SAID WAS--
BECAUSE YOU'RE A CAN'T-DO GUY, AND WE'RE A CAN-DO OPERATION. THERE'S NO ROOM FOR YOU HERE, BUDDY.
THIS TOWN IS CRAWLING WITH STUDIO REPTILES WHO SPECIALIZE IN TELLING PEOPLE WHAT CAN'T BE DONE. GO FIND ONE THAT'S HIRING.
NOW, WE NEED TO GET TO WORK, KIDS.
FIRST WE'RE GOING TO HIRE THE HOTTEST SCREENWRITERS IN THE BUSINESS.
BY CLOSE OF PLAY TODAY, I WANT AT LEAST A DOZEN PITCH MEETINGS SET UP FOR FIRST THING NEXT WEEK.
LET'S GO, PEOPLE. WE'RE ALREADY WAY BEHIND SCHEDULE.
IF YOU'RE NOT THE TYPE WHO CAN HIT THE GROUND RUNNING, YOU CAN FOLLOW WHAT'S-HIS-NAME OUT THE DOOR.

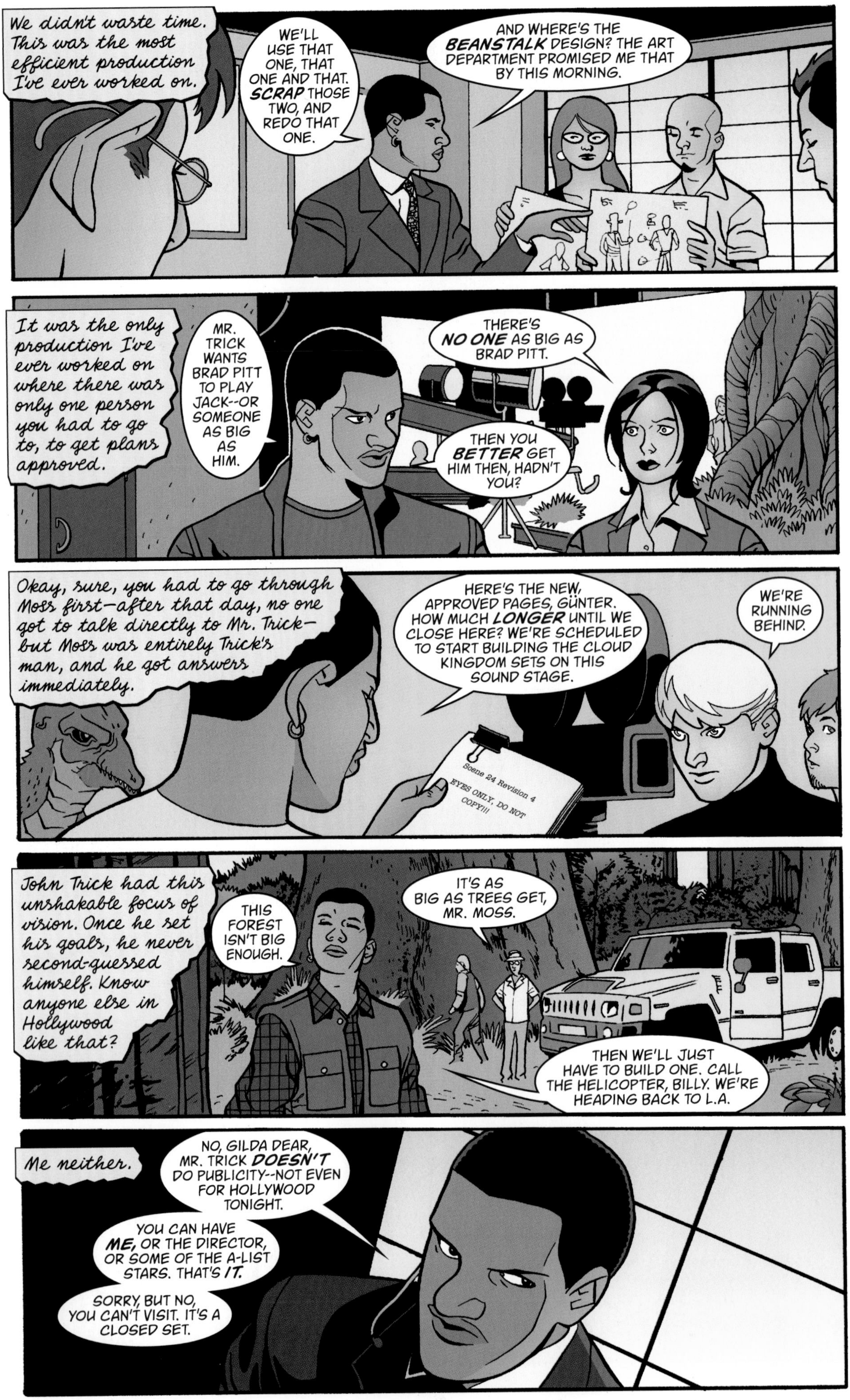
We didn't waste time. This was the most efficient production I've ever worked on.
WE'LL USE THAT ONE, THAT ONE AND THAT. SCRAP THOSE TWO, AND REDO THAT ONE.
AND WHERE'S THE BEANSTALK DESIGN? THE ART DEPARTMENT PROMISED ME THAT BY THIS MORNING.
It was the only production I've ever worked on where there was only one person you had to go to, to get plans approved.
MR. TRICK WANTS BRAD PITT TO PLAY JACK--OR SOMEONE AS BIG AS HIM.
THERE'S NO ONE AS BIG AS BRAD PITT.
THEN YOU BETTER GET HIM THEN, HADN'T YOU?
Okay, sure, you had to go through Moss first—after that day, no one got to talk directly to Mr. Trick—but Moss was entirely Trick's man, and he got answers immediately.
HERE'S THE NEW, APPROVED PAGES, GÜNTER. HOW MUCH LONGER UNTIL WE CLOSE HERE? WE'RE SCHEDULED TO START BUILDING THE CLOUD KINGDOM SETS ON THIS SOUND STAGE.
WE'RE RUNNING BEHIND.
Scene 24 Revision 4
EYES ONLY, DO NOT COPY!!!
John Trick had this unshakable focus of vision. Once he set his goals, he never second-guessed himself. Know anyone else in Hollywood like that?
THIS FOREST ISN'T BIG ENOUGH.
IT'S AS BIG AS TREES GET, MR. MOSS.
THEN WE'LL JUST HAVE TO BUILD ONE. CALL THE HELICOPTER, BILLY. WE'RE HEADING BACK TO L.A.
Me neither.
NO, GILDA DEAR, MR. TRICK DOESN'T DO PUBLICITY--NOT EVEN FOR HOLLYWOOD TONIGHT.
YOU CAN HAVE ME, OR THE DIRECTOR, OR SOME OF THE A-LIST STARS. THAT'S IT.
SORRY, BUT NO, YOU CAN'T VISIT. IT'S A CLOSED SET.

CHAPTER FIVE: OTHER TESTIMONIALS

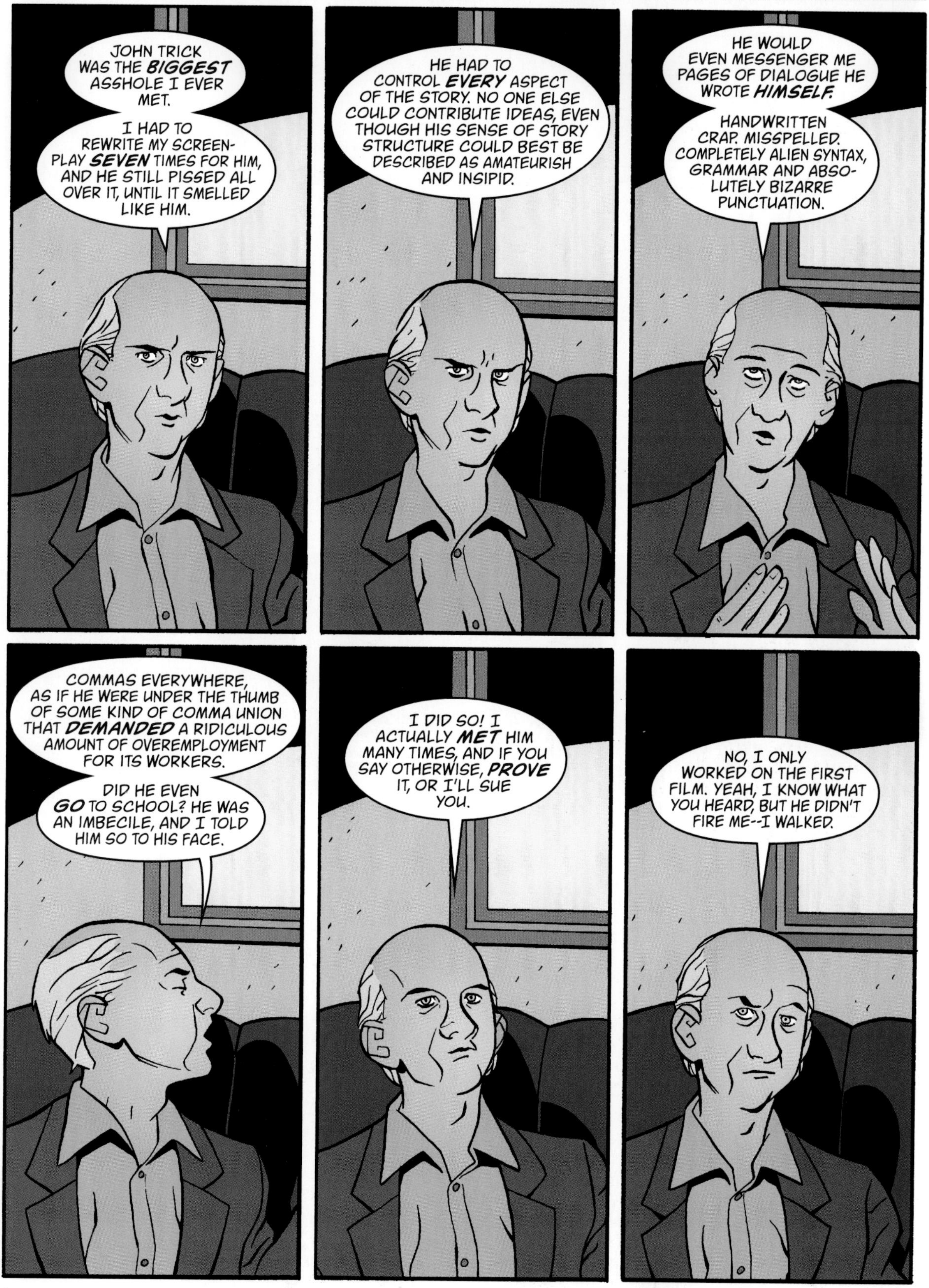

JOHN TRICK WAS THE BIGGEST ASSHOLE I EVER MET.
I HAD TO REWRITE MY SCREEN-PLAY SEVEN TIMES FOR HIM, AND HE STILL PISSED ALL OVER IT, UNTIL IT SMELLED LIKE HIM.
HE HAD TO CONTROL EVERY ASPECT OF THE STORY. NO ONE ELSE COULD CONTRIBUTE IDEAS, EVEN THOUGH HIS SENSE OF STORY STRUCTURE COULD BEST BE DESCRIBED AS AMATEURISH AND INSIPID.
HE WOULD EVEN MESSENGER ME PAGES OF DIALOGUE HE WROTE HIMSELF.
HANDWRITTEN CRAP. MISSPELLED. COMPLETELY ALIEN SYNTAX, GRAMMAR AND ABSO-LUTELY BIZARRE PUNCTUATION.
COMMAS EVERYWHERE, AS IF HE WERE UNDER THE THUMB OF SOME KIND OF COMMA UNION THAT DEMANDED A RIDICULOUS AMOUNT OF OVEREMPLOYMENT FOR ITS WORKERS.
DID HE EVEN GO TO SCHOOL? HE WAS AN IMBECILE, AND I TOLD HIM SO TO HIS FACE.
I DID SO! I ACTUALLY MET HIM MANY TIMES, AND IF YOU SAY OTHERWISE, PROVE IT, OR I'LL SUE YOU.
NO, I ONLY WORKED ON THE FIRST FILM. YEAH, I KNOW WHAT YOU HEARD, BUT HE DIDN'T FIRE ME--I WALKED.

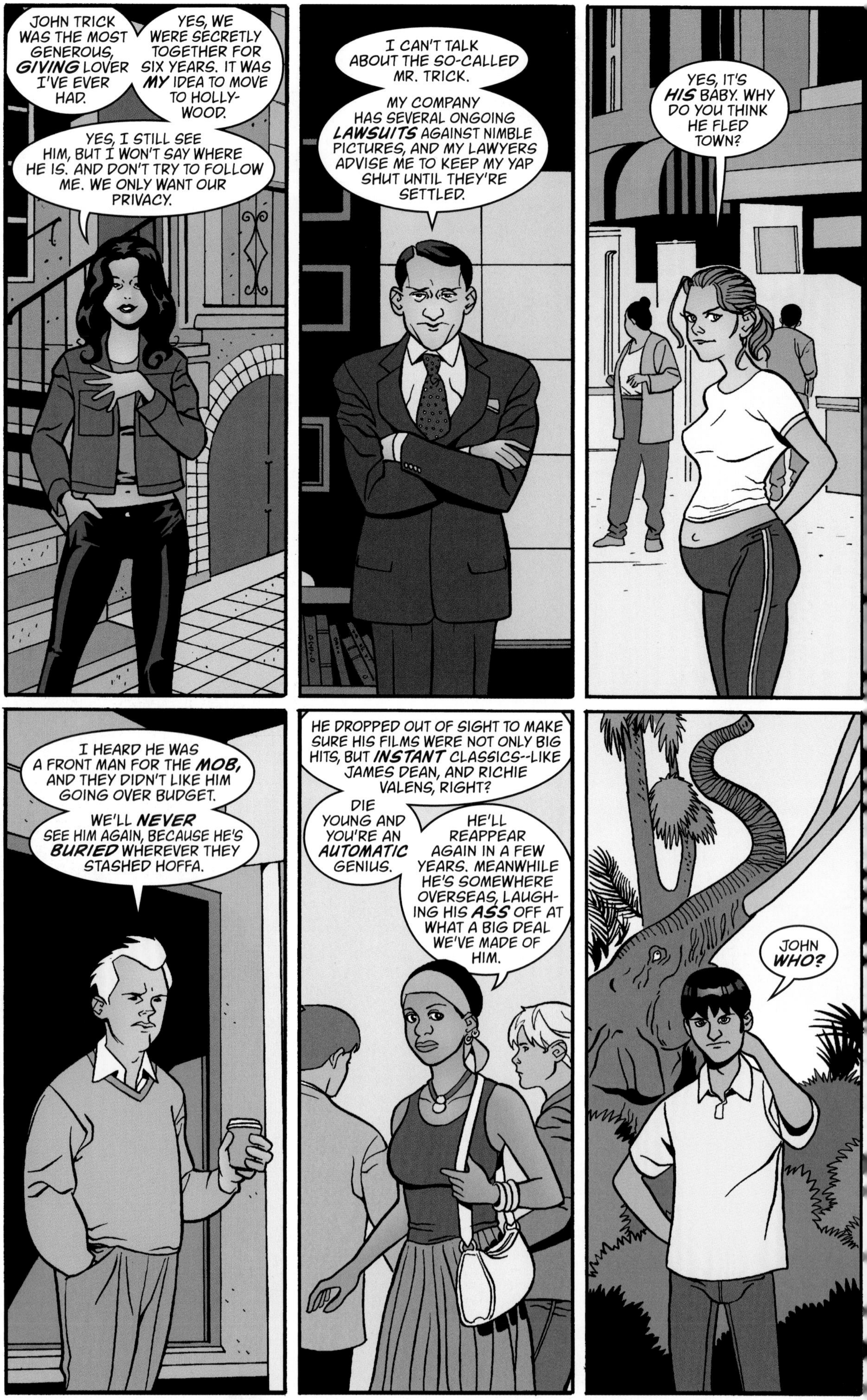
JOHN TRICK WAS THE MOST GENEROUS, GIVING LOVER I'VE EVER HAD.
YES, WE WERE SECRETLY TOGETHER FOR SIX YEARS. IT WAS MY IDEA TO MOVE TO HOLLY-WOOD.
YES, I STILL SEE HIM, BUT I WON'T SAY WHERE HE IS. AND DON'T TRY TO FOLLOW ME. WE ONLY WANT OUR PRIVACY.
I CAN'T TALK ABOUT THE SO-CALLED MR. TRICK.
MY COMPANY HAS SEVERAL ONGOING LAWSUITS AGAINST NIMBLE PICTURES, AND MY LAWYERS ADVISE ME TO KEEP MY YAP SHUT UNTIL THEY'RE SETTLED.
YES, IT'S HIS BABY. WHY DO YOU THINK HE FLED TOWN?
I HEARD HE WAS A FRONT MAN FOR THE MOB, AND THEY DIDN'T LIKE HIM GOING OVER BUDGET.
WE'LL NEVER SEE HIM AGAIN, BECAUSE HE'S BURIED WHEREVER THEY STASHED HOFFA.
HE DROPPED OUT OF SIGHT TO MAKE SURE HIS FILMS WERE NOT ONLY BIG HITS, BUT INSTANT CLASSICS--LIKE JAMES DEAN, AND RICHIE VALENS, RIGHT?
DIE YOUNG AND YOU'RE AN AUTOMATIC GENIUS.
HE'LL REAPPEAR AGAIN IN A FEW YEARS. MEANWHILE HE'S SOMEWHERE OVERSEAS, LAUGH-ING HIS ASS OFF AT WHAT A BIG DEAL WE'VE MADE OF HIM.
JOHN WHO?

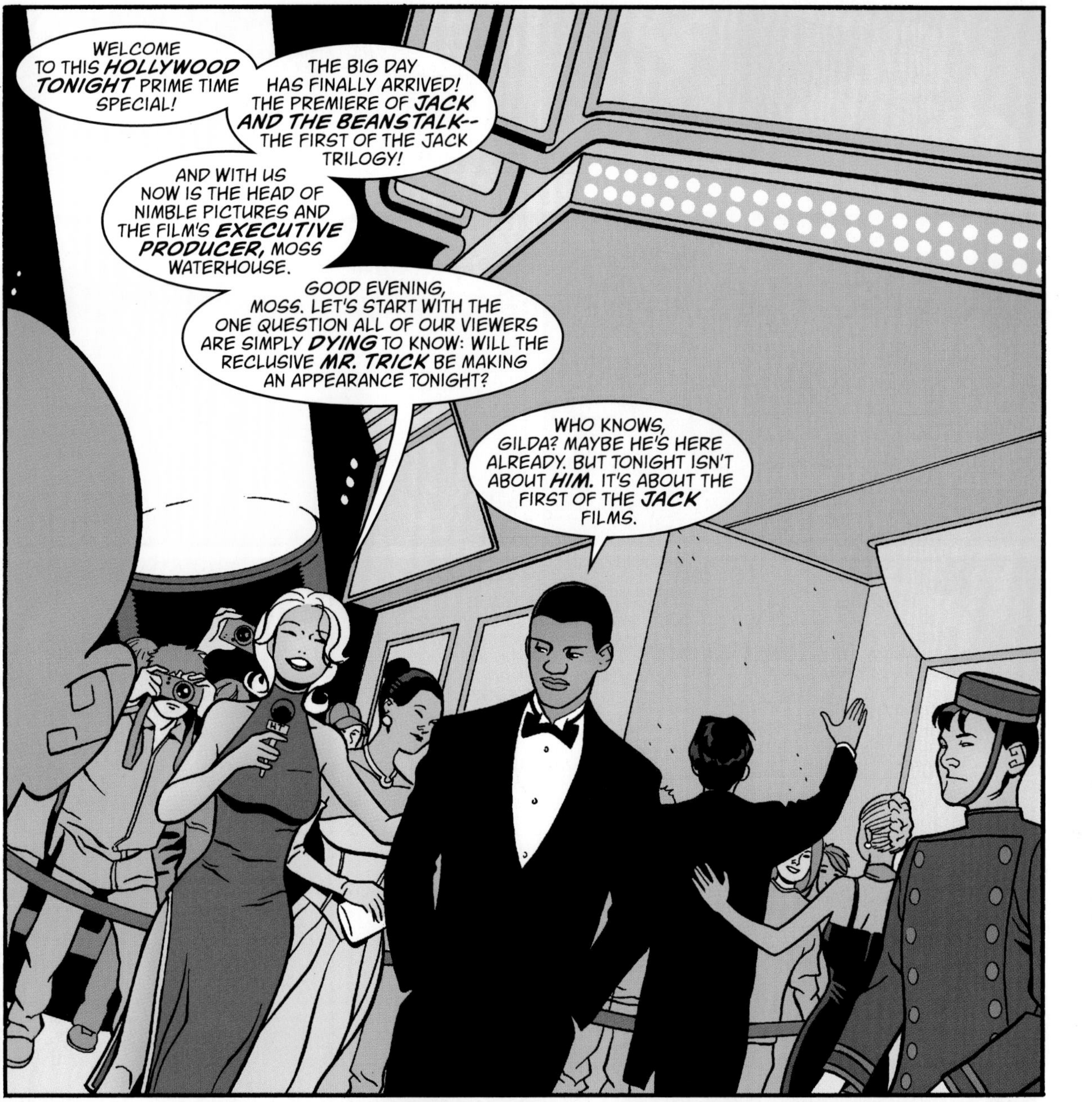
WELCOME TO THIS HOLLYWOOD TONIGHT PRIME TIME SPECIAL!
THE BIG DAY HAS FINALLY ARRIVED! THE PREMIERE OF JACK AND THE BEANSTALK-- THE FIRST OF THE JACK TRILOGY!
AND WITH US NOW IS THE HEAD OF NIMBLE PICTURES AND THE FILM'S EXECUTIVE PRODUCER, MOSS WATERHOUSE.
GOOD EVENING, MOSS. LET'S START WITH THE ONE QUESTION ALL OF OUR VIEWERS ARE SIMPLY DYING TO KNOW: WILL THE RECLUSIVE MR. TRICK BE MAKING AN APPEARANCE TONIGHT?
WHO KNOWS, GILDA? MAYBE HE'S HERE ALREADY. BUT TONIGHT ISN'T ABOUT HIM. IT'S ABOUT THE FIRST OF THE JACK FILMS.

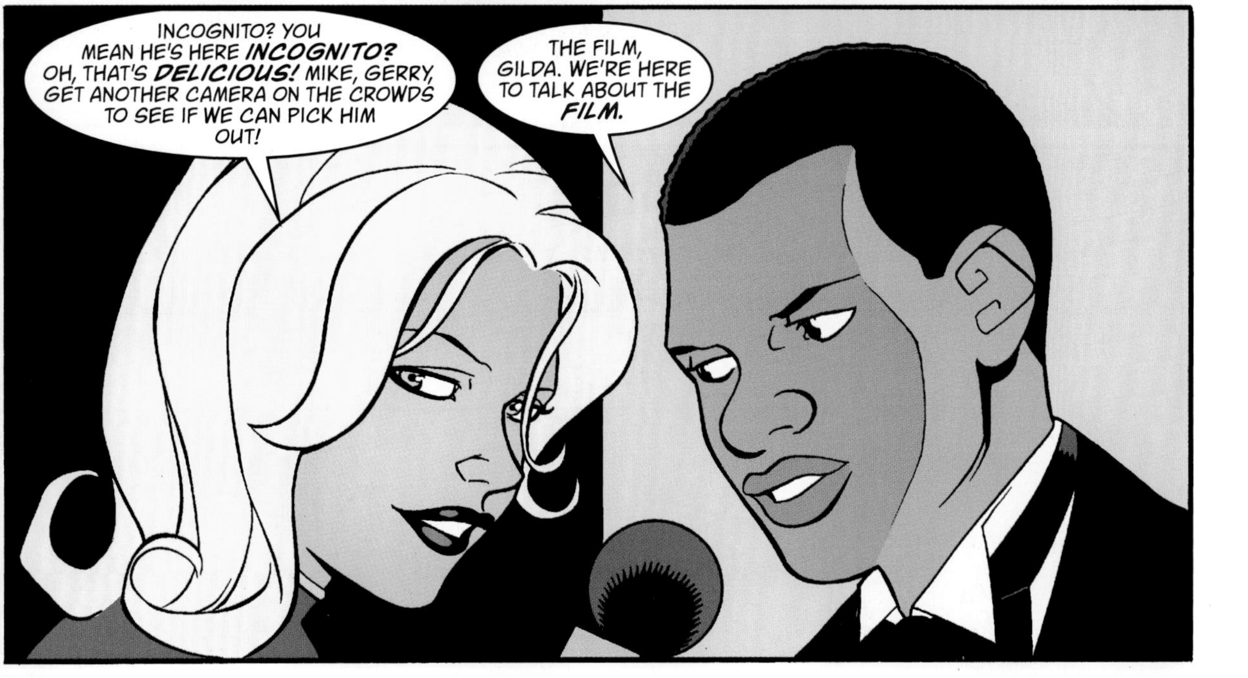
INCOGNITO? YOU MEAN HE'S HERE INCOGNITO? OH, THAT'S DELICIOUS! MIKE, GERRY, GET ANOTHER CAMERA ON THE CROWDS TO SEE IF WE CAN PICK HIM OUT!
THE FILM, GILDA. WE'RE HERE TO TALK ABOUT THE FILM.

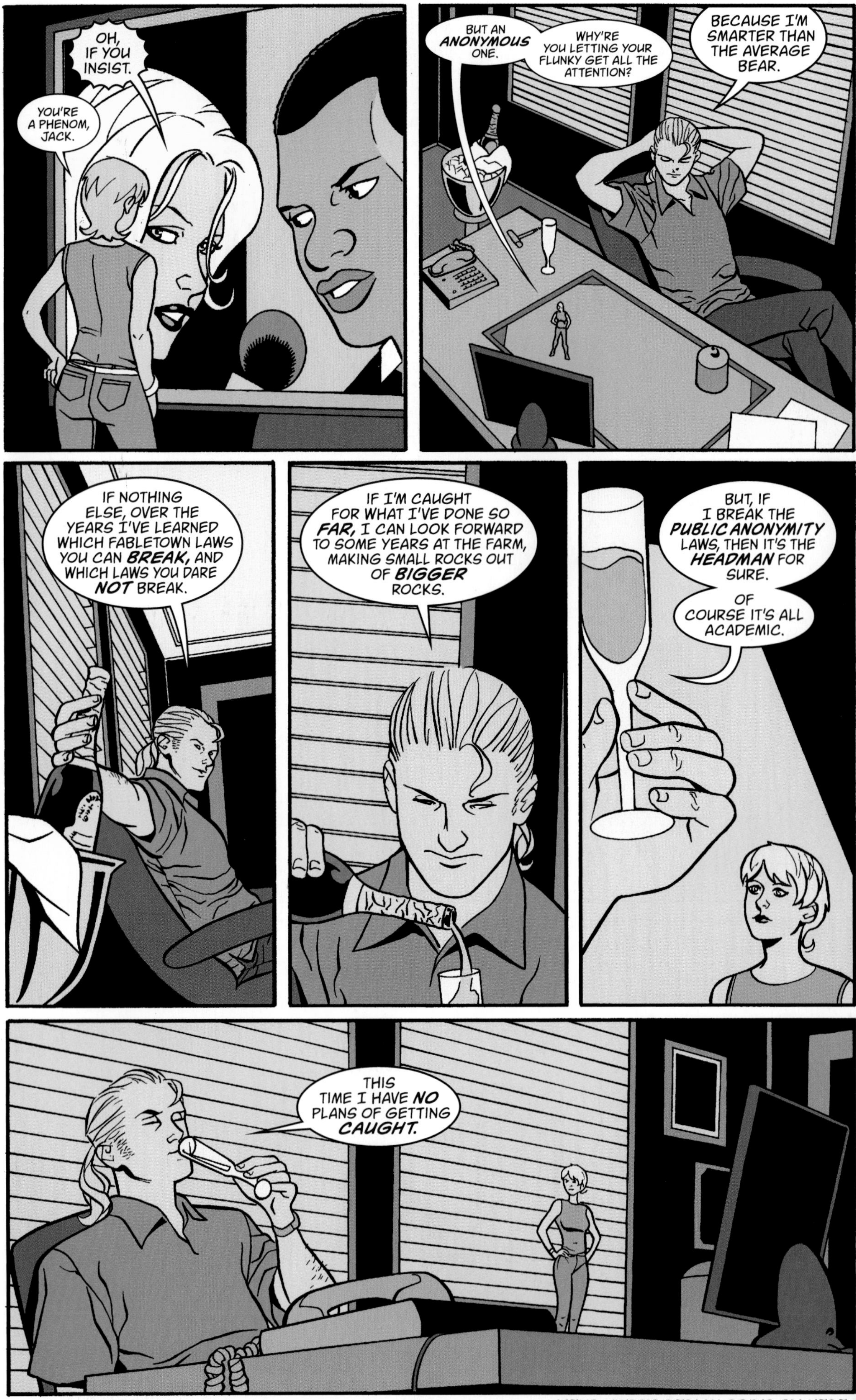
YOU'RE A PHENOM, JACK.
OH, IF YOU INSIST.
BUT AN ANONYMOUS ONE.
WHY'RE YOU LETTING YOUR FLUNKY GET ALL THE ATTENTION?
BECAUSE I'M SMARTER THAN THE AVERAGE BEAR.
IF NOTHING ELSE, OVER THE YEARS I'VE LEARNED WHICH FABLETOWN LAWS YOU CAN BREAK, AND WHICH LAWS YOU DARE NOT BREAK.
IF I'M CAUGHT FOR WHAT I'VE DONE SO FAR, I CAN LOOK FORWARD TO SOME YEARS AT THE FARM, MAKING SMALL ROCKS OUT OF BIGGER ROCKS.
BUT, IF I BREAK THE PUBLIC ANONYMITY LAWS, THEN IT'S THE HEADMAN FOR SURE.
OF COURSE IT'S ALL ACADEMIC.
THIS TIME I HAVE NO PLANS OF GETTING CAUGHT.

NEXT: WHAT'S REALLY GOING ON HERE.

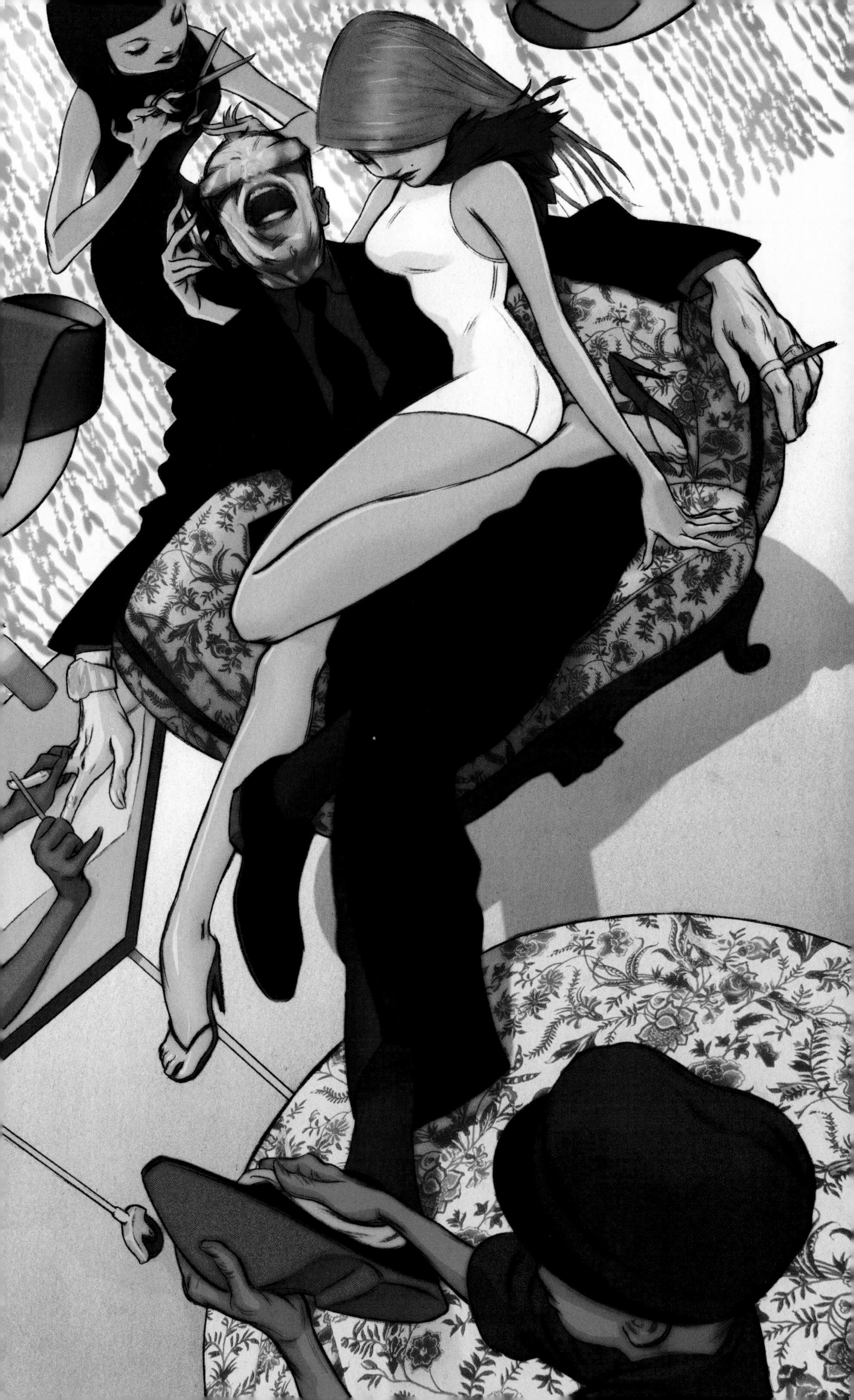

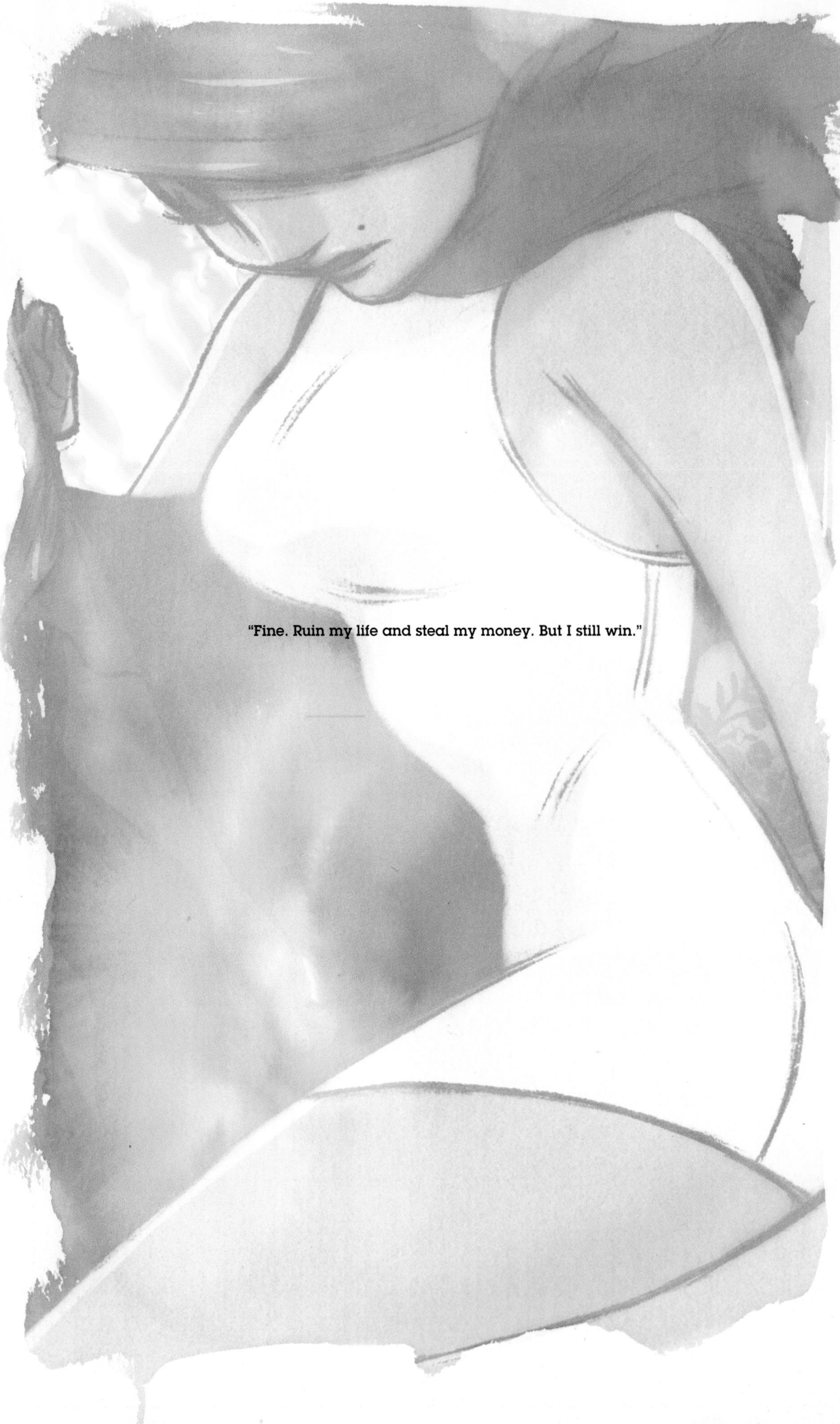

"Fine. Ruin my life and steal my money. But I still win."

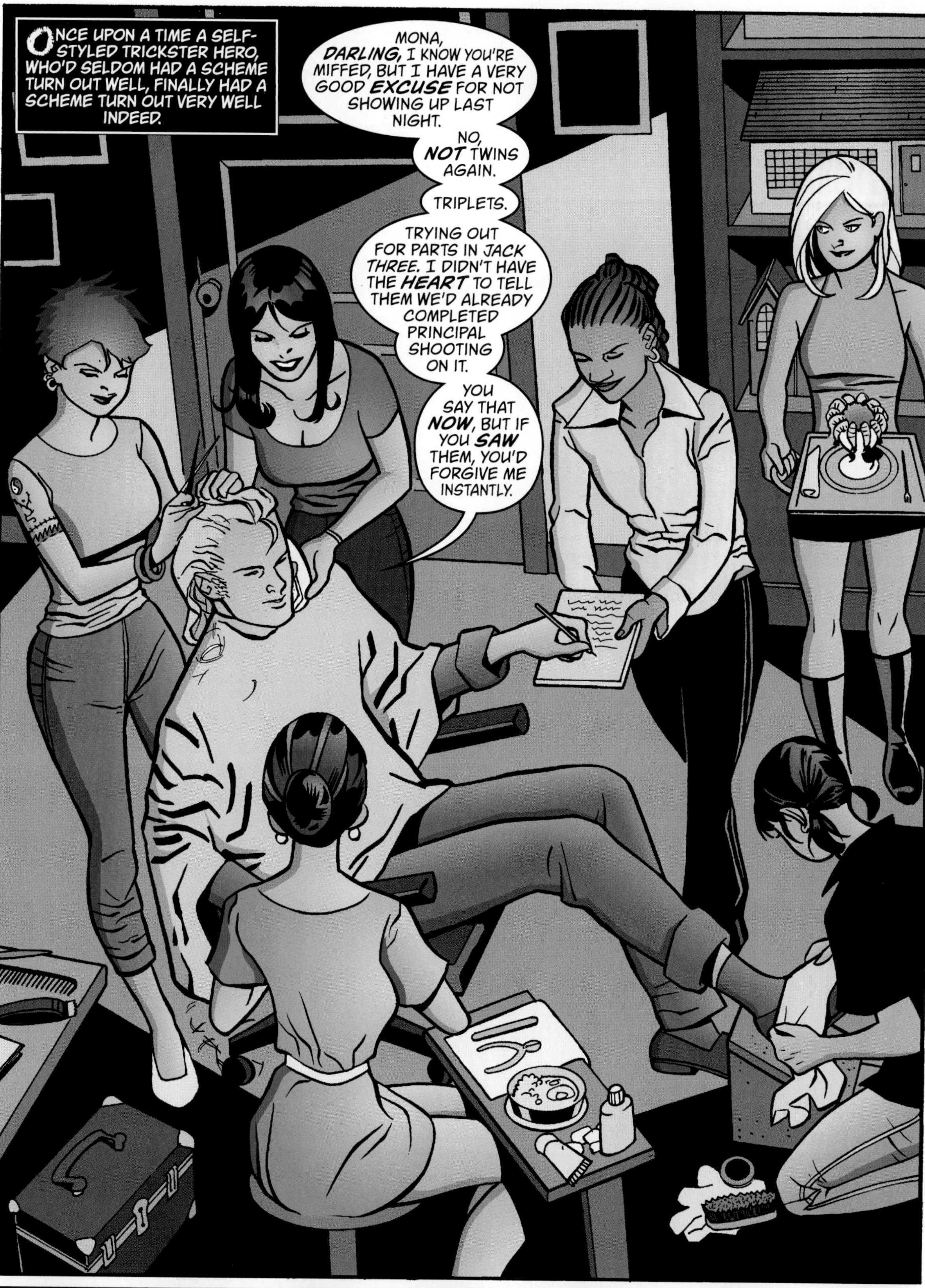

ONCE UPON A TIME A SELF-STYLED TRICKSTER HERO, WHO'D SELDOM HAD A SCHEME TURN OUT WELL, FINALLY HAD A SCHEME TURN OUT VERY WELL INDEED.
MONA, **DARLING,** I KNOW YOU'RE MIFFED, BUT I HAVE A VERY GOOD **EXCUSE** FOR NOT SHOWING UP LAST NIGHT.
NO, **NOT** TWINS AGAIN.
TRIPLETS.
TRYING OUT FOR PARTS IN *JACK THREE.* I DIDN'T HAVE THE **HEART** TO TELL THEM WE'D ALREADY COMPLETED PRINCIPAL SHOOTING ON IT.
YOU SAY THAT **NOW**, BUT IF YOU **SAW** THEM, YOU'D FORGIVE ME INSTANTLY.

BILL WILLINGHAM, WRITER/CREATOR PRESENTS

JACK BE NIMBLE

PART TWO OF TWO

DAVID HAHN, PENCILS & INKS
TODD KLEIN, LETTERS
DANIEL VOZZO, COLORS
JAMES JEAN, COVER ART
MARIAH HUEHNER, ASST. ED
SHELLY BOND, EDITOR

CHAPTER SIX: THE MOSS TRIBULATIONS

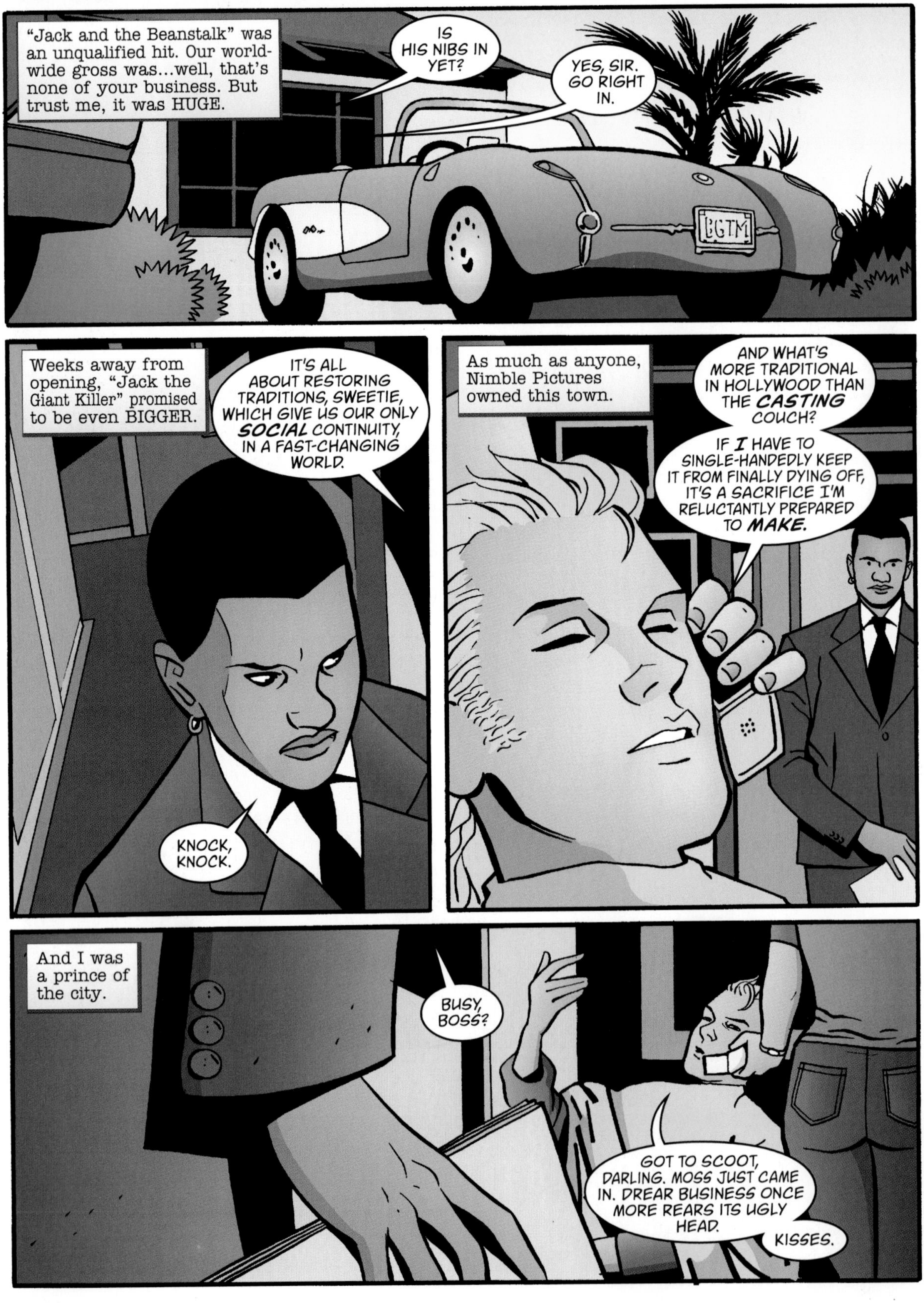

"Jack and the Beanstalk" was an unqualified hit. Our world-wide gross was...well, that's none of your business. But trust me, it was HUGE.
IS HIS NIBS IN YET?
YES, SIR. GO RIGHT IN.
BGTM
Weeks away from opening, "Jack the Giant Killer" promised to be even BIGGER.
IT'S ALL ABOUT RESTORING TRADITIONS, SWEETIE, WHICH GIVE US OUR ONLY *SOCIAL* CONTINUITY, IN A FAST-CHANGING WORLD.
KNOCK, KNOCK.
As much as anyone, Nimble Pictures owned this town.
AND WHAT'S MORE TRADITIONAL IN HOLLYWOOD THAN THE *CASTING* COUCH?
IF *I* HAVE TO SINGLE-HANDEDLY KEEP IT FROM FINALLY DYING OFF, IT'S A SACRIFICE I'M RELUCTANTLY PREPARED TO *MAKE.*
And I was a prince of the city.
BUSY, BOSS?
GOT TO SCOOT, DARLING. MOSS JUST CAME IN. DREAR BUSINESS ONCE MORE REARS ITS UGLY HEAD.
KISSES.

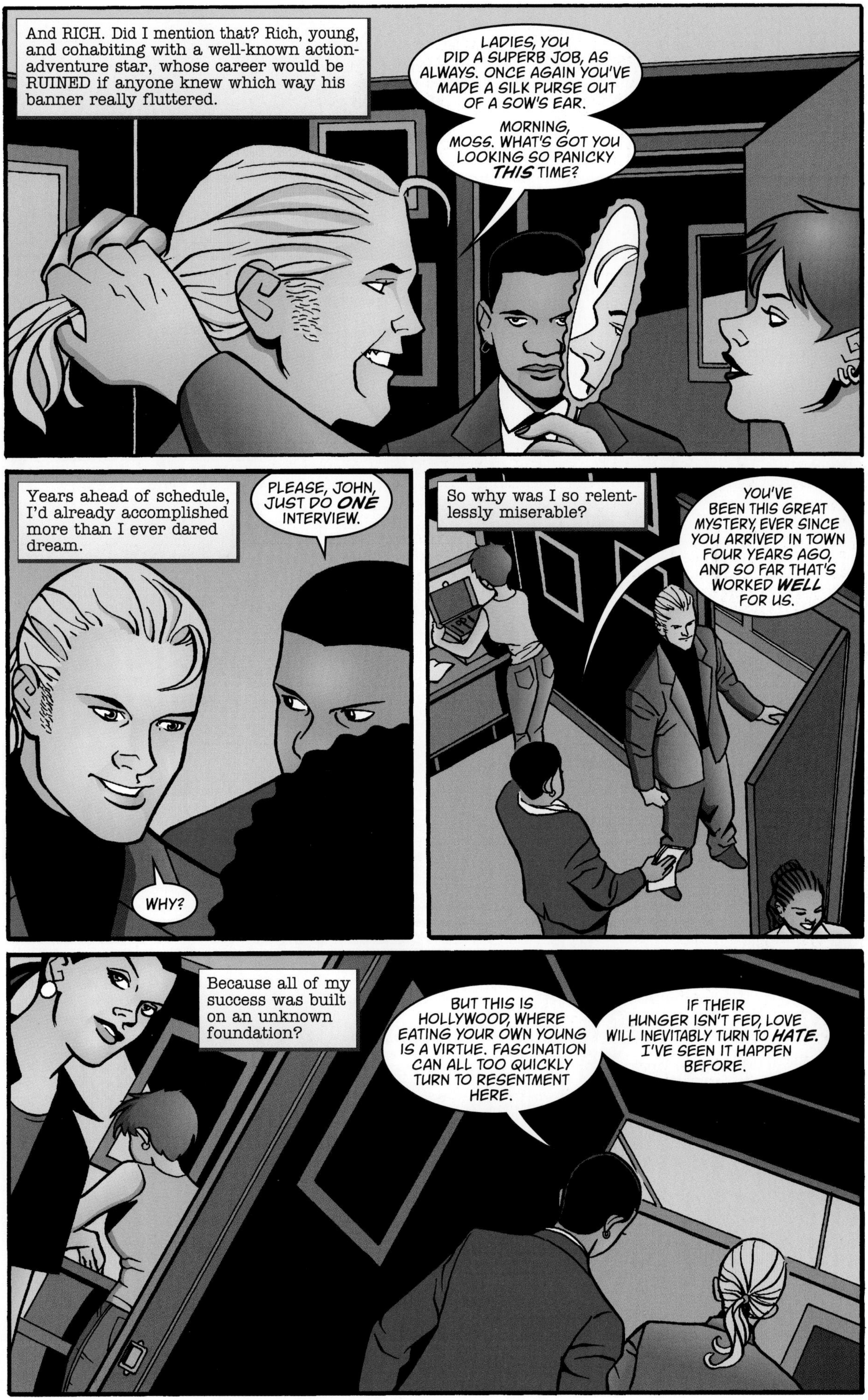
And RICH. Did I mention that? Rich, young, and cohabiting with a well-known action-adventure star, whose career would be RUINED if anyone knew which way his banner really fluttered.
LADIES, YOU DID A SUPERB JOB, AS ALWAYS. ONCE AGAIN YOU'VE MADE A SILK PURSE OUT OF A SOW'S EAR.
MORNING, MOSS. WHAT'S GOT YOU LOOKING SO PANICKY THIS TIME?
Years ahead of schedule, I'd already accomplished more than I ever dared dream.
PLEASE, JOHN, JUST DO ONE INTERVIEW.
WHY?
So why was I so relentlessly miserable?
YOU'VE BEEN THIS GREAT MYSTERY, EVER SINCE YOU ARRIVED IN TOWN FOUR YEARS AGO, AND SO FAR THAT'S WORKED WELL FOR US.
Because all of my success was built on an unknown foundation?
BUT THIS IS HOLLYWOOD, WHERE EATING YOUR OWN YOUNG IS A VIRTUE. FASCINATION CAN ALL TOO QUICKLY TURN TO RESENTMENT HERE.
IF THEIR HUNGER ISN'T FED, LOVE WILL INEVITABLY TURN TO HATE. I'VE SEEN IT HAPPEN BEFORE.

AND YOUR SOLUTION IS...?

WE NEED TO CONSIDER GETTING AHEAD OF THAT CURVE BY DEFLATING THE BUBBLE *BEFORE* IT BURSTS.

PEOPLE ARE BASICALLY RACCOONS. AS LONG AS YOU REMAIN SOME TWINKLY THING, JUST OUT OF THE CORNER OF THEIR EYES, THEY CAN'T HELP BUT BE INFATUATED.

NIMBLE PICTURES, CAN YOU HOLD PLEASE?

THANK YOU.

NIMBLE PICTURES, CAN YOU HOLD PLEASE?

THANK YOU.

NIMBLE PICTURES, CAN YOU HOLD PLEASE?

THANK YOU.

SO WE LET THEM GET ONE GOOD *LOOK* AT YOU, AND THEY'LL DUTIFULLY RESPOND BY FINDING SOME *OTHER* SHINY BAUBLE TO FIX THEIR ATTENTION ON.

THOSE ARE PRETTY GOOD ARGUMENTS, MOSS.

BUT I HIRED *YOU* TO BE THE PUBLIC FACE OF NIMBLE PICTURES. AND I PAY YOU A *KING'S RANSOM* TO DO IT.

IF YOU'RE NOT *UP* TO THE JOB, HELP ME FIND YOUR *REPLACE-MENT.*

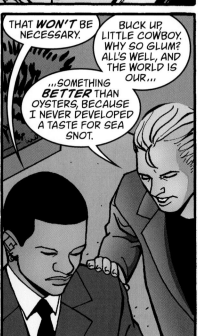

THAT *WON'T* BE NECESSARY.

BUCK UP, LITTLE COWBOY. WHY SO GLUM? ALL'S WELL, AND THE WORLD IS *OUR...*

...SOMETHING *BETTER* THAN OYSTERS, BECAUSE I NEVER DEVELOPED A TASTE FOR SEA SNOT.

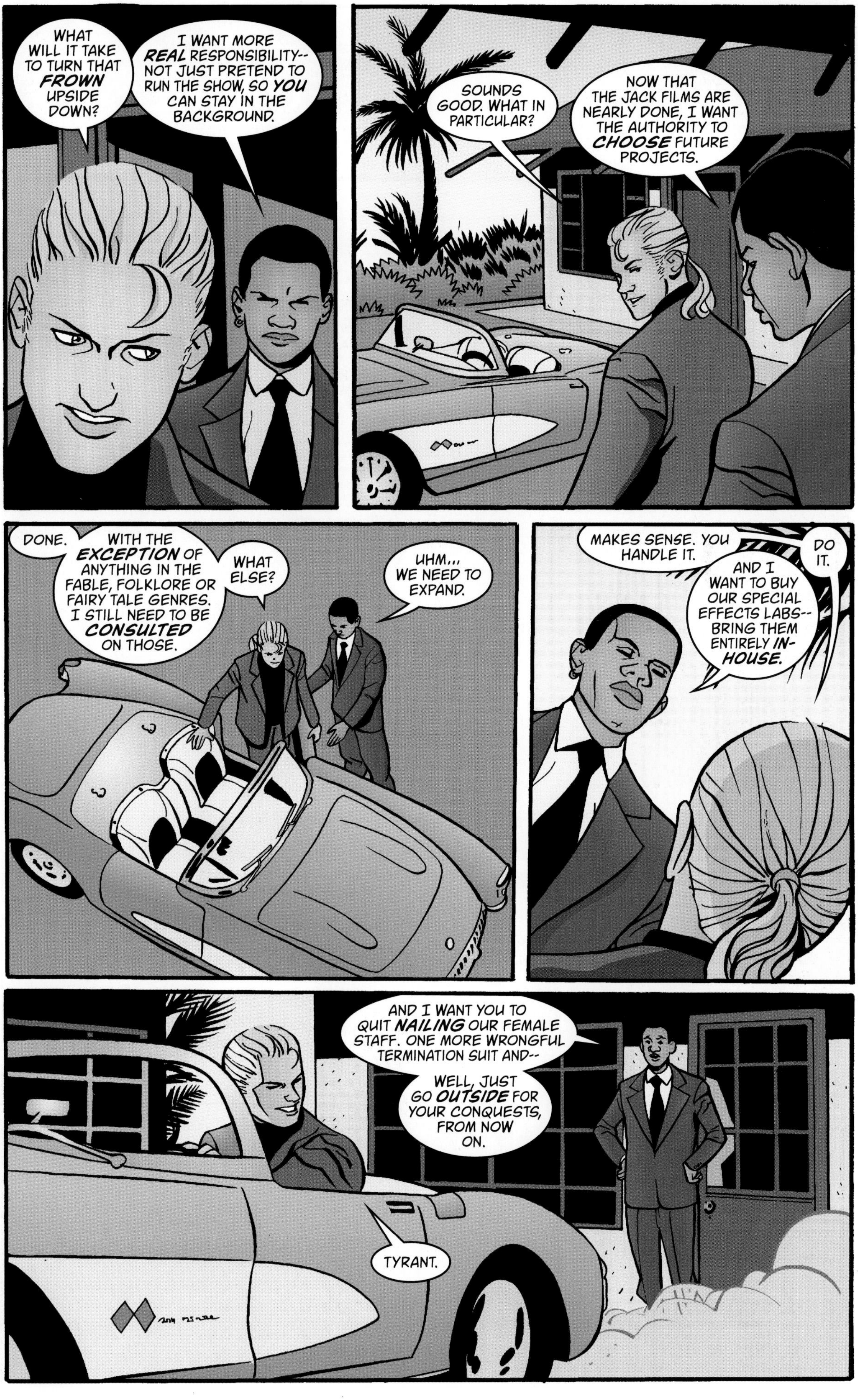
WHAT WILL IT TAKE TO TURN THAT FROWN UPSIDE DOWN?
I WANT MORE REAL RESPONSIBILITY-- NOT JUST PRETEND TO RUN THE SHOW, SO YOU CAN STAY IN THE BACKGROUND.
SOUNDS GOOD. WHAT IN PARTICULAR?
NOW THAT THE JACK FILMS ARE NEARLY DONE, I WANT THE AUTHORITY TO CHOOSE FUTURE PROJECTS.
DONE.
WITH THE EXCEPTION OF ANYTHING IN THE FABLE, FOLKLORE OR FAIRY TALE GENRES. I STILL NEED TO BE CONSULTED ON THOSE.
WHAT ELSE?
UHM... WE NEED TO EXPAND.
MAKES SENSE. YOU HANDLE IT.
AND I WANT TO BUY OUR SPECIAL EFFECTS LABS-- BRING THEM ENTIRELY IN-HOUSE.
DO IT.
AND I WANT YOU TO QUIT NAILING OUR FEMALE STAFF. ONE MORE WRONGFUL TERMINATION SUIT AND--
WELL, JUST GO OUTSIDE FOR YOUR CONQUESTS, FROM NOW ON.
TYRANT.

CHAPTER SEVEN: THE FURTHER ADVENTURES OF JILL

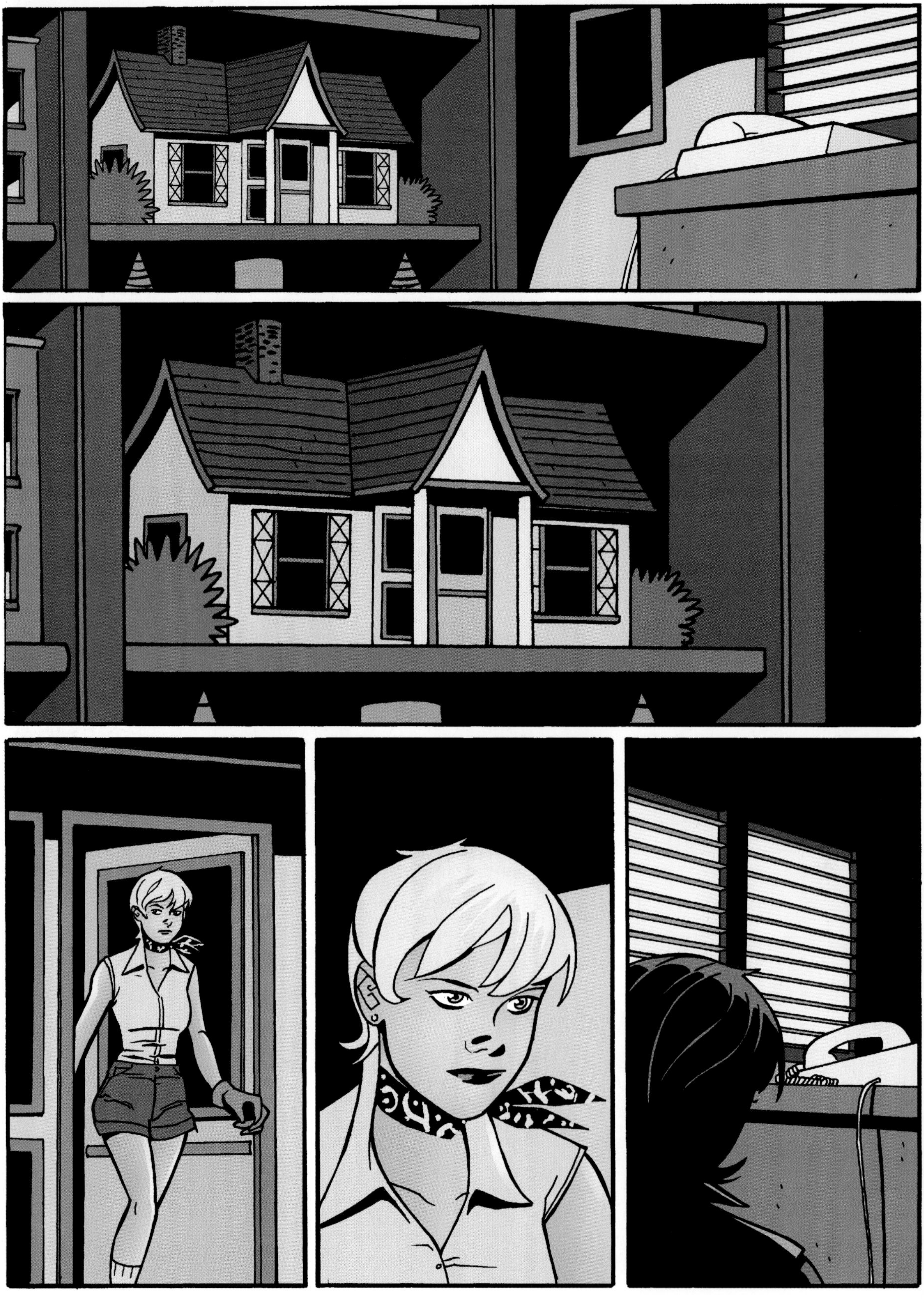

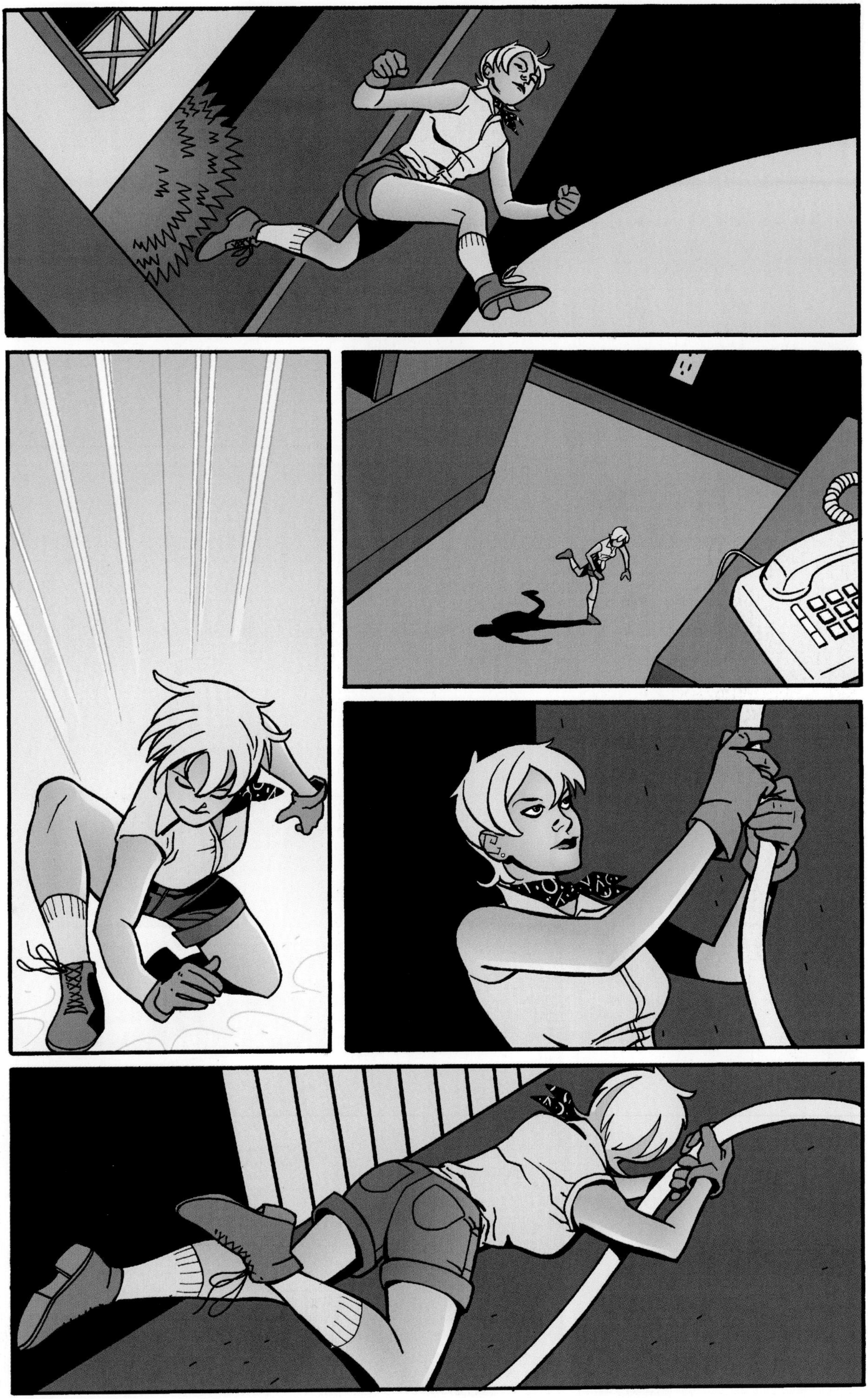

OKAY, LIFT, GIRL!

AND PUSH!

WAY TO GO, HOT MAMA!

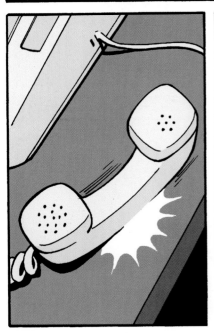

NOW FOR THE TRICKY PART--

--DIALING.

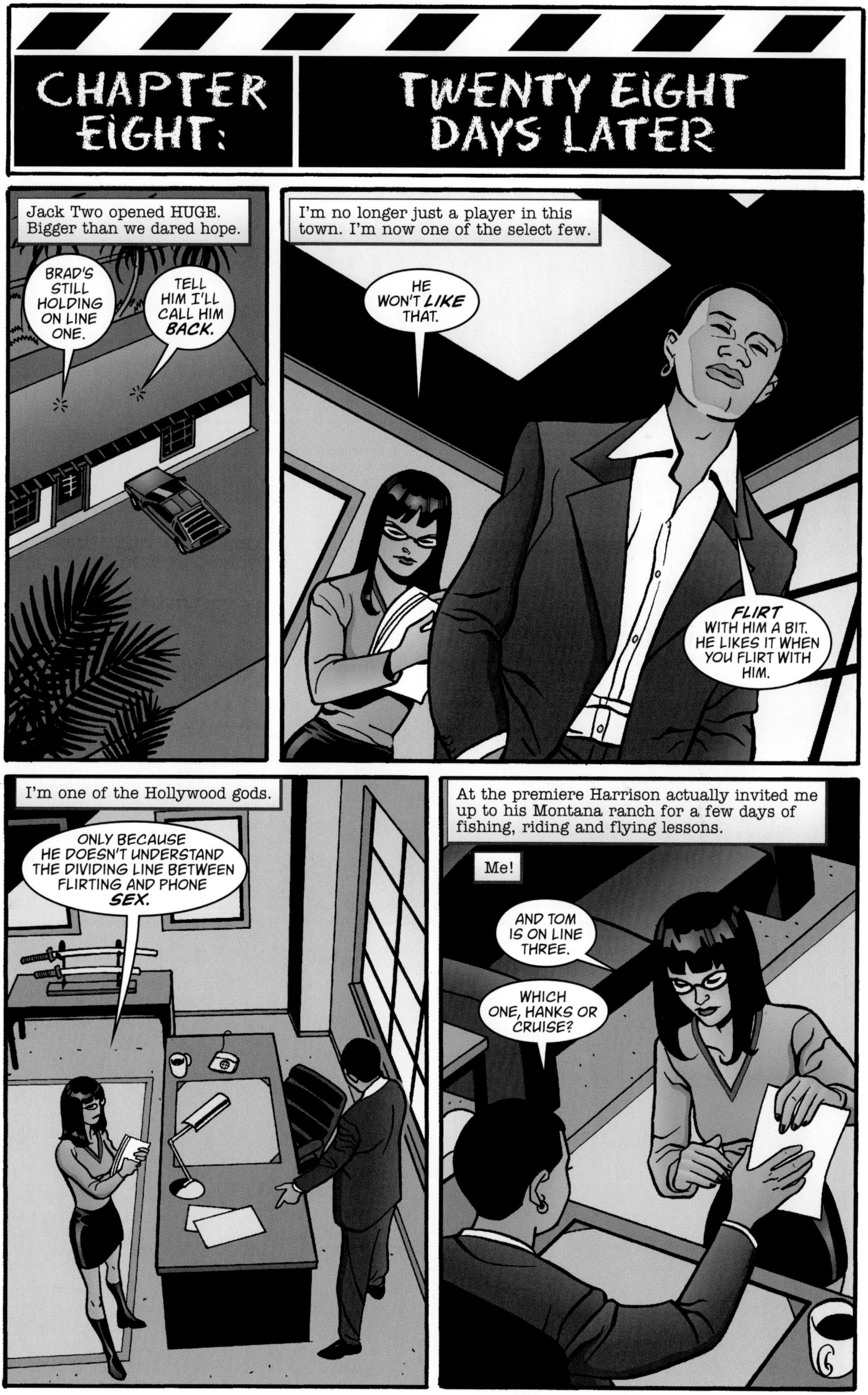
CHAPTER EIGHT:
TWENTY EIGHT DAYS LATER
Jack Two opened HUGE. Bigger than we dared hope.
BRAD'S STILL HOLDING ON LINE ONE.
TELL HIM I'LL CALL HIM BACK.
I'm no longer just a player in this town. I'm now one of the select few.
HE WON'T LIKE THAT.
FLIRT WITH HIM A BIT. HE LIKES IT WHEN YOU FLIRT WITH HIM.
I'm one of the Hollywood gods.
ONLY BECAUSE HE DOESN'T UNDERSTAND THE DIVIDING LINE BETWEEN FLIRTING AND PHONE SEX.
At the premiere Harrison actually invited me up to his Montana ranch for a few days of fishing, riding and flying lessons.
Me!
AND TOM IS ON LINE THREE.
WHICH ONE, HANKS OR CRUISE?

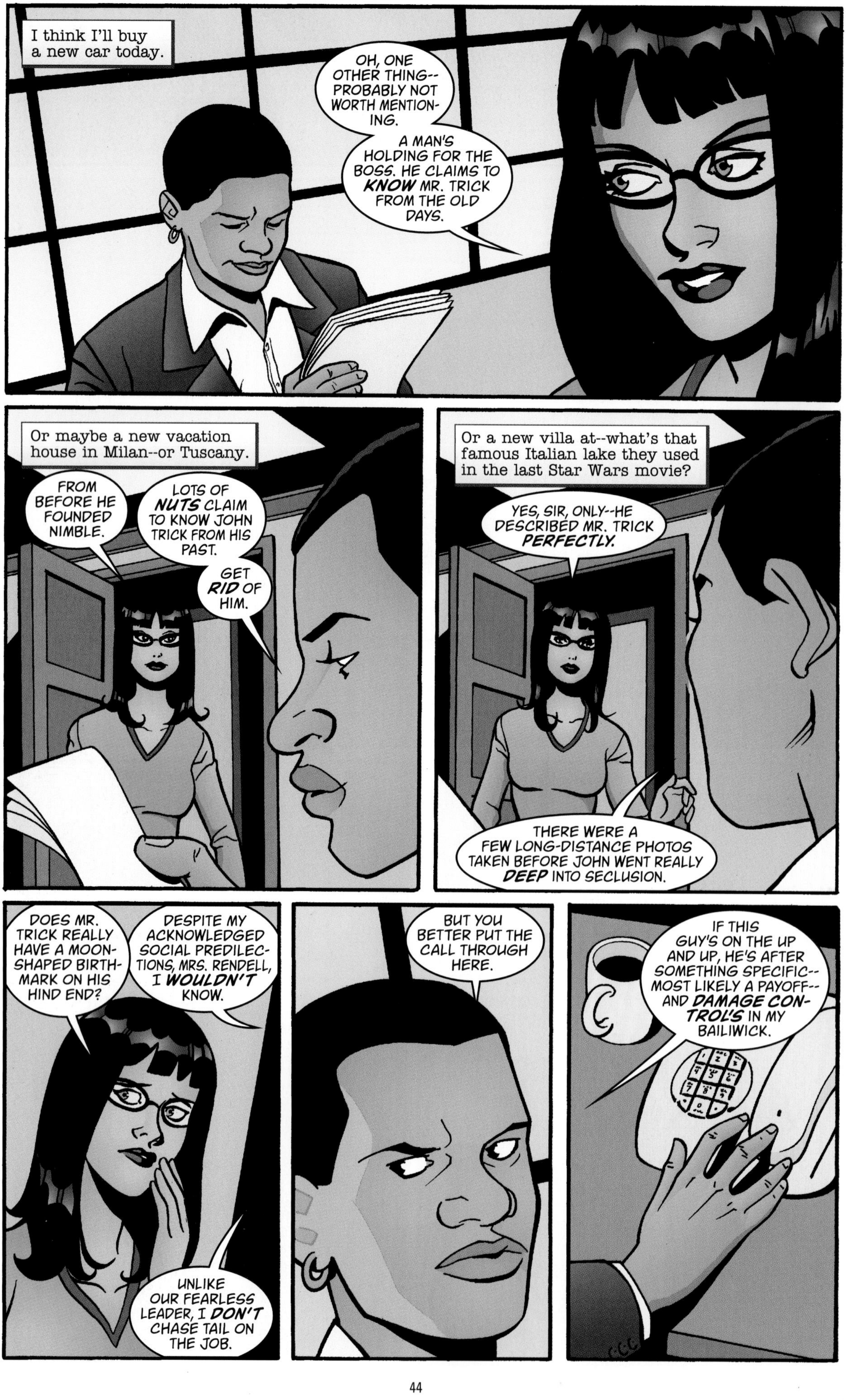
I think I'll buy a new car today.
OH, ONE OTHER THING--PROBABLY NOT WORTH MENTIONING.
A MAN'S HOLDING FOR THE BOSS. HE CLAIMS TO KNOW MR. TRICK FROM THE OLD DAYS.
Or maybe a new vacation house in Milan--or Tuscany.
FROM BEFORE HE FOUNDED NIMBLE.
LOTS OF NUTS CLAIM TO KNOW JOHN TRICK FROM HIS PAST.
GET RID OF HIM.
Or a new villa at--what's that famous Italian lake they used in the last Star Wars movie?
YES, SIR, ONLY--HE DESCRIBED MR. TRICK PERFECTLY.
THERE WERE A FEW LONG-DISTANCE PHOTOS TAKEN BEFORE JOHN WENT REALLY DEEP INTO SECLUSION.
DOES MR. TRICK REALLY HAVE A MOON-SHAPED BIRTHMARK ON HIS HIND END?
DESPITE MY ACKNOWLEDGED SOCIAL PREDILECTIONS, MRS. RENDELL, I WOULDN'T KNOW.
UNLIKE OUR FEARLESS LEADER, I DON'T CHASE TAIL ON THE JOB.
BUT YOU BETTER PUT THE CALL THROUGH HERE.
IF THIS GUY'S ON THE UP AND UP, HE'S AFTER SOMETHING SPECIFIC--MOST LIKELY A PAYOFF--AND DAMAGE CONTROL'S IN MY BAILIWICK.

CHAPTER NINE: TUMBLING AFTER

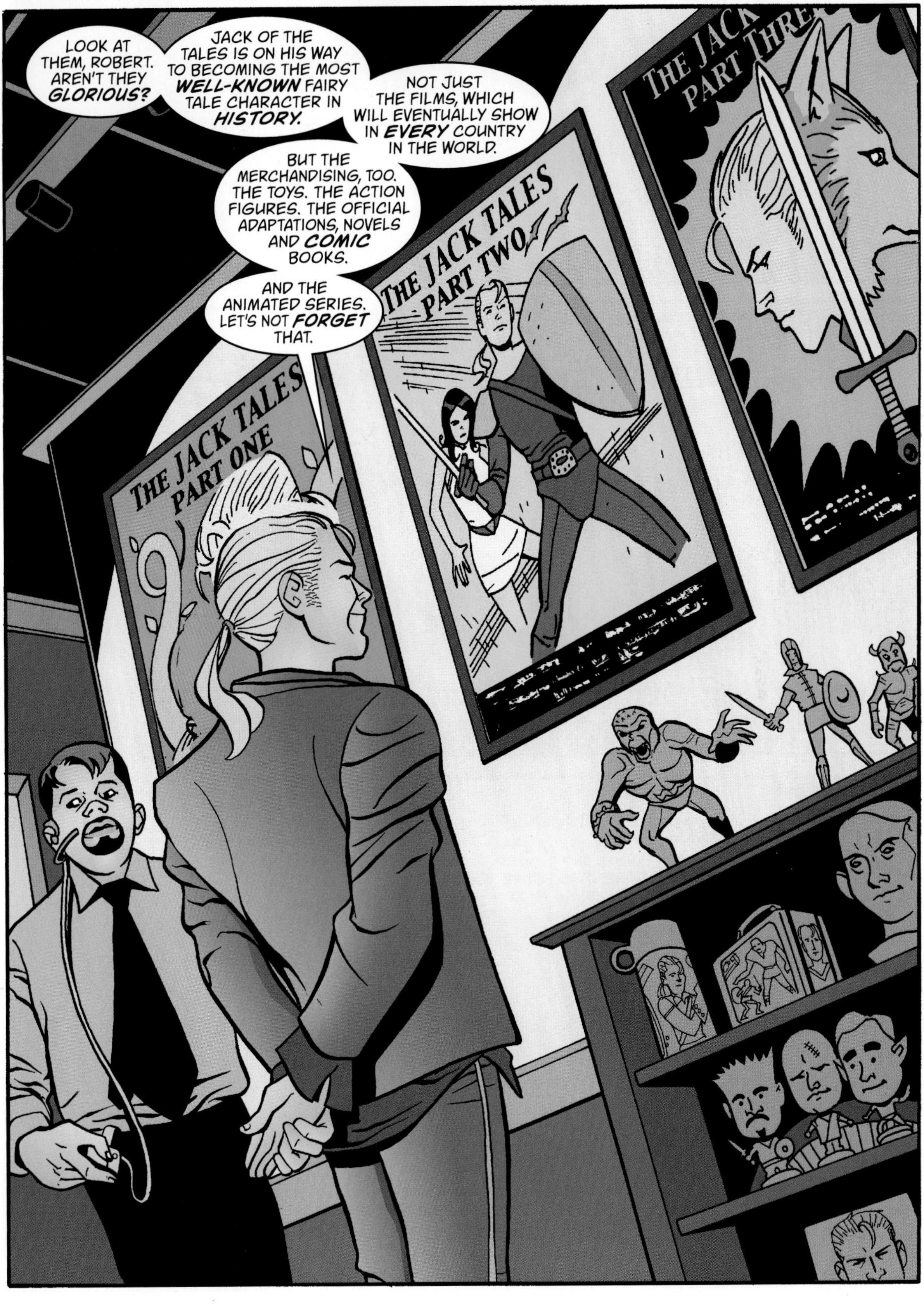
LOOK AT THEM, ROBERT. AREN'T THEY GLORIOUS?
JACK OF THE TALES IS ON HIS WAY TO BECOMING THE MOST WELL-KNOWN FAIRY TALE CHARACTER IN HISTORY.
NOT JUST THE FILMS, WHICH WILL EVENTUALLY SHOW IN EVERY COUNTRY IN THE WORLD.
BUT THE MERCHANDISING, TOO. THE TOYS. THE ACTION FIGURES. THE OFFICIAL ADAPTATIONS, NOVELS AND COMIC BOOKS.
AND THE ANIMATED SERIES. LET'S NOT FORGET THAT.
THE JACK TALES PART ONE
THE JACK TALES PART TWO
THE JACK PART THREE

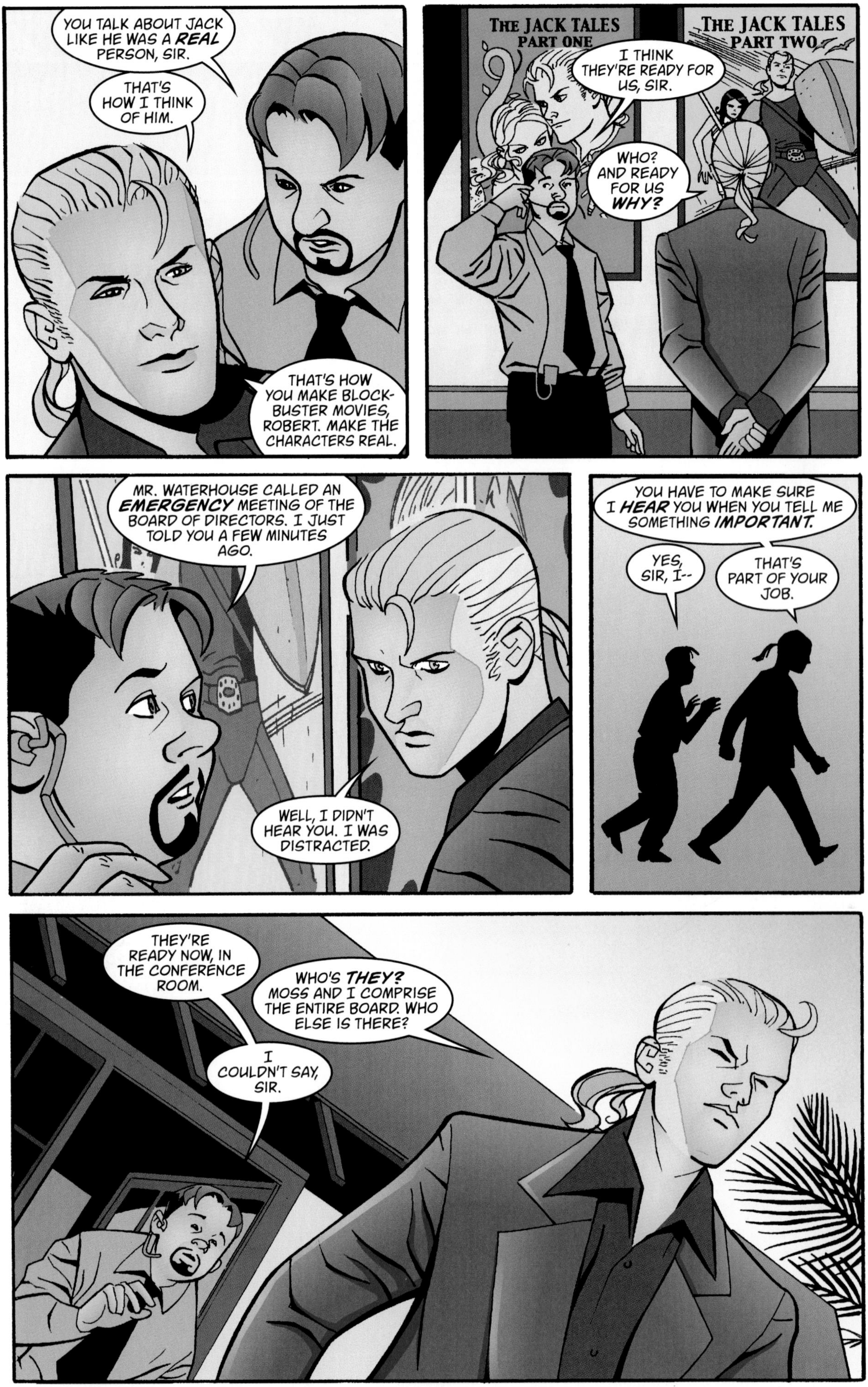

YOU TALK ABOUT JACK LIKE HE WAS A *REAL* PERSON, SIR.
THAT'S HOW I THINK OF HIM.
THAT'S HOW YOU MAKE BLOCK-BUSTER MOVIES, ROBERT. MAKE THE CHARACTERS REAL.
THE JACK TALES PART ONE
THE JACK TALES PART TWO
I THINK THEY'RE READY FOR US, SIR.
WHO? AND READY FOR US *WHY?*
MR. WATERHOUSE CALLED AN *EMERGENCY* MEETING OF THE BOARD OF DIRECTORS. I JUST TOLD YOU A FEW MINUTES AGO.
WELL, I DIDN'T HEAR YOU. I WAS DISTRACTED.
YOU HAVE TO MAKE SURE I *HEAR* YOU WHEN YOU TELL ME SOMETHING *IMPORTANT.*
YES, SIR, I--
THAT'S PART OF YOUR JOB.
THEY'RE READY NOW, IN THE CONFERENCE ROOM.
WHO'S *THEY?* MOSS AND I COMPRISE THE ENTIRE BOARD. WHO ELSE IS THERE?
I COULDN'T SAY, SIR.

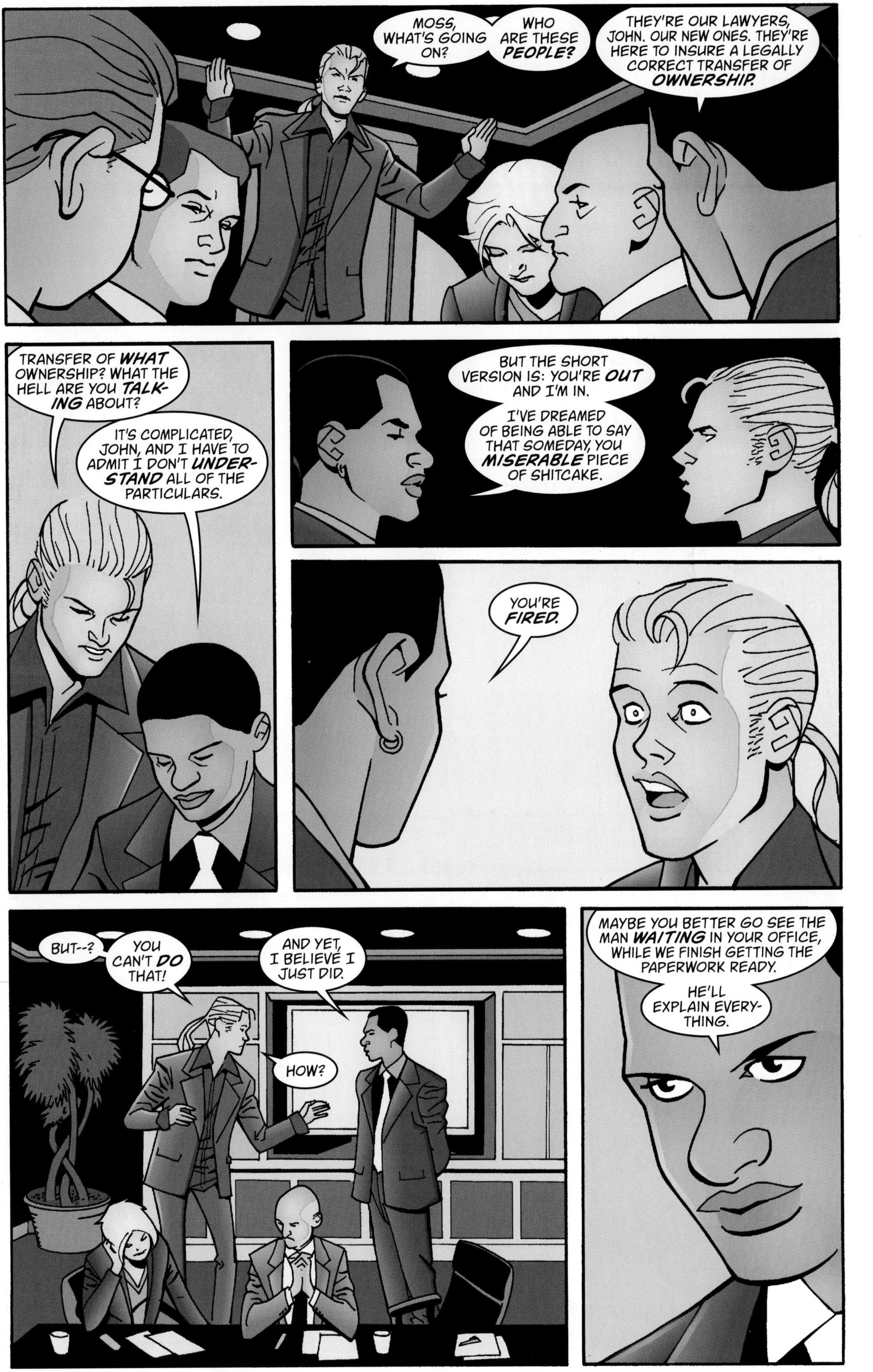

MOSS, WHAT'S GOING ON?
WHO ARE THESE *PEOPLE?*
THEY'RE OUR LAWYERS, JOHN. OUR NEW ONES. THEY'RE HERE TO INSURE A LEGALLY CORRECT TRANSFER OF *OWNERSHIP.*
TRANSFER OF *WHAT* OWNERSHIP? WHAT THE HELL ARE YOU *TALKING* ABOUT?
IT'S COMPLICATED, JOHN, AND I HAVE TO ADMIT I DON'T *UNDERSTAND* ALL OF THE PARTICULARS.
BUT THE SHORT VERSION IS: YOU'RE *OUT* AND I'M IN.
I'VE DREAMED OF BEING ABLE TO SAY THAT SOMEDAY, YOU *MISERABLE* PIECE OF SHITCAKE.
YOU'RE *FIRED.*
BUT--?
YOU CAN'T *DO* THAT!
AND YET, I BELIEVE I JUST DID.
HOW?
MAYBE YOU BETTER GO SEE THE MAN *WAITING* IN YOUR OFFICE, WHILE WE FINISH GETTING THE PAPERWORK READY.
HE'LL EXPLAIN EVERYTHING.

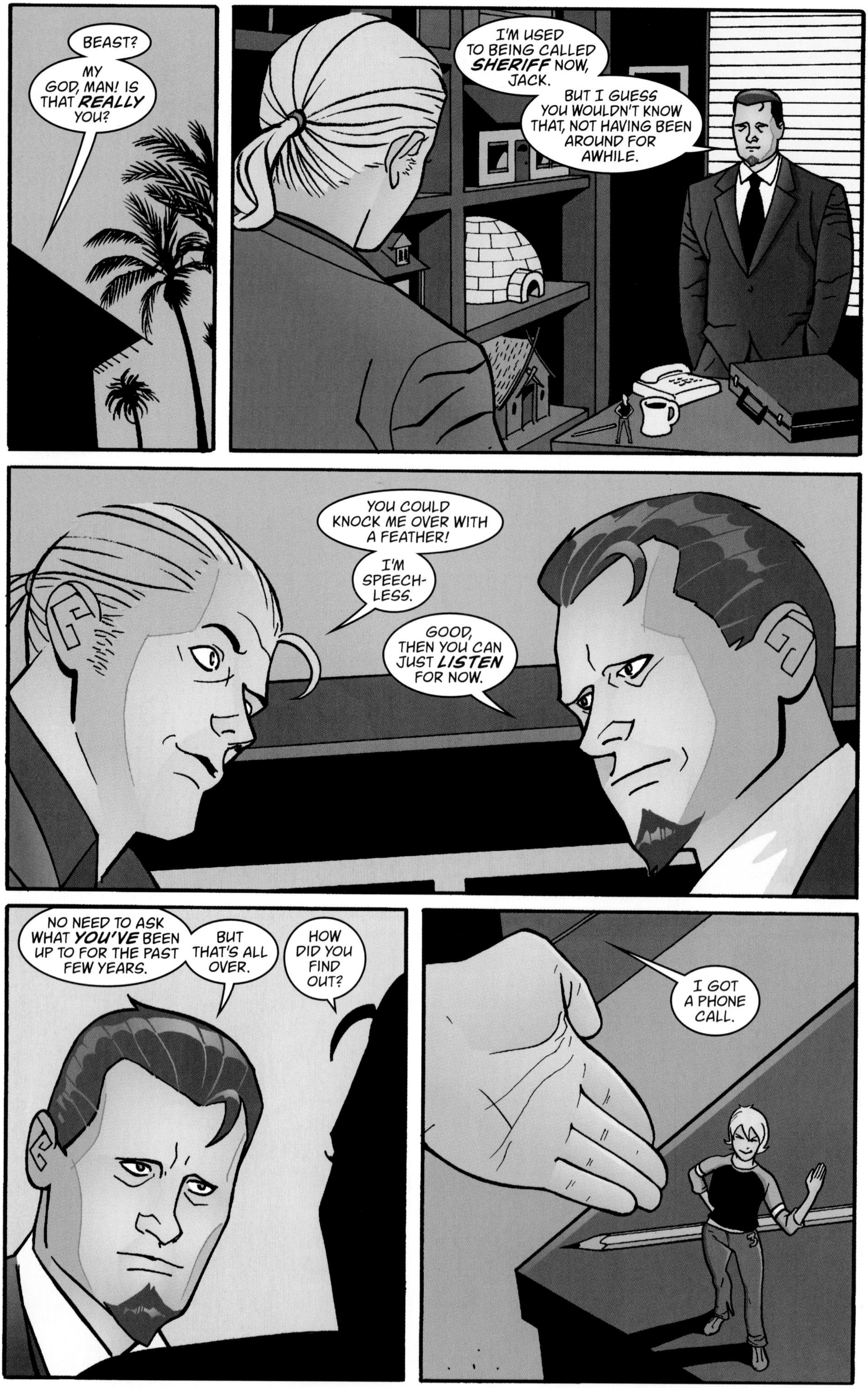

BEAST?
MY GOD, MAN! IS THAT REALLY YOU?
I'M USED TO BEING CALLED SHERIFF NOW, JACK.
BUT I GUESS YOU WOULDN'T KNOW THAT, NOT HAVING BEEN AROUND FOR AWHILE.
YOU COULD KNOCK ME OVER WITH A FEATHER!
I'M SPEECH-LESS.
GOOD, THEN YOU CAN JUST LISTEN FOR NOW.
NO NEED TO ASK WHAT YOU'VE BEEN UP TO FOR THE PAST FEW YEARS.
BUT THAT'S ALL OVER.
HOW DID YOU FIND OUT?
I GOT A PHONE CALL.

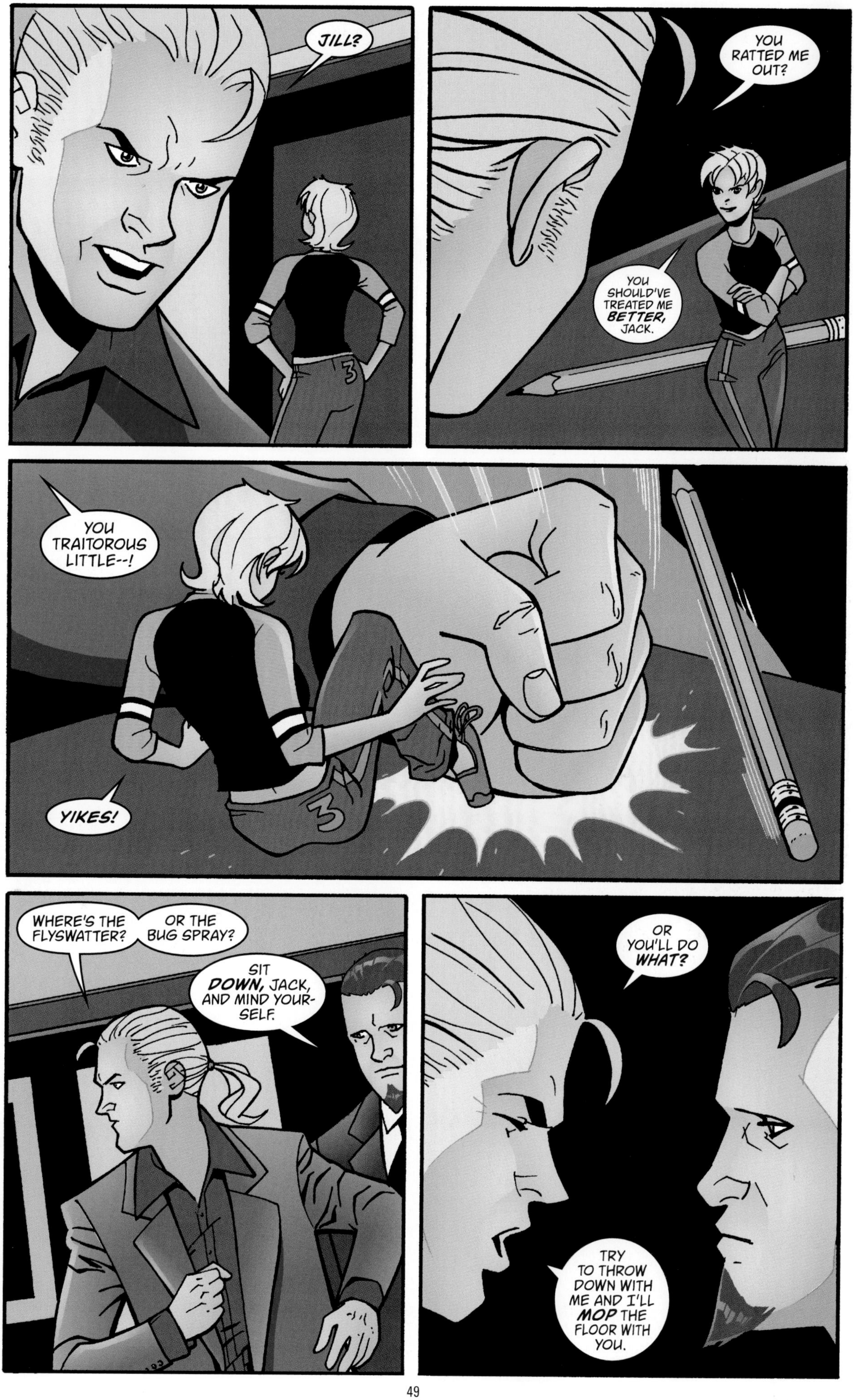
JILL?
YOU RATTED ME OUT?
YOU SHOULD'VE TREATED ME BETTER, JACK.
YOU TRAITOROUS LITTLE--!
YIKES!
WHERE'S THE FLYSWATTER?
OR THE BUG SPRAY?
SIT DOWN, JACK, AND MIND YOURSELF.
OR YOU'LL DO WHAT?
TRY TO THROW DOWN WITH ME AND I'LL MOP THE FLOOR WITH YOU.

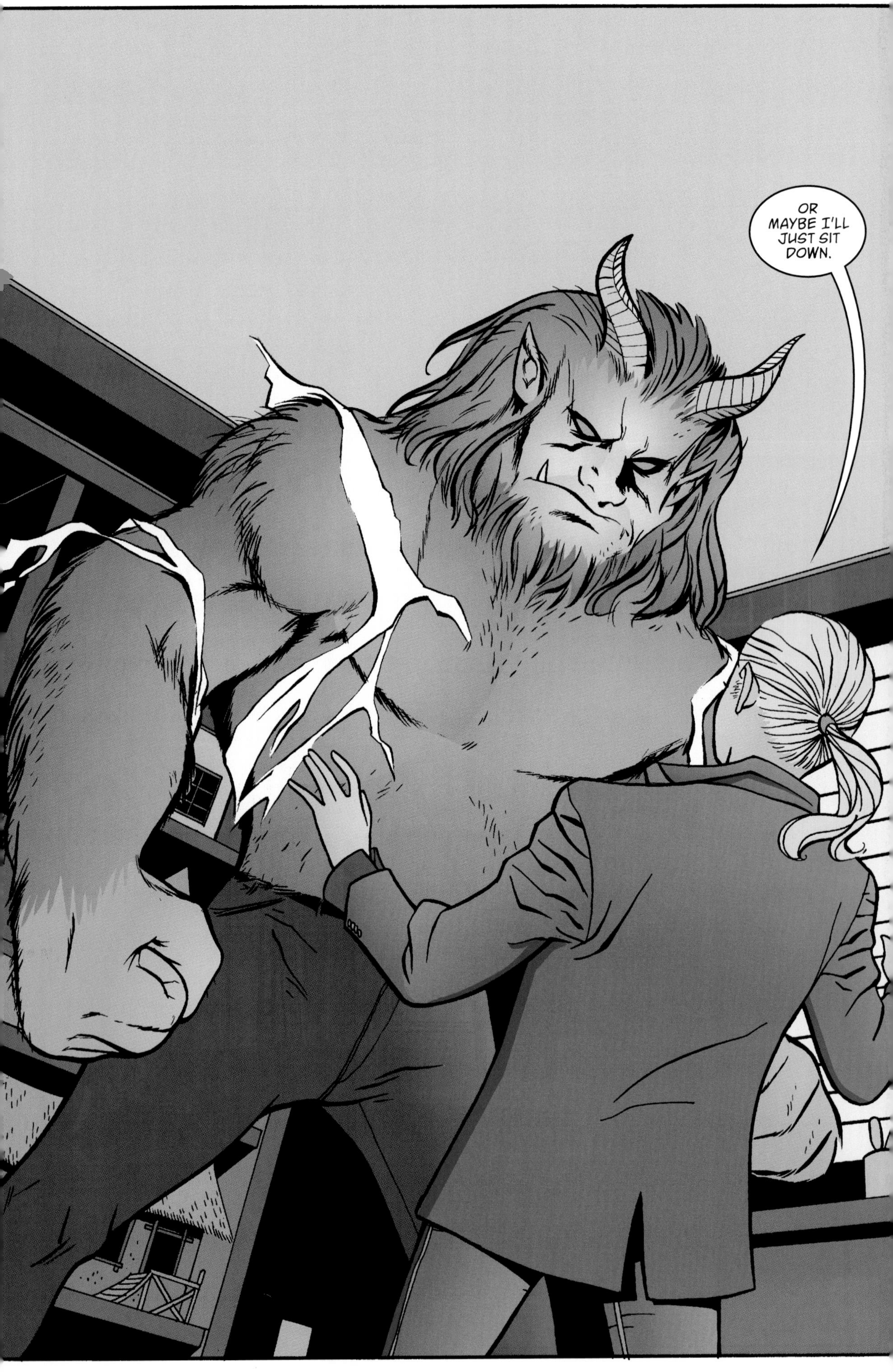
OR MAYBE I'LL JUST SIT DOWN.

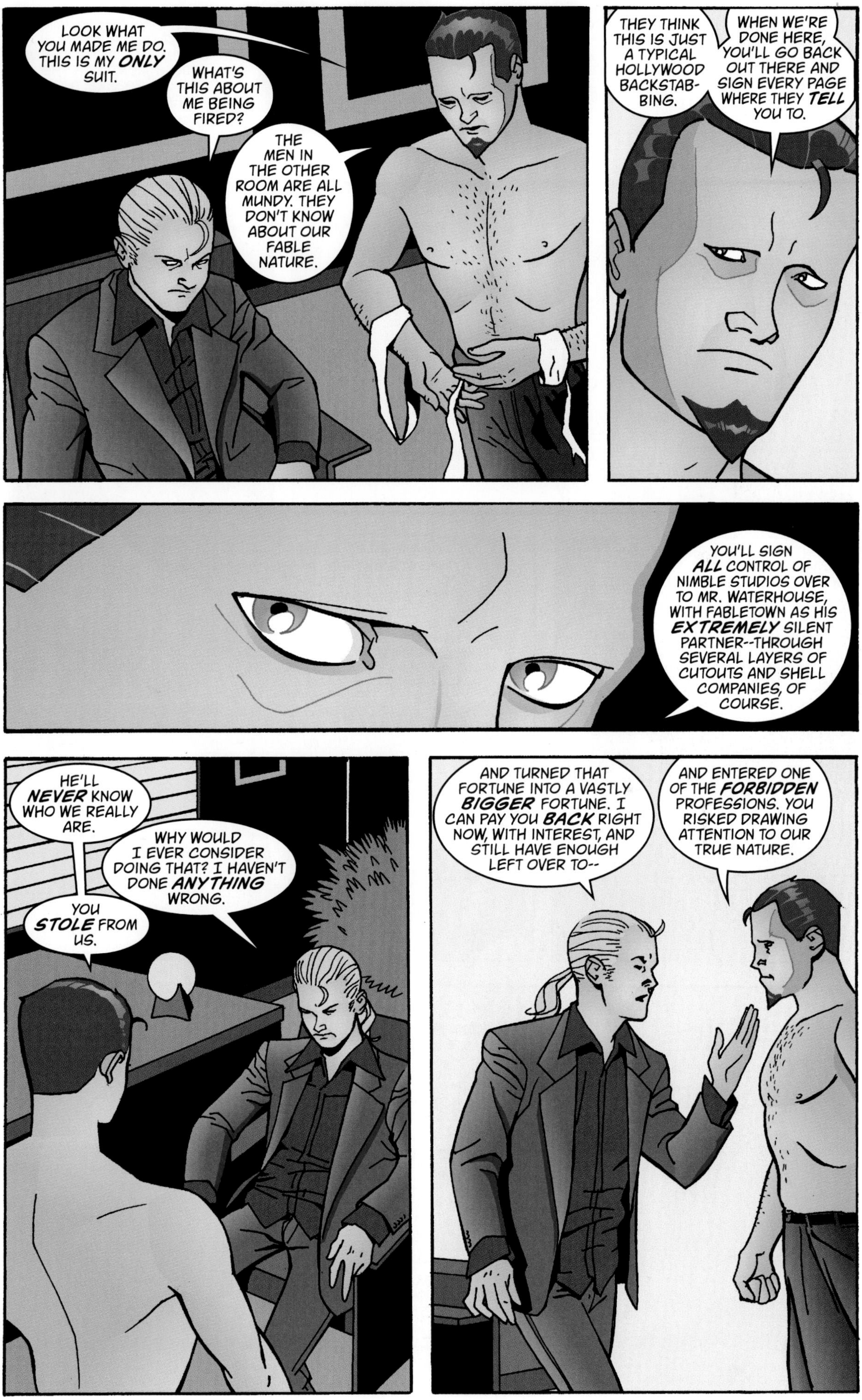
LOOK WHAT YOU MADE ME DO. THIS IS MY ONLY SUIT.
WHAT'S THIS ABOUT ME BEING FIRED?
THE MEN IN THE OTHER ROOM ARE ALL MUNDY. THEY DON'T KNOW ABOUT OUR FABLE NATURE.
THEY THINK THIS IS JUST A TYPICAL HOLLYWOOD BACKSTAB-BING.
WHEN WE'RE DONE HERE, YOU'LL GO BACK OUT THERE AND SIGN EVERY PAGE WHERE THEY TELL YOU TO.
YOU'LL SIGN ALL CONTROL OF NIMBLE STUDIOS OVER TO MR. WATERHOUSE, WITH FABLETOWN AS HIS EXTREMELY SILENT PARTNER--THROUGH SEVERAL LAYERS OF CUTOUTS AND SHELL COMPANIES, OF COURSE.
HE'LL NEVER KNOW WHO WE REALLY ARE.
WHY WOULD I EVER CONSIDER DOING THAT? I HAVEN'T DONE ANYTHING WRONG.
YOU STOLE FROM US.
AND TURNED THAT FORTUNE INTO A VASTLY BIGGER FORTUNE. I CAN PAY YOU BACK RIGHT NOW, WITH INTEREST, AND STILL HAVE ENOUGH LEFT OVER TO--
AND ENTERED ONE OF THE FORBIDDEN PROFESSIONS. YOU RISKED DRAWING ATTENTION TO OUR TRUE NATURE.

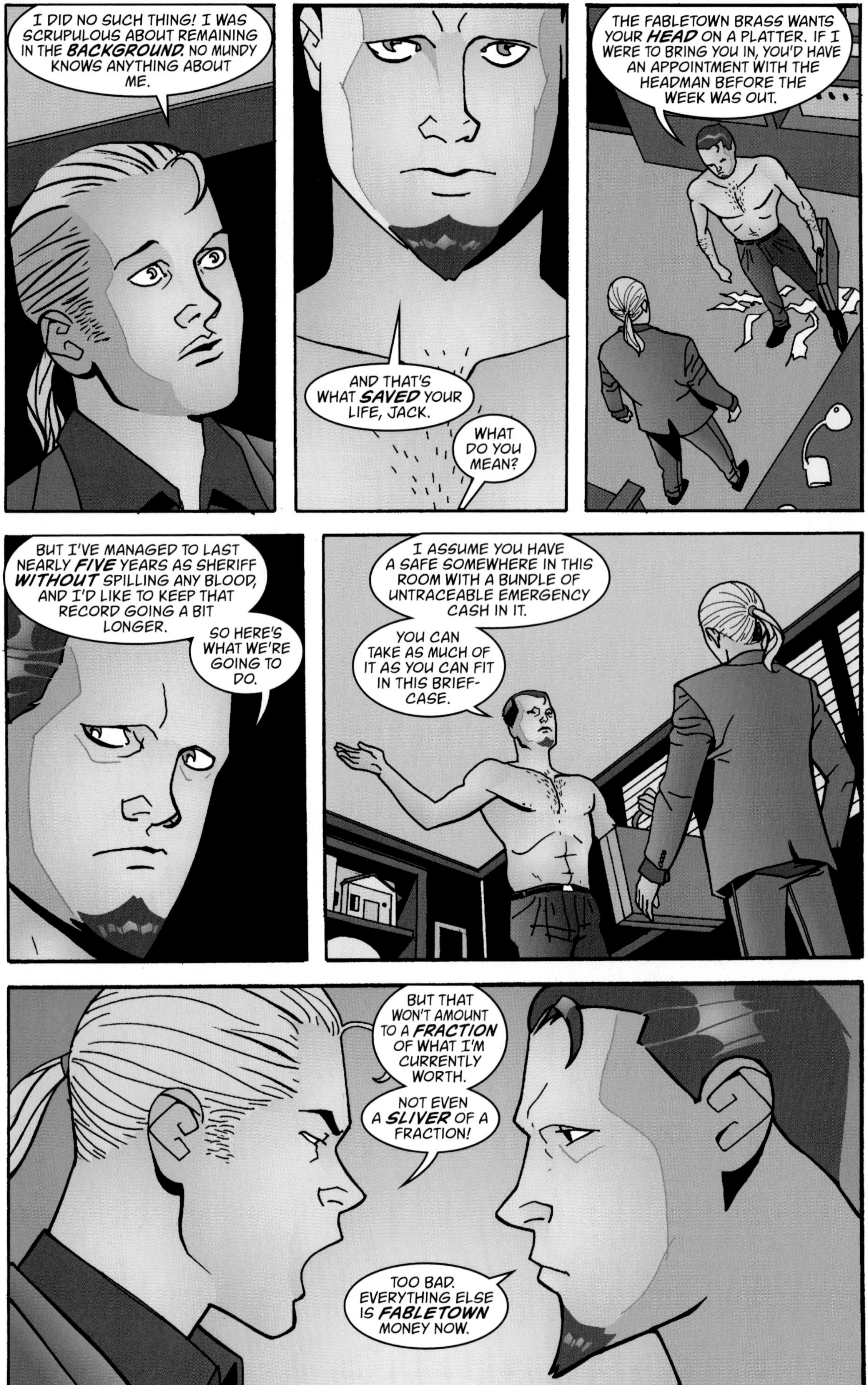

I DID NO SUCH THING! I WAS SCRUPULOUS ABOUT REMAINING IN THE BACKGROUND. NO MUNDY KNOWS ANYTHING ABOUT ME.
AND THAT'S WHAT SAVED YOUR LIFE, JACK.
WHAT DO YOU MEAN?
THE FABLETOWN BRASS WANTS YOUR HEAD ON A PLATTER. IF I WERE TO BRING YOU IN, YOU'D HAVE AN APPOINTMENT WITH THE HEADMAN BEFORE THE WEEK WAS OUT.
BUT I'VE MANAGED TO LAST NEARLY FIVE YEARS AS SHERIFF WITHOUT SPILLING ANY BLOOD, AND I'D LIKE TO KEEP THAT RECORD GOING A BIT LONGER.
SO HERE'S WHAT WE'RE GOING TO DO.
I ASSUME YOU HAVE A SAFE SOMEWHERE IN THIS ROOM WITH A BUNDLE OF UNTRACEABLE EMERGENCY CASH IN IT.
YOU CAN TAKE AS MUCH OF IT AS YOU CAN FIT IN THIS BRIEF-CASE.
BUT THAT WON'T AMOUNT TO A FRACTION OF WHAT I'M CURRENTLY WORTH.
NOT EVEN A SLIVER OF A FRACTION!
TOO BAD. EVERYTHING ELSE IS FABLETOWN MONEY NOW.

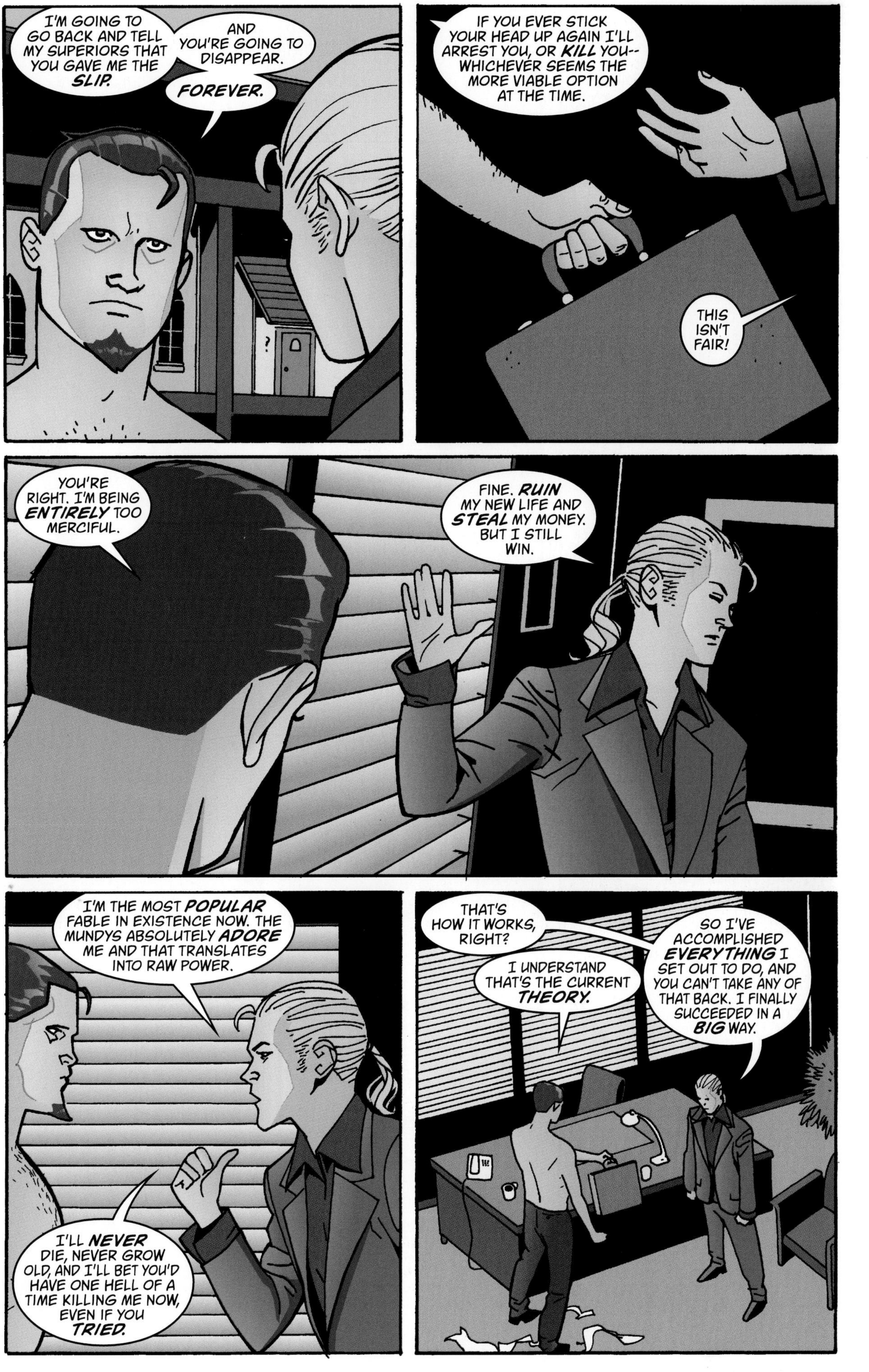
I'M GOING TO GO BACK AND TELL MY SUPERIORS THAT YOU GAVE ME THE SLIP.
AND YOU'RE GOING TO DISAPPEAR.
FOREVER.
IF YOU EVER STICK YOUR HEAD UP AGAIN I'LL ARREST YOU, OR KILL YOU-- WHICHEVER SEEMS THE MORE VIABLE OPTION AT THE TIME.
THIS ISN'T FAIR!
YOU'RE RIGHT. I'M BEING ENTIRELY TOO MERCIFUL.
FINE. RUIN MY NEW LIFE AND STEAL MY MONEY. BUT I STILL WIN.
I'M THE MOST POPULAR FABLE IN EXISTENCE NOW. THE MUNDYS ABSOLUTELY ADORE ME AND THAT TRANSLATES INTO RAW POWER.
I'LL NEVER DIE, NEVER GROW OLD, AND I'LL BET YOU'D HAVE ONE HELL OF A TIME KILLING ME NOW, EVEN IF YOU TRIED.
THAT'S HOW IT WORKS, RIGHT?
I UNDERSTAND THAT'S THE CURRENT THEORY.
SO I'VE ACCOMPLISHED EVERYTHING I SET OUT TO DO, AND YOU CAN'T TAKE ANY OF THAT BACK. I FINALLY SUCCEEDED IN A BIG WAY.

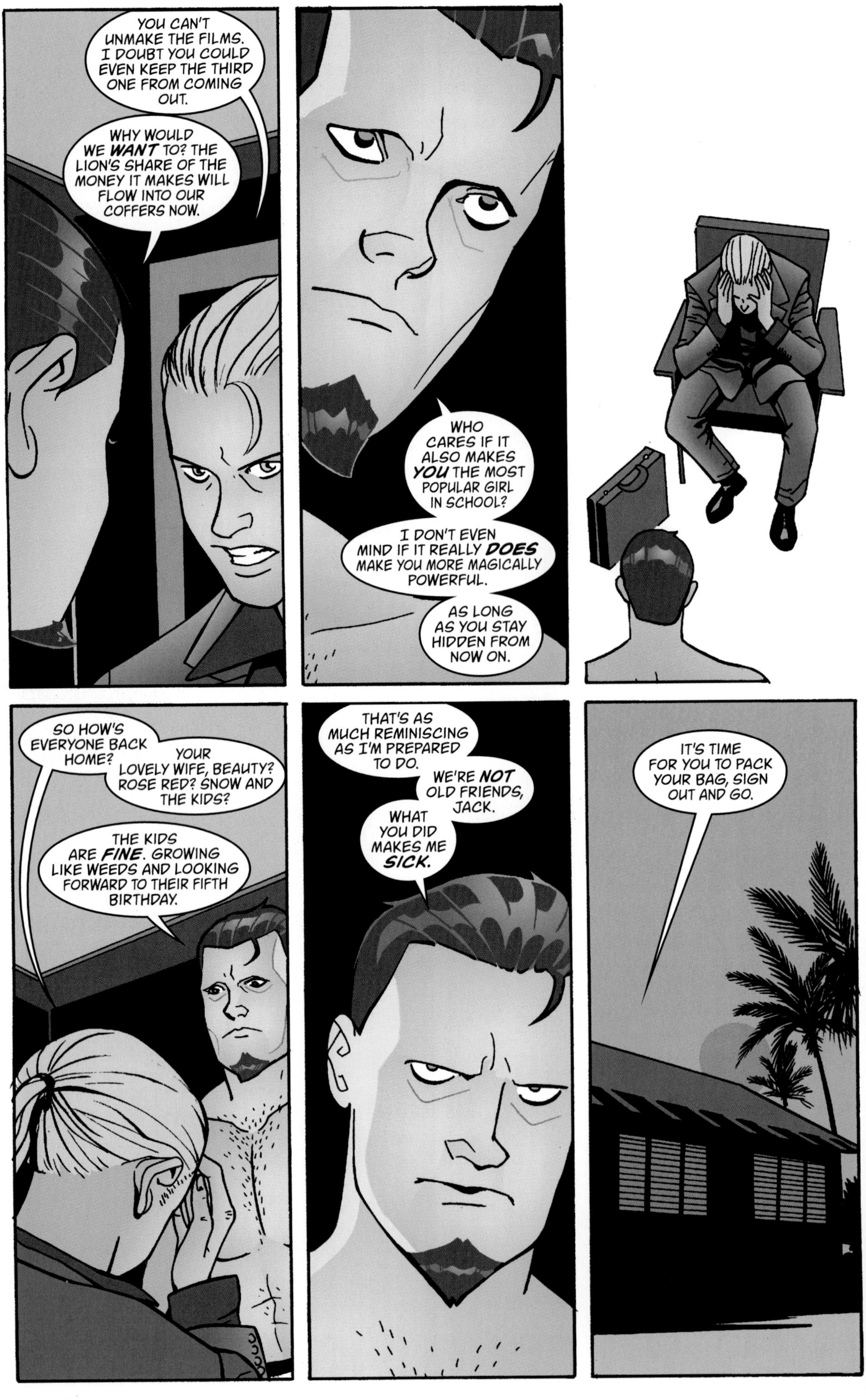
YOU CAN'T UNMAKE THE FILMS. I DOUBT YOU COULD EVEN KEEP THE THIRD ONE FROM COMING OUT.
WHY WOULD WE WANT TO? THE LION'S SHARE OF THE MONEY IT MAKES WILL FLOW INTO OUR COFFERS NOW.
WHO CARES IF IT ALSO MAKES YOU THE MOST POPULAR GIRL IN SCHOOL?
I DON'T EVEN MIND IF IT REALLY DOES MAKE YOU MORE MAGICALLY POWERFUL.
AS LONG AS YOU STAY HIDDEN FROM NOW ON.
SO HOW'S EVERYONE BACK HOME?
YOUR LOVELY WIFE, BEAUTY? ROSE RED? SNOW AND THE KIDS?
THE KIDS ARE FINE. GROWING LIKE WEEDS AND LOOKING FORWARD TO THEIR FIFTH BIRTHDAY.
THAT'S AS MUCH REMINISCING AS I'M PREPARED TO DO.
WE'RE NOT OLD FRIENDS, JACK.
WHAT YOU DID MAKES ME SICK.
IT'S TIME FOR YOU TO PACK YOUR BAG, SIGN OUT AND GO.

CHAPTER TEN: BROKEN CROWNS AND CANDLESTICKS

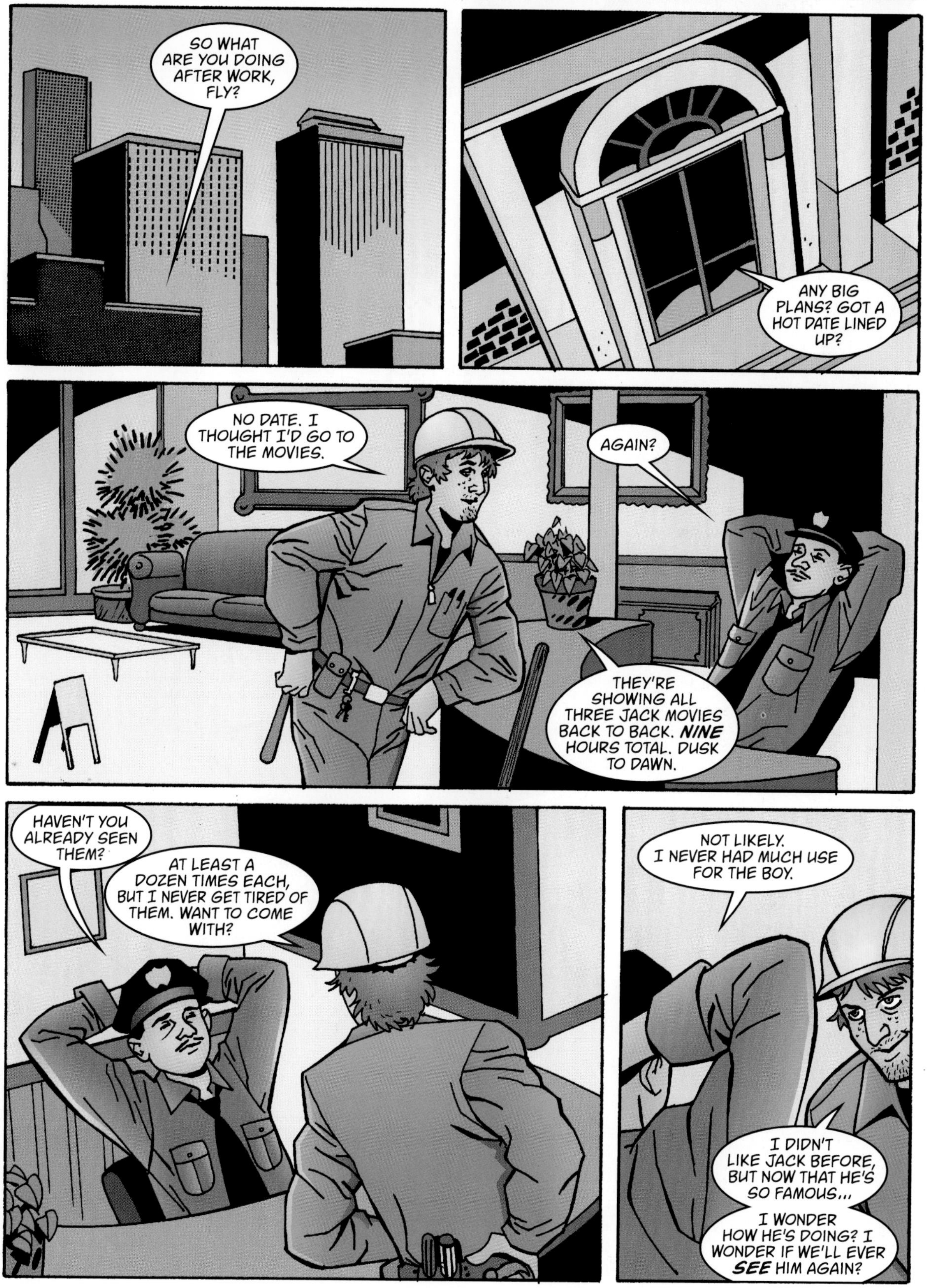

SO WHAT ARE YOU DOING AFTER WORK, FLY?
ANY BIG PLANS? GOT A HOT DATE LINED UP?
NO DATE. I THOUGHT I'D GO TO THE MOVIES.
AGAIN?
THEY'RE SHOWING ALL THREE JACK MOVIES BACK TO BACK. *NINE* HOURS TOTAL. DUSK TO DAWN.
HAVEN'T YOU ALREADY SEEN THEM?
AT LEAST A DOZEN TIMES EACH, BUT I NEVER GET TIRED OF THEM. WANT TO COME WITH?
NOT LIKELY. I NEVER HAD MUCH USE FOR THE BOY.
I DIDN'T LIKE JACK BEFORE, BUT NOW THAT HE'S SO FAMOUS...
I WONDER HOW HE'S DOING? I WONDER IF WE'LL EVER *SEE* HIM AGAIN?

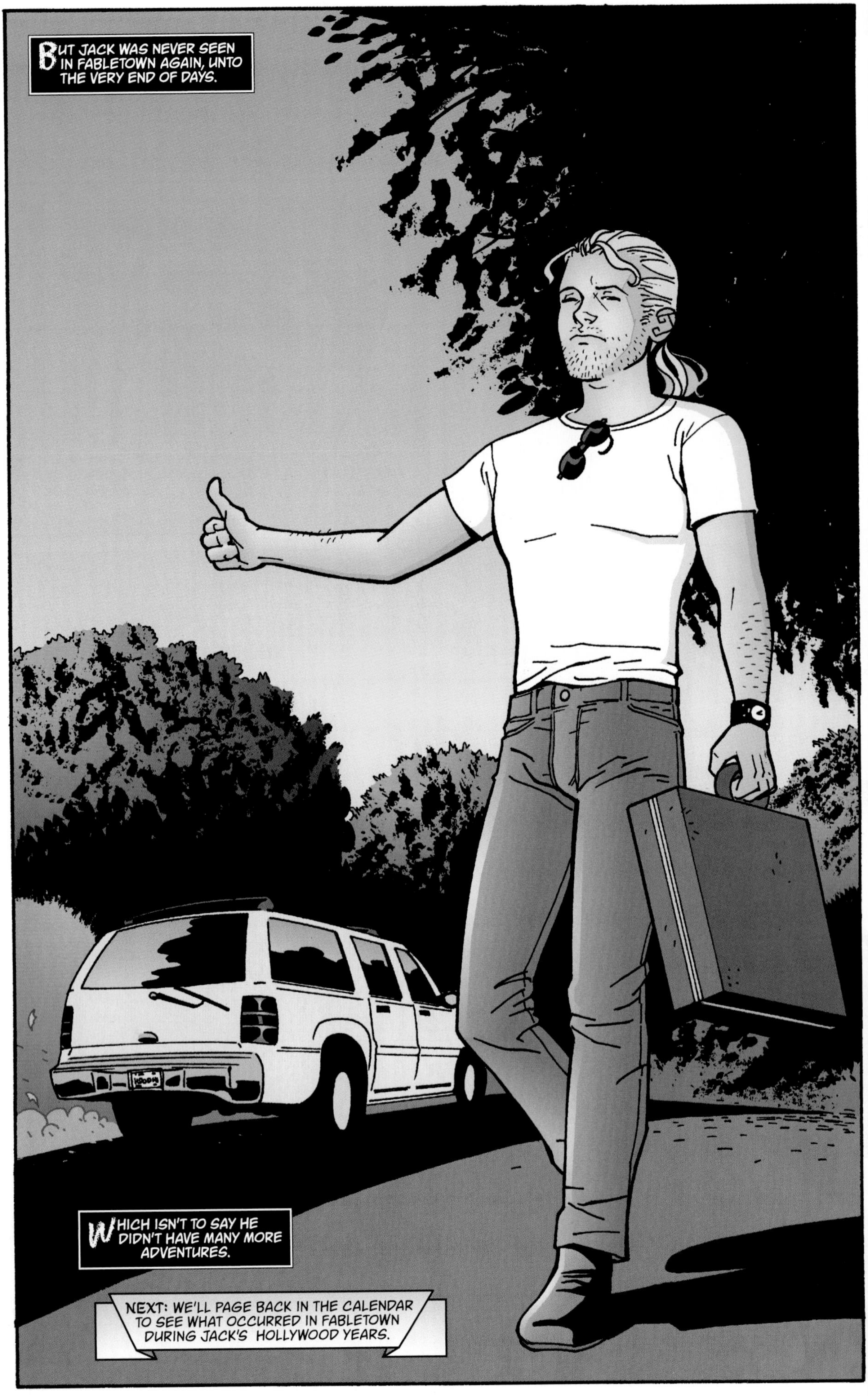

BUT JACK WAS NEVER SEEN IN FABLETOWN AGAIN, UNTO THE VERY END OF DAYS.
WHICH ISN'T TO SAY HE DIDN'T HAVE MANY MORE ADVENTURES.
NEXT: WE'LL PAGE BACK IN THE CALENDAR TO SEE WHAT OCCURRED IN FABLETOWN DURING JACK'S HOLLYWOOD YEARS.

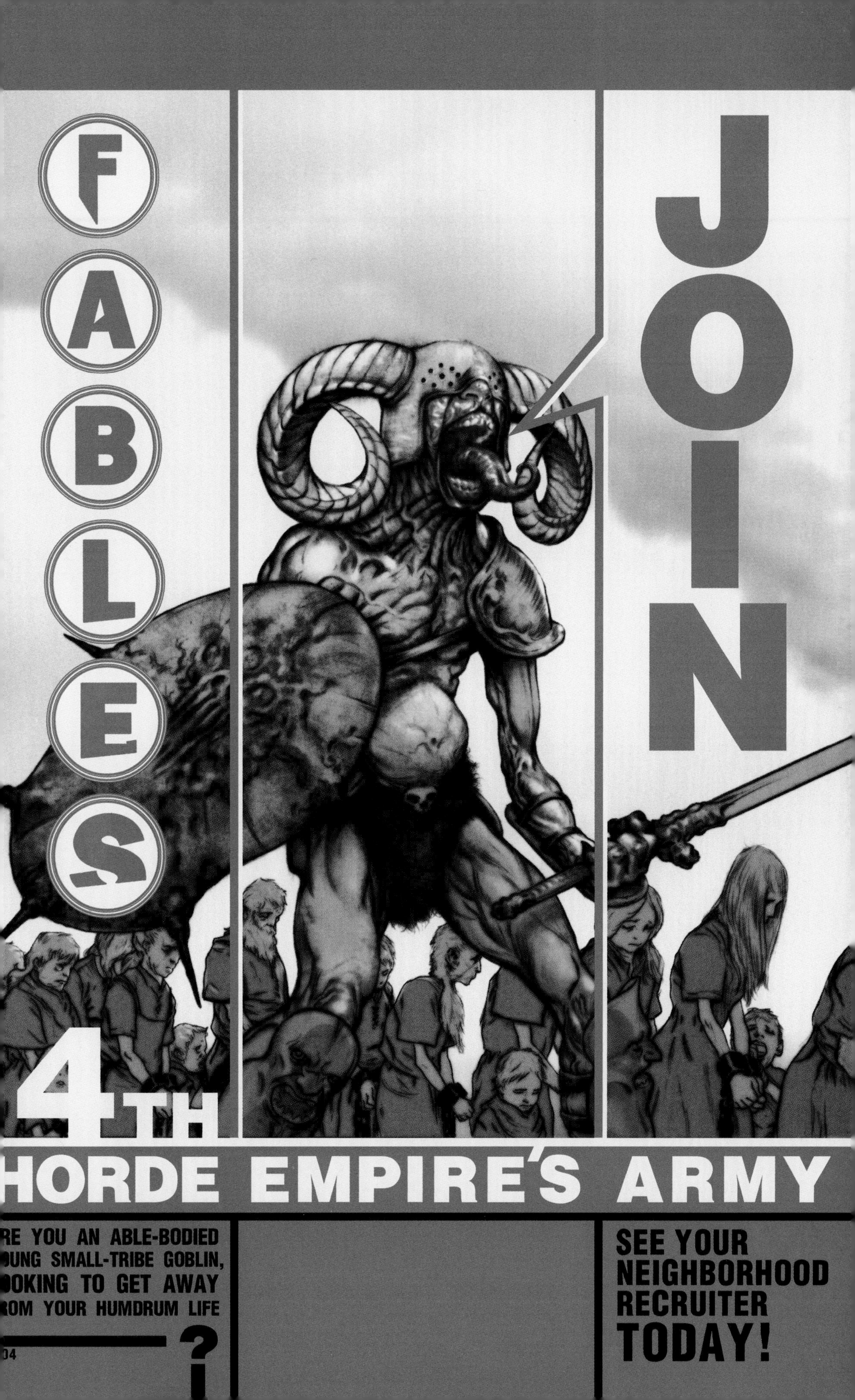
FABLES
JOIN
4TH
HORDE EMPIRE'S ARMY
RE YOU AN ABLE-BODIED
OUNG SMALL-TRIBE GOBLIN,
OOKING TO GET AWAY
ROM YOUR HUMDRUM LIFE
?
SEE YOUR NEIGHBORHOOD RECRUITER TODAY!

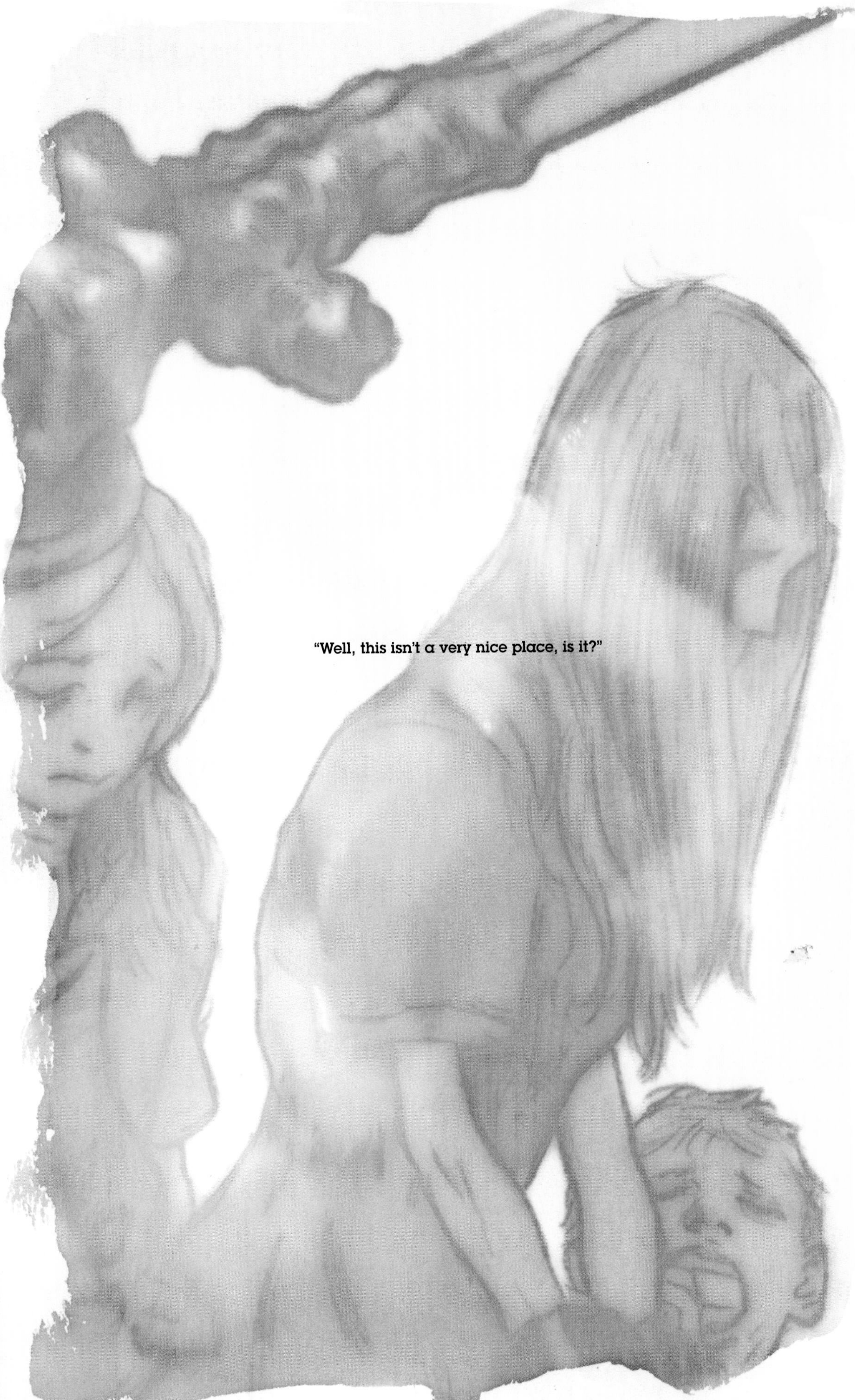

"Well, this isn't a very nice place, is it?"

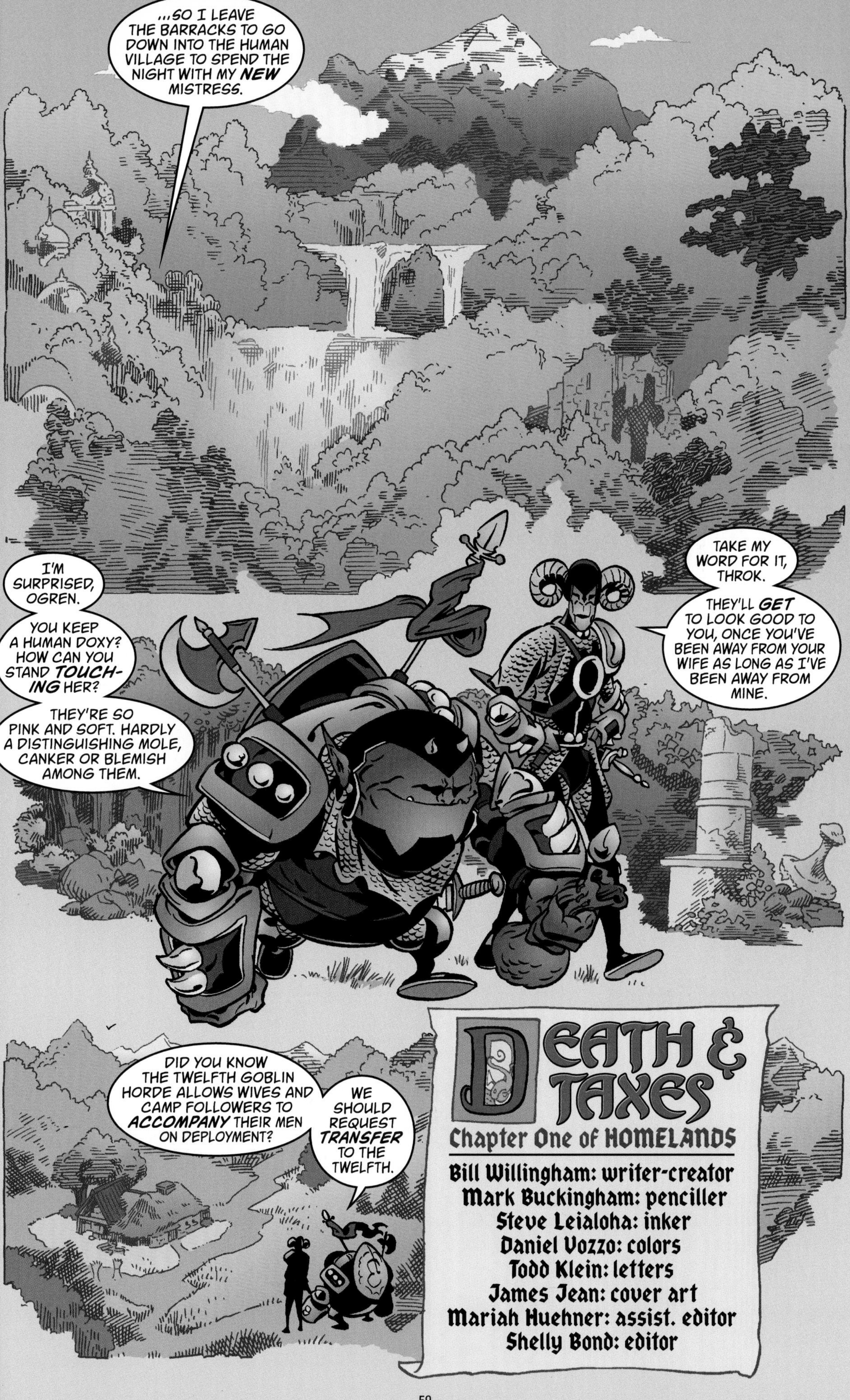
...SO I LEAVE THE BARRACKS TO GO DOWN INTO THE HUMAN VILLAGE TO SPEND THE NIGHT WITH MY NEW MISTRESS.
I'M SURPRISED, OGREN.
YOU KEEP A HUMAN DOXY? HOW CAN YOU STAND TOUCHING HER?
THEY'RE SO PINK AND SOFT. HARDLY A DISTINGUISHING MOLE, CANKER OR BLEMISH AMONG THEM.
TAKE MY WORD FOR IT, THROK.
THEY'LL GET TO LOOK GOOD TO YOU, ONCE YOU'VE BEEN AWAY FROM YOUR WIFE AS LONG AS I'VE BEEN AWAY FROM MINE.
DID YOU KNOW THE TWELFTH GOBLIN HORDE ALLOWS WIVES AND CAMP FOLLOWERS TO ACCOMPANY THEIR MEN ON DEPLOYMENT?
WE SHOULD REQUEST TRANSFER TO THE TWELFTH.
DEATH & TAXES
Chapter One of HOMELANDS
Bill Willingham: writer-creator
Mark Buckingham: penciller
Steve Leialoha: inker
Daniel Vozzo: colors
Todd Klein: letters
James Jean: cover art
Mariah Huehner: assist. editor
Shelly Bond: editor

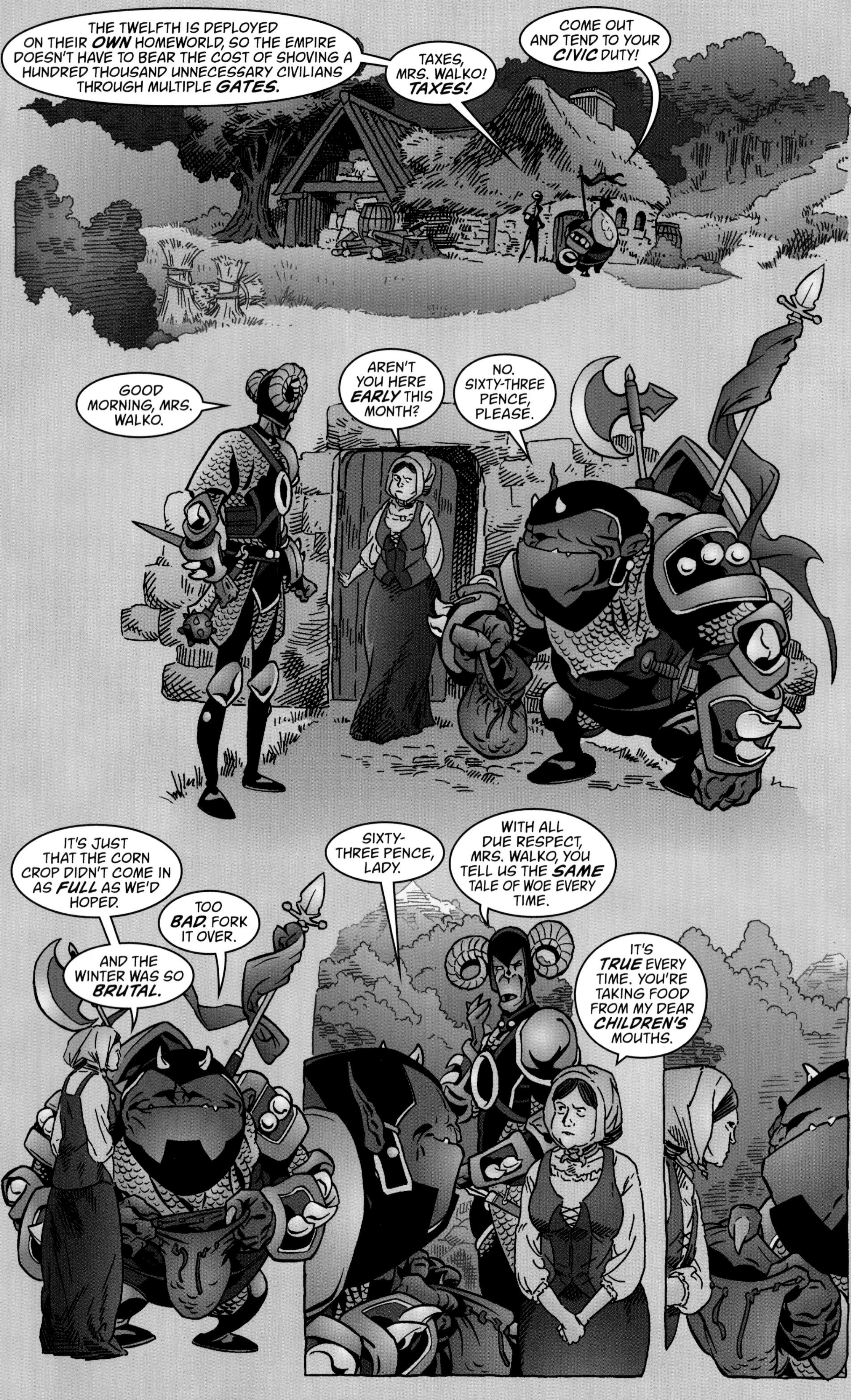
THE TWELFTH IS DEPLOYED ON THEIR *OWN* HOMEWORLD, SO THE EMPIRE DOESN'T HAVE TO BEAR THE COST OF SHOVING A HUNDRED THOUSAND UNNECESSARY CIVILIANS THROUGH MULTIPLE *GATES.*
TAXES, MRS. WALKO! *TAXES!*
COME OUT AND TEND TO YOUR *CIVIC* DUTY!
GOOD MORNING, MRS. WALKO.
AREN'T YOU HERE *EARLY* THIS MONTH?
NO. SIXTY-THREE PENCE, PLEASE.
IT'S JUST THAT THE CORN CROP DIDN'T COME IN AS *FULL* AS WE'D HOPED.
TOO *BAD.* FORK IT OVER.
AND THE WINTER WAS SO *BRUTAL.*
SIXTY-THREE PENCE, LADY.
WITH ALL DUE RESPECT, MRS. WALKO, YOU TELL US THE *SAME* TALE OF WOE EVERY TIME.
IT'S *TRUE* EVERY TIME. YOU'RE TAKING FOOD FROM MY DEAR *CHILDREN'S* MOUTHS.

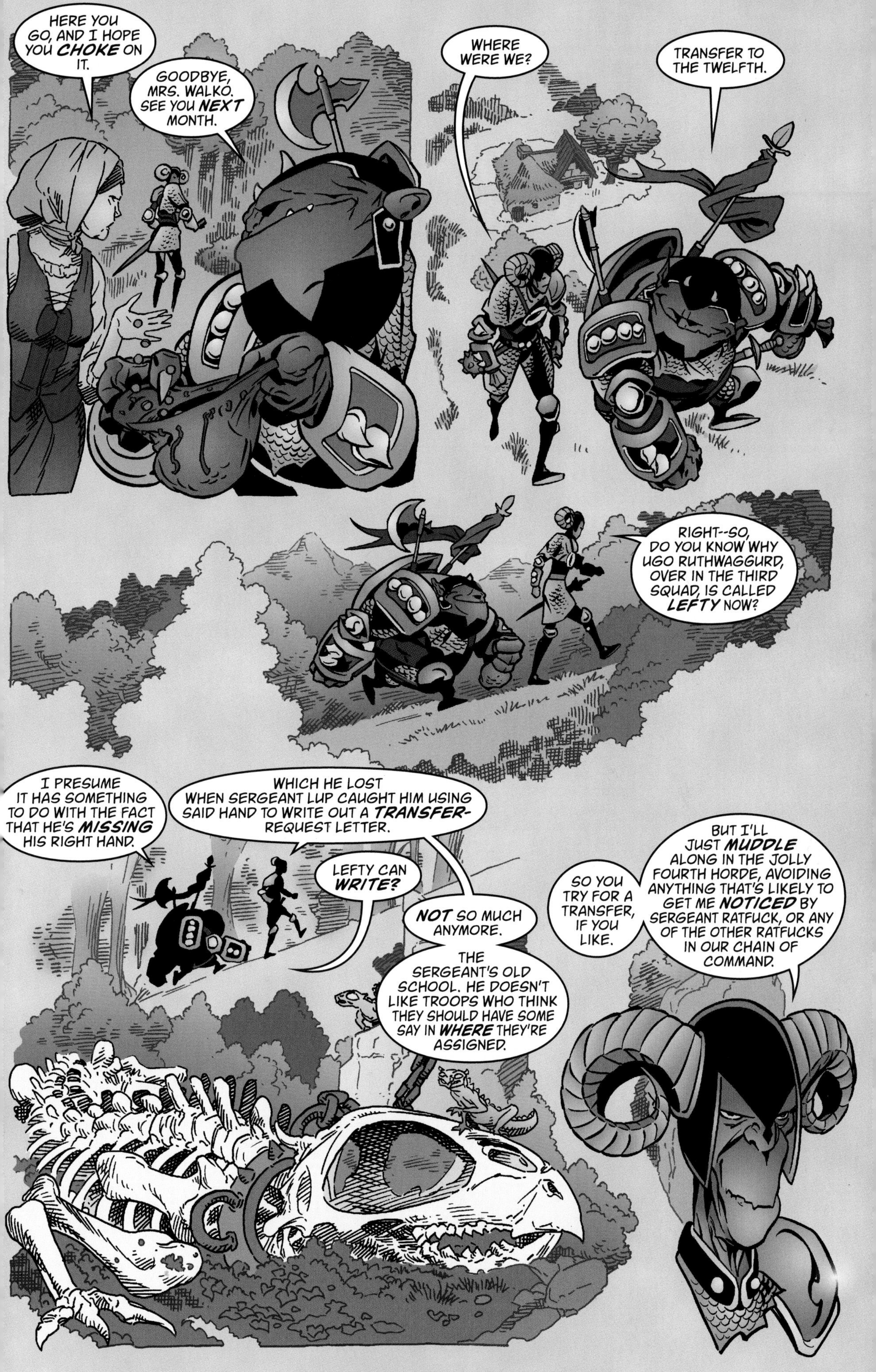
HERE YOU GO, AND I HOPE YOU CHOKE ON IT.
GOODBYE, MRS. WALKO. SEE YOU NEXT MONTH.
WHERE WERE WE?
TRANSFER TO THE TWELFTH.
RIGHT--SO, DO YOU KNOW WHY UGO RUTHWAGGURD, OVER IN THE THIRD SQUAD, IS CALLED LEFTY NOW?
I PRESUME IT HAS SOMETHING TO DO WITH THE FACT THAT HE'S MISSING HIS RIGHT HAND.
WHICH HE LOST WHEN SERGEANT LUP CAUGHT HIM USING SAID HAND TO WRITE OUT A TRANSFER-REQUEST LETTER.
LEFTY CAN WRITE?
NOT SO MUCH ANYMORE.
THE SERGEANT'S OLD SCHOOL. HE DOESN'T LIKE TROOPS WHO THINK THEY SHOULD HAVE SOME SAY IN WHERE THEY'RE ASSIGNED.
SO YOU TRY FOR A TRANSFER, IF YOU LIKE.
BUT I'LL JUST MUDDLE ALONG IN THE JOLLY FOURTH HORDE, AVOIDING ANYTHING THAT'S LIKELY TO GET ME NOTICED BY SERGEANT RATFUCK, OR ANY OF THE OTHER RATFUCKS IN OUR CHAIN OF COMMAND.

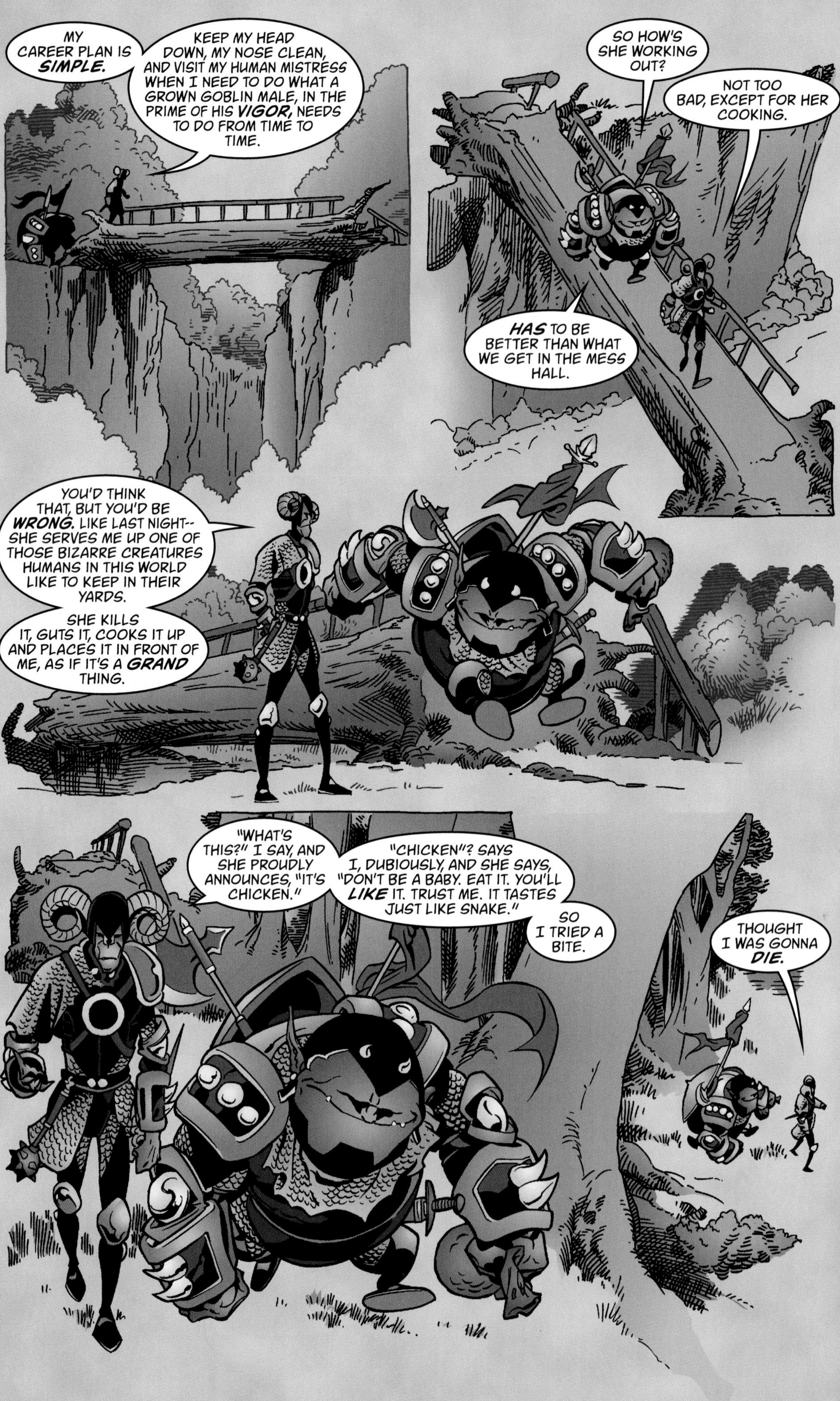
MY CAREER PLAN IS **SIMPLE.**
KEEP MY HEAD DOWN, MY NOSE CLEAN, AND VISIT MY HUMAN MISTRESS WHEN I NEED TO DO WHAT A GROWN GOBLIN MALE, IN THE PRIME OF HIS **VIGOR,** NEEDS TO DO FROM TIME TO TIME.
SO HOW'S SHE WORKING OUT?
NOT TOO BAD, EXCEPT FOR HER COOKING.
HAS TO BE BETTER THAN WHAT WE GET IN THE MESS HALL.
YOU'D THINK THAT, BUT YOU'D BE **WRONG.** LIKE LAST NIGHT-- SHE SERVES ME UP ONE OF THOSE BIZARRE CREATURES HUMANS IN THIS WORLD LIKE TO KEEP IN THEIR YARDS.
SHE KILLS IT, GUTS IT, COOKS IT UP AND PLACES IT IN FRONT OF ME, AS IF IT'S A **GRAND** THING.
"WHAT'S THIS?" I SAY, AND SHE PROUDLY ANNOUNCES, "IT'S CHICKEN."
"CHICKEN"? SAYS I, DUBIOUSLY, AND SHE SAYS, "DON'T BE A BABY. EAT IT. YOU'LL **LIKE** IT. TRUST ME. IT TASTES JUST LIKE SNAKE."
SO I TRIED A BITE.
THOUGHT I WAS GONNA **DIE.**

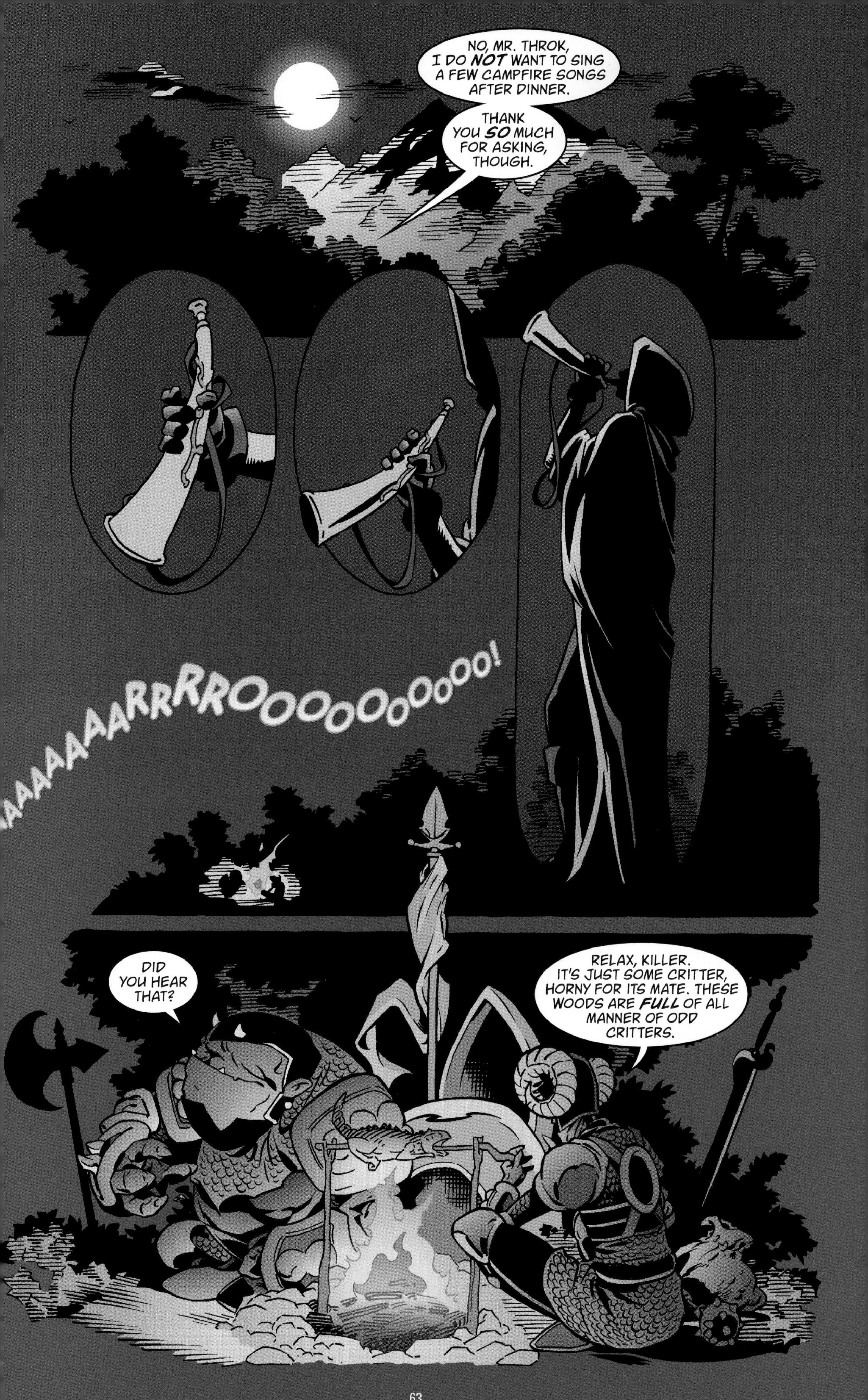
NO, MR. THROK, I DO NOT WANT TO SING A FEW CAMPFIRE SONGS AFTER DINNER.
THANK YOU SO MUCH FOR ASKING, THOUGH.
AAAAAARRRROOOOOOOOOOO!
DID YOU HEAR THAT?
RELAX, KILLER. IT'S JUST SOME CRITTER, HORNY FOR ITS MATE. THESE WOODS ARE FULL OF ALL MANNER OF ODD CRITTERS.

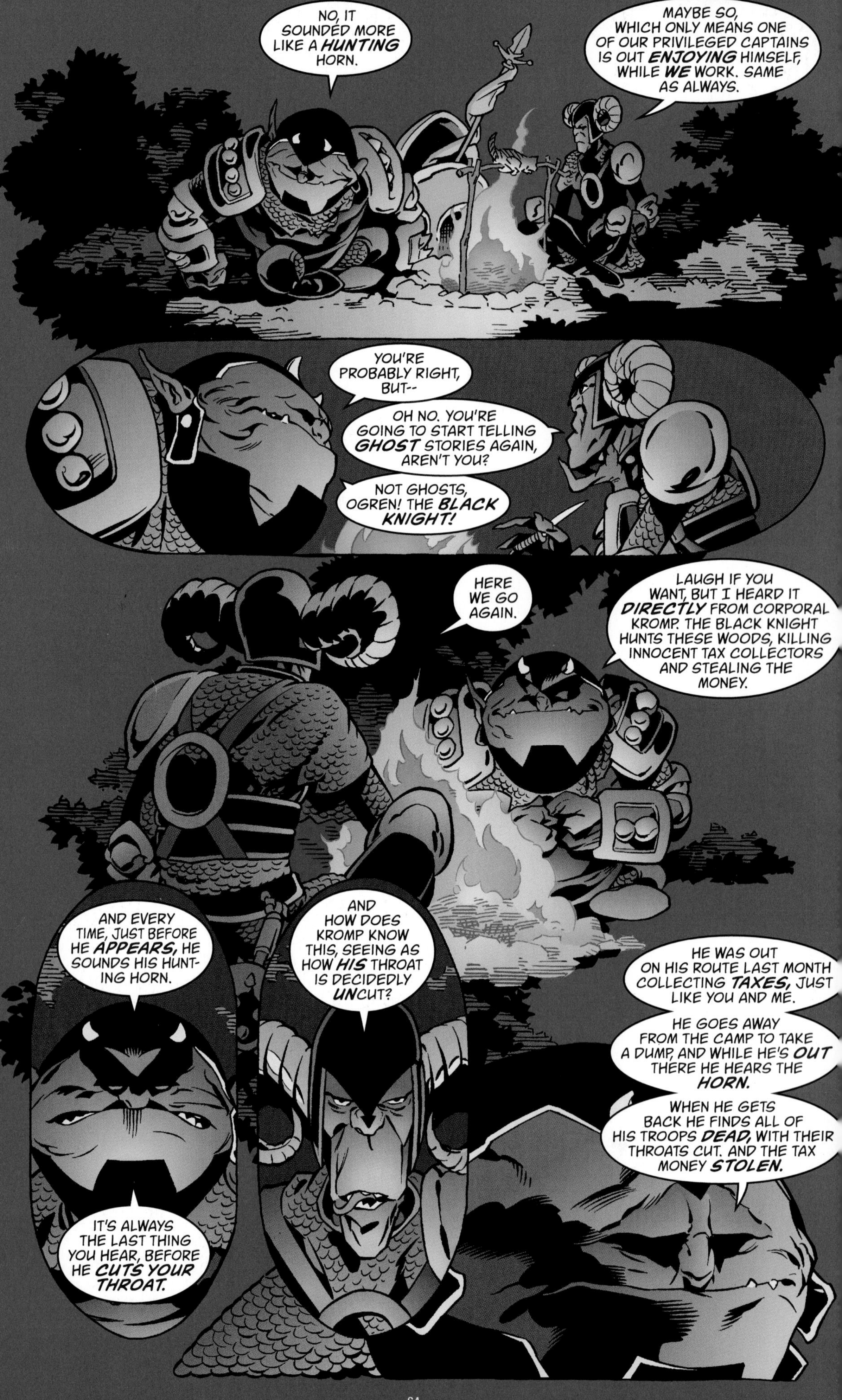
NO, IT SOUNDED MORE LIKE A HUNTING HORN.
MAYBE SO, WHICH ONLY MEANS ONE OF OUR PRIVILEGED CAPTAINS IS OUT ENJOYING HIMSELF, WHILE WE WORK. SAME AS ALWAYS.
YOU'RE PROBABLY RIGHT, BUT--
OH NO. YOU'RE GOING TO START TELLING GHOST STORIES AGAIN, AREN'T YOU?
NOT GHOSTS, OGREN! THE BLACK KNIGHT!
HERE WE GO AGAIN.
LAUGH IF YOU WANT, BUT I HEARD IT DIRECTLY FROM CORPORAL KROMP. THE BLACK KNIGHT HUNTS THESE WOODS, KILLING INNOCENT TAX COLLECTORS AND STEALING THE MONEY.
AND EVERY TIME, JUST BEFORE HE APPEARS, HE SOUNDS HIS HUNTING HORN.
IT'S ALWAYS THE LAST THING YOU HEAR, BEFORE HE CUTS YOUR THROAT.
AND HOW DOES KROMP KNOW THIS, SEEING AS HOW HIS THROAT IS DECIDEDLY UNCUT?
HE WAS OUT ON HIS ROUTE LAST MONTH COLLECTING TAXES, JUST LIKE YOU AND ME.
HE GOES AWAY FROM THE CAMP TO TAKE A DUMP, AND WHILE HE'S OUT THERE HE HEARS THE HORN.
WHEN HE GETS BACK HE FINDS ALL OF HIS TROOPS DEAD, WITH THEIR THROATS CUT. AND THE TAX MONEY STOLEN.

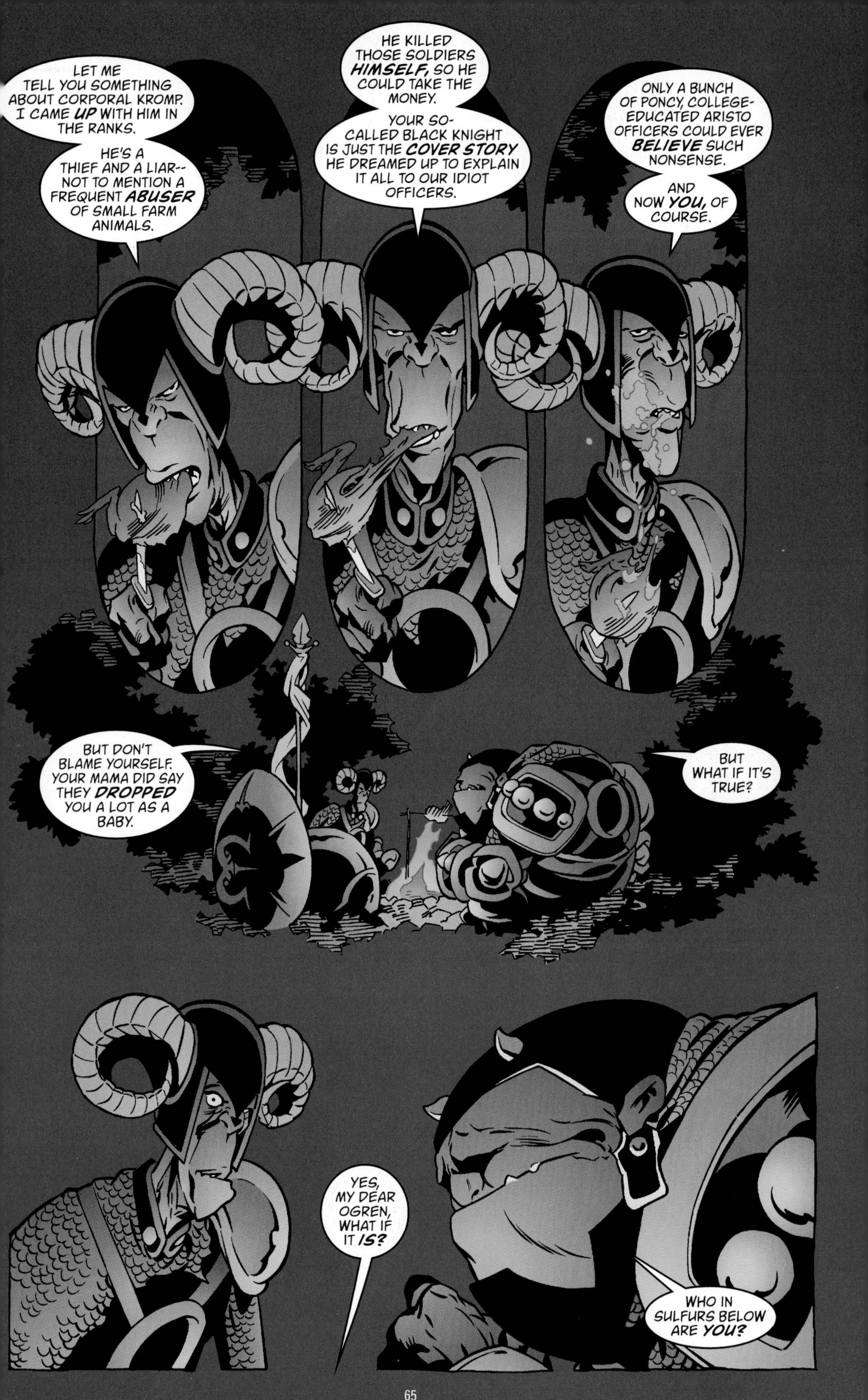
LET ME TELL YOU SOMETHING ABOUT CORPORAL KROMP. I CAME UP WITH HIM IN THE RANKS.
HE'S A THIEF AND A LIAR-- NOT TO MENTION A FREQUENT ABUSER OF SMALL FARM ANIMALS.
HE KILLED THOSE SOLDIERS HIMSELF, SO HE COULD TAKE THE MONEY.
YOUR SO-CALLED BLACK KNIGHT IS JUST THE COVER STORY HE DREAMED UP TO EXPLAIN IT ALL TO OUR IDIOT OFFICERS.
ONLY A BUNCH OF PONCY, COLLEGE-EDUCATED ARISTO OFFICERS COULD EVER BELIEVE SUCH NONSENSE.
AND NOW YOU, OF COURSE.
BUT DON'T BLAME YOURSELF. YOUR MAMA DID SAY THEY DROPPED YOU A LOT AS A BABY.
BUT WHAT IF IT'S TRUE?
YES, MY DEAR OGREN, WHAT IF IT IS?
WHO IN SULFURS BELOW ARE YOU?

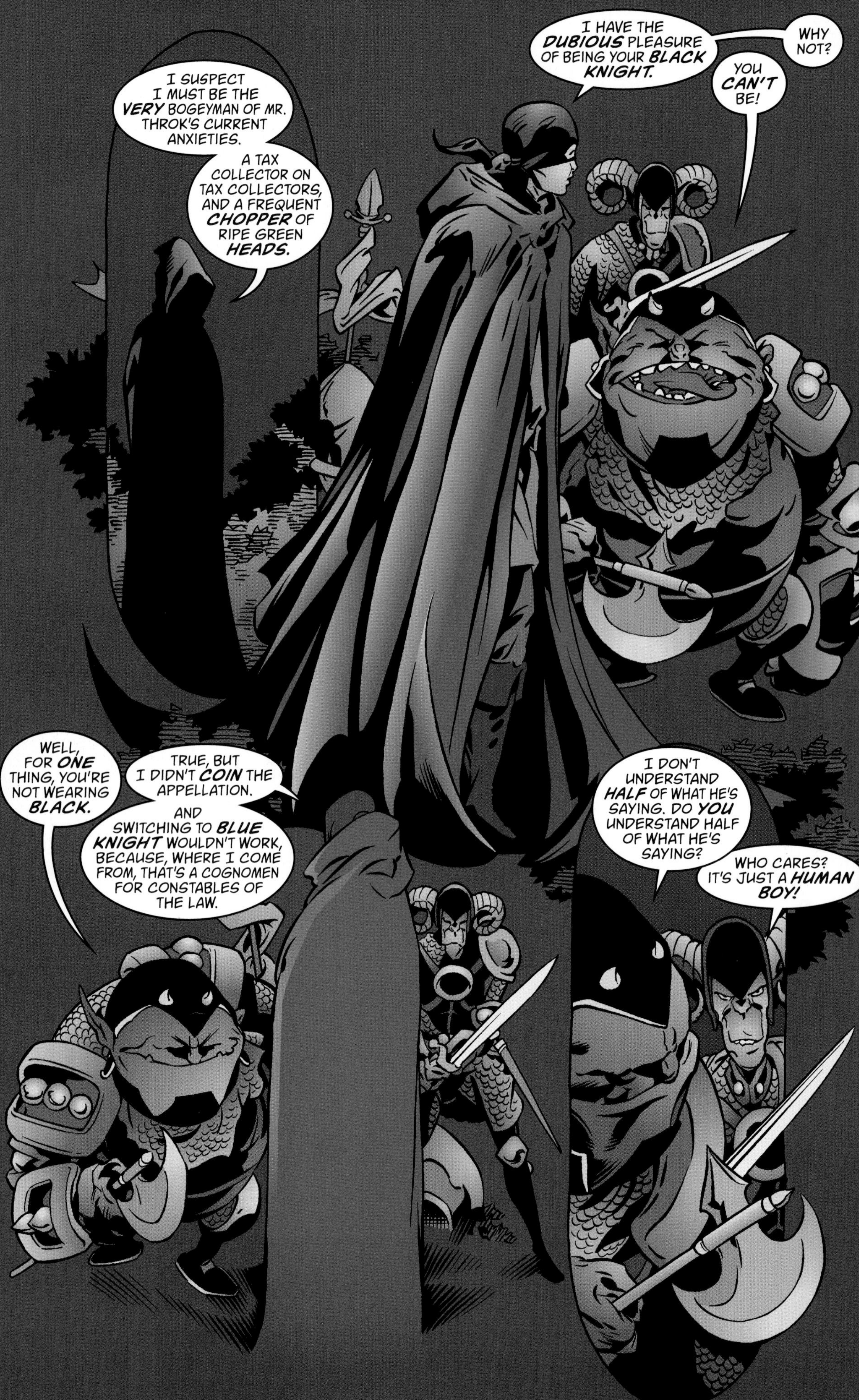
I SUSPECT I MUST BE THE VERY BOGEYMAN OF MR. THROK'S CURRENT ANXIETIES.
A TAX COLLECTOR ON TAX COLLECTORS, AND A FREQUENT CHOPPER OF RIPE GREEN HEADS.
I HAVE THE DUBIOUS PLEASURE OF BEING YOUR BLACK KNIGHT.
WHY NOT?
YOU CAN'T BE!
WELL, FOR ONE THING, YOU'RE NOT WEARING BLACK.
TRUE, BUT I DIDN'T COIN THE APPELLATION.
AND SWITCHING TO BLUE KNIGHT WOULDN'T WORK, BECAUSE, WHERE I COME FROM, THAT'S A COGNOMEN FOR CONSTABLES OF THE LAW.
I DON'T UNDERSTAND HALF OF WHAT HE'S SAYING. DO YOU UNDERSTAND HALF OF WHAT HE'S SAYING?
WHO CARES? IT'S JUST A HUMAN BOY!

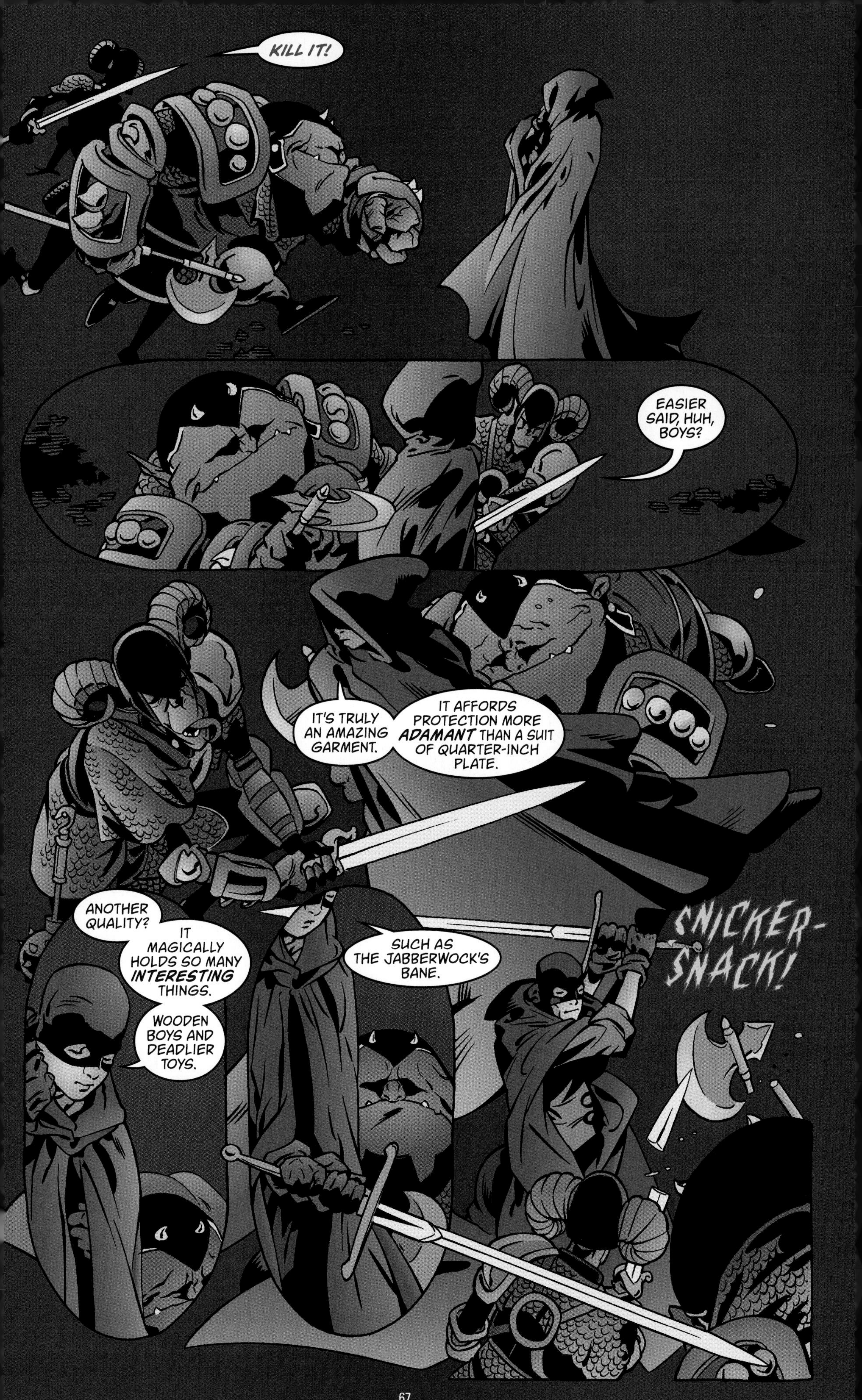
KILL IT!
EASIER SAID, HUH, BOYS?
IT'S TRULY AN AMAZING GARMENT.
IT AFFORDS PROTECTION MORE ADAMANT THAN A SUIT OF QUARTER-INCH PLATE.
ANOTHER QUALITY?
IT MAGICALLY HOLDS SO MANY INTERESTING THINGS.
WOODEN BOYS AND DEADLIER TOYS.
SUCH AS THE JABBERWOCK'S BANE.
SNICKER-SNACK!

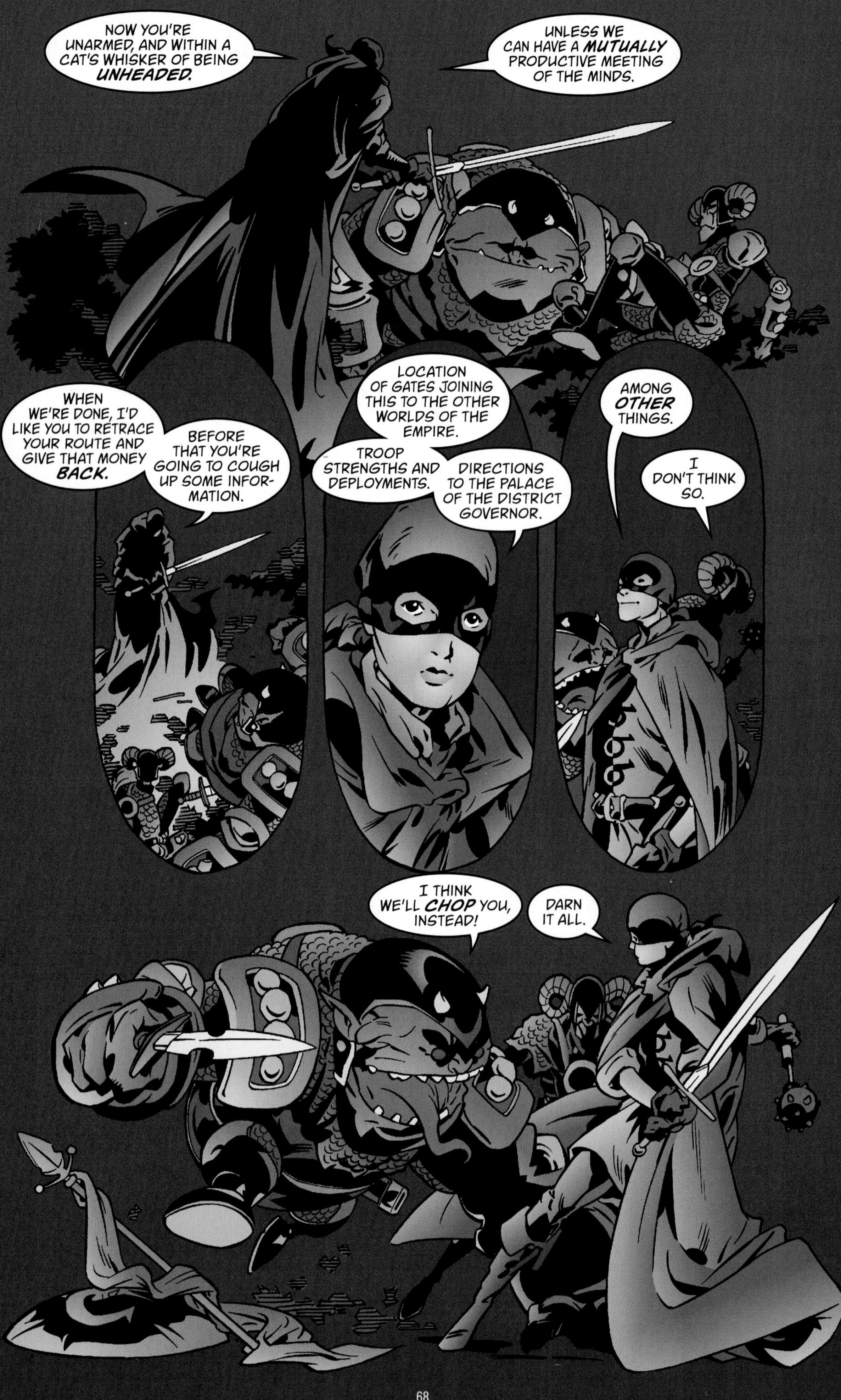
NOW YOU'RE UNARMED, AND WITHIN A CAT'S WHISKER OF BEING UNHEADED.
UNLESS WE CAN HAVE A MUTUALLY PRODUCTIVE MEETING OF THE MINDS.
WHEN WE'RE DONE, I'D LIKE YOU TO RETRACE YOUR ROUTE AND GIVE THAT MONEY BACK.
BEFORE THAT YOU'RE GOING TO COUGH UP SOME INFOR-MATION.
LOCATION OF GATES JOINING THIS TO THE OTHER WORLDS OF THE EMPIRE.
TROOP STRENGTHS AND DEPLOYMENTS.
DIRECTIONS TO THE PALACE OF THE DISTRICT GOVERNOR.
AMONG OTHER THINGS.
I DON'T THINK SO.
I THINK WE'LL CHOP YOU, INSTEAD!
DARN IT ALL.

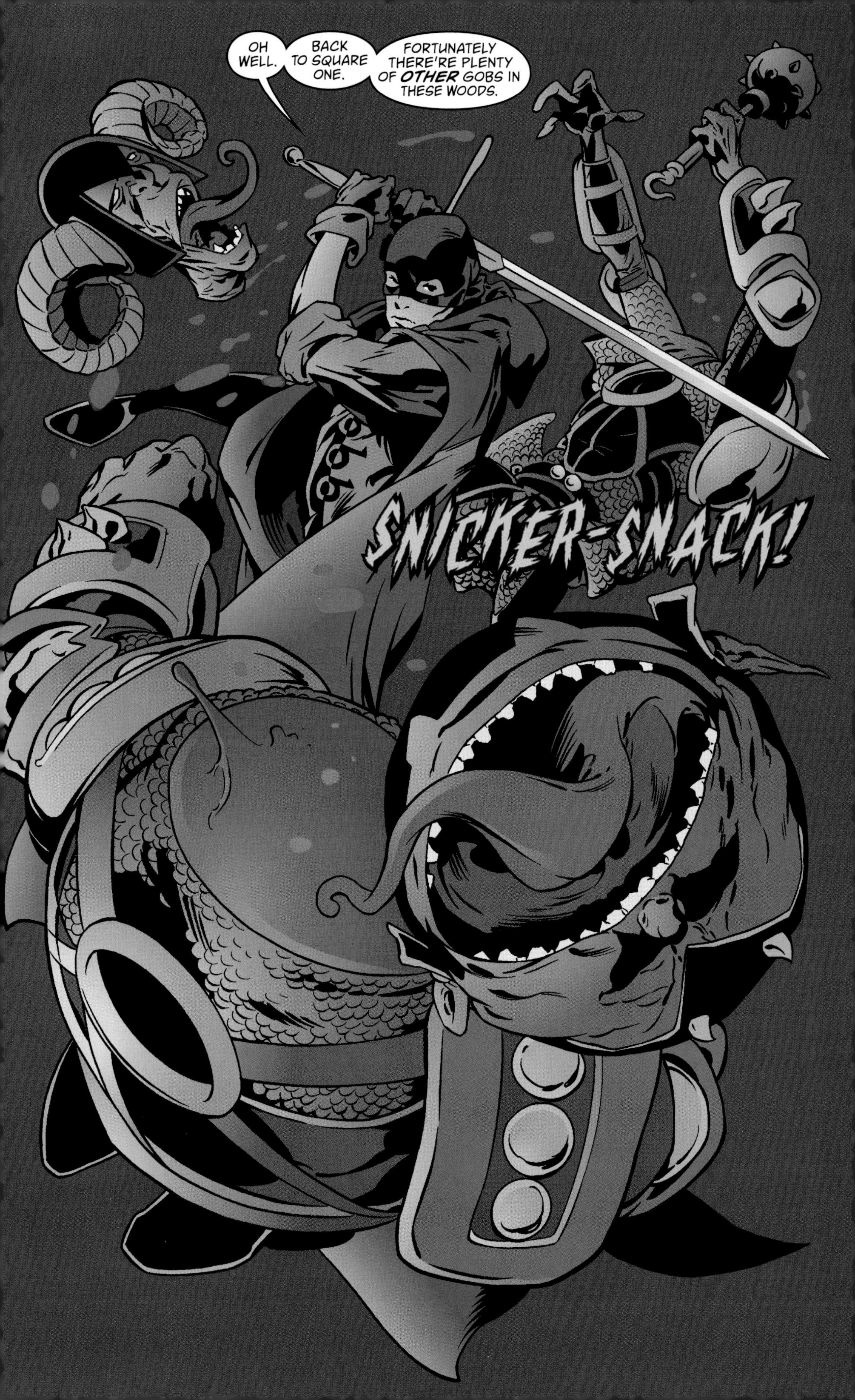
OH WELL.
BACK TO SQUARE ONE.
FORTUNATELY THERE'RE PLENTY OF OTHER GOBS IN THESE WOODS.
SNICKER-SNACK!

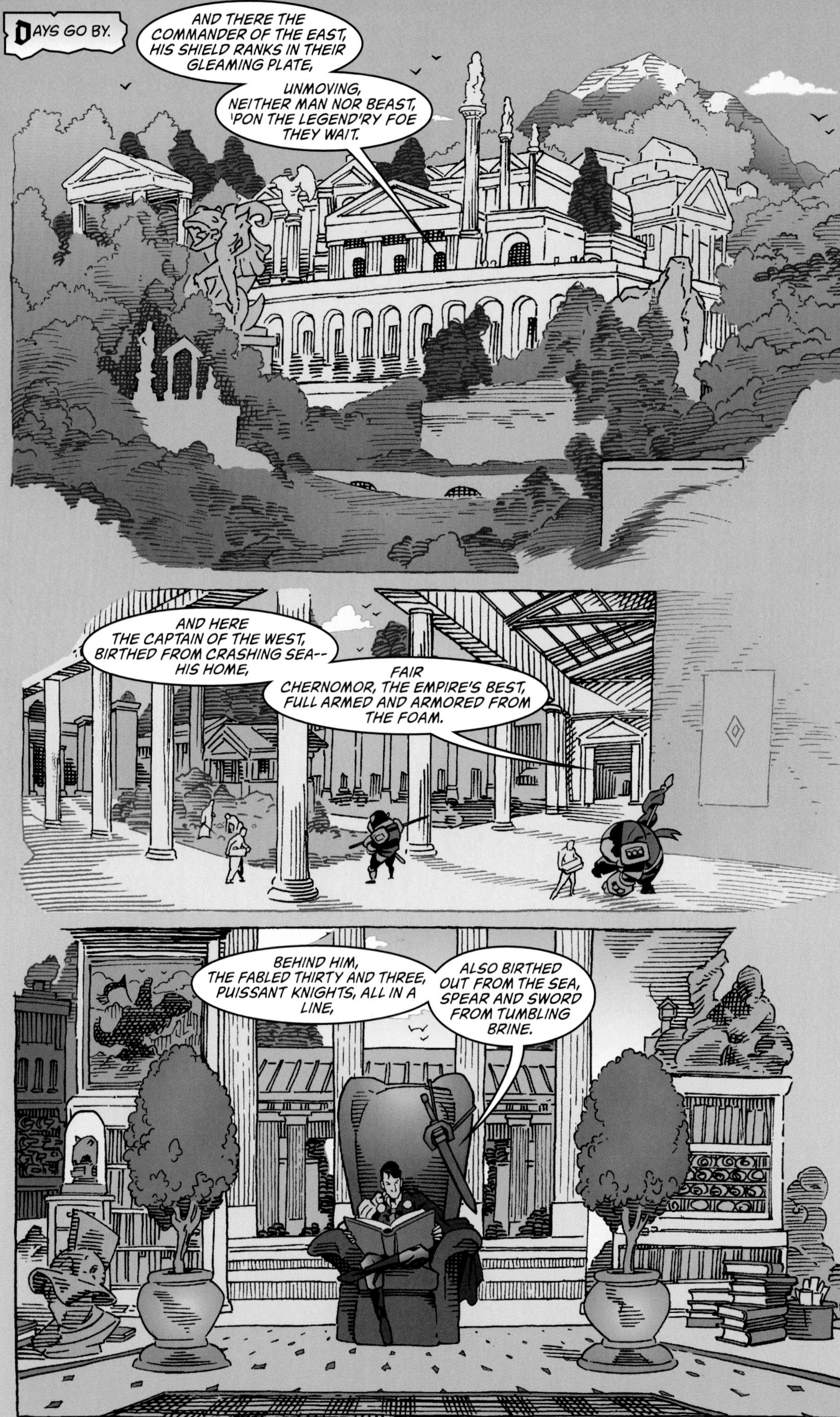
DAYS GO BY.
AND THERE THE COMMANDER OF THE EAST, HIS SHIELD RANKS IN THEIR GLEAMING PLATE,
UNMOVING, NEITHER MAN NOR BEAST, 'PON THE LEGEND'RY FOE THEY WAIT.
AND HERE THE CAPTAIN OF THE WEST, BIRTHED FROM CRASHING SEA-- HIS HOME,
FAIR CHERNOMOR, THE EMPIRE'S BEST, FULL ARMED AND ARMORED FROM THE FOAM.
BEHIND HIM, THE FABLED THIRTY AND THREE, PUISSANT KNIGHTS, ALL IN A LINE,
ALSO BIRTHED OUT FROM THE SEA, SPEAR AND SWORD FROM TUMBLING BRINE.

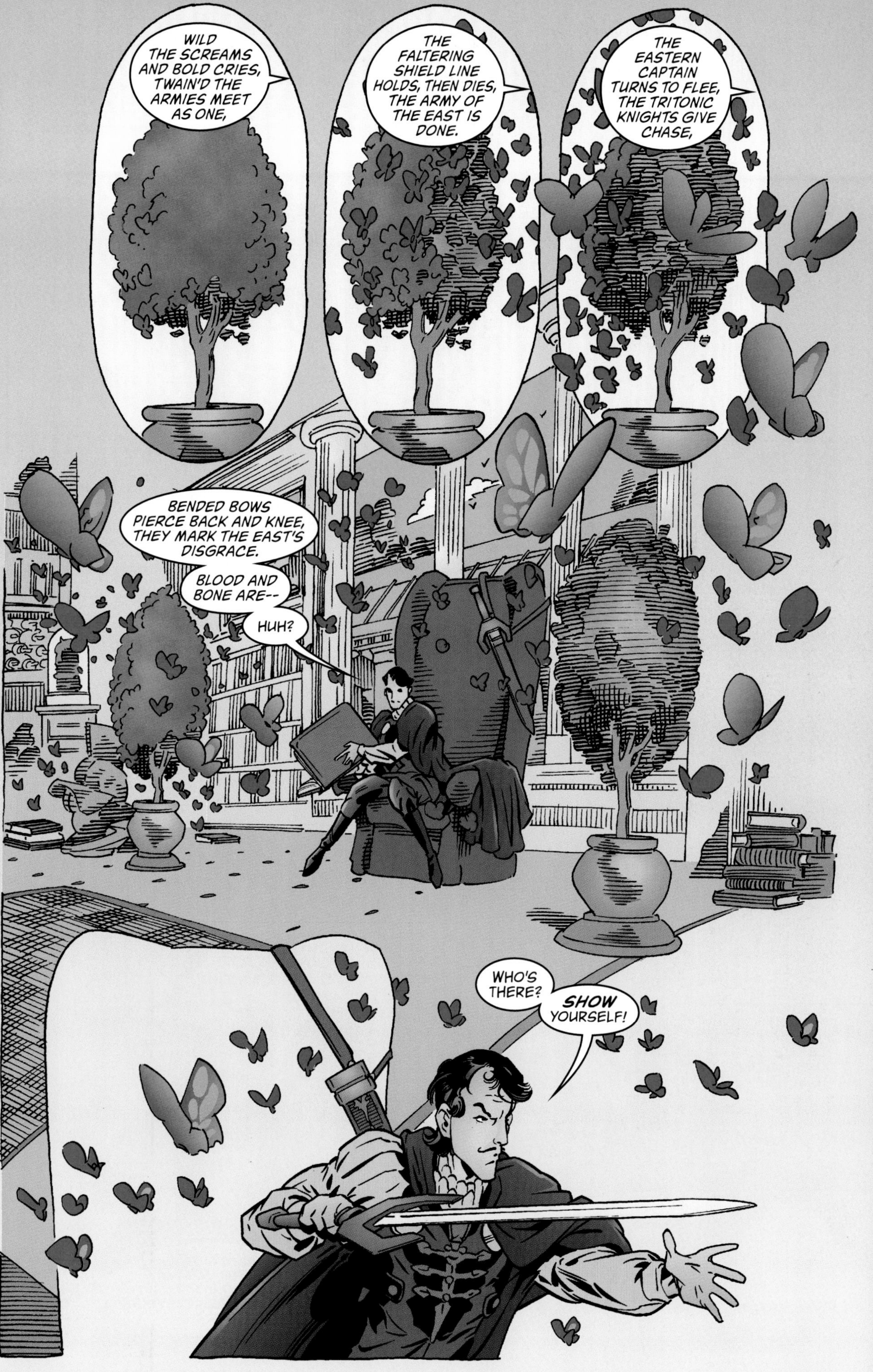
WILD THE SCREAMS AND BOLD CRIES, TWAIN'D THE ARMIES MEET AS ONE,
THE FALTERING SHIELD LINE HOLDS, THEN DIES, THE ARMY OF THE EAST IS DONE.
THE EASTERN CAPTAIN TURNS TO FLEE, THE TRITONIC KNIGHTS GIVE CHASE,
BENDED BOWS PIERCE BACK AND KNEE, THEY MARK THE EAST'S DISGRACE.
BLOOD AND BONE ARE--
HUH?
WHO'S THERE?
SHOW YOURSELF!

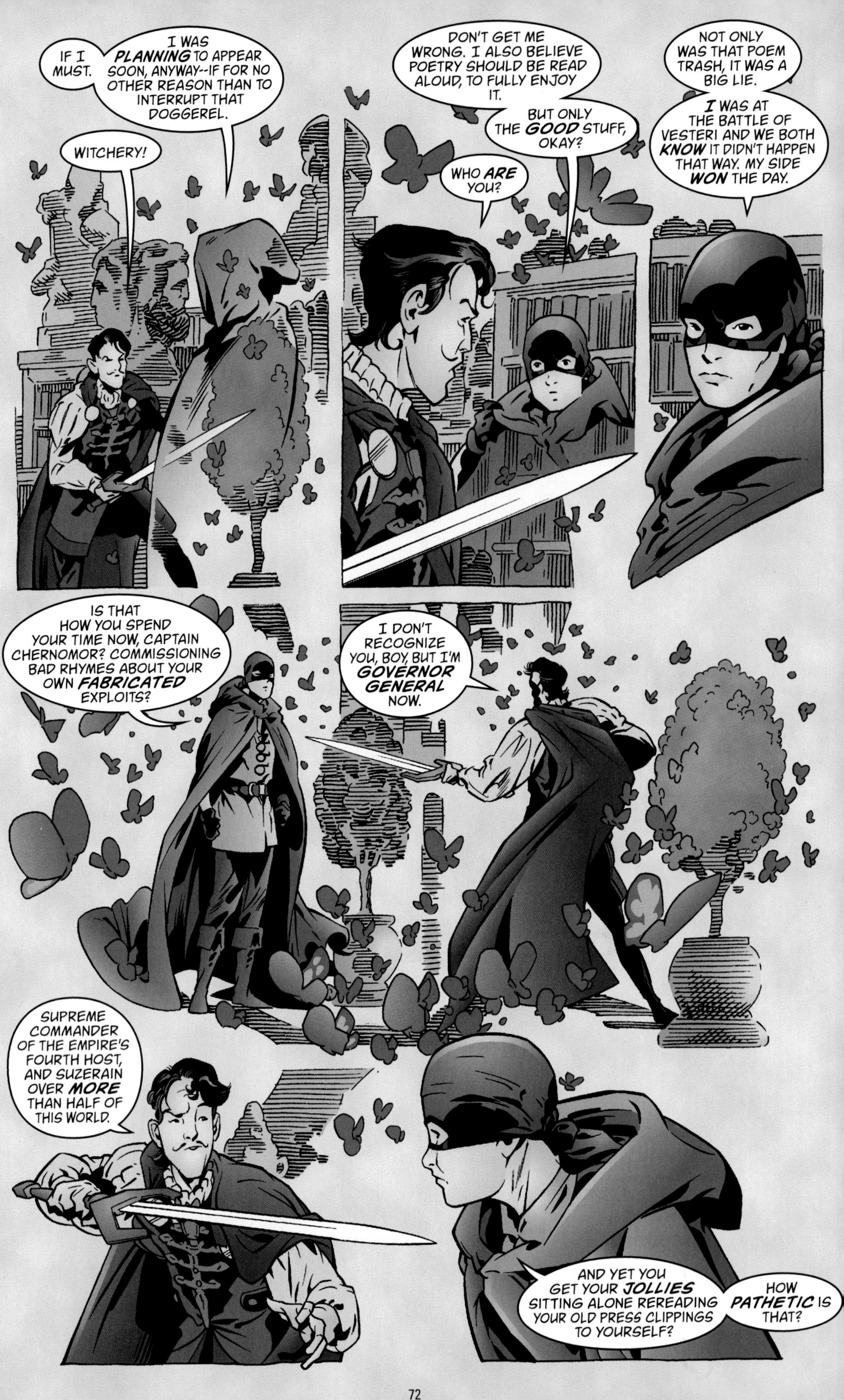
IF I MUST.
I WAS PLANNING TO APPEAR SOON, ANYWAY--IF FOR NO OTHER REASON THAN TO INTERRUPT THAT DOGGEREL.
WITCHERY!
DON'T GET ME WRONG. I ALSO BELIEVE POETRY SHOULD BE READ ALOUD, TO FULLY ENJOY IT.
BUT ONLY THE GOOD STUFF, OKAY?
WHO ARE YOU?
NOT ONLY WAS THAT POEM TRASH, IT WAS A BIG LIE.
I WAS AT THE BATTLE OF VESTERI AND WE BOTH KNOW IT DIDN'T HAPPEN THAT WAY. MY SIDE WON THE DAY.
IS THAT HOW YOU SPEND YOUR TIME NOW, CAPTAIN CHERNOMOR? COMMISSIONING BAD RHYMES ABOUT YOUR OWN FABRICATED EXPLOITS?
I DON'T RECOGNIZE YOU, BOY, BUT I'M GOVERNOR GENERAL NOW.
SUPREME COMMANDER OF THE EMPIRE'S FOURTH HOST, AND SUZERAIN OVER MORE THAN HALF OF THIS WORLD.
AND YET YOU GET YOUR JOLLIES SITTING ALONE REREADING YOUR OLD PRESS CLIPPINGS TO YOURSELF?
HOW PATHETIC IS THAT?

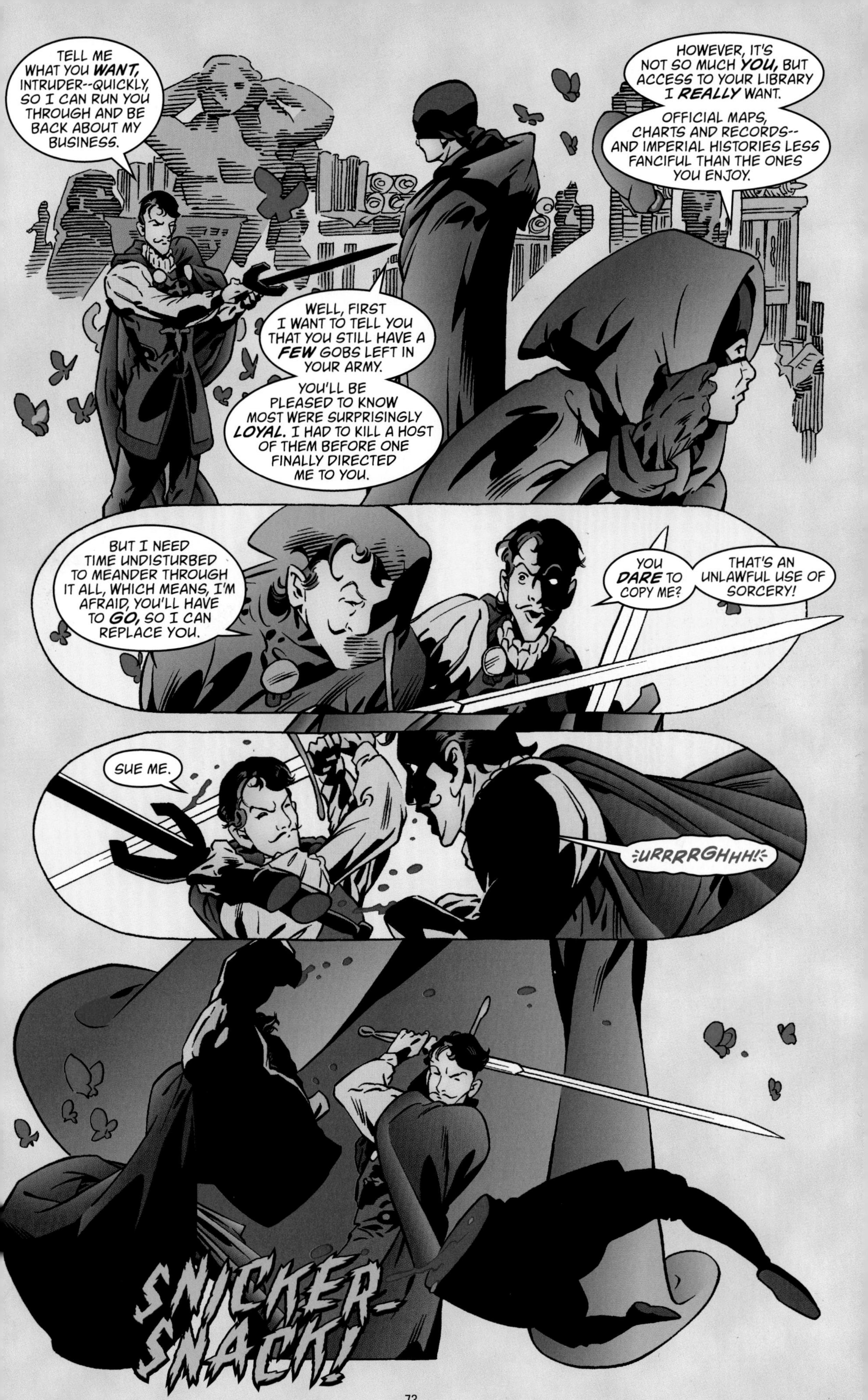
TELL ME WHAT YOU WANT, INTRUDER--QUICKLY, SO I CAN RUN YOU THROUGH AND BE BACK ABOUT MY BUSINESS.
HOWEVER, IT'S NOT SO MUCH YOU, BUT ACCESS TO YOUR LIBRARY I REALLY WANT.
OFFICIAL MAPS, CHARTS AND RECORDS--AND IMPERIAL HISTORIES LESS FANCIFUL THAN THE ONES YOU ENJOY.
WELL, FIRST I WANT TO TELL YOU THAT YOU STILL HAVE A FEW GOBS LEFT IN YOUR ARMY.
YOU'LL BE PLEASED TO KNOW MOST WERE SURPRISINGLY LOYAL. I HAD TO KILL A HOST OF THEM BEFORE ONE FINALLY DIRECTED ME TO YOU.
BUT I NEED TIME UNDISTURBED TO MEANDER THROUGH IT ALL, WHICH MEANS, I'M AFRAID, YOU'LL HAVE TO GO, SO I CAN REPLACE YOU.
YOU DARE TO COPY ME?
THAT'S AN UNLAWFUL USE OF SORCERY!
SUE ME.
URRRRGHHH!
SNICKER-SNACK!

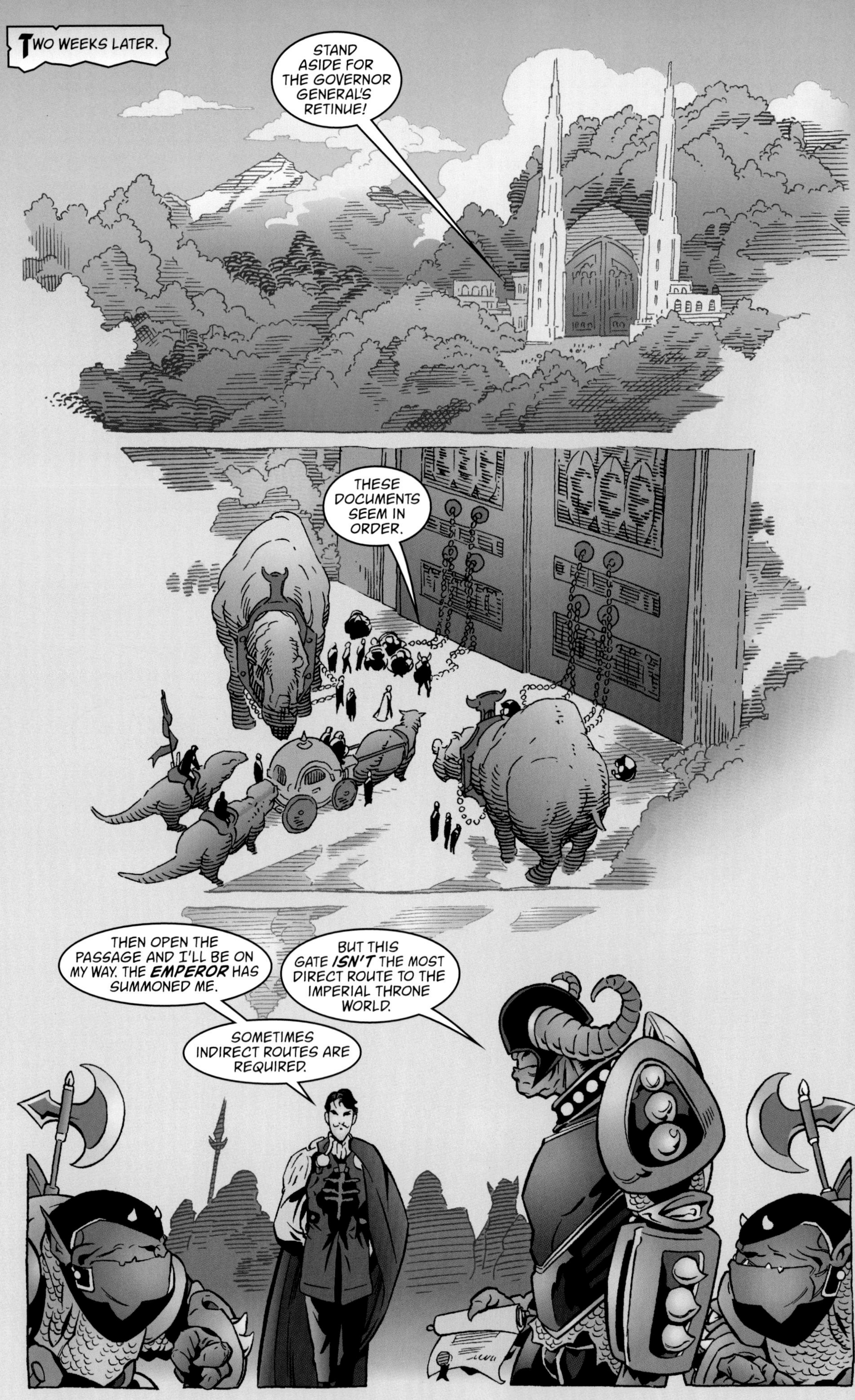
TWO WEEKS LATER.
STAND ASIDE FOR THE GOVERNOR GENERAL'S RETINUE!
THESE DOCUMENTS SEEM IN ORDER.
THEN OPEN THE PASSAGE AND I'LL BE ON MY WAY. THE EMPEROR HAS SUMMONED ME.
BUT THIS GATE ISN'T THE MOST DIRECT ROUTE TO THE IMPERIAL THRONE WORLD.
SOMETIMES INDIRECT ROUTES ARE REQUIRED.

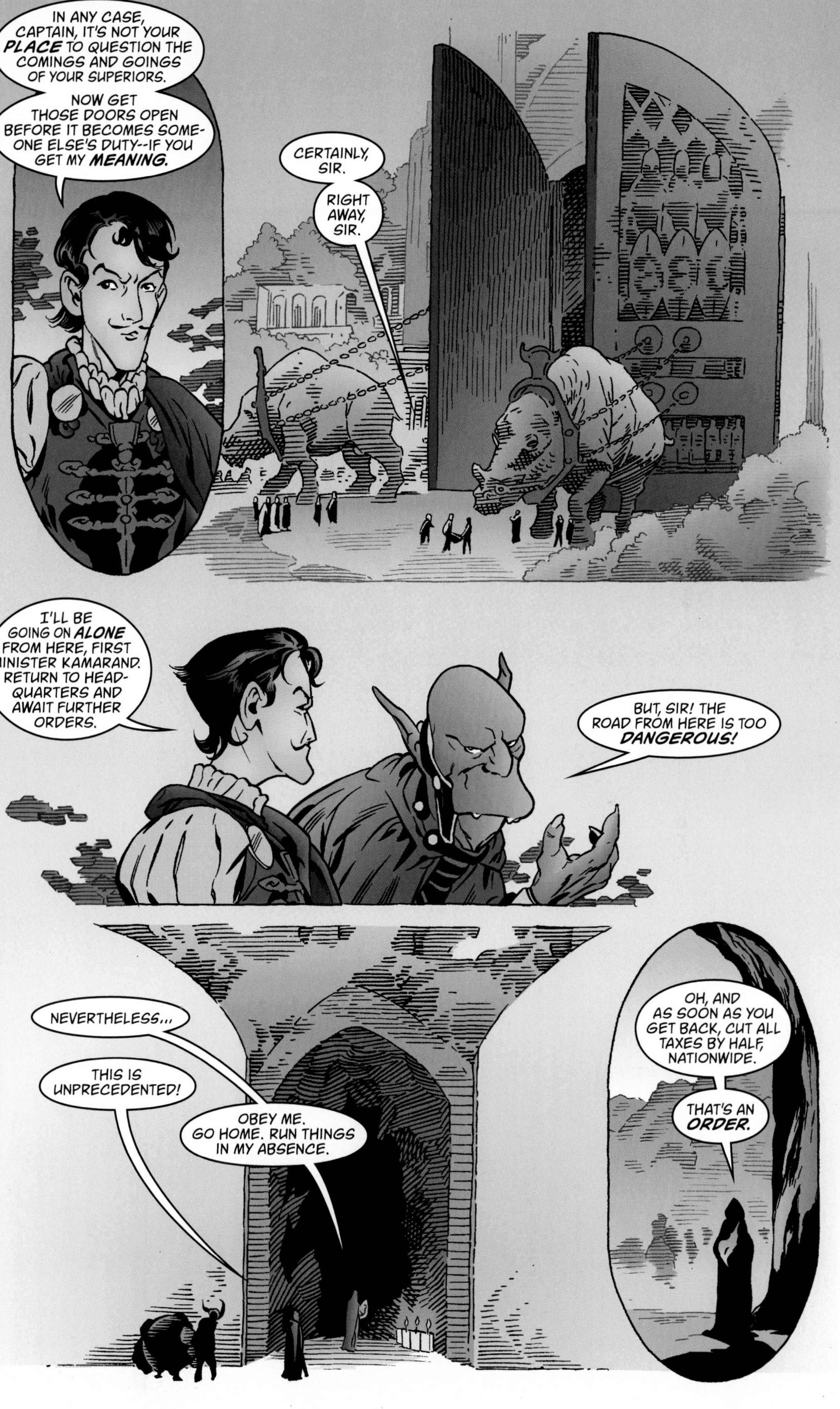
IN ANY CASE, CAPTAIN, IT'S NOT YOUR PLACE TO QUESTION THE COMINGS AND GOINGS OF YOUR SUPERIORS.
NOW GET THOSE DOORS OPEN BEFORE IT BECOMES SOME-ONE ELSE'S DUTY--IF YOU GET MY MEANING.
CERTAINLY, SIR.
RIGHT AWAY, SIR.
I'LL BE GOING ON ALONE FROM HERE, FIRST MINISTER KAMARAND. RETURN TO HEAD-QUARTERS AND AWAIT FURTHER ORDERS.
BUT, SIR! THE ROAD FROM HERE IS TOO DANGEROUS!
NEVERTHELESS...
THIS IS UNPRECEDENTED!
OBEY ME. GO HOME. RUN THINGS IN MY ABSENCE.
OH, AND AS SOON AS YOU GET BACK, CUT ALL TAXES BY HALF, NATIONWIDE.
THAT'S AN ORDER.

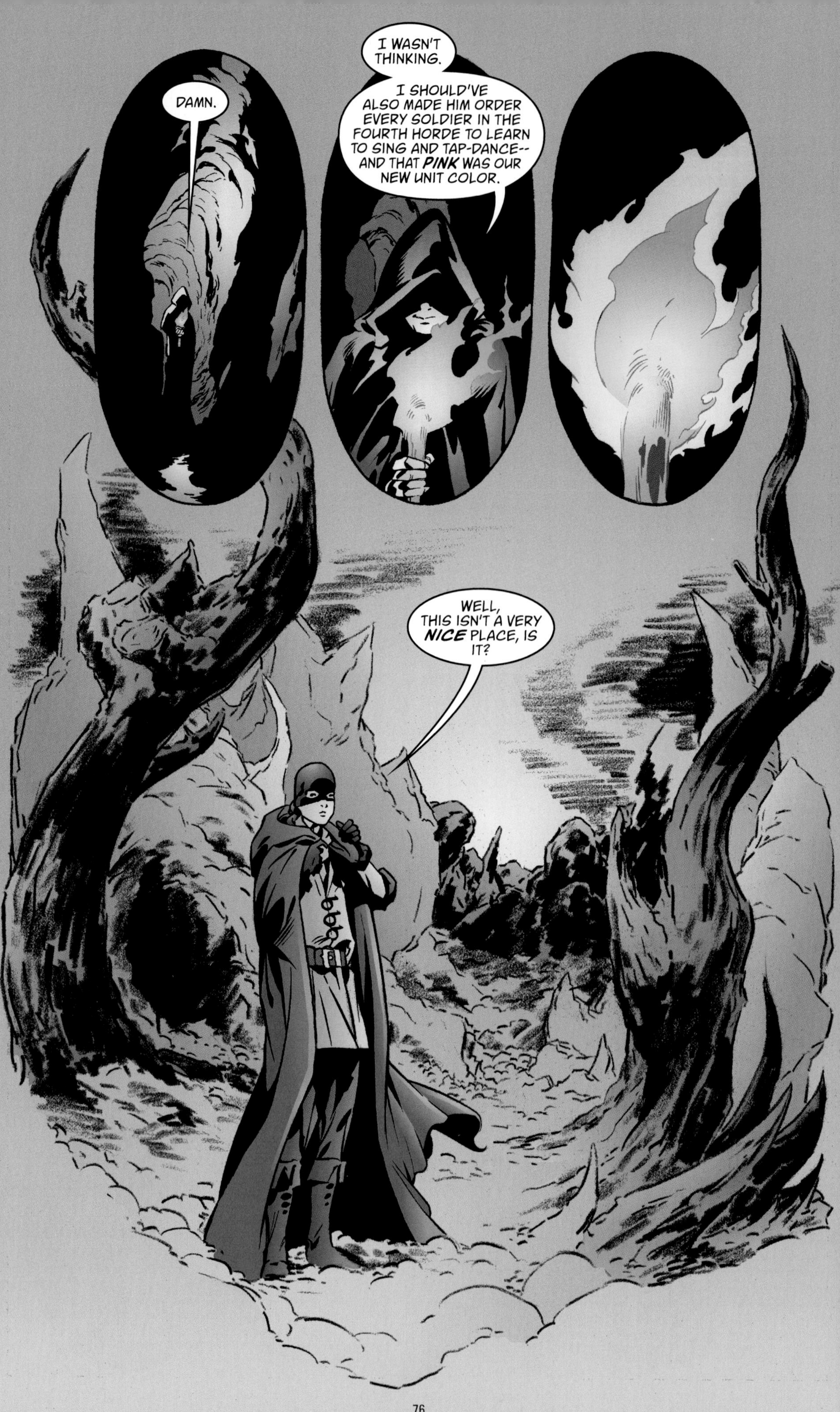
DAMN.
I WASN'T THINKING.
I SHOULD'VE ALSO MADE HIM ORDER EVERY SOLDIER IN THE FOURTH HORDE TO LEARN TO SING AND TAP-DANCE-- AND THAT PINK WAS OUR NEW UNIT COLOR.
WELL, THIS ISN'T A VERY NICE PLACE, IS IT?

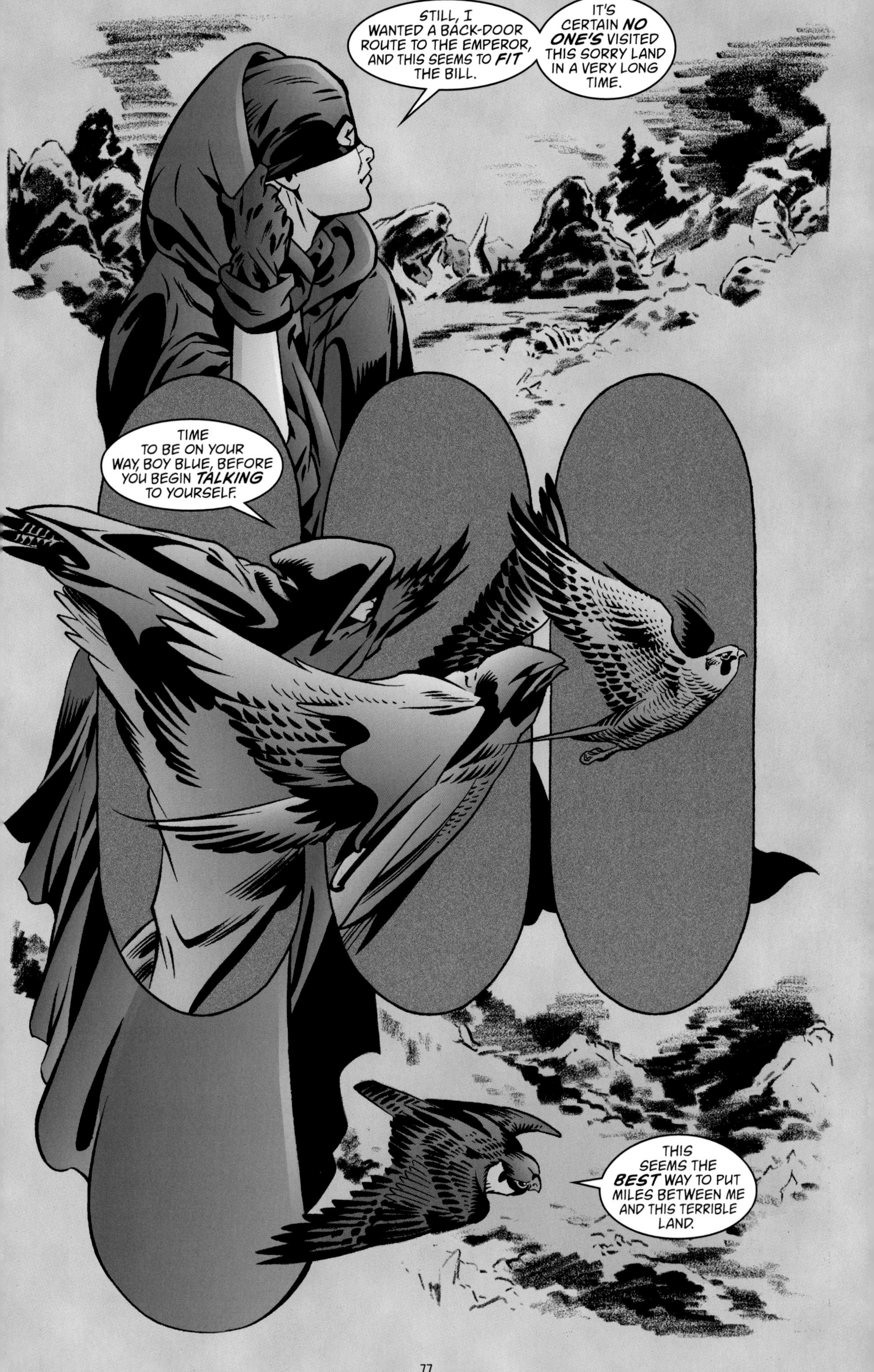
STILL, I WANTED A BACK-DOOR ROUTE TO THE EMPEROR, AND THIS SEEMS TO FIT THE BILL.
IT'S CERTAIN NO ONE'S VISITED THIS SORRY LAND IN A VERY LONG TIME.
TIME TO BE ON YOUR WAY, BOY BLUE, BEFORE YOU BEGIN TALKING TO YOURSELF.
THIS SEEMS THE BEST WAY TO PUT MILES BETWEEN ME AND THIS TERRIBLE LAND.

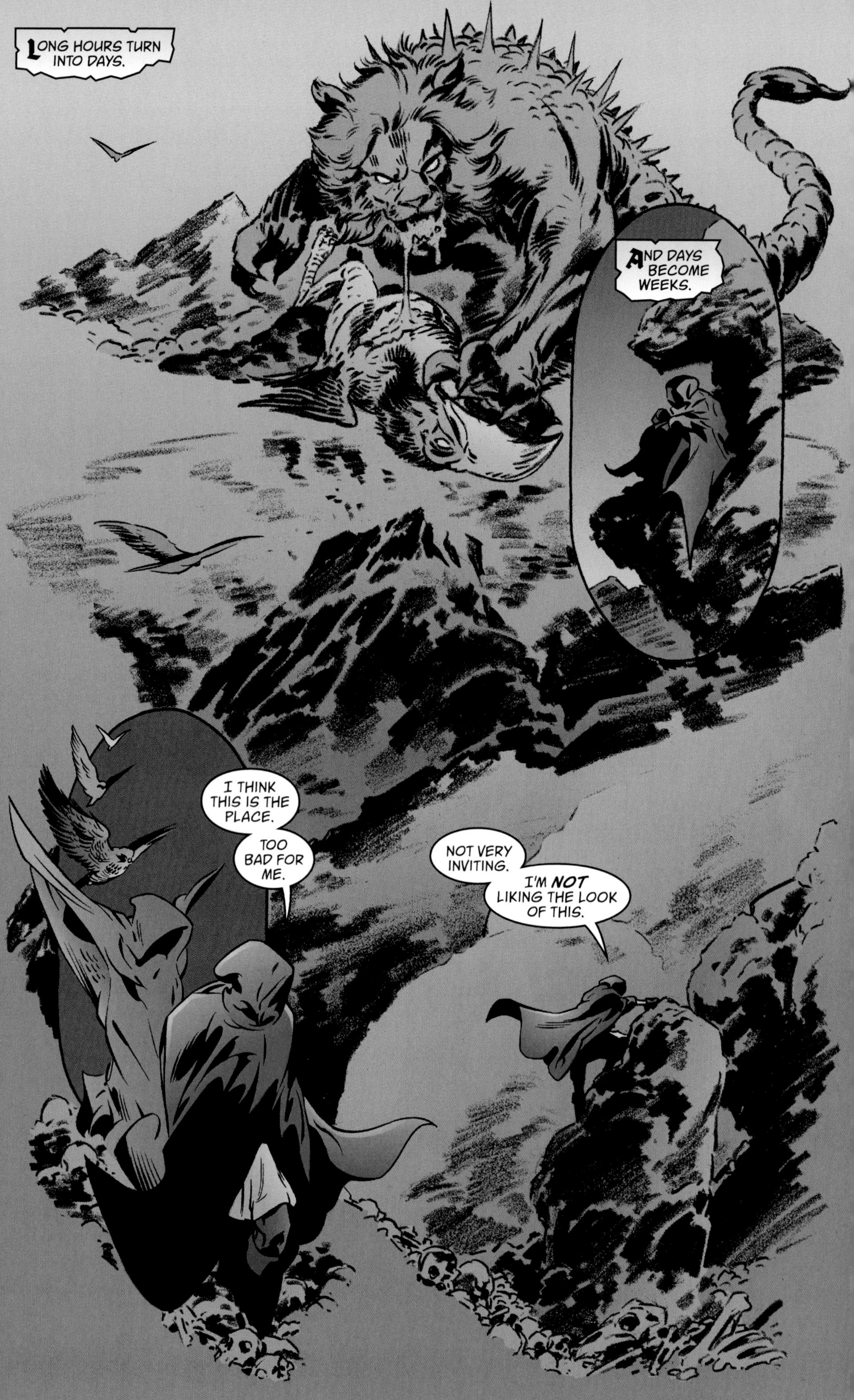
LONG HOURS TURN INTO DAYS.
AND DAYS BECOME WEEKS.
I THINK THIS IS THE PLACE.
TOO BAD FOR ME.
NOT VERY INVITING.
I'M **NOT** LIKING THE LOOK OF THIS.

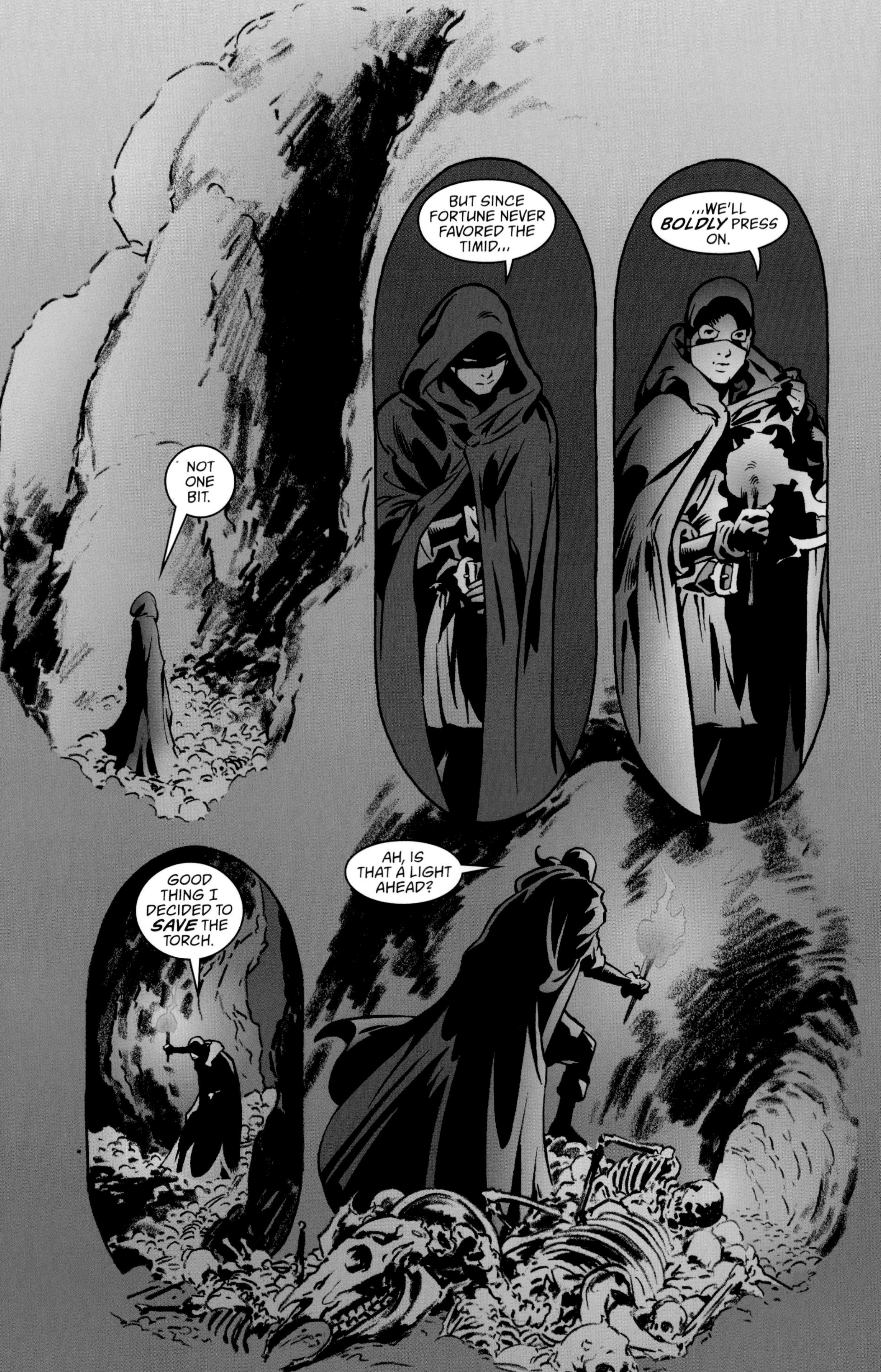
NOT ONE BIT.
BUT SINCE FORTUNE NEVER FAVORED THE TIMID...
...WE'LL BOLDLY PRESS ON.
GOOD THING I DECIDED TO SAVE THE TORCH.
AH, IS THAT A LIGHT AHEAD?

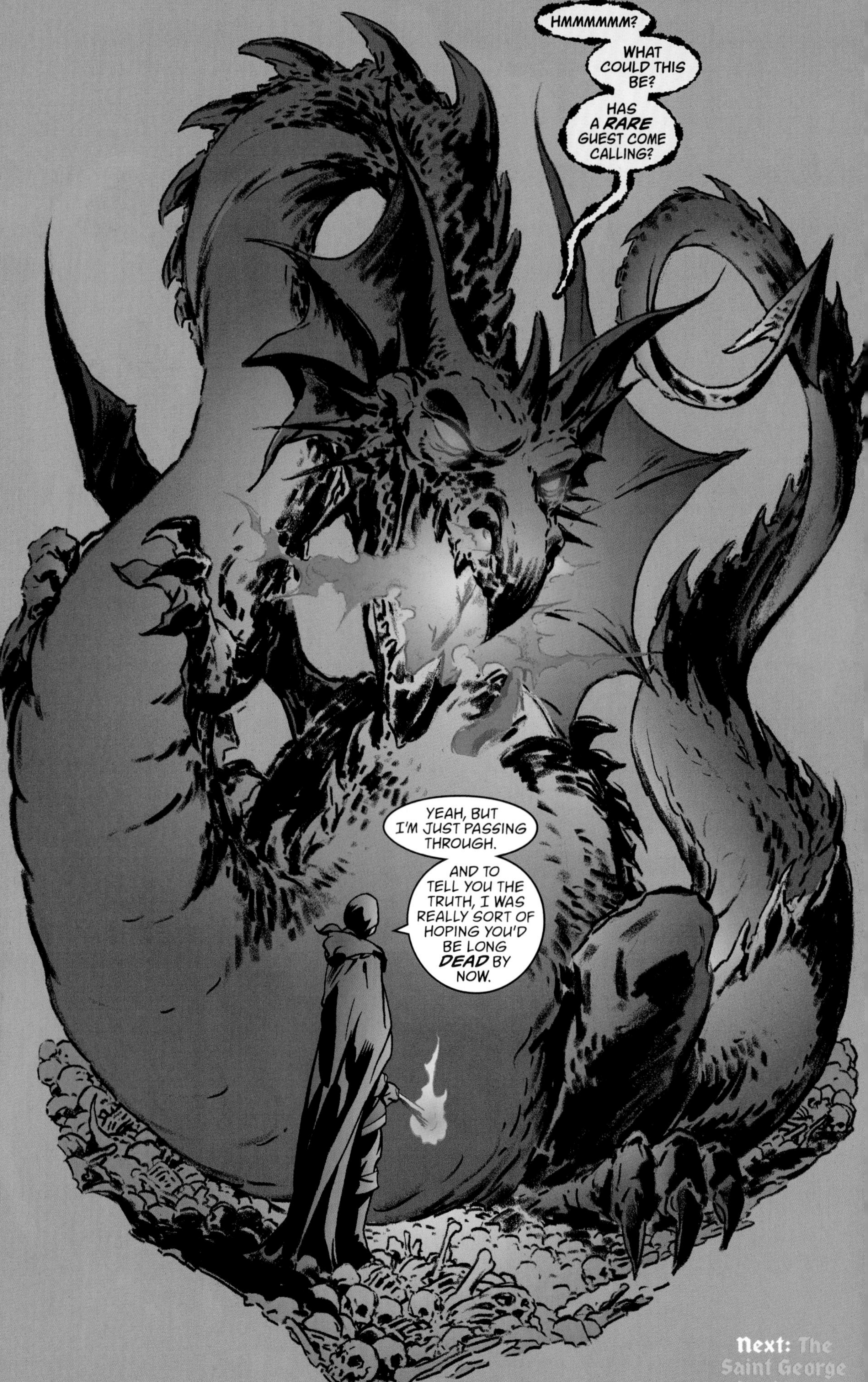
HMMMMMM?
WHAT COULD THIS BE?
HAS A RARE GUEST COME CALLING?
YEAH, BUT I'M JUST PASSING THROUGH.
AND TO TELL YOU THE TRUTH, I WAS REALLY SORT OF HOPING YOU'D BE LONG DEAD BY NOW.

Next: The Saint George Syndrome

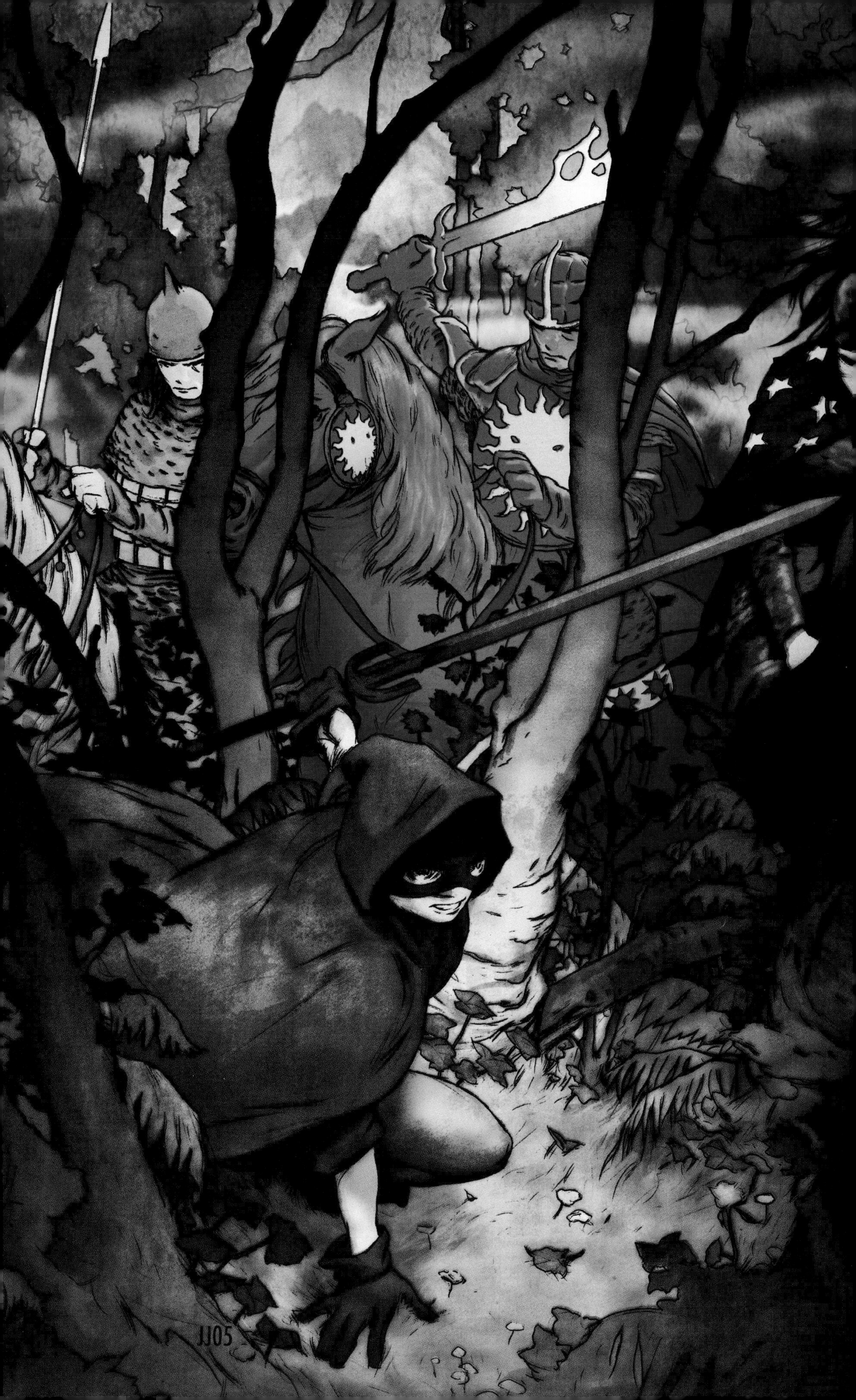
JJ05

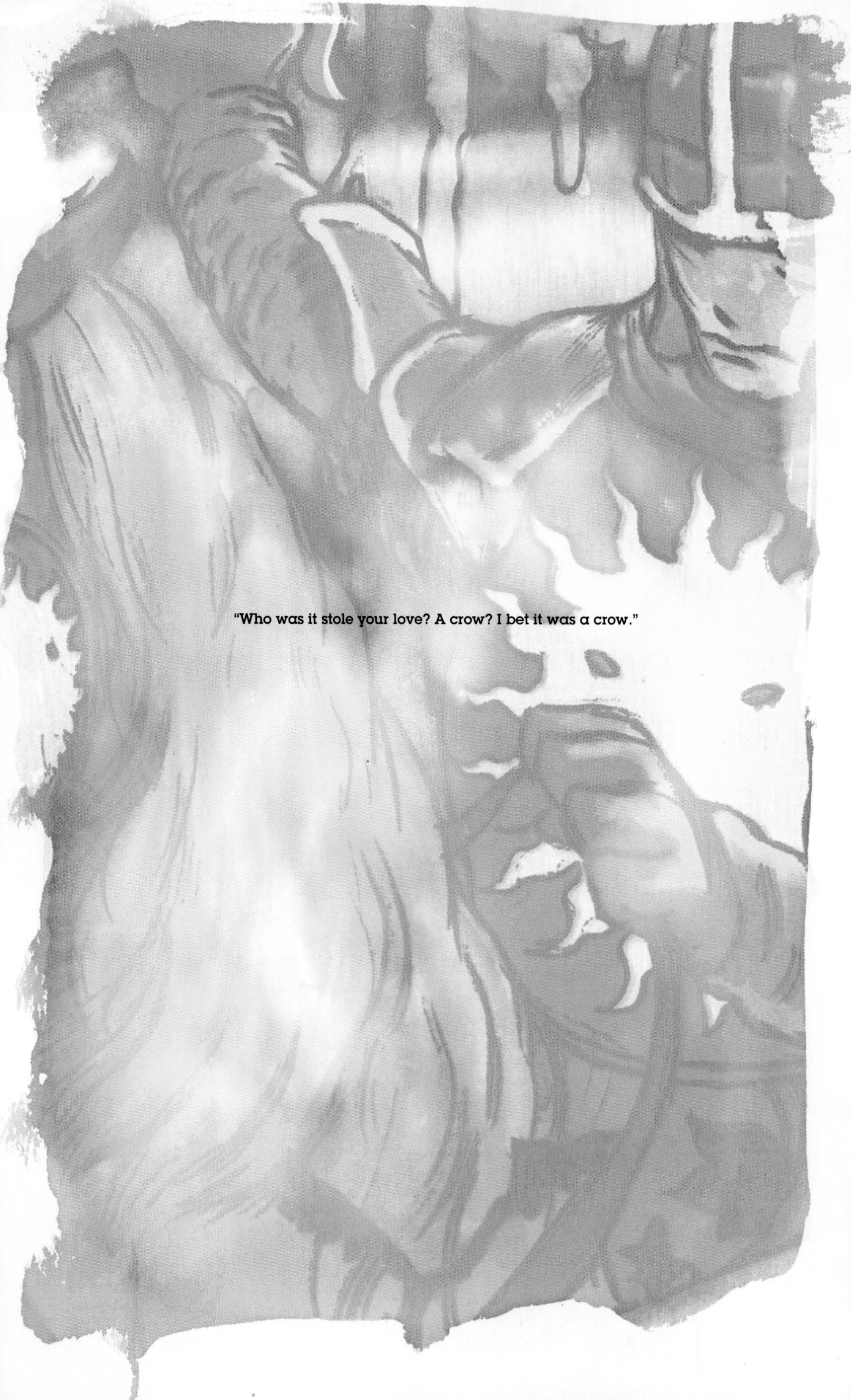

"Who was it stole your love? A crow? I bet it was a crow."

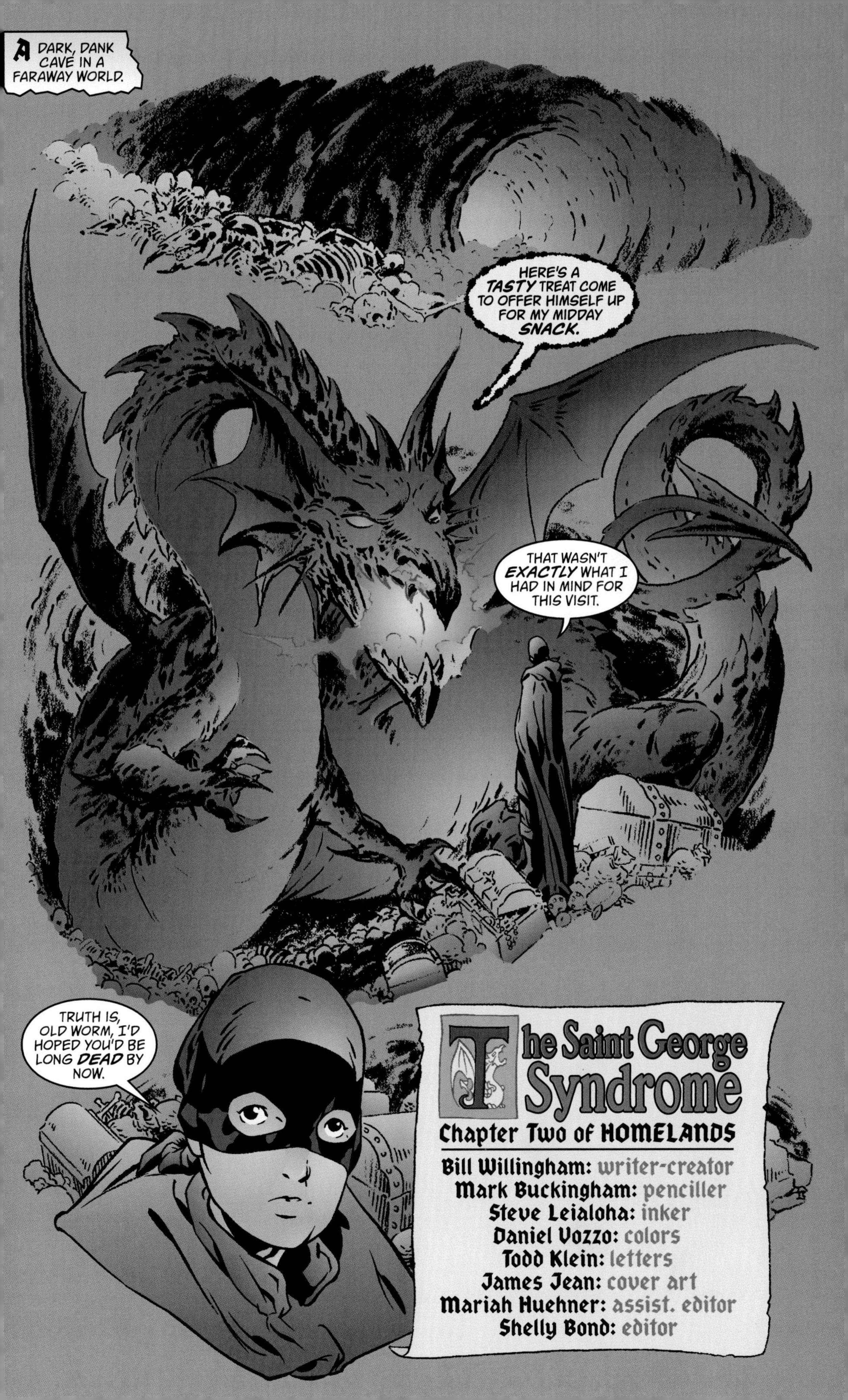
A DARK, DANK CAVE IN A FARAWAY WORLD.
HERE'S A TASTY TREAT COME TO OFFER HIMSELF UP FOR MY MIDDAY SNACK.
THAT WASN'T EXACTLY WHAT I HAD IN MIND FOR THIS VISIT.
TRUTH IS, OLD WORM, I'D HOPED YOU'D BE LONG DEAD BY NOW.
The Saint George Syndrome
Chapter Two of HOMELANDS
Bill Willingham: writer-creator
Mark Buckingham: penciller
Steve Leialoha: inker
Daniel Vozzo: colors
Todd Klein: letters
James Jean: cover art
Mariah Huehner: assist. editor
Shelly Bond: editor

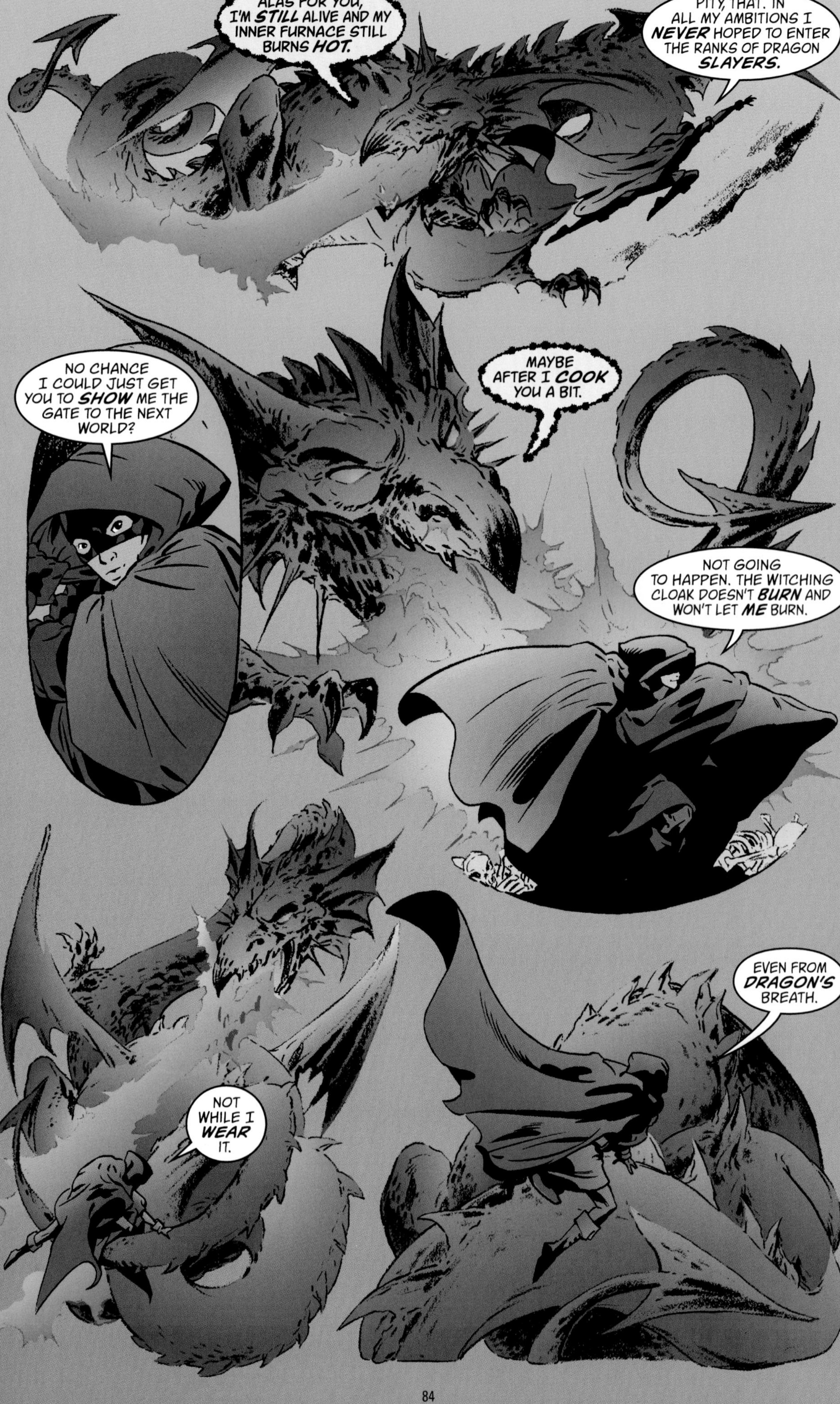
ALAS FOR YOU, I'M STILL ALIVE AND MY INNER FURNACE STILL BURNS HOT.
PITY, THAT. IN ALL MY AMBITIONS I NEVER HOPED TO ENTER THE RANKS OF DRAGON SLAYERS.
NO CHANCE I COULD JUST GET YOU TO SHOW ME THE GATE TO THE NEXT WORLD?
MAYBE AFTER I COOK YOU A BIT.
NOT GOING TO HAPPEN. THE WITCHING CLOAK DOESN'T BURN AND WON'T LET ME BURN.
EVEN FROM DRAGON'S BREATH.
NOT WHILE I WEAR IT.

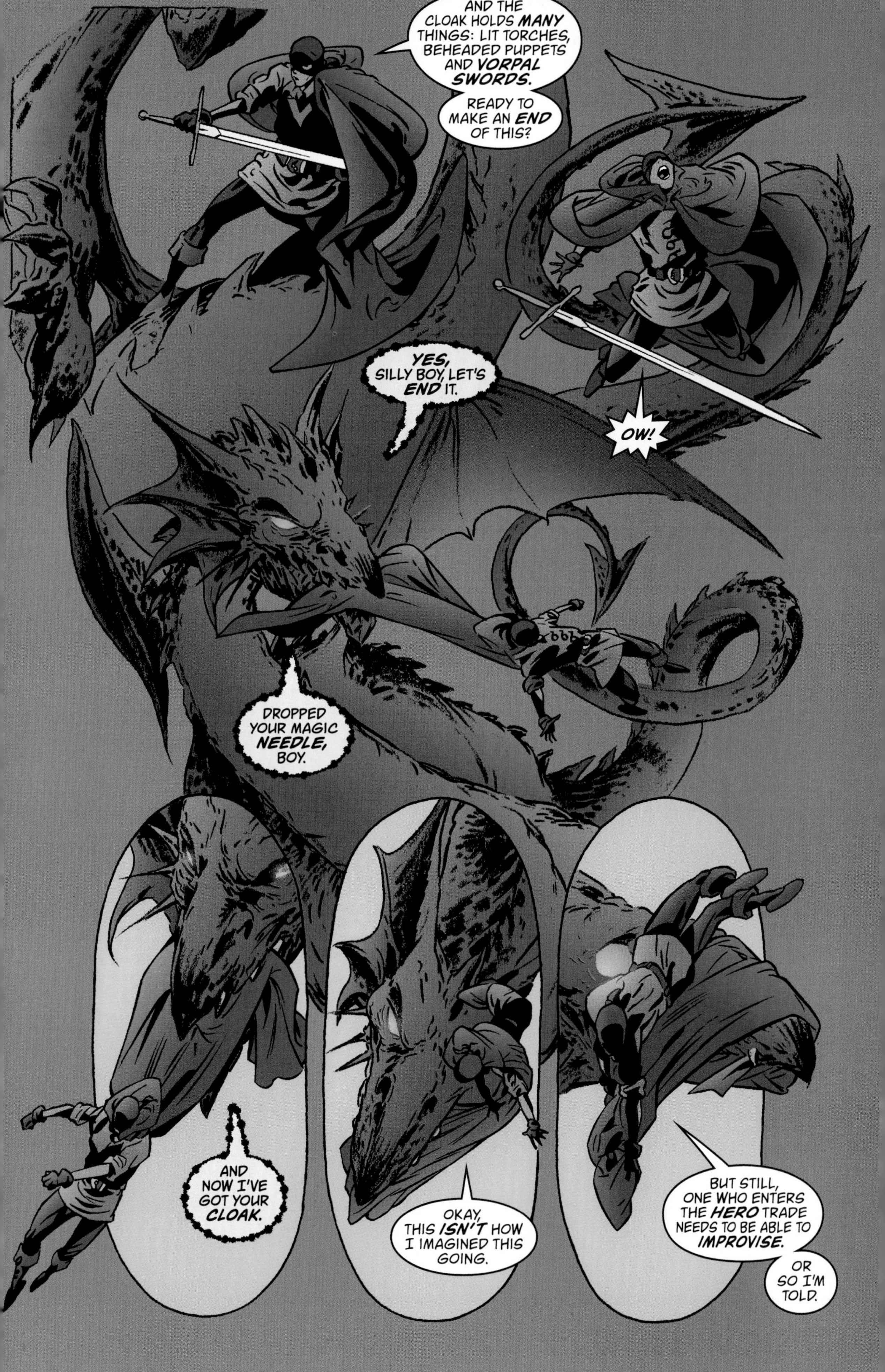
AND THE CLOAK HOLDS MANY THINGS: LIT TORCHES, BEHEADED PUPPETS AND VORPAL SWORDS.
READY TO MAKE AN END OF THIS?
YES, SILLY BOY, LET'S END IT.
OW!
DROPPED YOUR MAGIC NEEDLE, BOY.
AND NOW I'VE GOT YOUR CLOAK.
OKAY, THIS ISN'T HOW I IMAGINED THIS GOING.
BUT STILL, ONE WHO ENTERS THE HERO TRADE NEEDS TO BE ABLE TO IMPROVISE.
OR SO I'M TOLD.

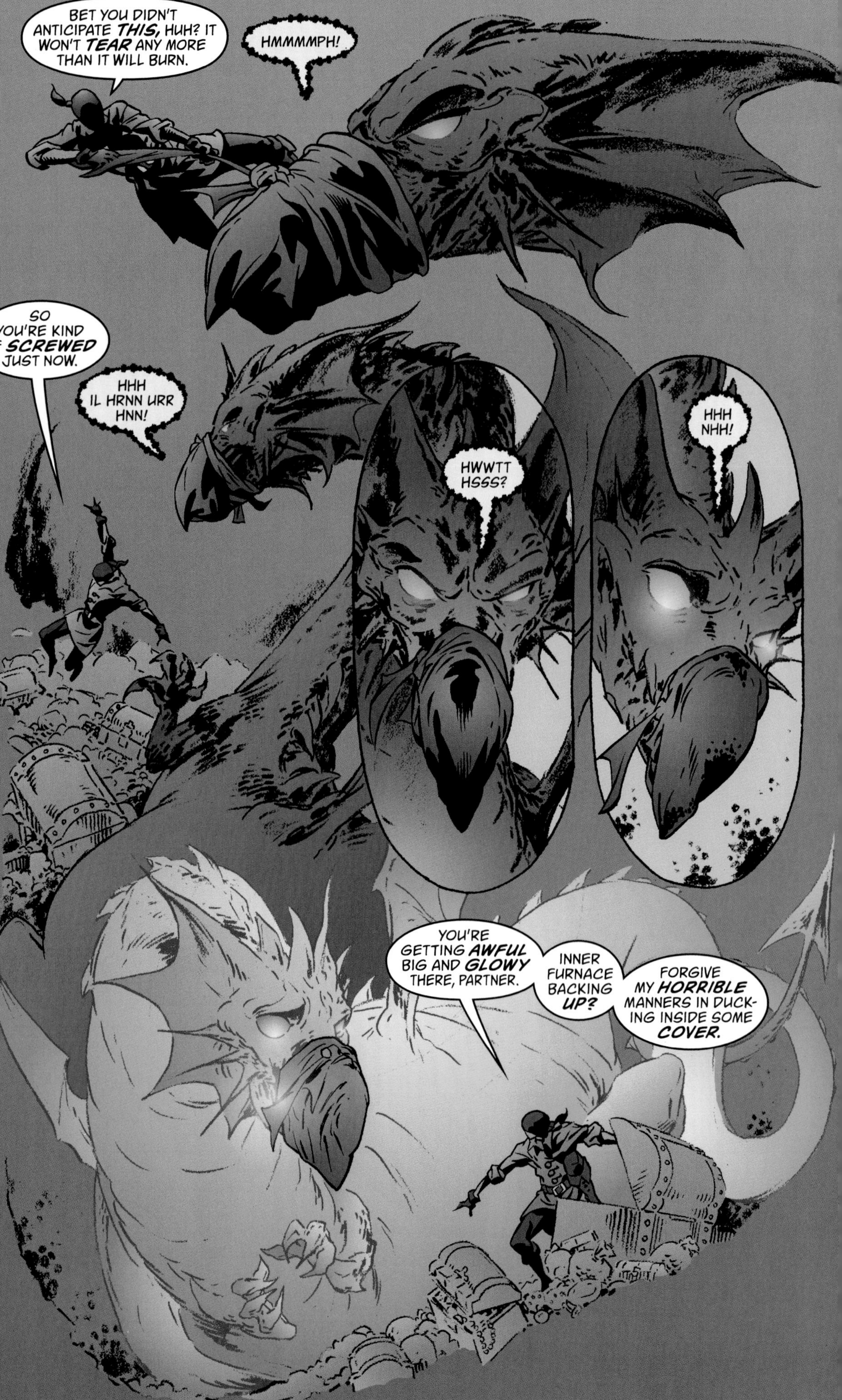

BET YOU DIDN'T ANTICIPATE THIS, HUH? IT WON'T TEAR ANY MORE THAN IT WILL BURN.
HMMMMPH!
SO YOU'RE KIND OF SCREWED JUST NOW.
HHH IL HRNN URR HNN!
HWWTT HSSS?
HHH NHH!
YOU'RE GETTING AWFUL BIG AND GLOWY THERE, PARTNER.
INNER FURNACE BACKING UP?
FORGIVE MY HORRIBLE MANNERS IN DUCKING INSIDE SOME COVER.

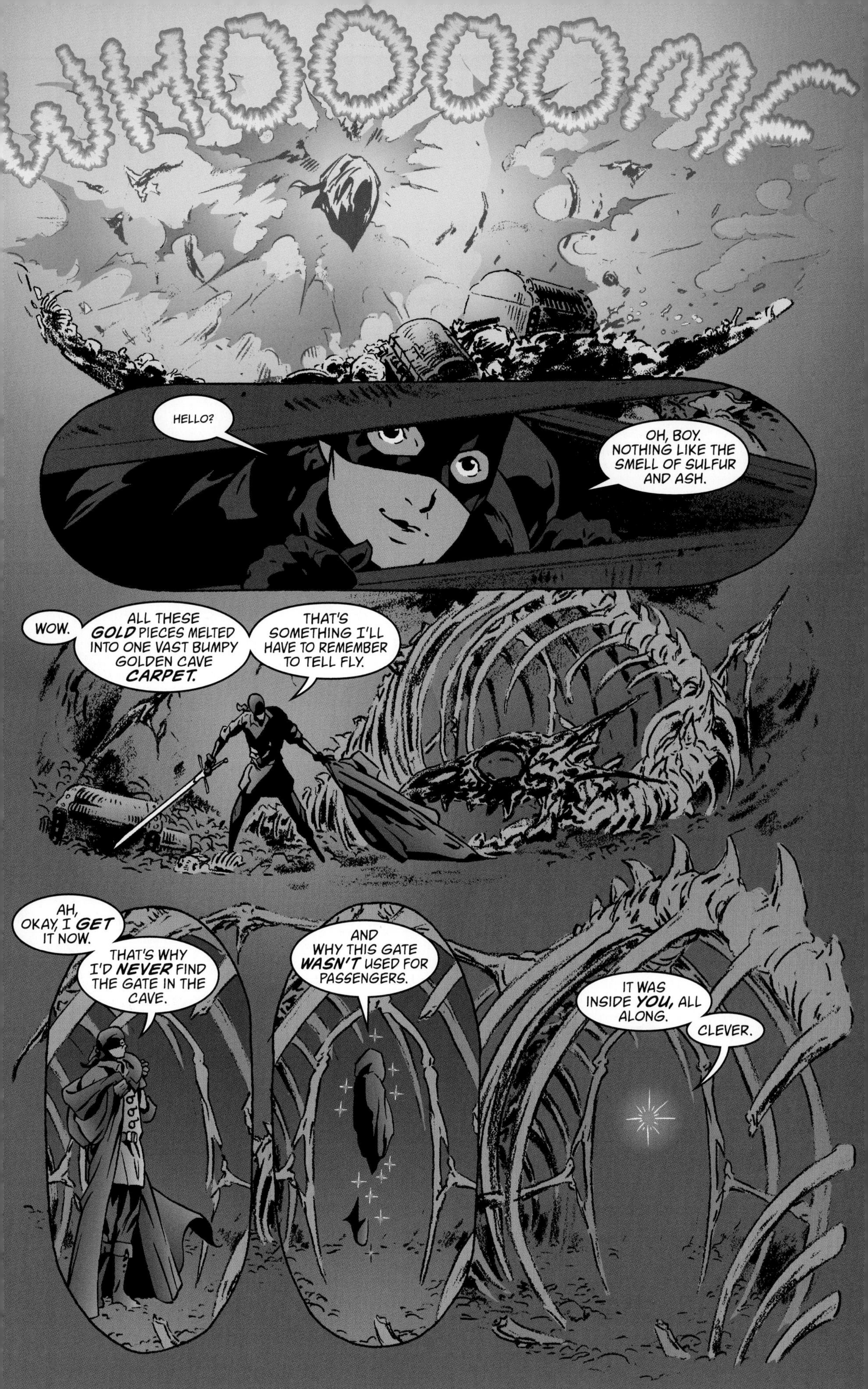
WHOOOOOMF
HELLO?
OH, BOY. NOTHING LIKE THE SMELL OF SULFUR AND ASH.
WOW.
ALL THESE **GOLD** PIECES MELTED INTO ONE VAST BUMPY GOLDEN CAVE **CARPET.**
THAT'S SOMETHING I'LL HAVE TO REMEMBER TO TELL FLY.
AH, OKAY, I ***GET*** IT NOW.
THAT'S WHY I'D ***NEVER*** FIND THE GATE IN THE CAVE.
AND WHY THIS GATE ***WASN'T*** USED FOR PASSENGERS.
IT WAS INSIDE ***YOU,*** ALL ALONG.
CLEVER.

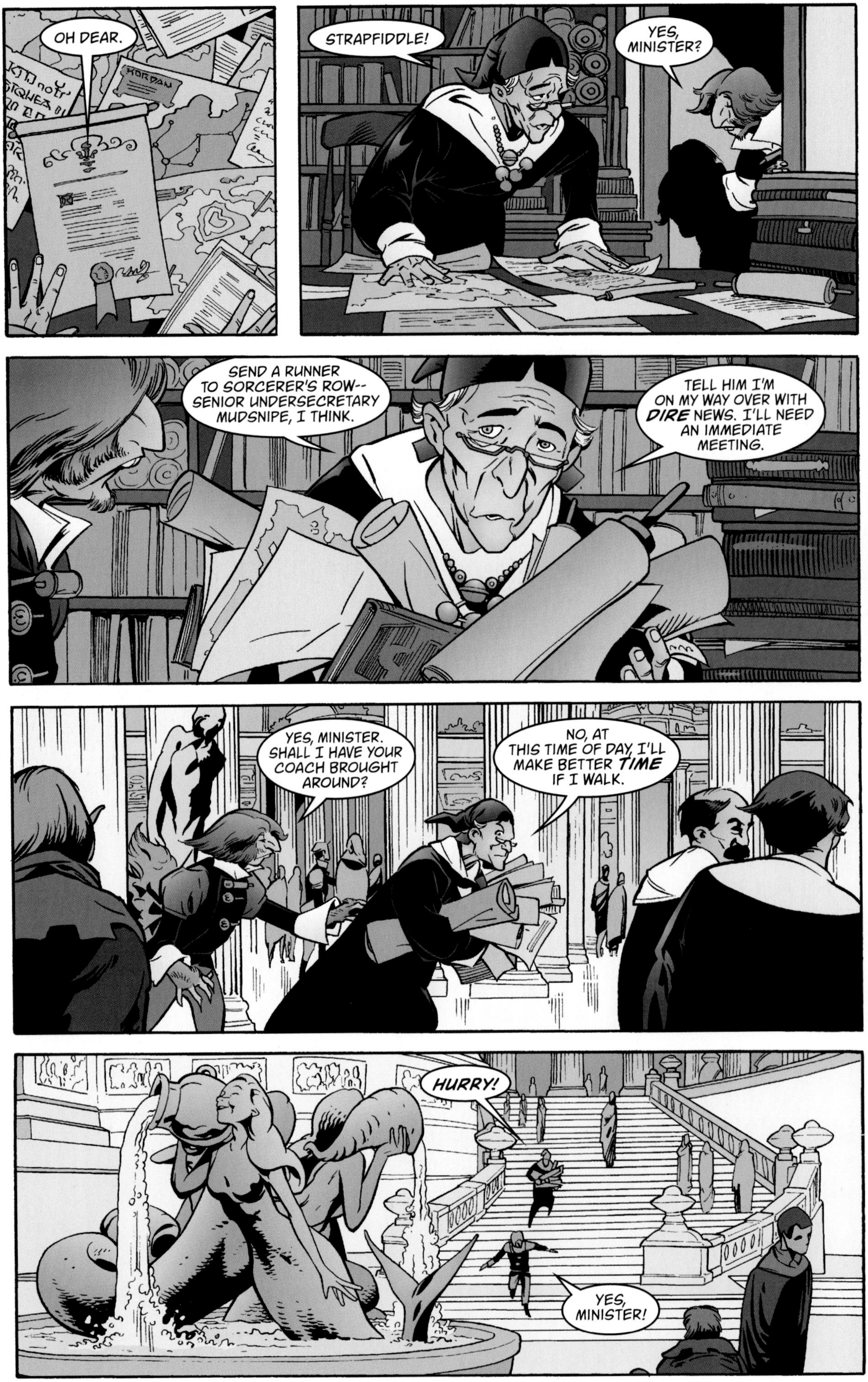
OH DEAR.
STRAPFIDDLE!
YES, MINISTER?
SEND A RUNNER TO SORCERER'S ROW-- SENIOR UNDERSECRETARY MUDSNIPE, I THINK.
TELL HIM I'M ON MY WAY OVER WITH ***DIRE*** NEWS. I'LL NEED AN IMMEDIATE MEETING.
YES, MINISTER. SHALL I HAVE YOUR COACH BROUGHT AROUND?
NO, AT THIS TIME OF DAY, I'LL MAKE BETTER ***TIME*** IF I WALK.
HURRY!
YES, MINISTER!

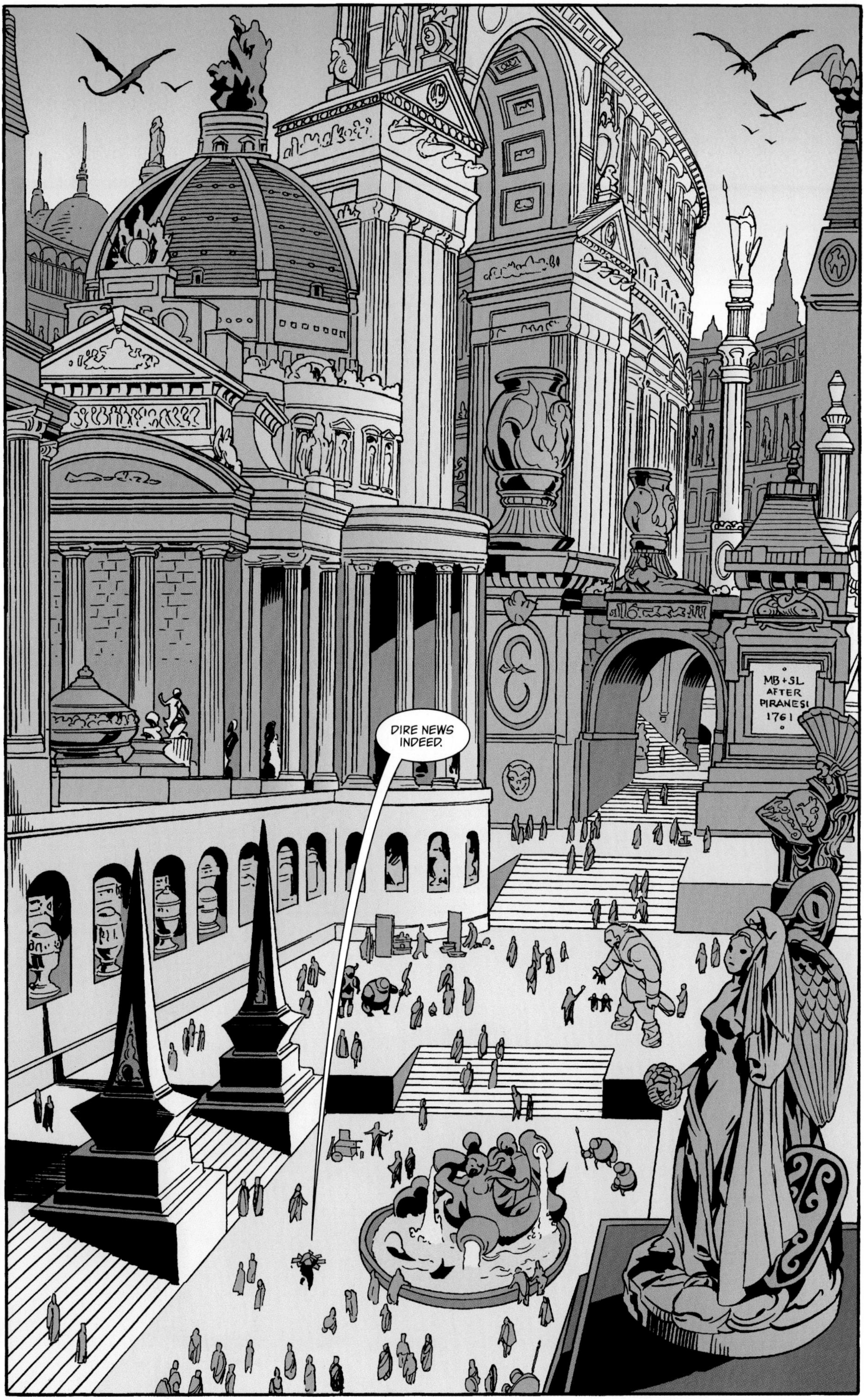
MB+SL
AFTER
PIRANESI
1761
DIRE NEWS
INDEED.

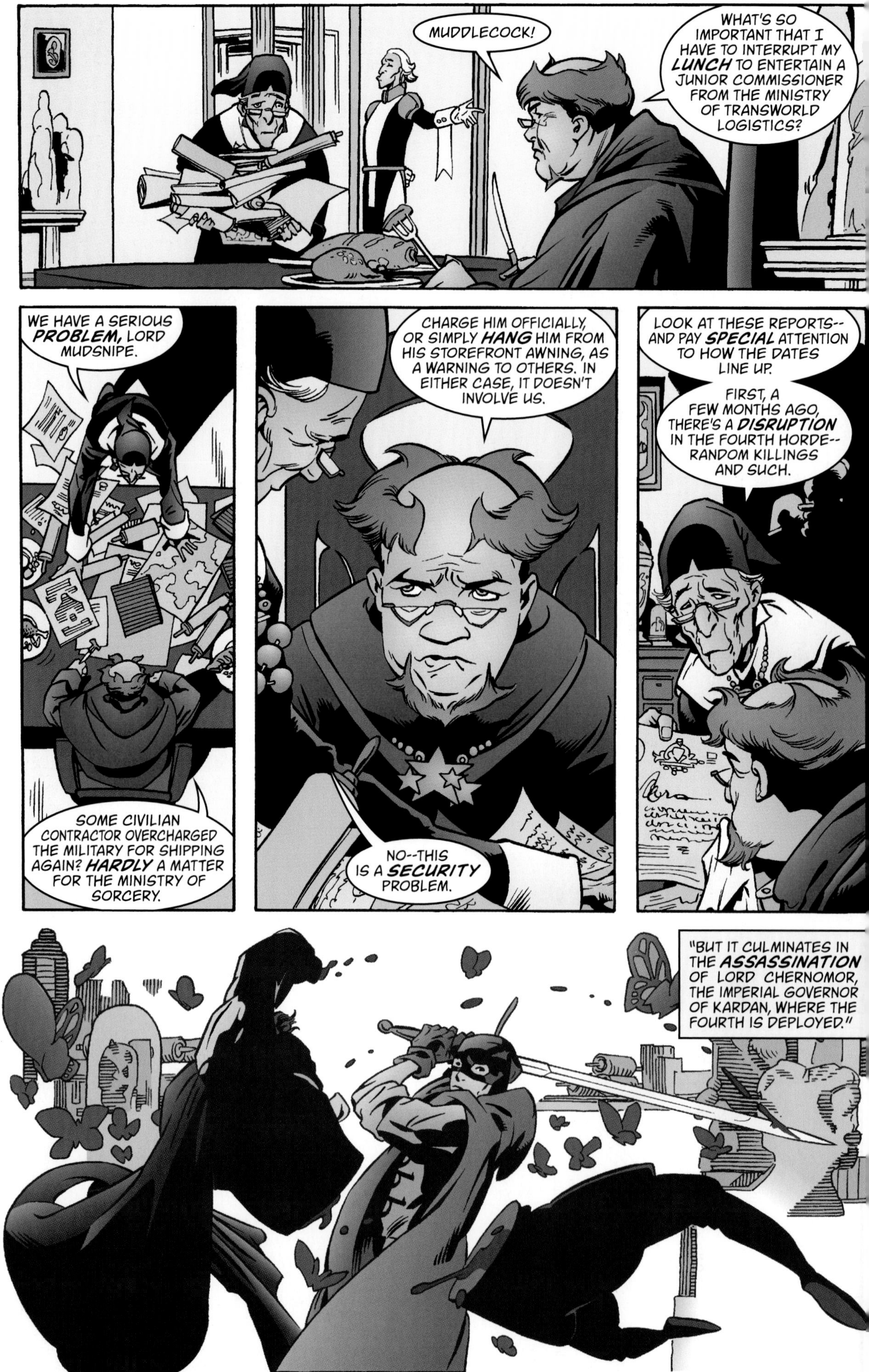

MUDDLECOCK!
WHAT'S SO IMPORTANT THAT I HAVE TO INTERRUPT MY LUNCH TO ENTERTAIN A JUNIOR COMMISSIONER FROM THE MINISTRY OF TRANSWORLD LOGISTICS?
WE HAVE A SERIOUS PROBLEM, LORD MUDSNIPE.
SOME CIVILIAN CONTRACTOR OVERCHARGED THE MILITARY FOR SHIPPING AGAIN? HARDLY A MATTER FOR THE MINISTRY OF SORCERY.
CHARGE HIM OFFICIALLY, OR SIMPLY HANG HIM FROM HIS STOREFRONT AWNING, AS A WARNING TO OTHERS. IN EITHER CASE, IT DOESN'T INVOLVE US.
NO--THIS IS A SECURITY PROBLEM.
LOOK AT THESE REPORTS--AND PAY SPECIAL ATTENTION TO HOW THE DATES LINE UP.
FIRST, A FEW MONTHS AGO, THERE'S A DISRUPTION IN THE FOURTH HORDE--RANDOM KILLINGS AND SUCH.
"BUT IT CULMINATES IN THE ASSASSINATION OF LORD CHERNOMOR, THE IMPERIAL GOVERNOR OF KARDAN, WHERE THE FOURTH IS DEPLOYED."

A LOCAL UPRISING?

I THOUGHT SO AT **FIRST**, BUT LOOK AT THIS. DAYS AFTER CHERNOMOR IS KILLED, SOMEONE OF HIS LIKENESS PASSES THROUGH THE GATE LINKING KARDAN TO THE WASTES OF SKOLD.

WASN'T A **DRAGON** KILLED THERE LAST MONTH?

I SEEM TO RECALL A REPORT--

EXACTLY.

"AND AFTER THAT, OUR KILLER SHOWS UP IN THE WORLD OF THE **RUS**, WHICH ONE CAN REACH FROM **SKOLD**."

OKAY, ONE OF THESE ROADS LEADS TO WHERE I WANT TO GO-- BUT **WHICH** ONE?

MB+CA after И. БИЛИБИНЪ ·1899·

ONLY IF YOU'RE WILLING TO CRAWL THROUGH A DRAGON'S **BELLY**.

CONVENIENT THEN TO HAVE A **DEAD** ONE, HMM?

"NOW LOOK AT THESE REPORTS FROM THE WORLD OF THE RUS. OUR KILLER IS UP TO SOME GRIM BUSINESS THERE."

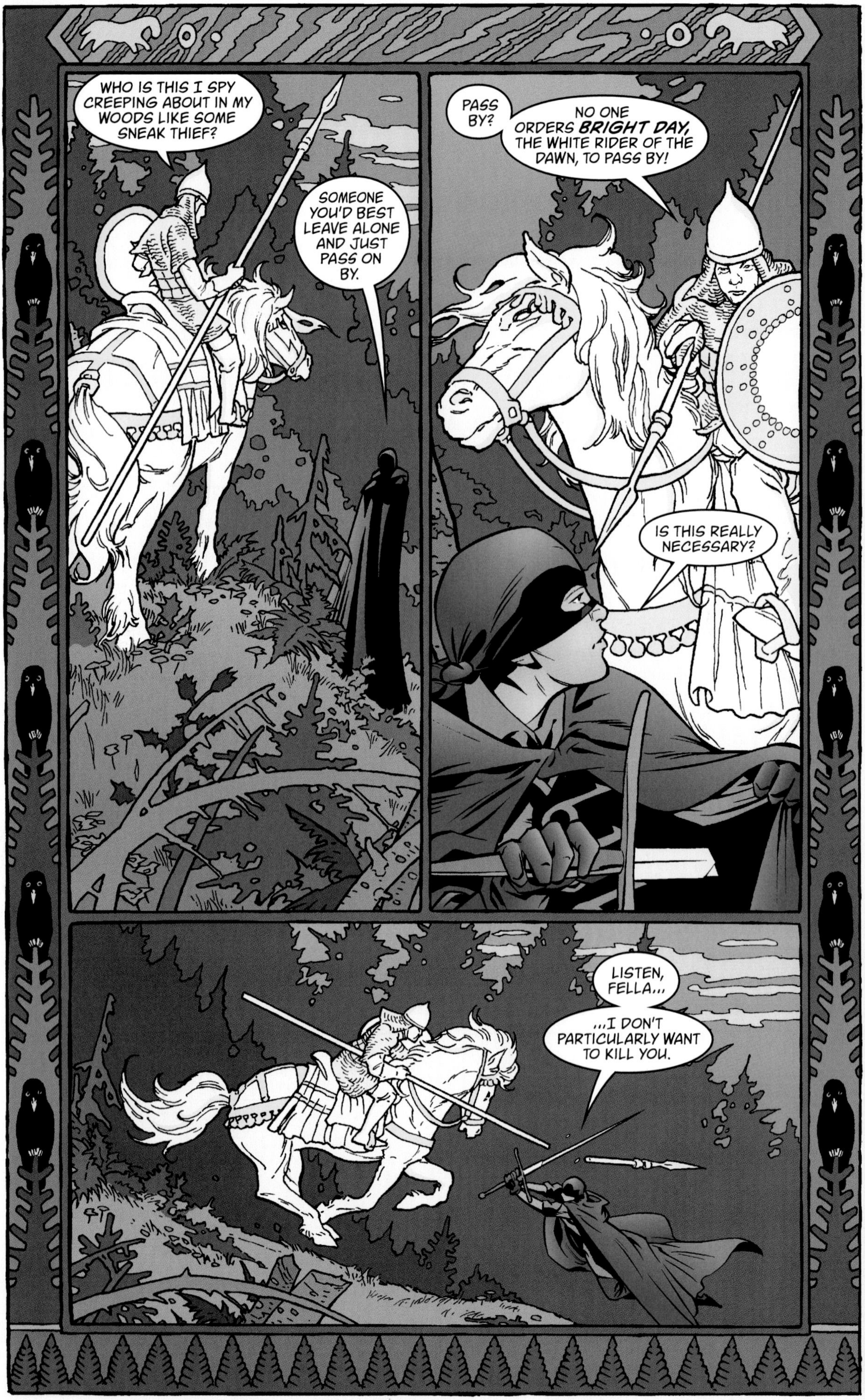
WHO IS THIS I SPY CREEPING ABOUT IN MY WOODS LIKE SOME SNEAK THIEF?
SOMEONE YOU'D BEST LEAVE ALONE AND JUST PASS ON BY.
PASS BY?
NO ONE ORDERS **BRIGHT DAY,** THE WHITE RIDER OF THE DAWN, TO PASS BY!
IS THIS REALLY NECESSARY?
LISTEN, FELLA...
...I DON'T PARTICULARLY WANT TO KILL YOU.

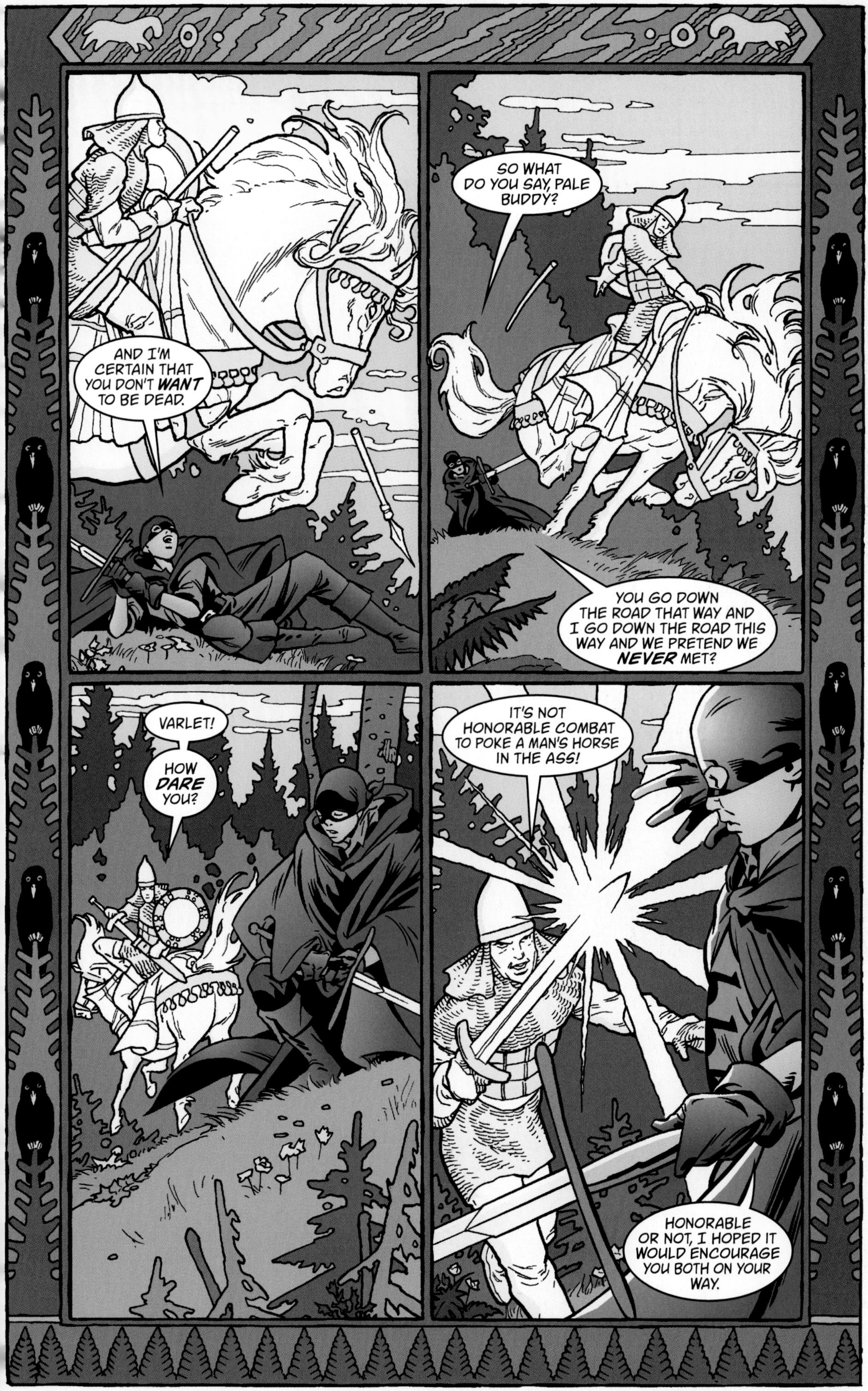
AND I'M CERTAIN THAT YOU DON'T *WANT* TO BE DEAD.
SO WHAT DO YOU SAY, PALE BUDDY?
YOU GO DOWN THE ROAD THAT WAY AND I GO DOWN THE ROAD THIS WAY AND WE PRETEND WE *NEVER* MET?
VARLET!
HOW *DARE* YOU?
IT'S NOT HONORABLE COMBAT TO POKE A MAN'S HORSE IN THE ASS!
HONORABLE OR NOT, I HOPED IT WOULD ENCOURAGE YOU BOTH ON YOUR WAY.

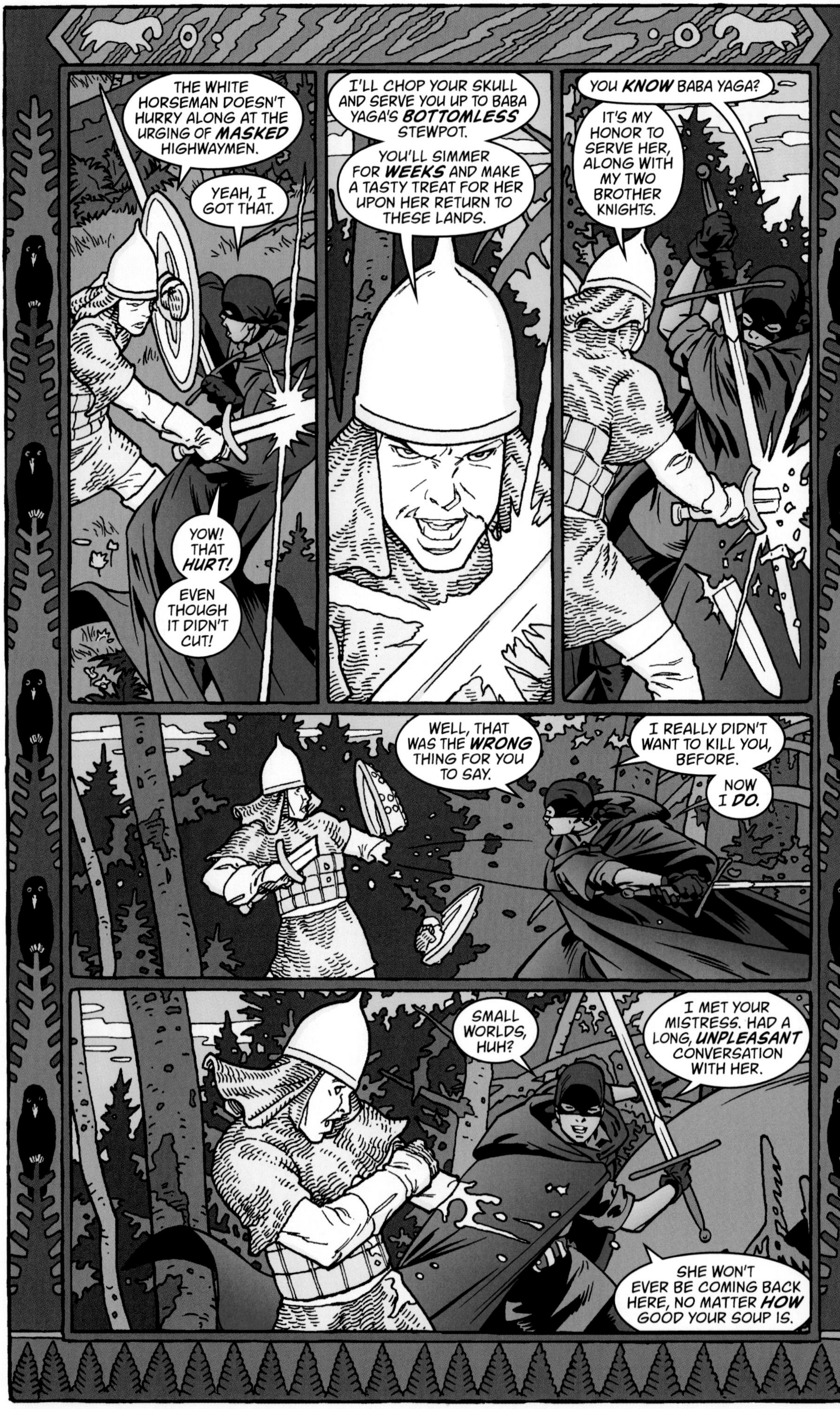
THE WHITE HORSEMAN DOESN'T HURRY ALONG AT THE URGING OF MASKED HIGHWAYMEN.
YEAH, I GOT THAT.
YOW! THAT HURT!
EVEN THOUGH IT DIDN'T CUT!
I'LL CHOP YOUR SKULL AND SERVE YOU UP TO BABA YAGA'S BOTTOMLESS STEWPOT.
YOU'LL SIMMER FOR WEEKS AND MAKE A TASTY TREAT FOR HER UPON HER RETURN TO THESE LANDS.
YOU KNOW BABA YAGA?
IT'S MY HONOR TO SERVE HER, ALONG WITH MY TWO BROTHER KNIGHTS.
WELL, THAT WAS THE WRONG THING FOR YOU TO SAY.
I REALLY DIDN'T WANT TO KILL YOU, BEFORE.
NOW I DO.
SMALL WORLDS, HUH?
I MET YOUR MISTRESS. HAD A LONG, UNPLEASANT CONVERSATION WITH HER.
SHE WON'T EVER BE COMING BACK HERE, NO MATTER HOW GOOD YOUR SOUP IS.

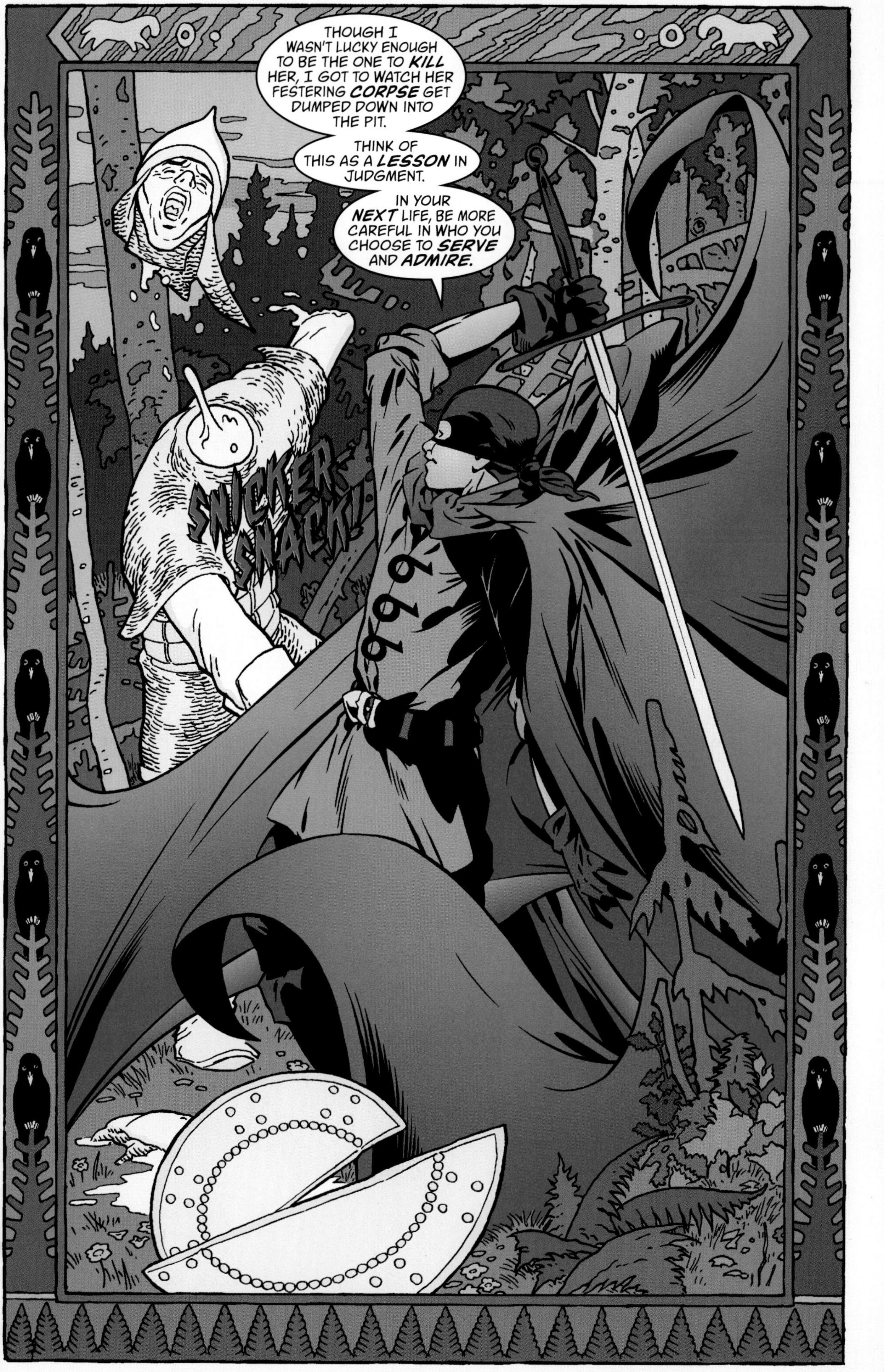
THOUGH I WASN'T LUCKY ENOUGH TO BE THE ONE TO KILL HER, I GOT TO WATCH HER FESTERING CORPSE GET DUMPED DOWN INTO THE PIT.
THINK OF THIS AS A LESSON IN JUDGMENT.
IN YOUR NEXT LIFE, BE MORE CAREFUL IN WHO YOU CHOOSE TO SERVE AND ADMIRE.
SNICKER-SNACK!!

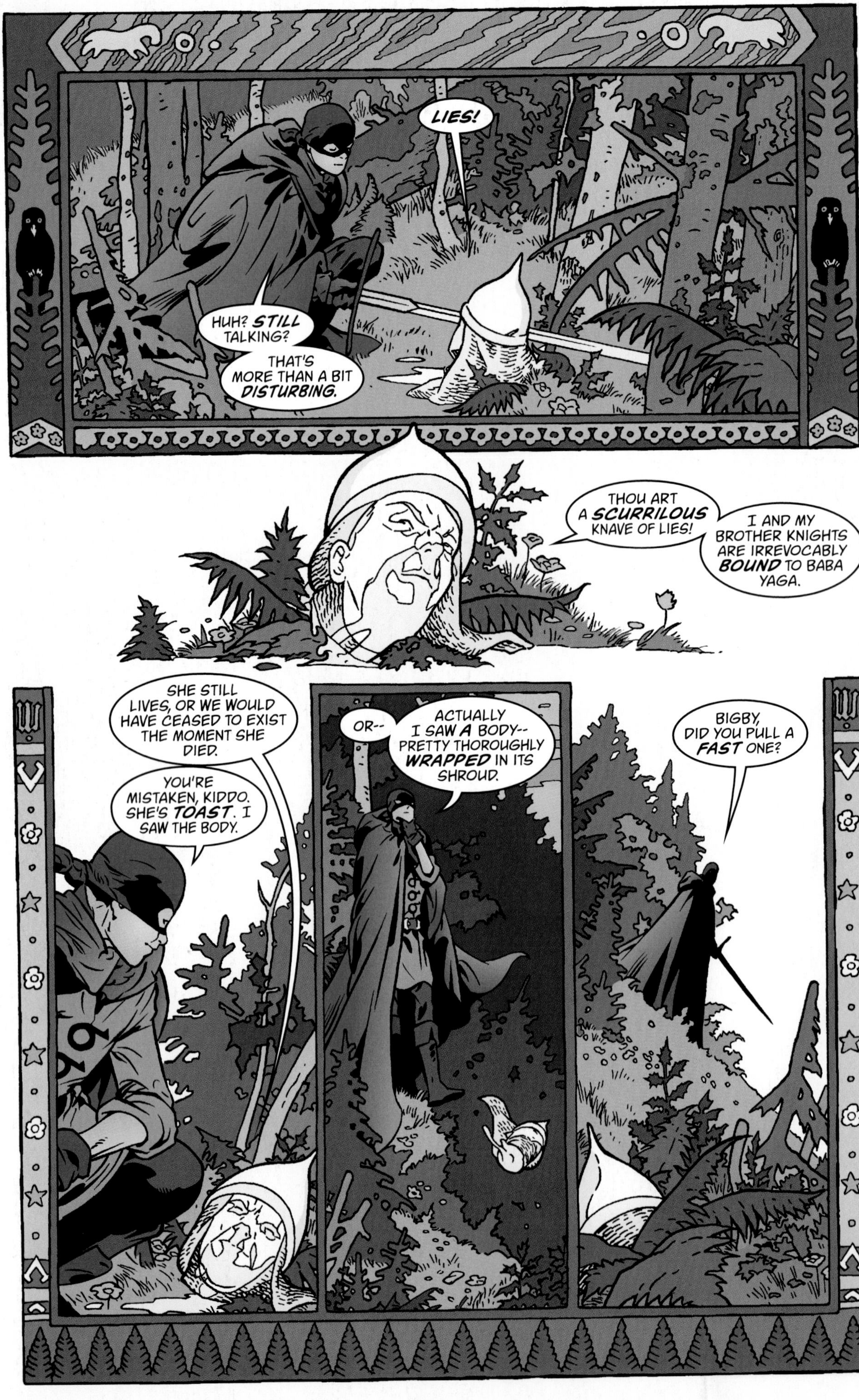

LIES!
HUH? STILL TALKING?
THAT'S MORE THAN A BIT DISTURBING.
THOU ART A SCURRILOUS KNAVE OF LIES!
I AND MY BROTHER KNIGHTS ARE IRREVOCABLY BOUND TO BABA YAGA.
SHE STILL LIVES, OR WE WOULD HAVE CEASED TO EXIST THE MOMENT SHE DIED.
YOU'RE MISTAKEN, KIDDO. SHE'S TOAST. I SAW THE BODY.
OR--
ACTUALLY I SAW A BODY-- PRETTY THOROUGHLY WRAPPED IN ITS SHROUD.
BIGBY, DID YOU PULL A FAST ONE?

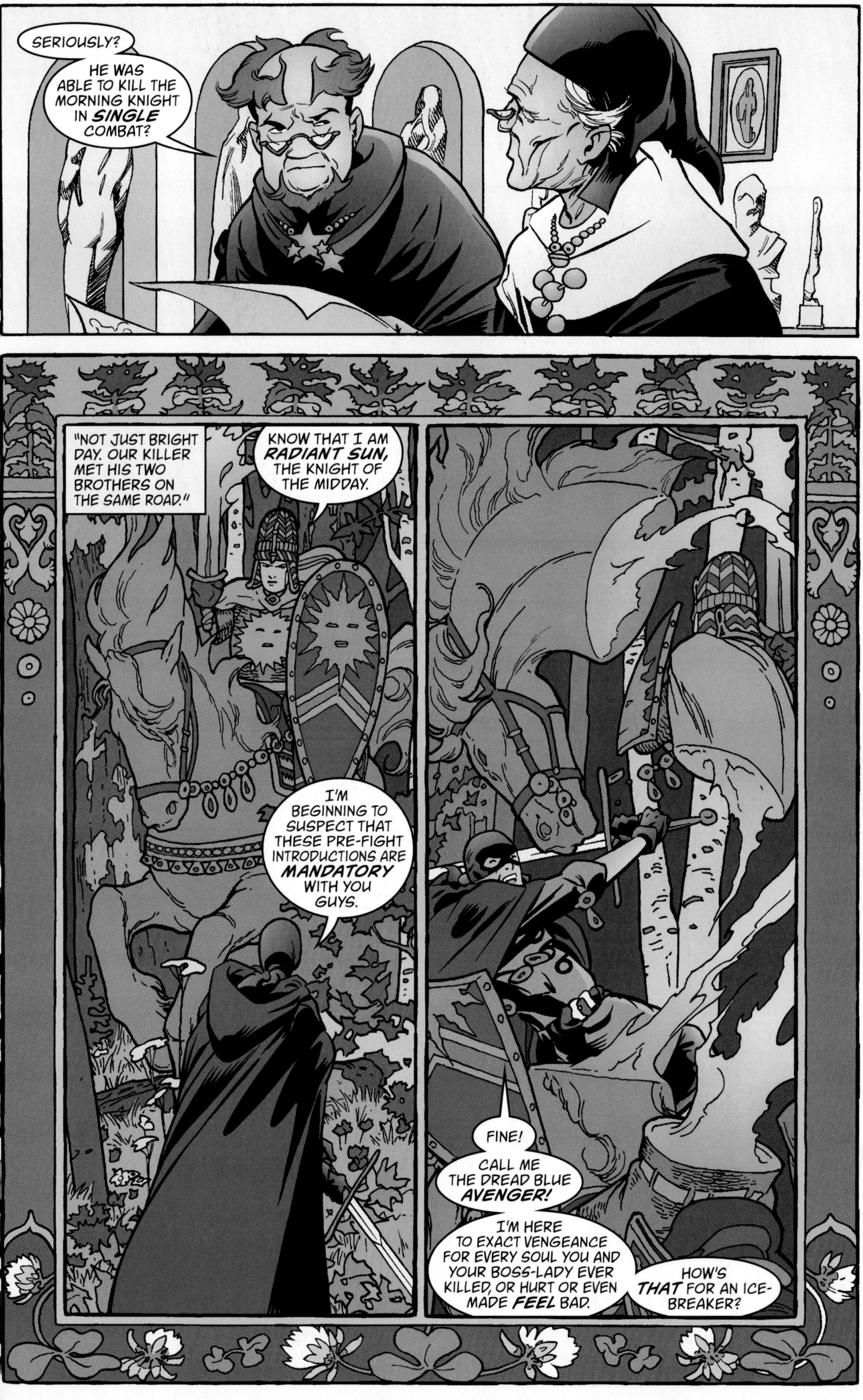
SERIOUSLY?
HE WAS ABLE TO KILL THE MORNING KNIGHT IN SINGLE COMBAT?
"NOT JUST BRIGHT DAY. OUR KILLER MET HIS TWO BROTHERS ON THE SAME ROAD."
KNOW THAT I AM RADIANT SUN, THE KNIGHT OF THE MIDDAY.
I'M BEGINNING TO SUSPECT THAT THESE PRE-FIGHT INTRODUCTIONS ARE MANDATORY WITH YOU GUYS.
FINE!
CALL ME THE DREAD BLUE AVENGER!
I'M HERE TO EXACT VENGEANCE FOR EVERY SOUL YOU AND YOUR BOSS-LADY EVER KILLED, OR HURT OR EVEN MADE FEEL BAD.
HOW'S THAT FOR AN ICE-BREAKER?

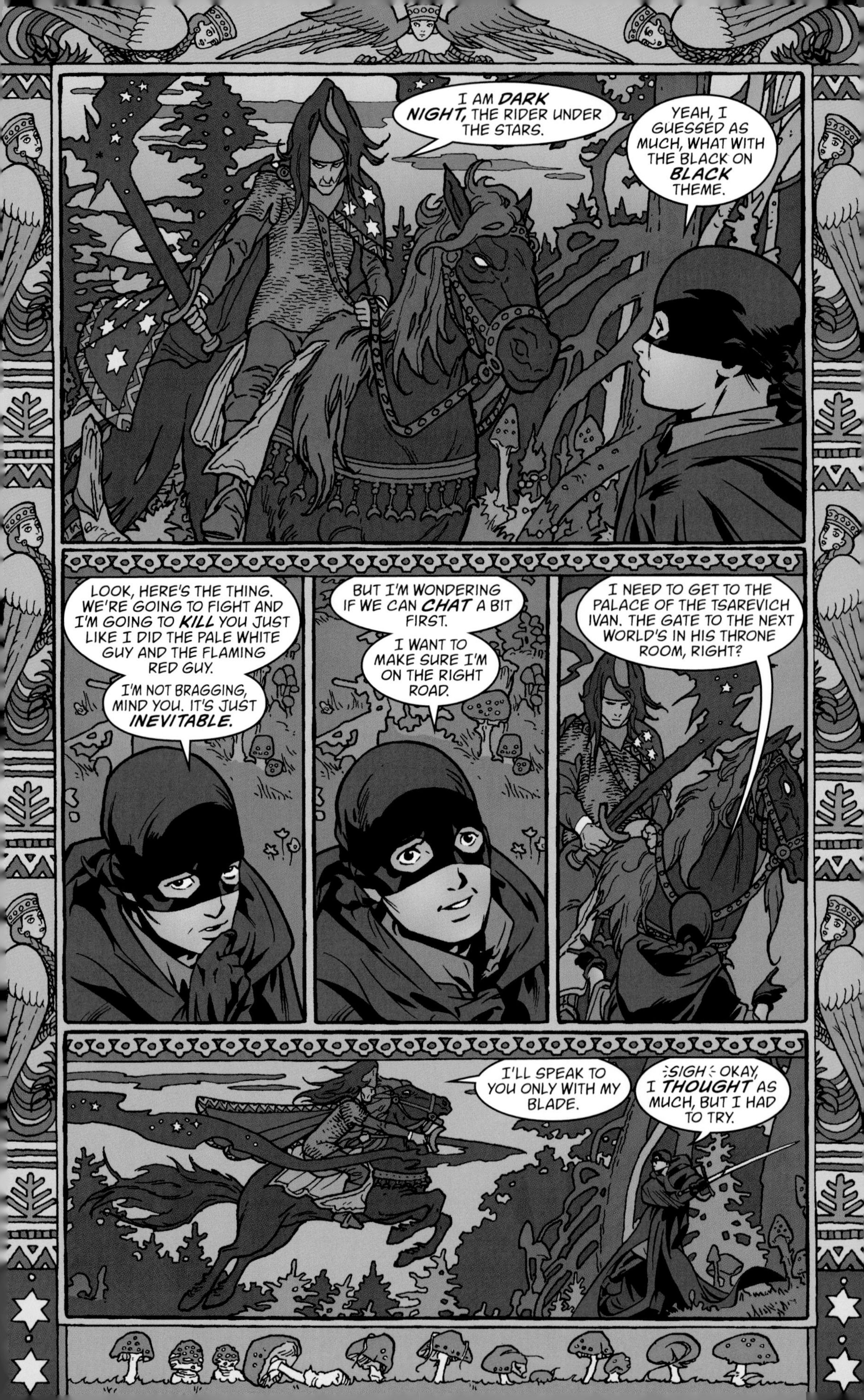
I AM DARK NIGHT, THE RIDER UNDER THE STARS.
YEAH, I GUESSED AS MUCH, WHAT WITH THE BLACK ON BLACK THEME.
LOOK, HERE'S THE THING. WE'RE GOING TO FIGHT AND I'M GOING TO KILL YOU JUST LIKE I DID THE PALE WHITE GUY AND THE FLAMING RED GUY.
I'M NOT BRAGGING, MIND YOU. IT'S JUST INEVITABLE.
BUT I'M WONDERING IF WE CAN CHAT A BIT FIRST.
I WANT TO MAKE SURE I'M ON THE RIGHT ROAD.
I NEED TO GET TO THE PALACE OF THE TSAREVICH IVAN. THE GATE TO THE NEXT WORLD'S IN HIS THRONE ROOM, RIGHT?
I'LL SPEAK TO YOU ONLY WITH MY BLADE.
SIGH OKAY, I THOUGHT AS MUCH, BUT I HAD TO TRY.

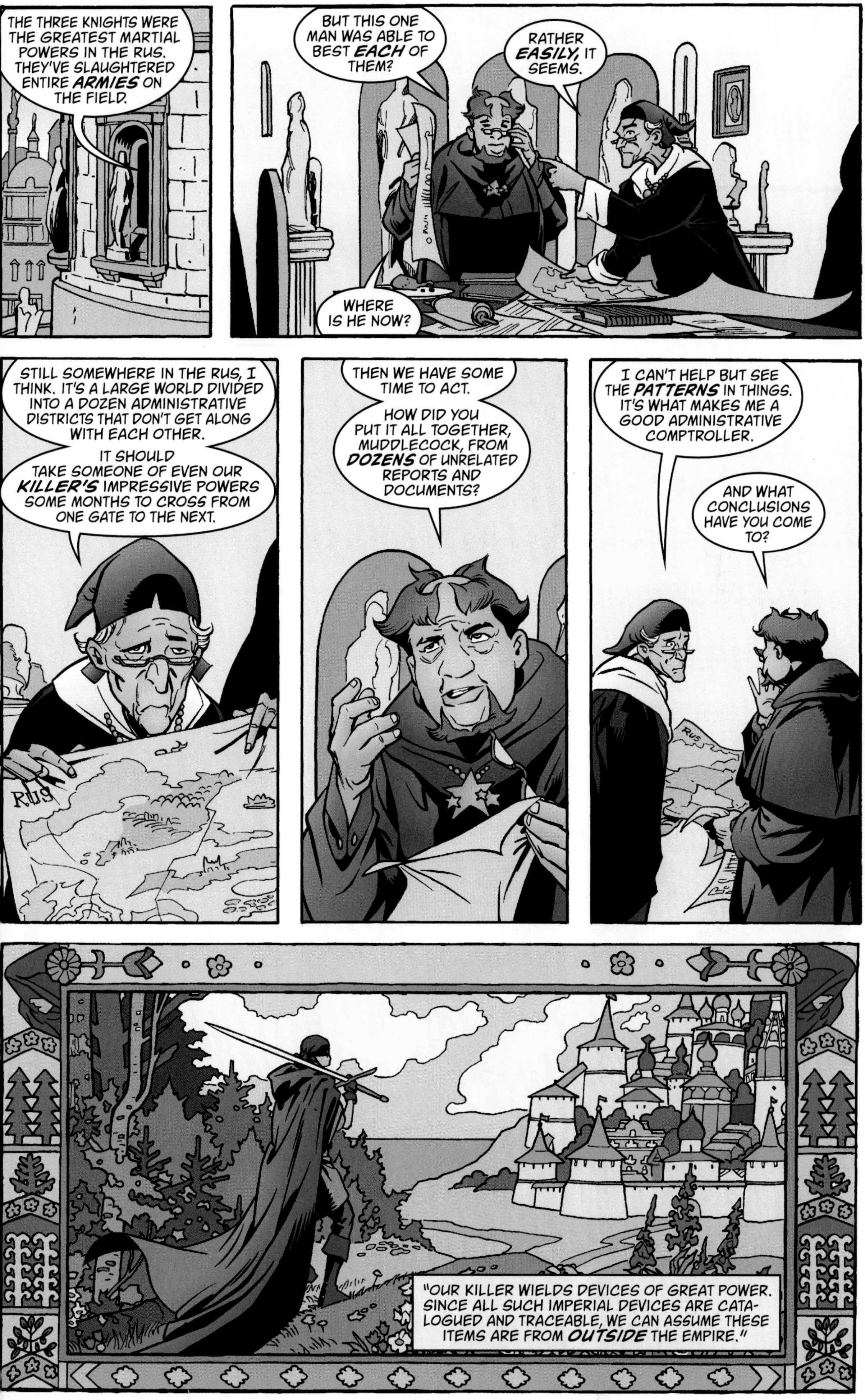
THE THREE KNIGHTS WERE THE GREATEST MARTIAL POWERS IN THE RUS. THEY'VE SLAUGHTERED ENTIRE ARMIES ON THE FIELD.
BUT THIS ONE MAN WAS ABLE TO BEST EACH OF THEM?
RATHER EASILY, IT SEEMS.
WHERE IS HE NOW?
STILL SOMEWHERE IN THE RUS, I THINK. IT'S A LARGE WORLD DIVIDED INTO A DOZEN ADMINISTRATIVE DISTRICTS THAT DON'T GET ALONG WITH EACH OTHER.
IT SHOULD TAKE SOMEONE OF EVEN OUR KILLER'S IMPRESSIVE POWERS SOME MONTHS TO CROSS FROM ONE GATE TO THE NEXT.
RUS
THEN WE HAVE SOME TIME TO ACT.
HOW DID YOU PUT IT ALL TOGETHER, MUDDLECOCK, FROM DOZENS OF UNRELATED REPORTS AND DOCUMENTS?
I CAN'T HELP BUT SEE THE PATTERNS IN THINGS. IT'S WHAT MAKES ME A GOOD ADMINISTRATIVE COMPTROLLER.
AND WHAT CONCLUSIONS HAVE YOU COME TO?
RUS
"OUR KILLER WIELDS DEVICES OF GREAT POWER. SINCE ALL SUCH IMPERIAL DEVICES ARE CATALOGUED AND TRACEABLE, WE CAN ASSUME THESE ITEMS ARE FROM OUTSIDE THE EMPIRE."

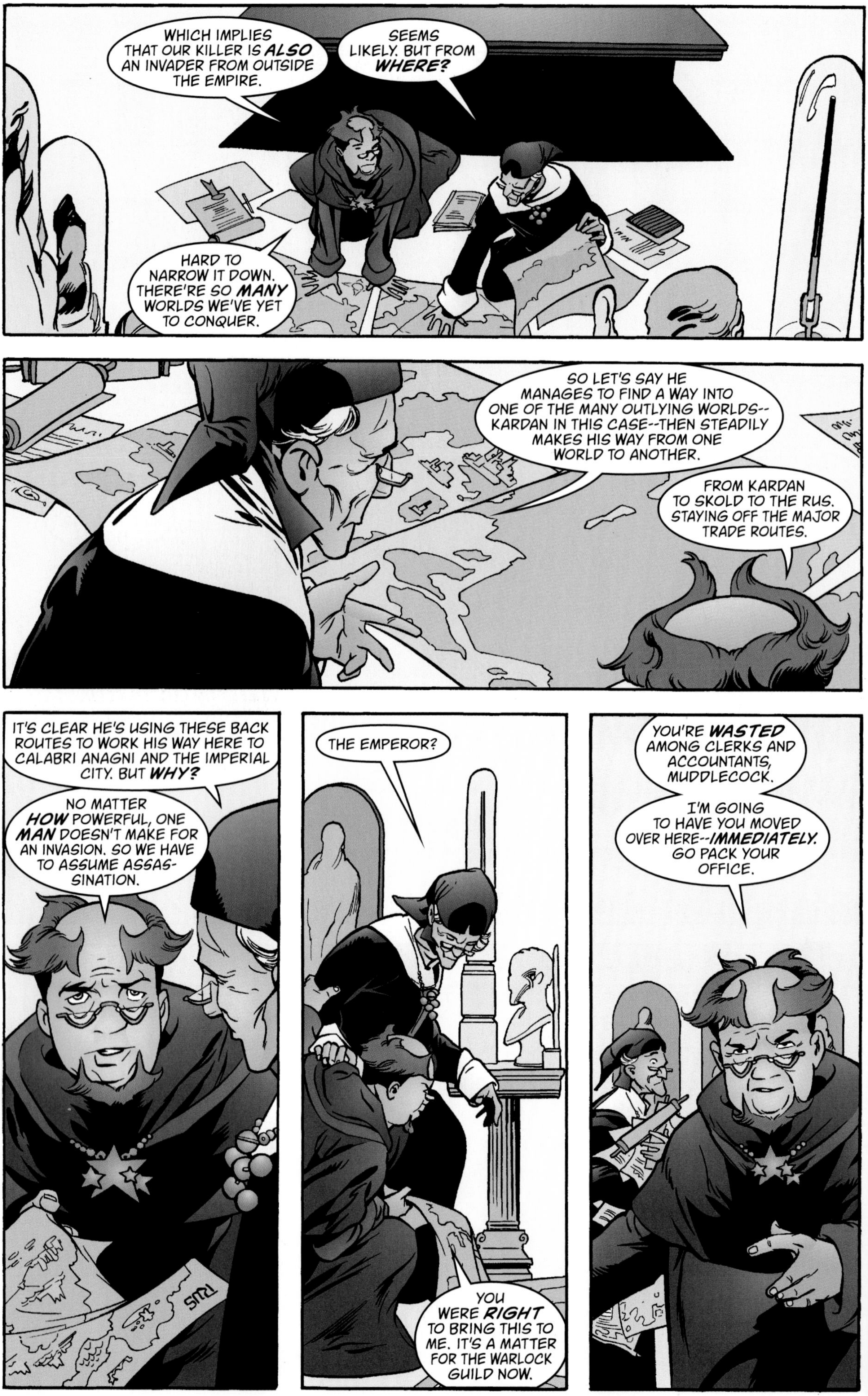
WHICH IMPLIES THAT OUR KILLER IS ALSO AN INVADER FROM OUTSIDE THE EMPIRE.
SEEMS LIKELY. BUT FROM WHERE?
HARD TO NARROW IT DOWN. THERE'RE SO MANY WORLDS WE'VE YET TO CONQUER.
SO LET'S SAY HE MANAGES TO FIND A WAY INTO ONE OF THE MANY OUTLYING WORLDS-- KARDAN IN THIS CASE--THEN STEADILY MAKES HIS WAY FROM ONE WORLD TO ANOTHER.
FROM KARDAN TO SKOLD TO THE RUS. STAYING OFF THE MAJOR TRADE ROUTES.
IT'S CLEAR HE'S USING THESE BACK ROUTES TO WORK HIS WAY HERE TO CALABRI ANAGNI AND THE IMPERIAL CITY. BUT WHY?
NO MATTER HOW POWERFUL, ONE MAN DOESN'T MAKE FOR AN INVASION. SO WE HAVE TO ASSUME ASSAS-SINATION.
RUS
THE EMPEROR?
YOU WERE RIGHT TO BRING THIS TO ME. IT'S A MATTER FOR THE WARLOCK GUILD NOW.
YOU'RE WASTED AMONG CLERKS AND ACCOUNTANTS, MUDDLECOCK.
I'M GOING TO HAVE YOU MOVED OVER HERE--IMMEDIATELY. GO PACK YOUR OFFICE.

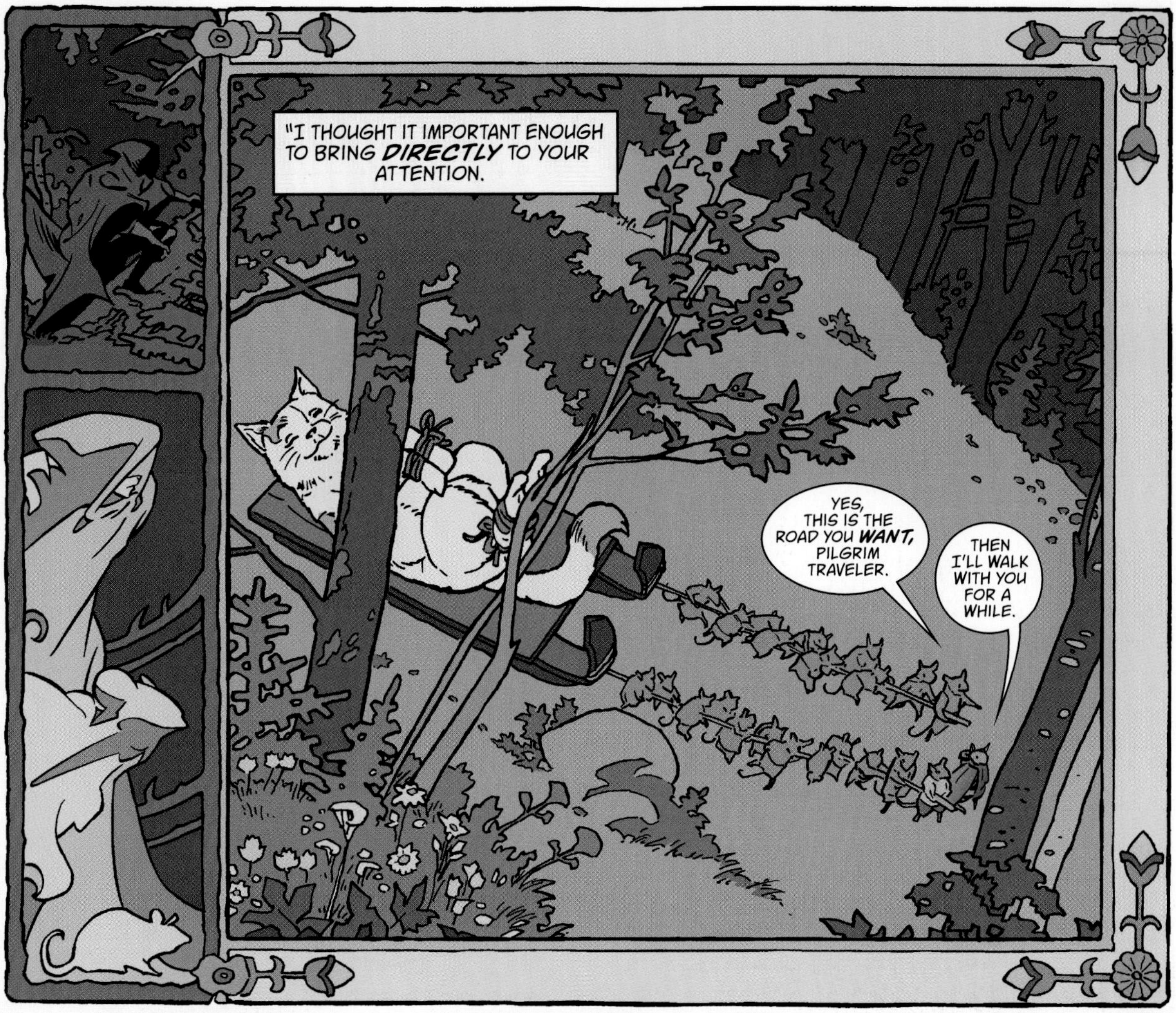
"I THOUGHT IT IMPORTANT ENOUGH TO BRING DIRECTLY TO YOUR ATTENTION.
YES, THIS IS THE ROAD YOU WANT, PILGRIM TRAVELER.
THEN I'LL WALK WITH YOU FOR A WHILE.

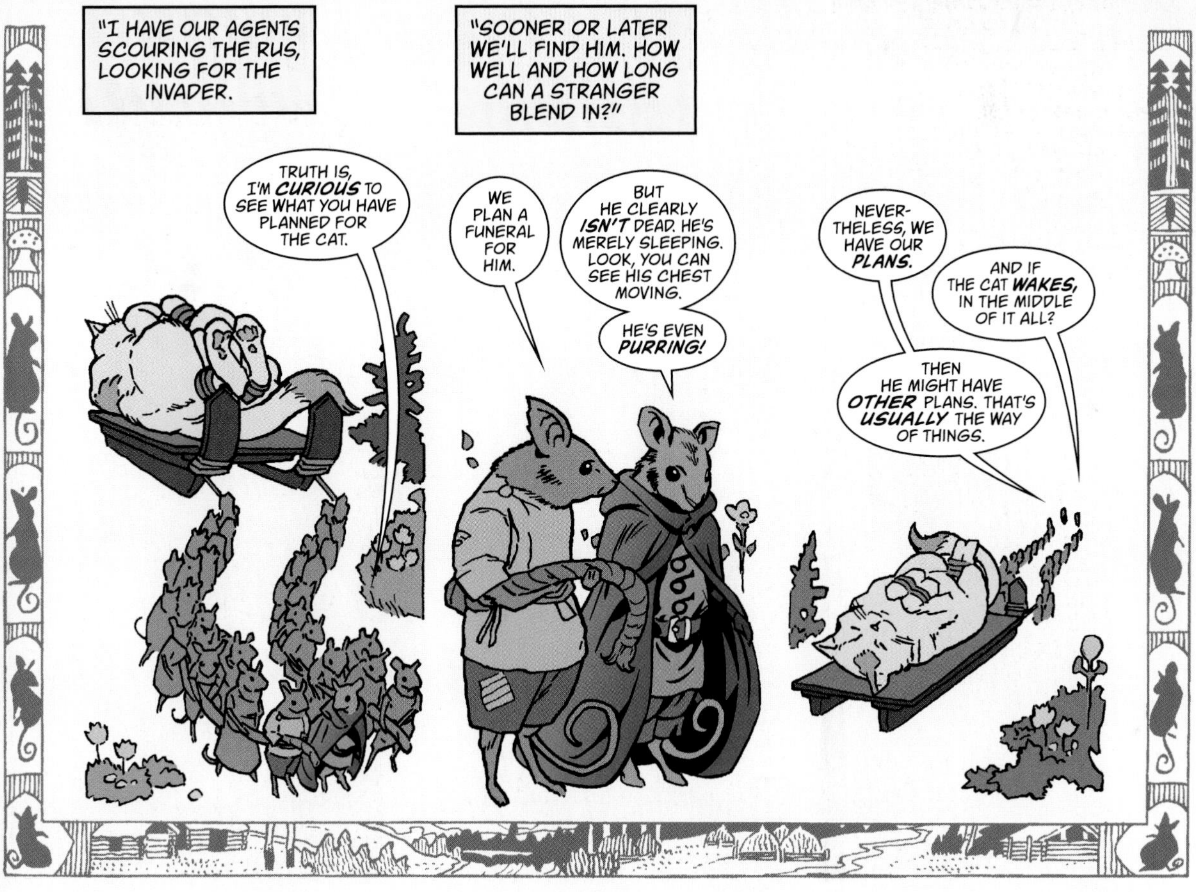
"I HAVE OUR AGENTS SCOURING THE RUS, LOOKING FOR THE INVADER.
"SOONER OR LATER WE'LL FIND HIM. HOW WELL AND HOW LONG CAN A STRANGER BLEND IN?"
TRUTH IS, I'M CURIOUS TO SEE WHAT YOU HAVE PLANNED FOR THE CAT.
WE PLAN A FUNERAL FOR HIM.
BUT HE CLEARLY ISN'T DEAD. HE'S MERELY SLEEPING. LOOK, YOU CAN SEE HIS CHEST MOVING.
HE'S EVEN PURRING!
NEVER-THELESS, WE HAVE OUR PLANS.
AND IF THE CAT WAKES, IN THE MIDDLE OF IT ALL?
THEN HE MIGHT HAVE OTHER PLANS. THAT'S USUALLY THE WAY OF THINGS.

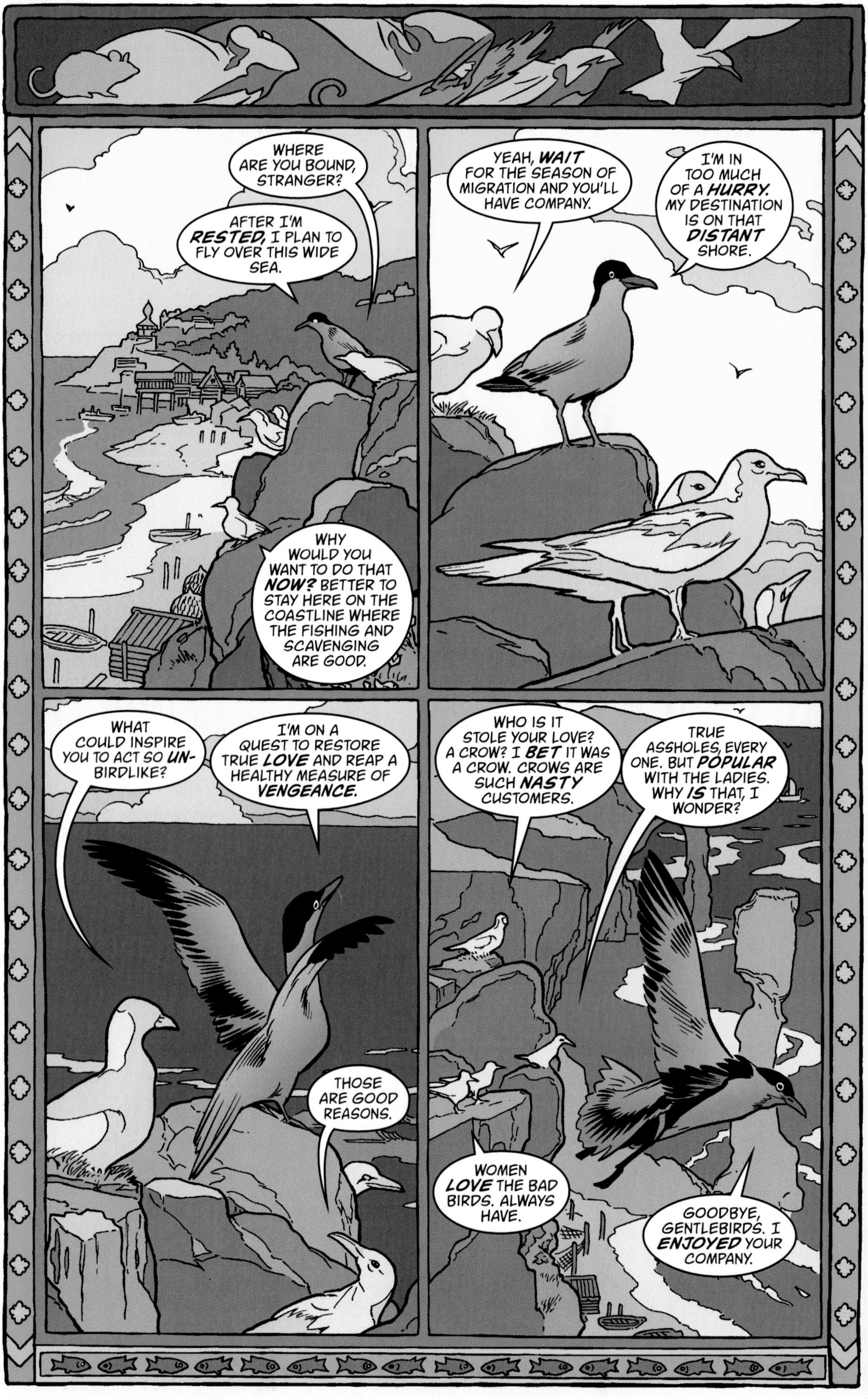
WHERE ARE YOU BOUND, STRANGER?
AFTER I'M RESTED, I PLAN TO FLY OVER THIS WIDE SEA.
WHY WOULD YOU WANT TO DO THAT NOW? BETTER TO STAY HERE ON THE COASTLINE WHERE THE FISHING AND SCAVENGING ARE GOOD.
YEAH, WAIT FOR THE SEASON OF MIGRATION AND YOU'LL HAVE COMPANY.
I'M IN TOO MUCH OF A HURRY. MY DESTINATION IS ON THAT DISTANT SHORE.
WHAT COULD INSPIRE YOU TO ACT SO UN-BIRDLIKE?
I'M ON A QUEST TO RESTORE TRUE LOVE AND REAP A HEALTHY MEASURE OF VENGEANCE.
THOSE ARE GOOD REASONS.
WHO IS IT STOLE YOUR LOVE? A CROW? I BET IT WAS A CROW. CROWS ARE SUCH NASTY CUSTOMERS.
TRUE ASSHOLES, EVERY ONE. BUT POPULAR WITH THE LADIES. WHY IS THAT, I WONDER?
WOMEN LOVE THE BAD BIRDS. ALWAYS HAVE.
GOODBYE, GENTLEBIRDS. I ENJOYED YOUR COMPANY.

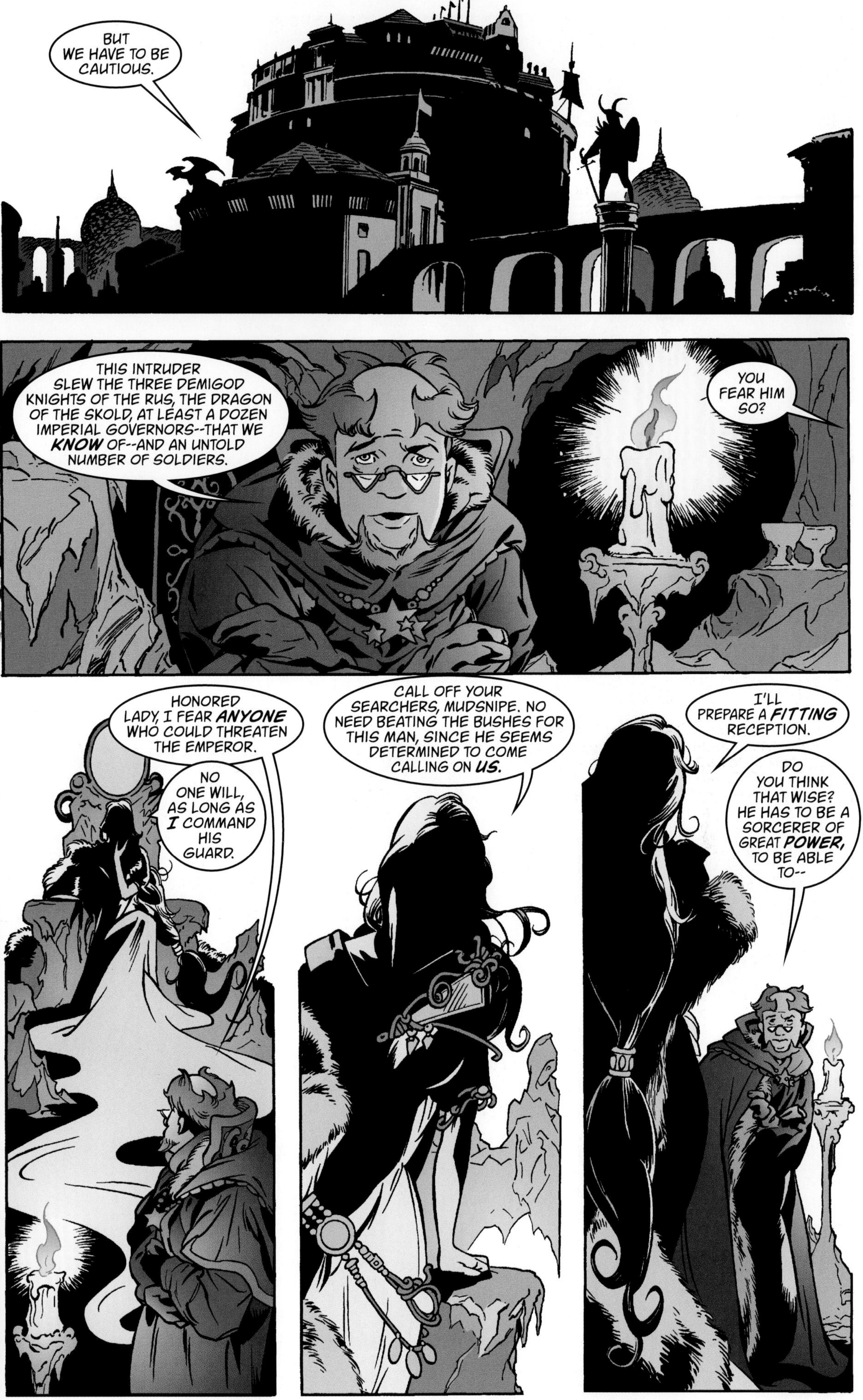
BUT WE HAVE TO BE CAUTIOUS.
THIS INTRUDER SLEW THE THREE DEMIGOD KNIGHTS OF THE RUS, THE DRAGON OF THE SKOLD, AT LEAST A DOZEN IMPERIAL GOVERNORS--THAT WE KNOW OF--AND AN UNTOLD NUMBER OF SOLDIERS.
YOU FEAR HIM SO?
HONORED LADY, I FEAR ANYONE WHO COULD THREATEN THE EMPEROR.
NO ONE WILL, AS LONG AS I COMMAND HIS GUARD.
CALL OFF YOUR SEARCHERS, MUDSNIPE. NO NEED BEATING THE BUSHES FOR THIS MAN, SINCE HE SEEMS DETERMINED TO COME CALLING ON US.
I'LL PREPARE A FITTING RECEPTION.
DO YOU THINK THAT WISE? HE HAS TO BE A SORCERER OF GREAT POWER, TO BE ABLE TO--

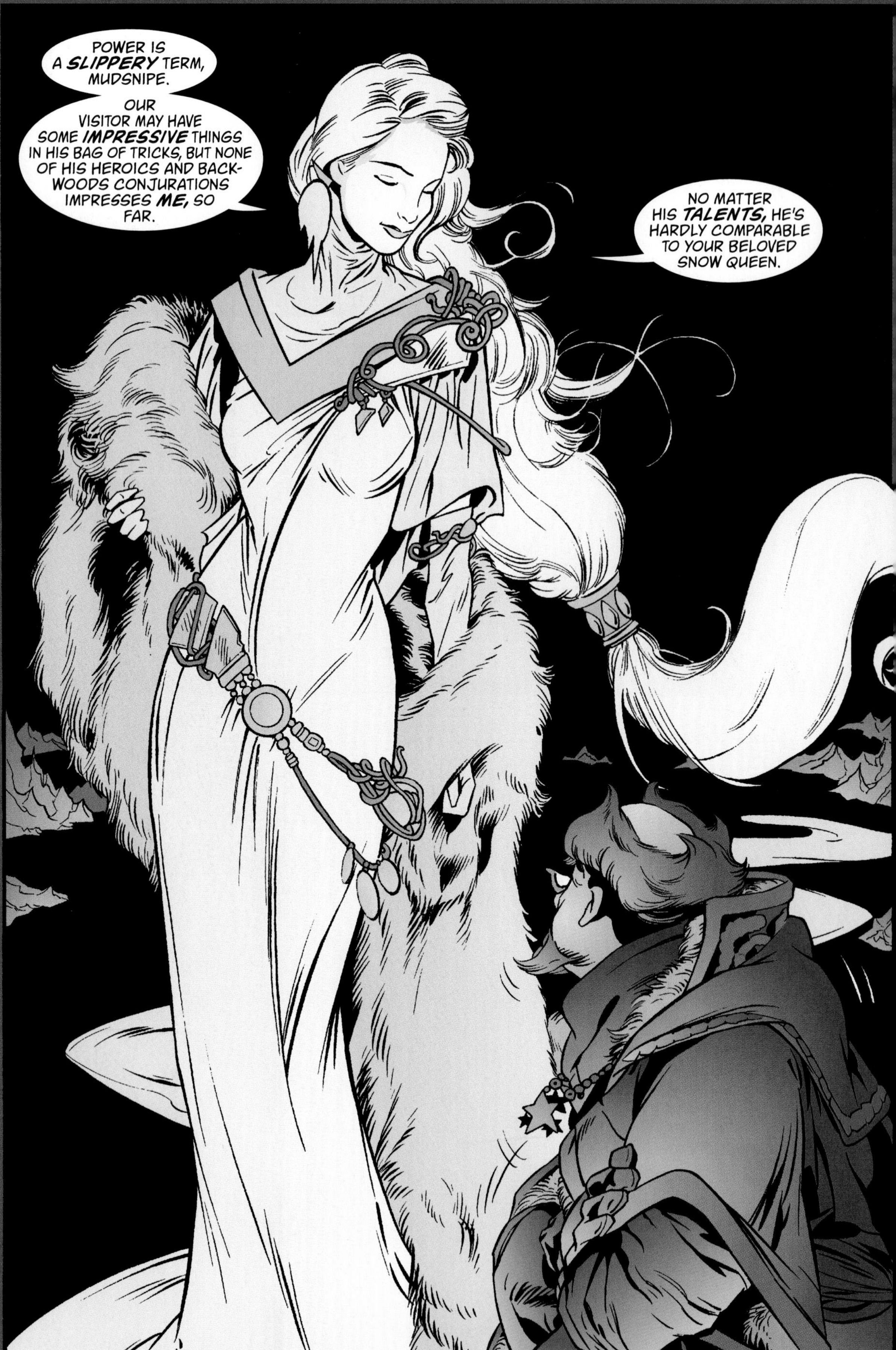
POWER IS A *SLIPPERY* TERM, MUDSNIPE.
OUR VISITOR MAY HAVE SOME *IMPRESSIVE* THINGS IN HIS BAG OF TRICKS, BUT NONE OF HIS HEROICS AND BACK-WOODS CONJURATIONS IMPRESSES *ME,* SO FAR.
NO MATTER HIS *TALENTS,* HE'S HARDLY COMPARABLE TO YOUR BELOVED SNOW QUEEN.

NEXT: THE ADVERSARY!

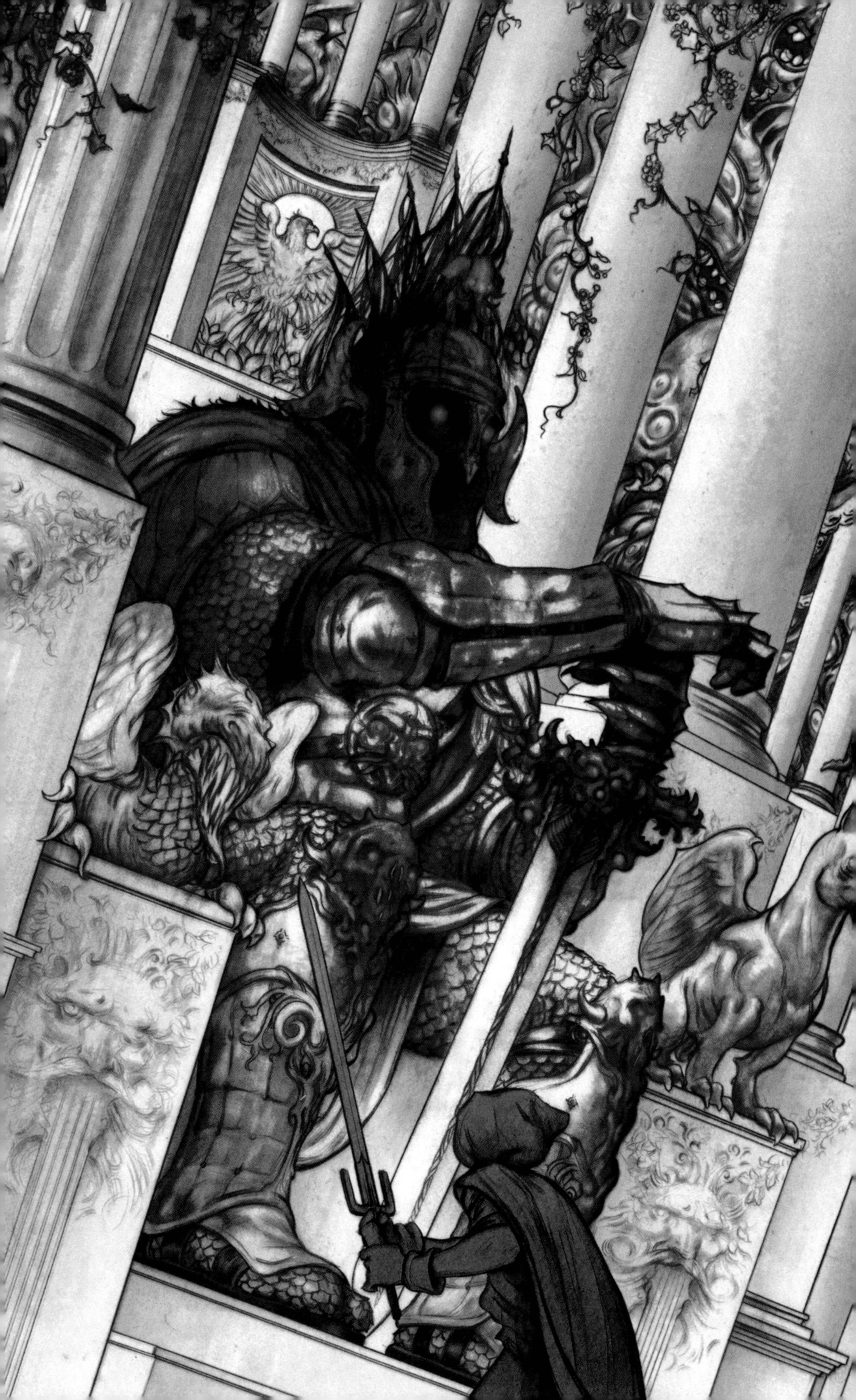

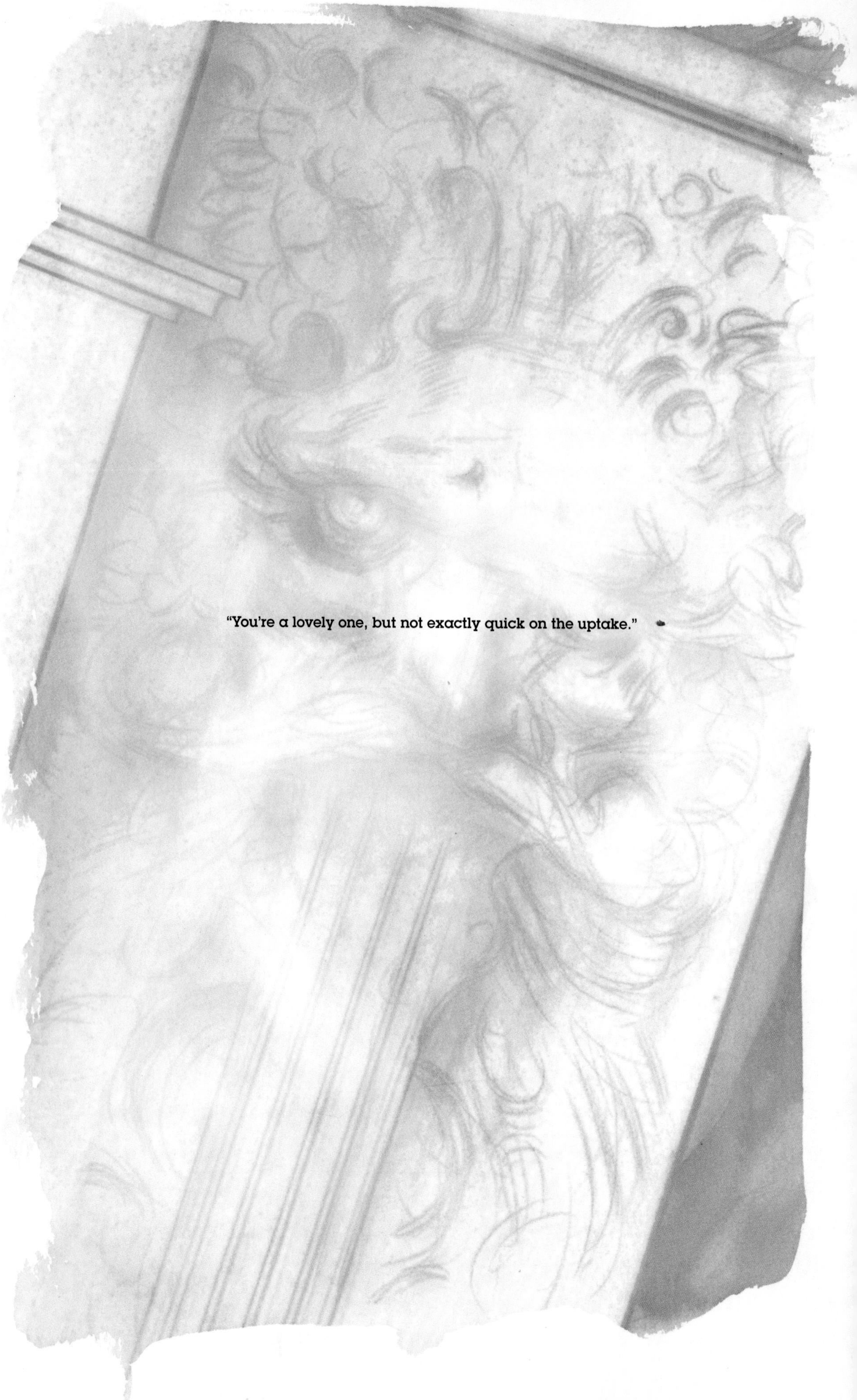

"You're a lovely one, but not exactly quick on the uptake."

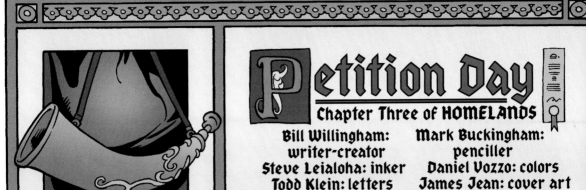

Petition Day
Chapter Three of HOMELANDS

Bill Willingham: writer-creator
Mark Buckingham: penciller
Steve Leialoha: inker
Daniel Vozzo: colors
Todd Klein: letters
James Jean: cover art
Mariah Huehner: asst. ed.
Shelly Bond: editor

GOOD **MORNING**, MY GOOD FELLOW. HOW FAR AM I FROM CALABRI ANAGNI?

OH, YOU'VE BEEN INSIDE THE CALABRI ANAGNI DISTRICT FOR SOME **TIME** NOW, SIR, BUT IF IT'S THE IMPERIAL CITY YOU'RE WANTING, YOU'RE NOT THREE LEAGUES DISTANT FROM IT ON THIS VERY ROAD.

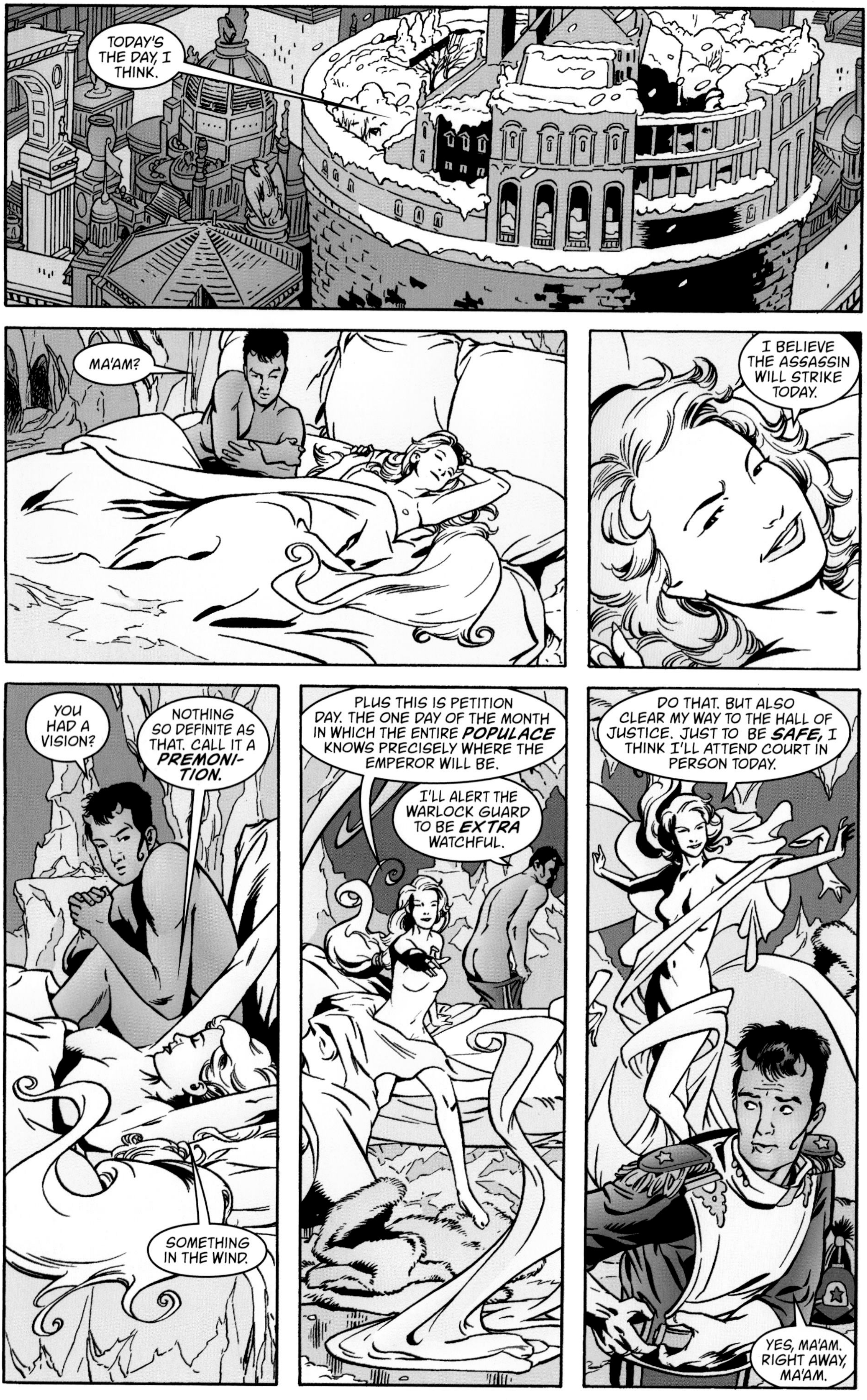
TODAY'S THE DAY, I THINK.
MA'AM?
I BELIEVE THE ASSASSIN WILL STRIKE TODAY.
YOU HAD A VISION?
NOTHING SO DEFINITE AS THAT. CALL IT A PREMONI-TION.
SOMETHING IN THE WIND.
PLUS THIS IS PETITION DAY. THE ONE DAY OF THE MONTH IN WHICH THE ENTIRE POPULACE KNOWS PRECISELY WHERE THE EMPEROR WILL BE.
I'LL ALERT THE WARLOCK GUARD TO BE EXTRA WATCHFUL.
DO THAT. BUT ALSO CLEAR MY WAY TO THE HALL OF JUSTICE. JUST TO BE SAFE, I THINK I'LL ATTEND COURT IN PERSON TODAY.
YES, MA'AM. RIGHT AWAY, MA'AM.

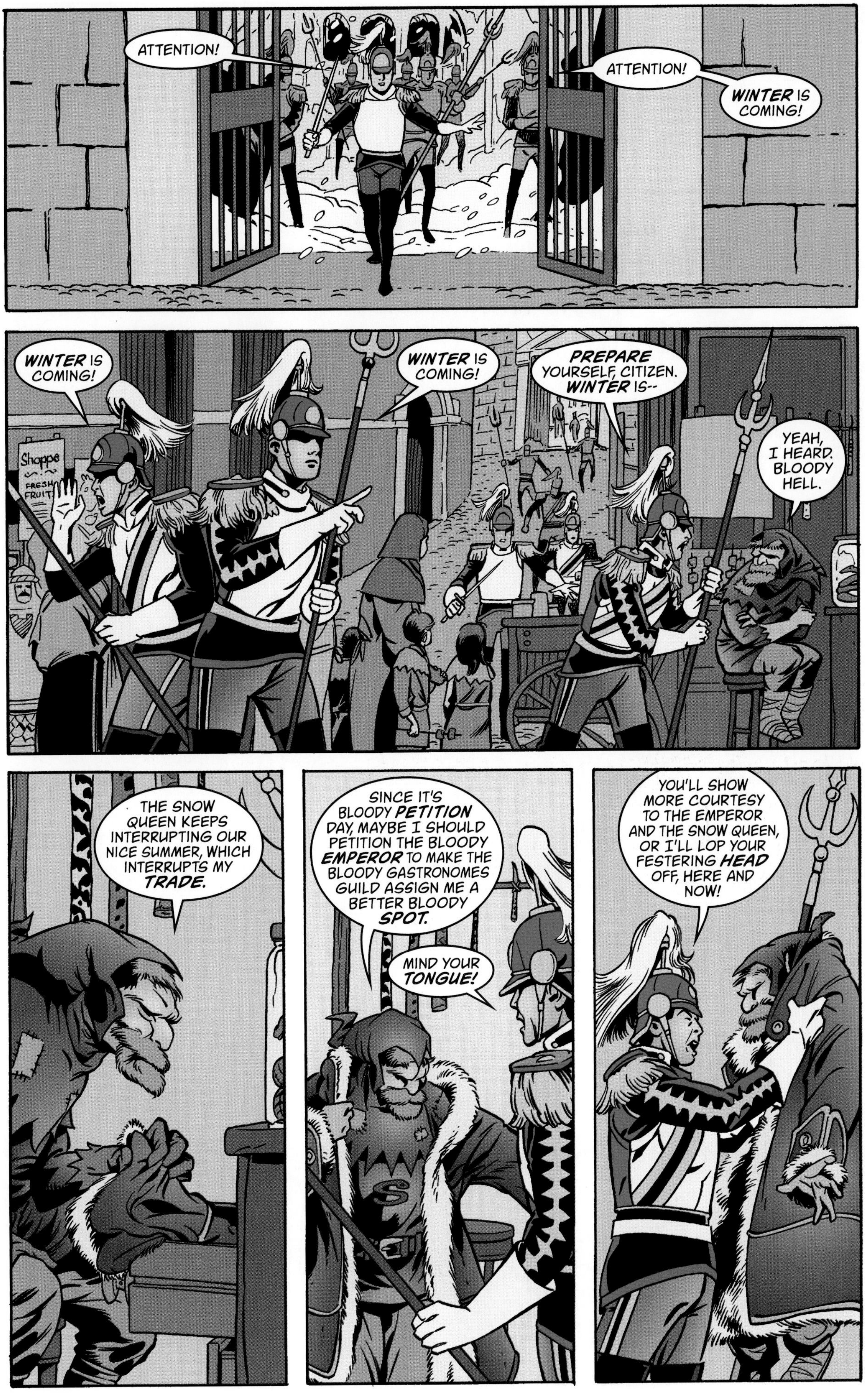
ATTENTION!
ATTENTION!
WINTER IS COMING!
WINTER IS COMING!
WINTER IS COMING!
PREPARE YOURSELF, CITIZEN. WINTER IS--
YEAH, I HEARD. BLOODY HELL.
Shoppe
FRESH FRUIT
THE SNOW QUEEN KEEPS INTERRUPTING OUR NICE SUMMER, WHICH INTERRUPTS MY TRADE.
SINCE IT'S BLOODY PETITION DAY, MAYBE I SHOULD PETITION THE BLOODY EMPEROR TO MAKE THE BLOODY GASTRONOMES GUILD ASSIGN ME A BETTER BLOODY SPOT.
MIND YOUR TONGUE!
YOU'LL SHOW MORE COURTESY TO THE EMPEROR AND THE SNOW QUEEN, OR I'LL LOP YOUR FESTERING HEAD OFF, HERE AND NOW!

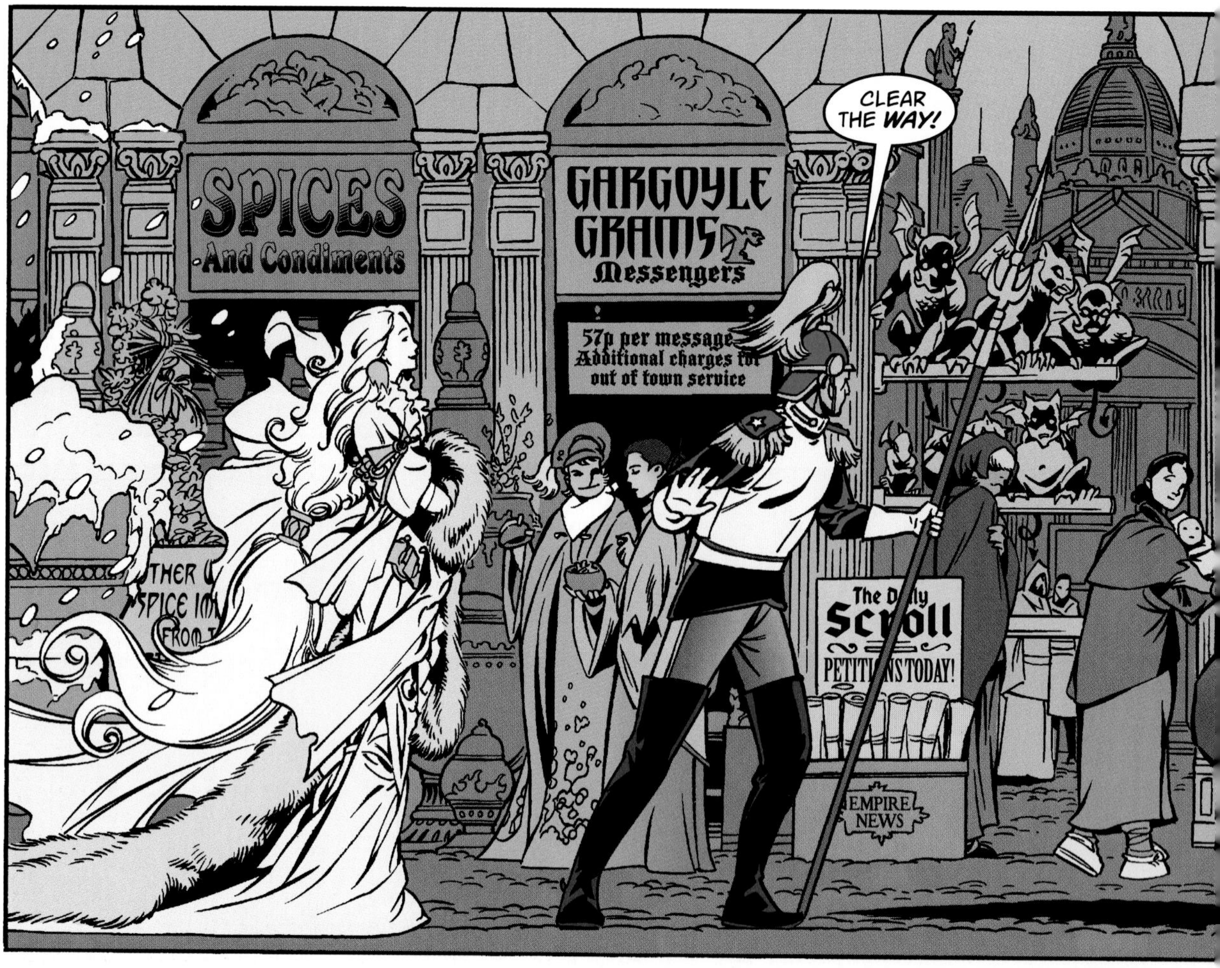
SPICES
And Condiments
GARGOYLE GRAMS
Messengers
57p per message. Additional charges for out of town service
CLEAR THE WAY!
The Daily Scroll
PETITIONS TODAY!
EMPIRE NEWS

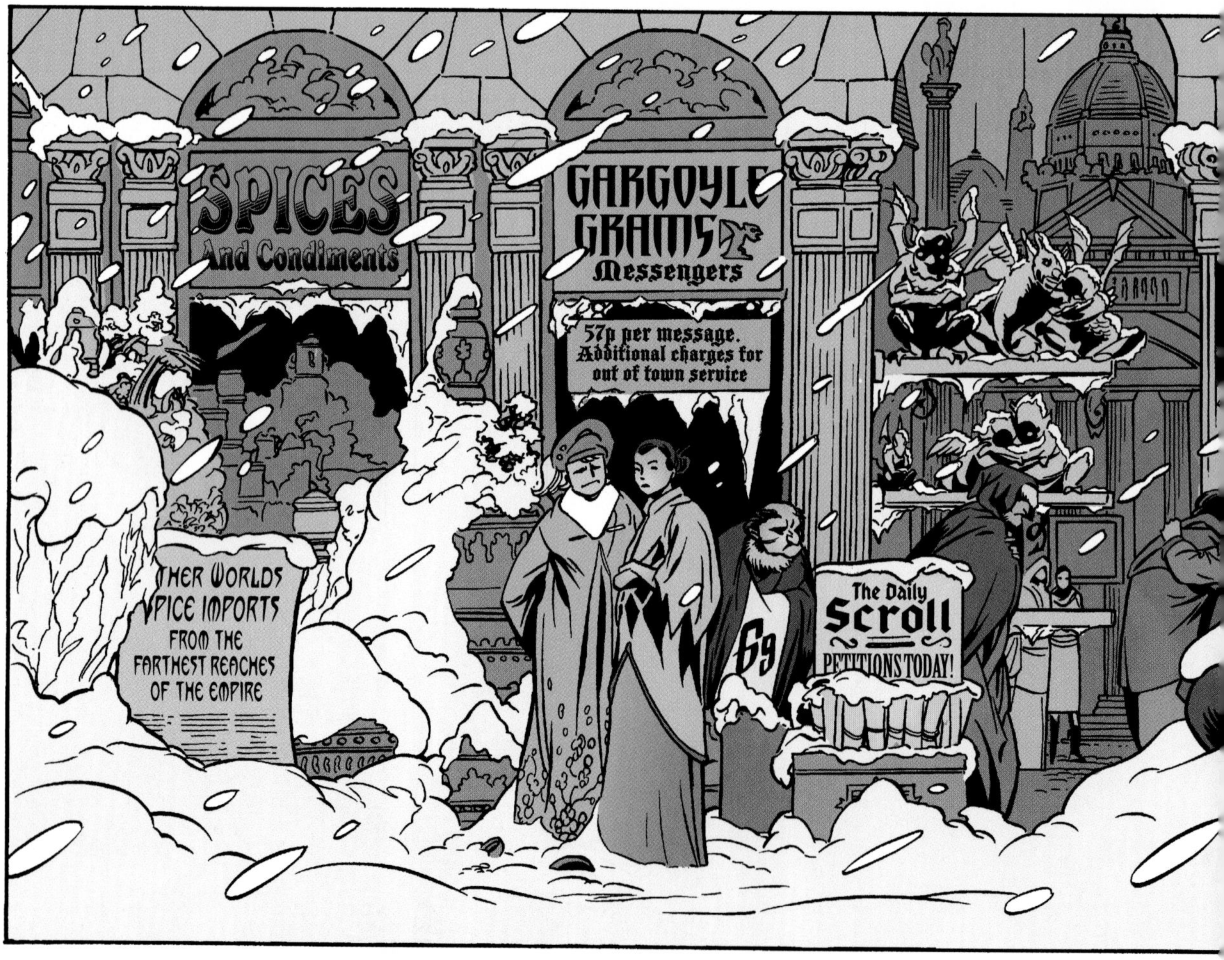
SPICES
And Condiments
GARGOYLE GRAMS
Messengers
57p per message. Additional charges for out of town service
THER WORLDS
PICE IMPORTS
FROM THE FARTHEST REACHES OF THE EMPIRE
69
The Daily Scroll
PETITIONS TODAY!

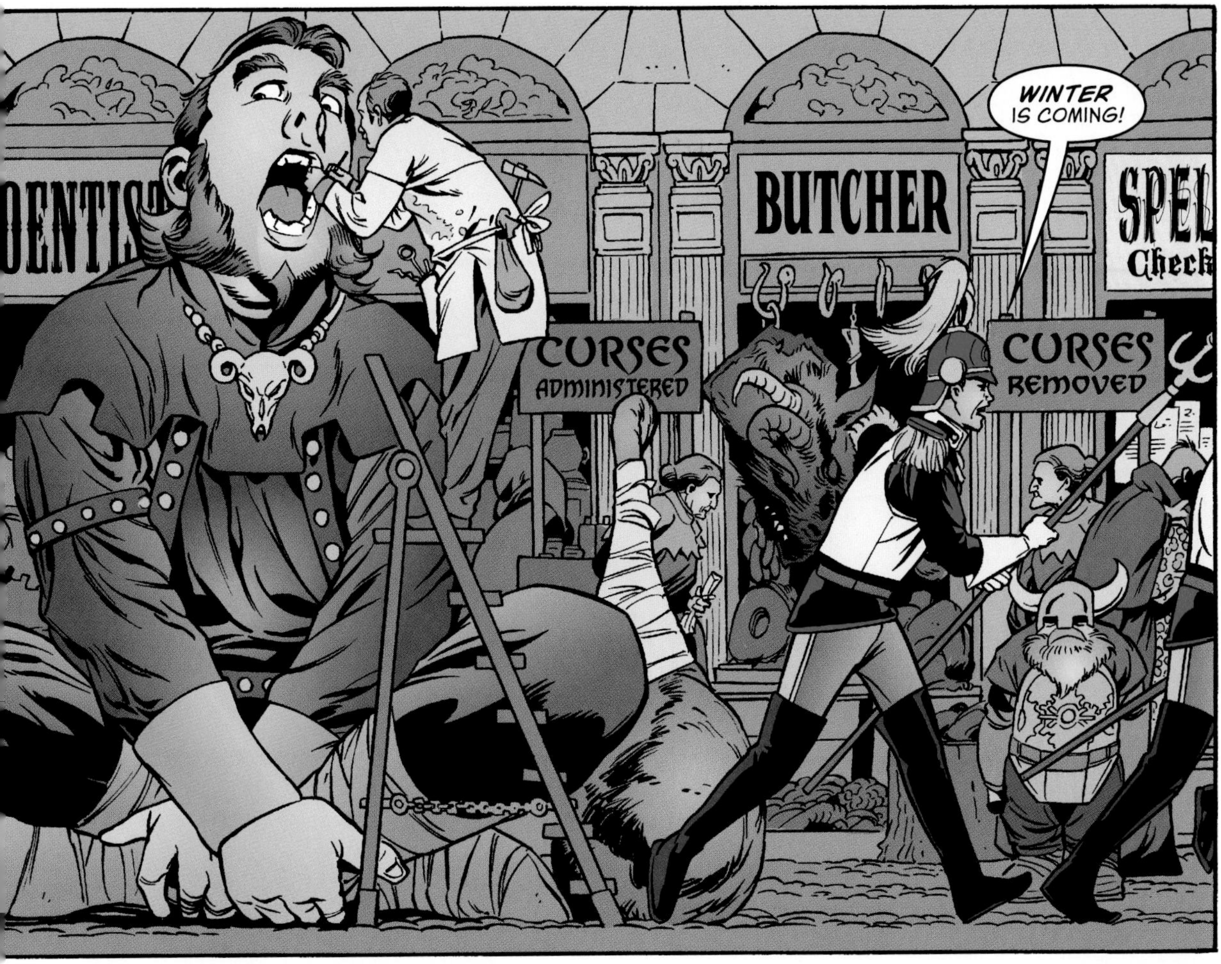
DENTIST
BUTCHER
SPEL
Check
CURSES ADMINISTERED
CURSES REMOVED
WINTER IS COMING!

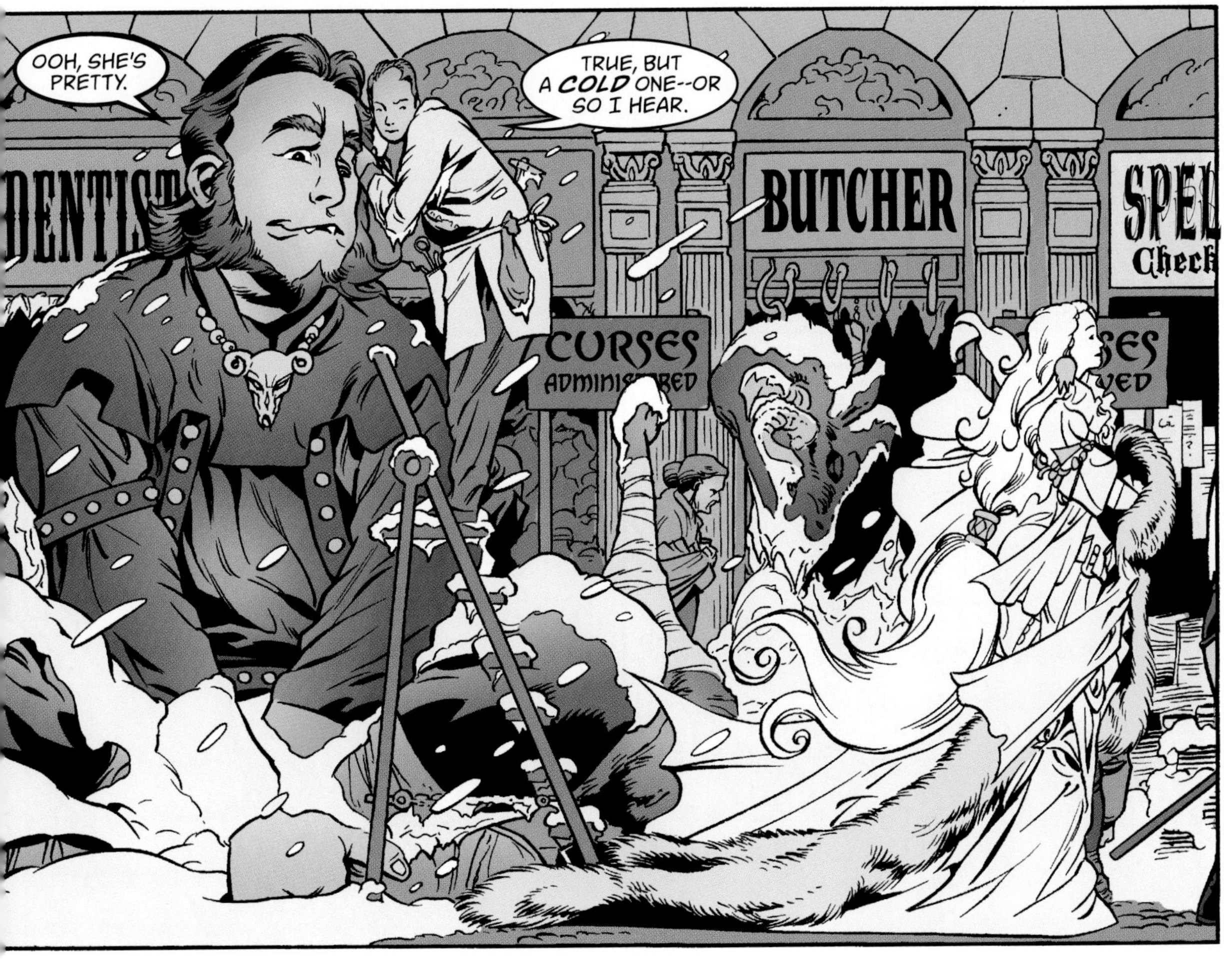
OOH, SHE'S PRETTY.
TRUE, BUT A COLD ONE--OR SO I HEAR.
DENTIST
BUTCHER
SPEL
Check

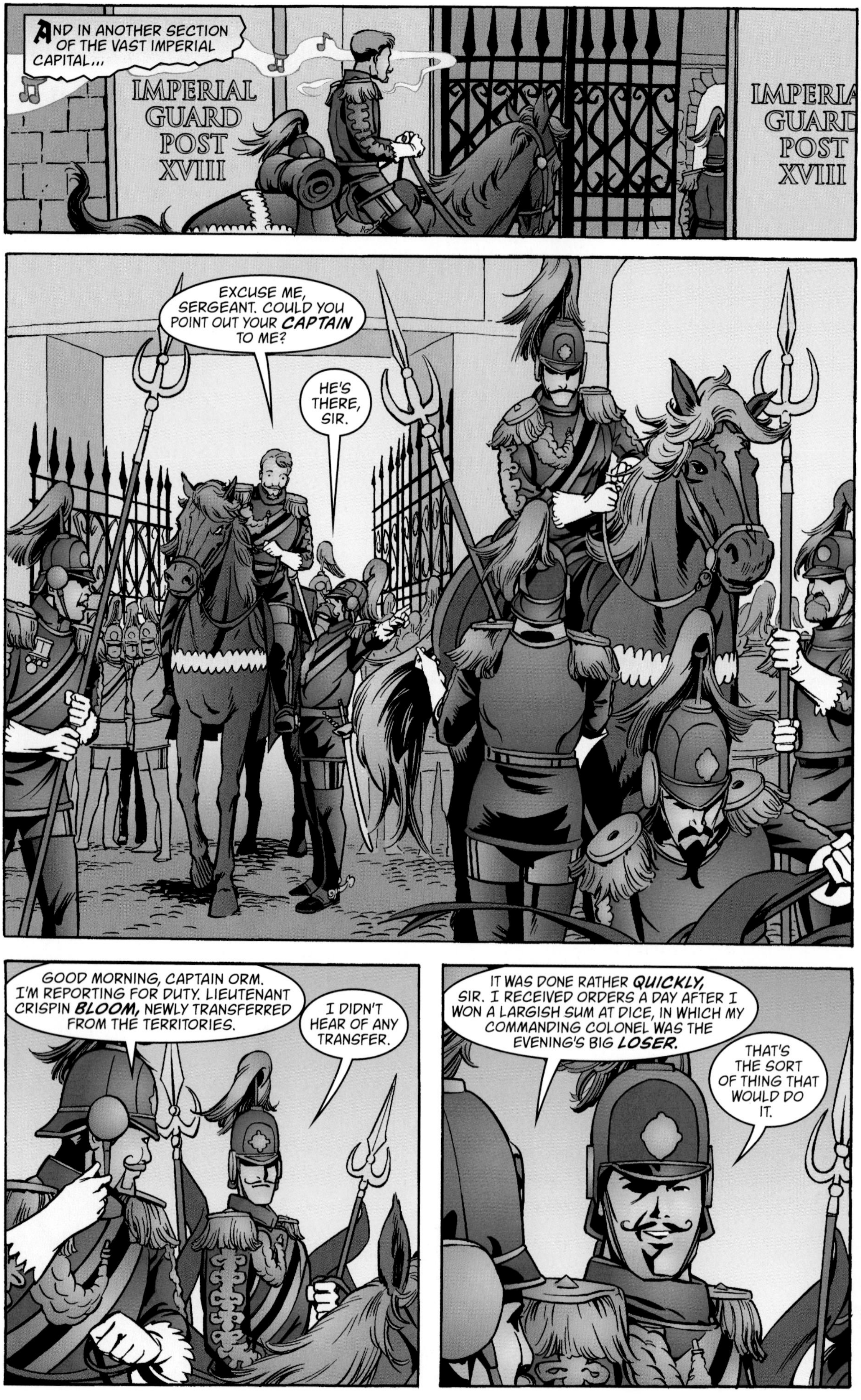
AND IN ANOTHER SECTION OF THE VAST IMPERIAL CAPITAL...
IMPERIAL GUARD POST XVIII
IMPERIAL GUARD POST XVIII
EXCUSE ME, SERGEANT. COULD YOU POINT OUT YOUR CAPTAIN TO ME?
HE'S THERE, SIR.
GOOD MORNING, CAPTAIN ORM. I'M REPORTING FOR DUTY. LIEUTENANT CRISPIN BLOOM, NEWLY TRANSFERRED FROM THE TERRITORIES.
I DIDN'T HEAR OF ANY TRANSFER.
IT WAS DONE RATHER QUICKLY, SIR. I RECEIVED ORDERS A DAY AFTER I WON A LARGISH SUM AT DICE, IN WHICH MY COMMANDING COLONEL WAS THE EVENING'S BIG LOSER.
THAT'S THE SORT OF THING THAT WOULD DO IT.

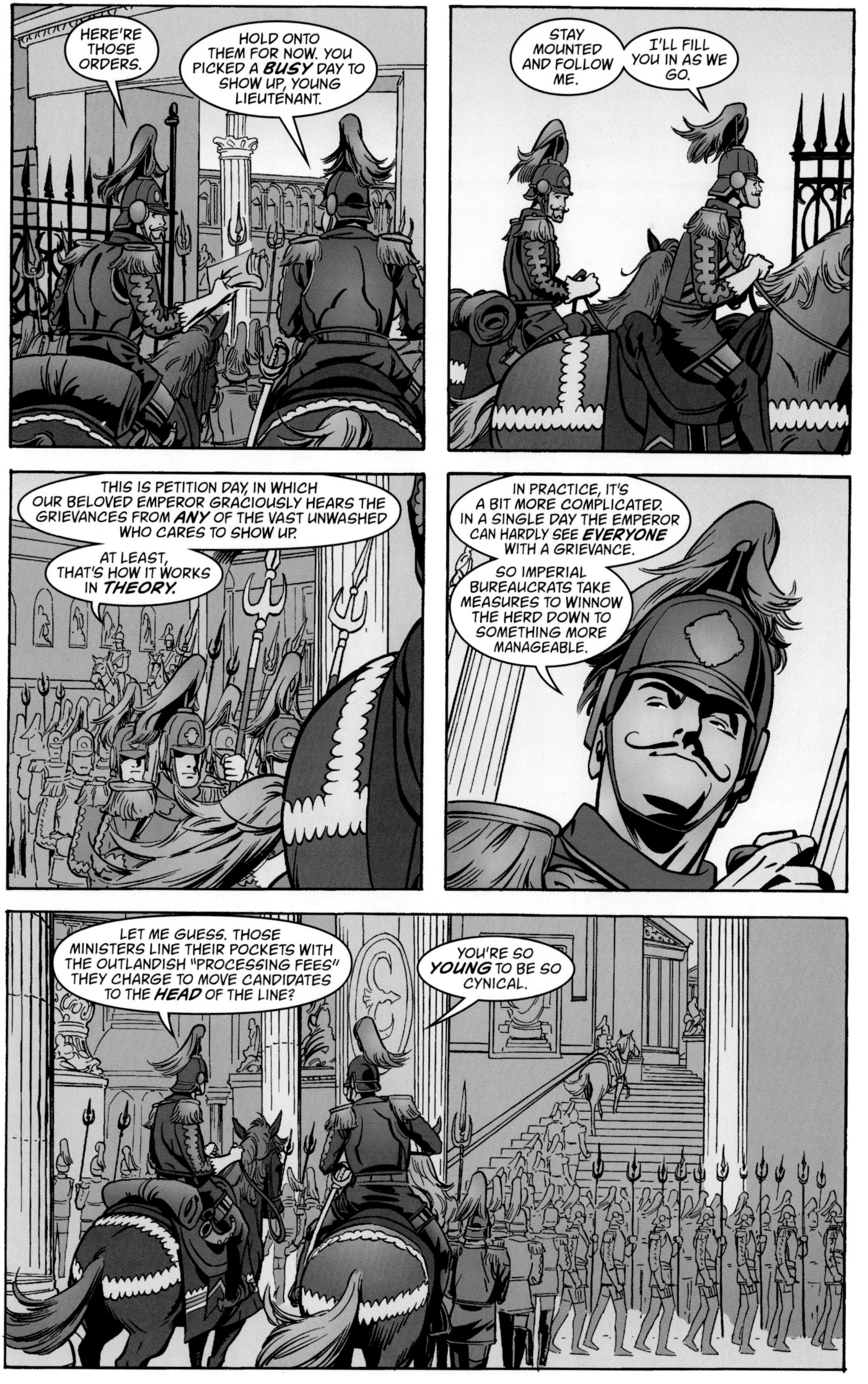
HERE'RE THOSE ORDERS.
HOLD ONTO THEM FOR NOW. YOU PICKED A BUSY DAY TO SHOW UP, YOUNG LIEUTENANT.
STAY MOUNTED AND FOLLOW ME.
I'LL FILL YOU IN AS WE GO.
THIS IS PETITION DAY, IN WHICH OUR BELOVED EMPEROR GRACIOUSLY HEARS THE GRIEVANCES FROM ANY OF THE VAST UNWASHED WHO CARES TO SHOW UP.
AT LEAST, THAT'S HOW IT WORKS IN THEORY.
IN PRACTICE, IT'S A BIT MORE COMPLICATED. IN A SINGLE DAY THE EMPEROR CAN HARDLY SEE EVERYONE WITH A GRIEVANCE.
SO IMPERIAL BUREAUCRATS TAKE MEASURES TO WINNOW THE HERD DOWN TO SOMETHING MORE MANAGEABLE.
LET ME GUESS. THOSE MINISTERS LINE THEIR POCKETS WITH THE OUTLANDISH "PROCESSING FEES" THEY CHARGE TO MOVE CANDIDATES TO THE HEAD OF THE LINE?
YOU'RE SO YOUNG TO BE SO CYNICAL.

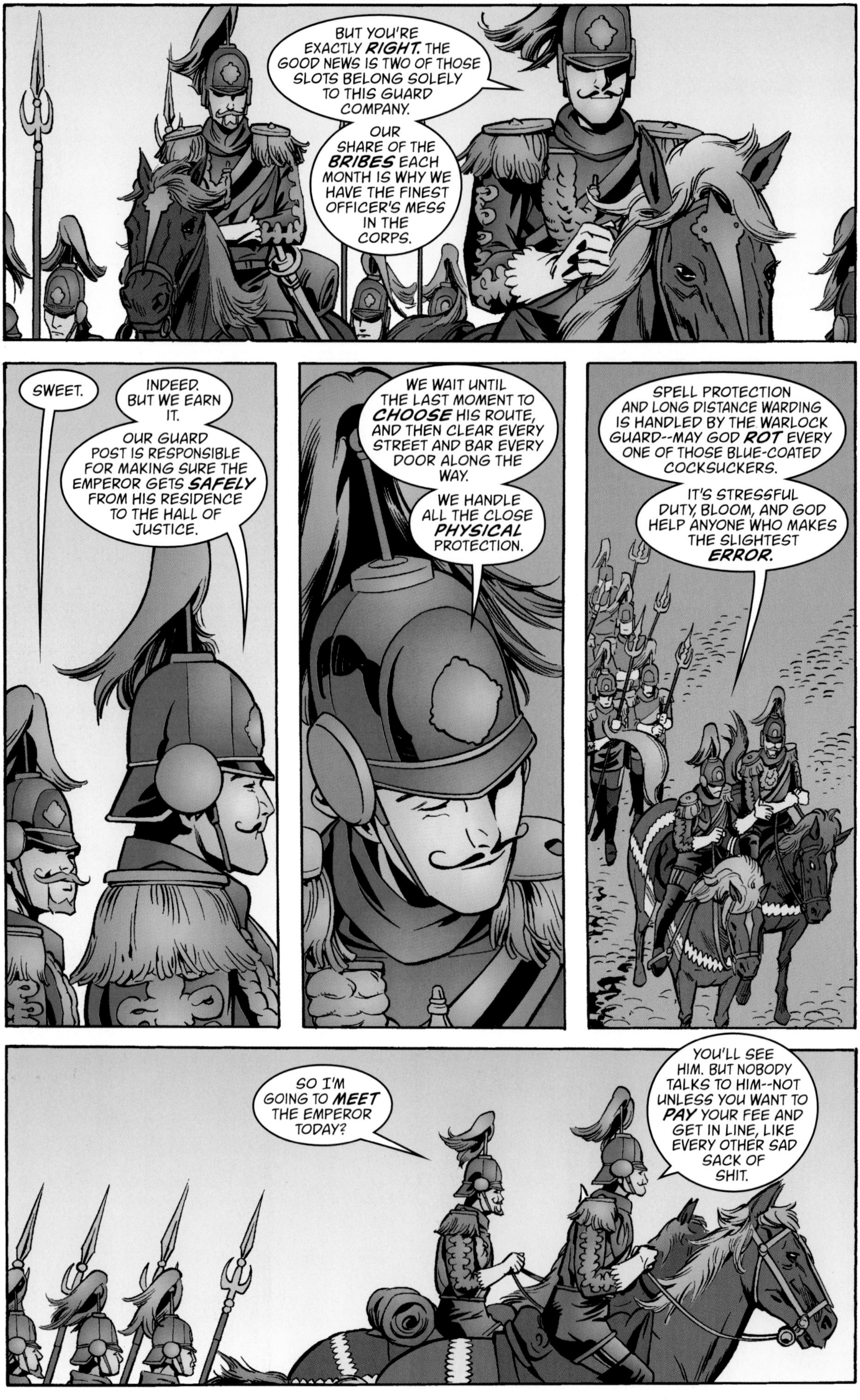
BUT YOU'RE EXACTLY RIGHT. THE GOOD NEWS IS TWO OF THOSE SLOTS BELONG SOLELY TO THIS GUARD COMPANY.
OUR SHARE OF THE BRIBES EACH MONTH IS WHY WE HAVE THE FINEST OFFICER'S MESS IN THE CORPS.
SWEET.
INDEED. BUT WE EARN IT.
OUR GUARD POST IS RESPONSIBLE FOR MAKING SURE THE EMPEROR GETS SAFELY FROM HIS RESIDENCE TO THE HALL OF JUSTICE.
WE WAIT UNTIL THE LAST MOMENT TO CHOOSE HIS ROUTE, AND THEN CLEAR EVERY STREET AND BAR EVERY DOOR ALONG THE WAY.
WE HANDLE ALL THE CLOSE PHYSICAL PROTECTION.
SPELL PROTECTION AND LONG DISTANCE WARDING IS HANDLED BY THE WARLOCK GUARD--MAY GOD ROT EVERY ONE OF THOSE BLUE-COATED COCKSUCKERS.
IT'S STRESSFUL DUTY, BLOOM, AND GOD HELP ANYONE WHO MAKES THE SLIGHTEST ERROR.
SO I'M GOING TO MEET THE EMPEROR TODAY?
YOU'LL SEE HIM. BUT NOBODY TALKS TO HIM--NOT UNLESS YOU WANT TO PAY YOUR FEE AND GET IN LINE, LIKE EVERY OTHER SAD SACK OF SHIT.

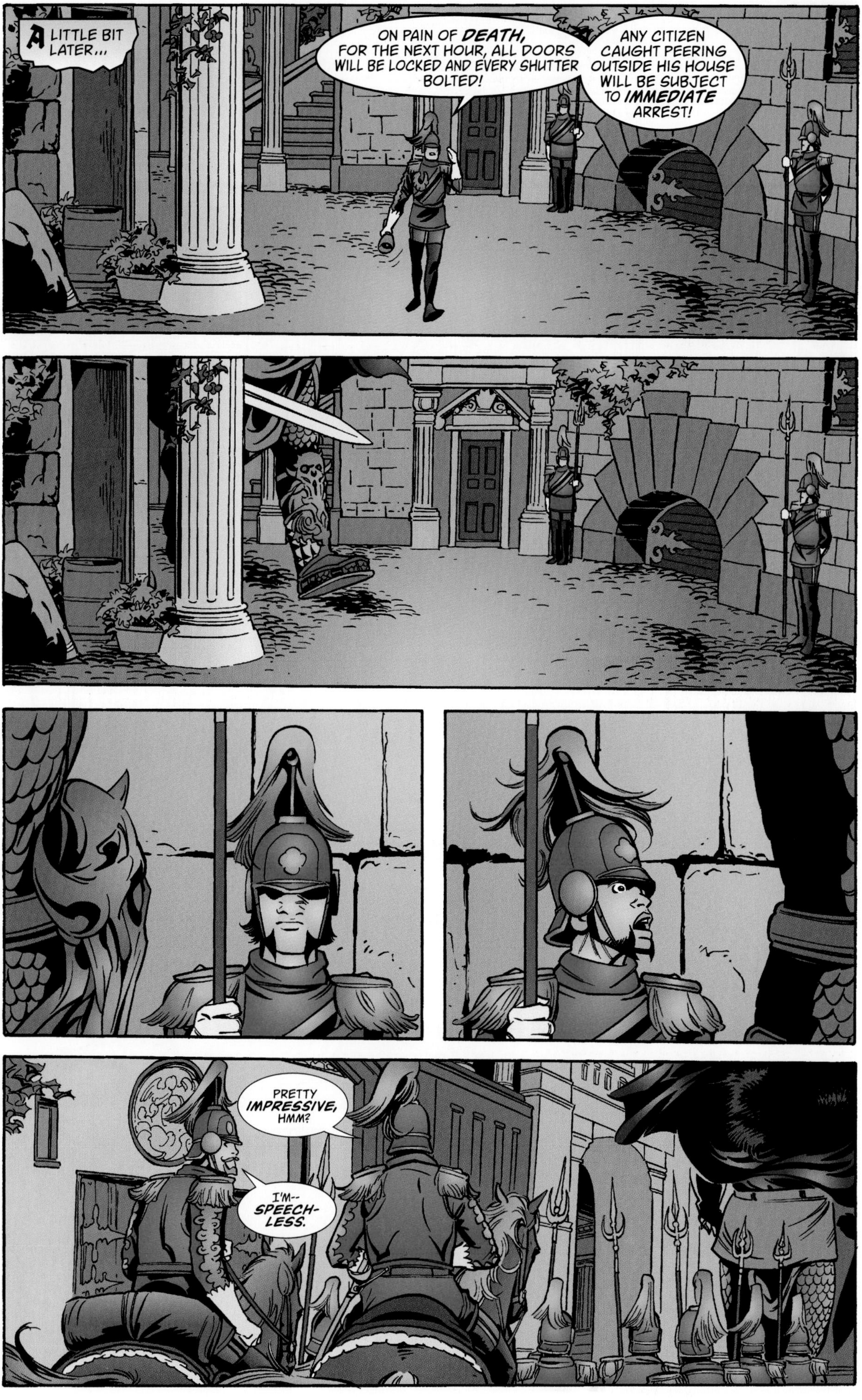
A LITTLE BIT LATER...
ON PAIN OF DEATH, FOR THE NEXT HOUR, ALL DOORS WILL BE LOCKED AND EVERY SHUTTER BOLTED!
ANY CITIZEN CAUGHT PEERING OUTSIDE HIS HOUSE WILL BE SUBJECT TO IMMEDIATE ARREST!
PRETTY IMPRESSIVE, HMM?
I'M-- SPEECH-LESS.

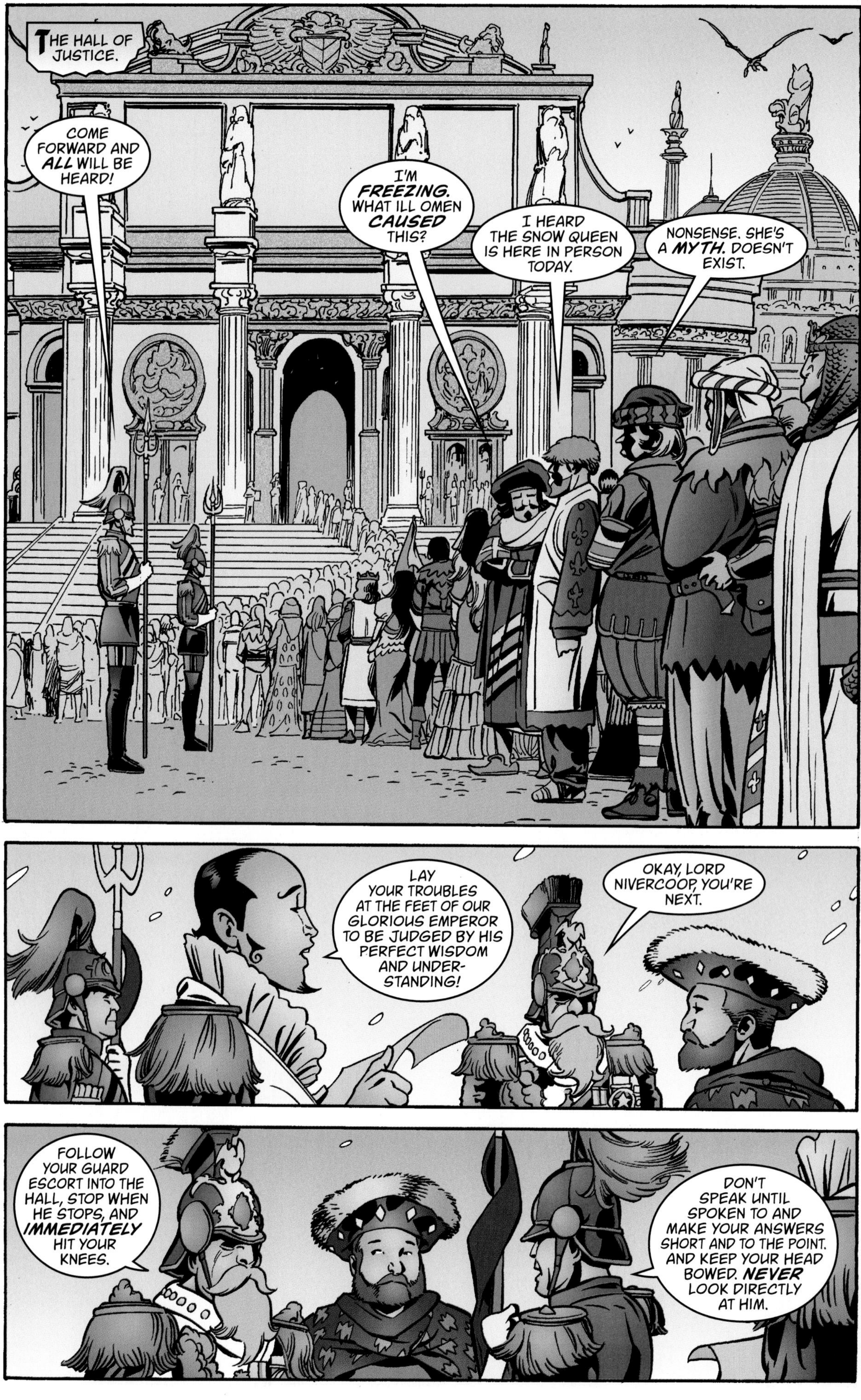
THE HALL OF JUSTICE.
COME FORWARD AND ALL WILL BE HEARD!
I'M FREEZING. WHAT ILL OMEN CAUSED THIS?
I HEARD THE SNOW QUEEN IS HERE IN PERSON TODAY.
NONSENSE. SHE'S A MYTH. DOESN'T EXIST.
LAY YOUR TROUBLES AT THE FEET OF OUR GLORIOUS EMPEROR TO BE JUDGED BY HIS PERFECT WISDOM AND UNDER-STANDING!
OKAY, LORD NIVERCOOP, YOU'RE NEXT.
FOLLOW YOUR GUARD ESCORT INTO THE HALL, STOP WHEN HE STOPS, AND IMMEDIATELY HIT YOUR KNEES.
DON'T SPEAK UNTIL SPOKEN TO AND MAKE YOUR ANSWERS SHORT AND TO THE POINT. AND KEEP YOUR HEAD BOWED. NEVER LOOK DIRECTLY AT HIM.

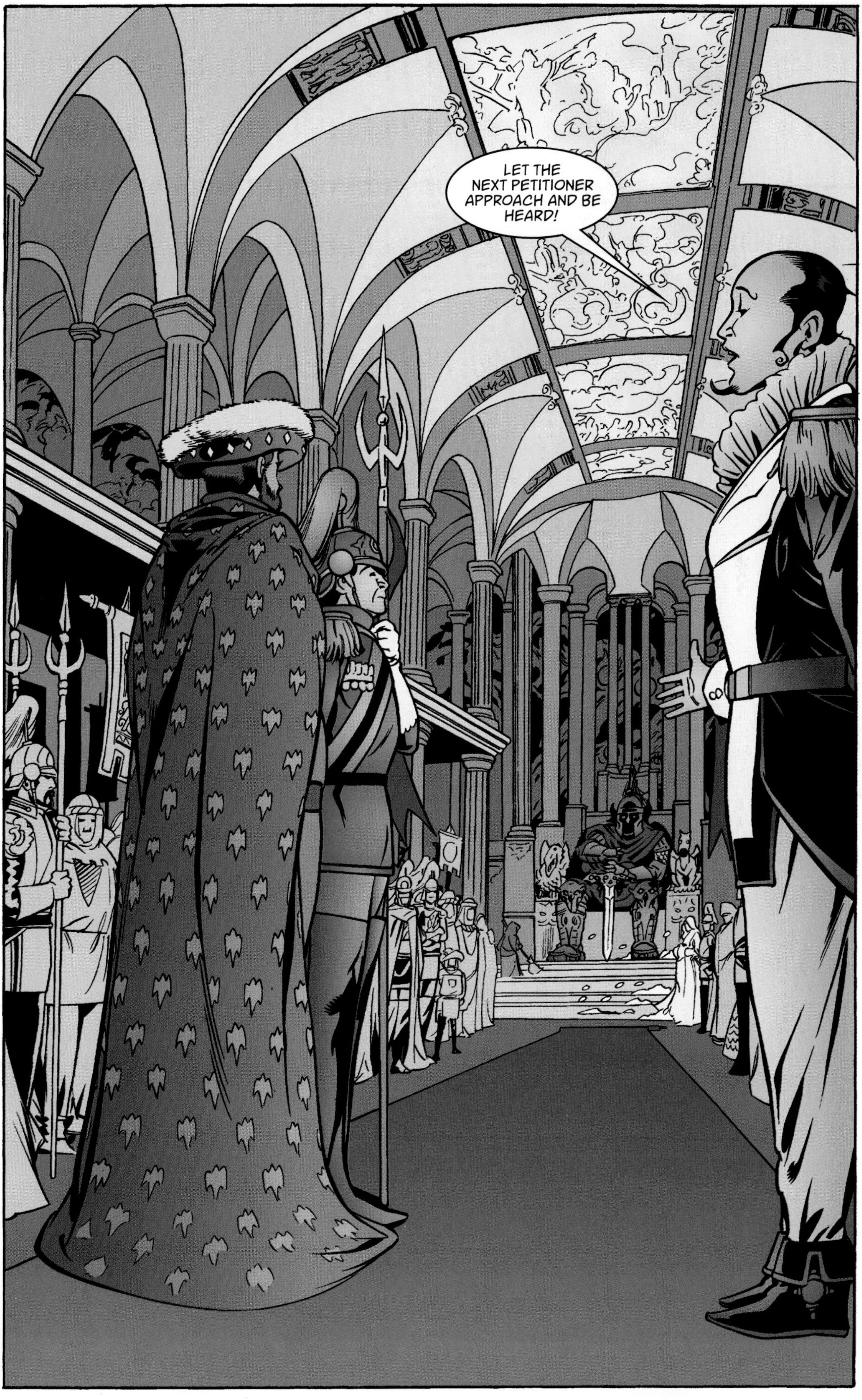
LET THE NEXT PETITIONER APPROACH AND BE HEARD!

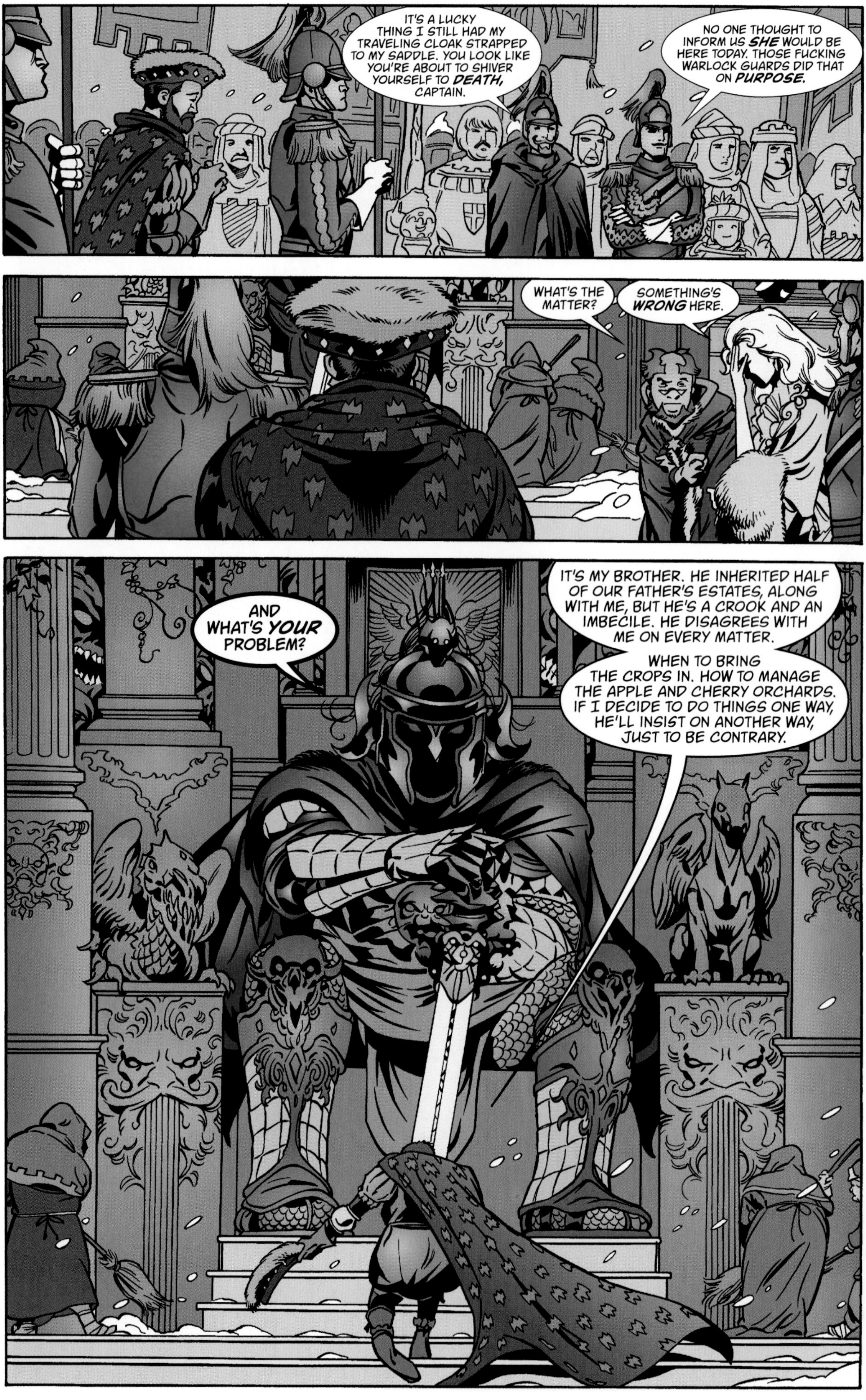
IT'S A LUCKY THING I STILL HAD MY TRAVELING CLOAK STRAPPED TO MY SADDLE. YOU LOOK LIKE YOU'RE ABOUT TO SHIVER YOURSELF TO **DEATH,** CAPTAIN.
NO ONE THOUGHT TO INFORM US **SHE** WOULD BE HERE TODAY. THOSE FUCKING WARLOCK GUARDS DID THAT ON **PURPOSE.**
WHAT'S THE MATTER?
SOMETHING'S **WRONG** HERE.
AND WHAT'S **YOUR** PROBLEM?
IT'S MY BROTHER. HE INHERITED HALF OF OUR FATHER'S ESTATES, ALONG WITH ME, BUT HE'S A CROOK AND AN IMBECILE. HE DISAGREES WITH ME ON EVERY MATTER.
WHEN TO BRING THE CROPS IN. HOW TO MANAGE THE APPLE AND CHERRY ORCHARDS. IF I DECIDE TO DO THINGS ONE WAY, HE'LL INSIST ON ANOTHER WAY, JUST TO BE CONTRARY.

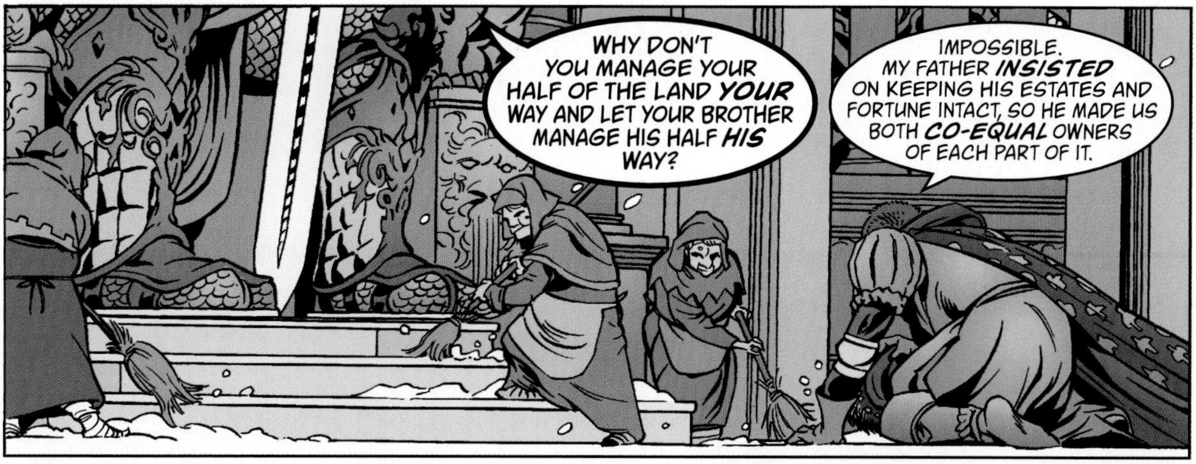
WHY DON'T YOU MANAGE YOUR HALF OF THE LAND YOUR WAY AND LET YOUR BROTHER MANAGE HIS HALF HIS WAY?
IMPOSSIBLE. MY FATHER INSISTED ON KEEPING HIS ESTATES AND FORTUNE INTACT, SO HE MADE US BOTH CO-EQUAL OWNERS OF EACH PART OF IT.

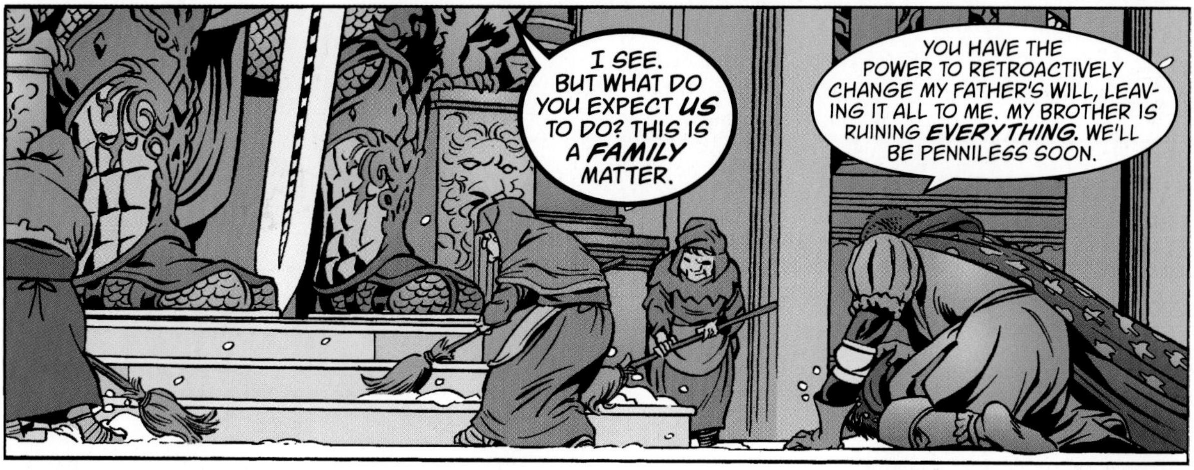
I SEE. BUT WHAT DO YOU EXPECT US TO DO? THIS IS A FAMILY MATTER.
YOU HAVE THE POWER TO RETROACTIVELY CHANGE MY FATHER'S WILL, LEAVING IT ALL TO ME. MY BROTHER IS RUINING EVERYTHING. WE'LL BE PENNILESS SOON.

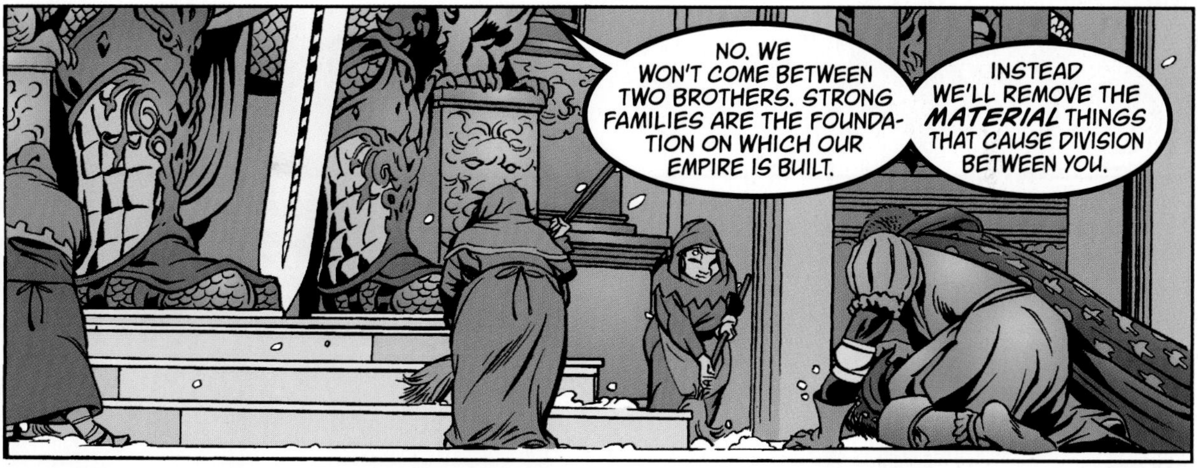
NO. WE WON'T COME BETWEEN TWO BROTHERS. STRONG FAMILIES ARE THE FOUNDATION ON WHICH OUR EMPIRE IS BUILT.
INSTEAD WE'LL REMOVE THE MATERIAL THINGS THAT CAUSE DIVISION BETWEEN YOU.

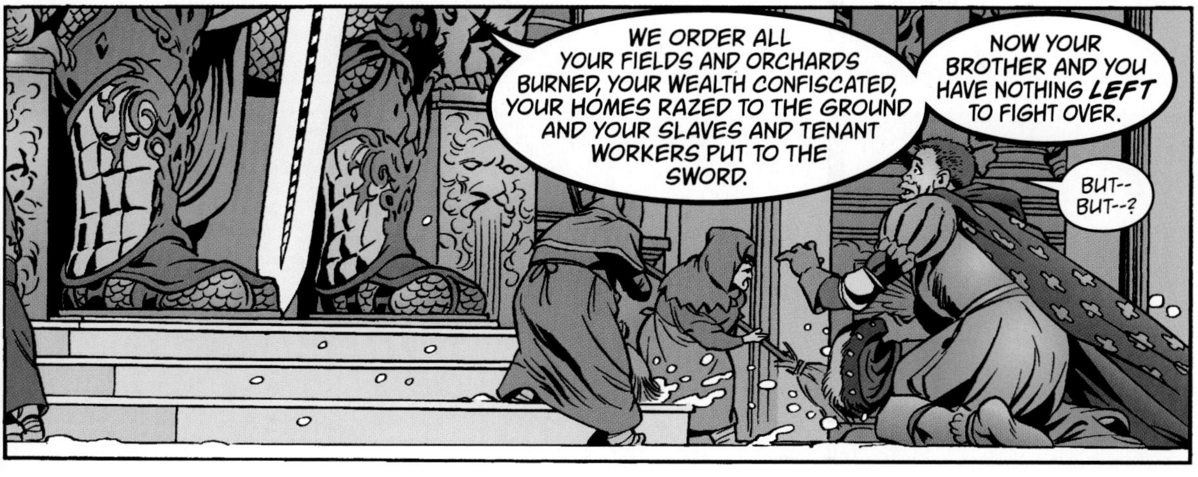
WE ORDER ALL YOUR FIELDS AND ORCHARDS BURNED, YOUR WEALTH CONFISCATED, YOUR HOMES RAZED TO THE GROUND AND YOUR SLAVES AND TENANT WORKERS PUT TO THE SWORD.
NOW YOUR BROTHER AND YOU HAVE NOTHING LEFT TO FIGHT OVER.
BUT-- BUT--?

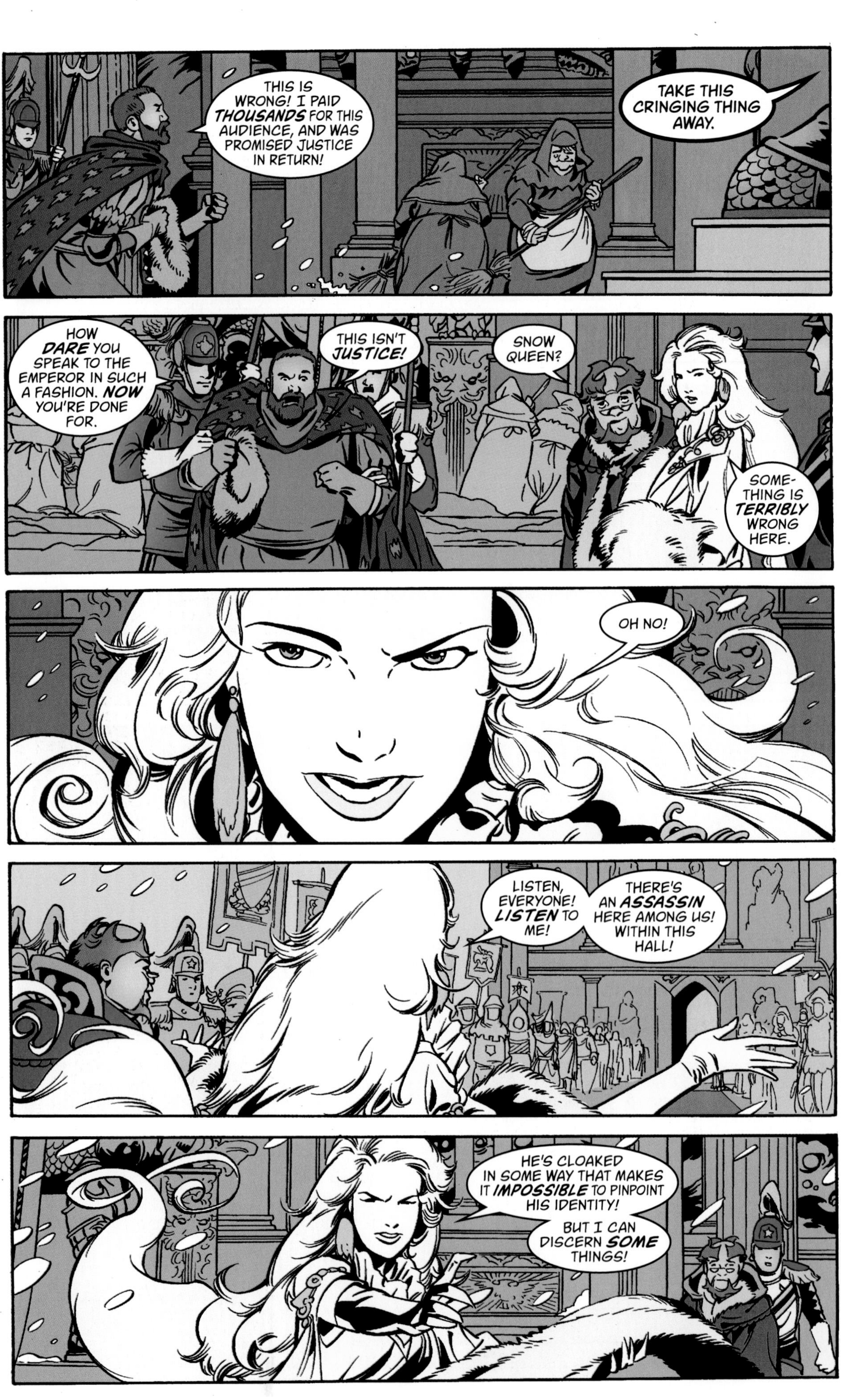
THIS IS WRONG! I PAID THOUSANDS FOR THIS AUDIENCE, AND WAS PROMISED JUSTICE IN RETURN!
TAKE THIS CRINGING THING AWAY.
HOW DARE YOU SPEAK TO THE EMPEROR IN SUCH A FASHION. NOW YOU'RE DONE FOR.
THIS ISN'T JUSTICE!
SNOW QUEEN?
SOME-THING IS TERRIBLY WRONG HERE.
OH NO!
LISTEN, EVERYONE! LISTEN TO ME!
THERE'S AN ASSASSIN HERE AMONG US! WITHIN THIS HALL!
HE'S CLOAKED IN SOME WAY THAT MAKES IT IMPOSSIBLE TO PINPOINT HIS IDENTITY!
BUT I CAN DISCERN SOME THINGS!

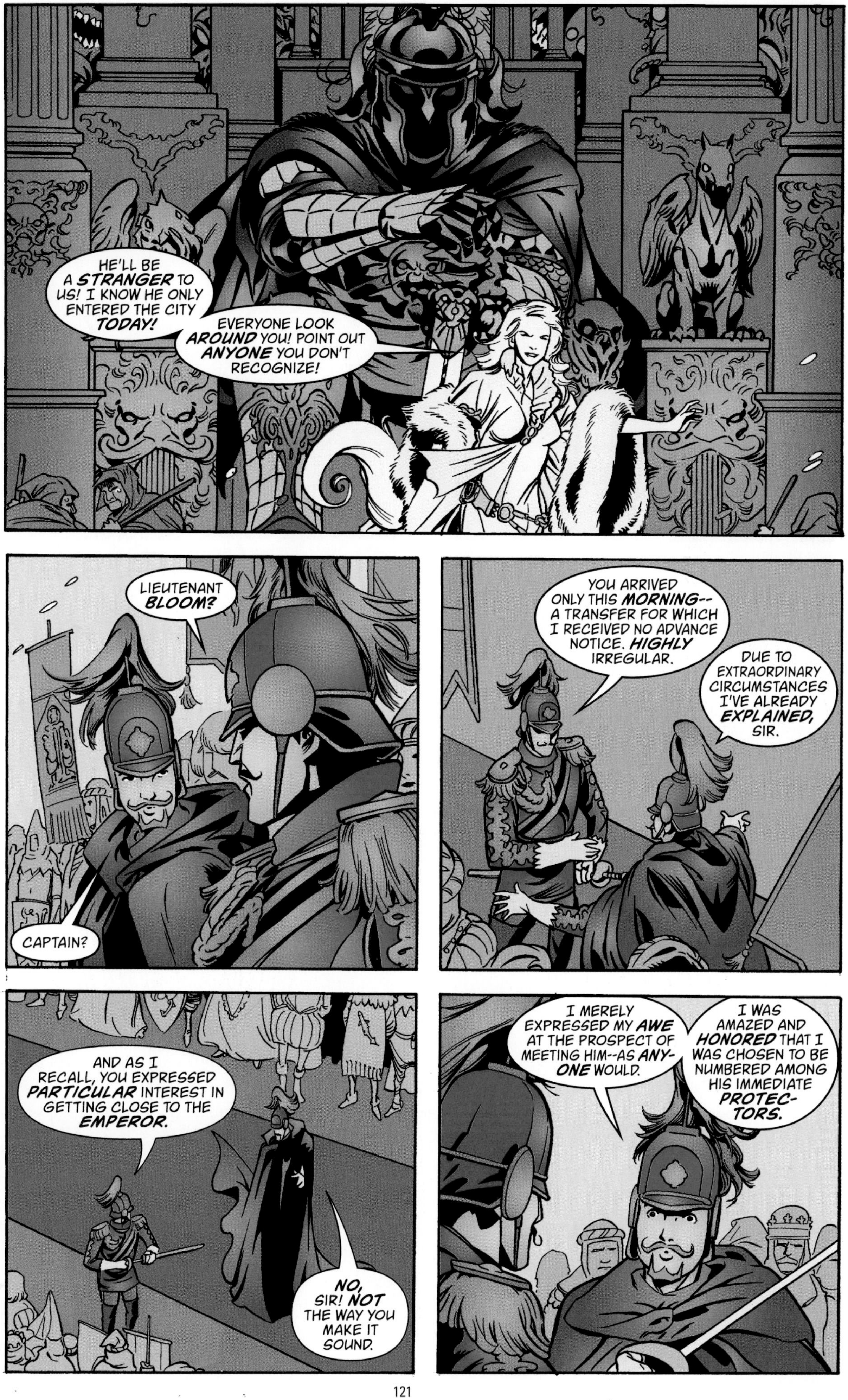
HE'LL BE A STRANGER TO US! I KNOW HE ONLY ENTERED THE CITY TODAY!
EVERYONE LOOK AROUND YOU! POINT OUT ANYONE YOU DON'T RECOGNIZE!
LIEUTENANT BLOOM?
CAPTAIN?
YOU ARRIVED ONLY THIS MORNING--A TRANSFER FOR WHICH I RECEIVED NO ADVANCE NOTICE. HIGHLY IRREGULAR.
DUE TO EXTRAORDINARY CIRCUMSTANCES I'VE ALREADY EXPLAINED, SIR.
AND AS I RECALL, YOU EXPRESSED PARTICULAR INTEREST IN GETTING CLOSE TO THE EMPEROR.
NO, SIR! NOT THE WAY YOU MAKE IT SOUND.
I MERELY EXPRESSED MY AWE AT THE PROSPECT OF MEETING HIM--AS ANYONE WOULD.
I WAS AMAZED AND HONORED THAT I WAS CHOSEN TO BE NUMBERED AMONG HIS IMMEDIATE PROTECTORS.

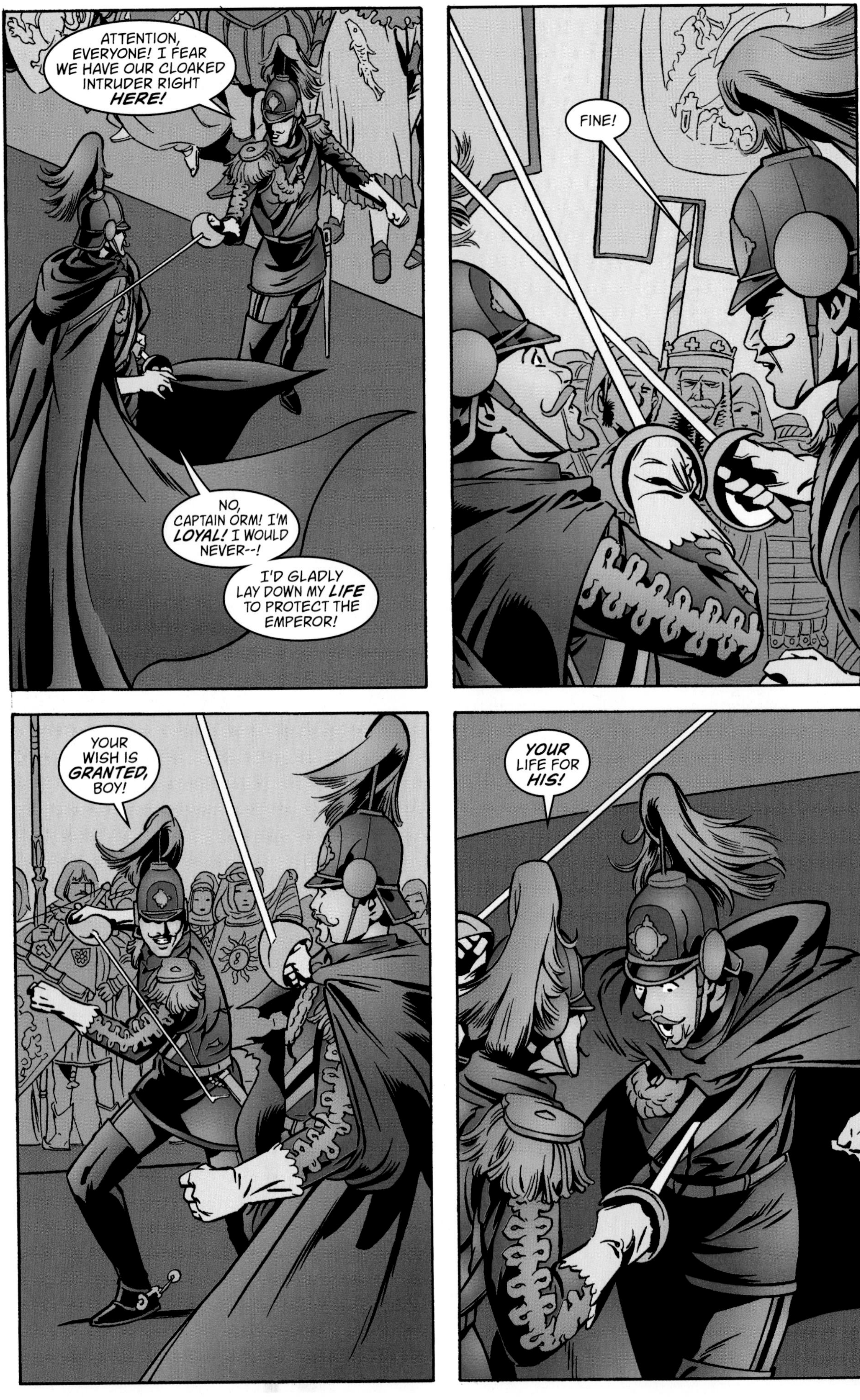
ATTENTION, EVERYONE! I FEAR WE HAVE OUR CLOAKED INTRUDER RIGHT HERE!
NO, CAPTAIN ORM! I'M LOYAL! I WOULD NEVER--!
I'D GLADLY LAY DOWN MY LIFE TO PROTECT THE EMPEROR!
FINE!
YOUR WISH IS GRANTED, BOY!
YOUR LIFE FOR HIS!

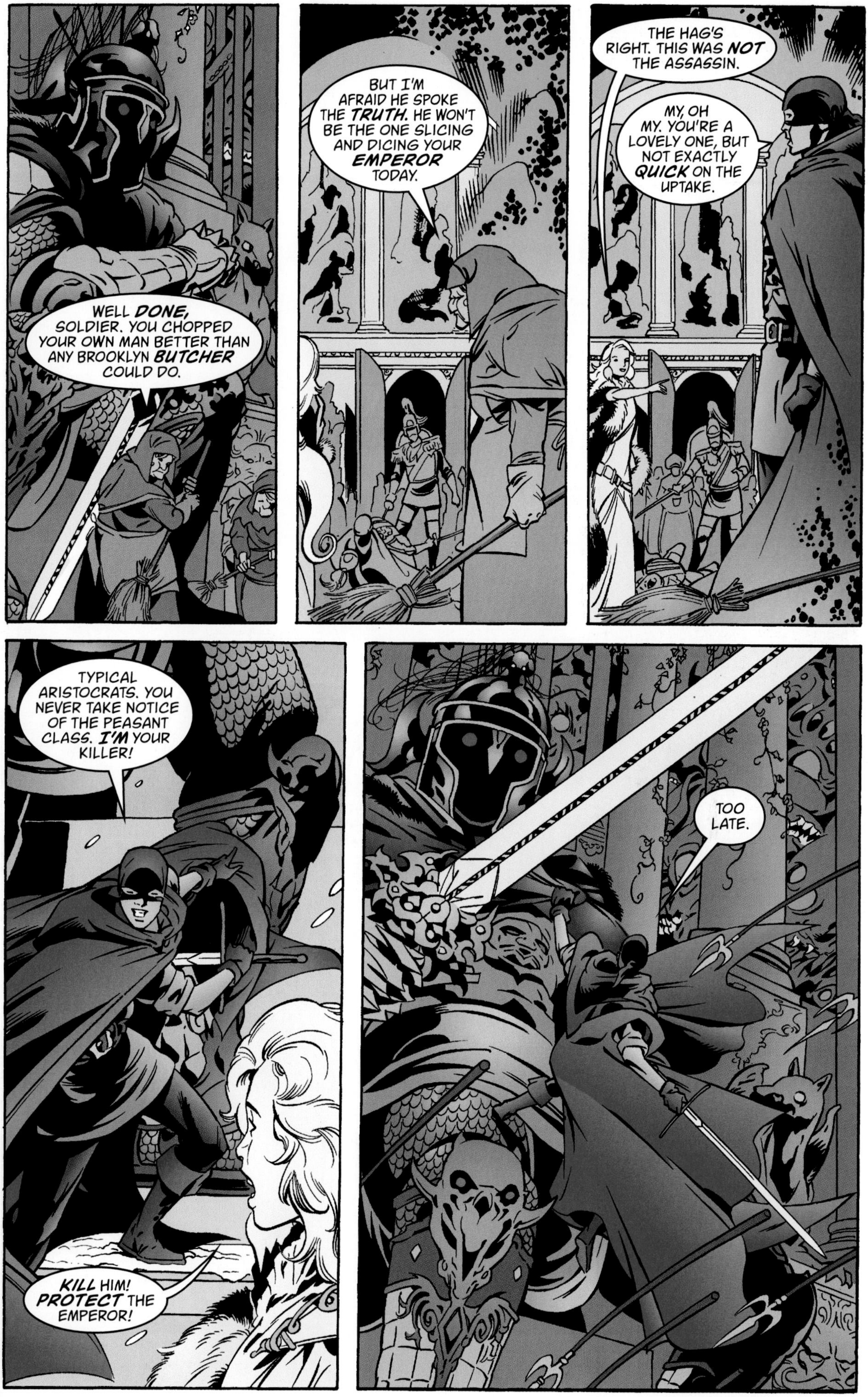
WELL DONE, SOLDIER. YOU CHOPPED YOUR OWN MAN BETTER THAN ANY BROOKLYN BUTCHER COULD DO.
BUT I'M AFRAID HE SPOKE THE TRUTH. HE WON'T BE THE ONE SLICING AND DICING YOUR EMPEROR TODAY.
THE HAG'S RIGHT. THIS WAS NOT THE ASSASSIN.
MY, OH MY. YOU'RE A LOVELY ONE, BUT NOT EXACTLY QUICK ON THE UPTAKE.
TYPICAL ARISTOCRATS. YOU NEVER TAKE NOTICE OF THE PEASANT CLASS. I'M YOUR KILLER!
KILL HIM! PROTECT THE EMPEROR!
TOO LATE.

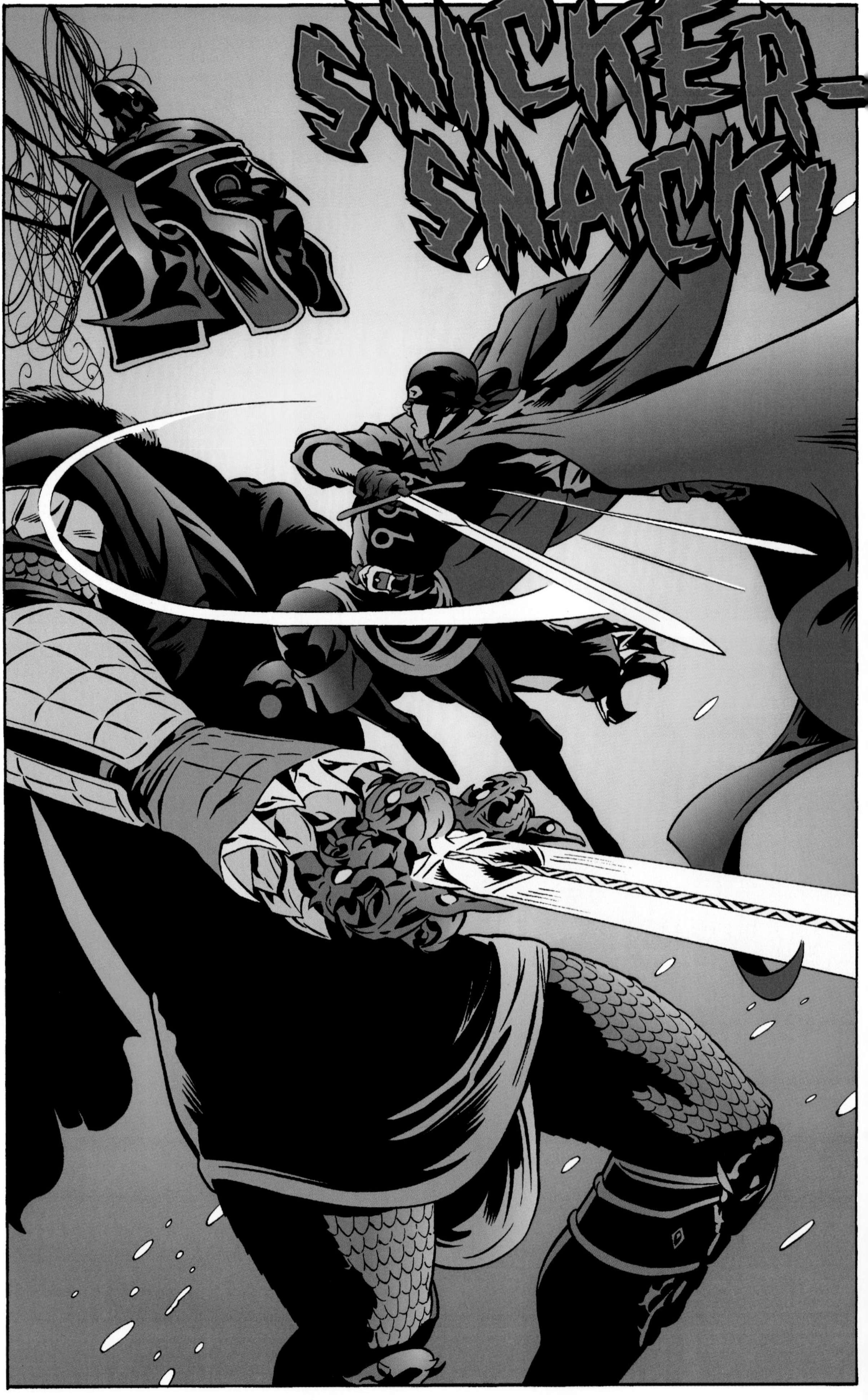
SNICKER-SNACK!

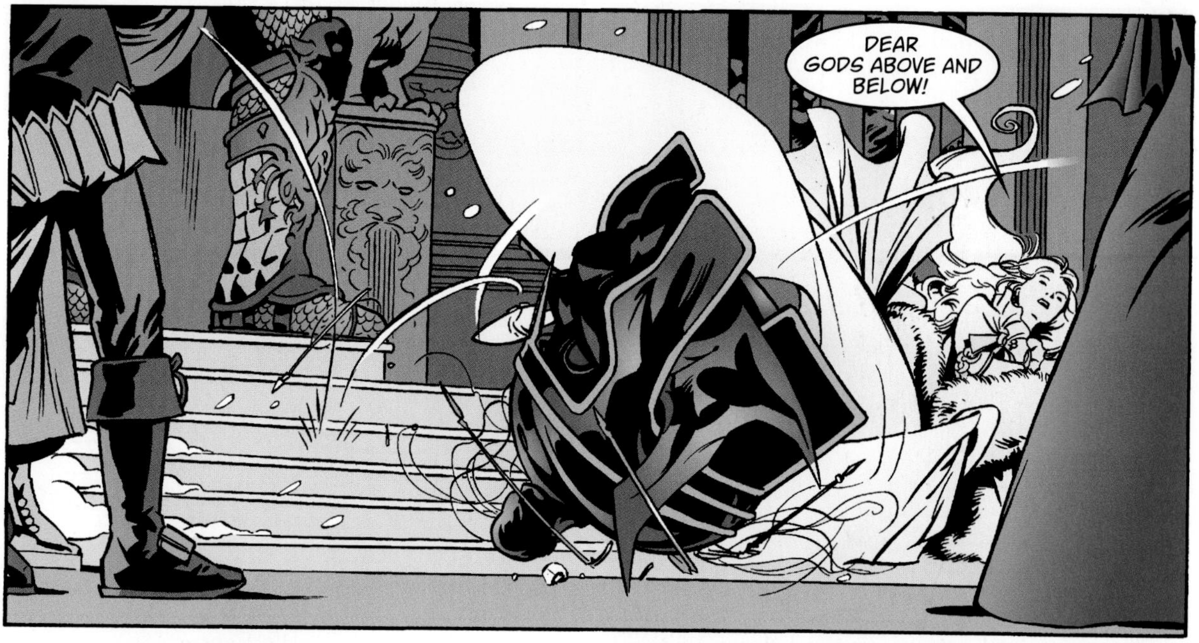
DEAR GODS ABOVE AND BELOW!

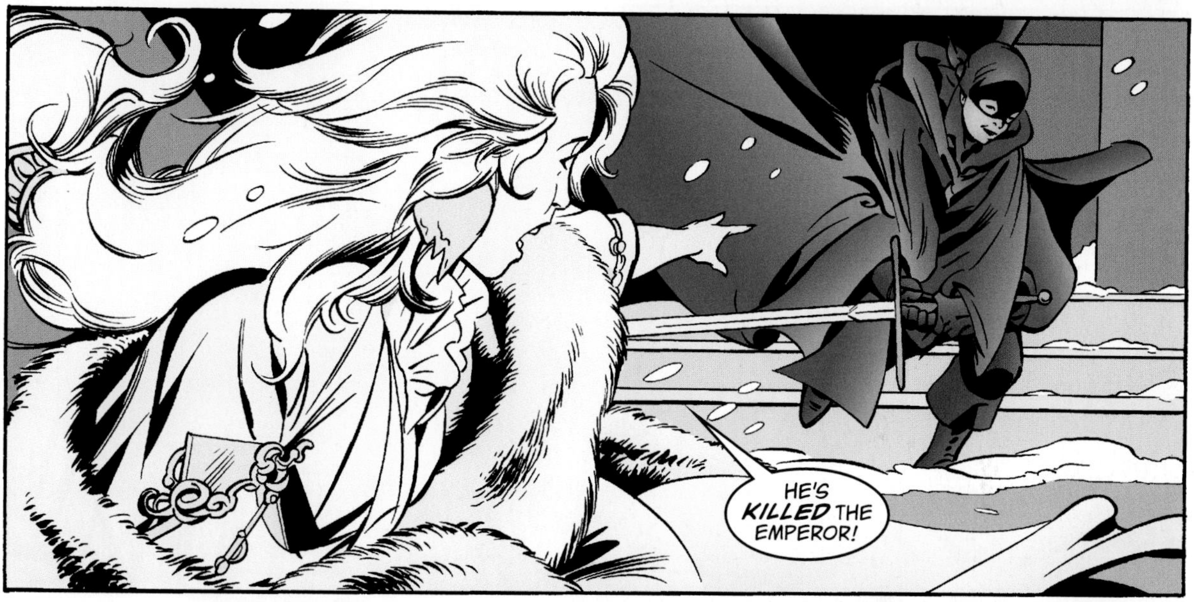
HE'S *KILLED* THE EMPEROR!

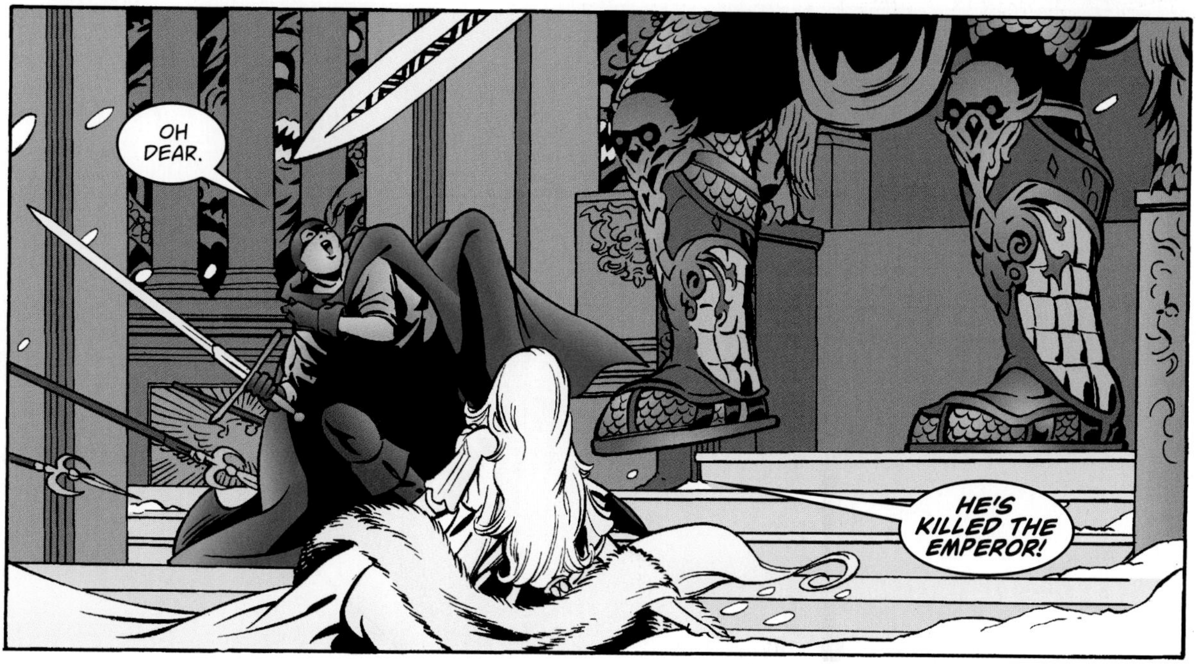
OH DEAR.
HE'S KILLED THE EMPEROR!

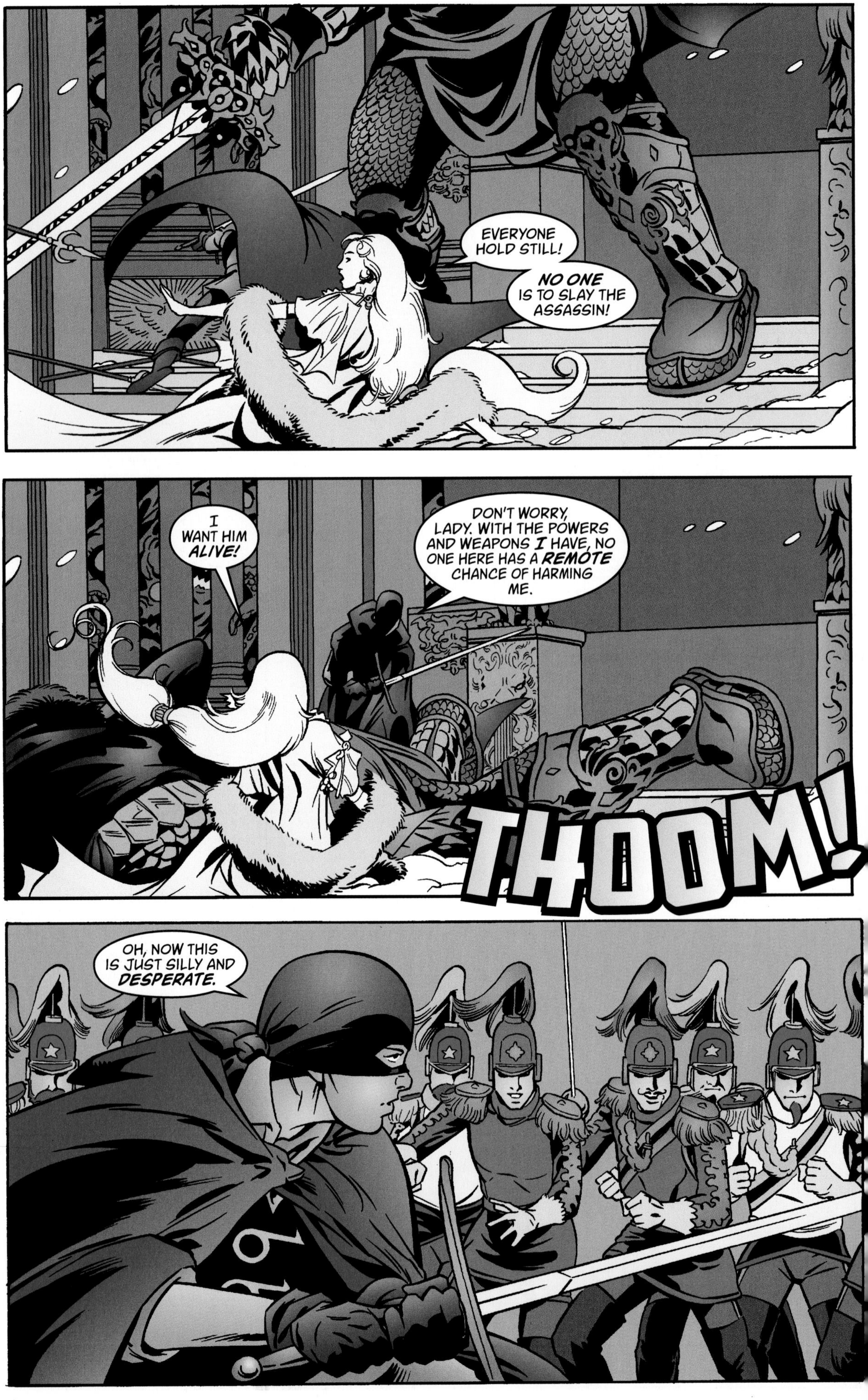
EVERYONE HOLD STILL!
NO ONE IS TO SLAY THE ASSASSIN!
I WANT HIM ALIVE!
DON'T WORRY, LADY. WITH THE POWERS AND WEAPONS I HAVE, NO ONE HERE HAS A REMOTE CHANCE OF HARMING ME.
THOOM!
OH, NOW THIS IS JUST SILLY AND DESPERATE.

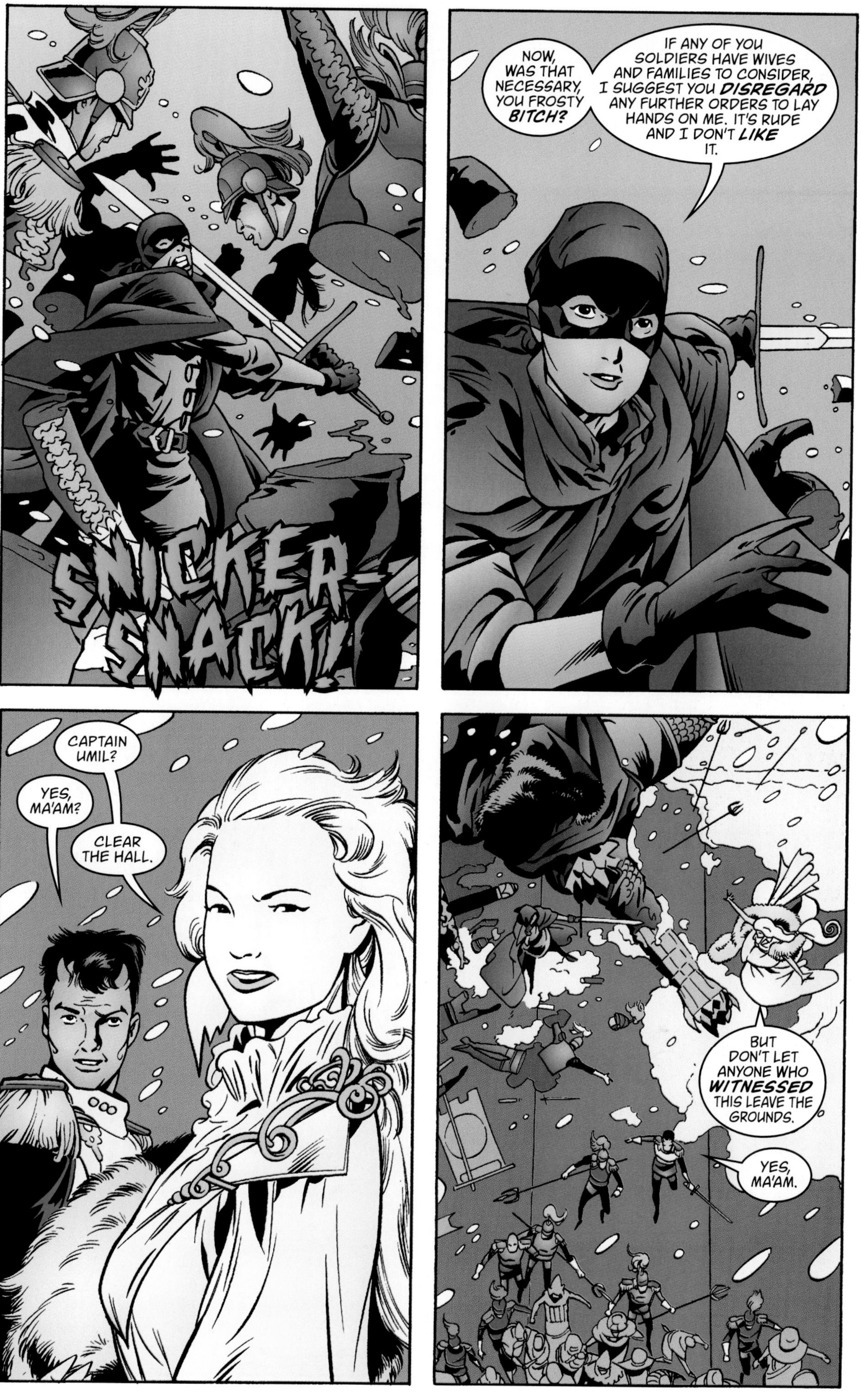
SNICKER-SNACK!
NOW, WAS THAT NECESSARY, YOU FROSTY BITCH?
IF ANY OF YOU SOLDIERS HAVE WIVES AND FAMILIES TO CONSIDER, I SUGGEST YOU DISREGARD ANY FURTHER ORDERS TO LAY HANDS ON ME. IT'S RUDE AND I DON'T LIKE IT.
CAPTAIN UMIL?
YES, MA'AM?
CLEAR THE HALL.
BUT DON'T LET ANYONE WHO WITNESSED THIS LEAVE THE GROUNDS.
YES, MA'AM.

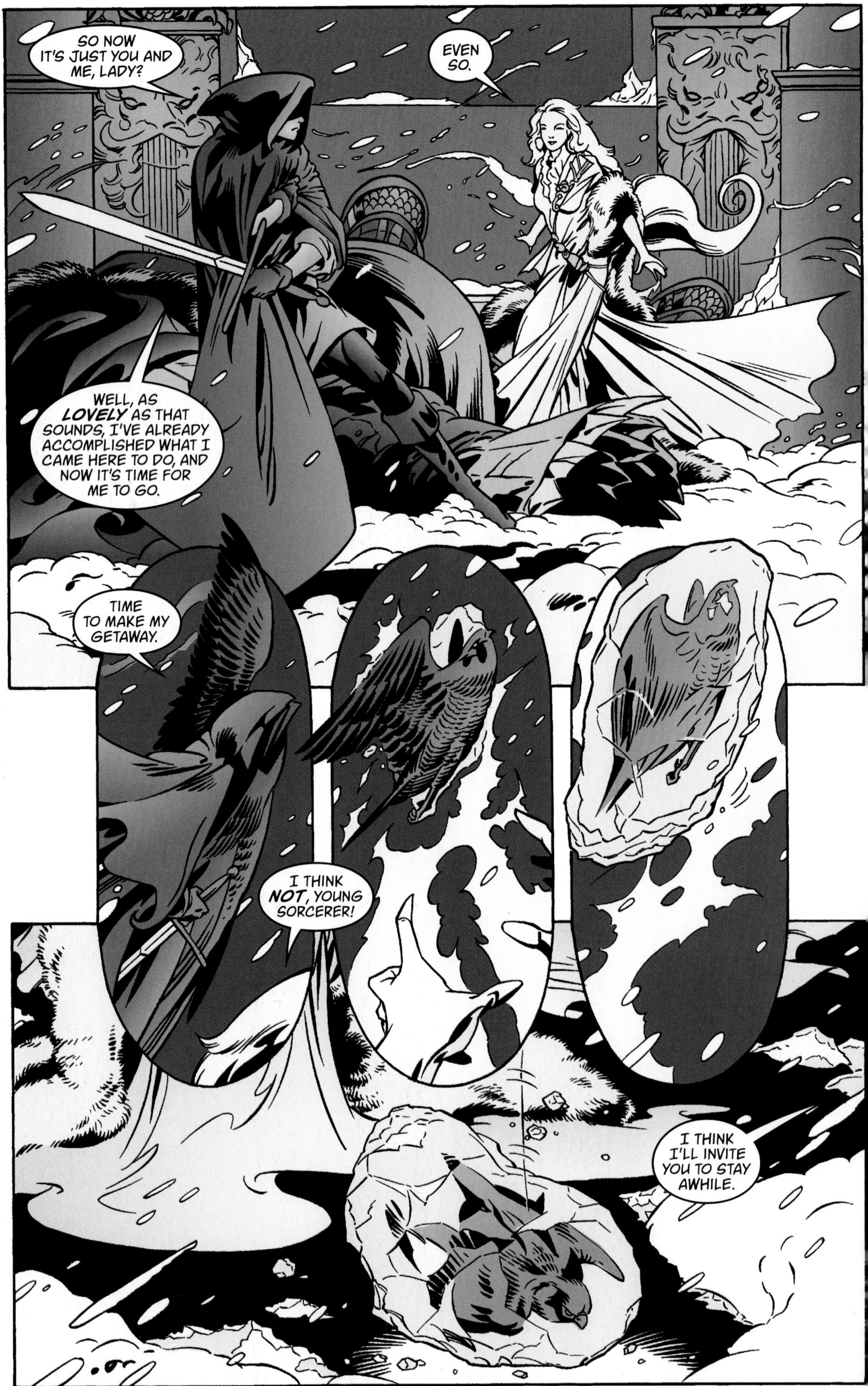
SO NOW IT'S JUST YOU AND ME, LADY?
EVEN SO.
WELL, AS LOVELY AS THAT SOUNDS, I'VE ALREADY ACCOMPLISHED WHAT I CAME HERE TO DO, AND NOW IT'S TIME FOR ME TO GO.
TIME TO MAKE MY GETAWAY.
I THINK NOT, YOUNG SORCERER!
I THINK I'LL INVITE YOU TO STAY AWHILE.

NEXT: RETURN TO FABLETOWN!

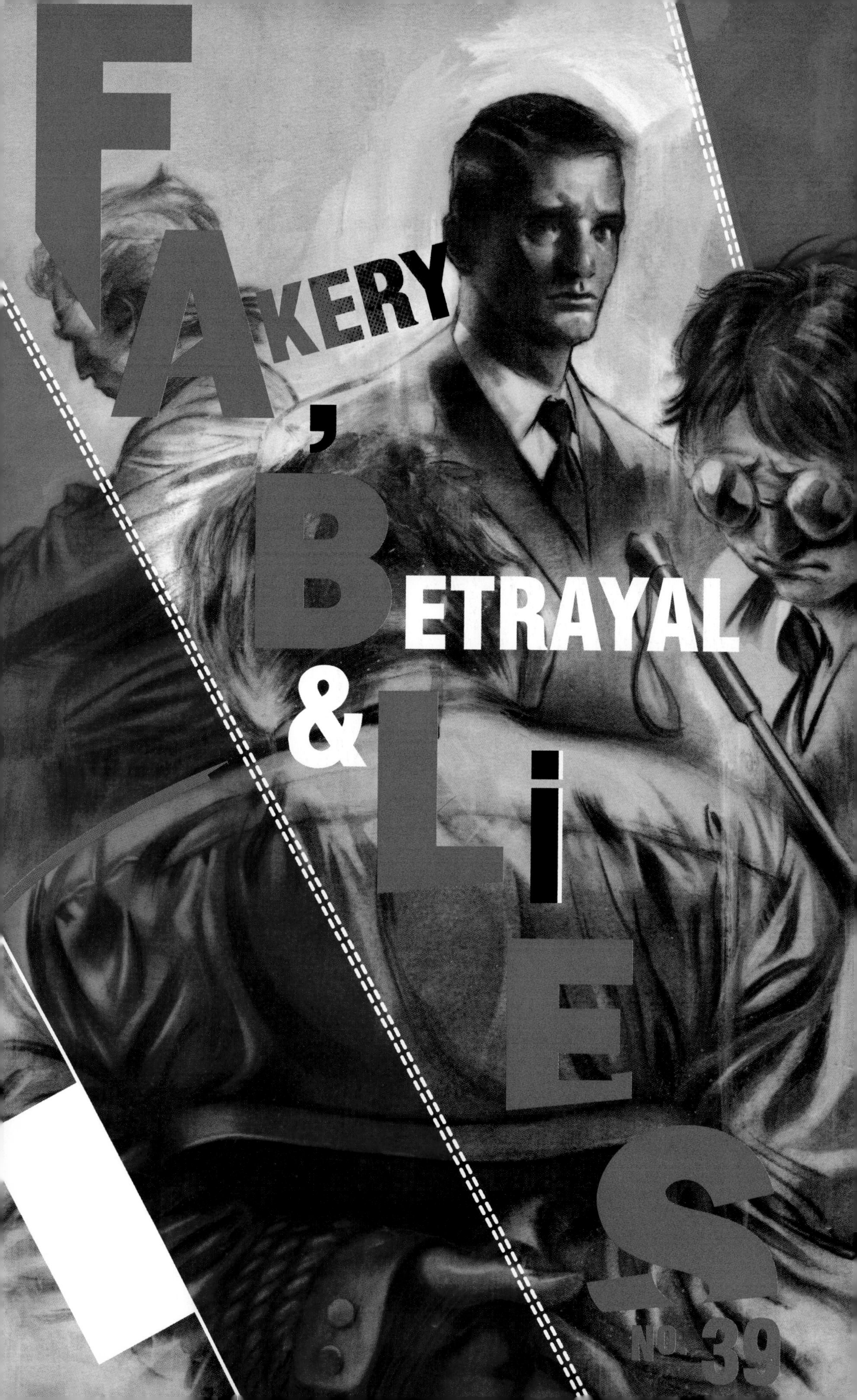
FAKERY, BETRAYAL & LIES
NO. 39

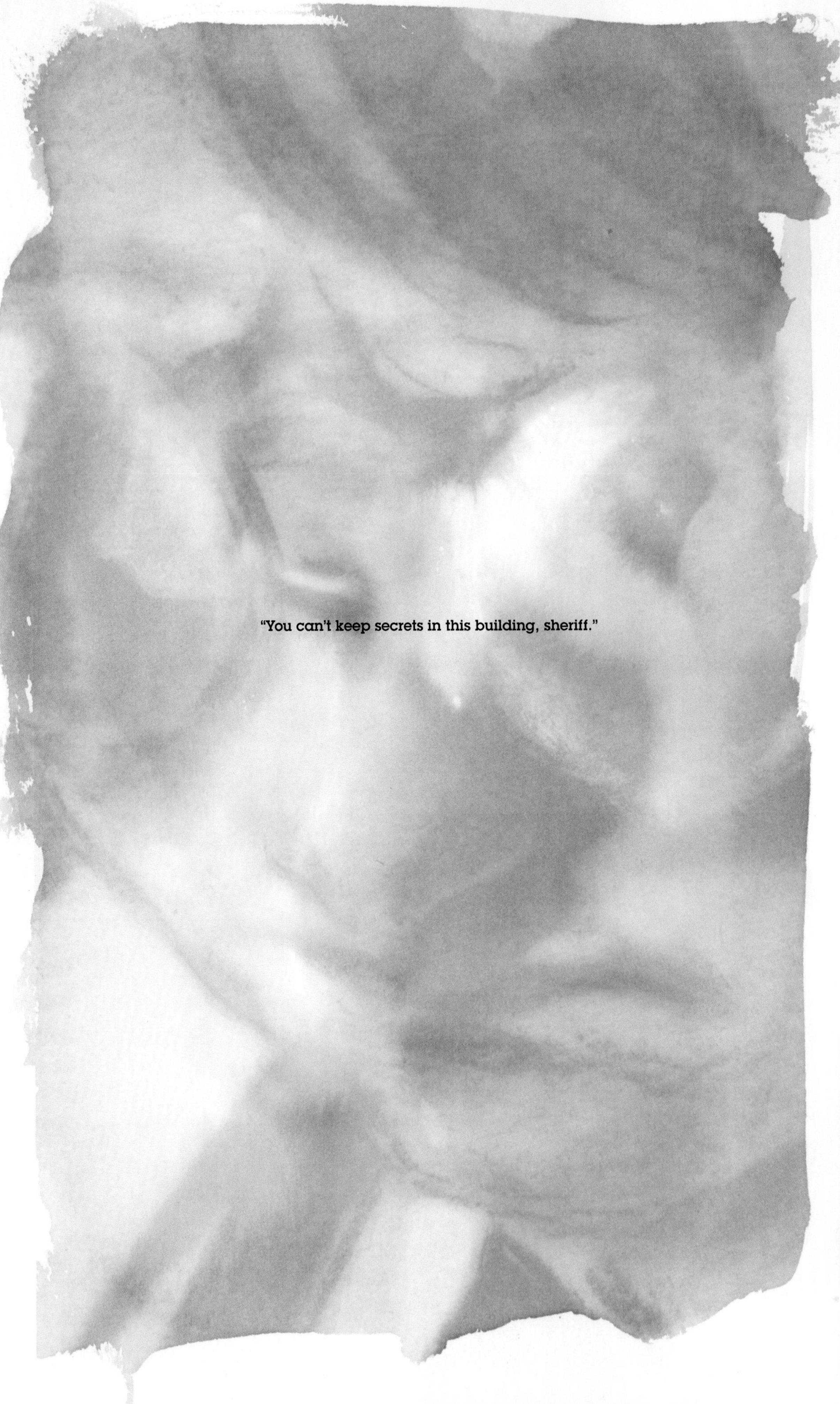
"You can't keep secrets in this building, sheriff."

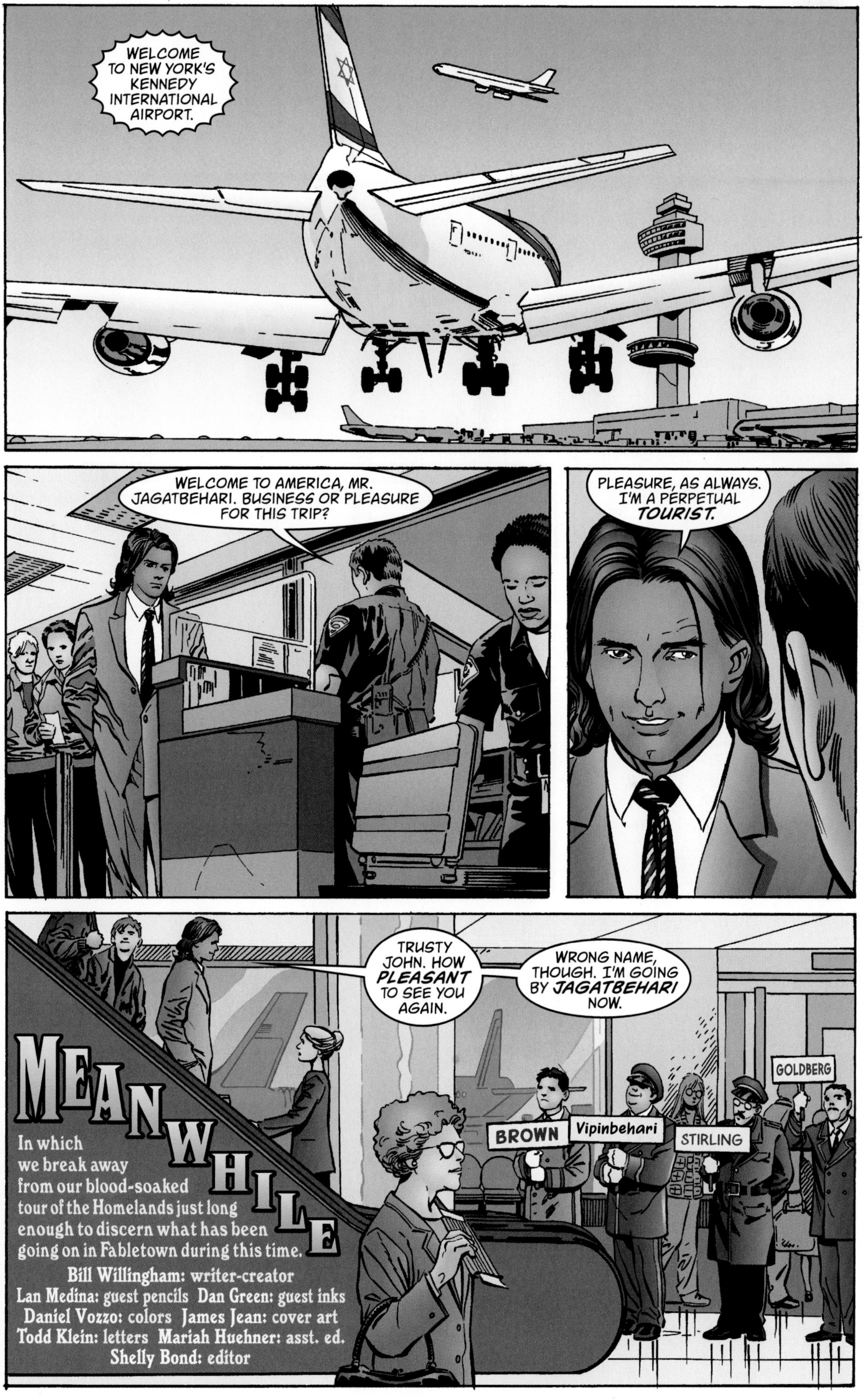
WELCOME TO NEW YORK'S KENNEDY INTERNATIONAL AIRPORT.
WELCOME TO AMERICA, MR. JAGATBEHARI. BUSINESS OR PLEASURE FOR THIS TRIP?
PLEASURE, AS ALWAYS. I'M A PERPETUAL *TOURIST.*
TRUSTY JOHN. HOW *PLEASANT* TO SEE YOU AGAIN.
WRONG NAME, THOUGH. I'M GOING BY *JAGATBEHARI* NOW.
GOLDBERG
BROWN
Vipinbehari
STIRLING
MEANWHILE
In which we break away from our blood-soaked tour of the Homelands just long enough to discern what has been going on in Fabletown during this time.
Bill Willingham: writer-creator
Lan Medina: guest pencils Dan Green: guest inks
Daniel Vozzo: colors James Jean: cover art
Todd Klein: letters Mariah Huehner: asst. ed.
Shelly Bond: editor

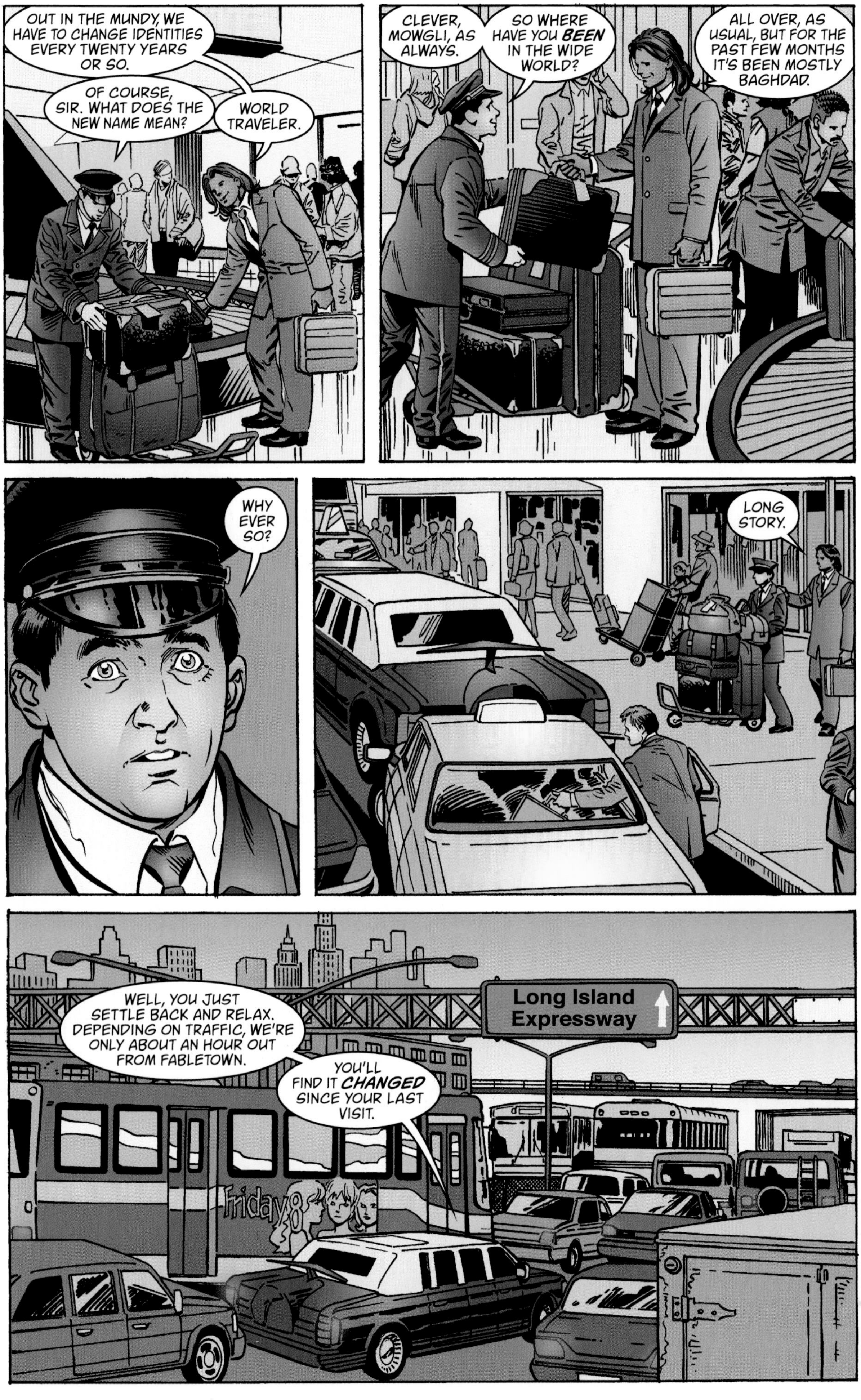

OUT IN THE MUNDY, WE HAVE TO CHANGE IDENTITIES EVERY TWENTY YEARS OR SO.
OF COURSE, SIR. WHAT DOES THE NEW NAME MEAN?
WORLD TRAVELER.
CLEVER, MOWGLI, AS ALWAYS.
SO WHERE HAVE YOU BEEN IN THE WIDE WORLD?
ALL OVER, AS USUAL, BUT FOR THE PAST FEW MONTHS IT'S BEEN MOSTLY BAGHDAD.
WHY EVER SO?
LONG STORY.
Long Island Expressway
WELL, YOU JUST SETTLE BACK AND RELAX. DEPENDING ON TRAFFIC, WE'RE ONLY ABOUT AN HOUR OUT FROM FABLETOWN.
YOU'LL FIND IT CHANGED SINCE YOUR LAST VISIT.
Friday 8

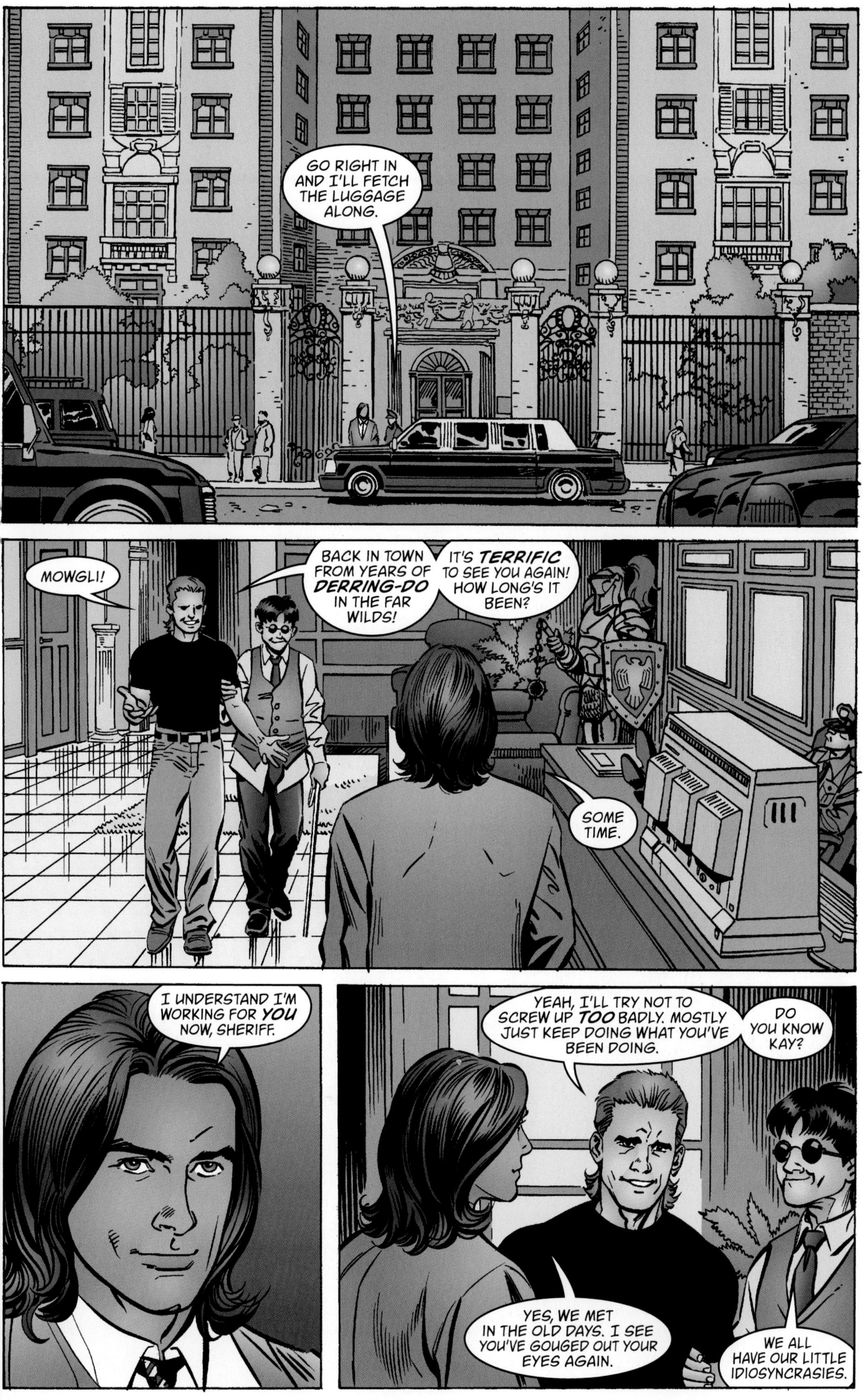
GO RIGHT IN AND I'LL FETCH THE LUGGAGE ALONG.
MOWGLI!
BACK IN TOWN FROM YEARS OF DERRING-DO IN THE FAR WILDS!
IT'S TERRIFIC TO SEE YOU AGAIN! HOW LONG'S IT BEEN?
SOME TIME.
I UNDERSTAND I'M WORKING FOR YOU NOW, SHERIFF.
YEAH, I'LL TRY NOT TO SCREW UP TOO BADLY. MOSTLY JUST KEEP DOING WHAT YOU'VE BEEN DOING.
DO YOU KNOW KAY?
YES, WE MET IN THE OLD DAYS. I SEE YOU'VE GOUGED OUT YOUR EYES AGAIN.
WE ALL HAVE OUR LITTLE IDIOSYNCRASIES.

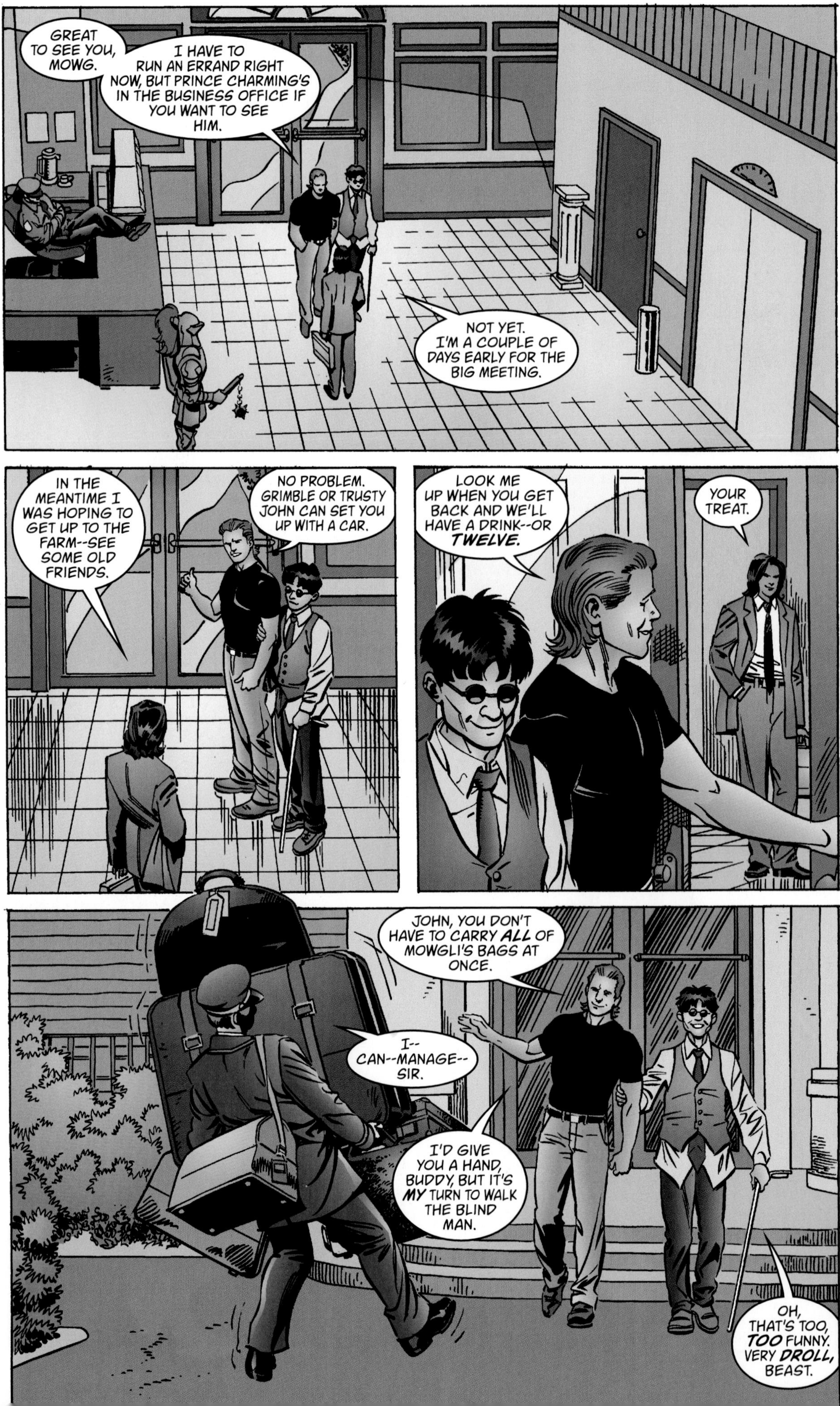
GREAT TO SEE YOU, MOWG.
I HAVE TO RUN AN ERRAND RIGHT NOW, BUT PRINCE CHARMING'S IN THE BUSINESS OFFICE IF YOU WANT TO SEE HIM.
NOT YET. I'M A COUPLE OF DAYS EARLY FOR THE BIG MEETING.
IN THE MEANTIME I WAS HOPING TO GET UP TO THE FARM--SEE SOME OLD FRIENDS.
NO PROBLEM. GRIMBLE OR TRUSTY JOHN CAN SET YOU UP WITH A CAR.
LOOK ME UP WHEN YOU GET BACK AND WE'LL HAVE A DRINK--OR **TWELVE.**
YOUR TREAT.
JOHN, YOU DON'T HAVE TO CARRY **ALL** OF MOWGLI'S BAGS AT ONCE.
I-- CAN--MANAGE-- SIR.
I'D GIVE YOU A HAND, BUDDY, BUT IT'S **MY** TURN TO WALK THE BLIND MAN.
OH, THAT'S TOO, **TOO** FUNNY. VERY **DROLL,** BEAST.

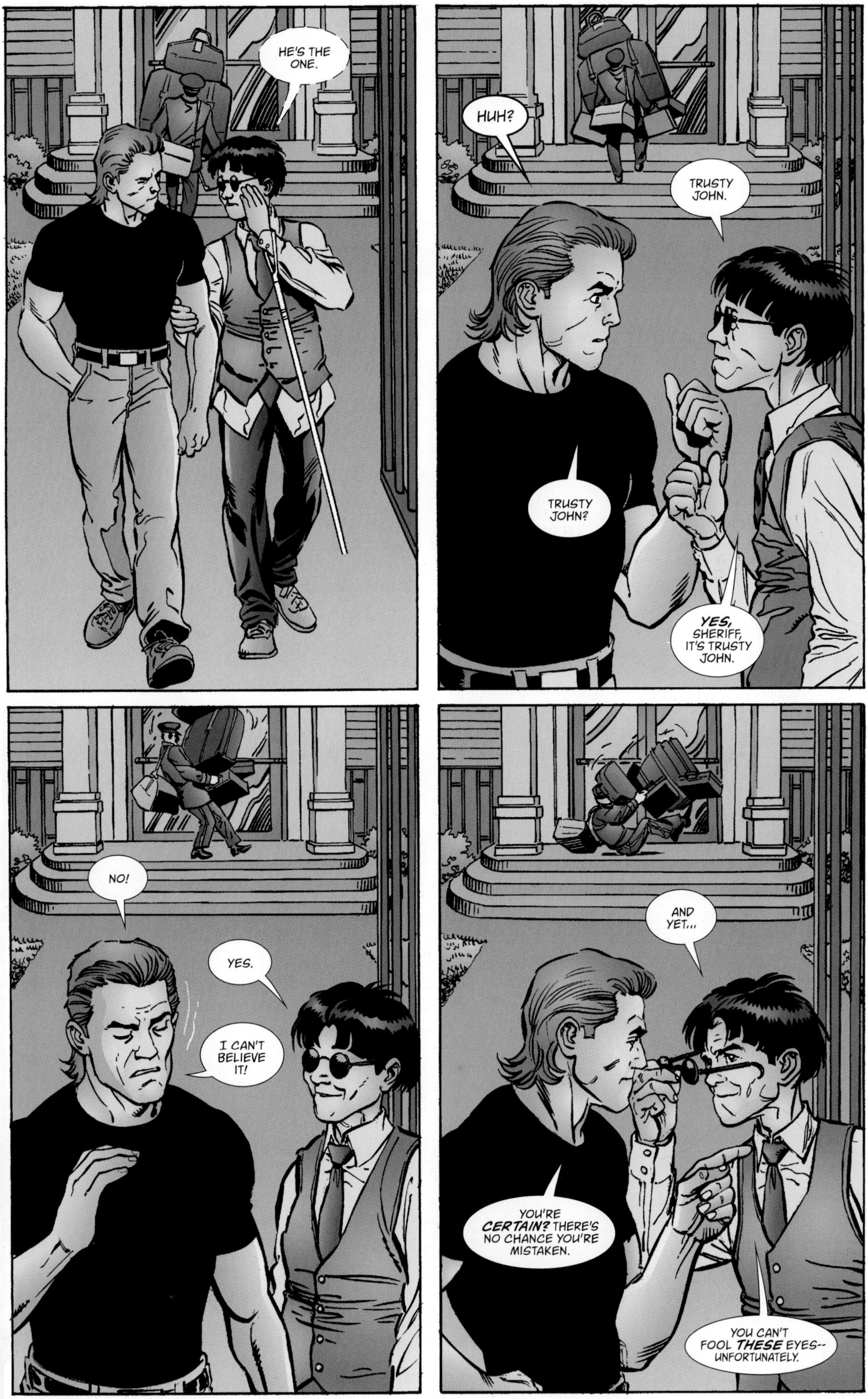
HE'S THE ONE.
HUH?
TRUSTY JOHN.
TRUSTY JOHN?
YES, SHERIFF, IT'S TRUSTY JOHN.
NO!
YES.
I CAN'T BELIEVE IT!
AND YET...
YOU'RE CERTAIN? THERE'S NO CHANCE YOU'RE MISTAKEN.
YOU CAN'T FOOL THESE EYES-- UNFORTUNATELY.

MOWGLI.

LITTLE BROTHER.

HELLO, BAGHEERA. IT'S BEEN *AGES*.

LITTLE FROG'S ALL GROWN UP NOW.

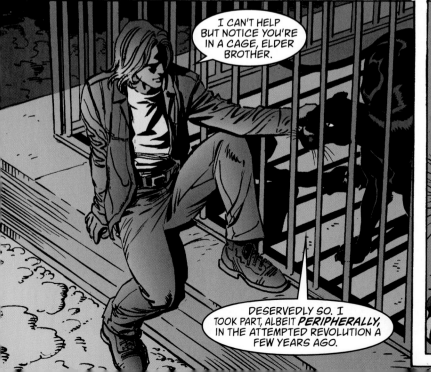

I CAN'T HELP BUT NOTICE YOU'RE IN A CAGE, ELDER BROTHER.

DESERVEDLY SO. I TOOK PART, ALBEIT *PERIPHERALLY*, IN THE ATTEMPTED REVOLUTION A FEW YEARS AGO.

THIS IS MY PUNISHMENT.

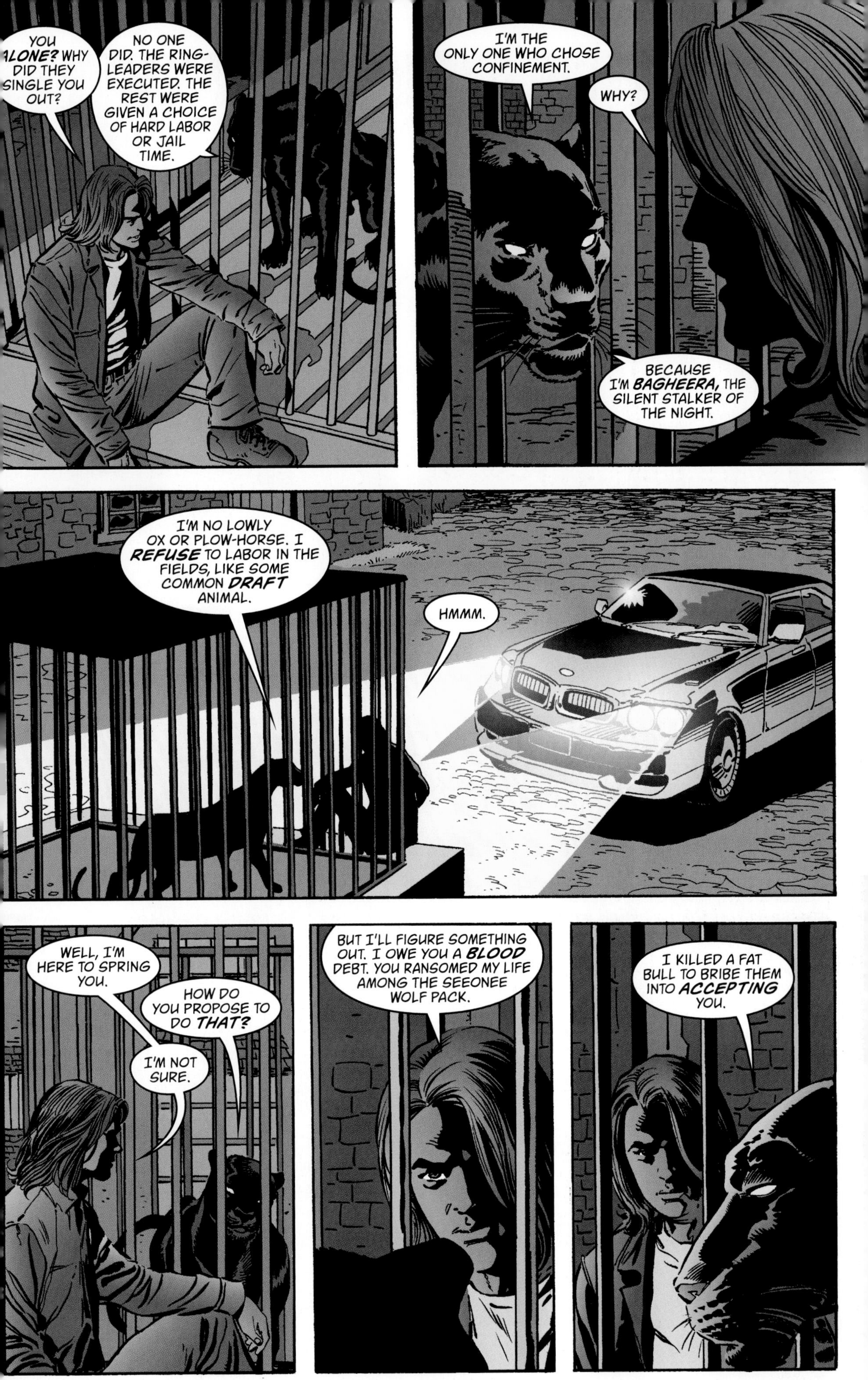

YOU ALONE? WHY DID THEY SINGLE YOU OUT?
NO ONE DID. THE RING-LEADERS WERE EXECUTED. THE REST WERE GIVEN A CHOICE OF HARD LABOR OR JAIL TIME.
I'M THE ONLY ONE WHO CHOSE CONFINEMENT.
WHY?
BECAUSE I'M BAGHEERA, THE SILENT STALKER OF THE NIGHT.
I'M NO LOWLY OX OR PLOW-HORSE. I REFUSE TO LABOR IN THE FIELDS, LIKE SOME COMMON DRAFT ANIMAL.
HMMM.
WELL, I'M HERE TO SPRING YOU.
HOW DO YOU PROPOSE TO DO THAT?
I'M NOT SURE.
BUT I'LL FIGURE SOMETHING OUT. I OWE YOU A BLOOD DEBT. YOU RANSOMED MY LIFE AMONG THE SEEONEE WOLF PACK.
I KILLED A FAT BULL TO BRIBE THEM INTO ACCEPTING YOU.

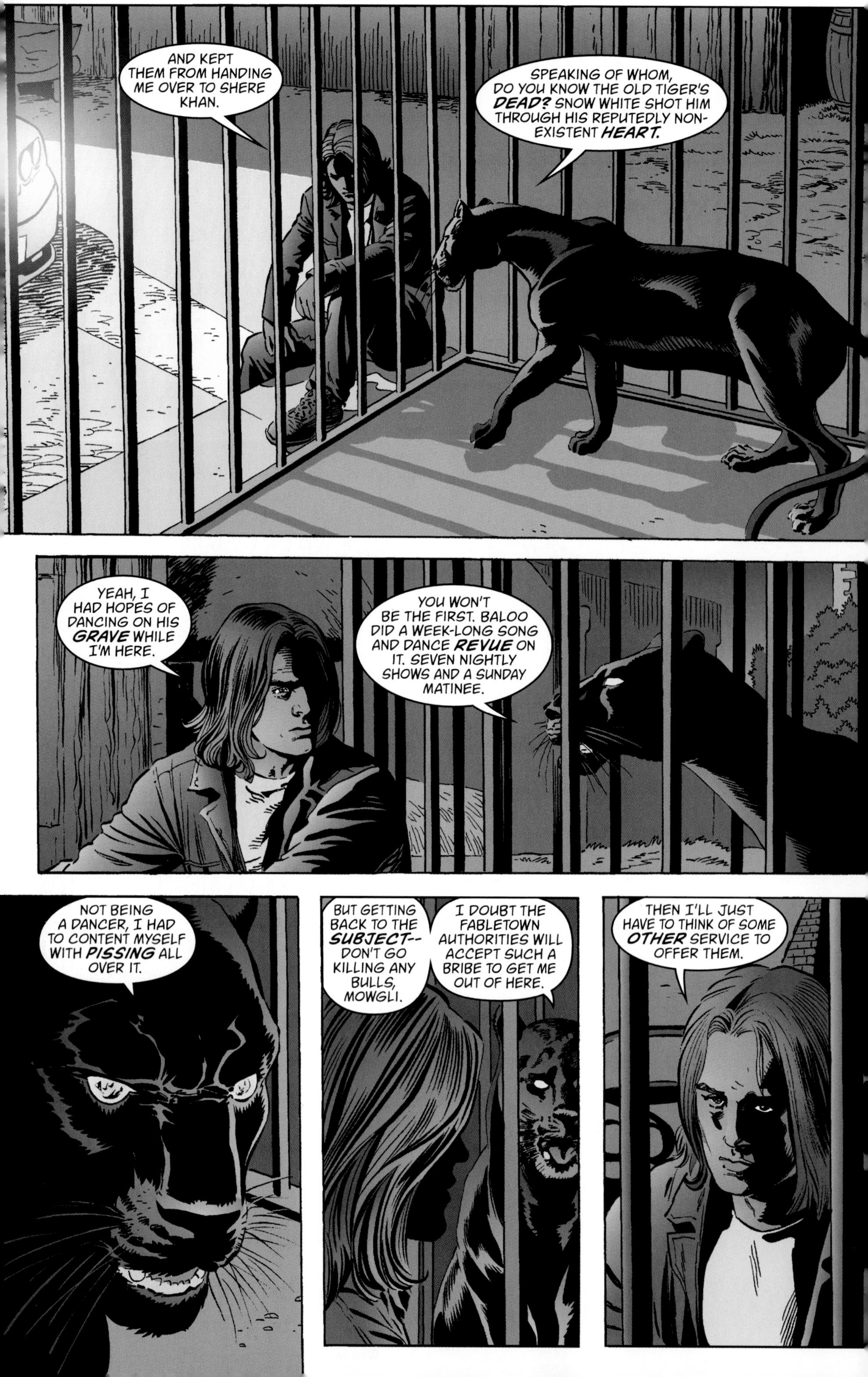
AND KEPT THEM FROM HANDING ME OVER TO SHERE KHAN.
SPEAKING OF WHOM, DO YOU KNOW THE OLD TIGER'S DEAD? SNOW WHITE SHOT HIM THROUGH HIS REPUTEDLY NON-EXISTENT HEART.
YEAH, I HAD HOPES OF DANCING ON HIS GRAVE WHILE I'M HERE.
YOU WON'T BE THE FIRST. BALOO DID A WEEK-LONG SONG AND DANCE REVUE ON IT. SEVEN NIGHTLY SHOWS AND A SUNDAY MATINEE.
NOT BEING A DANCER, I HAD TO CONTENT MYSELF WITH PISSING ALL OVER IT.
BUT GETTING BACK TO THE SUBJECT-- DON'T GO KILLING ANY BULLS, MOWGLI.
I DOUBT THE FABLETOWN AUTHORITIES WILL ACCEPT SUCH A BRIBE TO GET ME OUT OF HERE.
THEN I'LL JUST HAVE TO THINK OF SOME OTHER SERVICE TO OFFER THEM.

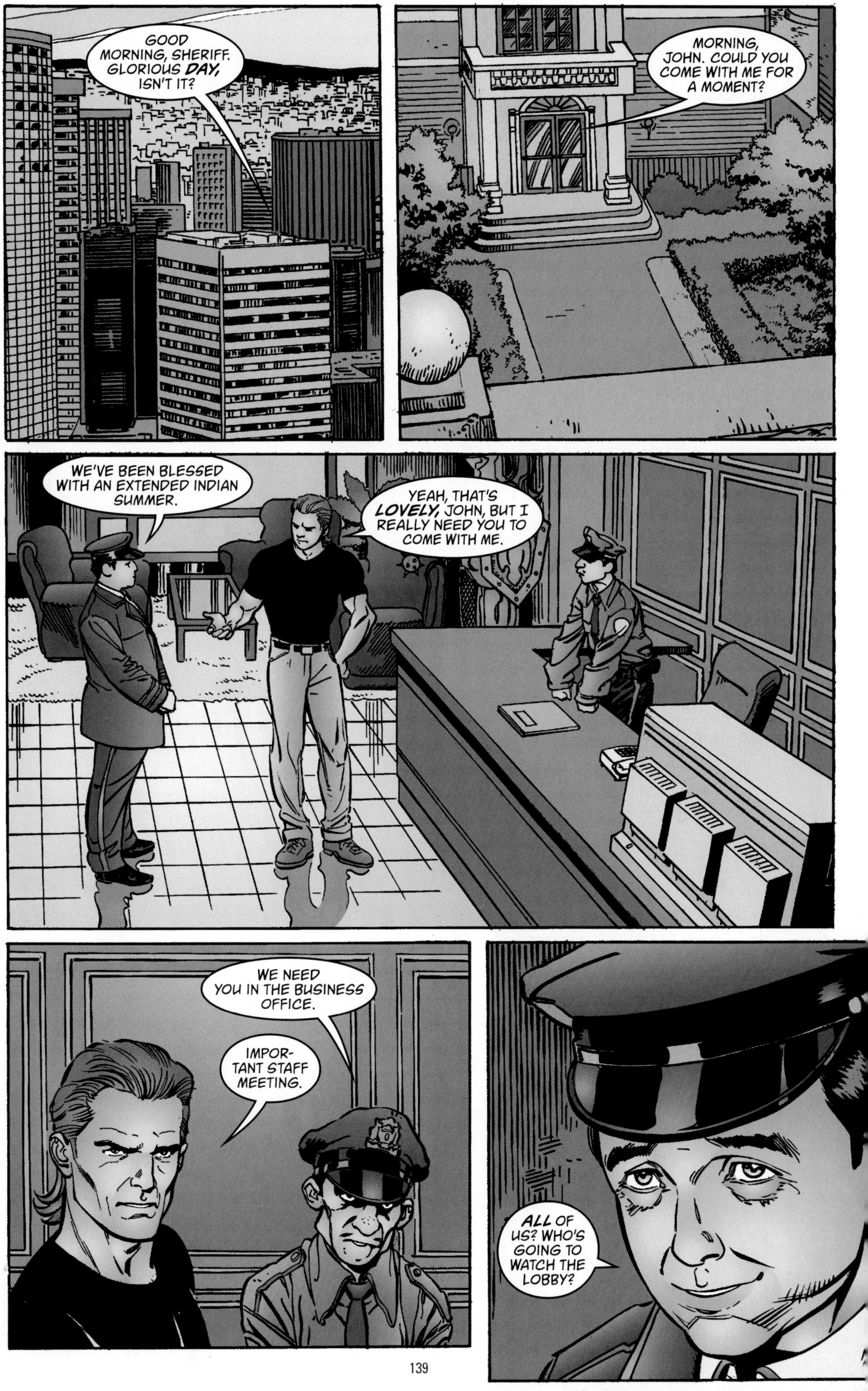
GOOD MORNING, SHERIFF. GLORIOUS DAY, ISN'T IT?
MORNING, JOHN. COULD YOU COME WITH ME FOR A MOMENT?
WE'VE BEEN BLESSED WITH AN EXTENDED INDIAN SUMMER.
YEAH, THAT'S LOVELY, JOHN, BUT I REALLY NEED YOU TO COME WITH ME.
WE NEED YOU IN THE BUSINESS OFFICE.
IMPOR-TANT STAFF MEETING.
ALL OF US? WHO'S GOING TO WATCH THE LOBBY?

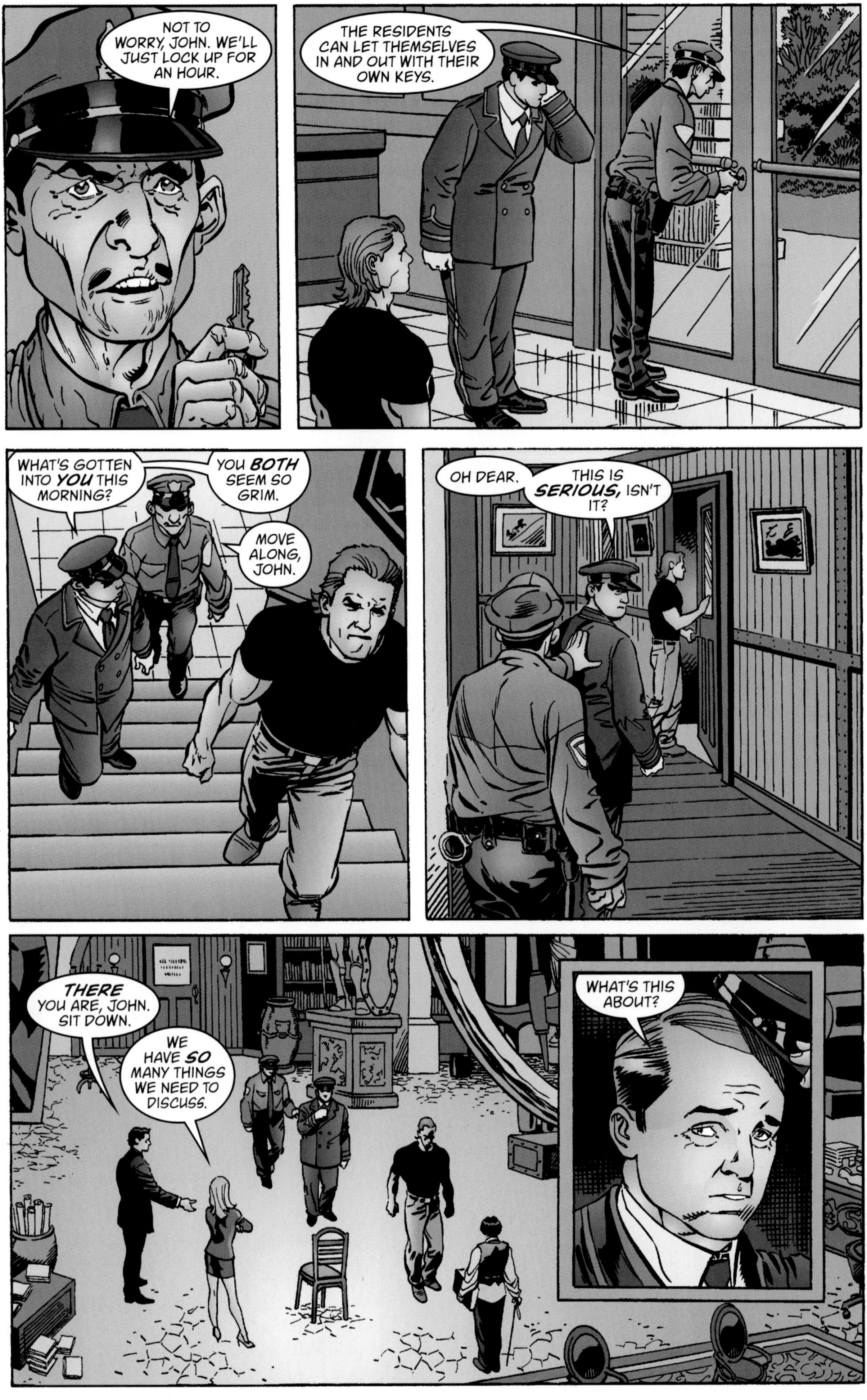
NOT TO WORRY, JOHN. WE'LL JUST LOCK UP FOR AN HOUR.
THE RESIDENTS CAN LET THEMSELVES IN AND OUT WITH THEIR OWN KEYS.
WHAT'S GOTTEN INTO YOU THIS MORNING?
YOU BOTH SEEM SO GRIM.
MOVE ALONG, JOHN.
OH DEAR.
THIS IS SERIOUS, ISN'T IT?
THERE YOU ARE, JOHN. SIT DOWN.
WE HAVE SO MANY THINGS WE NEED TO DISCUSS.
WHAT'S THIS ABOUT?

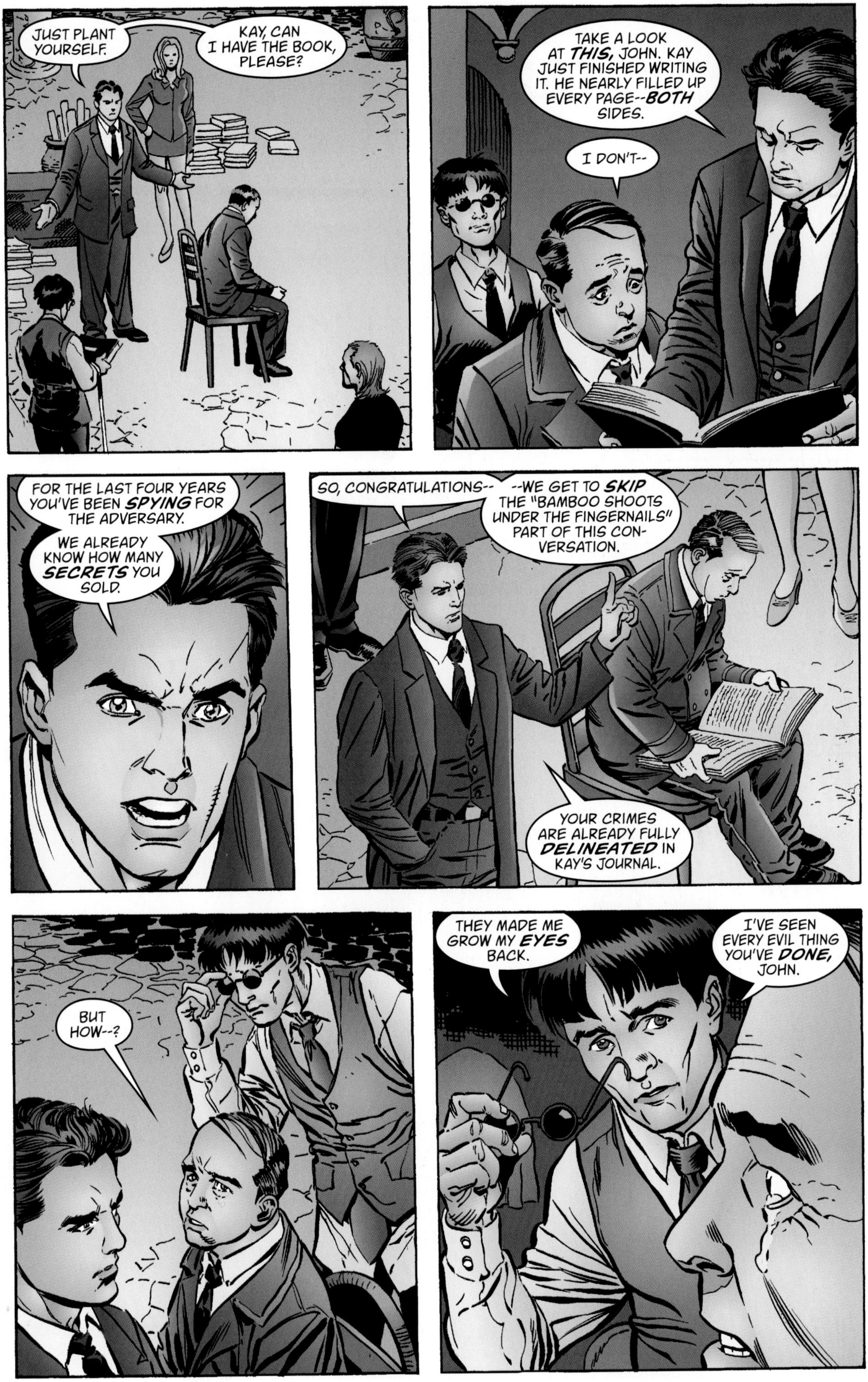
JUST PLANT YOURSELF.
KAY, CAN I HAVE THE BOOK, PLEASE?
TAKE A LOOK AT THIS, JOHN. KAY JUST FINISHED WRITING IT. HE NEARLY FILLED UP EVERY PAGE--BOTH SIDES.
I DON'T--
FOR THE LAST FOUR YEARS YOU'VE BEEN SPYING FOR THE ADVERSARY.
WE ALREADY KNOW HOW MANY SECRETS YOU SOLD.
SO, CONGRATULATIONS--
--WE GET TO SKIP THE "BAMBOO SHOOTS UNDER THE FINGERNAILS" PART OF THIS CON-VERSATION.
YOUR CRIMES ARE ALREADY FULLY DELINEATED IN KAY'S JOURNAL.
BUT HOW--?
THEY MADE ME GROW MY EYES BACK.
I'VE SEEN EVERY EVIL THING YOU'VE DONE, JOHN.

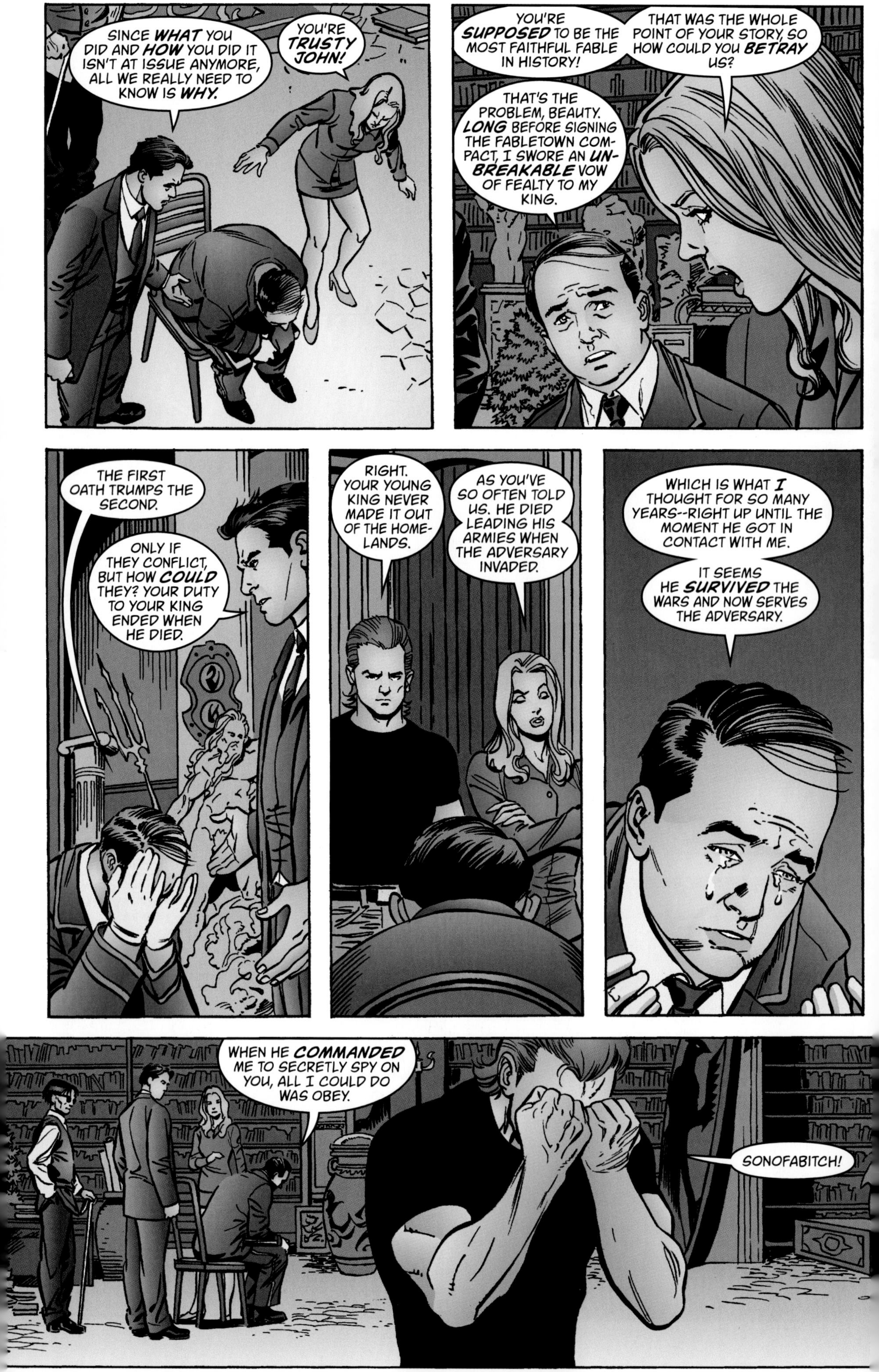
SINCE WHAT YOU DID AND HOW YOU DID IT ISN'T AT ISSUE ANYMORE, ALL WE REALLY NEED TO KNOW IS WHY.
YOU'RE TRUSTY JOHN!
YOU'RE SUPPOSED TO BE THE MOST FAITHFUL FABLE IN HISTORY!
THAT WAS THE WHOLE POINT OF YOUR STORY, SO HOW COULD YOU BETRAY US?
THAT'S THE PROBLEM, BEAUTY. LONG BEFORE SIGNING THE FABLETOWN COMPACT, I SWORE AN UNBREAKABLE VOW OF FEALTY TO MY KING.
THE FIRST OATH TRUMPS THE SECOND.
ONLY IF THEY CONFLICT, BUT HOW COULD THEY? YOUR DUTY TO YOUR KING ENDED WHEN HE DIED.
RIGHT. YOUR YOUNG KING NEVER MADE IT OUT OF THE HOMELANDS.
AS YOU'VE SO OFTEN TOLD US. HE DIED LEADING HIS ARMIES WHEN THE ADVERSARY INVADED.
WHICH IS WHAT I THOUGHT FOR SO MANY YEARS--RIGHT UP UNTIL THE MOMENT HE GOT IN CONTACT WITH ME.
IT SEEMS HE SURVIVED THE WARS AND NOW SERVES THE ADVERSARY.
WHEN HE COMMANDED ME TO SECRETLY SPY ON YOU, ALL I COULD DO WAS OBEY.
SONOFABITCH!

DO YOU STILL PRACTICE THE HUNTER'S DISCIPLINE OUT IN THE WORLD OF MAN, LITTLE FROG?

I SURE DO, OLD BALOO.

FEET THAT MAKE NO NOISE.

EYES THAT CAN SEE IN THE DARK.

EARS THAT CAN HEAR THE WINDS IN THEIR LAIRS.

AND SHARP WHITE TEETH.

WELL, WE CAN'T REALLY IMPROVE ON YOUR *TEETH*, MAN CUB.

YOU'RE STUCK WITH WHAT NATURE GAVE YOU.

AH, BUT, IN ADDITION TO LITTLE FROG OF SEEONEE WOLF PACK, I'M IN THE WORLD OF MAN NOW.

AND WE MAKE UP FOR HOW NATURE SHORTED US BY MANUFACTURING OUR *OWN* TEETH AND CLAWS.

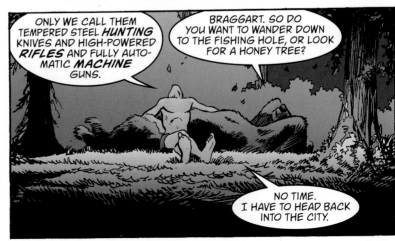

ONLY WE CALL THEM TEMPERED STEEL *HUNTING* KNIVES AND HIGH-POWERED *RIFLES* AND FULLY AUTO-MATIC *MACHINE* GUNS.

BRAGGART. SO DO YOU WANT TO WANDER DOWN TO THE FISHING HOLE, OR LOOK FOR A HONEY TREE?

NO TIME. I HAVE TO HEAD BACK INTO THE CITY.

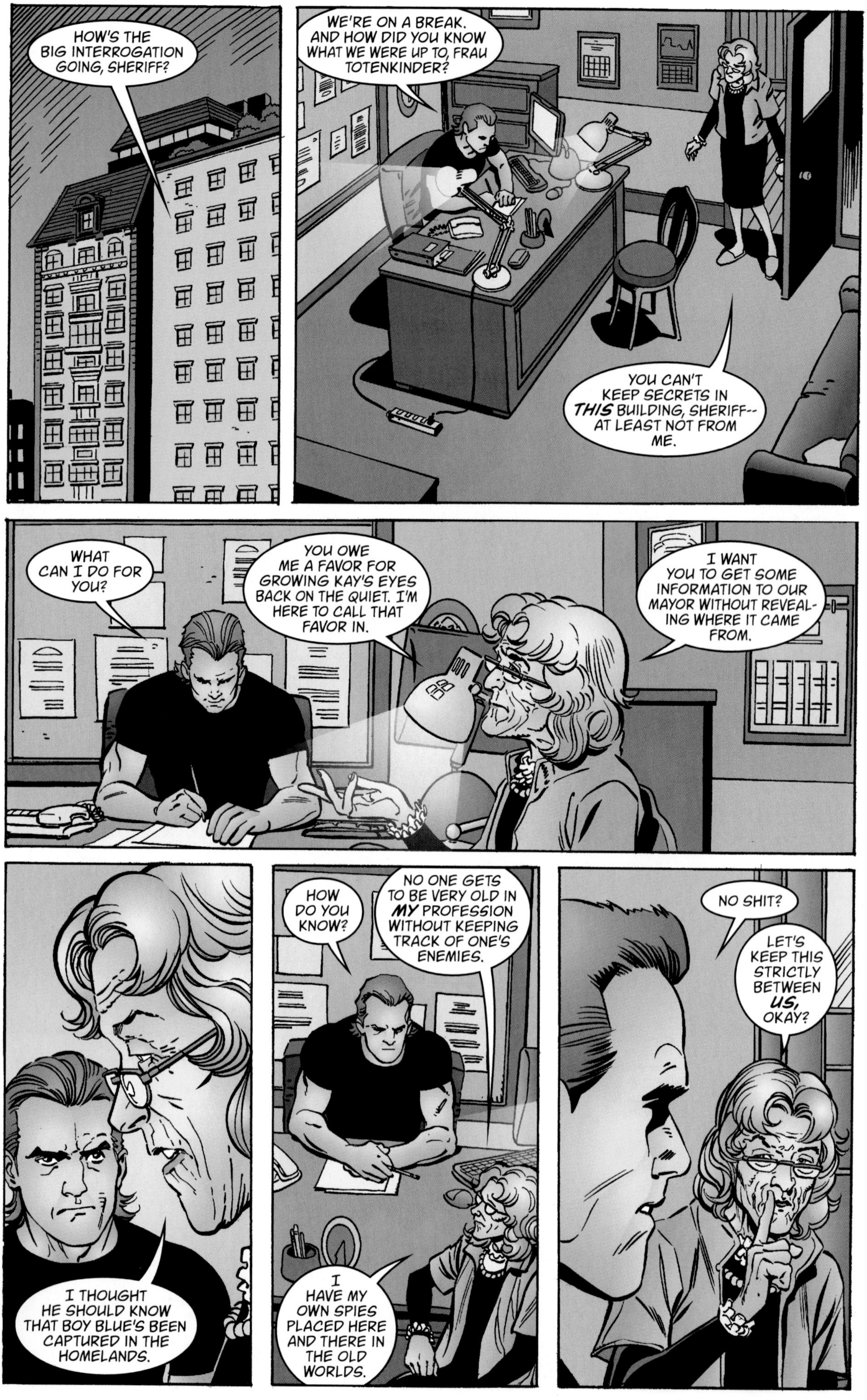
HOW'S THE BIG INTERROGATION GOING, SHERIFF?
WE'RE ON A BREAK. AND HOW DID YOU KNOW WHAT WE WERE UP TO, FRAU TOTENKINDER?
YOU CAN'T KEEP SECRETS IN THIS BUILDING, SHERIFF-- AT LEAST NOT FROM ME.
WHAT CAN I DO FOR YOU?
YOU OWE ME A FAVOR FOR GROWING KAY'S EYES BACK ON THE QUIET. I'M HERE TO CALL THAT FAVOR IN.
I WANT YOU TO GET SOME INFORMATION TO OUR MAYOR WITHOUT REVEALING WHERE IT CAME FROM.
I THOUGHT HE SHOULD KNOW THAT BOY BLUE'S BEEN CAPTURED IN THE HOMELANDS.
HOW DO YOU KNOW?
NO ONE GETS TO BE VERY OLD IN MY PROFESSION WITHOUT KEEPING TRACK OF ONE'S ENEMIES.
I HAVE MY OWN SPIES PLACED HERE AND THERE IN THE OLD WORLDS.
NO SHIT?
LET'S KEEP THIS STRICTLY BETWEEN US, OKAY?

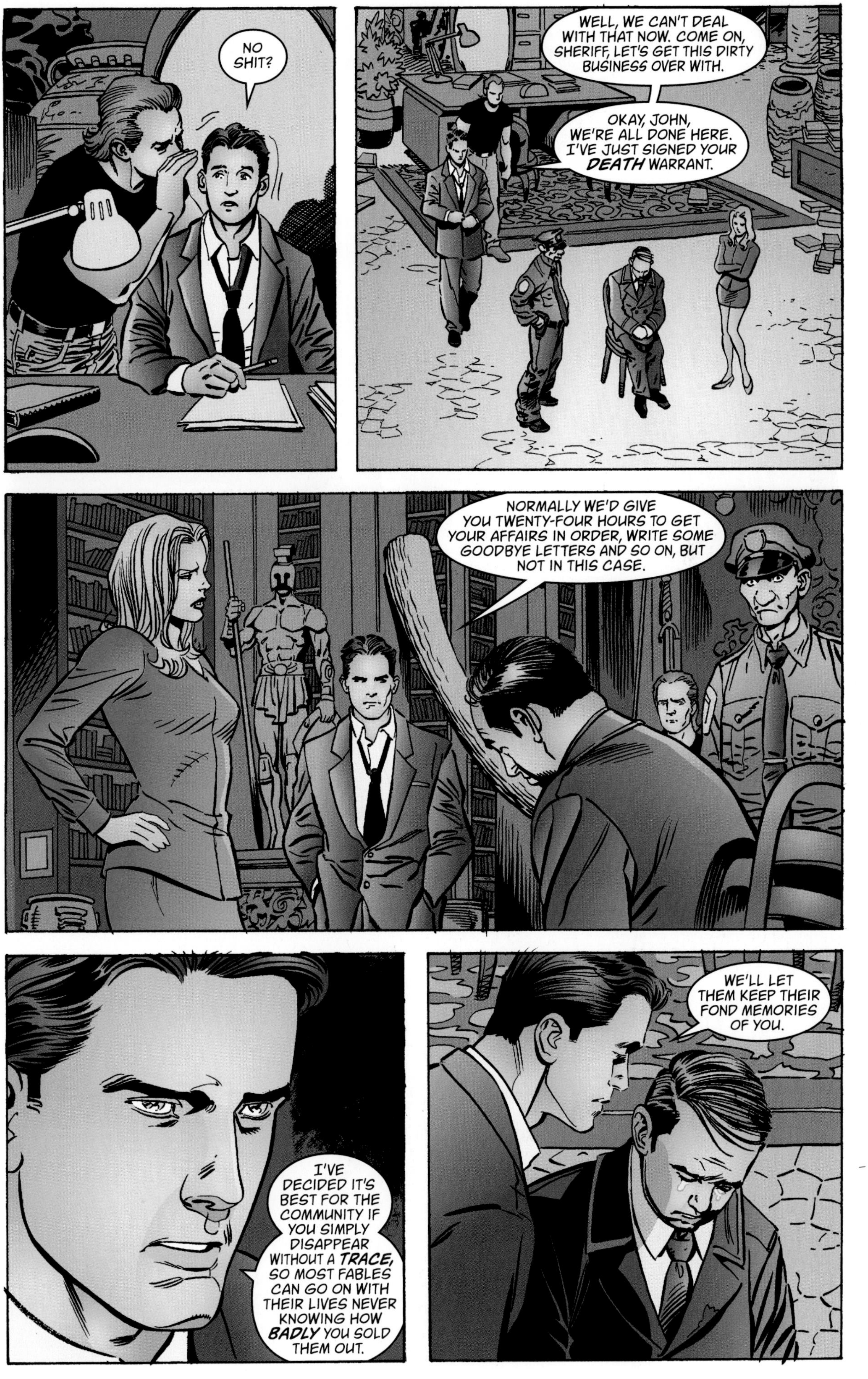
NO SHIT?
WELL, WE CAN'T DEAL WITH THAT NOW. COME ON, SHERIFF, LET'S GET THIS DIRTY BUSINESS OVER WITH.
OKAY, JOHN, WE'RE ALL DONE HERE. I'VE JUST SIGNED YOUR *DEATH* WARRANT.
NORMALLY WE'D GIVE YOU TWENTY-FOUR HOURS TO GET YOUR AFFAIRS IN ORDER, WRITE SOME GOODBYE LETTERS AND SO ON, BUT NOT IN THIS CASE.
I'VE DECIDED IT'S BEST FOR THE COMMUNITY IF YOU SIMPLY DISAPPEAR WITHOUT A *TRACE,* SO MOST FABLES CAN GO ON WITH THEIR LIVES NEVER KNOWING HOW *BADLY* YOU SOLD THEM OUT.
WE'LL LET THEM KEEP THEIR FOND MEMORIES OF YOU.

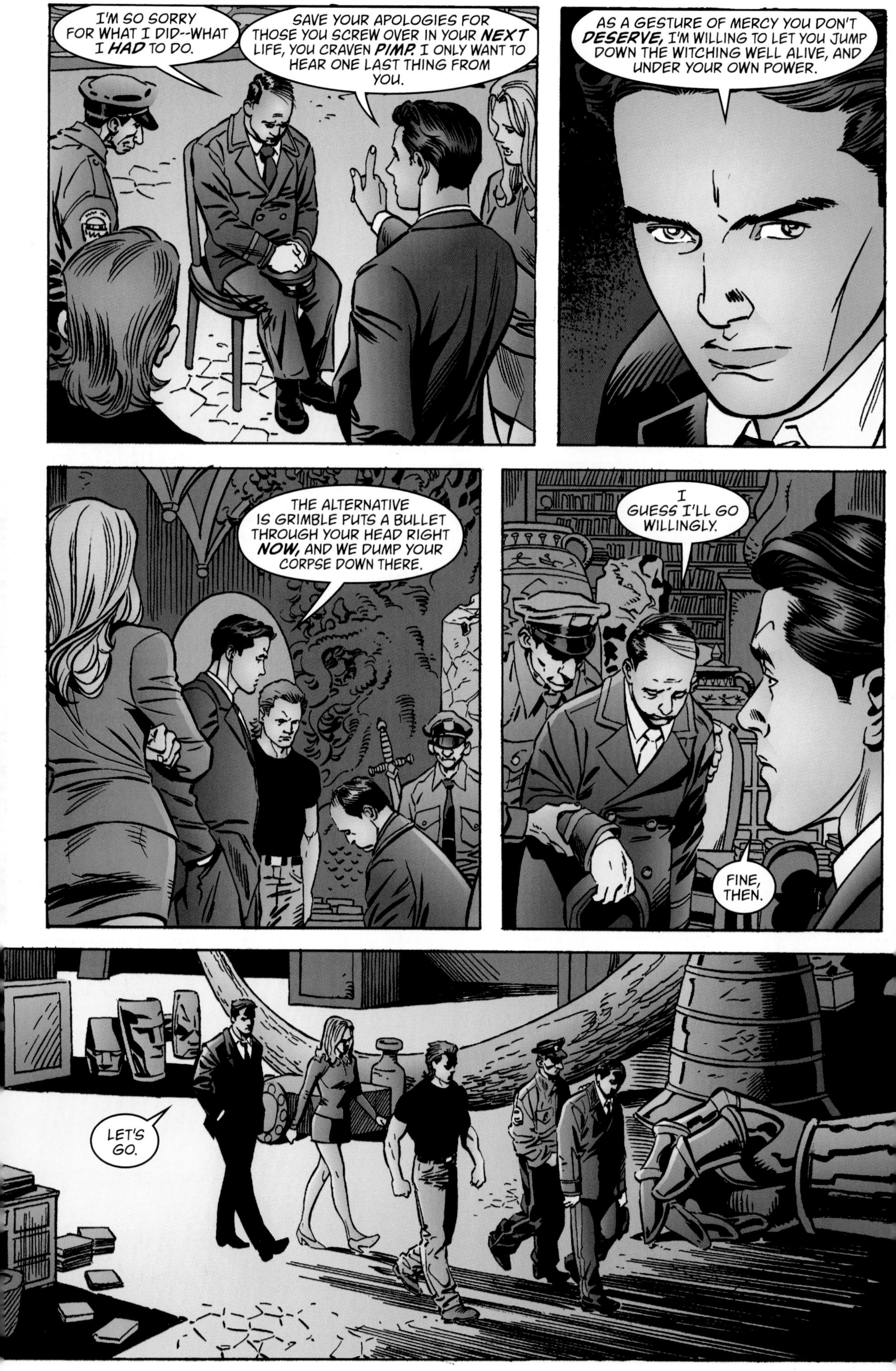
I'M SO SORRY FOR WHAT I DID--WHAT I HAD TO DO.
SAVE YOUR APOLOGIES FOR THOSE YOU SCREW OVER IN YOUR NEXT LIFE, YOU CRAVEN PIMP. I ONLY WANT TO HEAR ONE LAST THING FROM YOU.
AS A GESTURE OF MERCY YOU DON'T DESERVE, I'M WILLING TO LET YOU JUMP DOWN THE WITCHING WELL ALIVE, AND UNDER YOUR OWN POWER.
THE ALTERNATIVE IS GRIMBLE PUTS A BULLET THROUGH YOUR HEAD RIGHT NOW, AND WE DUMP YOUR CORPSE DOWN THERE.
I GUESS I'LL GO WILLINGLY.
FINE, THEN.
LET'S GO.

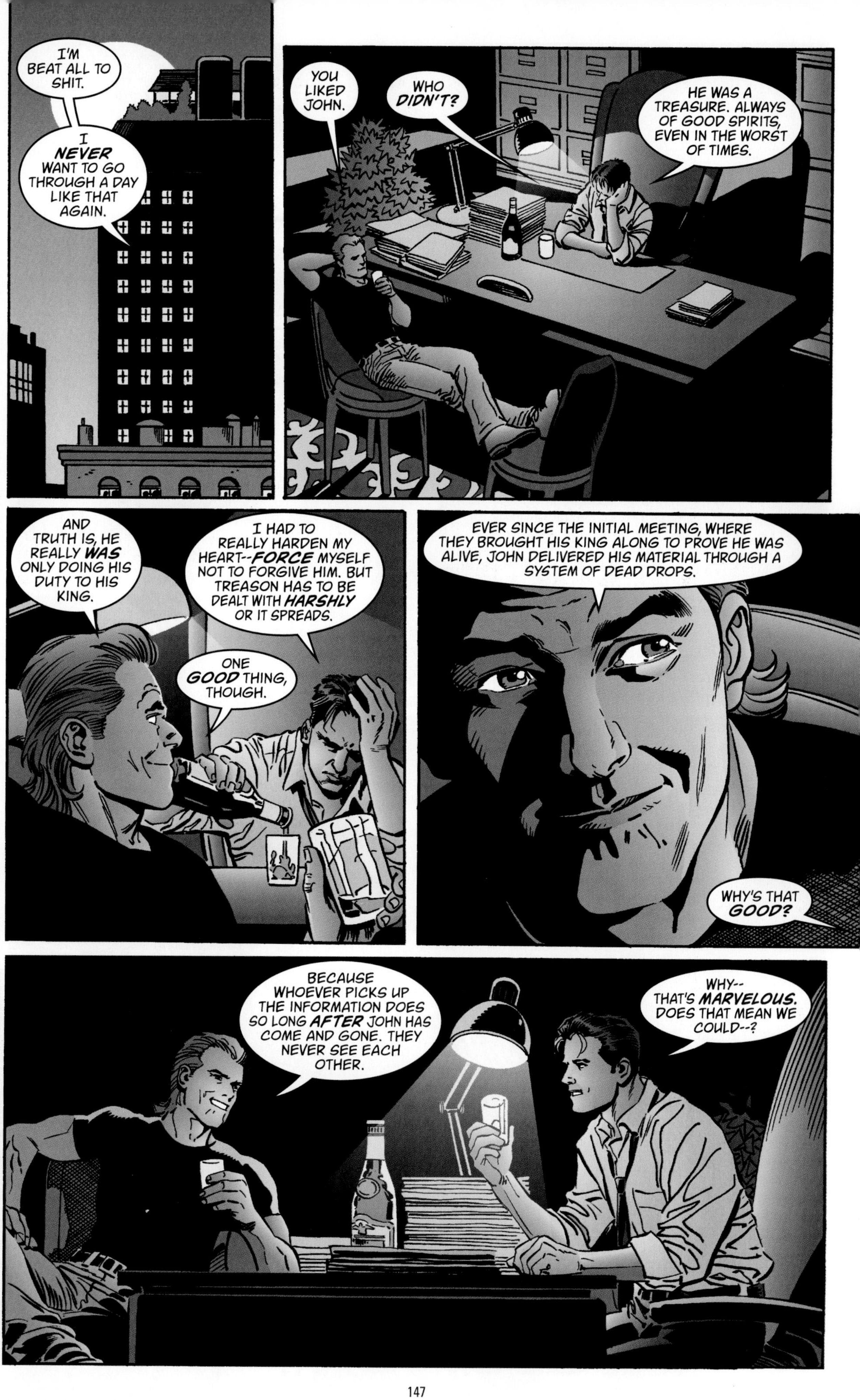
I'M BEAT ALL TO SHIT.
I NEVER WANT TO GO THROUGH A DAY LIKE THAT AGAIN.
YOU LIKED JOHN.
WHO DIDN'T?
HE WAS A TREASURE. ALWAYS OF GOOD SPIRITS, EVEN IN THE WORST OF TIMES.
AND TRUTH IS, HE REALLY WAS ONLY DOING HIS DUTY TO HIS KING.
I HAD TO REALLY HARDEN MY HEART--FORCE MYSELF NOT TO FORGIVE HIM. BUT TREASON HAS TO BE DEALT WITH HARSHLY OR IT SPREADS.
ONE GOOD THING, THOUGH.
EVER SINCE THE INITIAL MEETING, WHERE THEY BROUGHT HIS KING ALONG TO PROVE HE WAS ALIVE, JOHN DELIVERED HIS MATERIAL THROUGH A SYSTEM OF DEAD DROPS.
WHY'S THAT GOOD?
BECAUSE WHOEVER PICKS UP THE INFORMATION DOES SO LONG AFTER JOHN HAS COME AND GONE. THEY NEVER SEE EACH OTHER.
WHY-- THAT'S MARVELOUS. DOES THAT MEAN WE COULD--?

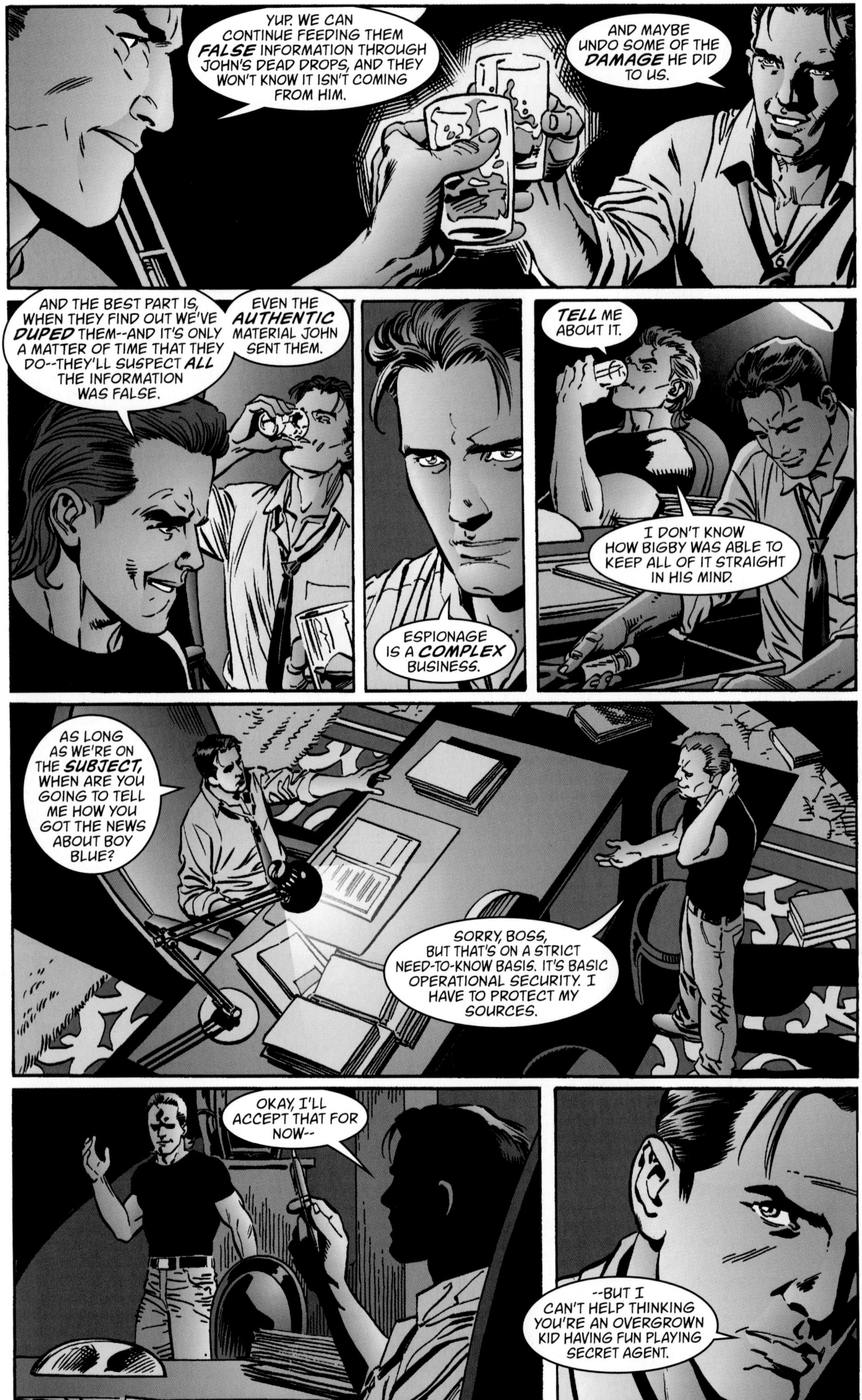
YUP. WE CAN CONTINUE FEEDING THEM FALSE INFORMATION THROUGH JOHN'S DEAD DROPS, AND THEY WON'T KNOW IT ISN'T COMING FROM HIM.
AND MAYBE UNDO SOME OF THE DAMAGE HE DID TO US.
AND THE BEST PART IS, WHEN THEY FIND OUT WE'VE DUPED THEM--AND IT'S ONLY A MATTER OF TIME THAT THEY DO--THEY'LL SUSPECT ALL THE INFORMATION WAS FALSE.
EVEN THE AUTHENTIC MATERIAL JOHN SENT THEM.
ESPIONAGE IS A COMPLEX BUSINESS.
TELL ME ABOUT IT.
I DON'T KNOW HOW BIGBY WAS ABLE TO KEEP ALL OF IT STRAIGHT IN HIS MIND.
AS LONG AS WE'RE ON THE SUBJECT, WHEN ARE YOU GOING TO TELL ME HOW YOU GOT THE NEWS ABOUT BOY BLUE?
SORRY, BOSS, BUT THAT'S ON A STRICT NEED-TO-KNOW BASIS. IT'S BASIC OPERATIONAL SECURITY. I HAVE TO PROTECT MY SOURCES.
OKAY, I'LL ACCEPT THAT FOR NOW--
--BUT I CAN'T HELP THINKING YOU'RE AN OVERGROWN KID HAVING FUN PLAYING SECRET AGENT.

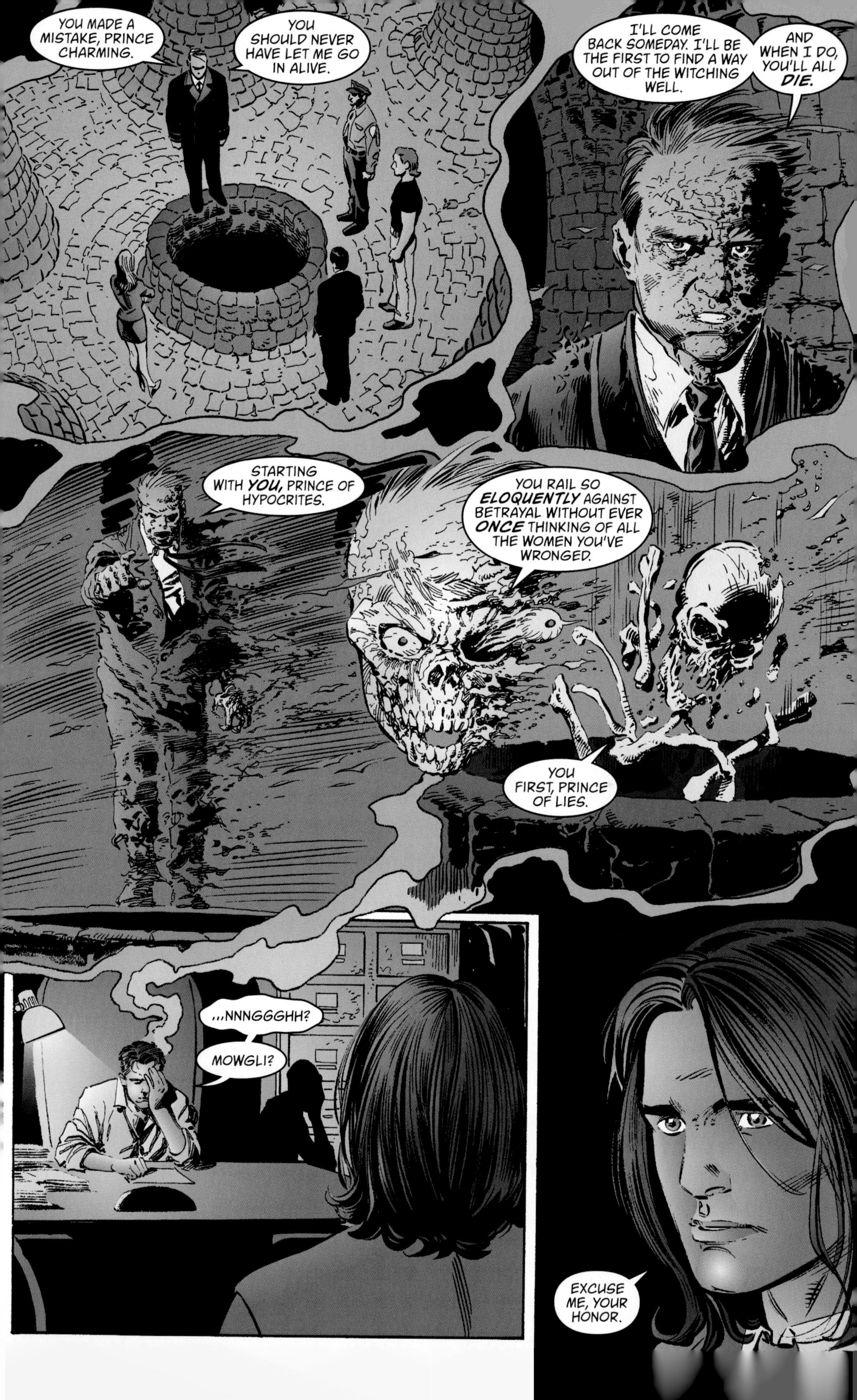
YOU MADE A MISTAKE, PRINCE CHARMING.
YOU SHOULD NEVER HAVE LET ME GO IN ALIVE.
I'LL COME BACK SOMEDAY. I'LL BE THE FIRST TO FIND A WAY OUT OF THE WITCHING WELL.
AND WHEN I DO, YOU'LL ALL DIE.
STARTING WITH YOU, PRINCE OF HYPOCRITES.
YOU RAIL SO ELOQUENTLY AGAINST BETRAYAL WITHOUT EVER ONCE THINKING OF ALL THE WOMEN YOU'VE WRONGED.
YOU FIRST, PRINCE OF LIES.
...NNNGGGHH?
MOWGLI?
EXCUSE ME, YOUR HONOR.

I'M SORRY TO WAKE YOU, BUT WE HAD A MEETING SCHEDULED.

UH--THAT'S OKAY, I HADN'T PLANNED TO SLEEP. TRYING TO GET CAUGHT UP ON *PAPERWORK* AND--

FROM THE SOUND OF IT ON *THIS* END YOU WEREN'T HAVING VERY PLEASANT DREAMS ANYWAY.

THAT'S AN *UNDERSTATEMENT*. I DON'T THINK I'VE HAD AN UNDISTURBED NIGHT SINCE I *TOOK* THIS ACCURSED JOB.

BUT LET'S GET TO THE POINT OF WHY I BROUGHT YOU HERE. YOU KNOW I HAD A MEETING LAST SPRING WITH THE OTHER TOURISTS.

YES, SIR. I'M SORRY I COULDN'T MAKE IT, BUT I WAS INVOLVED WITH A BIT OF BUSINESS I SIMPLY COULDN'T BREAK AWAY FROM.

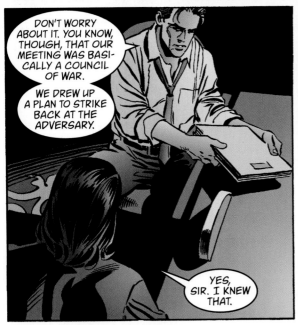

DON'T WORRY ABOUT IT. YOU KNOW, THOUGH, THAT OUR MEETING WAS BASICALLY A COUNCIL OF WAR.

WE DREW UP A PLAN TO STRIKE BACK AT THE ADVERSARY.

YES, SIR. I KNEW THAT.

WELL, HERE'S THE PLAN, AND IT'S A GOOD ONE. I THINK IT CAN DO THE JOB, EXCEPT THAT NO ONE HERE IS REMOTELY QUALIFIED TO CARRY IT OUT.

THAT'S WHERE *YOU* COME IN.

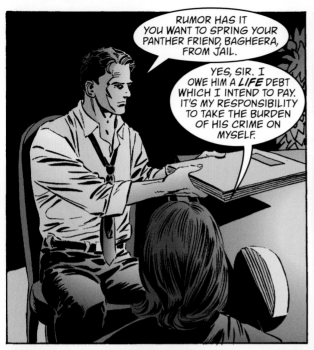

RUMOR HAS IT YOU WANT TO SPRING YOUR PANTHER FRIEND, BAGHEERA, FROM JAIL.

YES, SIR. I OWE HIM A *LIFE* DEBT WHICH I INTEND TO PAY. IT'S MY RESPONSIBILITY TO TAKE THE BURDEN OF HIS CRIME ON MYSELF.

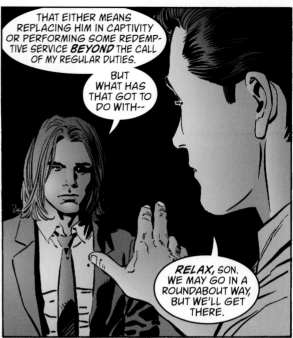

THAT EITHER MEANS REPLACING HIM IN CAPTIVITY OR PERFORMING SOME REDEMPTIVE SERVICE *BEYOND* THE CALL OF MY REGULAR DUTIES.

BUT WHAT HAS THAT GOT TO DO WITH--

RELAX, SON. WE MAY GO IN A ROUNDABOUT WAY, BUT WE'LL GET THERE.

IS IT TRUE YOU WERE RAISED BY WOLVES OR IS THAT JUST STORYBOOK NON-SENSE?

YES. THE FIRST DOZEN YEARS OF MY LIFE I WAS FULLY ENCULTURATED INTO THE SEEONEE WOLF PACK.

AND NOW YOU'VE HAD MANY YEARS' EXPERIENCE IN THE ESPIONAGE FIELD, AS ONE OF THE *TOURISTS*.

YOU KNOW HOW TO TRACK DOWN SOMEONE WHO DOESN'T *WANT* TO BE FOUND?

YOU WANT ME TO CARRY OUT THIS RETALIATORY MISSION IN THE HOMELANDS?

NOPE. BUT I WANT YOU TO FIND THE *ONE* MAN WHO CAN.

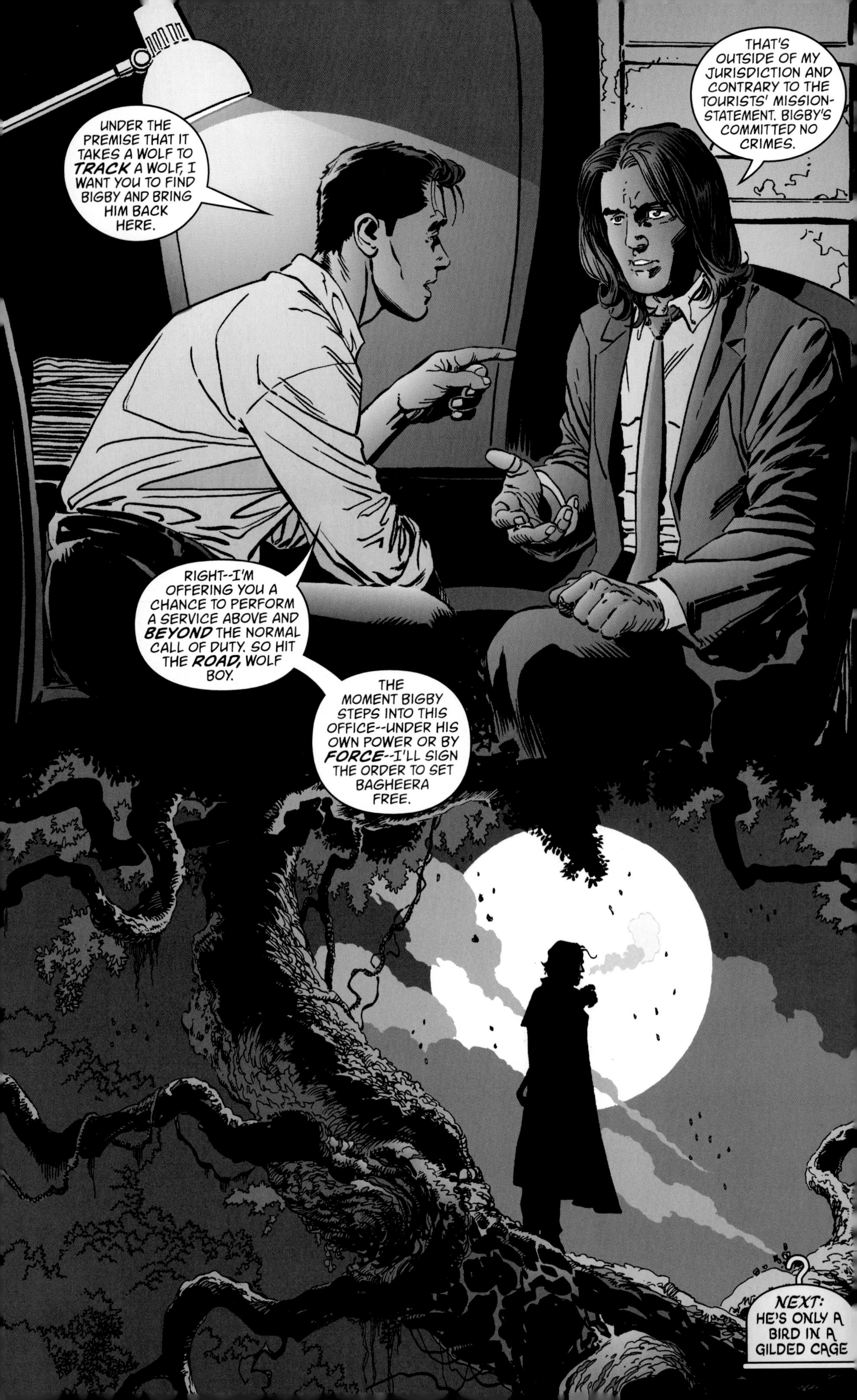
UNDER THE PREMISE THAT IT TAKES A WOLF TO TRACK A WOLF, I WANT YOU TO FIND BIGBY AND BRING HIM BACK HERE.
THAT'S OUTSIDE OF MY JURISDICTION AND CONTRARY TO THE TOURISTS' MISSION-STATEMENT. BIGBY'S COMMITTED NO CRIMES.
RIGHT--I'M OFFERING YOU A CHANCE TO PERFORM A SERVICE ABOVE AND BEYOND THE NORMAL CALL OF DUTY. SO HIT THE ROAD, WOLF BOY.
THE MOMENT BIGBY STEPS INTO THIS OFFICE--UNDER HIS OWN POWER OR BY FORCE--I'LL SIGN THE ORDER TO SET BAGHEERA FREE.
NEXT: HE'S ONLY A BIRD IN A GILDED CAGE

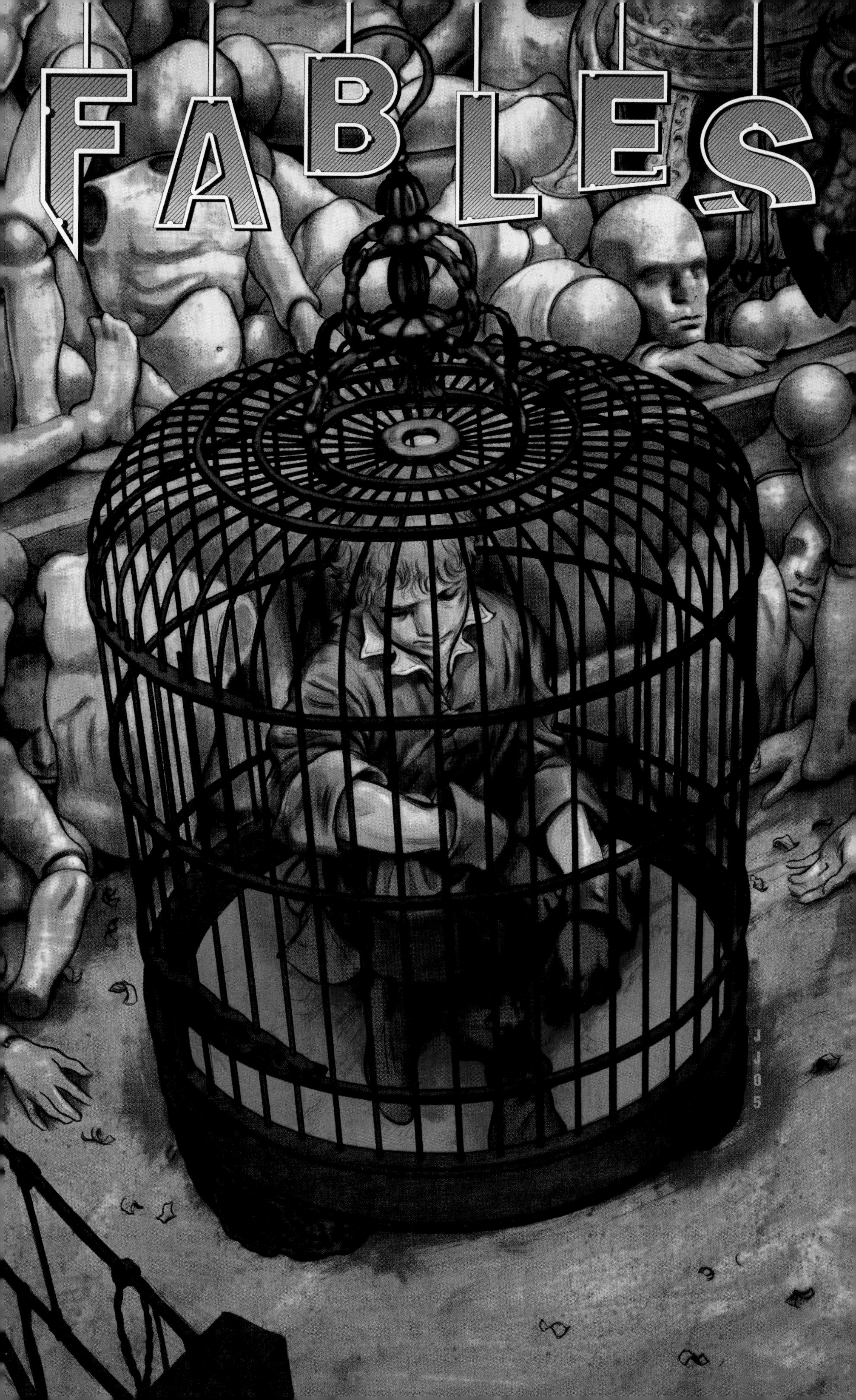
FABLES
JJ05

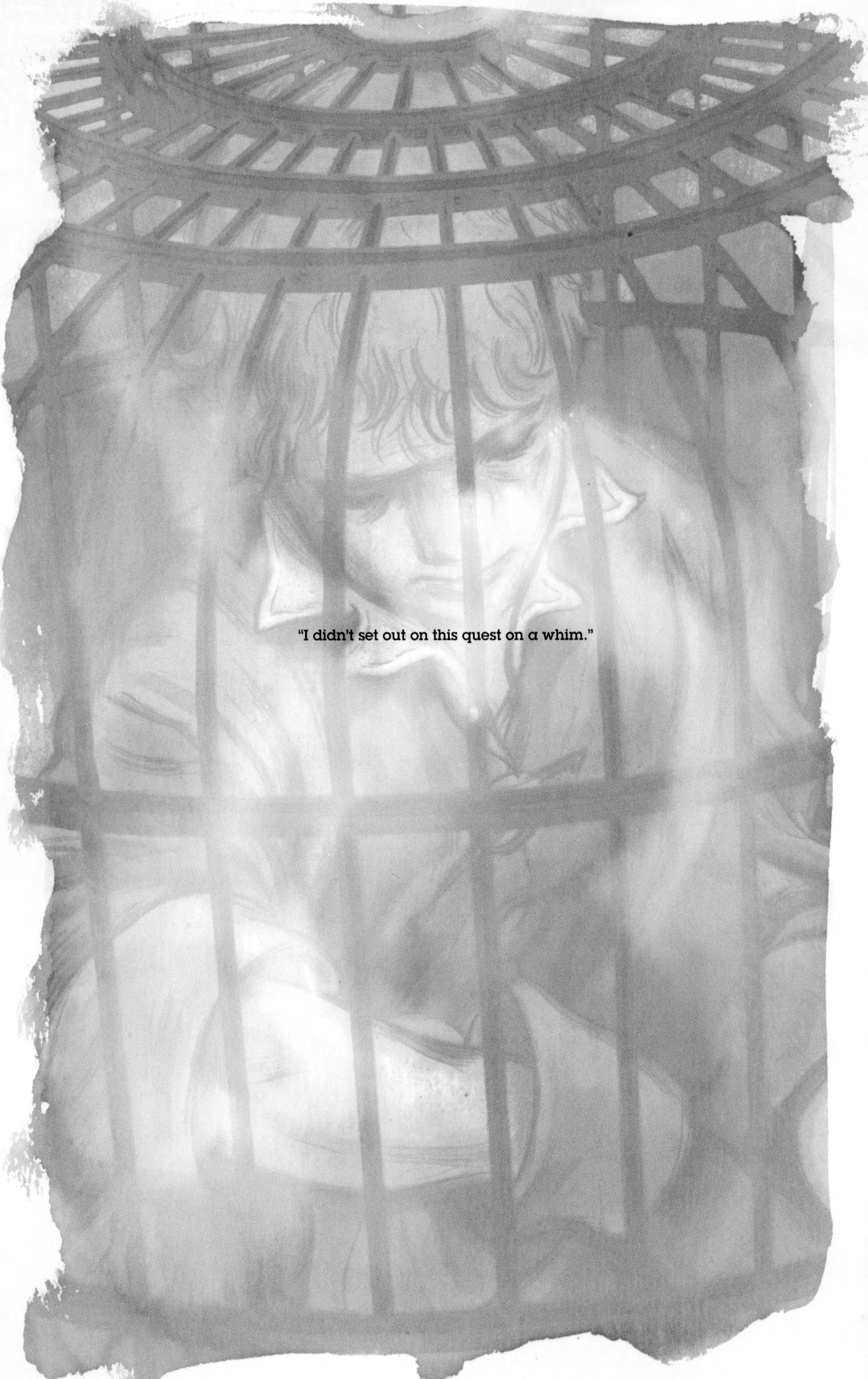

"I didn't set out on this quest on a whim."

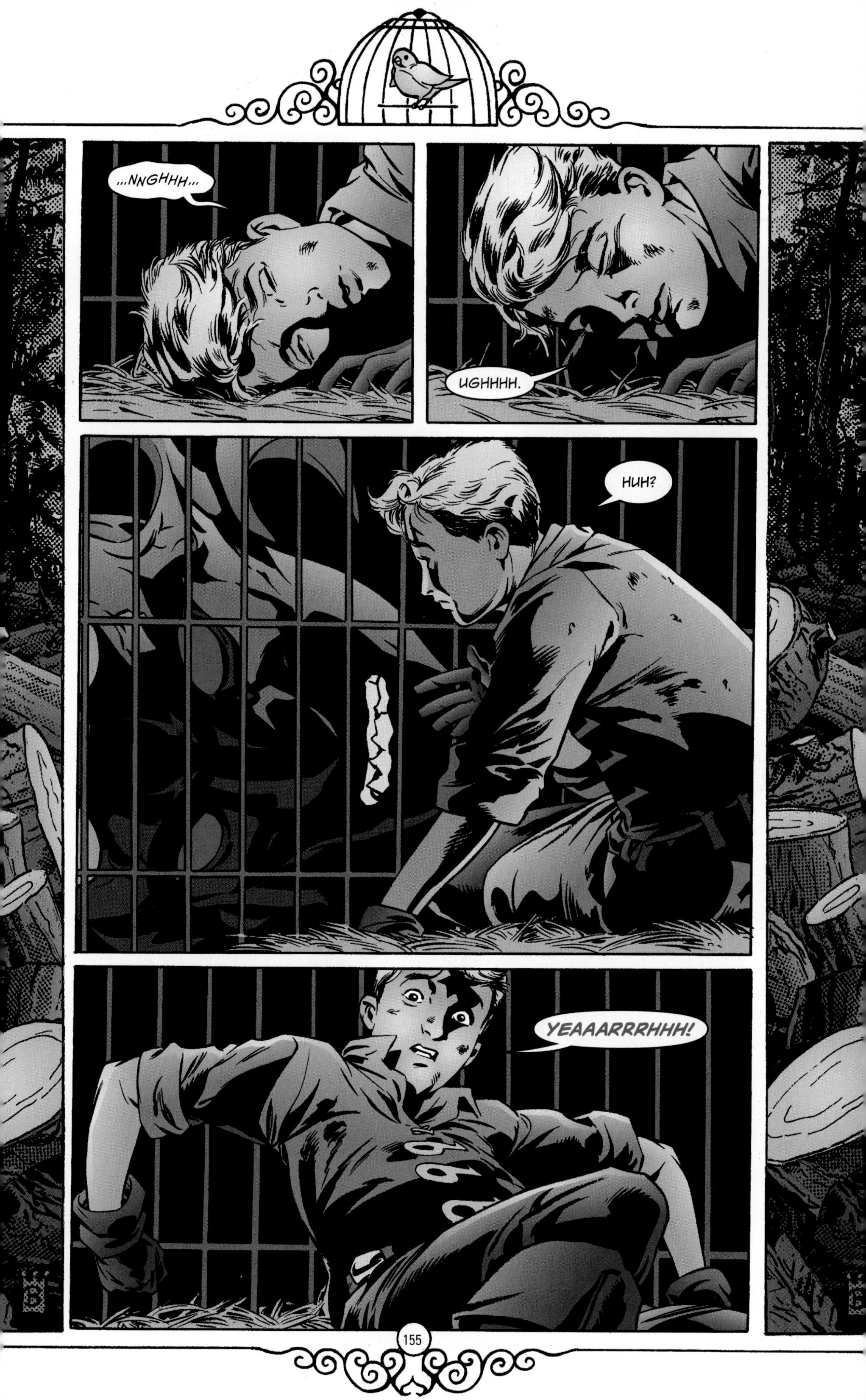
...NNGHHH...
UGHHHH.
HUH?
YEAAARRRHHH!

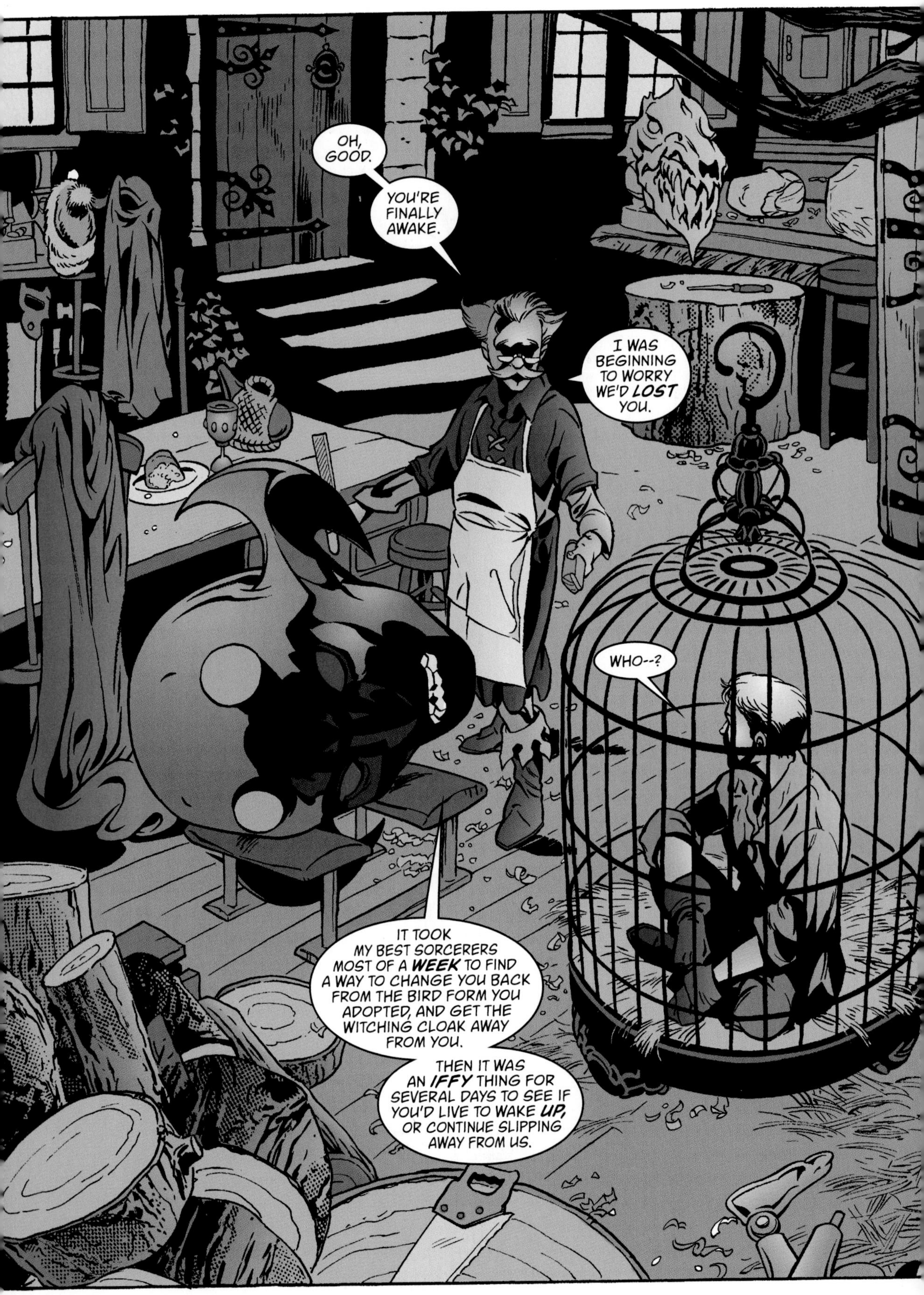
OH, GOOD.
YOU'RE FINALLY AWAKE.
I WAS BEGINNING TO WORRY WE'D LOST YOU.
WHO--?
IT TOOK MY BEST SORCERERS MOST OF A WEEK TO FIND A WAY TO CHANGE YOU BACK FROM THE BIRD FORM YOU ADOPTED, AND GET THE WITCHING CLOAK AWAY FROM YOU.
THEN IT WAS AN IFFY THING FOR SEVERAL DAYS TO SEE IF YOU'D LIVE TO WAKE UP, OR CONTINUE SLIPPING AWAY FROM US.

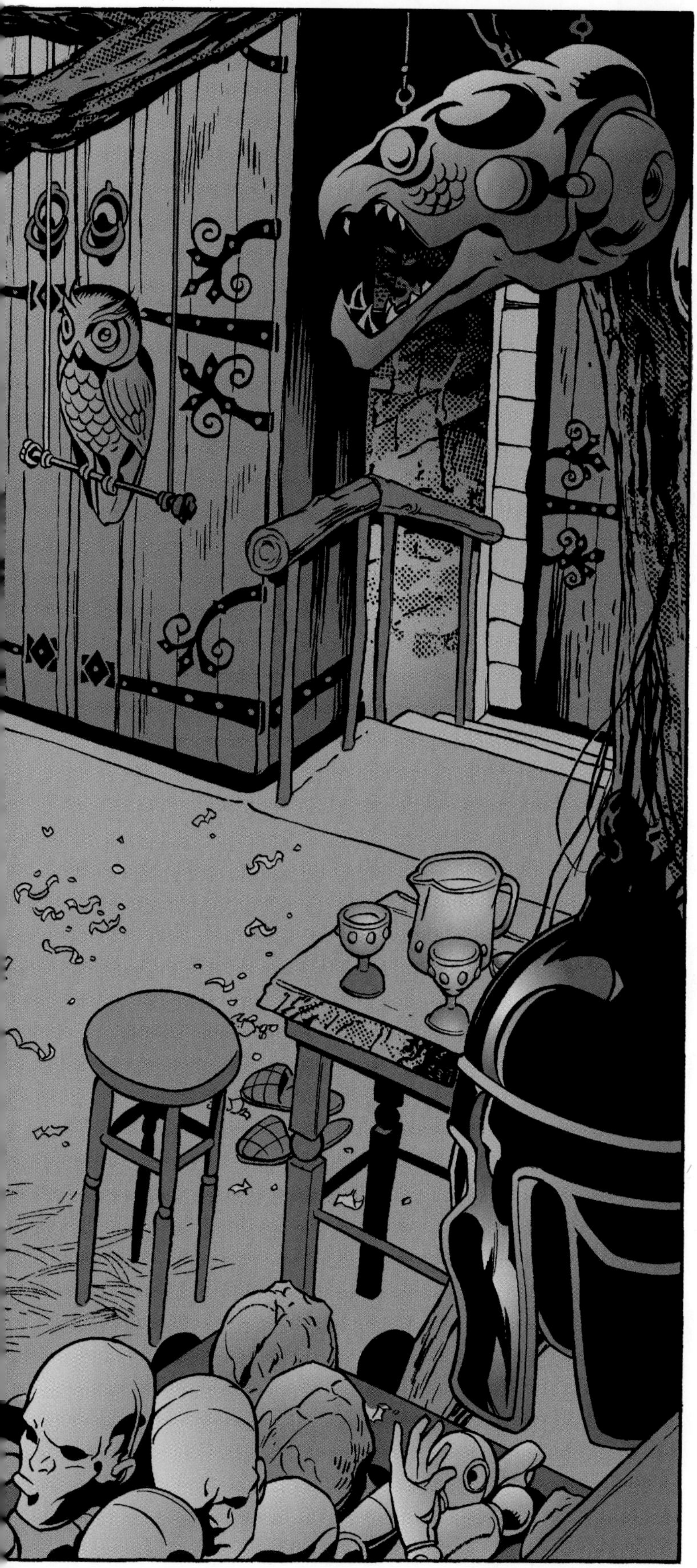

He's Only a Bird in a Gilded Cage

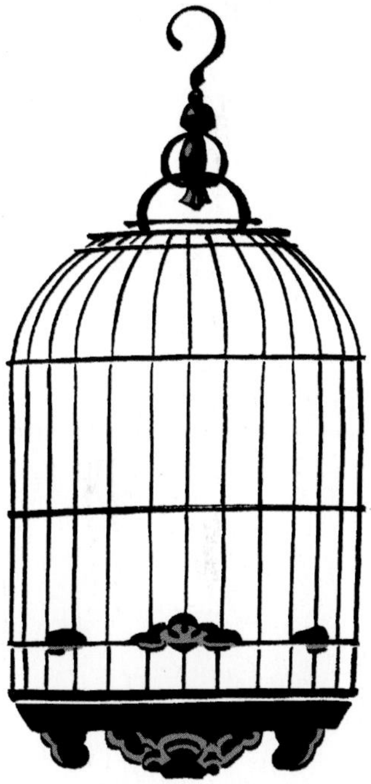

Chapter Four of
HOMELANDS

Bill Willingham: writer-creator
Mark Buckingham: penciller
Steve Leialoha: inker
Daniel Vozzo: colors
James Jean: cover art
Todd Klein: letters
Mariah Huehner: assistant editor
Shelly Bond: editor

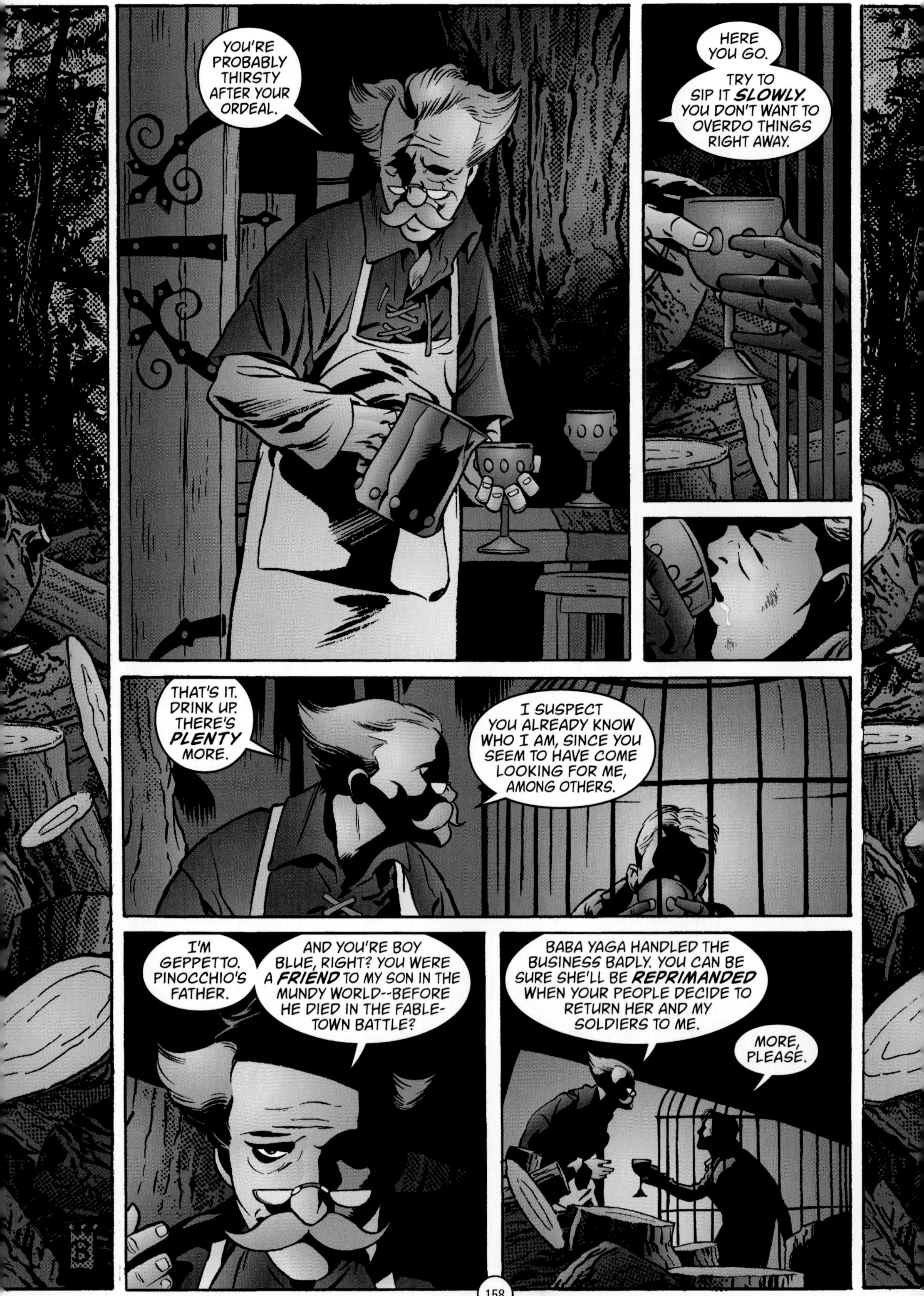

YOU'RE PROBABLY THIRSTY AFTER YOUR ORDEAL.
HERE YOU GO.
TRY TO SIP IT SLOWLY. YOU DON'T WANT TO OVERDO THINGS RIGHT AWAY.
THAT'S IT. DRINK UP. THERE'S PLENTY MORE.
I SUSPECT YOU ALREADY KNOW WHO I AM, SINCE YOU SEEM TO HAVE COME LOOKING FOR ME, AMONG OTHERS.
I'M GEPPETTO. PINOCCHIO'S FATHER.
AND YOU'RE BOY BLUE, RIGHT? YOU WERE A FRIEND TO MY SON IN THE MUNDY WORLD--BEFORE HE DIED IN THE FABLE-TOWN BATTLE?
BABA YAGA HANDLED THE BUSINESS BADLY. YOU CAN BE SURE SHE'LL BE REPRIMANDED WHEN YOUR PEOPLE DECIDE TO RETURN HER AND MY SOLDIERS TO ME.
MORE, PLEASE.

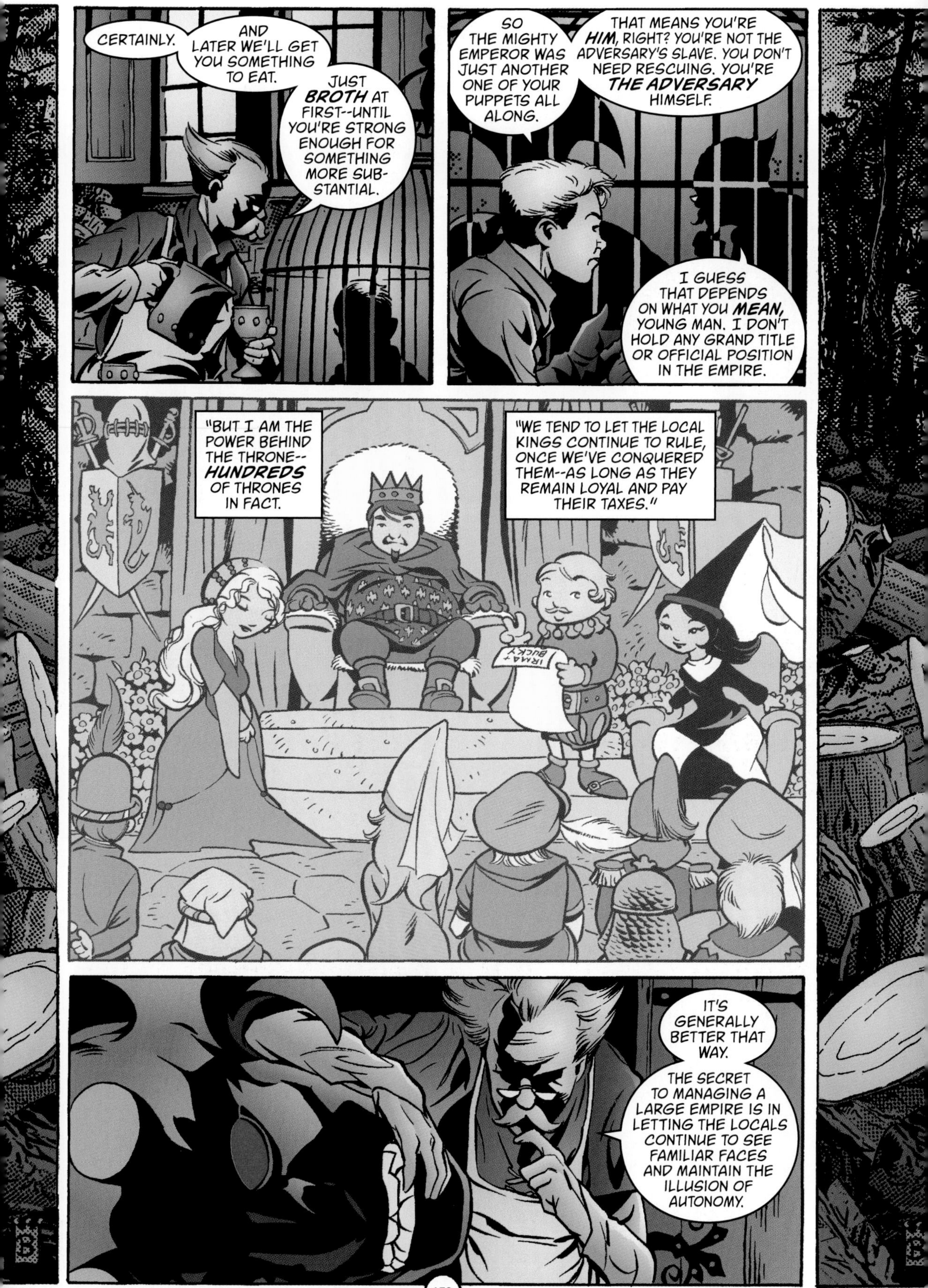

CERTAINLY.
AND LATER WE'LL GET YOU SOMETHING TO EAT.
JUST **BROTH** AT FIRST--UNTIL YOU'RE STRONG ENOUGH FOR SOMETHING MORE SUB-STANTIAL.
SO THE MIGHTY EMPEROR WAS JUST ANOTHER ONE OF YOUR PUPPETS ALL ALONG.
THAT MEANS YOU'RE ***HIM***, RIGHT? YOU'RE NOT THE ADVERSARY'S SLAVE. YOU DON'T NEED RESCUING. YOU'RE ***THE ADVERSARY*** HIMSELF.
I GUESS THAT DEPENDS ON WHAT YOU ***MEAN***, YOUNG MAN. I DON'T HOLD ANY GRAND TITLE OR OFFICIAL POSITION IN THE EMPIRE.
"BUT I AM THE POWER BEHIND THE THRONE-- ***HUNDREDS*** OF THRONES IN FACT.
"WE TEND TO LET THE LOCAL KINGS CONTINUE TO RULE, ONCE WE'VE CONQUERED THEM--AS LONG AS THEY REMAIN LOYAL AND PAY THEIR TAXES."
IT'S GENERALLY BETTER THAT WAY.
THE SECRET TO MANAGING A LARGE EMPIRE IS IN LETTING THE LOCALS CONTINUE TO SEE FAMILIAR FACES AND MAINTAIN THE ILLUSION OF AUTONOMY.

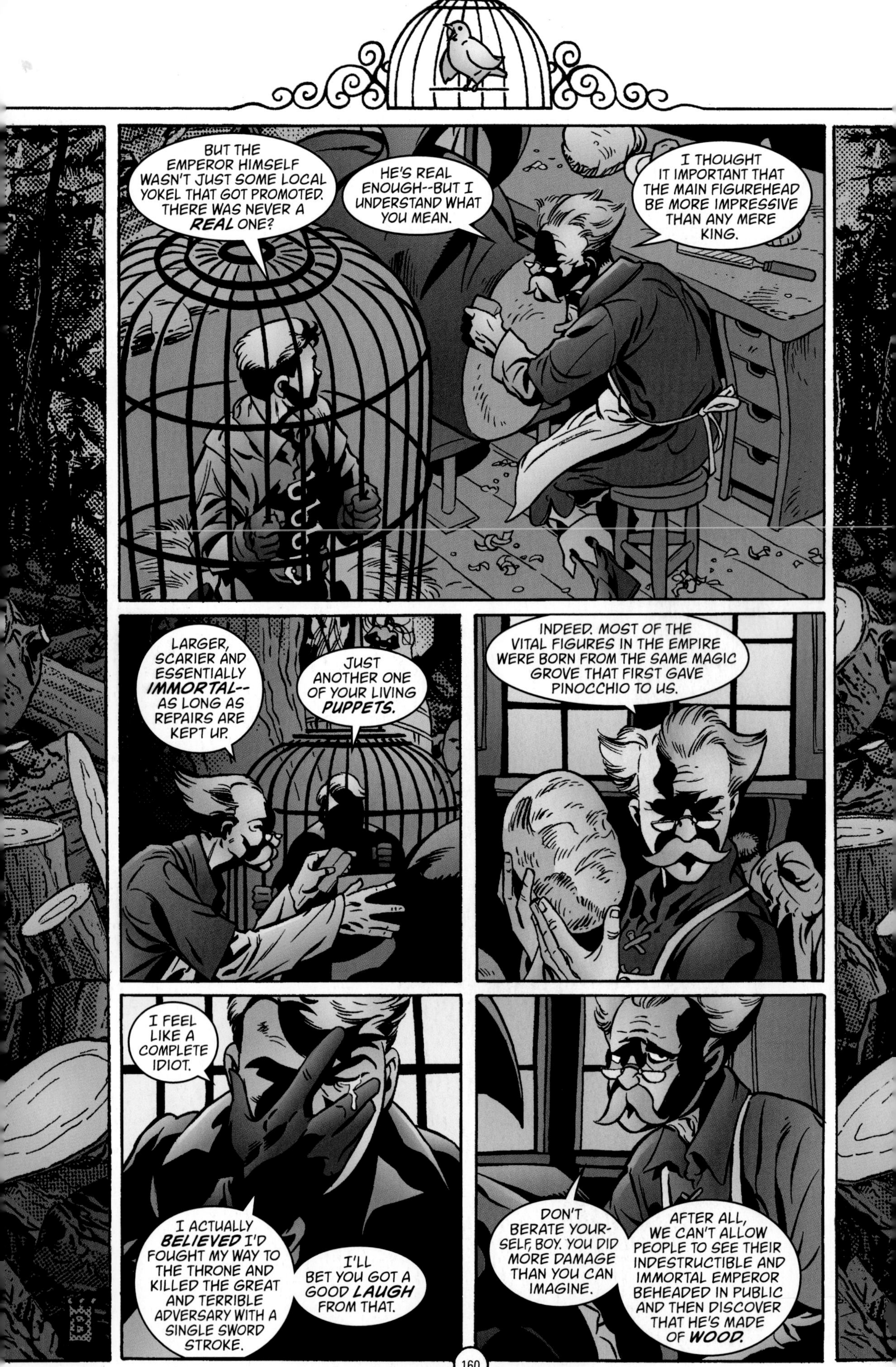
BUT THE EMPEROR HIMSELF WASN'T JUST SOME LOCAL YOKEL THAT GOT PROMOTED. THERE WAS NEVER A REAL ONE?
HE'S REAL ENOUGH--BUT I UNDERSTAND WHAT YOU MEAN.
I THOUGHT IT IMPORTANT THAT THE MAIN FIGUREHEAD BE MORE IMPRESSIVE THAN ANY MERE KING.
LARGER, SCARIER AND ESSENTIALLY IMMORTAL-- AS LONG AS REPAIRS ARE KEPT UP.
JUST ANOTHER ONE OF YOUR LIVING PUPPETS.
INDEED. MOST OF THE VITAL FIGURES IN THE EMPIRE WERE BORN FROM THE SAME MAGIC GROVE THAT FIRST GAVE PINOCCHIO TO US.
I FEEL LIKE A COMPLETE IDIOT.
I ACTUALLY BELIEVED I'D FOUGHT MY WAY TO THE THRONE AND KILLED THE GREAT AND TERRIBLE ADVERSARY WITH A SINGLE SWORD STROKE.
I'LL BET YOU GOT A GOOD LAUGH FROM THAT.
DON'T BERATE YOURSELF, BOY. YOU DID MORE DAMAGE THAN YOU CAN IMAGINE.
AFTER ALL, WE CAN'T ALLOW PEOPLE TO SEE THEIR INDESTRUCTIBLE AND IMMORTAL EMPEROR BEHEADED IN PUBLIC AND THEN DISCOVER THAT HE'S MADE OF WOOD.

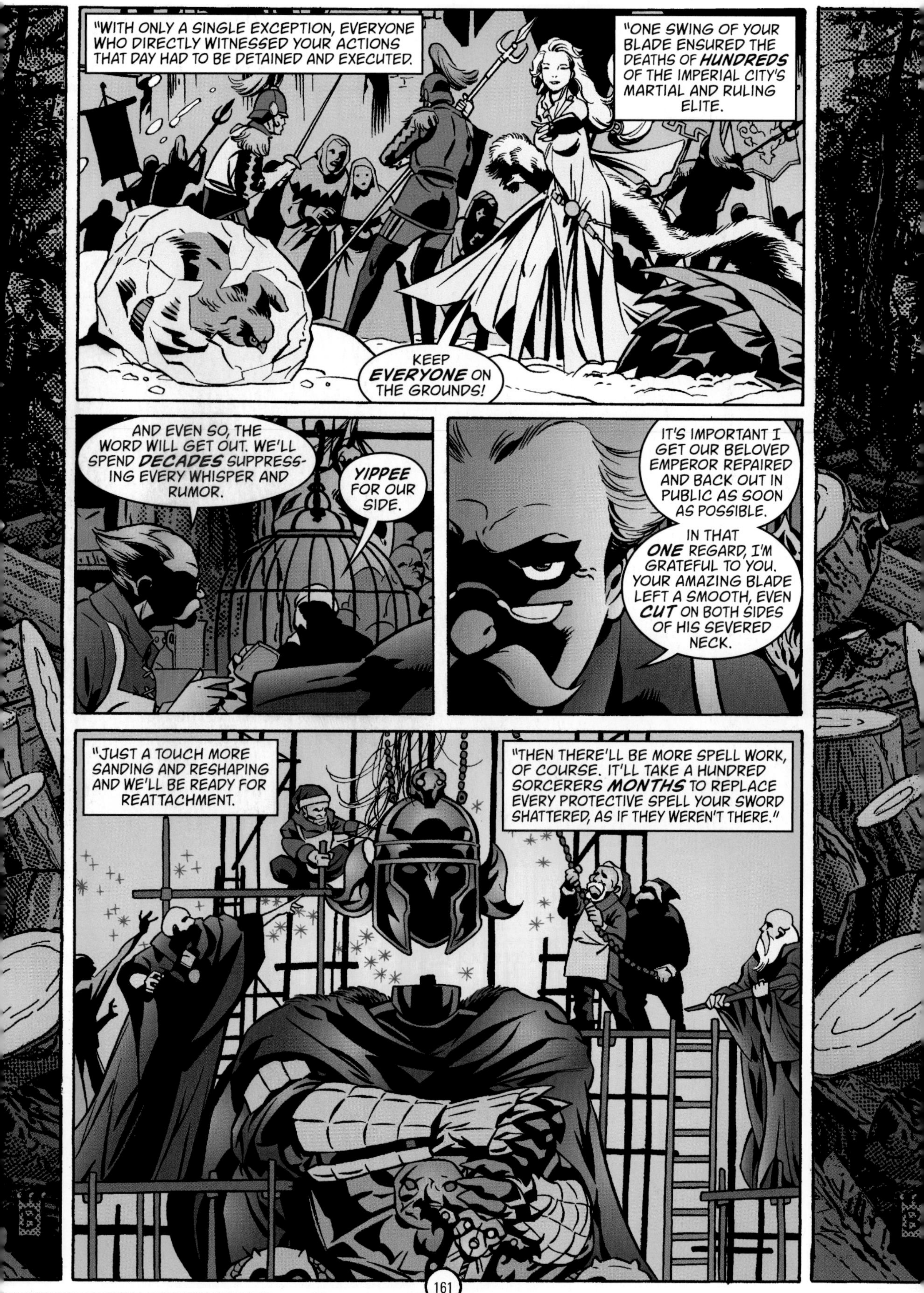
"WITH ONLY A SINGLE EXCEPTION, EVERYONE WHO DIRECTLY WITNESSED YOUR ACTIONS THAT DAY HAD TO BE DETAINED AND EXECUTED.
"ONE SWING OF YOUR BLADE ENSURED THE DEATHS OF HUNDREDS OF THE IMPERIAL CITY'S MARTIAL AND RULING ELITE.
KEEP EVERYONE ON THE GROUNDS!
AND EVEN SO, THE WORD WILL GET OUT. WE'LL SPEND DECADES SUPPRESSING EVERY WHISPER AND RUMOR.
YIPPEE FOR OUR SIDE.
IT'S IMPORTANT I GET OUR BELOVED EMPEROR REPAIRED AND BACK OUT IN PUBLIC AS SOON AS POSSIBLE.
IN THAT ONE REGARD, I'M GRATEFUL TO YOU. YOUR AMAZING BLADE LEFT A SMOOTH, EVEN CUT ON BOTH SIDES OF HIS SEVERED NECK.
"JUST A TOUCH MORE SANDING AND RESHAPING AND WE'LL BE READY FOR REATTACHMENT.
"THEN THERE'LL BE MORE SPELL WORK, OF COURSE. IT'LL TAKE A HUNDRED SORCERERS MONTHS TO REPLACE EVERY PROTECTIVE SPELL YOUR SWORD SHATTERED, AS IF THEY WEREN'T THERE."

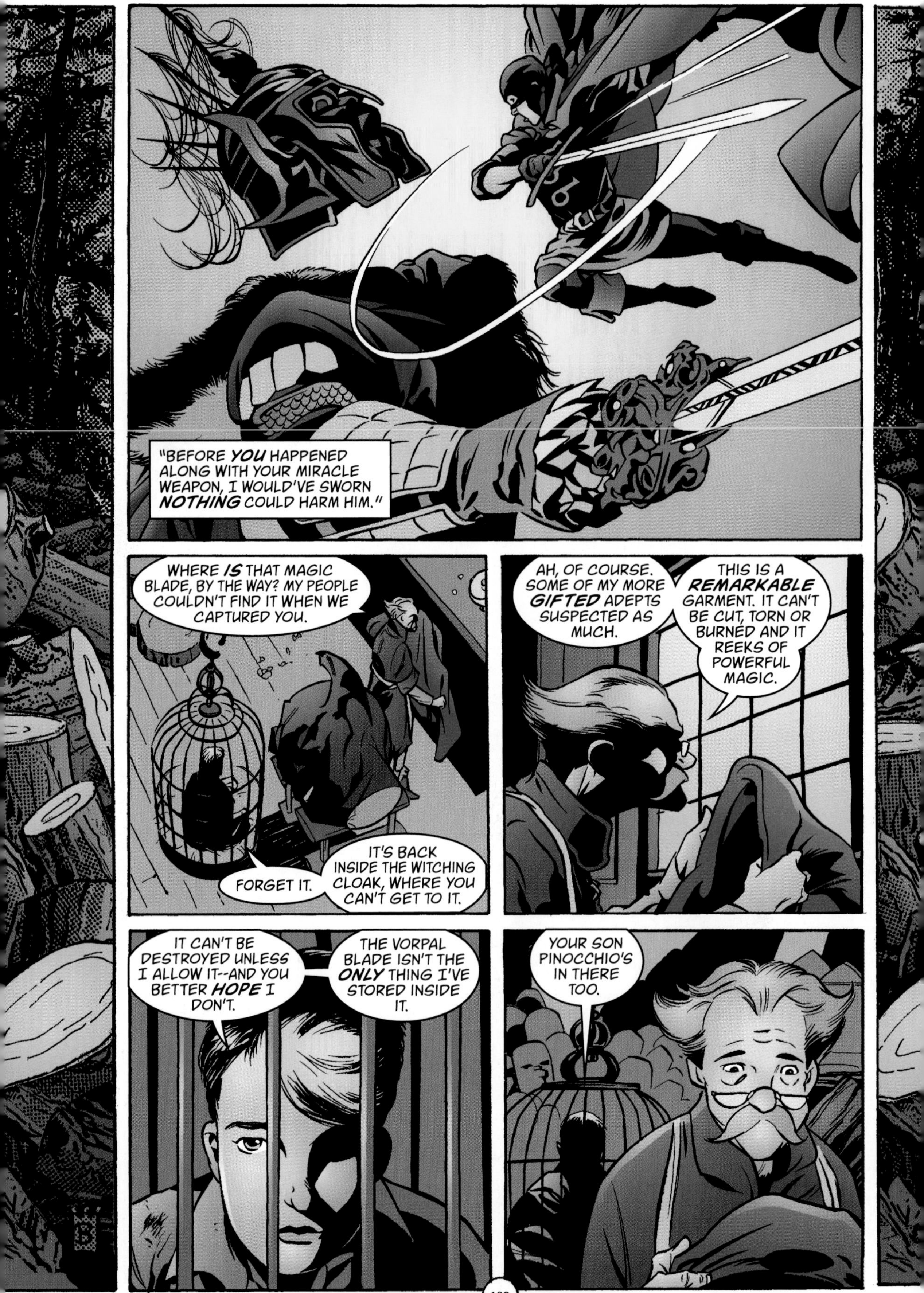
"BEFORE YOU HAPPENED ALONG WITH YOUR MIRACLE WEAPON, I WOULD'VE SWORN NOTHING COULD HARM HIM."
WHERE IS THAT MAGIC BLADE, BY THE WAY? MY PEOPLE COULDN'T FIND IT WHEN WE CAPTURED YOU.
FORGET IT.
IT'S BACK INSIDE THE WITCHING CLOAK, WHERE YOU CAN'T GET TO IT.
AH, OF COURSE. SOME OF MY MORE GIFTED ADEPTS SUSPECTED AS MUCH.
THIS IS A REMARKABLE GARMENT. IT CAN'T BE CUT, TORN OR BURNED AND IT REEKS OF POWERFUL MAGIC.
IT CAN'T BE DESTROYED UNLESS I ALLOW IT--AND YOU BETTER HOPE I DON'T.
THE VORPAL BLADE ISN'T THE ONLY THING I'VE STORED INSIDE IT.
YOUR SON PINOCCHIO'S IN THERE TOO.

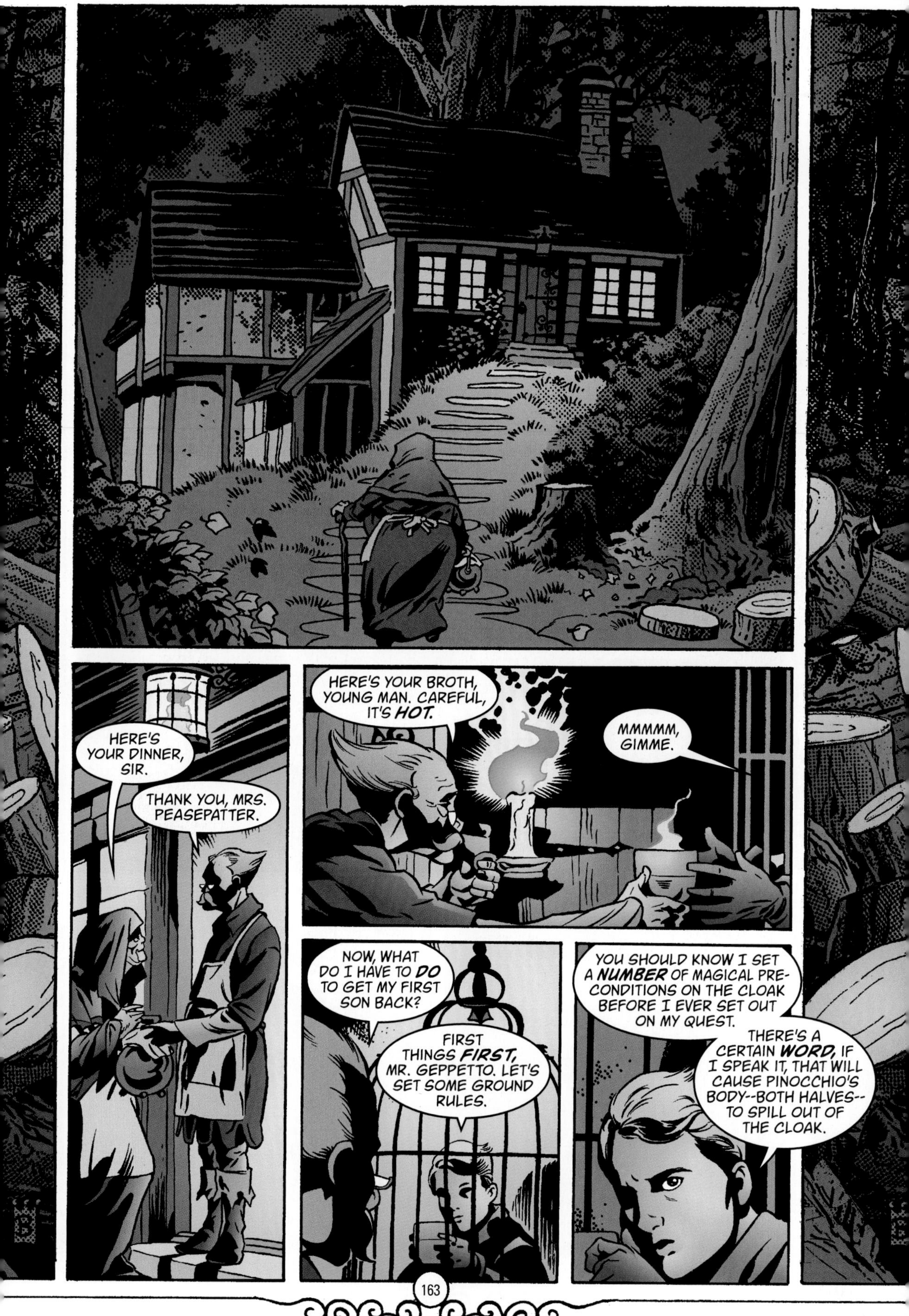
HERE'S YOUR DINNER, SIR.
THANK YOU, MRS. PEASEPATTER.
HERE'S YOUR BROTH, YOUNG MAN. CAREFUL, IT'S HOT.
MMMMM, GIMME.
NOW, WHAT DO I HAVE TO DO TO GET MY FIRST SON BACK?
FIRST THINGS FIRST, MR. GEPPETTO. LET'S SET SOME GROUND RULES.
YOU SHOULD KNOW I SET A NUMBER OF MAGICAL PRE-CONDITIONS ON THE CLOAK BEFORE I EVER SET OUT ON MY QUEST.
THERE'S A CERTAIN WORD, IF I SPEAK IT, THAT WILL CAUSE PINOCCHIO'S BODY--BOTH HALVES--TO SPILL OUT OF THE CLOAK.

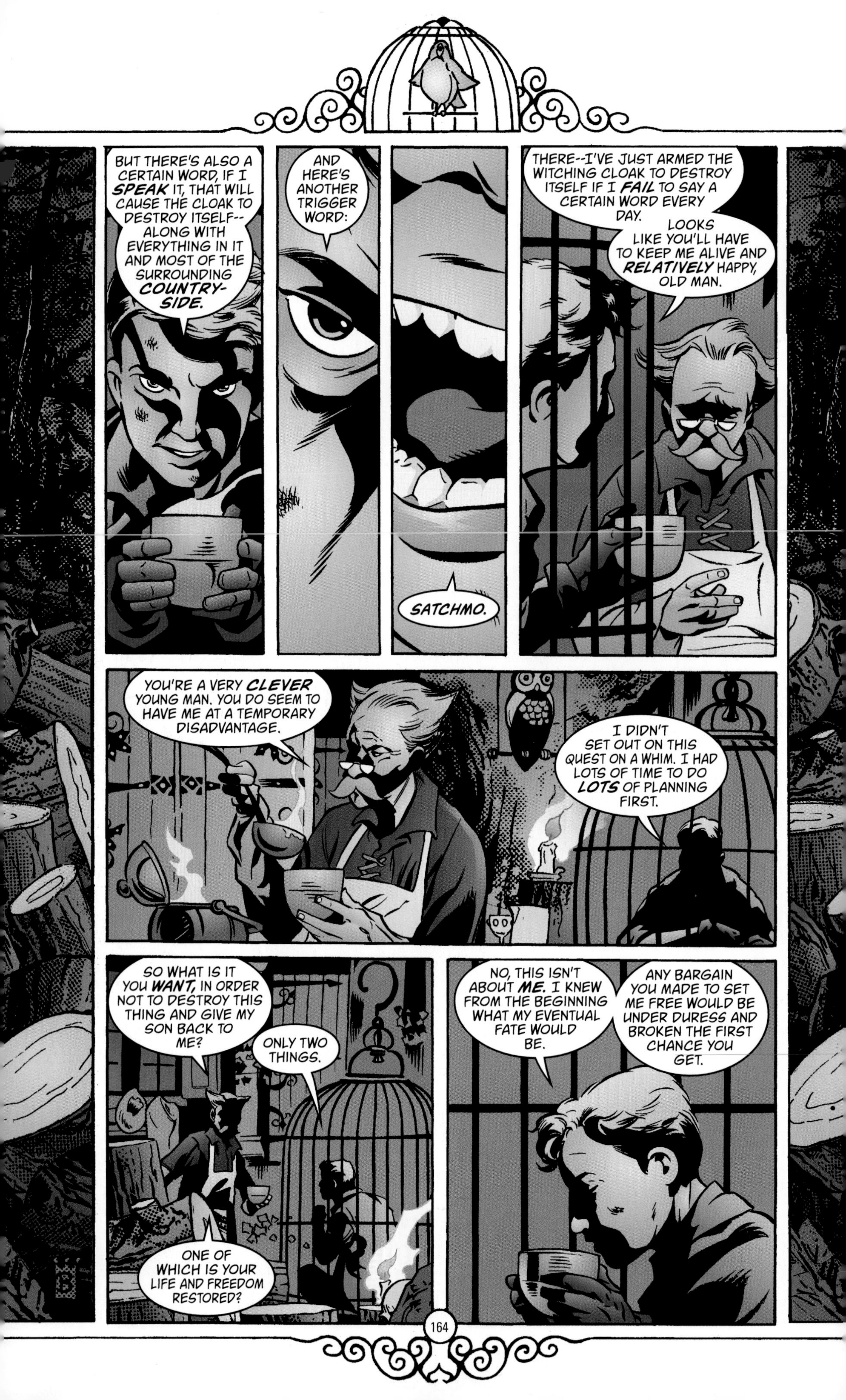

BUT THERE'S ALSO A CERTAIN WORD, IF I SPEAK IT, THAT WILL CAUSE THE CLOAK TO DESTROY ITSELF-- ALONG WITH EVERYTHING IN IT AND MOST OF THE SURROUNDING COUNTRY-SIDE.
AND HERE'S ANOTHER TRIGGER WORD:
SATCHMO.
THERE--I'VE JUST ARMED THE WITCHING CLOAK TO DESTROY ITSELF IF I FAIL TO SAY A CERTAIN WORD EVERY DAY.
LOOKS LIKE YOU'LL HAVE TO KEEP ME ALIVE AND RELATIVELY HAPPY, OLD MAN.
YOU'RE A VERY CLEVER YOUNG MAN. YOU DO SEEM TO HAVE ME AT A TEMPORARY DISADVANTAGE.
I DIDN'T SET OUT ON THIS QUEST ON A WHIM. I HAD LOTS OF TIME TO DO LOTS OF PLANNING FIRST.
SO WHAT IS IT YOU WANT, IN ORDER NOT TO DESTROY THIS THING AND GIVE MY SON BACK TO ME?
ONLY TWO THINGS.
ONE OF WHICH IS YOUR LIFE AND FREEDOM RESTORED?
NO, THIS ISN'T ABOUT ME. I KNEW FROM THE BEGINNING WHAT MY EVENTUAL FATE WOULD BE.
ANY BARGAIN YOU MADE TO SET ME FREE WOULD BE UNDER DURESS AND BROKEN THE FIRST CHANCE YOU GET.

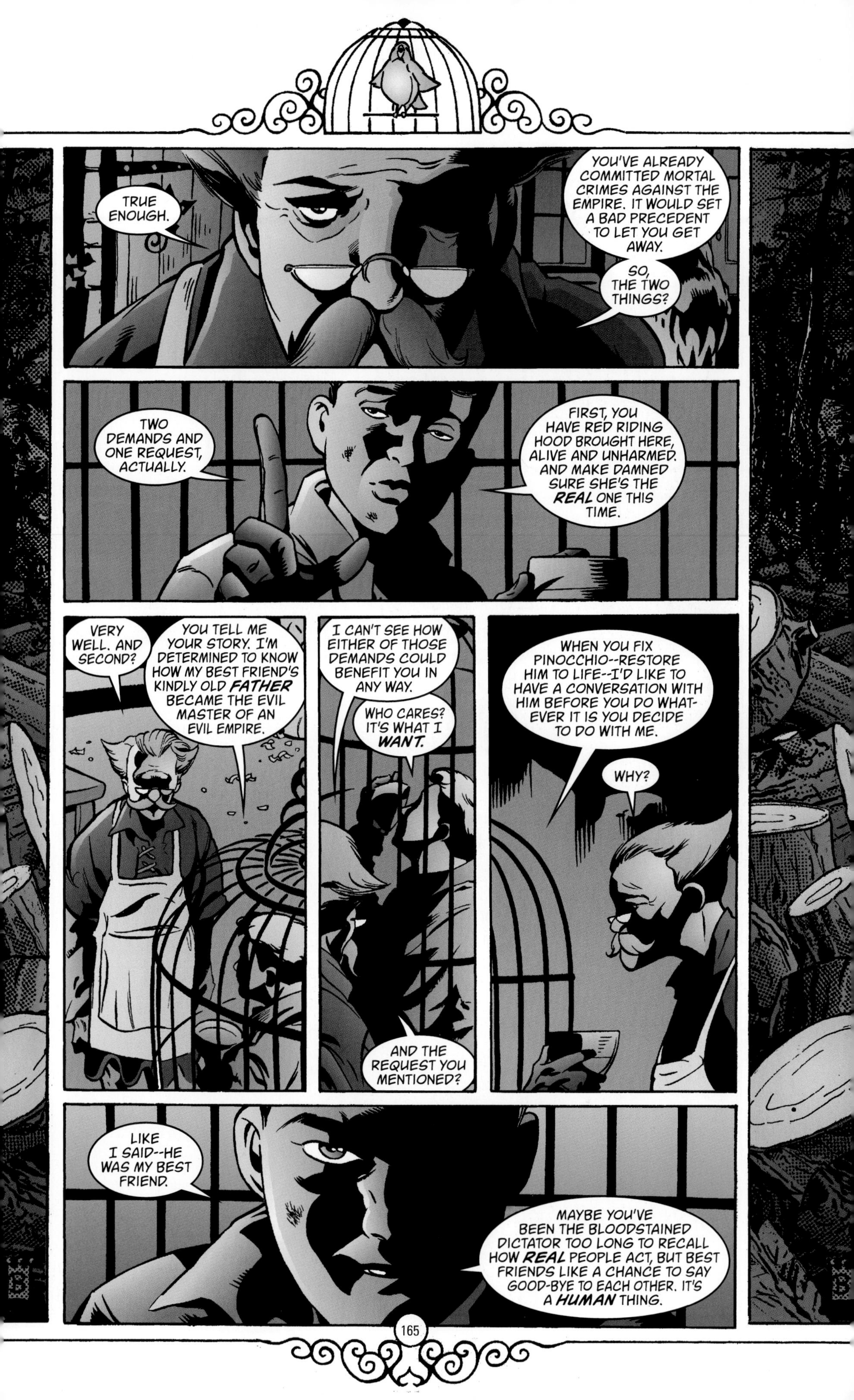
TRUE ENOUGH.
YOU'VE ALREADY COMMITTED MORTAL CRIMES AGAINST THE EMPIRE. IT WOULD SET A BAD PRECEDENT TO LET YOU GET AWAY.
SO, THE TWO THINGS?
TWO DEMANDS AND ONE REQUEST, ACTUALLY.
FIRST, YOU HAVE RED RIDING HOOD BROUGHT HERE, ALIVE AND UNHARMED. AND MAKE DAMNED SURE SHE'S THE REAL ONE THIS TIME.
VERY WELL. AND SECOND?
YOU TELL ME YOUR STORY. I'M DETERMINED TO KNOW HOW MY BEST FRIEND'S KINDLY OLD FATHER BECAME THE EVIL MASTER OF AN EVIL EMPIRE.
I CAN'T SEE HOW EITHER OF THOSE DEMANDS COULD BENEFIT YOU IN ANY WAY.
WHO CARES? IT'S WHAT I WANT.
AND THE REQUEST YOU MENTIONED?
WHEN YOU FIX PINOCCHIO--RESTORE HIM TO LIFE--I'D LIKE TO HAVE A CONVERSATION WITH HIM BEFORE YOU DO WHAT-EVER IT IS YOU DECIDE TO DO WITH ME.
WHY?
LIKE I SAID--HE WAS MY BEST FRIEND.
MAYBE YOU'VE BEEN THE BLOODSTAINED DICTATOR TOO LONG TO RECALL HOW REAL PEOPLE ACT, BUT BEST FRIENDS LIKE A CHANCE TO SAY GOOD-BYE TO EACH OTHER. IT'S A HUMAN THING.

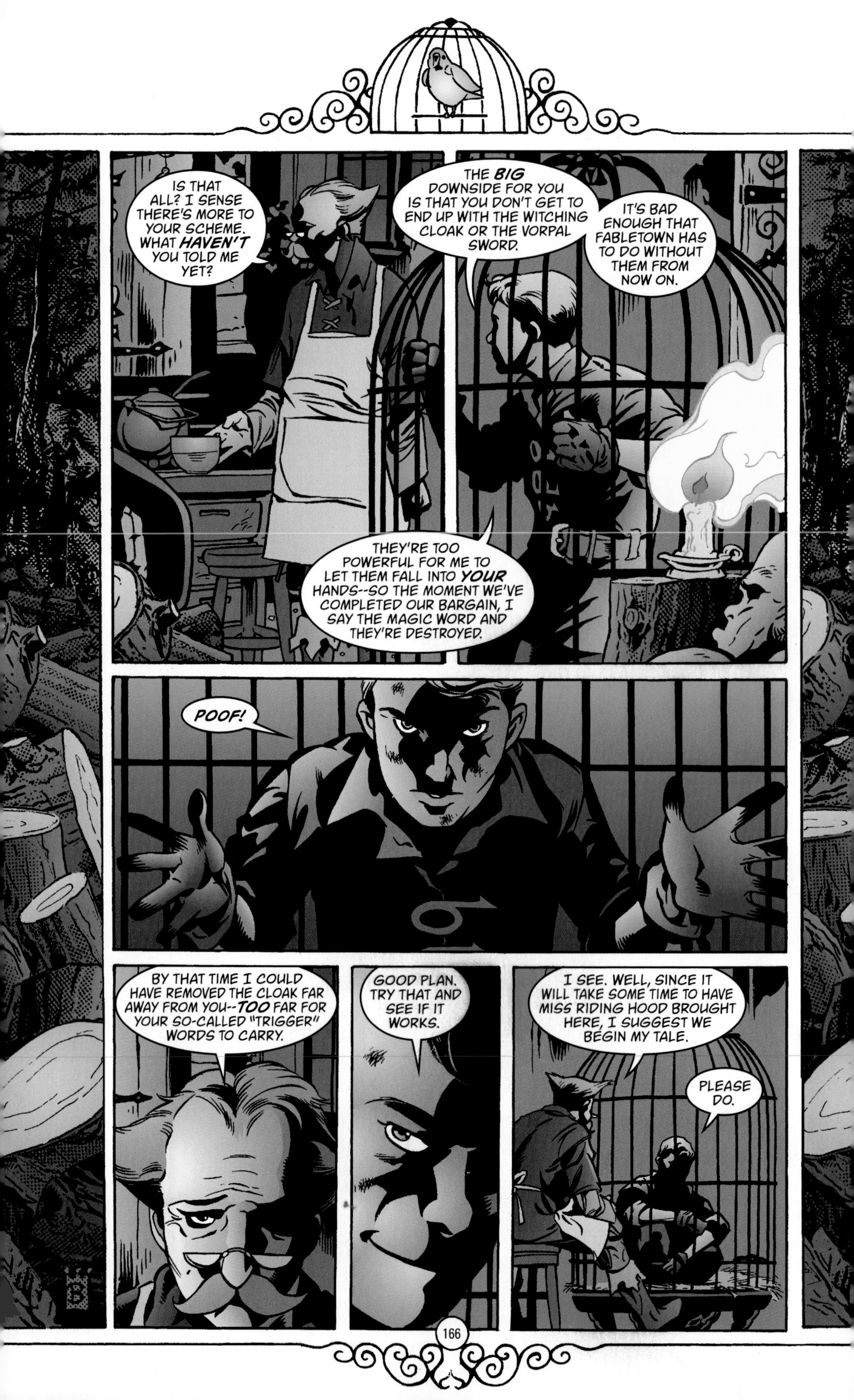

IS THAT ALL? I SENSE THERE'S MORE TO YOUR SCHEME. WHAT HAVEN'T YOU TOLD ME YET?
THE BIG DOWNSIDE FOR YOU IS THAT YOU DON'T GET TO END UP WITH THE WITCHING CLOAK OR THE VORPAL SWORD.
IT'S BAD ENOUGH THAT FABLETOWN HAS TO DO WITHOUT THEM FROM NOW ON.
THEY'RE TOO POWERFUL FOR ME TO LET THEM FALL INTO YOUR HANDS--SO THE MOMENT WE'VE COMPLETED OUR BARGAIN, I SAY THE MAGIC WORD AND THEY'RE DESTROYED.
POOF!
BY THAT TIME I COULD HAVE REMOVED THE CLOAK FAR AWAY FROM YOU--TOO FAR FOR YOUR SO-CALLED "TRIGGER" WORDS TO CARRY.
GOOD PLAN. TRY THAT AND SEE IF IT WORKS.
I SEE. WELL, SINCE IT WILL TAKE SOME TIME TO HAVE MISS RIDING HOOD BROUGHT HERE, I SUGGEST WE BEGIN MY TALE.
PLEASE DO.

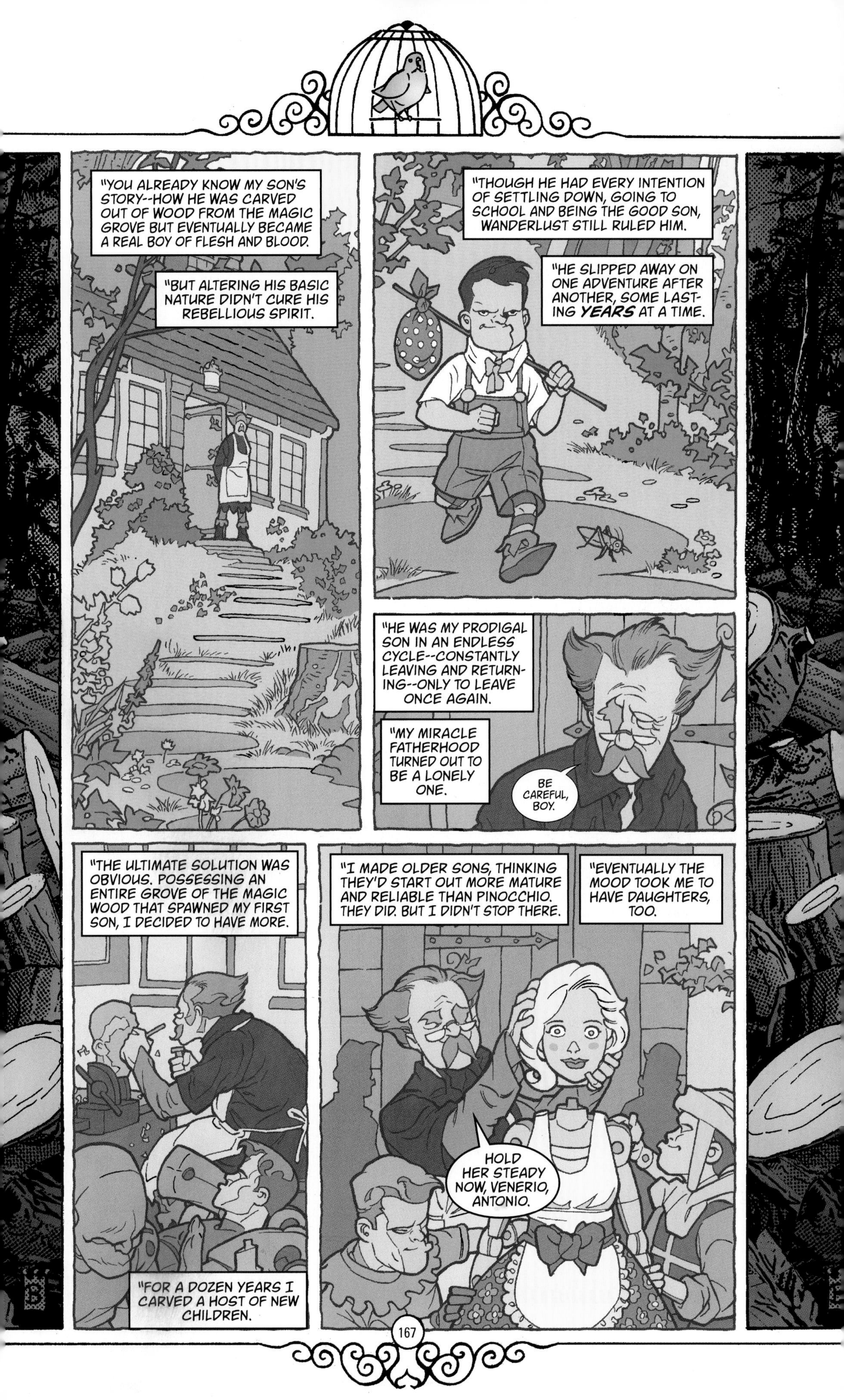
"YOU ALREADY KNOW MY SON'S STORY--HOW HE WAS CARVED OUT OF WOOD FROM THE MAGIC GROVE BUT EVENTUALLY BECAME A REAL BOY OF FLESH AND BLOOD.
"BUT ALTERING HIS BASIC NATURE DIDN'T CURE HIS REBELLIOUS SPIRIT.
"THOUGH HE HAD EVERY INTENTION OF SETTLING DOWN, GOING TO SCHOOL AND BEING THE GOOD SON, WANDERLUST STILL RULED HIM.
"HE SLIPPED AWAY ON ONE ADVENTURE AFTER ANOTHER, SOME LASTING **YEARS** AT A TIME.
"HE WAS MY PRODIGAL SON IN AN ENDLESS CYCLE--CONSTANTLY LEAVING AND RETURNING--ONLY TO LEAVE ONCE AGAIN.
"MY MIRACLE FATHERHOOD TURNED OUT TO BE A LONELY ONE.
BE CAREFUL, BOY.
"THE ULTIMATE SOLUTION WAS OBVIOUS. POSSESSING AN ENTIRE GROVE OF THE MAGIC WOOD THAT SPAWNED MY FIRST SON, I DECIDED TO HAVE MORE.
"FOR A DOZEN YEARS I CARVED A HOST OF NEW CHILDREN.
"I MADE OLDER SONS, THINKING THEY'D START OUT MORE MATURE AND RELIABLE THAN PINOCCHIO. THEY DID. BUT I DIDN'T STOP THERE.
"EVENTUALLY THE MOOD TOOK ME TO HAVE DAUGHTERS, TOO.
HOLD HER STEADY NOW, VENERIO, ANTONIO.

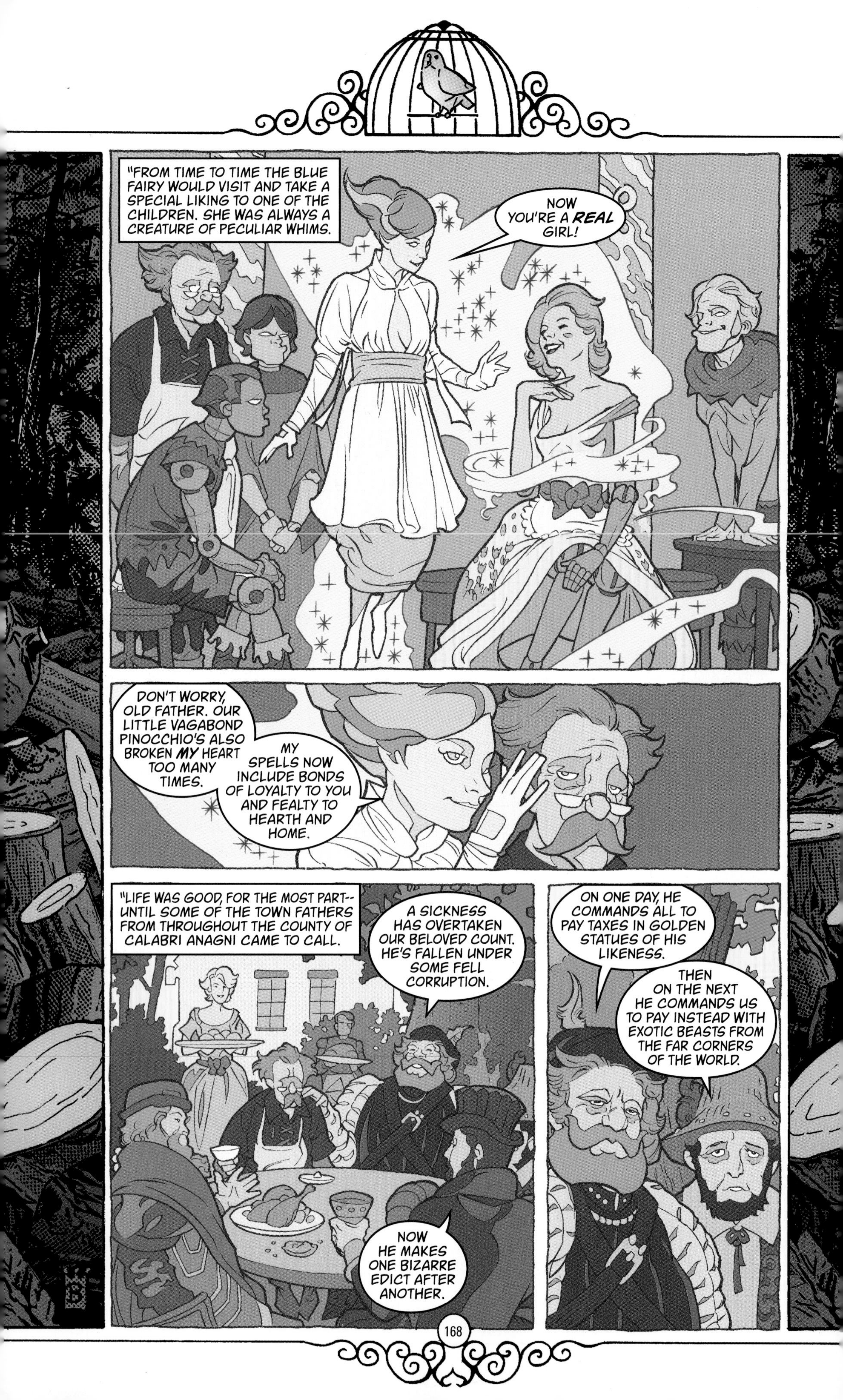
"FROM TIME TO TIME THE BLUE FAIRY WOULD VISIT AND TAKE A SPECIAL LIKING TO ONE OF THE CHILDREN. SHE WAS ALWAYS A CREATURE OF PECULIAR WHIMS.
NOW YOU'RE A *REAL* GIRL!
DON'T WORRY, OLD FATHER. OUR LITTLE VAGABOND PINOCCHIO'S ALSO BROKEN *MY* HEART TOO MANY TIMES.
MY SPELLS NOW INCLUDE BONDS OF LOYALTY TO YOU AND FEALTY TO HEARTH AND HOME.
"LIFE WAS GOOD, FOR THE MOST PART-- UNTIL SOME OF THE TOWN FATHERS FROM THROUGHOUT THE COUNTY OF CALABRI ANAGNI CAME TO CALL.
A SICKNESS HAS OVERTAKEN OUR BELOVED COUNT. HE'S FALLEN UNDER SOME FELL CORRUPTION.
NOW HE MAKES ONE BIZARRE EDICT AFTER ANOTHER.
ON ONE DAY, HE COMMANDS ALL TO PAY TAXES IN GOLDEN STATUES OF HIS LIKENESS.
THEN ON THE NEXT HE COMMANDS US TO PAY INSTEAD WITH EXOTIC BEASTS FROM THE FAR CORNERS OF THE WORLD.

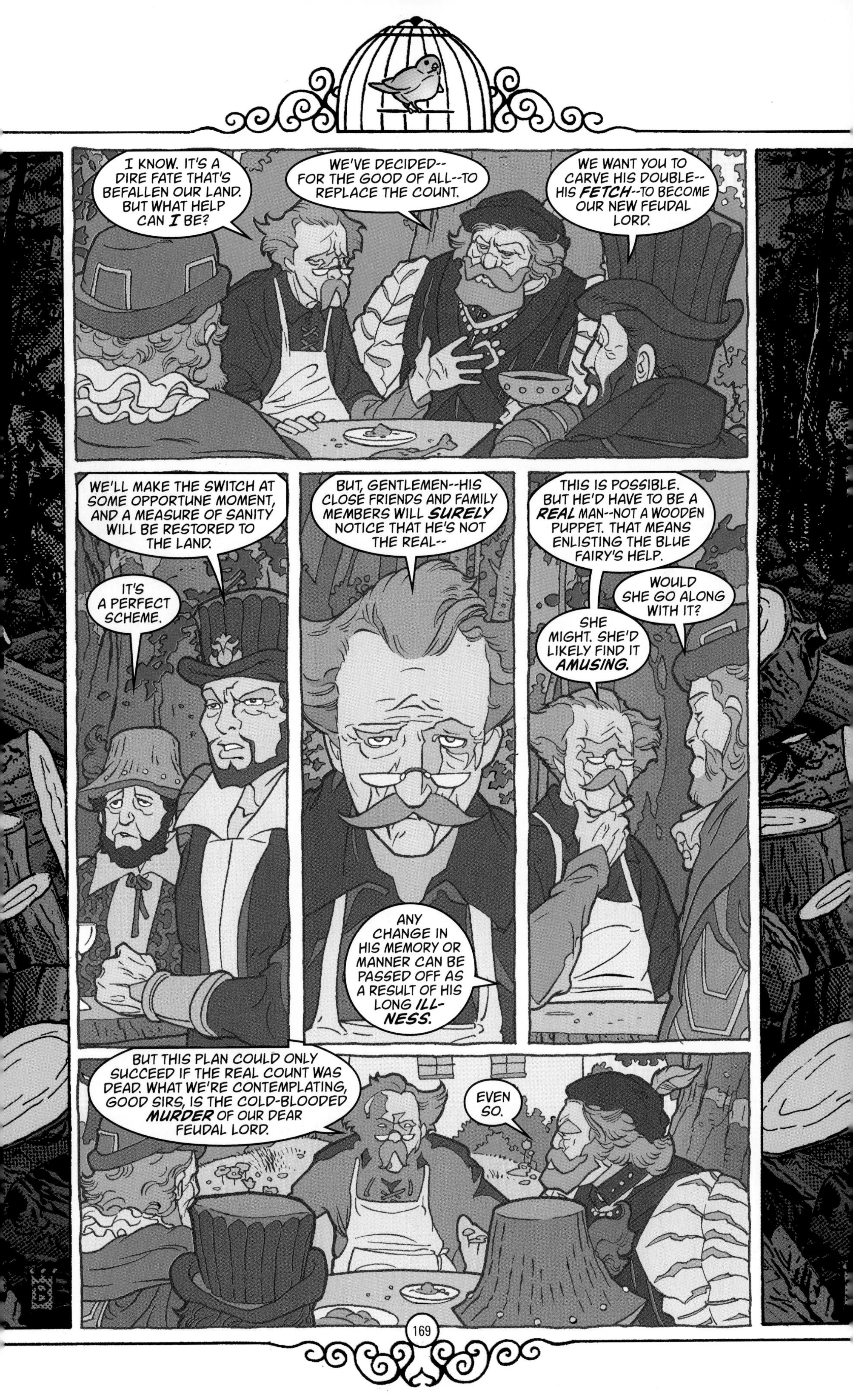
I KNOW. IT'S A DIRE FATE THAT'S BEFALLEN OUR LAND. BUT WHAT HELP CAN I BE?
WE'VE DECIDED-- FOR THE GOOD OF ALL--TO REPLACE THE COUNT.
WE WANT YOU TO CARVE HIS DOUBLE-- HIS FETCH--TO BECOME OUR NEW FEUDAL LORD.
WE'LL MAKE THE SWITCH AT SOME OPPORTUNE MOMENT, AND A MEASURE OF SANITY WILL BE RESTORED TO THE LAND.
IT'S A PERFECT SCHEME.
BUT, GENTLEMEN--HIS CLOSE FRIENDS AND FAMILY MEMBERS WILL SURELY NOTICE THAT HE'S NOT THE REAL--
ANY CHANGE IN HIS MEMORY OR MANNER CAN BE PASSED OFF AS A RESULT OF HIS LONG ILLNESS.
THIS IS POSSIBLE. BUT HE'D HAVE TO BE A REAL MAN--NOT A WOODEN PUPPET. THAT MEANS ENLISTING THE BLUE FAIRY'S HELP.
WOULD SHE GO ALONG WITH IT?
SHE MIGHT. SHE'D LIKELY FIND IT AMUSING.
BUT THIS PLAN COULD ONLY SUCCEED IF THE REAL COUNT WAS DEAD. WHAT WE'RE CONTEMPLATING, GOOD SIRS, IS THE COLD-BLOODED MURDER OF OUR DEAR FEUDAL LORD.
EVEN SO.

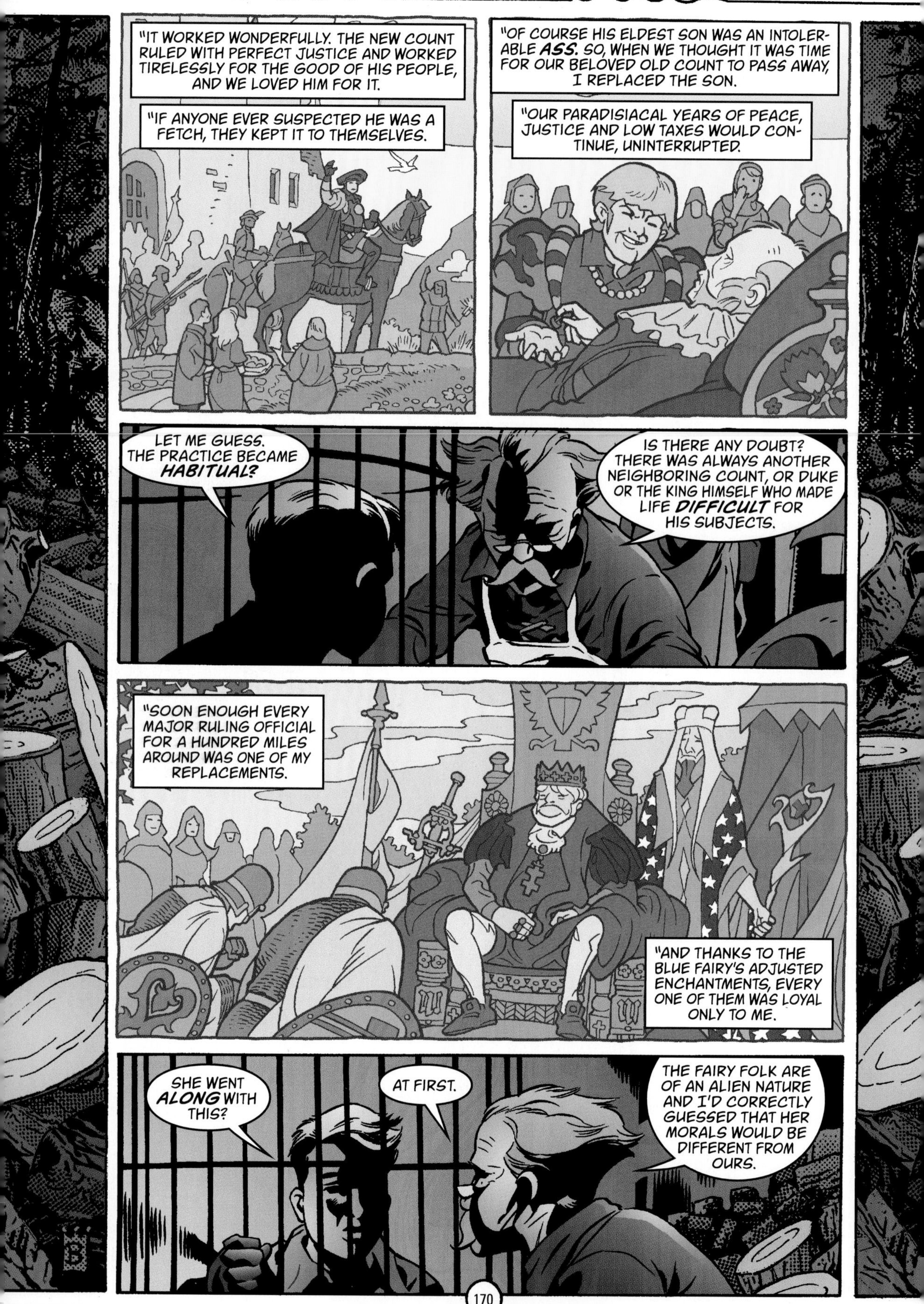
"IT WORKED WONDERFULLY. THE NEW COUNT RULED WITH PERFECT JUSTICE AND WORKED TIRELESSLY FOR THE GOOD OF HIS PEOPLE, AND WE LOVED HIM FOR IT.
"IF ANYONE EVER SUSPECTED HE WAS A FETCH, THEY KEPT IT TO THEMSELVES.
"OF COURSE HIS ELDEST SON WAS AN INTOLERABLE ASS. SO, WHEN WE THOUGHT IT WAS TIME FOR OUR BELOVED OLD COUNT TO PASS AWAY, I REPLACED THE SON.
"OUR PARADISIACAL YEARS OF PEACE, JUSTICE AND LOW TAXES WOULD CONTINUE, UNINTERRUPTED.
LET ME GUESS. THE PRACTICE BECAME HABITUAL?
IS THERE ANY DOUBT? THERE WAS ALWAYS ANOTHER NEIGHBORING COUNT, OR DUKE OR THE KING HIMSELF WHO MADE LIFE DIFFICULT FOR HIS SUBJECTS.
"SOON ENOUGH EVERY MAJOR RULING OFFICIAL FOR A HUNDRED MILES AROUND WAS ONE OF MY REPLACEMENTS.
"AND THANKS TO THE BLUE FAIRY'S ADJUSTED ENCHANTMENTS, EVERY ONE OF THEM WAS LOYAL ONLY TO ME.
SHE WENT ALONG WITH THIS?
AT FIRST.
THE FAIRY FOLK ARE OF AN ALIEN NATURE AND I'D CORRECTLY GUESSED THAT HER MORALS WOULD BE DIFFERENT FROM OURS.

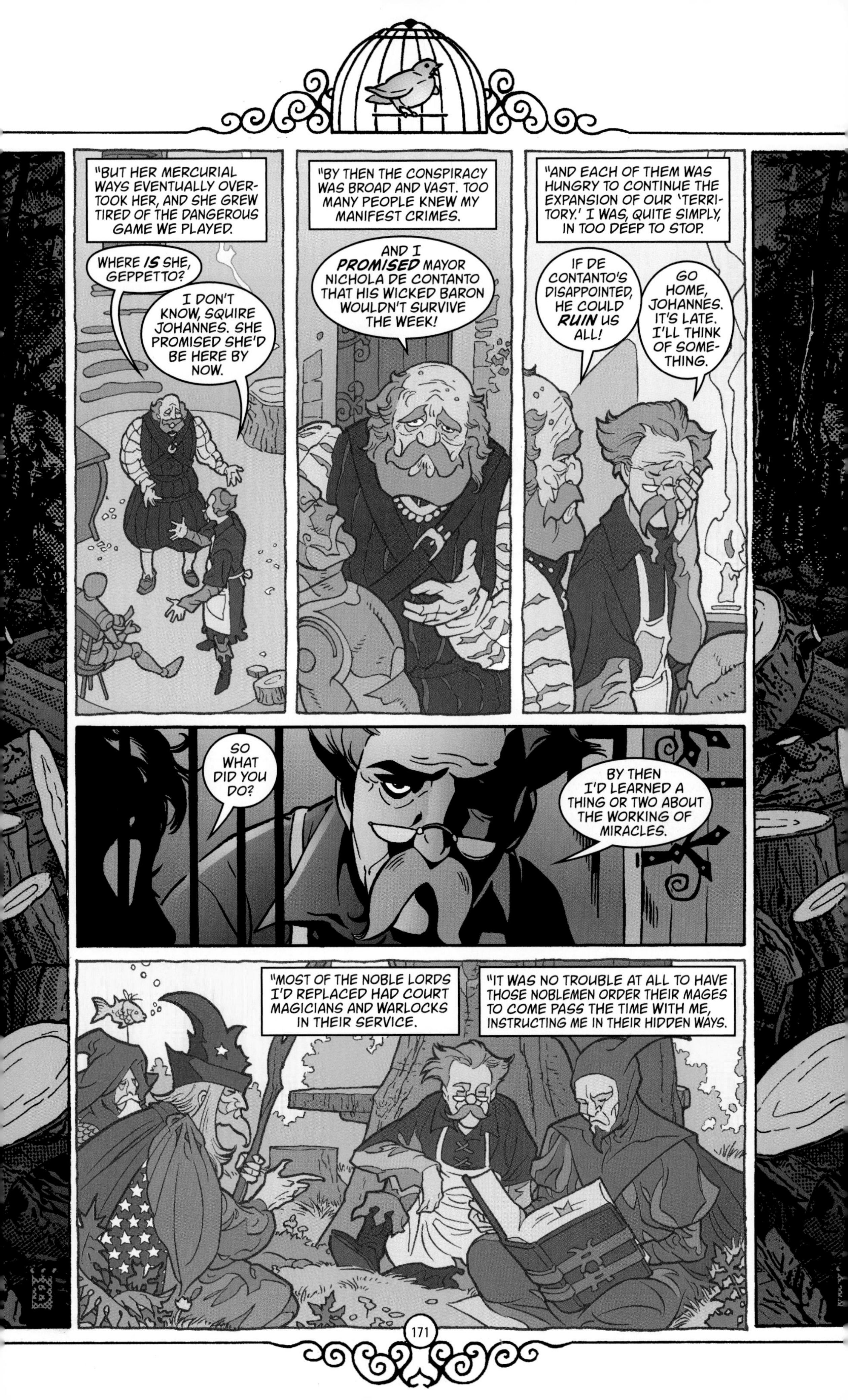

"BUT HER MERCURIAL WAYS EVENTUALLY OVERTOOK HER, AND SHE GREW TIRED OF THE DANGEROUS GAME WE PLAYED.
WHERE *IS* SHE, GEPPETTO?
I DON'T KNOW, SQUIRE JOHANNES. SHE PROMISED SHE'D BE HERE BY NOW.
"BY THEN THE CONSPIRACY WAS BROAD AND VAST. TOO MANY PEOPLE KNEW MY MANIFEST CRIMES.
AND I *PROMISED* MAYOR NICHOLA DE CONTANTO THAT HIS WICKED BARON WOULDN'T SURVIVE THE WEEK!
"AND EACH OF THEM WAS HUNGRY TO CONTINUE THE EXPANSION OF OUR 'TERRITORY.' I WAS, QUITE SIMPLY, IN TOO DEEP TO STOP.
IF DE CONTANTO'S DISAPPOINTED, HE COULD *RUIN* US ALL!
GO HOME, JOHANNES. IT'S LATE. I'LL THINK OF SOMETHING.
SO WHAT DID YOU DO?
BY THEN I'D LEARNED A THING OR TWO ABOUT THE WORKING OF MIRACLES.
"MOST OF THE NOBLE LORDS I'D REPLACED HAD COURT MAGICIANS AND WARLOCKS IN THEIR SERVICE.
"IT WAS NO TROUBLE AT ALL TO HAVE THOSE NOBLEMEN ORDER THEIR MAGES TO COME PASS THE TIME WITH ME, INSTRUCTING ME IN THEIR HIDDEN WAYS.

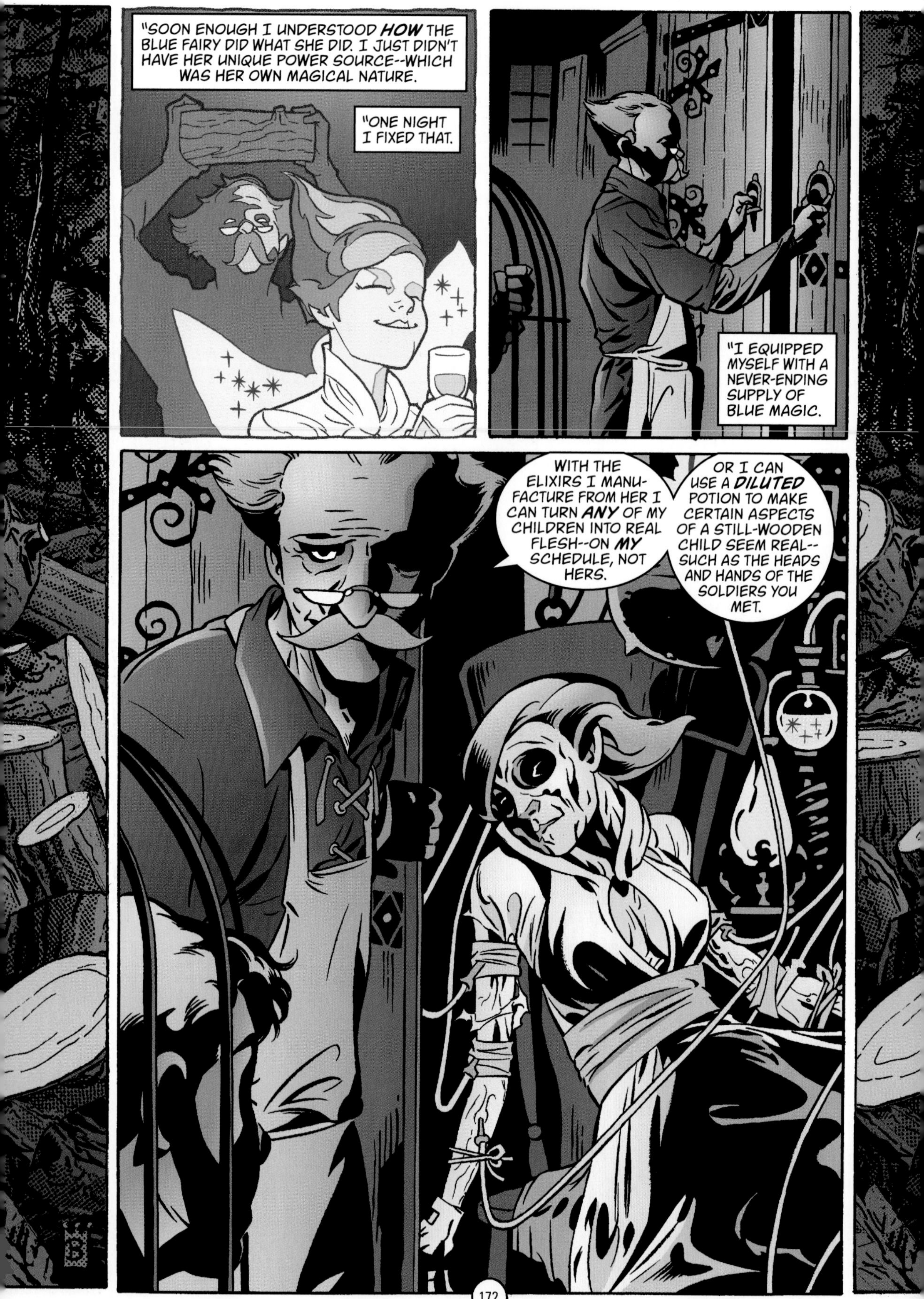

"SOON ENOUGH I UNDERSTOOD HOW THE BLUE FAIRY DID WHAT SHE DID. I JUST DIDN'T HAVE HER UNIQUE POWER SOURCE--WHICH WAS HER OWN MAGICAL NATURE.
"ONE NIGHT I FIXED THAT.
"I EQUIPPED MYSELF WITH A NEVER-ENDING SUPPLY OF BLUE MAGIC.
WITH THE ELIXIRS I MANUFACTURE FROM HER I CAN TURN ANY OF MY CHILDREN INTO REAL FLESH--ON MY SCHEDULE, NOT HERS.
OR I CAN USE A DILUTED POTION TO MAKE CERTAIN ASPECTS OF A STILL-WOODEN CHILD SEEM REAL--SUCH AS THE HEADS AND HANDS OF THE SOLDIERS YOU MET.

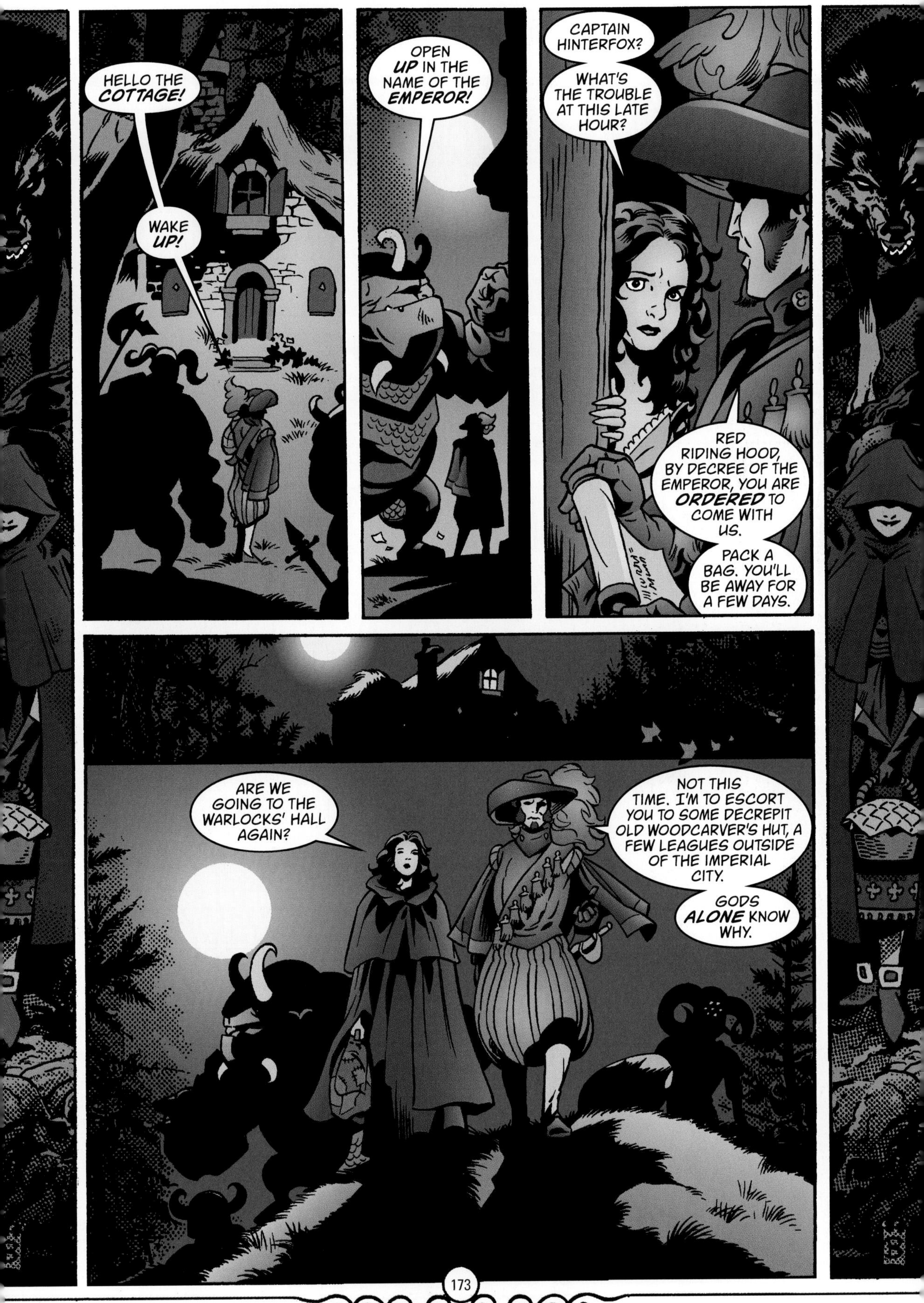

HELLO THE COTTAGE!
WAKE UP!
OPEN UP IN THE NAME OF THE EMPEROR!
CAPTAIN HINTERFOX?
WHAT'S THE TROUBLE AT THIS LATE HOUR?
RED RIDING HOOD, BY DECREE OF THE EMPEROR, YOU ARE ORDERED TO COME WITH US.
PACK A BAG. YOU'LL BE AWAY FOR A FEW DAYS.
ARE WE GOING TO THE WARLOCKS' HALL AGAIN?
NOT THIS TIME. I'M TO ESCORT YOU TO SOME DECREPIT OLD WOODCARVER'S HUT, A FEW LEAGUES OUTSIDE OF THE IMPERIAL CITY.
GODS ALONE KNOW WHY.

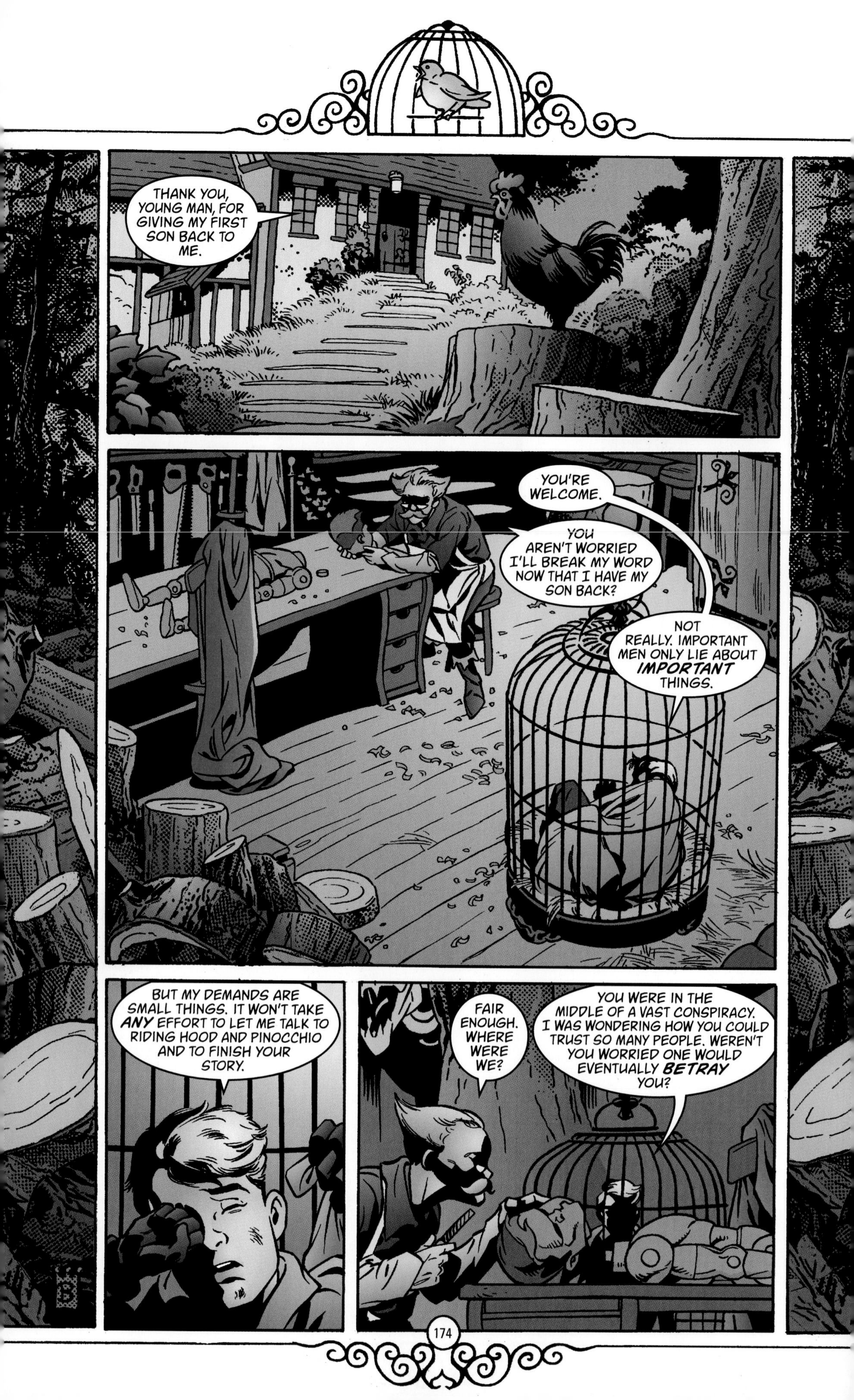
THANK YOU, YOUNG MAN, FOR GIVING MY FIRST SON BACK TO ME.
YOU'RE WELCOME.
YOU AREN'T WORRIED I'LL BREAK MY WORD NOW THAT I HAVE MY SON BACK?
NOT REALLY. IMPORTANT MEN ONLY LIE ABOUT IMPORTANT THINGS.
BUT MY DEMANDS ARE SMALL THINGS. IT WON'T TAKE ANY EFFORT TO LET ME TALK TO RIDING HOOD AND PINOCCHIO AND TO FINISH YOUR STORY.
FAIR ENOUGH. WHERE WERE WE?
YOU WERE IN THE MIDDLE OF A VAST CONSPIRACY. I WAS WONDERING HOW YOU COULD TRUST SO MANY PEOPLE. WEREN'T YOU WORRIED ONE WOULD EVENTUALLY BETRAY YOU?

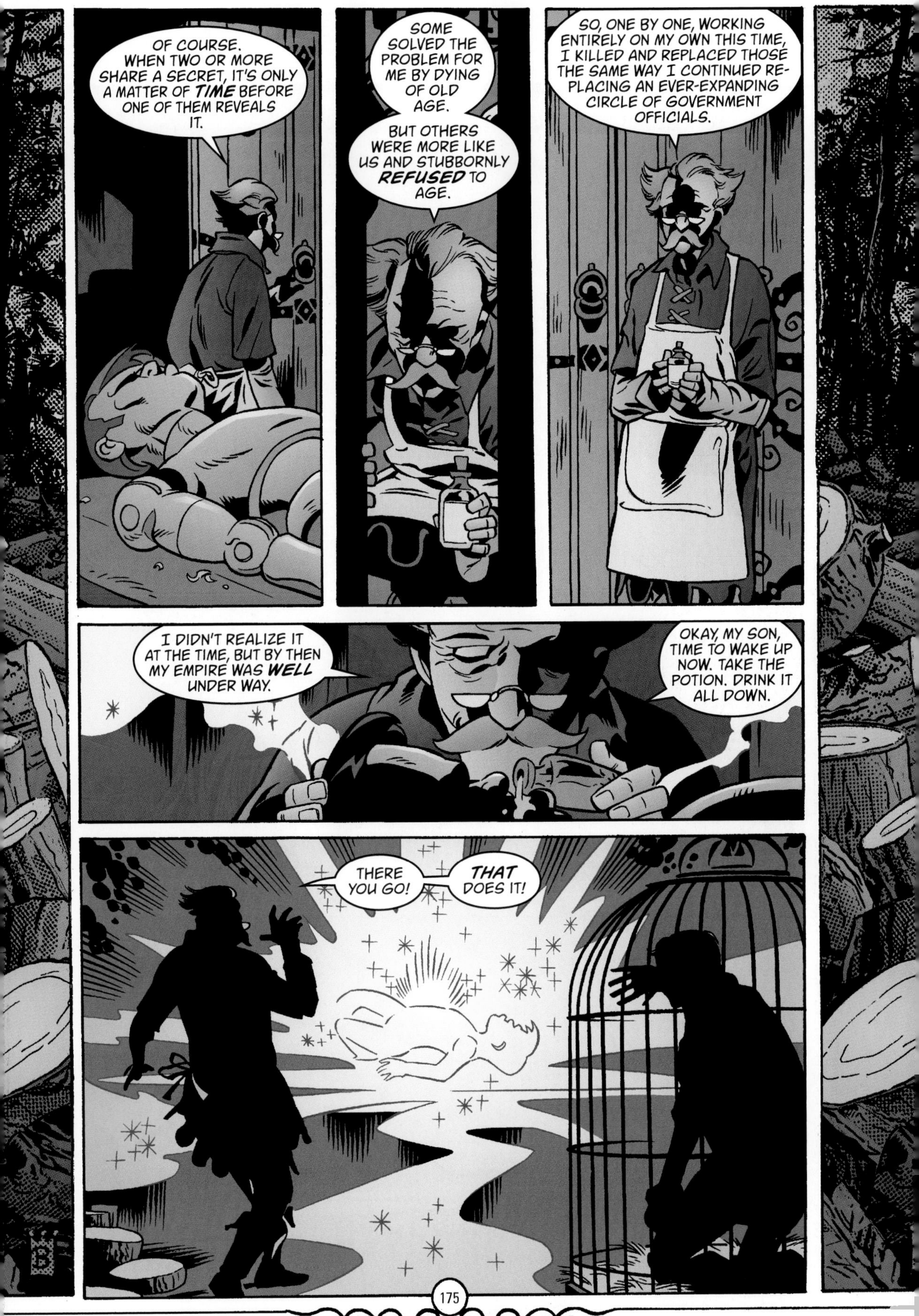
OF COURSE. WHEN TWO OR MORE SHARE A SECRET, IT'S ONLY A MATTER OF TIME BEFORE ONE OF THEM REVEALS IT.
SOME SOLVED THE PROBLEM FOR ME BY DYING OF OLD AGE.
BUT OTHERS WERE MORE LIKE US AND STUBBORNLY REFUSED TO AGE.
SO, ONE BY ONE, WORKING ENTIRELY ON MY OWN THIS TIME, I KILLED AND REPLACED THOSE THE SAME WAY I CONTINUED REPLACING AN EVER-EXPANDING CIRCLE OF GOVERNMENT OFFICIALS.
I DIDN'T REALIZE IT AT THE TIME, BUT BY THEN MY EMPIRE WAS WELL UNDER WAY.
OKAY, MY SON, TIME TO WAKE UP NOW. TAKE THE POTION. DRINK IT ALL DOWN.
THERE YOU GO!
THAT DOES IT!

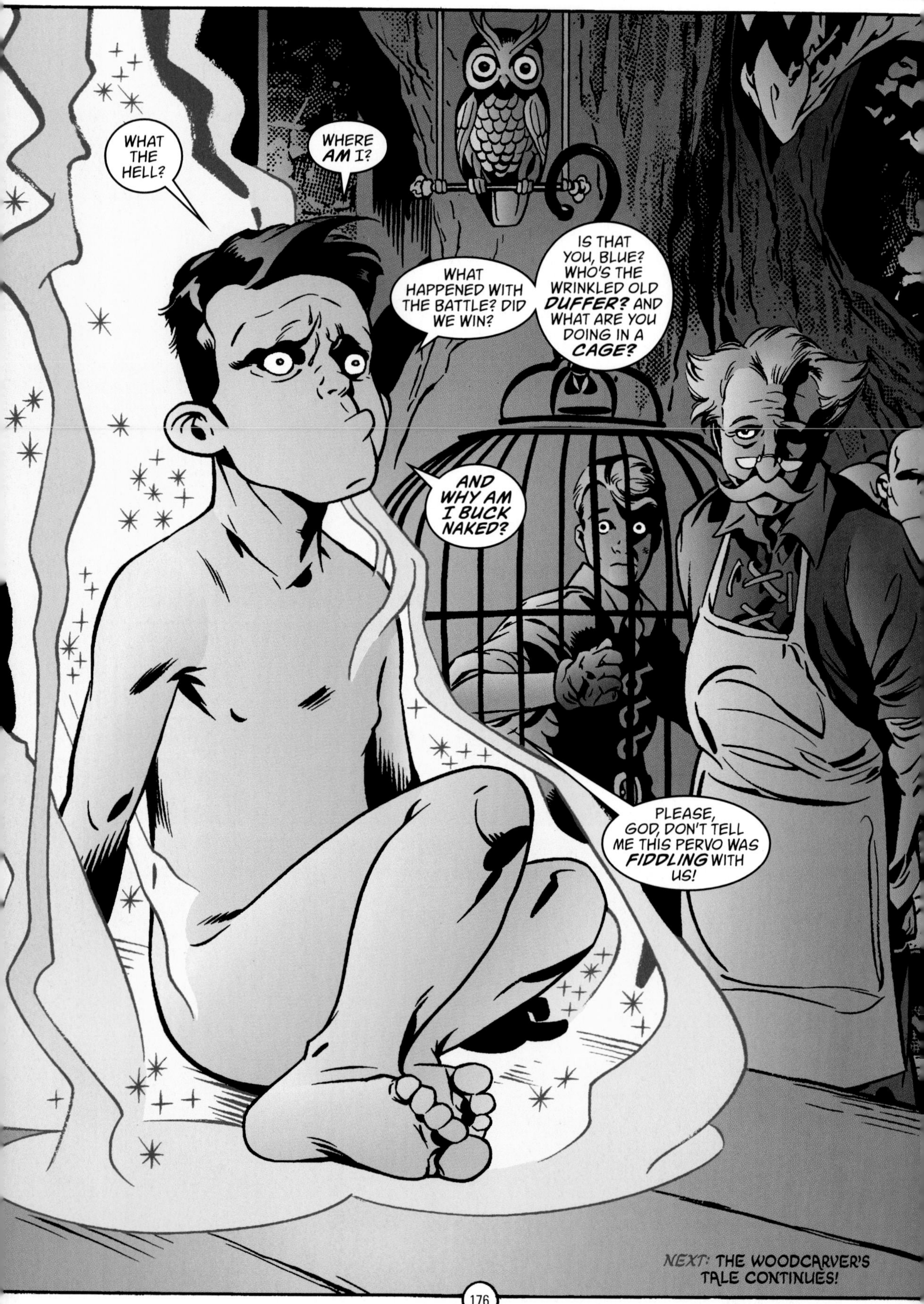
WHAT THE HELL?
WHERE AM I?
WHAT HAPPENED WITH THE BATTLE? DID WE WIN?
IS THAT YOU, BLUE? WHO'S THE WRINKLED OLD DUFFER? AND WHAT ARE YOU DOING IN A CAGE?
AND WHY AM I BUCK NAKED?
PLEASE, GOD, DON'T TELL ME THIS PERVO WAS FIDDLING WITH US!
NEXT: THE WOODCARVER'S TALE CONTINUES!

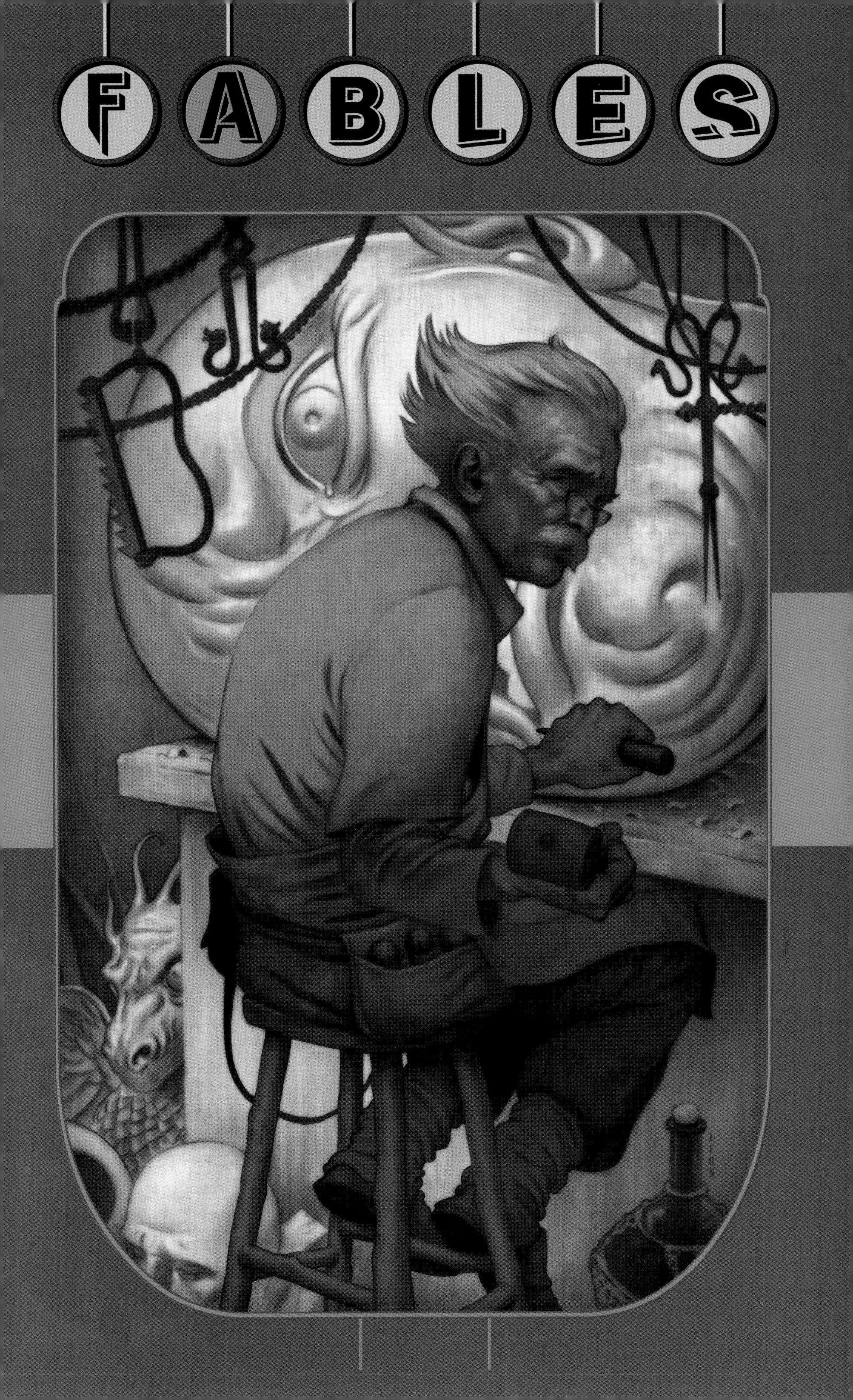
FABLES

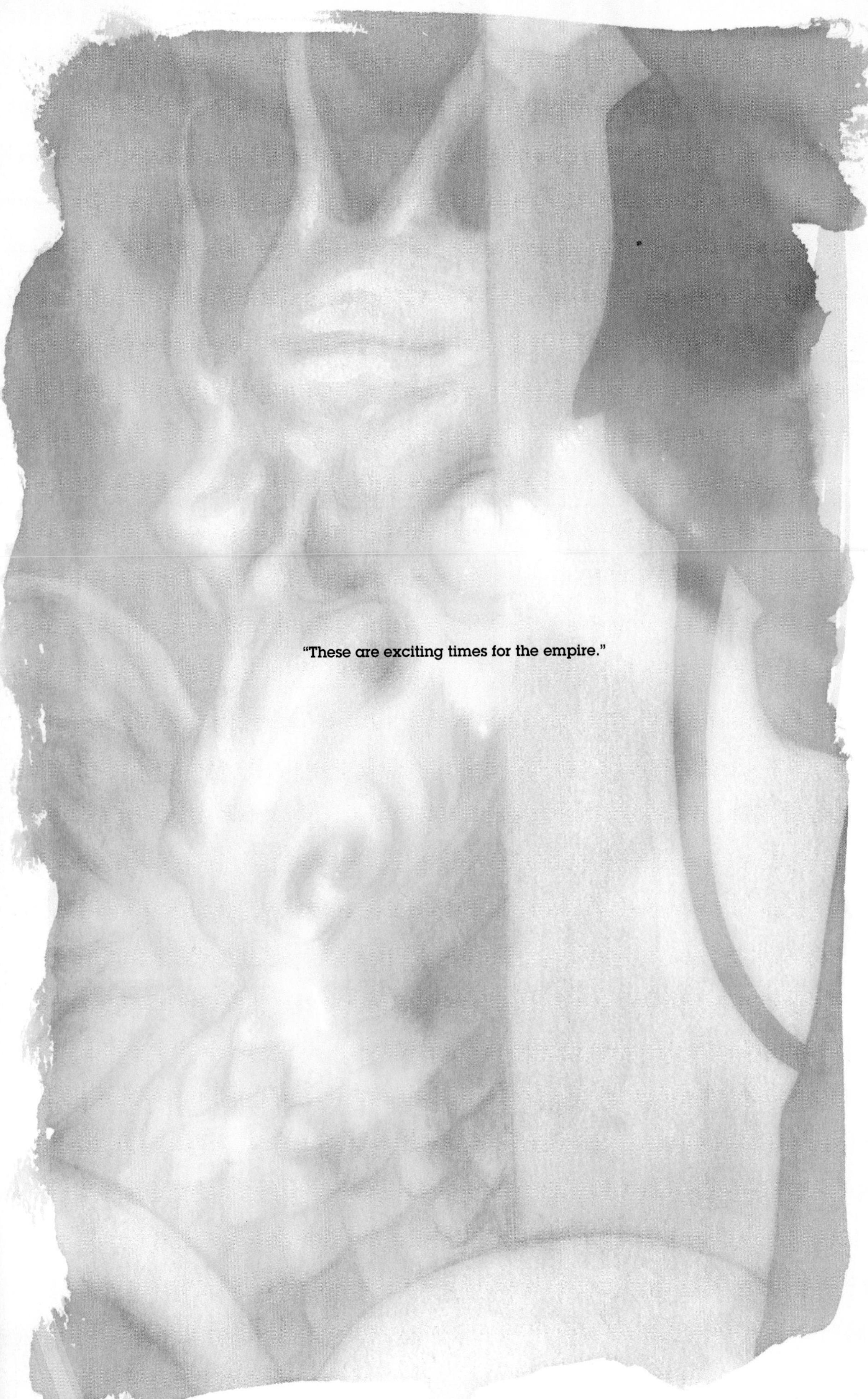

"These are exciting times for the empire."

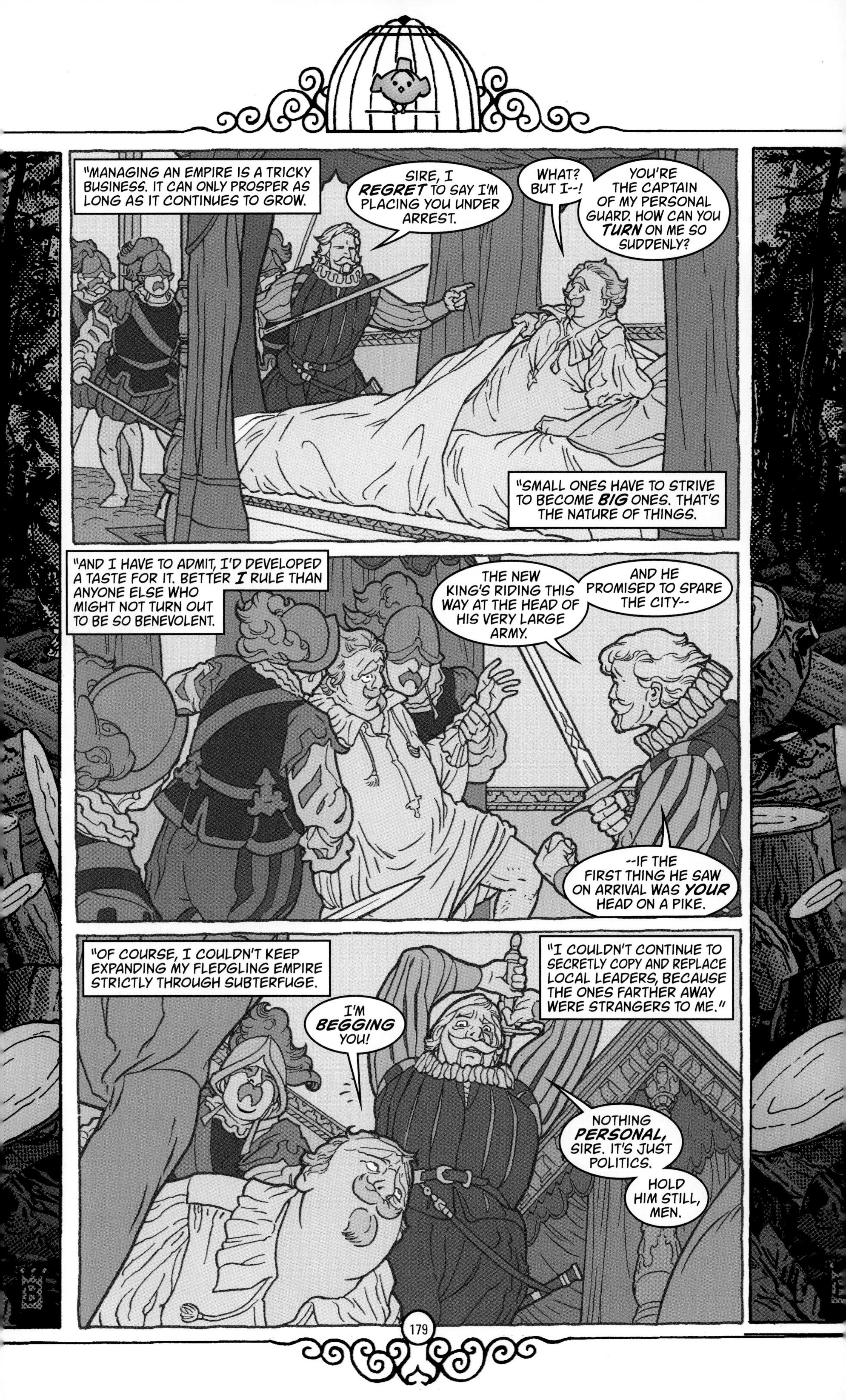
"MANAGING AN EMPIRE IS A TRICKY BUSINESS. IT CAN ONLY PROSPER AS LONG AS IT CONTINUES TO GROW.
SIRE, I REGRET TO SAY I'M PLACING YOU UNDER ARREST.
WHAT? BUT I--!
YOU'RE THE CAPTAIN OF MY PERSONAL GUARD. HOW CAN YOU TURN ON ME SO SUDDENLY?
"SMALL ONES HAVE TO STRIVE TO BECOME BIG ONES. THAT'S THE NATURE OF THINGS.
"AND I HAVE TO ADMIT, I'D DEVELOPED A TASTE FOR IT. BETTER I RULE THAN ANYONE ELSE WHO MIGHT NOT TURN OUT TO BE SO BENEVOLENT.
THE NEW KING'S RIDING THIS WAY AT THE HEAD OF HIS VERY LARGE ARMY.
AND HE PROMISED TO SPARE THE CITY--
--IF THE FIRST THING HE SAW ON ARRIVAL WAS YOUR HEAD ON A PIKE.
"OF COURSE, I COULDN'T KEEP EXPANDING MY FLEDGLING EMPIRE STRICTLY THROUGH SUBTERFUGE.
"I COULDN'T CONTINUE TO SECRETLY COPY AND REPLACE LOCAL LEADERS, BECAUSE THE ONES FARTHER AWAY WERE STRANGERS TO ME."
I'M BEGGING YOU!
NOTHING PERSONAL, SIRE. IT'S JUST POLITICS.
HOLD HIM STILL, MEN.

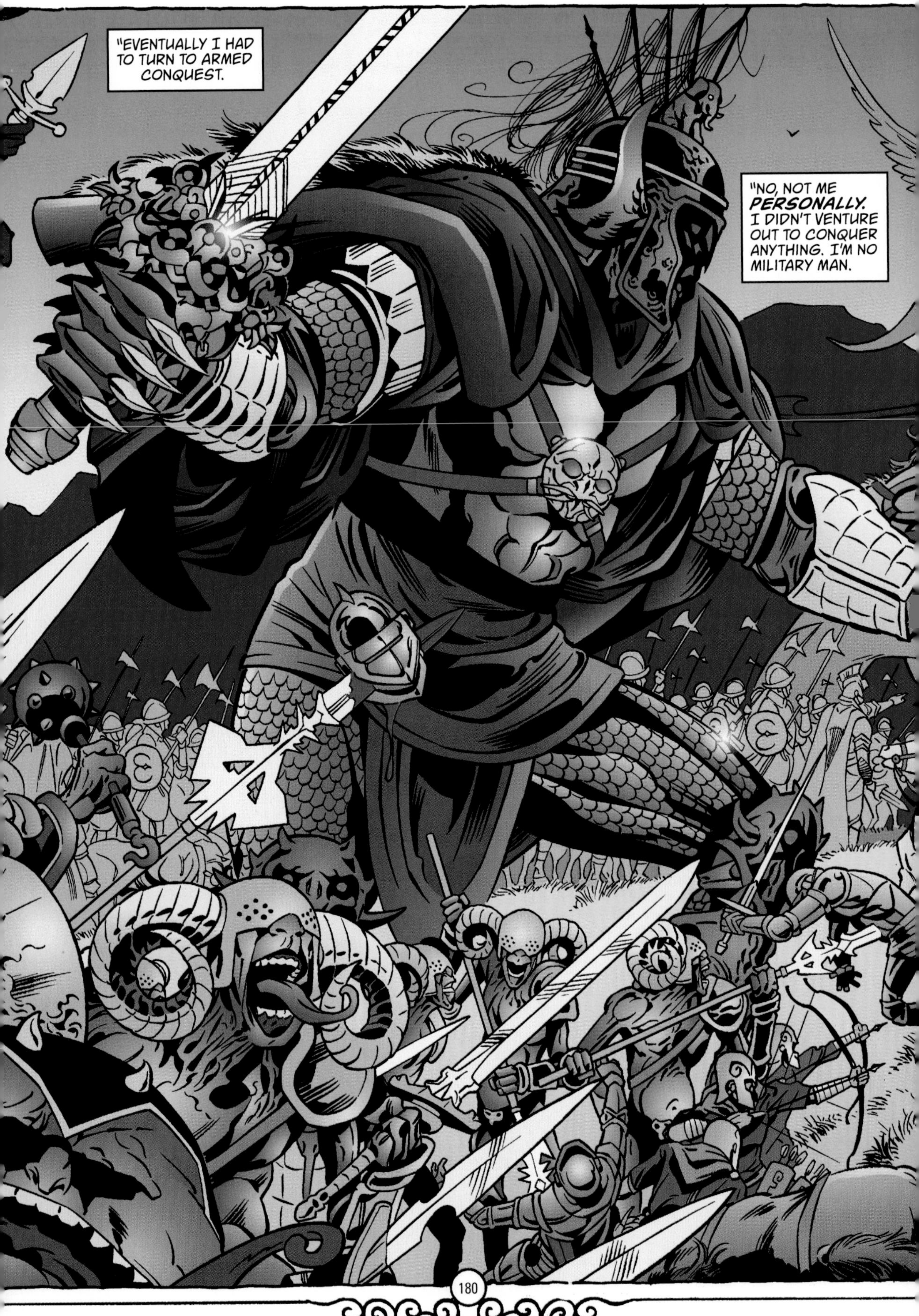
"EVENTUALLY I HAD TO TURN TO ARMED CONQUEST.
"NO, NOT ME **PERSONALLY.** I DIDN'T VENTURE OUT TO CONQUER ANYTHING. I'M NO MILITARY MAN.

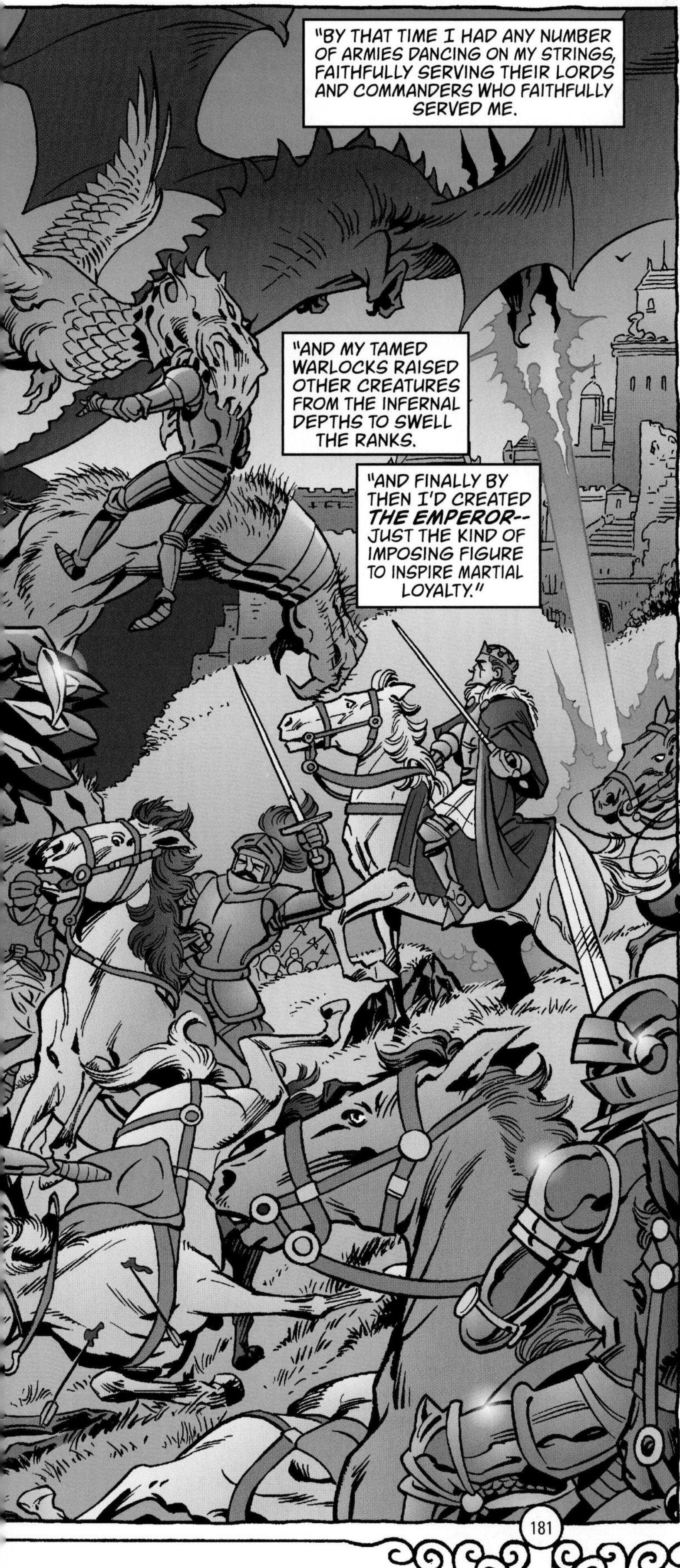
"BY THAT TIME I HAD ANY NUMBER OF ARMIES DANCING ON MY STRINGS, FAITHFULLY SERVING THEIR LORDS AND COMMANDERS WHO FAITHFULLY SERVED ME.
"AND MY TAMED WARLOCKS RAISED OTHER CREATURES FROM THE INFERNAL DEPTHS TO SWELL THE RANKS.
"AND FINALLY BY THEN I'D CREATED *THE EMPEROR*-- JUST THE KIND OF IMPOSING FIGURE TO INSPIRE MARTIAL LOYALTY."

PAX IMPERIUM

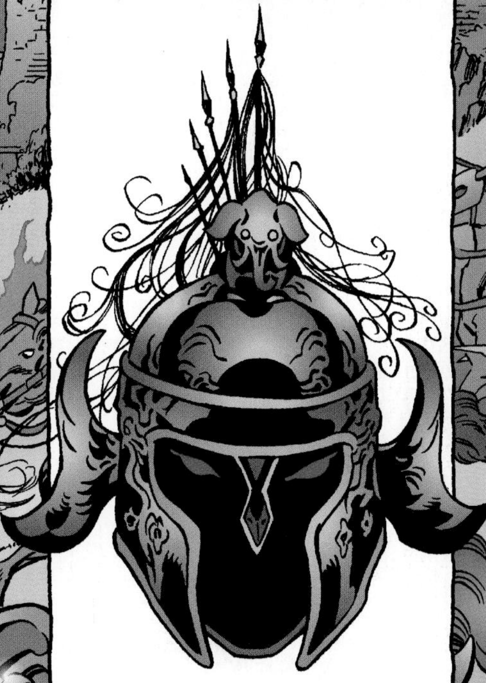

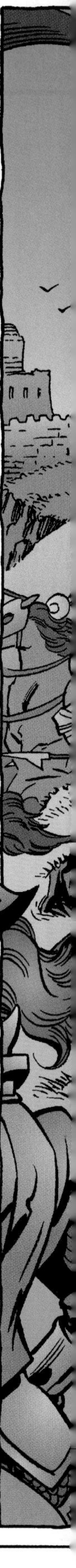

Chapter Five of HOMELANDS

Bill Willingham: writer-creator

Mark Buckingham: penciller

Steve Leialoha: inker

Daniel Vozzo: colors

James Jean: cover art

Todd Klein: letters

Angela Rufino: assistant editor

Shelly Bond: editor

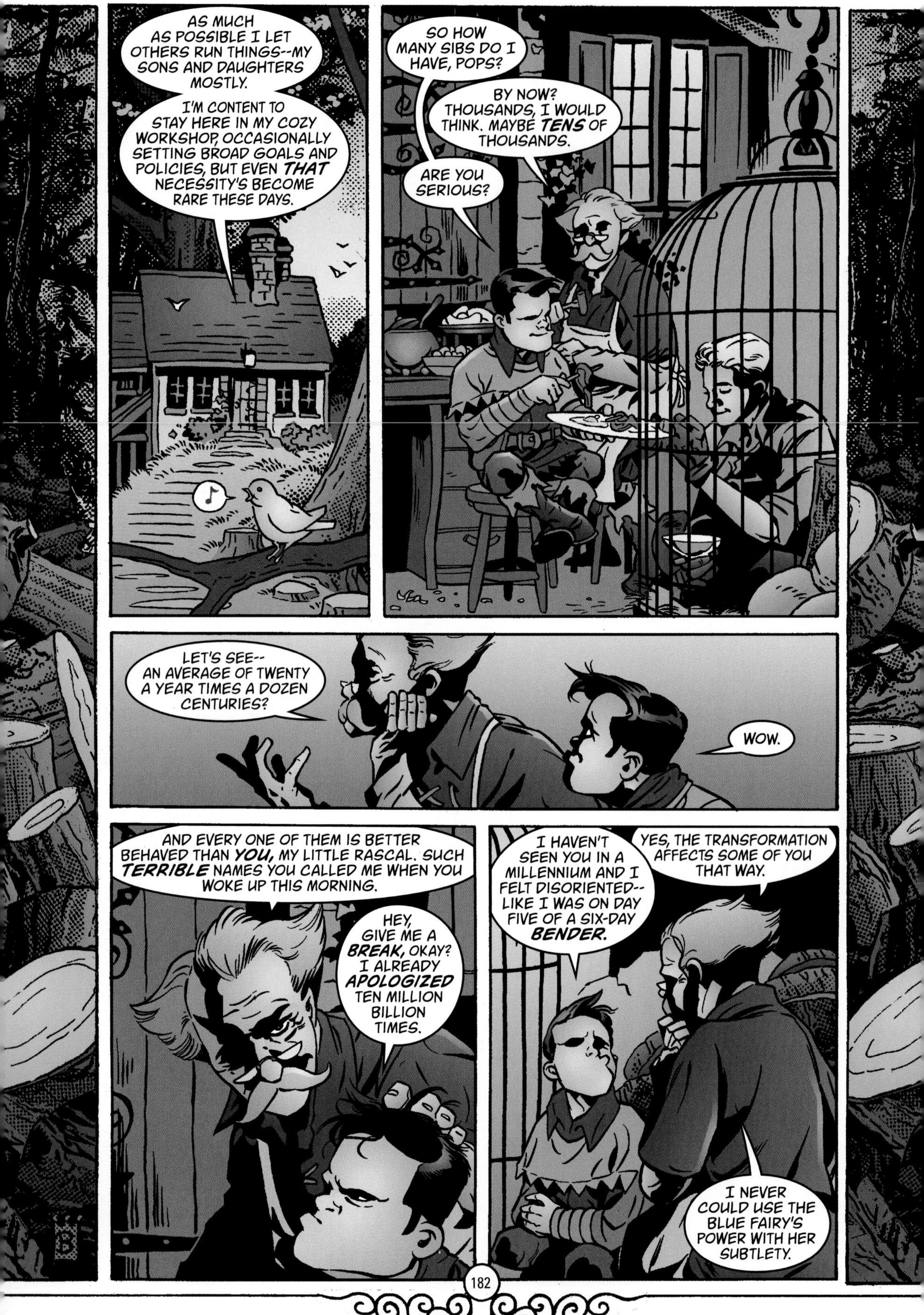
AS MUCH AS POSSIBLE I LET OTHERS RUN THINGS--MY SONS AND DAUGHTERS MOSTLY.
I'M CONTENT TO STAY HERE IN MY COZY WORKSHOP, OCCASIONALLY SETTING BROAD GOALS AND POLICIES, BUT EVEN THAT NECESSITY'S BECOME RARE THESE DAYS.
SO HOW MANY SIBS DO I HAVE, POPS?
BY NOW? THOUSANDS, I WOULD THINK. MAYBE TENS OF THOUSANDS.
ARE YOU SERIOUS?
LET'S SEE-- AN AVERAGE OF TWENTY A YEAR TIMES A DOZEN CENTURIES?
WOW.
AND EVERY ONE OF THEM IS BETTER BEHAVED THAN YOU, MY LITTLE RASCAL. SUCH TERRIBLE NAMES YOU CALLED ME WHEN YOU WOKE UP THIS MORNING.
HEY, GIVE ME A BREAK, OKAY? I ALREADY APOLOGIZED TEN MILLION BILLION TIMES.
I HAVEN'T SEEN YOU IN A MILLENNIUM AND I FELT DISORIENTED-- LIKE I WAS ON DAY FIVE OF A SIX-DAY BENDER.
YES, THE TRANSFORMATION AFFECTS SOME OF YOU THAT WAY.
I NEVER COULD USE THE BLUE FAIRY'S POWER WITH HER SUBTLETY.

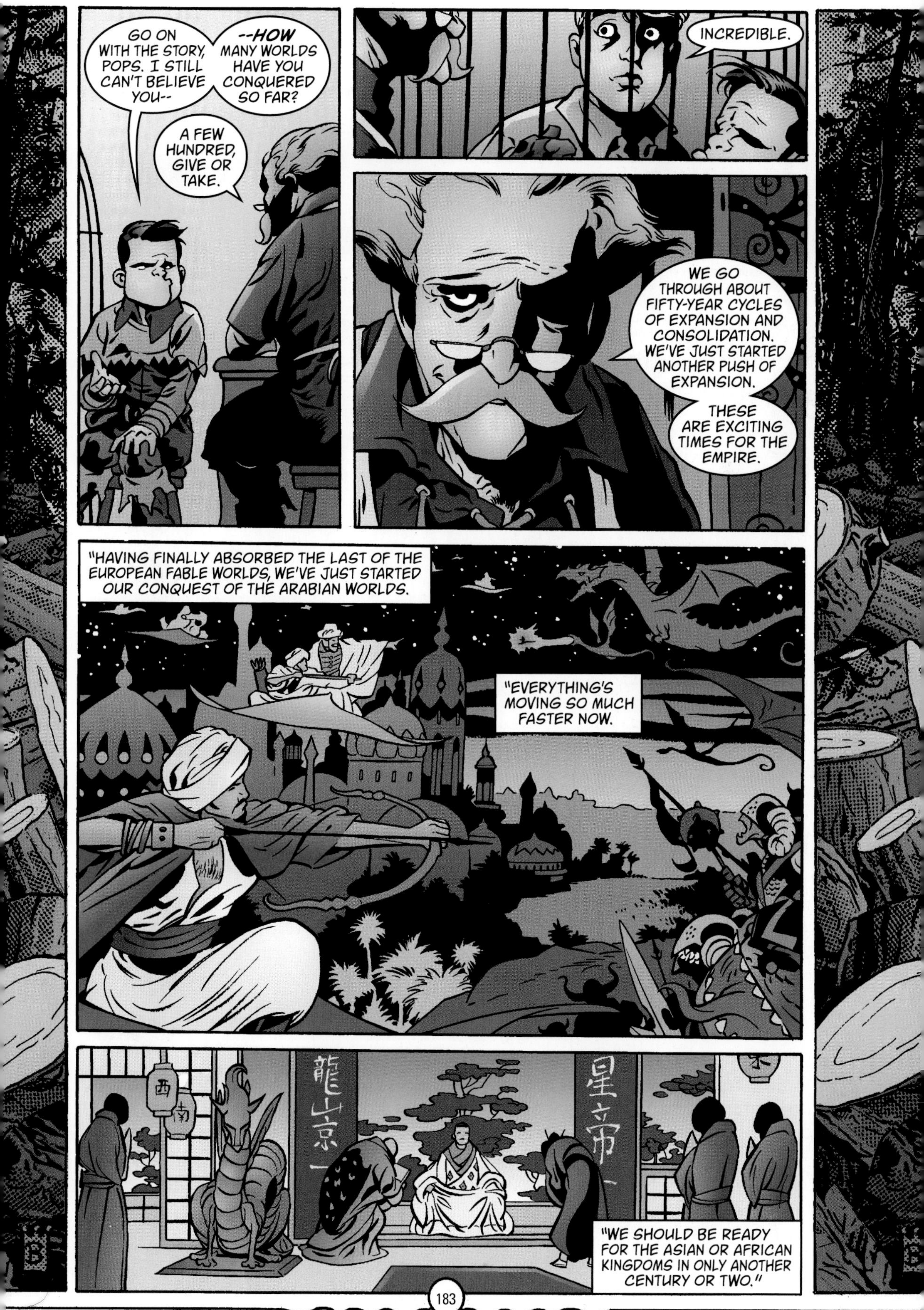
GO ON WITH THE STORY, POPS. I STILL CAN'T BELIEVE YOU--
--HOW MANY WORLDS HAVE YOU CONQUERED SO FAR?
A FEW HUNDRED, GIVE OR TAKE.
INCREDIBLE.
WE GO THROUGH ABOUT FIFTY-YEAR CYCLES OF EXPANSION AND CONSOLIDATION. WE'VE JUST STARTED ANOTHER PUSH OF EXPANSION.
THESE ARE EXCITING TIMES FOR THE EMPIRE.
"HAVING FINALLY ABSORBED THE LAST OF THE EUROPEAN FABLE WORLDS, WE'VE JUST STARTED OUR CONQUEST OF THE ARABIAN WORLDS.
"EVERYTHING'S MOVING SO MUCH FASTER NOW.
"WE SHOULD BE READY FOR THE ASIAN OR AFRICAN KINGDOMS IN ONLY ANOTHER CENTURY OR TWO."

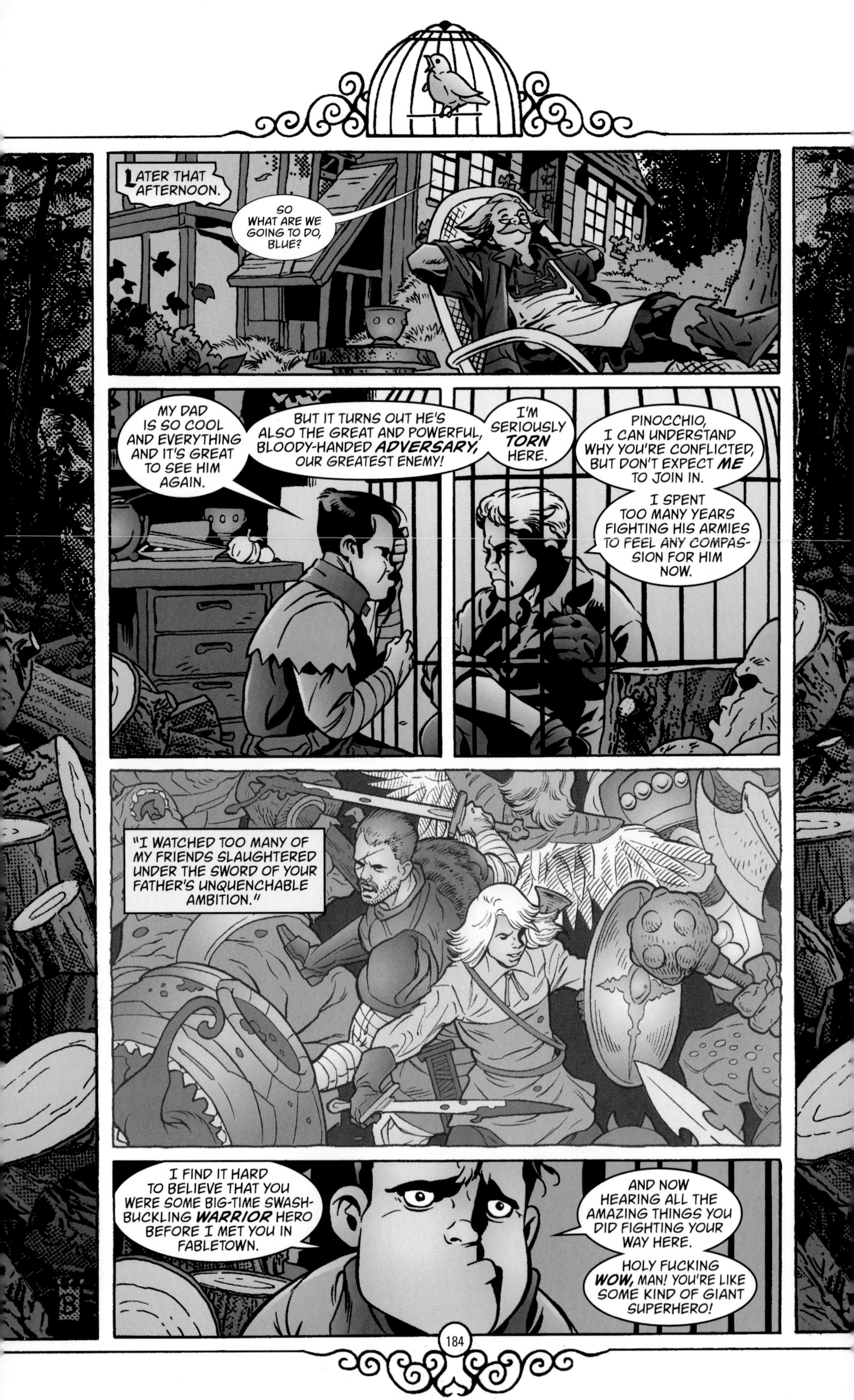

LATER THAT AFTERNOON.
SO WHAT ARE WE GOING TO DO, BLUE?
MY DAD IS SO COOL AND EVERYTHING AND IT'S GREAT TO SEE HIM AGAIN.
BUT IT TURNS OUT HE'S ALSO THE GREAT AND POWERFUL, BLOODY-HANDED ADVERSARY, OUR GREATEST ENEMY!
I'M SERIOUSLY TORN HERE.
PINOCCHIO, I CAN UNDERSTAND WHY YOU'RE CONFLICTED, BUT DON'T EXPECT ME TO JOIN IN.
I SPENT TOO MANY YEARS FIGHTING HIS ARMIES TO FEEL ANY COMPASSION FOR HIM NOW.
"I WATCHED TOO MANY OF MY FRIENDS SLAUGHTERED UNDER THE SWORD OF YOUR FATHER'S UNQUENCHABLE AMBITION."
I FIND IT HARD TO BELIEVE THAT YOU WERE SOME BIG-TIME SWASHBUCKLING WARRIOR HERO BEFORE I MET YOU IN FABLETOWN.
AND NOW HEARING ALL THE AMAZING THINGS YOU DID FIGHTING YOUR WAY HERE.
HOLY FUCKING WOW, MAN! YOU'RE LIKE SOME KIND OF GIANT SUPERHERO!

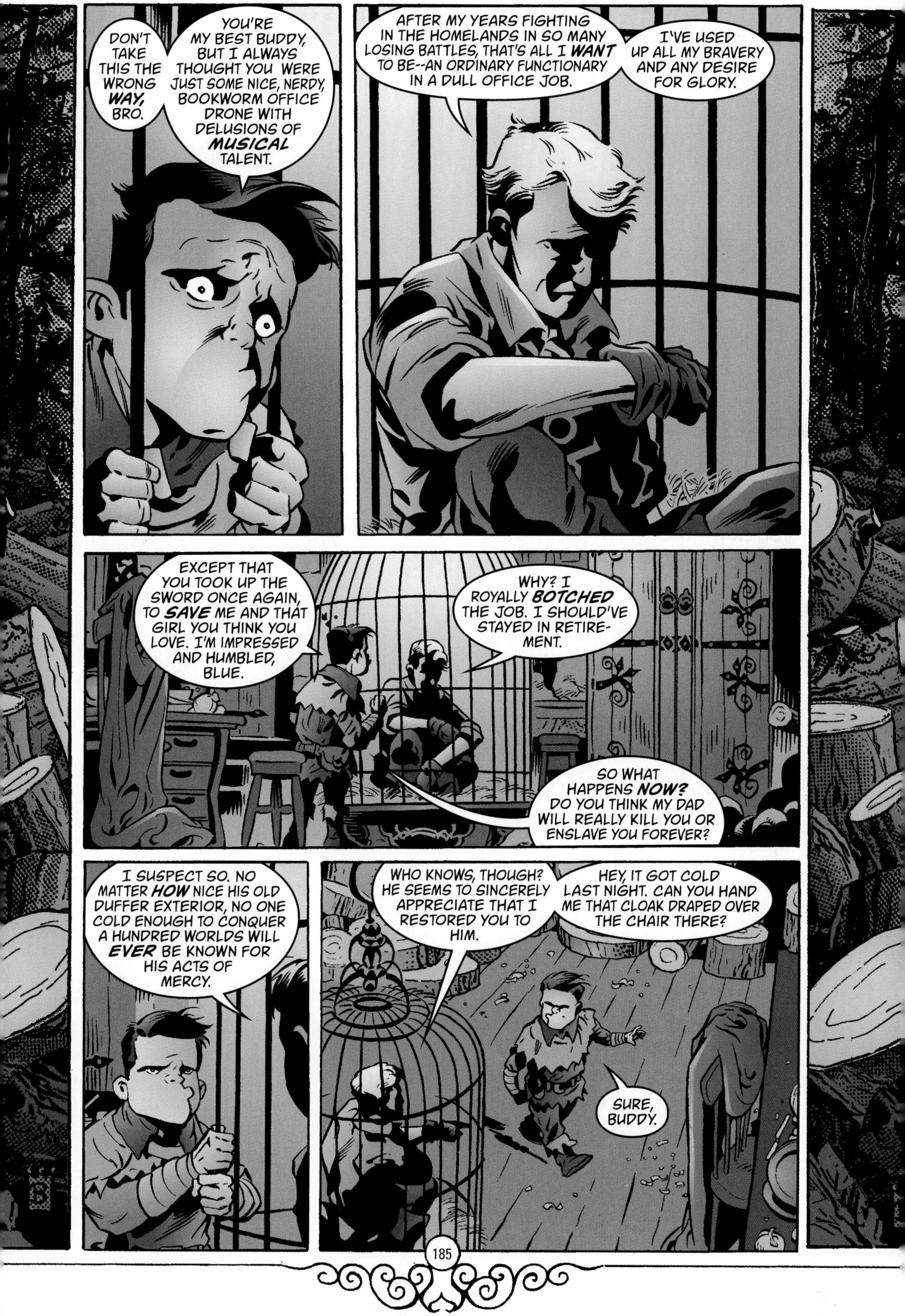
DON'T TAKE THIS THE WRONG WAY, BRO.
YOU'RE MY BEST BUDDY, BUT I ALWAYS THOUGHT YOU WERE JUST SOME NICE, NERDY, BOOKWORM OFFICE DRONE WITH DELUSIONS OF MUSICAL TALENT.
AFTER MY YEARS FIGHTING IN THE HOMELANDS IN SO MANY LOSING BATTLES, THAT'S ALL I WANT TO BE--AN ORDINARY FUNCTIONARY IN A DULL OFFICE JOB.
I'VE USED UP ALL MY BRAVERY AND ANY DESIRE FOR GLORY.
EXCEPT THAT YOU TOOK UP THE SWORD ONCE AGAIN, TO SAVE ME AND THAT GIRL YOU THINK YOU LOVE. I'M IMPRESSED AND HUMBLED, BLUE.
WHY? I ROYALLY BOTCHED THE JOB. I SHOULD'VE STAYED IN RETIRE-MENT.
SO WHAT HAPPENS NOW? DO YOU THINK MY DAD WILL REALLY KILL YOU OR ENSLAVE YOU FOREVER?
I SUSPECT SO. NO MATTER HOW NICE HIS OLD DUFFER EXTERIOR, NO ONE COLD ENOUGH TO CONQUER A HUNDRED WORLDS WILL EVER BE KNOWN FOR HIS ACTS OF MERCY.
WHO KNOWS, THOUGH? HE SEEMS TO SINCERELY APPRECIATE THAT I RESTORED YOU TO HIM.
HEY, IT GOT COLD LAST NIGHT. CAN YOU HAND ME THAT CLOAK DRAPED OVER THE CHAIR THERE?
SURE, BUDDY.

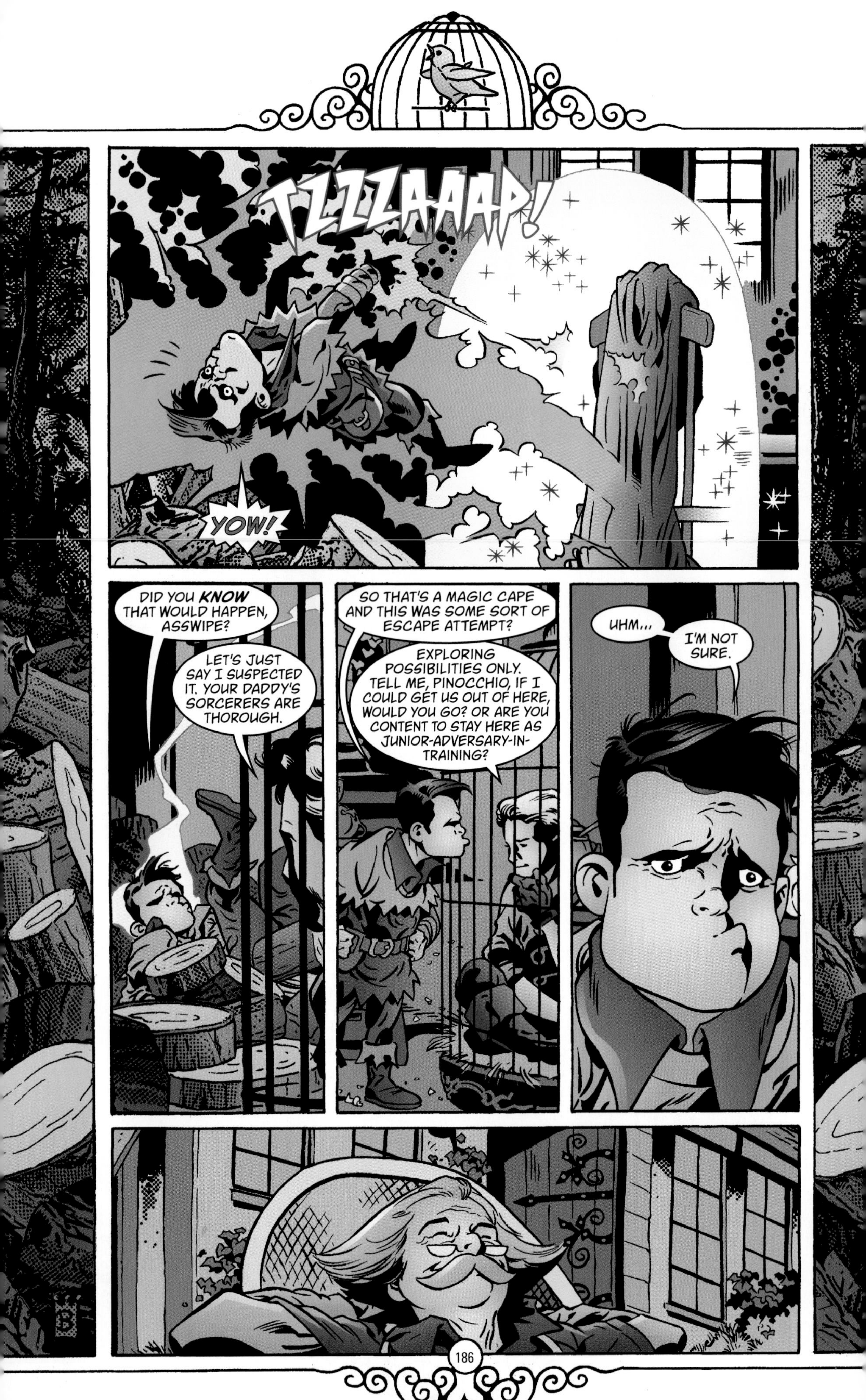

TZZZAAAP!
YOW!
DID YOU KNOW THAT WOULD HAPPEN, ASSWIPE?
LET'S JUST SAY I SUSPECTED IT. YOUR DADDY'S SORCERERS ARE THOROUGH.
SO THAT'S A MAGIC CAPE AND THIS WAS SOME SORT OF ESCAPE ATTEMPT?
EXPLORING POSSIBILITIES ONLY. TELL ME, PINOCCHIO, IF I COULD GET US OUT OF HERE, WOULD YOU GO? OR ARE YOU CONTENT TO STAY HERE AS JUNIOR-ADVERSARY-IN-TRAINING?
UHM...
I'M NOT SURE.

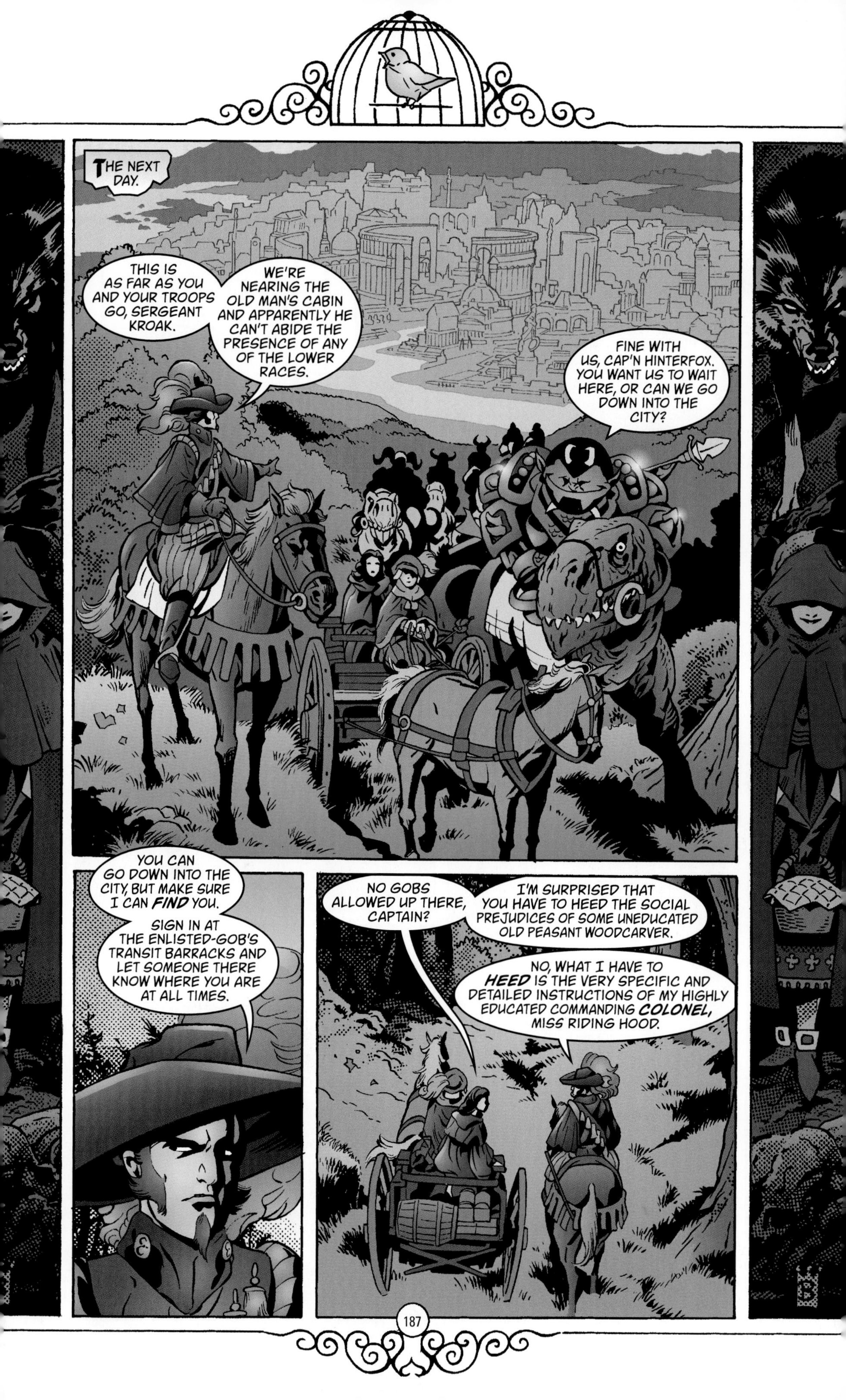
THE NEXT DAY.
THIS IS AS FAR AS YOU AND YOUR TROOPS GO, SERGEANT KROAK.
WE'RE NEARING THE OLD MAN'S CABIN AND APPARENTLY HE CAN'T ABIDE THE PRESENCE OF ANY OF THE LOWER RACES.
FINE WITH US, CAP'N HINTERFOX. YOU WANT US TO WAIT HERE, OR CAN WE GO DOWN INTO THE CITY?
YOU CAN GO DOWN INTO THE CITY, BUT MAKE SURE I CAN FIND YOU.
SIGN IN AT THE ENLISTED-GOB'S TRANSIT BARRACKS AND LET SOMEONE THERE KNOW WHERE YOU ARE AT ALL TIMES.
NO GOBS ALLOWED UP THERE, CAPTAIN?
I'M SURPRISED THAT YOU HAVE TO HEED THE SOCIAL PREJUDICES OF SOME UNEDUCATED OLD PEASANT WOODCARVER.
NO, WHAT I HAVE TO HEED IS THE VERY SPECIFIC AND DETAILED INSTRUCTIONS OF MY HIGHLY EDUCATED COMMANDING COLONEL, MISS RIDING HOOD.

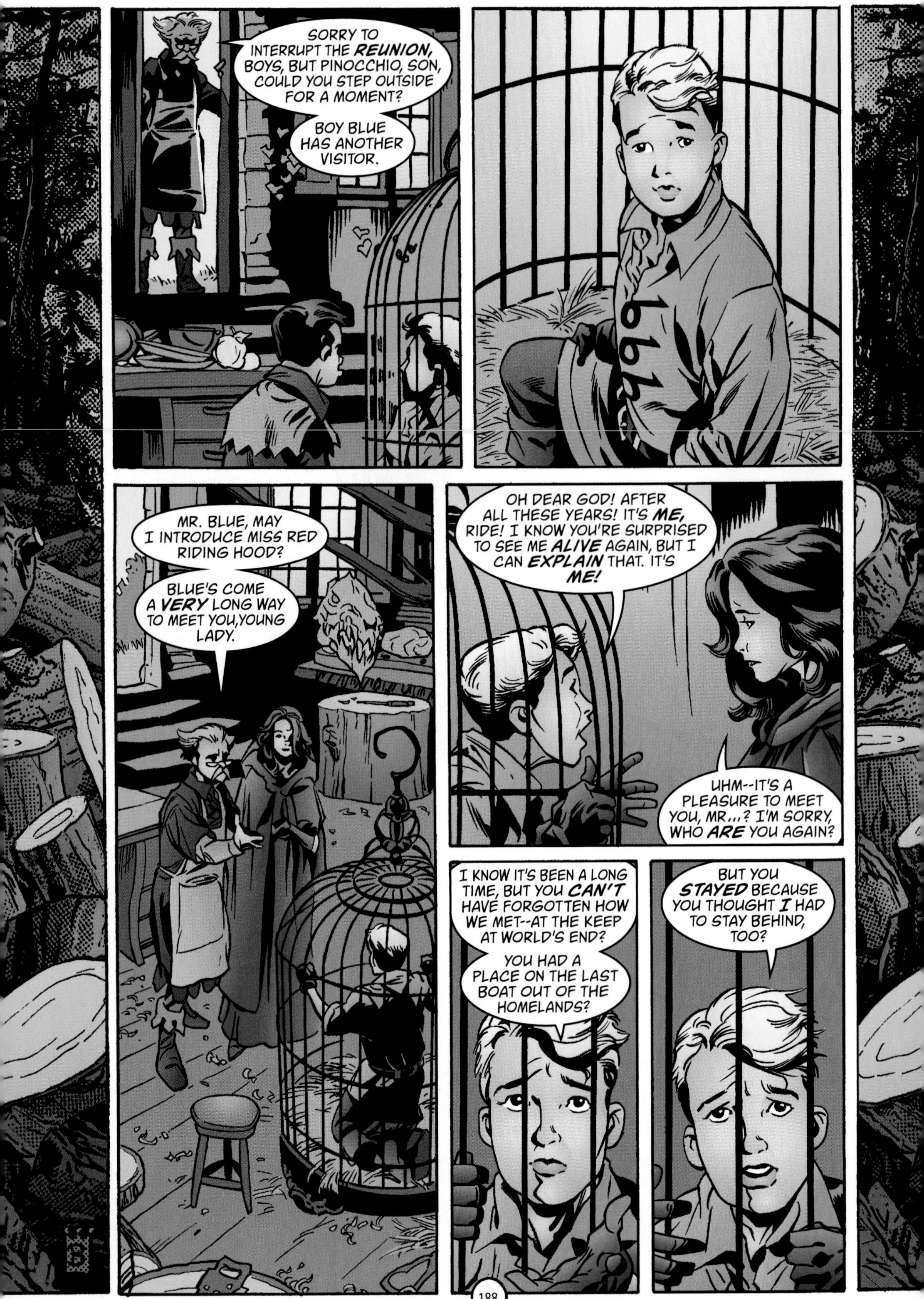
SORRY TO INTERRUPT THE REUNION, BOYS, BUT PINOCCHIO, SON, COULD YOU STEP OUTSIDE FOR A MOMENT?
BOY BLUE HAS ANOTHER VISITOR.
MR. BLUE, MAY I INTRODUCE MISS RED RIDING HOOD?
BLUE'S COME A VERY LONG WAY TO MEET YOU,YOUNG LADY.
OH DEAR GOD! AFTER ALL THESE YEARS! IT'S ME, RIDE! I KNOW YOU'RE SURPRISED TO SEE ME ALIVE AGAIN, BUT I CAN EXPLAIN THAT. IT'S ME!
UHM--IT'S A PLEASURE TO MEET YOU, MR...? I'M SORRY, WHO ARE YOU AGAIN?
I KNOW IT'S BEEN A LONG TIME, BUT YOU CAN'T HAVE FORGOTTEN HOW WE MET--AT THE KEEP AT WORLD'S END?
YOU HAD A PLACE ON THE LAST BOAT OUT OF THE HOMELANDS?
BUT YOU STAYED BECAUSE YOU THOUGHT I HAD TO STAY BEHIND, TOO?

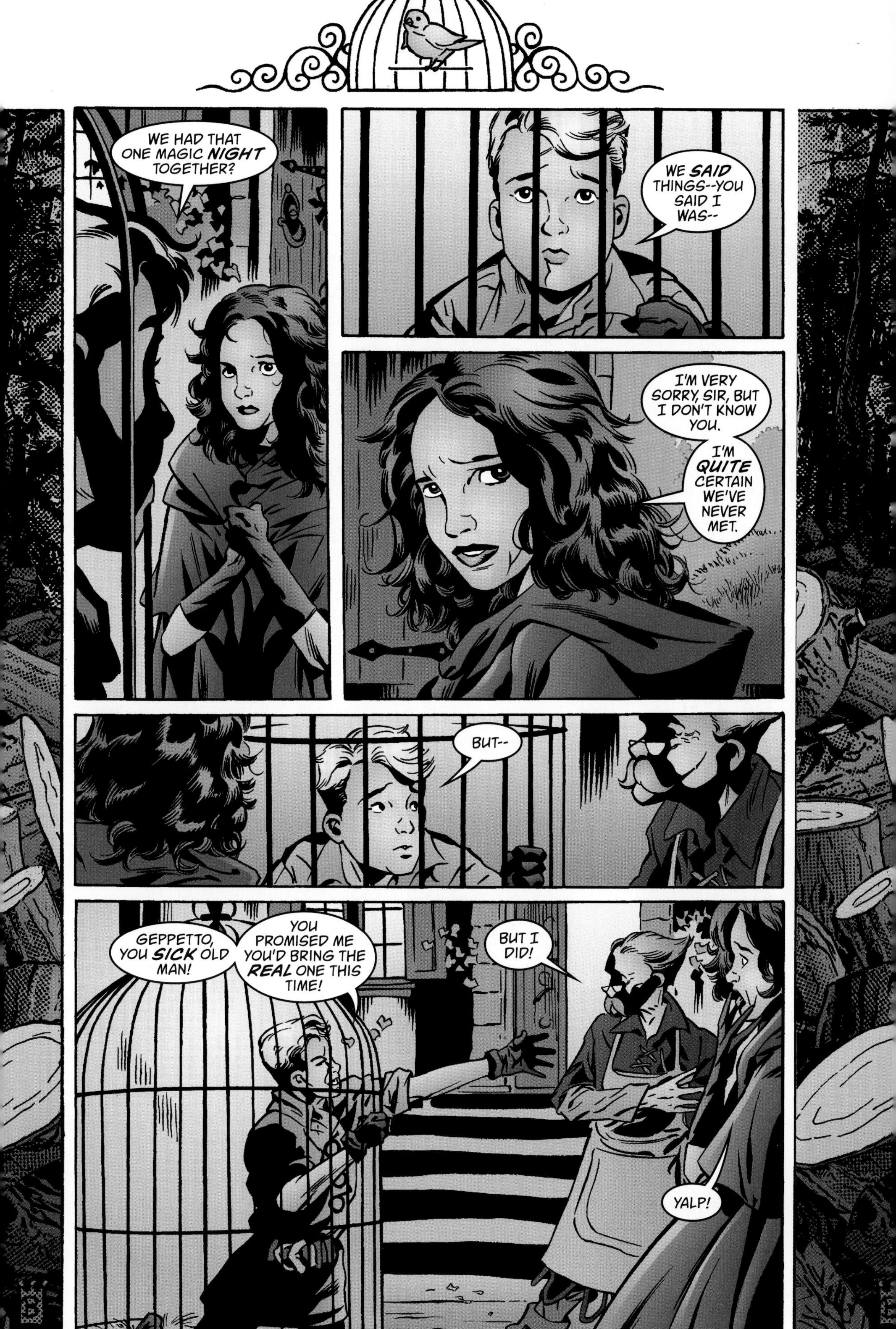
WE HAD THAT ONE MAGIC NIGHT TOGETHER?
WE SAID THINGS--YOU SAID I WAS--
I'M VERY SORRY, SIR, BUT I DON'T KNOW YOU.
I'M QUITE CERTAIN WE'VE NEVER MET.
BUT--
GEPPETTO, YOU SICK OLD MAN!
YOU PROMISED ME YOU'D BRING THE REAL ONE THIS TIME!
BUT I DID!
YALP!

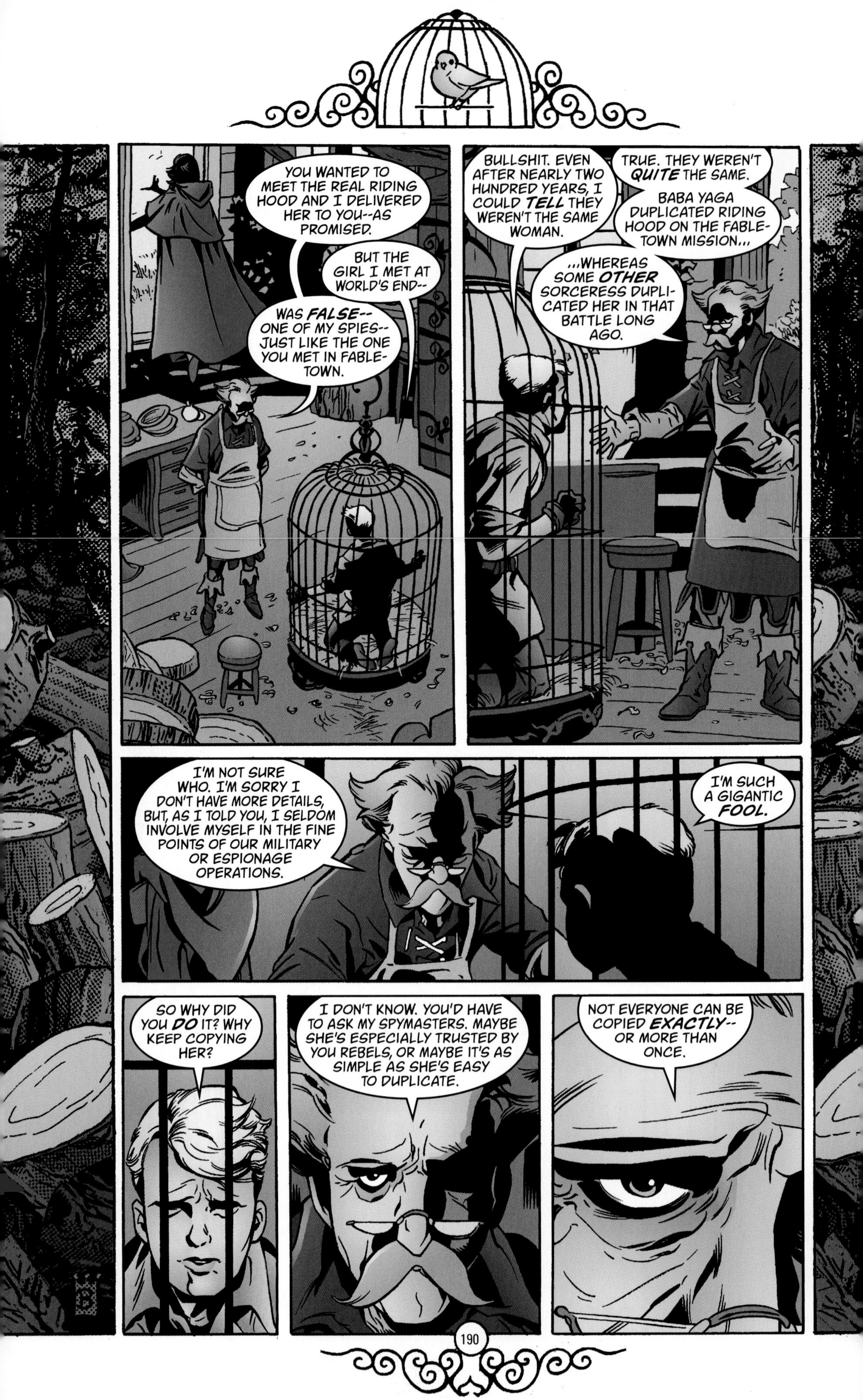
YOU WANTED TO MEET THE REAL RIDING HOOD AND I DELIVERED HER TO YOU--AS PROMISED.
BUT THE GIRL I MET AT WORLD'S END--
WAS FALSE-- ONE OF MY SPIES-- JUST LIKE THE ONE YOU MET IN FABLE-TOWN.
BULLSHIT. EVEN AFTER NEARLY TWO HUNDRED YEARS, I COULD TELL THEY WEREN'T THE SAME WOMAN.
TRUE. THEY WEREN'T QUITE THE SAME.
BABA YAGA DUPLICATED RIDING HOOD ON THE FABLE-TOWN MISSION...
...WHEREAS SOME OTHER SORCERESS DUPLICATED HER IN THAT BATTLE LONG AGO.
I'M NOT SURE WHO. I'M SORRY I DON'T HAVE MORE DETAILS, BUT, AS I TOLD YOU, I SELDOM INVOLVE MYSELF IN THE FINE POINTS OF OUR MILITARY OR ESPIONAGE OPERATIONS.
I'M SUCH A GIGANTIC FOOL.
SO WHY DID YOU DO IT? WHY KEEP COPYING HER?
I DON'T KNOW. YOU'D HAVE TO ASK MY SPYMASTERS. MAYBE SHE'S ESPECIALLY TRUSTED BY YOU REBELS, OR MAYBE IT'S AS SIMPLE AS SHE'S EASY TO DUPLICATE.
NOT EVERYONE CAN BE COPIED EXACTLY-- OR MORE THAN ONCE.

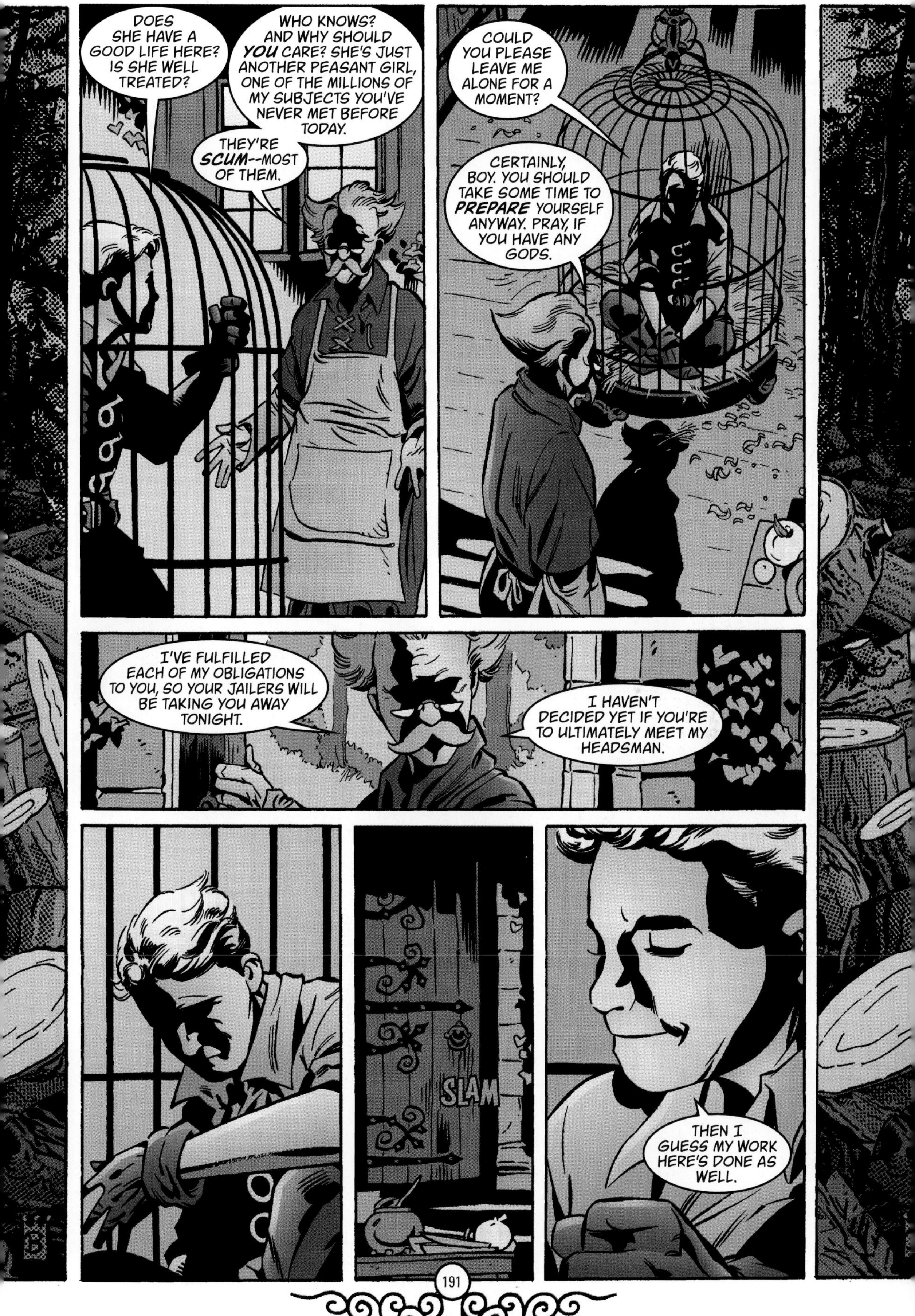
DOES SHE HAVE A GOOD LIFE HERE? IS SHE WELL TREATED?
WHO KNOWS? AND WHY SHOULD YOU CARE? SHE'S JUST ANOTHER PEASANT GIRL, ONE OF THE MILLIONS OF MY SUBJECTS YOU'VE NEVER MET BEFORE TODAY.
THEY'RE SCUM--MOST OF THEM.
COULD YOU PLEASE LEAVE ME ALONE FOR A MOMENT?
CERTAINLY, BOY. YOU SHOULD TAKE SOME TIME TO PREPARE YOURSELF ANYWAY. PRAY, IF YOU HAVE ANY GODS.
I'VE FULFILLED EACH OF MY OBLIGATIONS TO YOU, SO YOUR JAILERS WILL BE TAKING YOU AWAY TONIGHT.
I HAVEN'T DECIDED YET IF YOU'RE TO ULTIMATELY MEET MY HEADSMAN.
SLAM
THEN I GUESS MY WORK HERE'S DONE AS WELL.

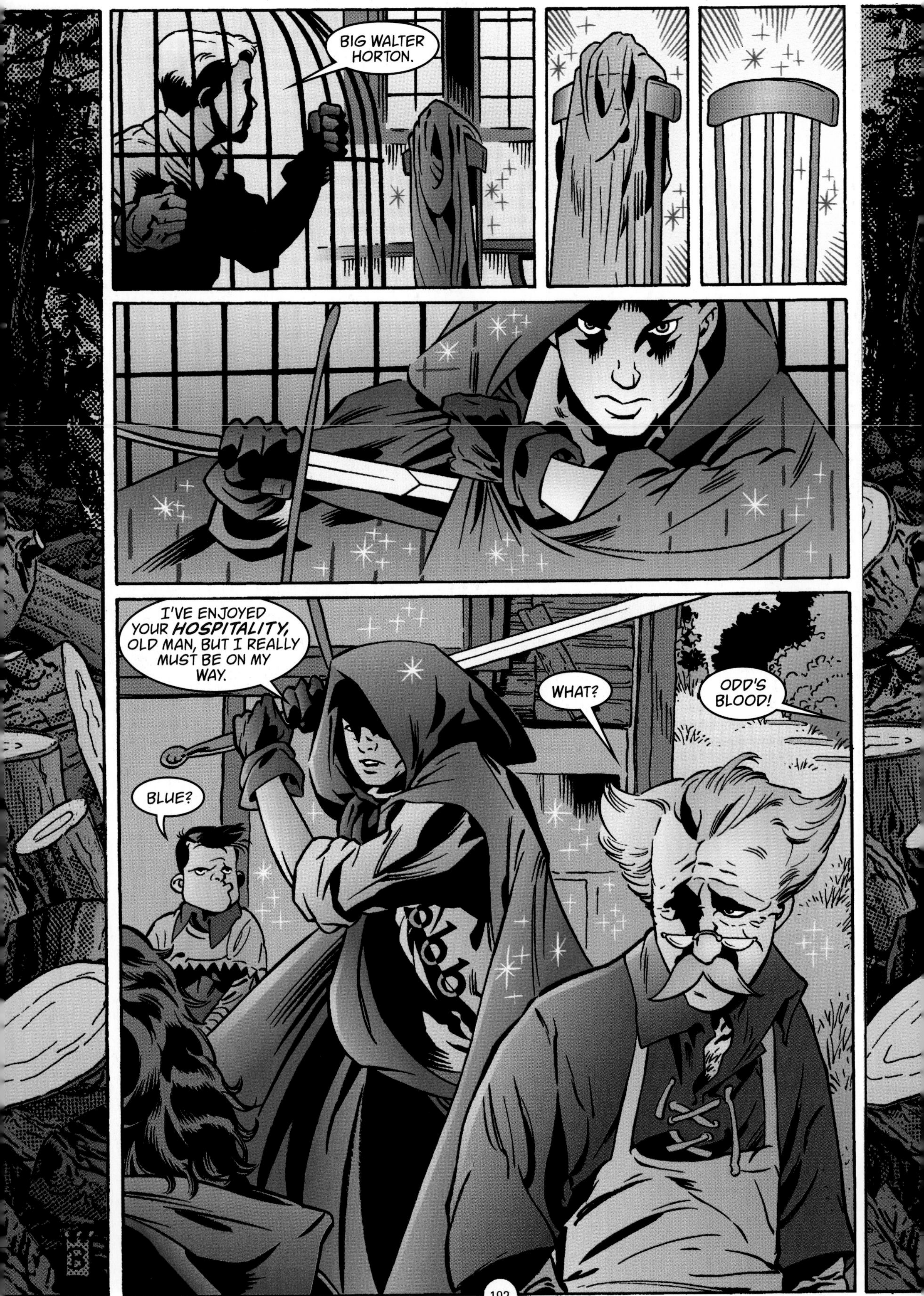

BIG WALTER HORTON.
I'VE ENJOYED YOUR HOSPITALITY, OLD MAN, BUT I REALLY MUST BE ON MY WAY.
BLUE?
WHAT?
ODD'S BLOOD!

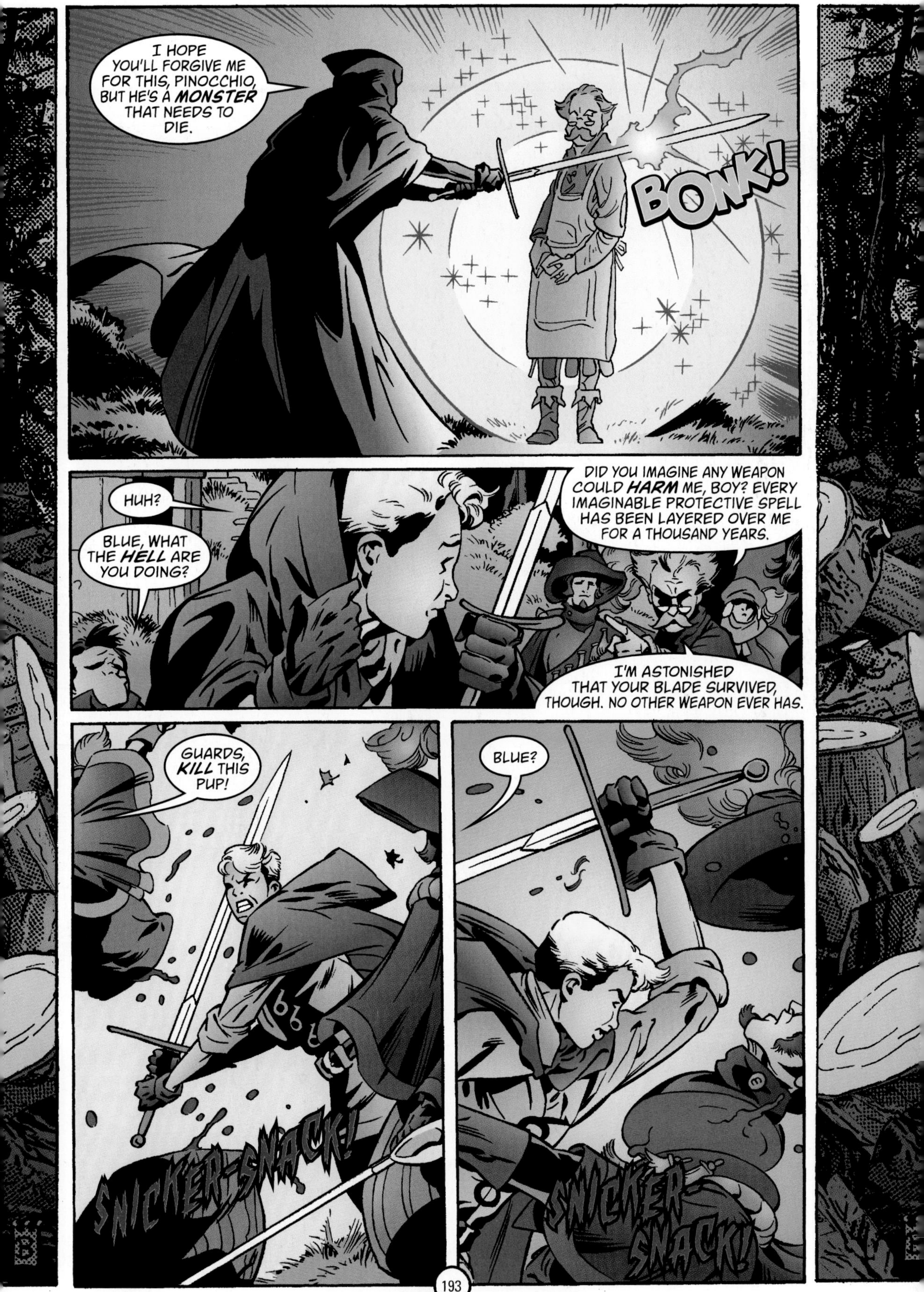
I HOPE YOU'LL FORGIVE ME FOR THIS, PINOCCHIO, BUT HE'S A ***MONSTER*** THAT NEEDS TO DIE.
BONK!
HUH?
BLUE, WHAT THE ***HELL*** ARE YOU DOING?
DID YOU IMAGINE ANY WEAPON COULD ***HARM*** ME, BOY? EVERY IMAGINABLE PROTECTIVE SPELL HAS BEEN LAYERED OVER ME FOR A THOUSAND YEARS.
I'M ASTONISHED THAT YOUR BLADE SURVIVED, THOUGH. NO OTHER WEAPON EVER HAS.
GUARDS, ***KILL*** THIS PUP!
SNICKER-SNACK!
BLUE?
SNICKER-SNACK!

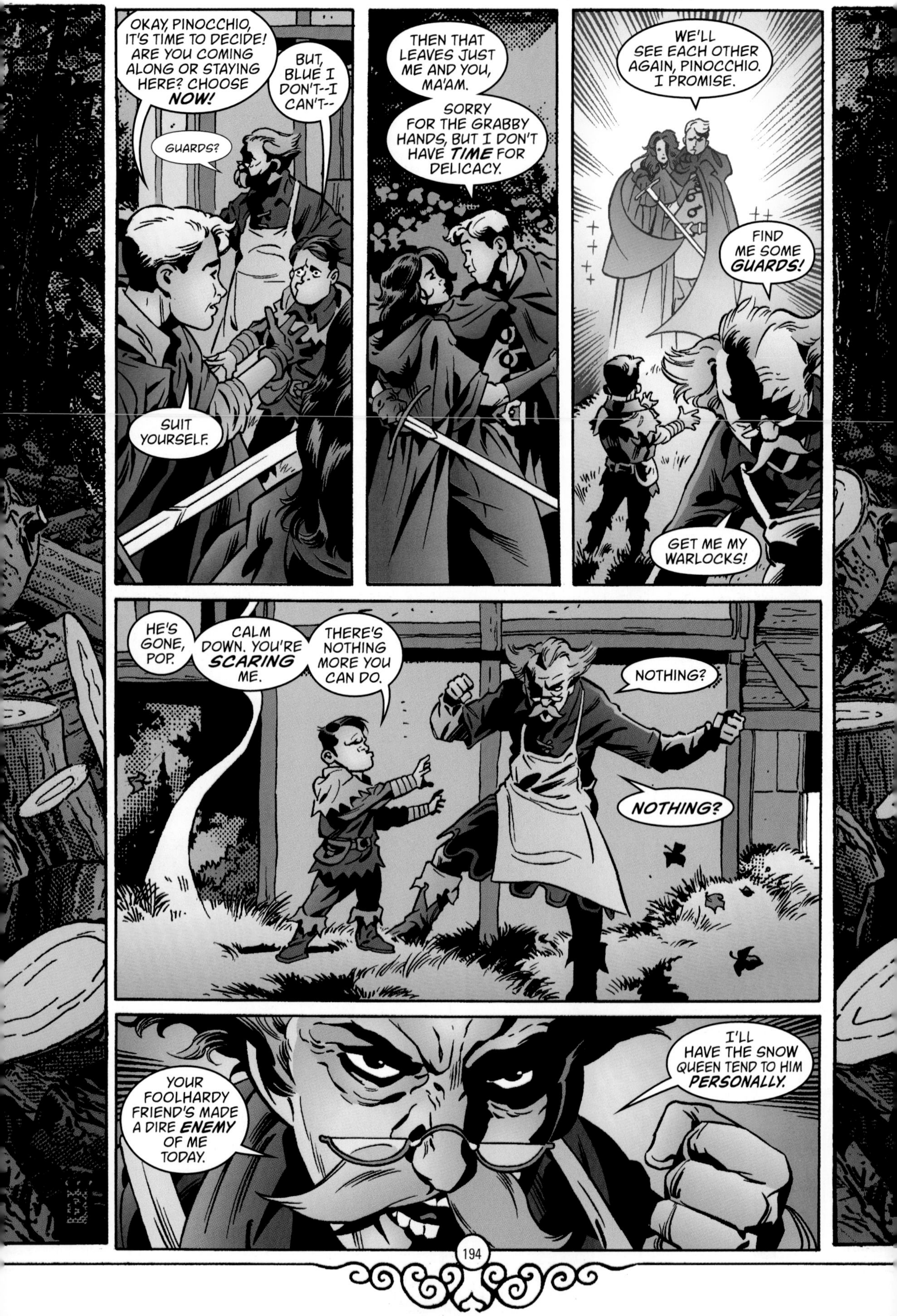
OKAY, PINOCCHIO, IT'S TIME TO DECIDE! ARE YOU COMING ALONG OR STAYING HERE? CHOOSE NOW!
BUT, BLUE I DON'T--I CAN'T--
GUARDS?
SUIT YOURSELF.
THEN THAT LEAVES JUST ME AND YOU, MA'AM.
SORRY FOR THE GRABBY HANDS, BUT I DON'T HAVE TIME FOR DELICACY.
WE'LL SEE EACH OTHER AGAIN, PINOCCHIO. I PROMISE.
FIND ME SOME GUARDS!
GET ME MY WARLOCKS!
HE'S GONE, POP.
CALM DOWN. YOU'RE SCARING ME.
THERE'S NOTHING MORE YOU CAN DO.
NOTHING?
NOTHING?
YOUR FOOLHARDY FRIEND'S MADE A DIRE ENEMY OF ME TODAY.
I'LL HAVE THE SNOW QUEEN TEND TO HIM PERSONALLY.

WILL YOU PLEASE **UNHAND** ME, SIR?!

YOU KILLED THOSE **MEN!**

THEY SORT OF FORCED THE ISSUE. I DIDN'T HAVE ENOUGH TIME TO FIND A LESS **BLOODY** SOLUTION TO OUR DILEMMA.

OUR **WHAT?** I TOLD YOU ONCE BEFORE, I HAVE NO **KNOWLEDGE** OF YOU AND NO BUSINESS WITH YOU!

YEAH, I KNOW. GEPPETTO FINALLY CONVINCED ME THAT YOU AND I NEVER MET. BUT I DID MEET TWO OF YOUR DOPPELGANGERS.

THAT'S WHAT THEY WERE DOING TO ME IN THE WARLOCKS' HALL ALL THOSE TIMES? MAKING **FETCHES** OF ME? THAT'S THE FOULEST SORT OF MAGIC!

TELL ME ABOUT IT.

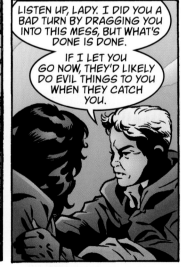

LISTEN UP, LADY. I DID YOU A BAD TURN BY DRAGGING YOU INTO THIS MESS, BUT WHAT'S DONE IS DONE.

IF I LET YOU GO NOW, THEY'D LIKELY DO EVIL THINGS TO YOU WHEN THEY CATCH YOU.

AND THEY **WILL** CATCH YOU.

WHAT DO **YOU** INTEND TO DO TO ME?

FOR BETTER OR WORSE, YOU'LL JUST HAVE TO COME WITH ME TO FABLETOWN. I'M SORRY I COULDN'T OFFER YOU A CHOICE IN THE MATTER.

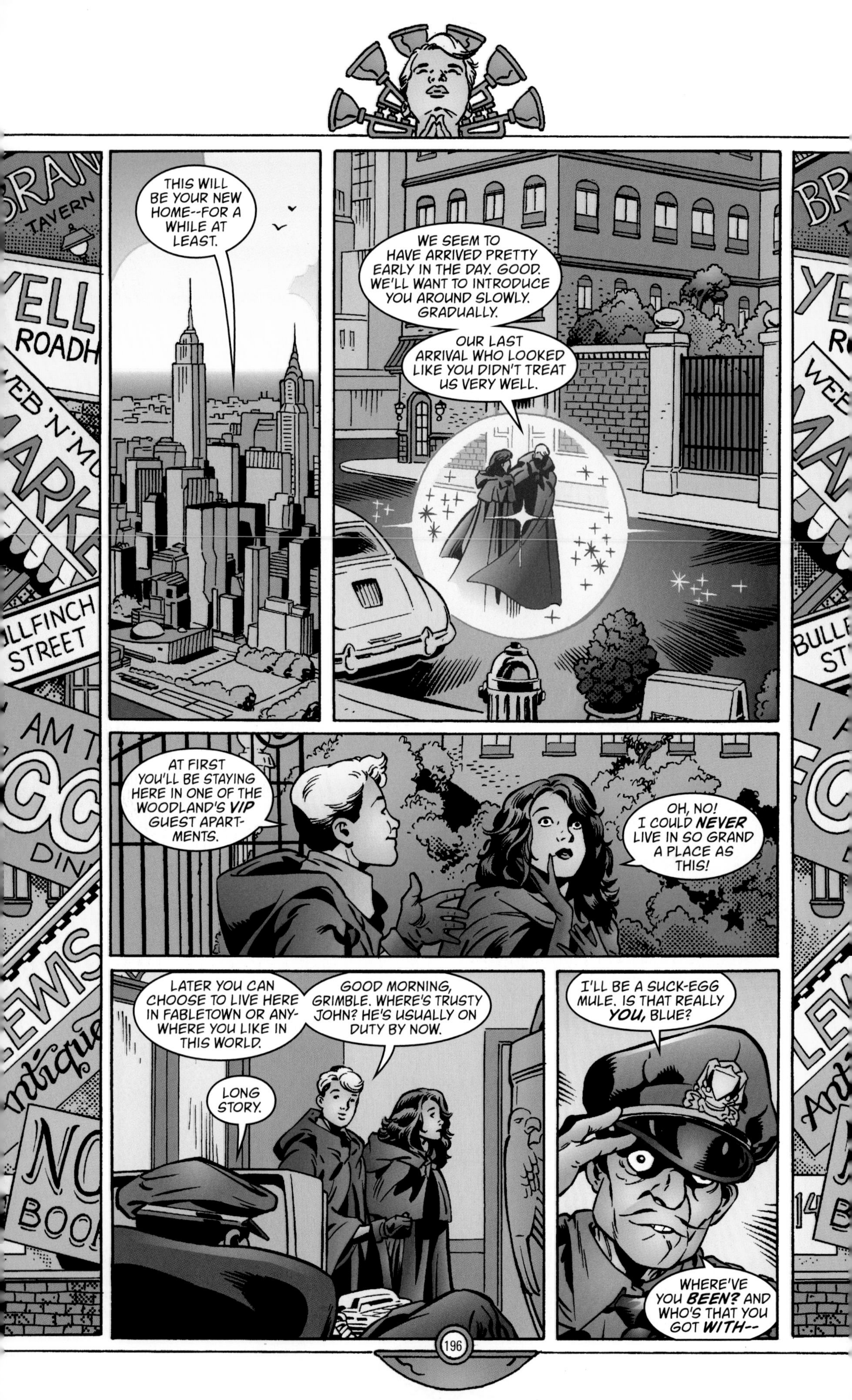
BRAN TAVERN
YELL ROADH
WEB 'N' MU
MARKE
BULLFINCH STREET
THIS WILL BE YOUR NEW HOME--FOR A WHILE AT LEAST.
WE SEEM TO HAVE ARRIVED PRETTY EARLY IN THE DAY. GOOD. WE'LL WANT TO INTRODUCE YOU AROUND SLOWLY. GRADUALLY.
OUR LAST ARRIVAL WHO LOOKED LIKE YOU DIDN'T TREAT US VERY WELL.
AT FIRST YOU'LL BE STAYING HERE IN ONE OF THE WOODLAND'S VIP GUEST APARTMENTS.
OH, NO! I COULD NEVER LIVE IN SO GRAND A PLACE AS THIS!
LATER YOU CAN CHOOSE TO LIVE HERE IN FABLETOWN OR ANYWHERE YOU LIKE IN THIS WORLD.
GOOD MORNING, GRIMBLE. WHERE'S TRUSTY JOHN? HE'S USUALLY ON DUTY BY NOW.
LONG STORY.
I'LL BE A SUCK-EGG MULE. IS THAT REALLY YOU, BLUE?
WHERE'VE YOU BEEN? AND WHO'S THAT YOU GOT WITH--

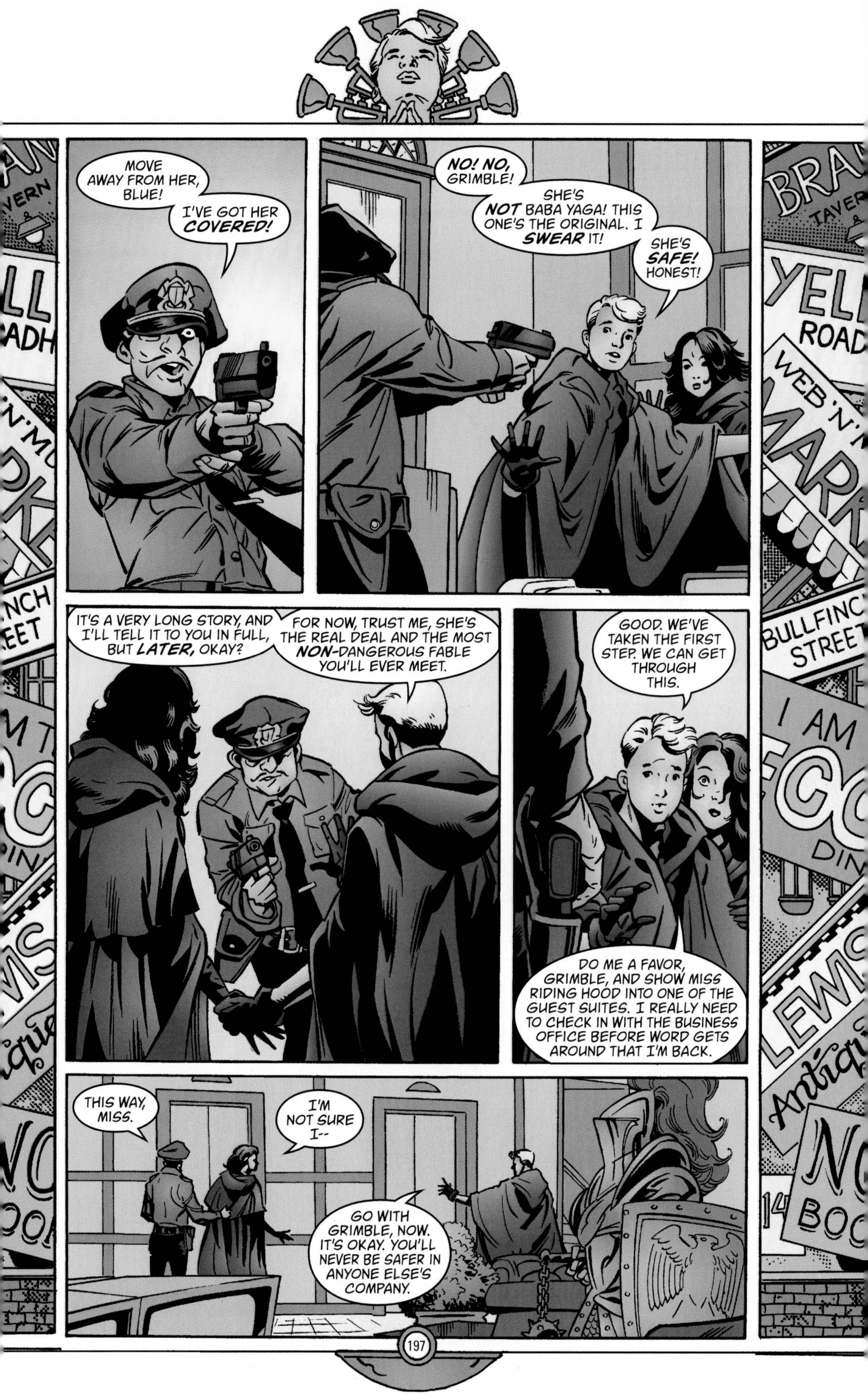

MOVE AWAY FROM HER, BLUE!
I'VE GOT HER COVERED!
NO! NO, GRIMBLE!
SHE'S NOT BABA YAGA! THIS ONE'S THE ORIGINAL. I SWEAR IT!
SHE'S SAFE! HONEST!
IT'S A VERY LONG STORY, AND I'LL TELL IT TO YOU IN FULL, BUT LATER, OKAY?
FOR NOW, TRUST ME, SHE'S THE REAL DEAL AND THE MOST NON-DANGEROUS FABLE YOU'LL EVER MEET.
GOOD. WE'VE TAKEN THE FIRST STEP. WE CAN GET THROUGH THIS.
DO ME A FAVOR, GRIMBLE, AND SHOW MISS RIDING HOOD INTO ONE OF THE GUEST SUITES. I REALLY NEED TO CHECK IN WITH THE BUSINESS OFFICE BEFORE WORD GETS AROUND THAT I'M BACK.
THIS WAY, MISS.
I'M NOT SURE I--
GO WITH GRIMBLE, NOW. IT'S OKAY. YOU'LL NEVER BE SAFER IN ANYONE ELSE'S COMPANY.

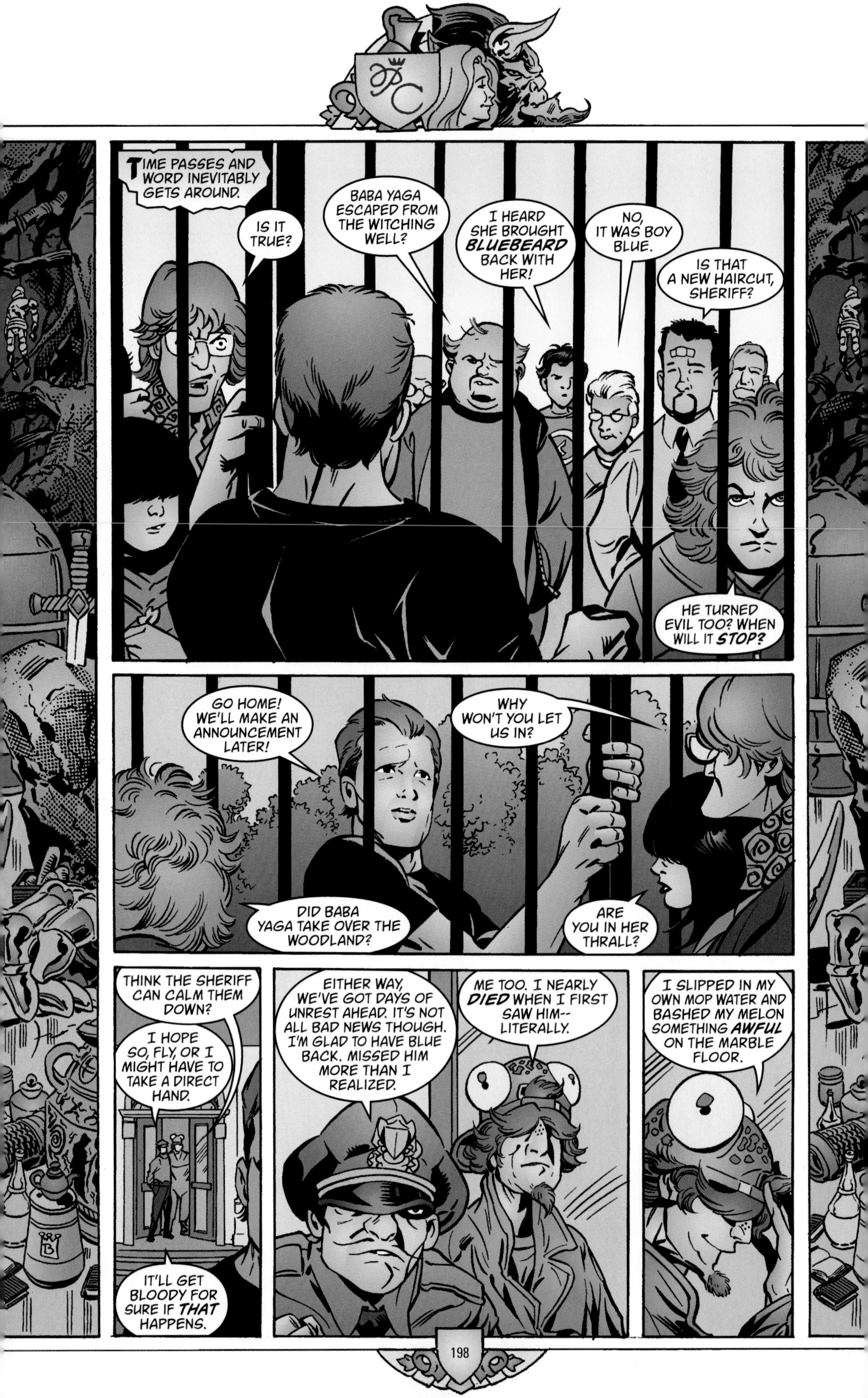
TIME PASSES AND WORD INEVITABLY GETS AROUND.
IS IT TRUE?
BABA YAGA ESCAPED FROM THE WITCHING WELL?
I HEARD SHE BROUGHT BLUEBEARD BACK WITH HER!
NO, IT WAS BOY BLUE.
IS THAT A NEW HAIRCUT, SHERIFF?
HE TURNED EVIL TOO? WHEN WILL IT STOP?
GO HOME! WE'LL MAKE AN ANNOUNCEMENT LATER!
WHY WON'T YOU LET US IN?
DID BABA YAGA TAKE OVER THE WOODLAND?
ARE YOU IN HER THRALL?
THINK THE SHERIFF CAN CALM THEM DOWN?
I HOPE SO, FLY, OR I MIGHT HAVE TO TAKE A DIRECT HAND.
IT'LL GET BLOODY FOR SURE IF THAT HAPPENS.
EITHER WAY, WE'VE GOT DAYS OF UNREST AHEAD. IT'S NOT ALL BAD NEWS THOUGH. I'M GLAD TO HAVE BLUE BACK. MISSED HIM MORE THAN I REALIZED.
ME TOO. I NEARLY DIED WHEN I FIRST SAW HIM--LITERALLY.
I SLIPPED IN MY OWN MOP WATER AND BASHED MY MELON SOMETHING AWFUL ON THE MARBLE FLOOR.

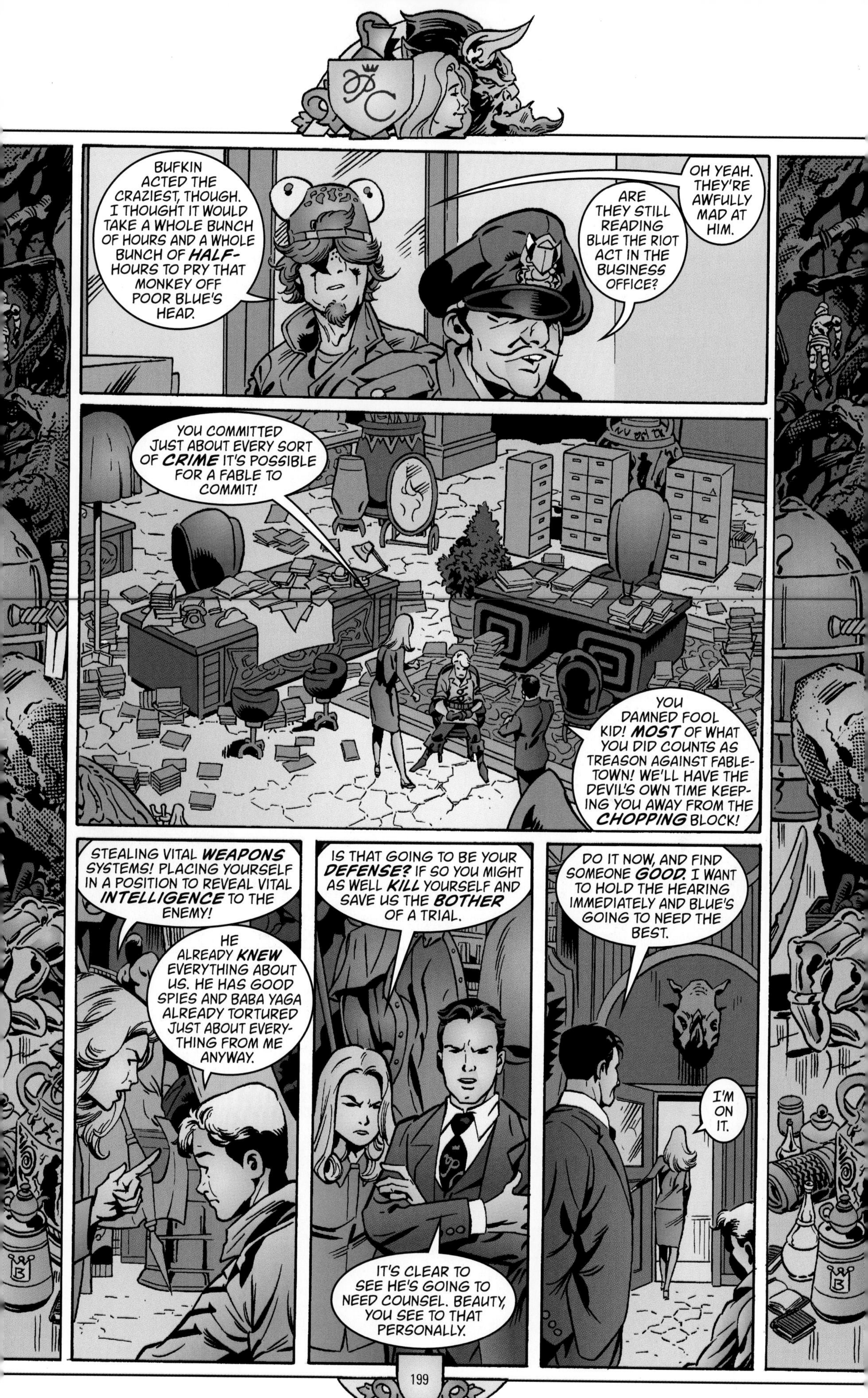
BUFKIN ACTED THE CRAZIEST, THOUGH. I THOUGHT IT WOULD TAKE A WHOLE BUNCH OF HOURS AND A WHOLE BUNCH OF HALF-HOURS TO PRY THAT MONKEY OFF POOR BLUE'S HEAD.
ARE THEY STILL READING BLUE THE RIOT ACT IN THE BUSINESS OFFICE?
OH YEAH. THEY'RE AWFULLY MAD AT HIM.
YOU COMMITTED JUST ABOUT EVERY SORT OF CRIME IT'S POSSIBLE FOR A FABLE TO COMMIT!
YOU DAMNED FOOL KID! MOST OF WHAT YOU DID COUNTS AS TREASON AGAINST FABLE-TOWN! WE'LL HAVE THE DEVIL'S OWN TIME KEEP-ING YOU AWAY FROM THE CHOPPING BLOCK!
STEALING VITAL WEAPONS SYSTEMS! PLACING YOURSELF IN A POSITION TO REVEAL VITAL INTELLIGENCE TO THE ENEMY!
HE ALREADY KNEW EVERYTHING ABOUT US. HE HAS GOOD SPIES AND BABA YAGA ALREADY TORTURED JUST ABOUT EVERY-THING FROM ME ANYWAY.
IS THAT GOING TO BE YOUR DEFENSE? IF SO YOU MIGHT AS WELL KILL YOURSELF AND SAVE US THE BOTHER OF A TRIAL.
IT'S CLEAR TO SEE HE'S GOING TO NEED COUNSEL. BEAUTY, YOU SEE TO THAT PERSONALLY.
DO IT NOW, AND FIND SOMEONE GOOD. I WANT TO HOLD THE HEARING IMMEDIATELY AND BLUE'S GOING TO NEED THE BEST.
I'M ON IT.

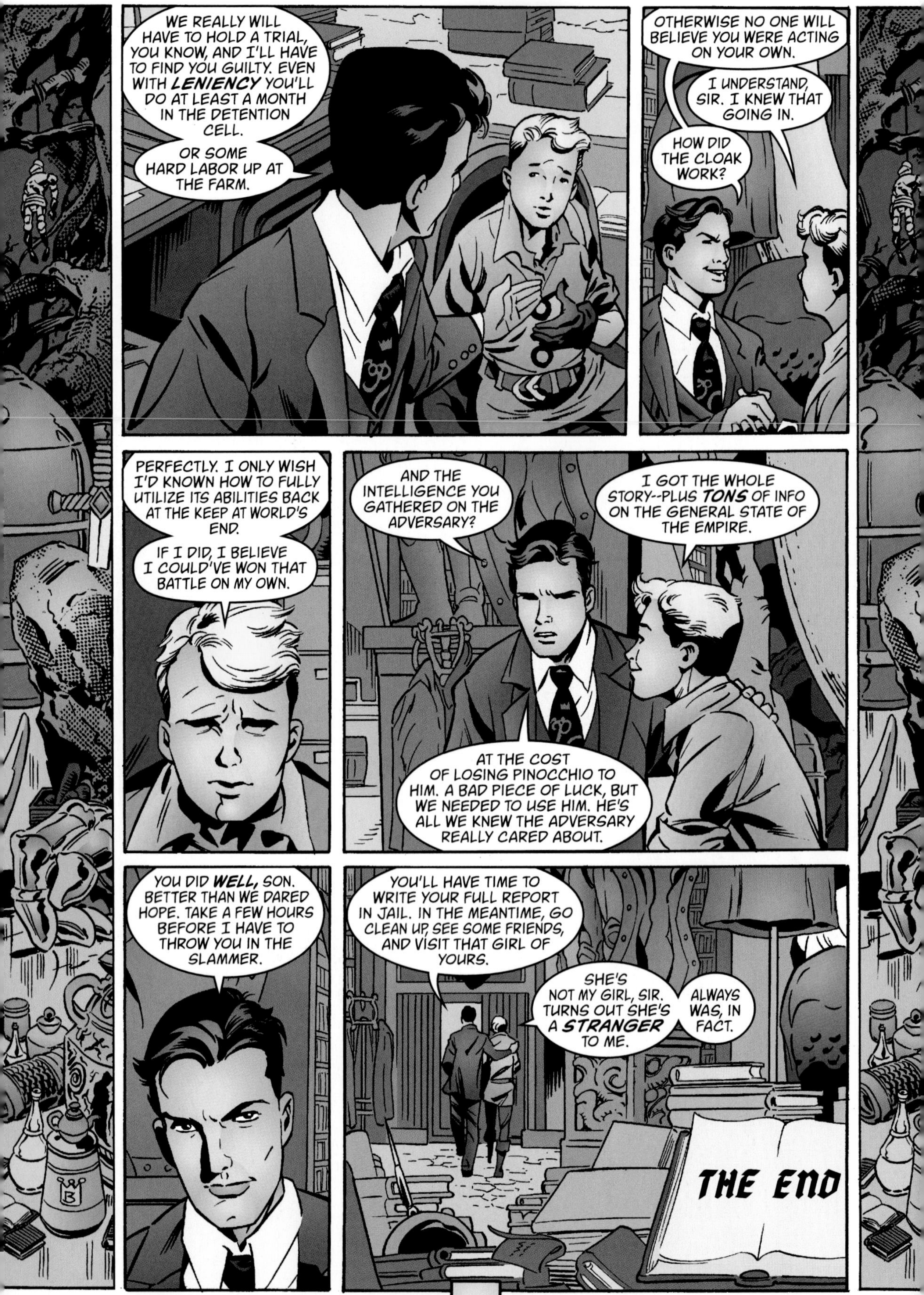

WE REALLY WILL HAVE TO HOLD A TRIAL, YOU KNOW, AND I'LL HAVE TO FIND YOU GUILTY. EVEN WITH LENIENCY YOU'LL DO AT LEAST A MONTH IN THE DETENTION CELL.
OR SOME HARD LABOR UP AT THE FARM.
OTHERWISE NO ONE WILL BELIEVE YOU WERE ACTING ON YOUR OWN.
I UNDERSTAND, SIR. I KNEW THAT GOING IN.
HOW DID THE CLOAK WORK?
PERFECTLY. I ONLY WISH I'D KNOWN HOW TO FULLY UTILIZE ITS ABILITIES BACK AT THE KEEP AT WORLD'S END.
IF I DID, I BELIEVE I COULD'VE WON THAT BATTLE ON MY OWN.
AND THE INTELLIGENCE YOU GATHERED ON THE ADVERSARY?
I GOT THE WHOLE STORY--PLUS TONS OF INFO ON THE GENERAL STATE OF THE EMPIRE.
AT THE COST OF LOSING PINOCCHIO TO HIM. A BAD PIECE OF LUCK, BUT WE NEEDED TO USE HIM. HE'S ALL WE KNEW THE ADVERSARY REALLY CARED ABOUT.
YOU DID WELL, SON. BETTER THAN WE DARED HOPE. TAKE A FEW HOURS BEFORE I HAVE TO THROW YOU IN THE SLAMMER.
YOU'LL HAVE TIME TO WRITE YOUR FULL REPORT IN JAIL. IN THE MEANTIME, GO CLEAN UP, SEE SOME FRIENDS, AND VISIT THAT GIRL OF YOURS.
SHE'S NOT MY GIRL, SIR. TURNS OUT SHE'S A STRANGER TO ME.
ALWAYS WAS, IN FACT.
THE END

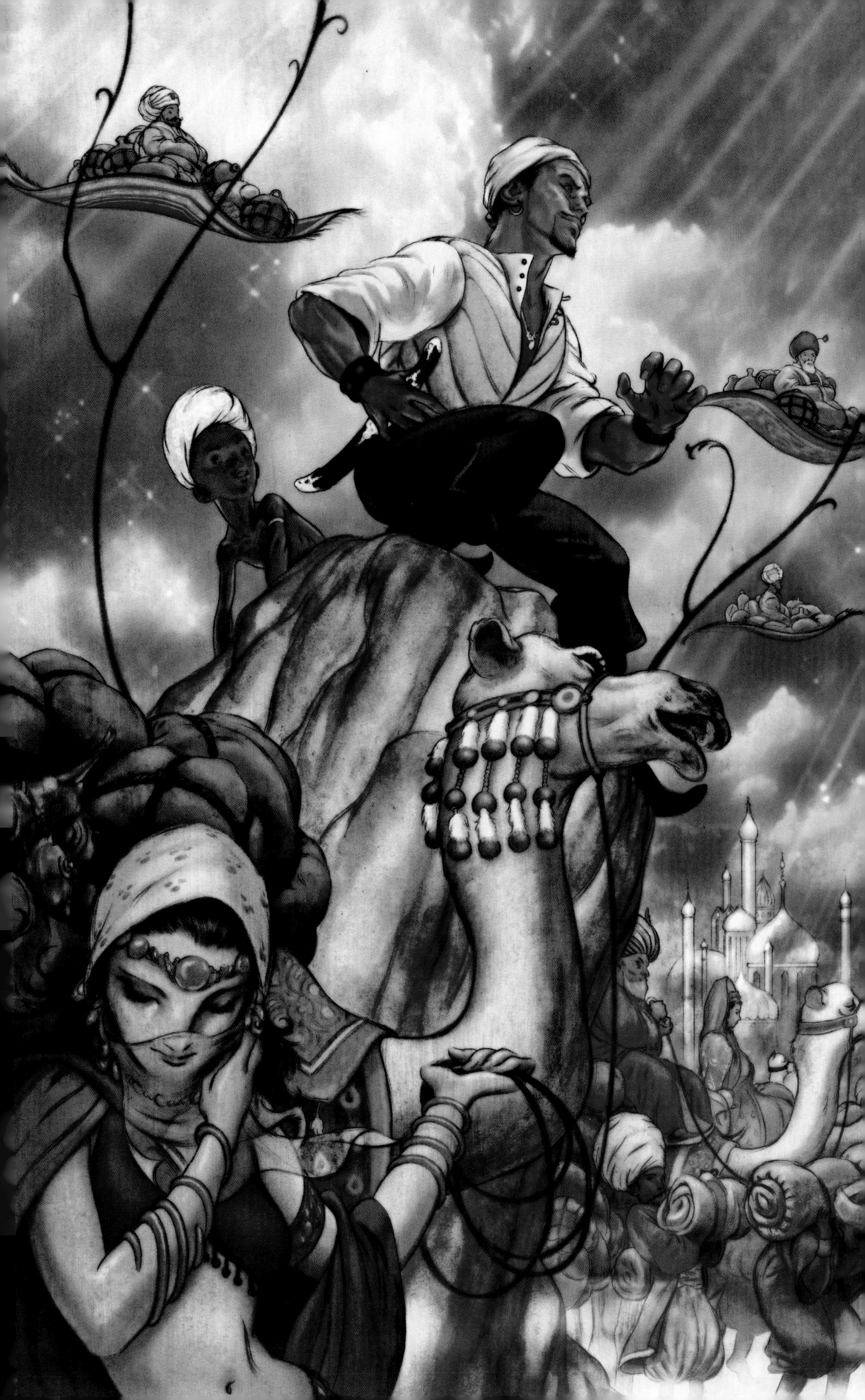

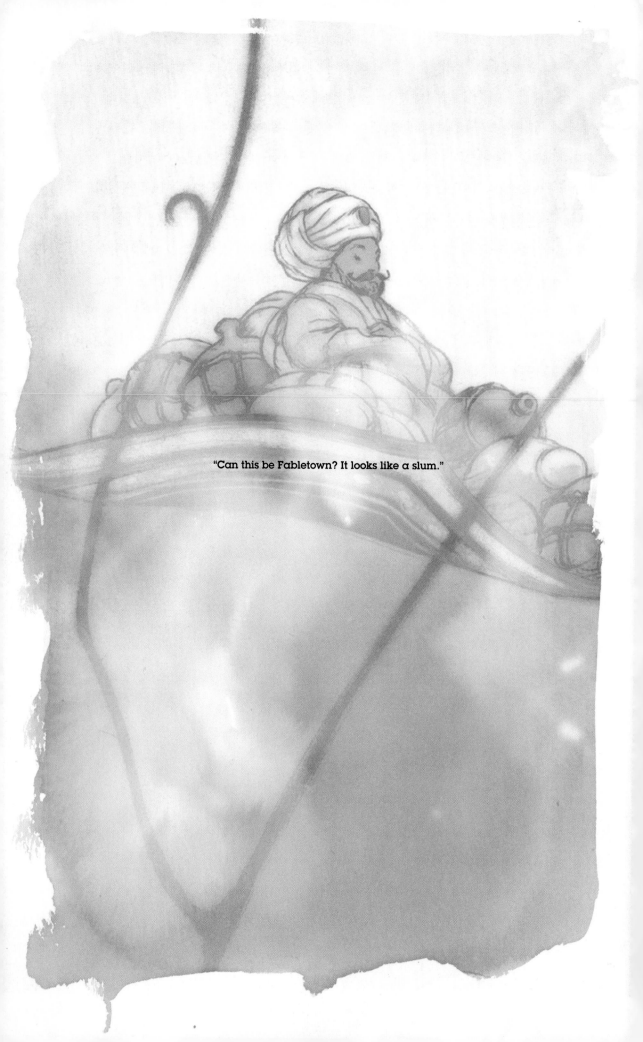

"Can this be Fabletown? It looks like a slum."

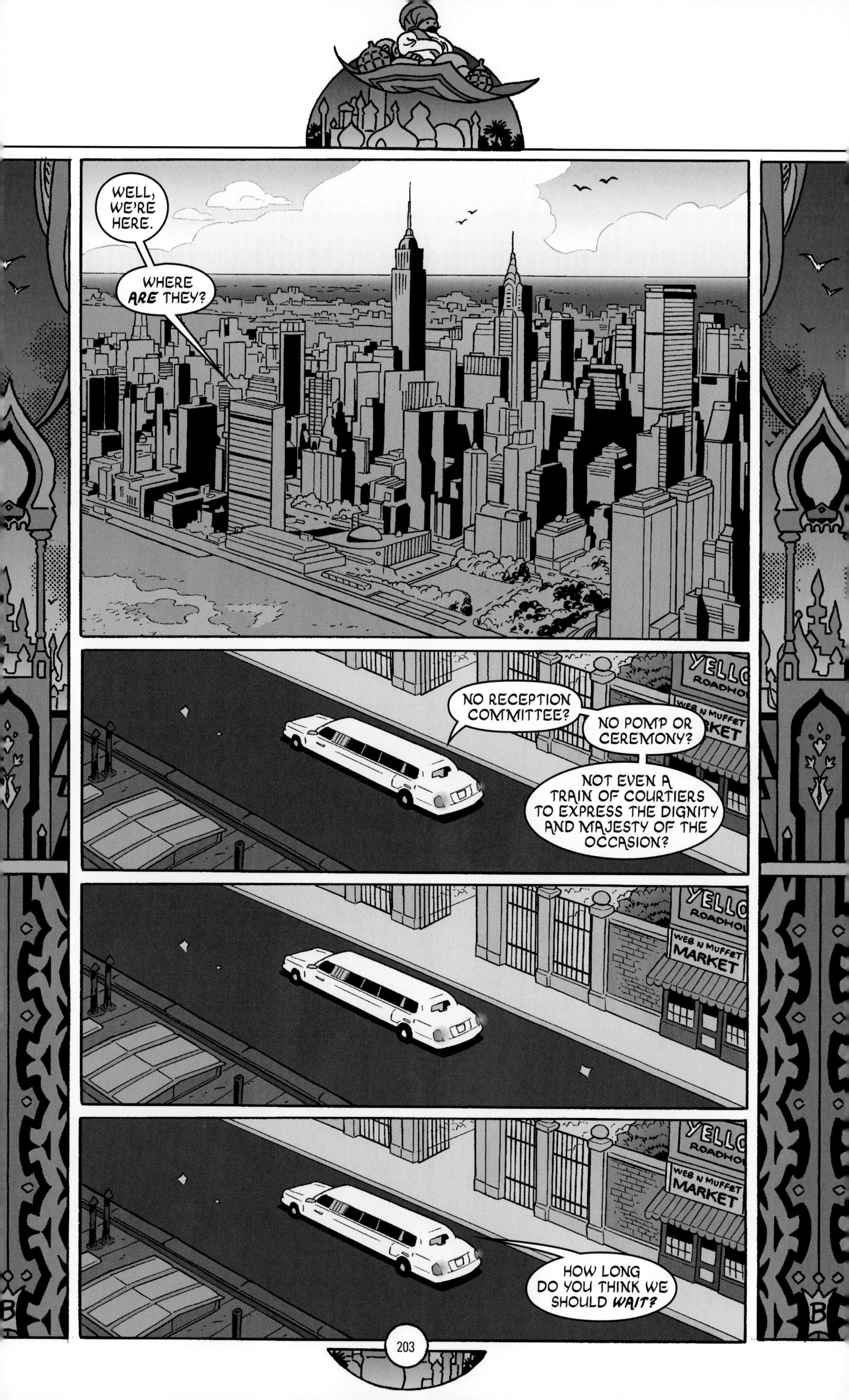
WELL, WE'RE HERE.
WHERE *ARE* THEY?
NO RECEPTION COMMITTEE?
NO POMP OR CEREMONY?
NOT EVEN A TRAIN OF COURTIERS TO EXPRESS THE DIGNITY AND MAJESTY OF THE OCCASION?
MARKET
HOW LONG DO YOU THINK WE SHOULD *WAIT?*

BROKEN ENGLISH
~❖~ Chapter ONE of ~❖~
Arabian Nights (and days)

~❖~~❖~~❖~~❖~~❖~~❖~~❖~~❖~~❖~~❖~~❖~

BILL WILLINGHAM: WRITER-CREATOR	MARK BUCKINGHAM: PENCILLER	STEVE LEIALOHA: INKER	DANIEL VOZZO: COLORS
JAMES JEAN: COVER ART	TODD KLEIN: LETTERS	ANGELA RUFINO ASST. EDITOR	SHELLY BOND EDITOR

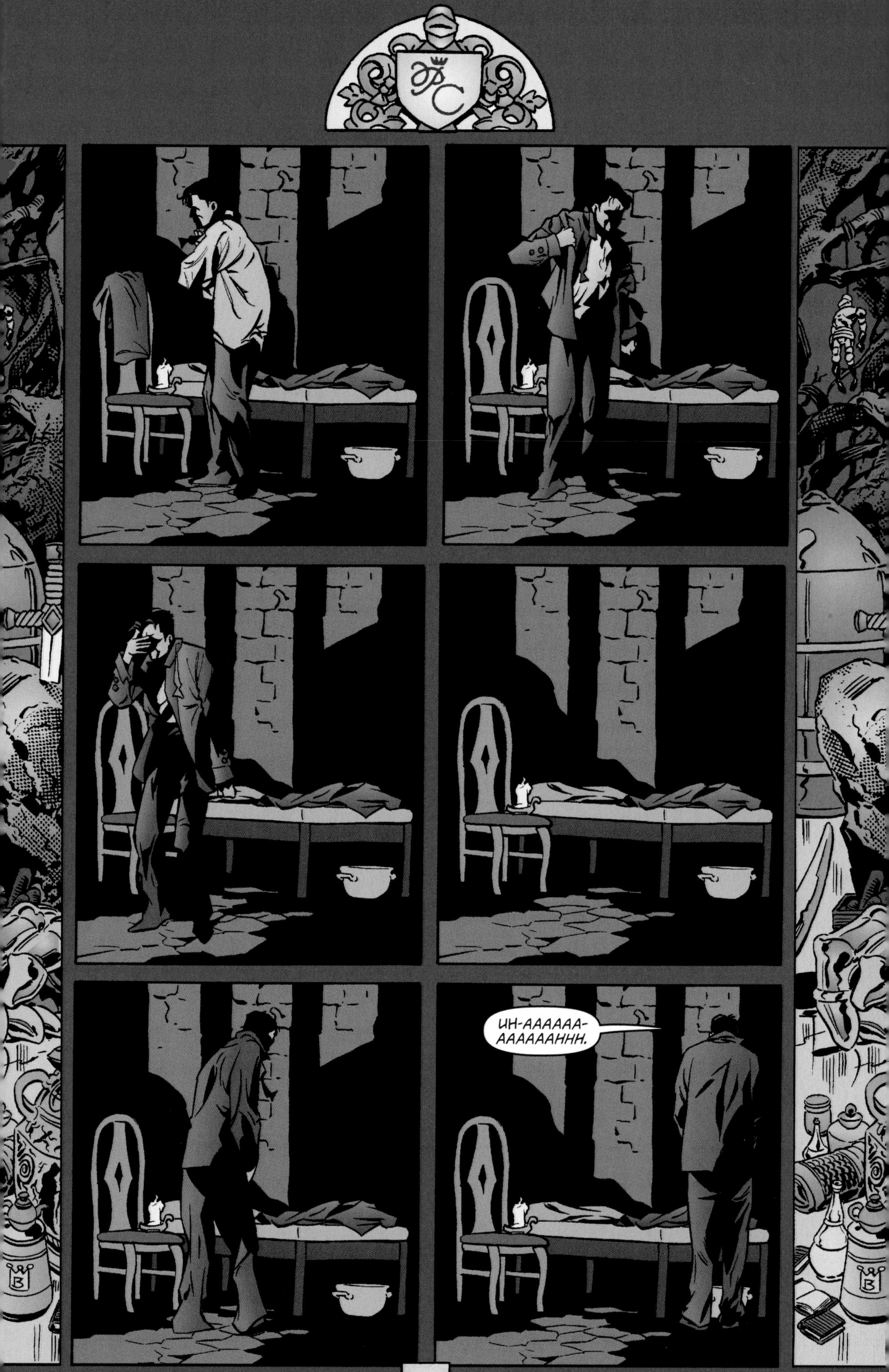
UH-AAAAAA-AAAAAAAHHH.

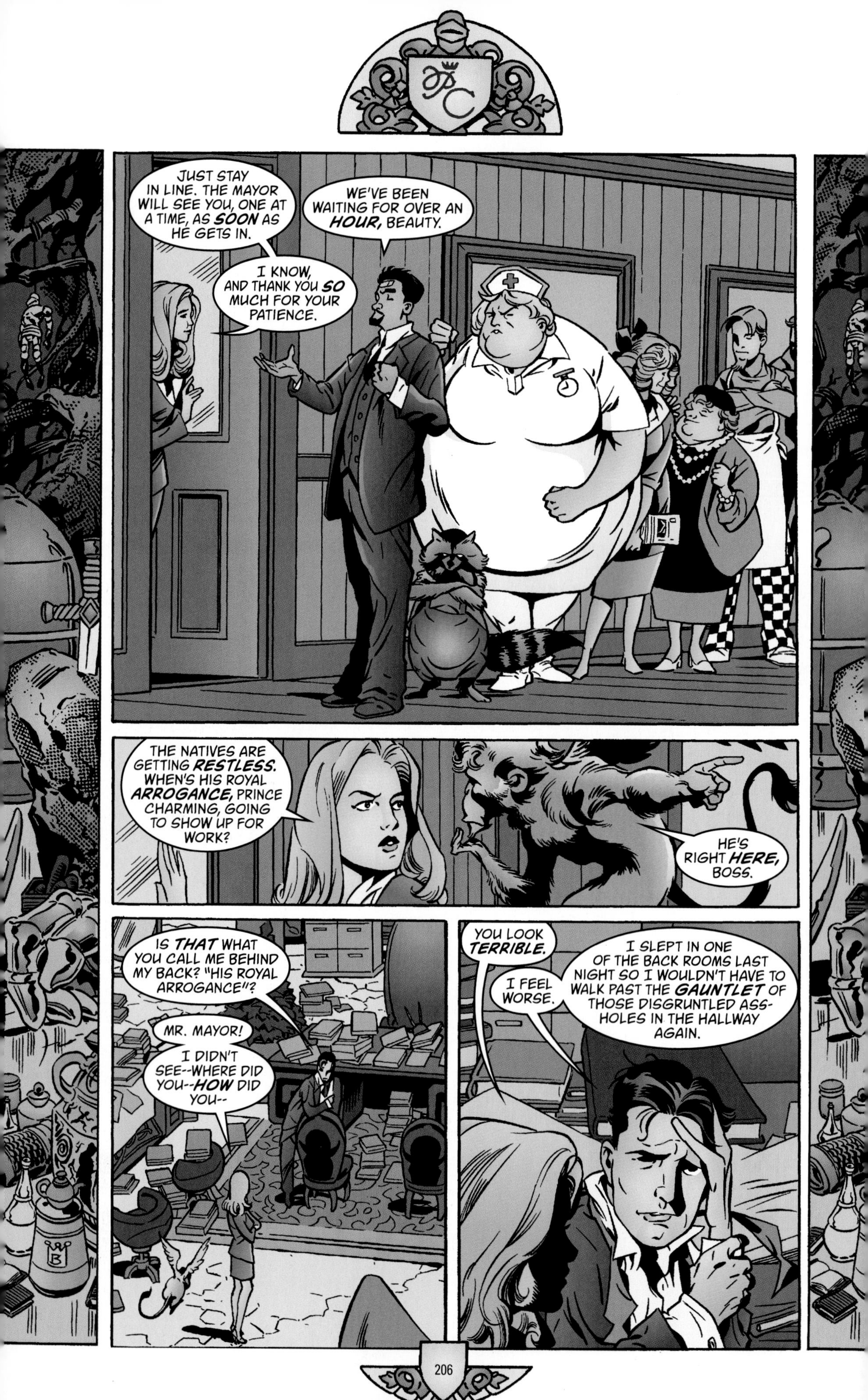
JUST STAY IN LINE. THE MAYOR WILL SEE YOU, ONE AT A TIME, AS SOON AS HE GETS IN.
WE'VE BEEN WAITING FOR OVER AN HOUR, BEAUTY.
I KNOW, AND THANK YOU SO MUCH FOR YOUR PATIENCE.
THE NATIVES ARE GETTING RESTLESS. WHEN'S HIS ROYAL ARROGANCE, PRINCE CHARMING, GOING TO SHOW UP FOR WORK?
HE'S RIGHT HERE, BOSS.
IS THAT WHAT YOU CALL ME BEHIND MY BACK? "HIS ROYAL ARROGANCE"?
MR. MAYOR!
I DIDN'T SEE--WHERE DID YOU--HOW DID YOU--
YOU LOOK TERRIBLE.
I FEEL WORSE.
I SLEPT IN ONE OF THE BACK ROOMS LAST NIGHT SO I WOULDN'T HAVE TO WALK PAST THE GAUNTLET OF THOSE DISGRUNTLED ASS-HOLES IN THE HALLWAY AGAIN.

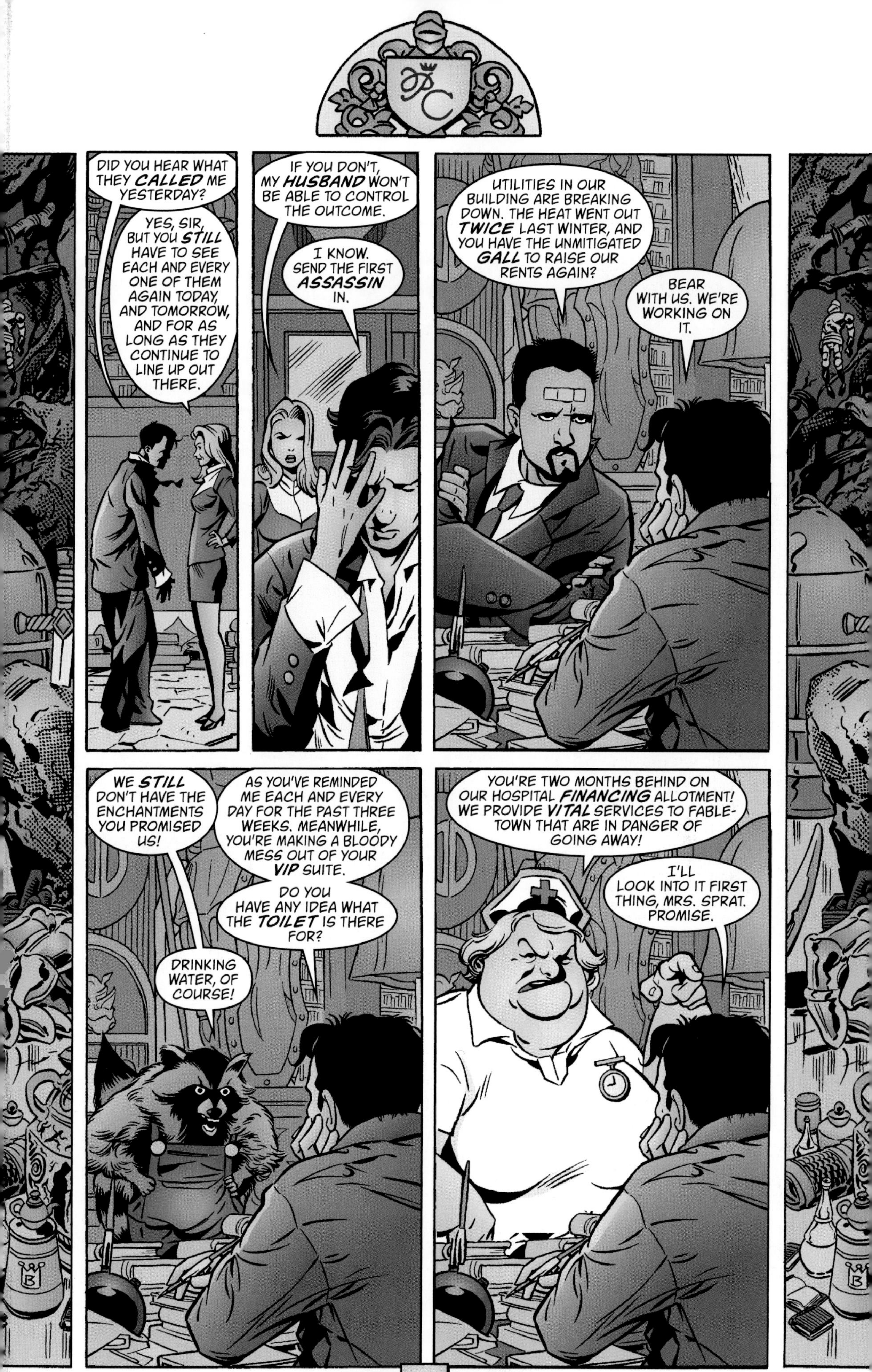
DID YOU HEAR WHAT THEY CALLED ME YESTERDAY?
YES, SIR, BUT YOU STILL HAVE TO SEE EACH AND EVERY ONE OF THEM AGAIN TODAY, AND TOMORROW, AND FOR AS LONG AS THEY CONTINUE TO LINE UP OUT THERE.
IF YOU DON'T, MY HUSBAND WON'T BE ABLE TO CONTROL THE OUTCOME.
I KNOW. SEND THE FIRST ASSASSIN IN.
UTILITIES IN OUR BUILDING ARE BREAKING DOWN. THE HEAT WENT OUT TWICE LAST WINTER, AND YOU HAVE THE UNMITIGATED GALL TO RAISE OUR RENTS AGAIN?
BEAR WITH US. WE'RE WORKING ON IT.
WE STILL DON'T HAVE THE ENCHANTMENTS YOU PROMISED US!
AS YOU'VE REMINDED ME EACH AND EVERY DAY FOR THE PAST THREE WEEKS. MEANWHILE, YOU'RE MAKING A BLOODY MESS OUT OF YOUR VIP SUITE.
DO YOU HAVE ANY IDEA WHAT THE TOILET IS THERE FOR?
DRINKING WATER, OF COURSE!
YOU'RE TWO MONTHS BEHIND ON OUR HOSPITAL FINANCING ALLOTMENT! WE PROVIDE VITAL SERVICES TO FABLE-TOWN THAT ARE IN DANGER OF GOING AWAY!
I'LL LOOK INTO IT FIRST THING, MRS. SPRAT. PROMISE.

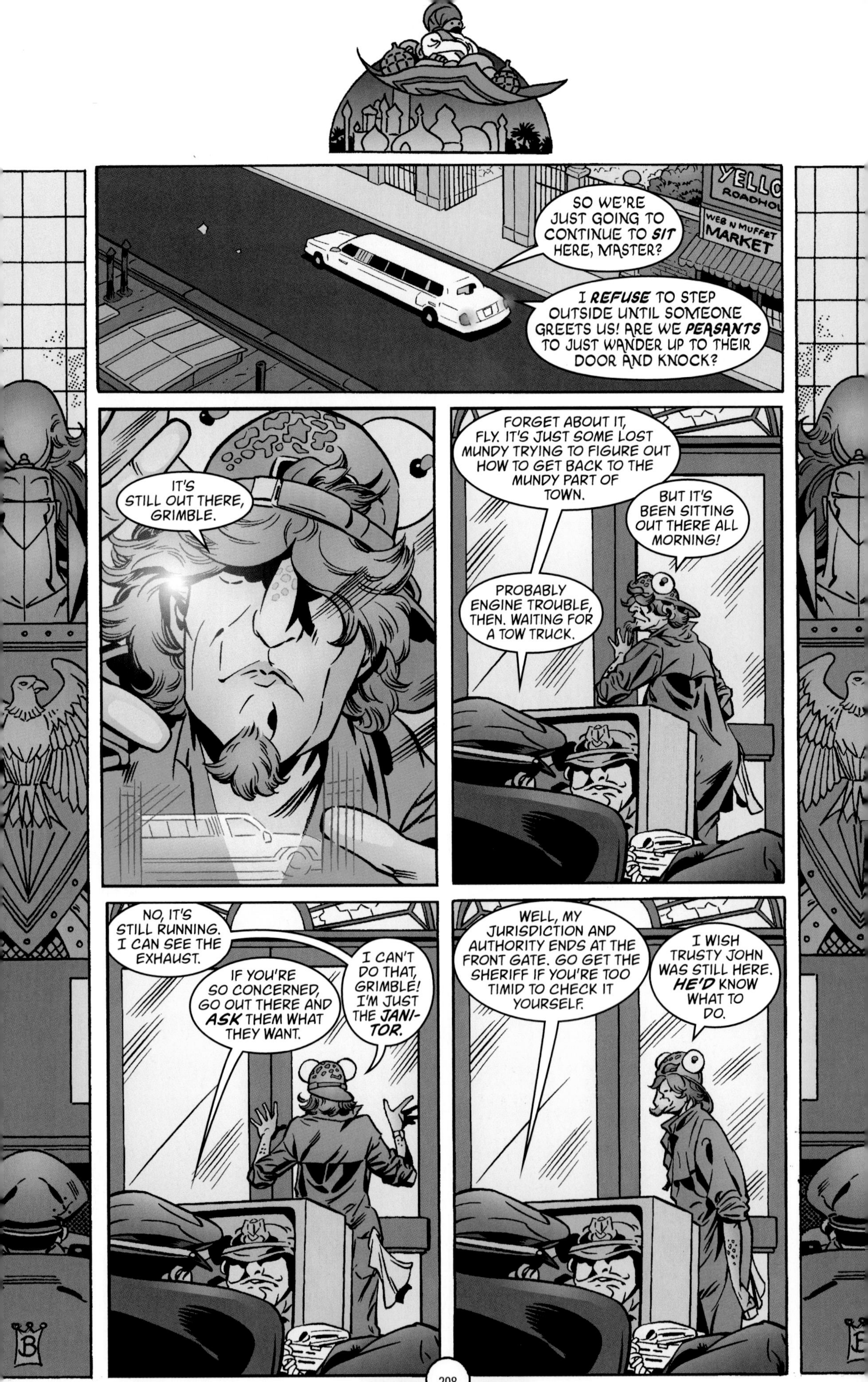
WEB N MUFFET
MARKET
SO WE'RE JUST GOING TO CONTINUE TO *SIT* HERE, MASTER?
I *REFUSE* TO STEP OUTSIDE UNTIL SOMEONE GREETS US! ARE WE *PEASANTS* TO JUST WANDER UP TO THEIR DOOR AND KNOCK?
IT'S STILL OUT THERE, GRIMBLE.
FORGET ABOUT IT, FLY. IT'S JUST SOME LOST MUNDY TRYING TO FIGURE OUT HOW TO GET BACK TO THE MUNDY PART OF TOWN.
BUT IT'S BEEN SITTING OUT THERE ALL MORNING!
PROBABLY ENGINE TROUBLE, THEN. WAITING FOR A TOW TRUCK.
NO, IT'S STILL RUNNING. I CAN SEE THE EXHAUST.
IF YOU'RE SO CONCERNED, GO OUT THERE AND *ASK* THEM WHAT THEY WANT.
I CAN'T DO THAT, GRIMBLE! I'M JUST THE *JANITOR.*
WELL, MY JURISDICTION AND AUTHORITY ENDS AT THE FRONT GATE. GO GET THE SHERIFF IF YOU'RE TOO TIMID TO CHECK IT YOURSELF.
I WISH TRUSTY JOHN WAS STILL HERE. *HE'D* KNOW WHAT TO DO.

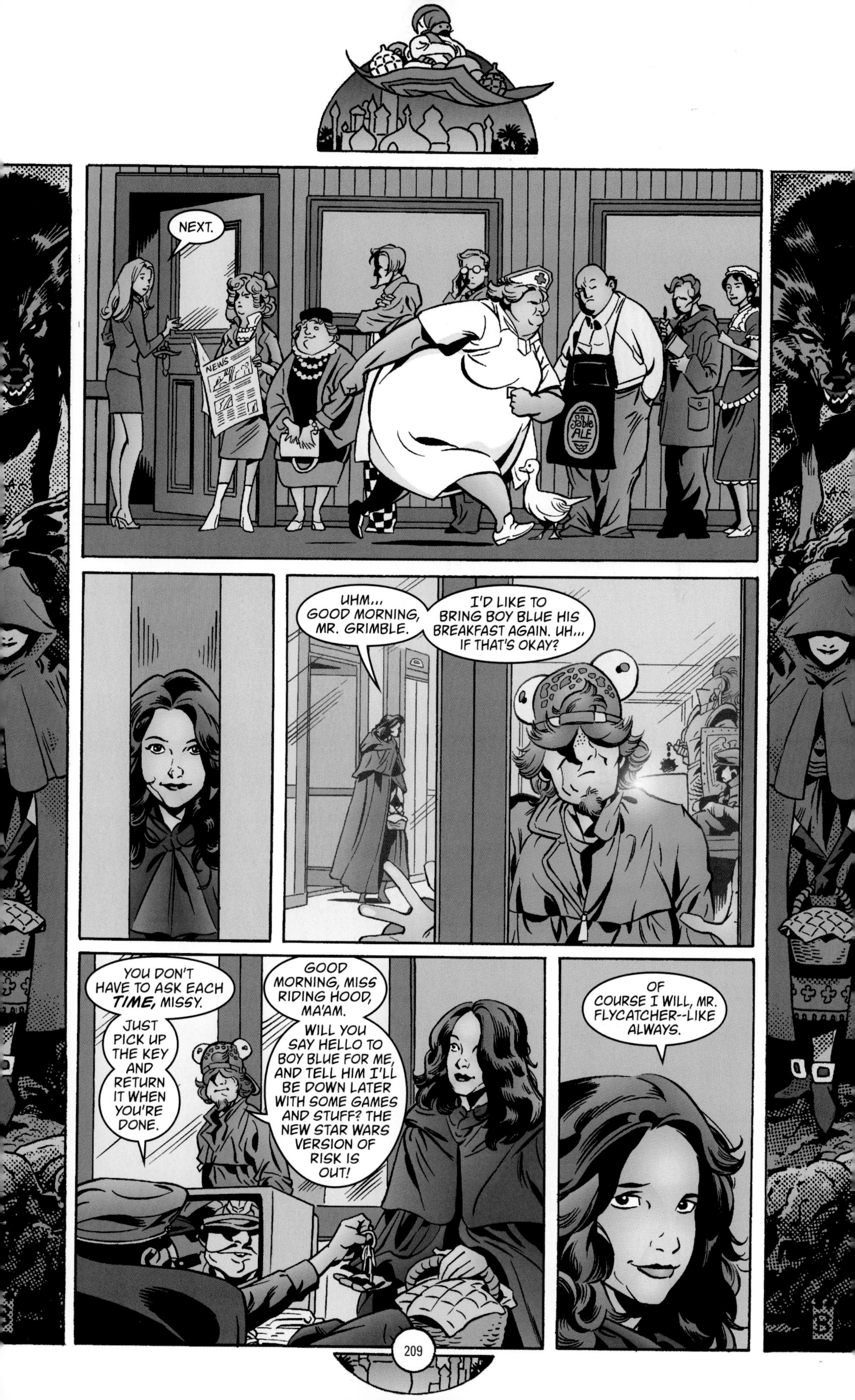

NEXT.
NEWS
Sable ALE
UHM... GOOD MORNING, MR. GRIMBLE.
I'D LIKE TO BRING BOY BLUE HIS BREAKFAST AGAIN. UH... IF THAT'S OKAY?
YOU DON'T HAVE TO ASK EACH *TIME,* MISSY.
JUST PICK UP THE KEY AND RETURN IT WHEN YOU'RE DONE.
GOOD MORNING, MISS RIDING HOOD, MA'AM.
WILL YOU SAY HELLO TO BOY BLUE FOR ME, AND TELL HIM I'LL BE DOWN LATER WITH SOME GAMES AND STUFF? THE NEW STAR WARS VERSION OF RISK IS OUT!
OF COURSE I WILL, MR. FLYCATCHER--LIKE ALWAYS.

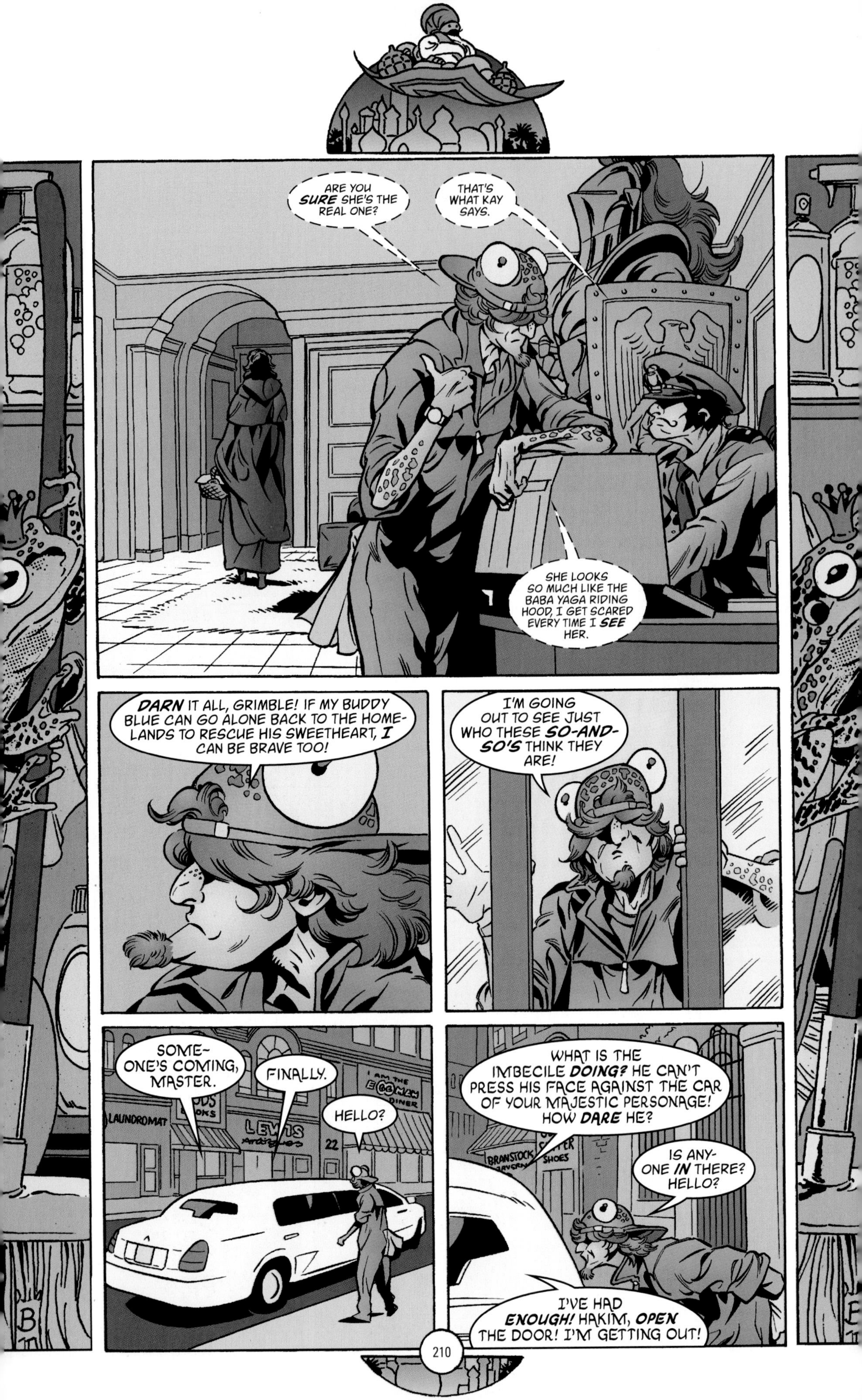

ARE YOU SURE SHE'S THE REAL ONE?
THAT'S WHAT KAY SAYS.
SHE LOOKS SO MUCH LIKE THE BABA YAGA RIDING HOOD, I GET SCARED EVERY TIME I SEE HER.
DARN IT ALL, GRIMBLE! IF MY BUDDY BLUE CAN GO ALONE BACK TO THE HOMELANDS TO RESCUE HIS SWEETHEART, I CAN BE BRAVE TOO!
I'M GOING OUT TO SEE JUST WHO THESE SO-AND-SO'S THINK THEY ARE!
SOMEONE'S COMING, MASTER.
FINALLY.
HELLO?
LAUNDROMAT
WHAT IS THE IMBECILE DOING? HE CAN'T PRESS HIS FACE AGAINST THE CAR OF YOUR MAJESTIC PERSONAGE! HOW DARE HE?
IS ANYONE IN THERE? HELLO?
I'VE HAD ENOUGH! HAKIM, OPEN THE DOOR! I'M GETTING OUT!

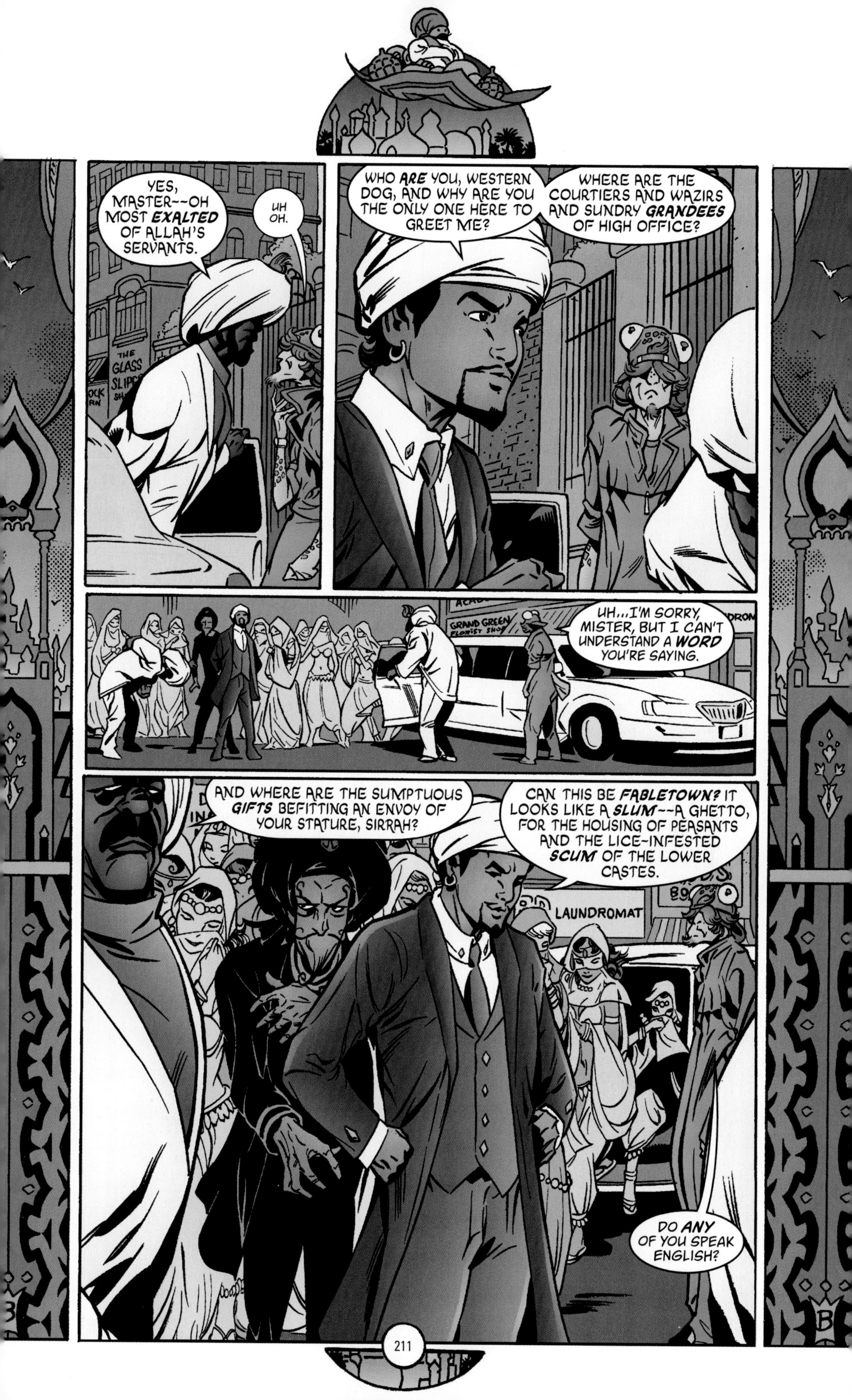
YES, MASTER--OH MOST EXALTED OF ALLAH'S SERVANTS.
UH OH.
THE GLASS SLIPP
WHO ARE YOU, WESTERN DOG, AND WHY ARE YOU THE ONLY ONE HERE TO GREET ME?
WHERE ARE THE COURTIERS AND WAZIRS AND SUNDRY GRANDEES OF HIGH OFFICE?
GRAND GREEN FLORIST SHOP
UH...I'M SORRY, MISTER, BUT I CAN'T UNDERSTAND A WORD YOU'RE SAYING.
AND WHERE ARE THE SUMPTUOUS GIFTS BEFITTING AN ENVOY OF YOUR STATURE, SIRRAH?
CAN THIS BE FABLETOWN? IT LOOKS LIKE A SLUM--A GHETTO, FOR THE HOUSING OF PEASANTS AND THE LICE-INFESTED SCUM OF THE LOWER CASTES.
LAUNDROMAT
DO ANY OF YOU SPEAK ENGLISH?

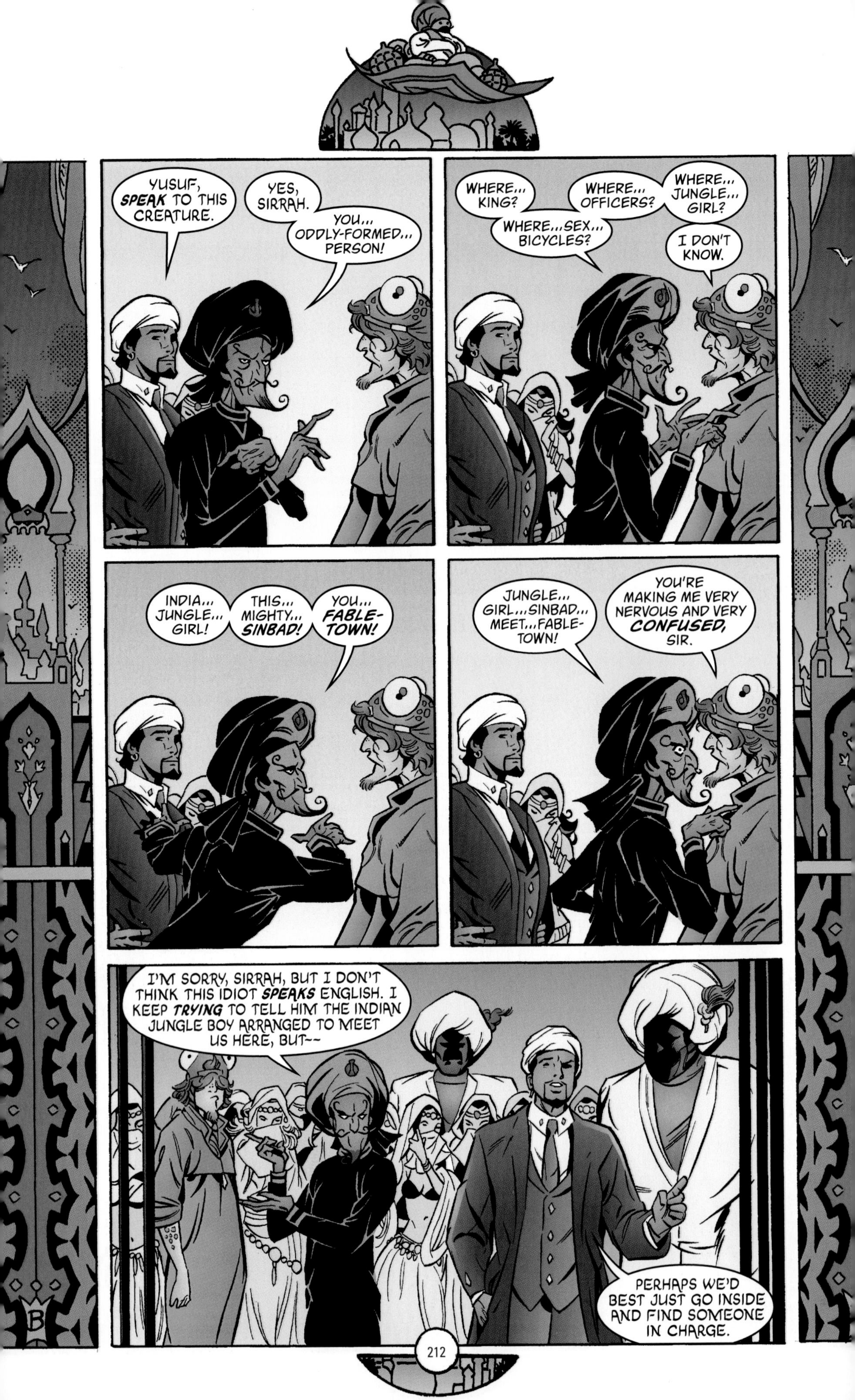
YUSUF, SPEAK TO THIS CREATURE.
YES, SIRRAH.
YOU... ODDLY-FORMED... PERSON!
WHERE... KING?
WHERE... SEX... BICYCLES?
WHERE... OFFICERS?
WHERE... JUNGLE... GIRL?
I DON'T KNOW.
INDIA... JUNGLE... GIRL!
THIS... MIGHTY... SINBAD!
YOU... FABLE-TOWN!
JUNGLE... GIRL... SINBAD... MEET... FABLE-TOWN!
YOU'RE MAKING ME VERY NERVOUS AND VERY CONFUSED, SIR.
I'M SORRY, SIRRAH, BUT I DON'T THINK THIS IDIOT SPEAKS ENGLISH. I KEEP TRYING TO TELL HIM THE INDIAN JUNGLE BOY ARRANGED TO MEET US HERE, BUT--
PERHAPS WE'D BEST JUST GO INSIDE AND FIND SOMEONE IN CHARGE.

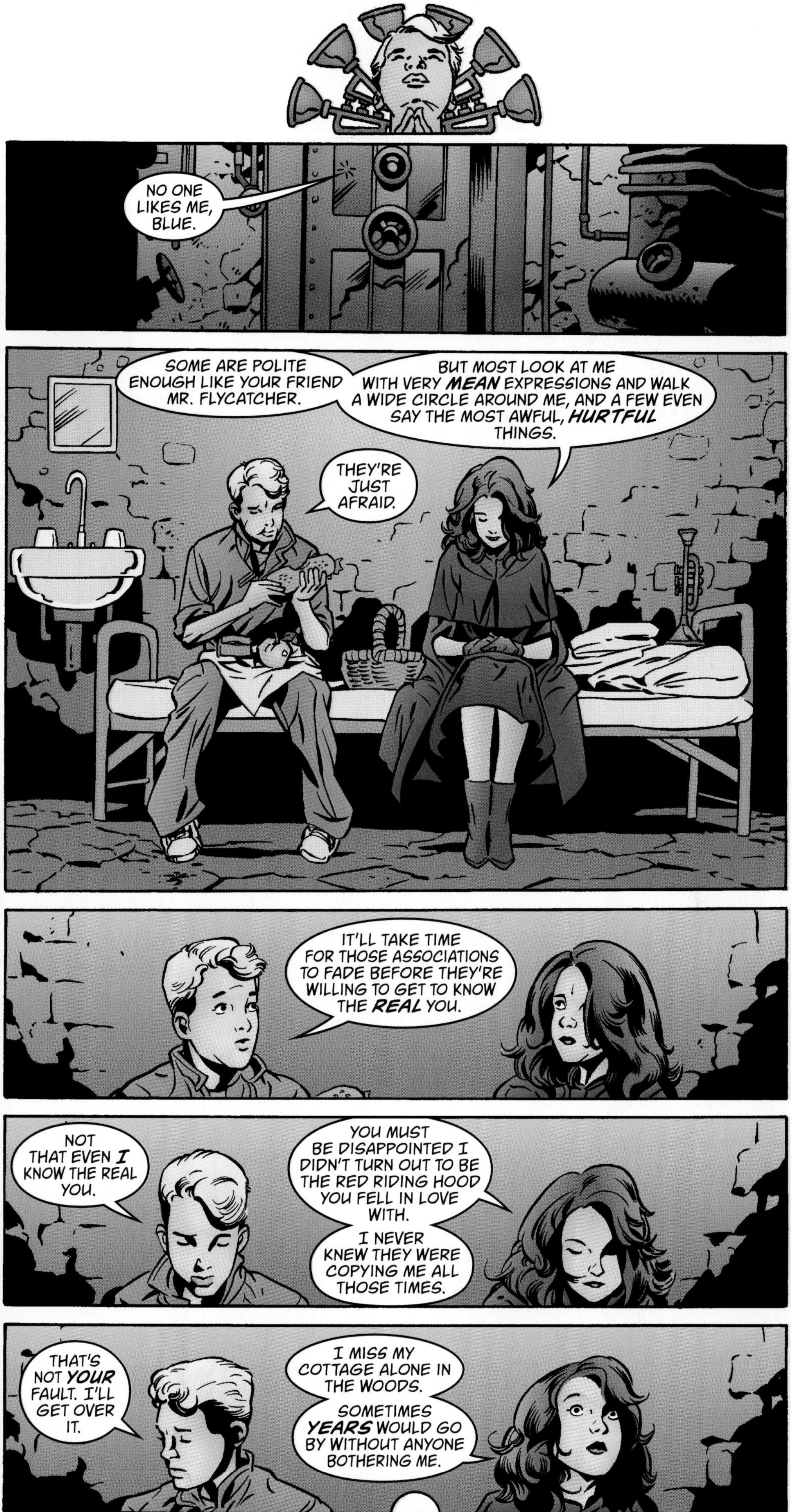
NO ONE LIKES ME, BLUE.
SOME ARE POLITE ENOUGH LIKE YOUR FRIEND MR. FLYCATCHER.
BUT MOST LOOK AT ME WITH VERY MEAN EXPRESSIONS AND WALK A WIDE CIRCLE AROUND ME, AND A FEW EVEN SAY THE MOST AWFUL, HURTFUL THINGS.
THEY'RE JUST AFRAID.
IT'LL TAKE TIME FOR THOSE ASSOCIATIONS TO FADE BEFORE THEY'RE WILLING TO GET TO KNOW THE REAL YOU.
NOT THAT EVEN I KNOW THE REAL YOU.
YOU MUST BE DISAPPOINTED I DIDN'T TURN OUT TO BE THE RED RIDING HOOD YOU FELL IN LOVE WITH.
I NEVER KNEW THEY WERE COPYING ME ALL THOSE TIMES.
THAT'S NOT YOUR FAULT. I'LL GET OVER IT.
I MISS MY COTTAGE ALONE IN THE WOODS.
SOMETIMES YEARS WOULD GO BY WITHOUT ANYONE BOTHERING ME.

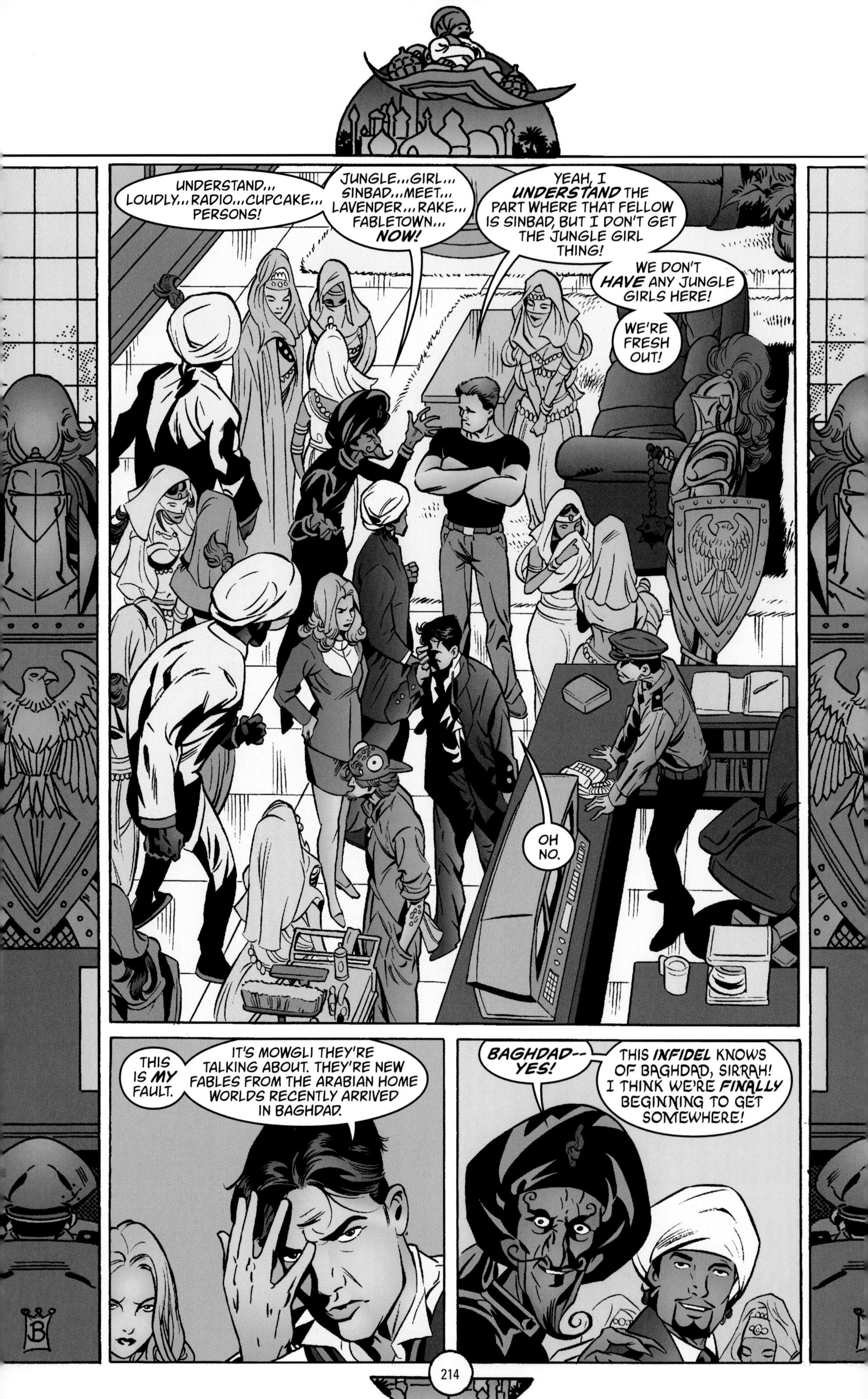
UNDERSTAND... LOUDLY... RADIO... CUPCAKE... PERSONS!
JUNGLE... GIRL... SINBAD... MEET... LAVENDER... RAKE... FABLETOWN... NOW!
YEAH, I UNDERSTAND THE PART WHERE THAT FELLOW IS SINBAD, BUT I DON'T GET THE JUNGLE GIRL THING!
WE DON'T HAVE ANY JUNGLE GIRLS HERE!
WE'RE FRESH OUT!
OH NO.
THIS IS MY FAULT.
IT'S MOWGLI THEY'RE TALKING ABOUT. THEY'RE NEW FABLES FROM THE ARABIAN HOME WORLDS RECENTLY ARRIVED IN BAGHDAD.
BAGHDAD-- YES!
THIS INFIDEL KNOWS OF BAGHDAD, SIRRAH! I THINK WE'RE FINALLY BEGINNING TO GET SOMEWHERE!

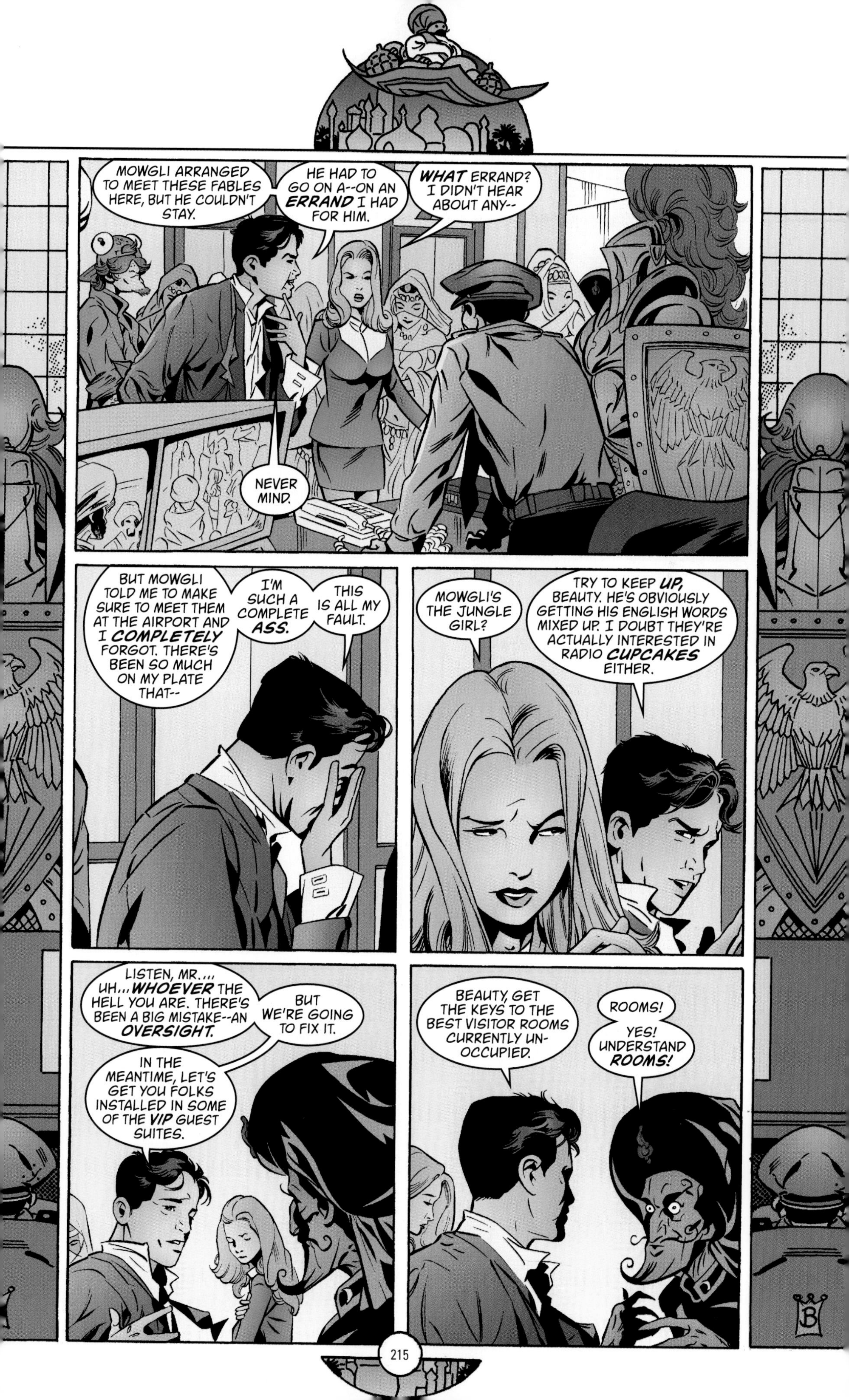

MOWGLI ARRANGED TO MEET THESE FABLES HERE, BUT HE COULDN'T STAY.
HE HAD TO GO ON A--ON AN ERRAND I HAD FOR HIM.
WHAT ERRAND? I DIDN'T HEAR ABOUT ANY--
NEVER MIND.
BUT MOWGLI TOLD ME TO MAKE SURE TO MEET THEM AT THE AIRPORT AND I COMPLETELY FORGOT. THERE'S BEEN SO MUCH ON MY PLATE THAT--
I'M SUCH A COMPLETE ASS.
THIS IS ALL MY FAULT.
MOWGLI'S THE JUNGLE GIRL?
TRY TO KEEP UP, BEAUTY. HE'S OBVIOUSLY GETTING HIS ENGLISH WORDS MIXED UP. I DOUBT THEY'RE ACTUALLY INTERESTED IN RADIO CUPCAKES EITHER.
LISTEN, MR...., UH...WHOEVER THE HELL YOU ARE. THERE'S BEEN A BIG MISTAKE--AN OVERSIGHT.
BUT WE'RE GOING TO FIX IT.
IN THE MEANTIME, LET'S GET YOU FOLKS INSTALLED IN SOME OF THE VIP GUEST SUITES.
BEAUTY, GET THE KEYS TO THE BEST VISITOR ROOMS CURRENTLY UN-OCCUPIED.
ROOMS!
YES! UNDERSTAND ROOMS!

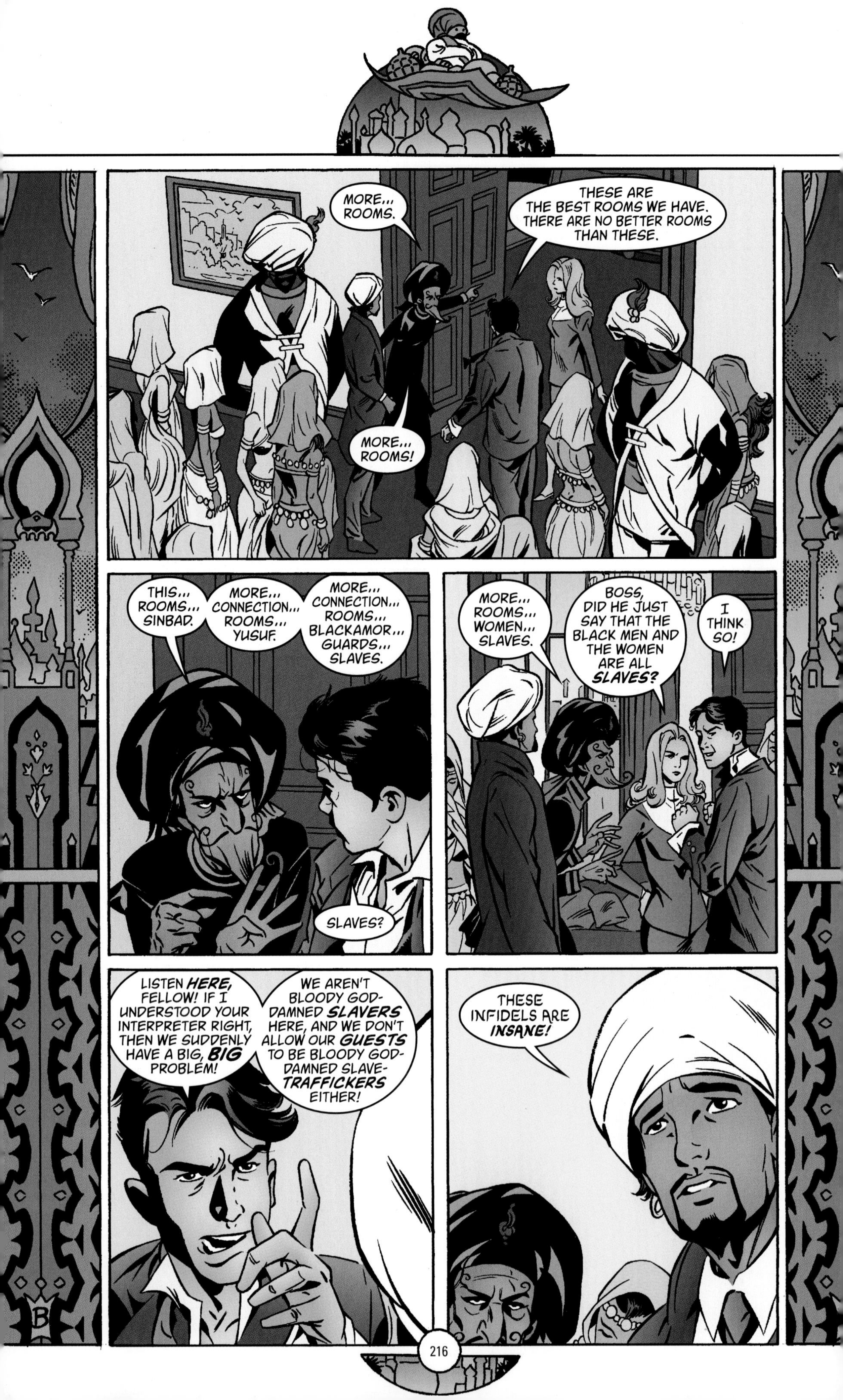

MORE... ROOMS.
THESE ARE THE BEST ROOMS WE HAVE. THERE ARE NO BETTER ROOMS THAN THESE.
MORE... ROOMS!
THIS... ROOMS... SINBAD.
MORE... CONNECTION... ROOMS... YUSUF.
MORE... CONNECTION... ROOMS... BLACKAMOR... GUARDS... SLAVES.
SLAVES?
MORE... ROOMS... WOMEN... SLAVES.
BOSS, DID HE JUST SAY THAT THE BLACK MEN AND THE WOMEN ARE ALL *SLAVES?*
I THINK SO!
LISTEN *HERE,* FELLOW! IF I UNDERSTOOD YOUR INTERPRETER RIGHT, THEN WE SUDDENLY HAVE A BIG, *BIG* PROBLEM!
WE AREN'T BLOODY GOD-DAMNED *SLAVERS* HERE, AND WE DON'T ALLOW OUR *GUESTS* TO BE BLOODY GOD-DAMNED SLAVE-*TRAFFICKERS* EITHER!
THESE INFIDELS ARE *INSANE!*

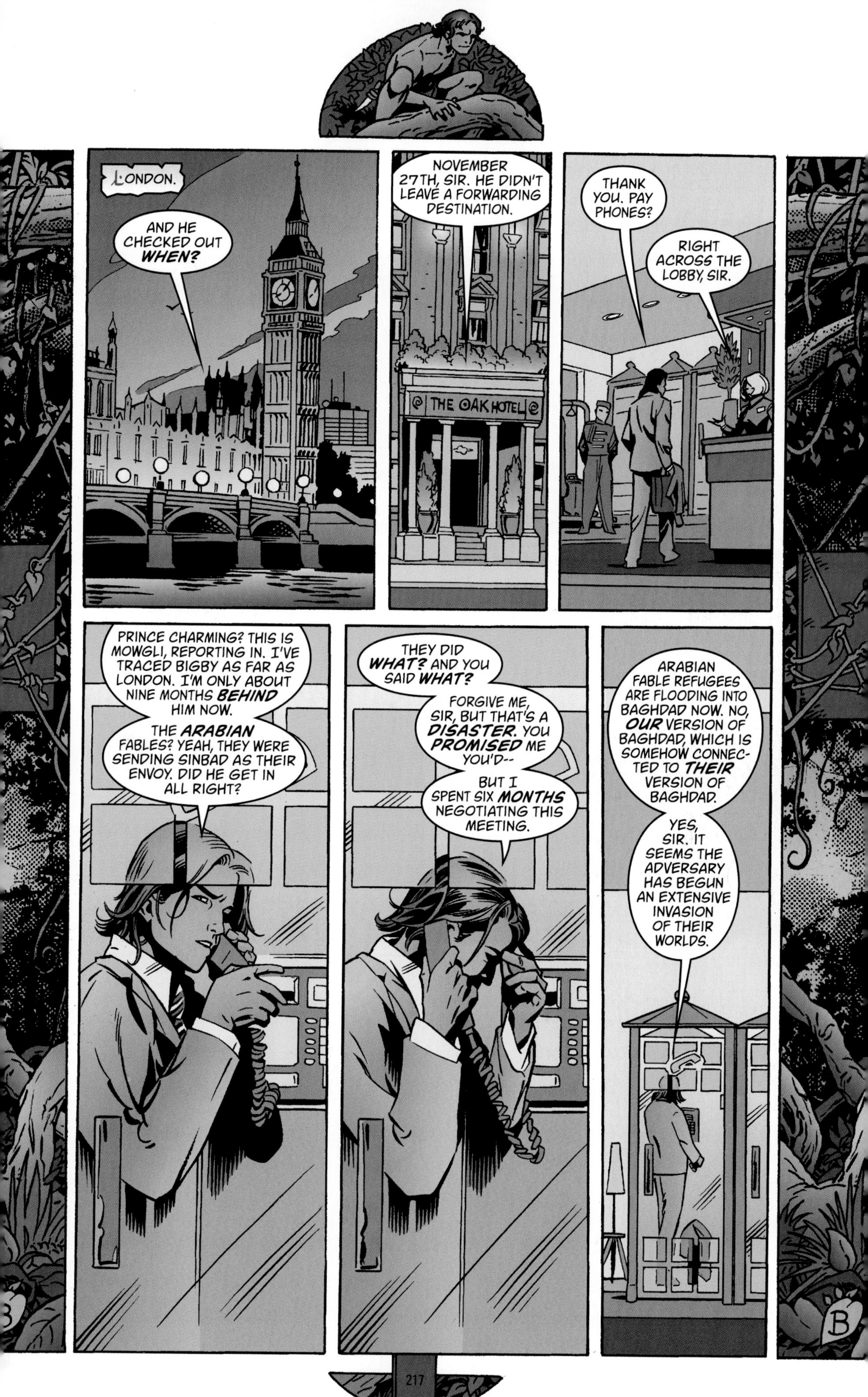
LONDON.
AND HE CHECKED OUT WHEN?
NOVEMBER 27TH, SIR. HE DIDN'T LEAVE A FORWARDING DESTINATION.
THE OAK HOTEL
THANK YOU. PAY PHONES?
RIGHT ACROSS THE LOBBY, SIR.
PRINCE CHARMING? THIS IS MOWGLI, REPORTING IN. I'VE TRACED BIGBY AS FAR AS LONDON. I'M ONLY ABOUT NINE MONTHS BEHIND HIM NOW.
THE ARABIAN FABLES? YEAH, THEY WERE SENDING SINBAD AS THEIR ENVOY. DID HE GET IN ALL RIGHT?
THEY DID WHAT? AND YOU SAID WHAT?
FORGIVE ME, SIR, BUT THAT'S A DISASTER. YOU PROMISED ME YOU'D--
BUT I SPENT SIX MONTHS NEGOTIATING THIS MEETING.
ARABIAN FABLE REFUGEES ARE FLOODING INTO BAGHDAD NOW. NO, OUR VERSION OF BAGHDAD, WHICH IS SOMEHOW CONNECTED TO THEIR VERSION OF BAGHDAD.
YES, SIR. IT SEEMS THE ADVERSARY HAS BEGUN AN EXTENSIVE INVASION OF THEIR WORLDS.

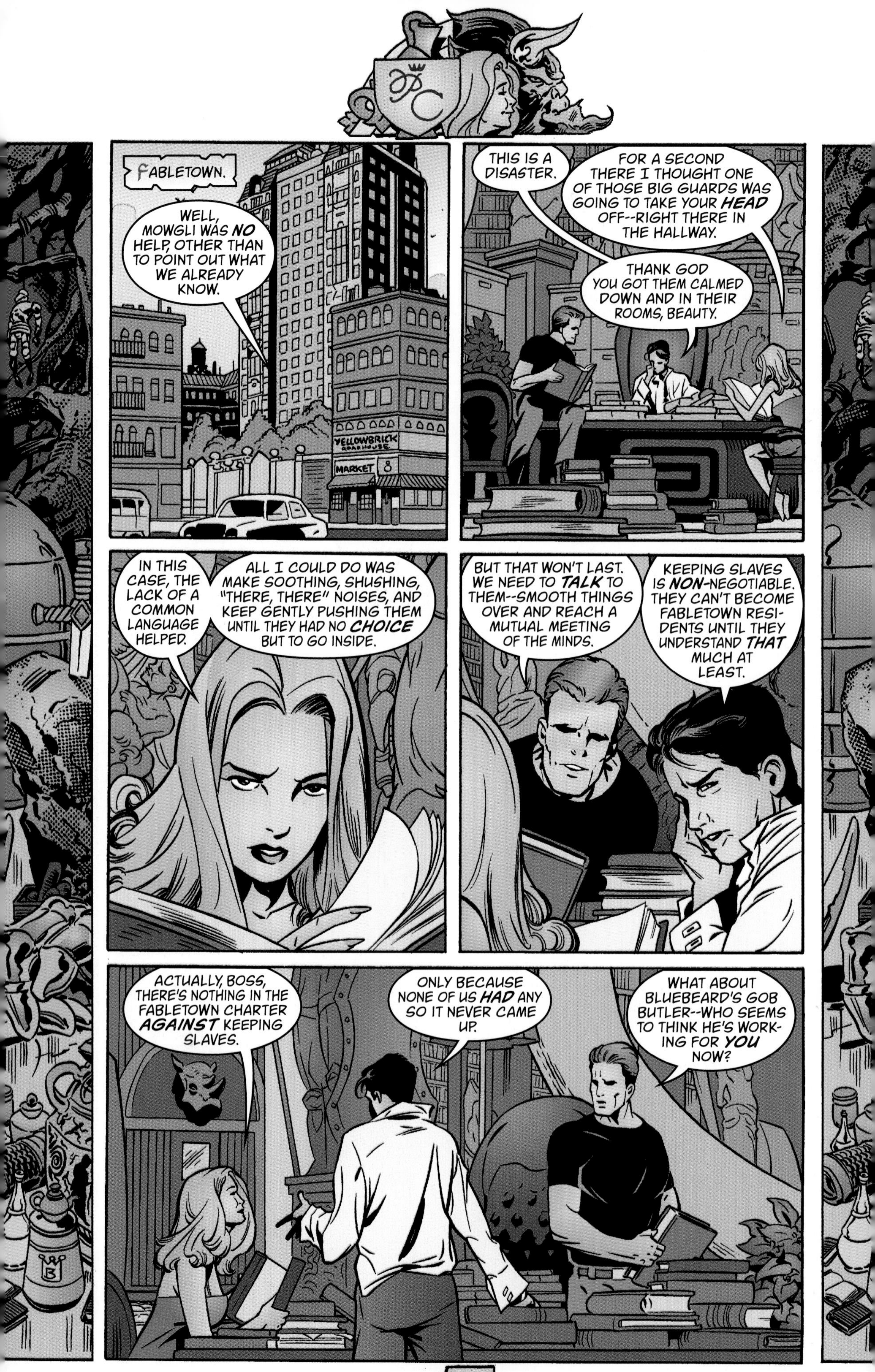
FABLETOWN.
WELL, MOWGLI WAS NO HELP, OTHER THAN TO POINT OUT WHAT WE ALREADY KNOW.
YELLOWBRICK ROADHOUSE.
MARKET
THIS IS A DISASTER.
FOR A SECOND THERE I THOUGHT ONE OF THOSE BIG GUARDS WAS GOING TO TAKE YOUR HEAD OFF--RIGHT THERE IN THE HALLWAY.
THANK GOD YOU GOT THEM CALMED DOWN AND IN THEIR ROOMS, BEAUTY.
IN THIS CASE, THE LACK OF A COMMON LANGUAGE HELPED.
ALL I COULD DO WAS MAKE SOOTHING, SHUSHING, "THERE, THERE" NOISES, AND KEEP GENTLY PUSHING THEM UNTIL THEY HAD NO CHOICE BUT TO GO INSIDE.
BUT THAT WON'T LAST. WE NEED TO TALK TO THEM--SMOOTH THINGS OVER AND REACH A MUTUAL MEETING OF THE MINDS.
KEEPING SLAVES IS NON-NEGOTIABLE. THEY CAN'T BECOME FABLETOWN RESI-DENTS UNTIL THEY UNDERSTAND THAT MUCH AT LEAST.
ACTUALLY, BOSS, THERE'S NOTHING IN THE FABLETOWN CHARTER AGAINST KEEPING SLAVES.
ONLY BECAUSE NONE OF US HAD ANY SO IT NEVER CAME UP.
WHAT ABOUT BLUEBEARD'S GOB BUTLER--WHO SEEMS TO THINK HE'S WORK-ING FOR YOU NOW?

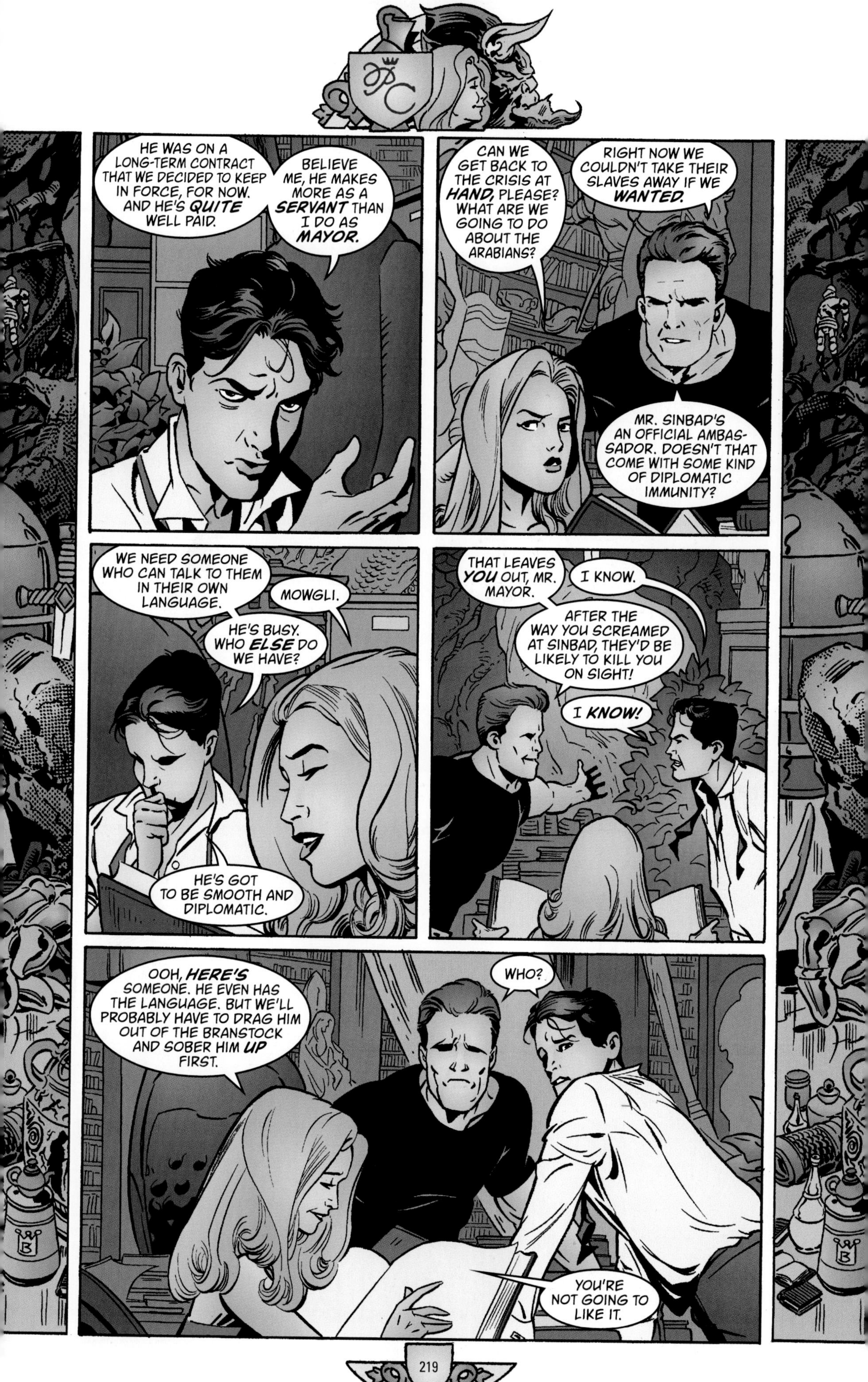

HE WAS ON A LONG-TERM CONTRACT THAT WE DECIDED TO KEEP IN FORCE, FOR NOW. AND HE'S **QUITE** WELL PAID.
BELIEVE ME, HE MAKES MORE AS A **SERVANT** THAN I DO AS **MAYOR.**
CAN WE GET BACK TO THE CRISIS AT **HAND,** PLEASE? WHAT ARE WE GOING TO DO ABOUT THE ARABIANS?
RIGHT NOW WE COULDN'T TAKE THEIR SLAVES AWAY IF WE **WANTED.**
MR. SINBAD'S AN OFFICIAL AMBASSADOR. DOESN'T THAT COME WITH SOME KIND OF DIPLOMATIC IMMUNITY?
WE NEED SOMEONE WHO CAN TALK TO THEM IN THEIR OWN LANGUAGE.
MOWGLI.
HE'S BUSY. WHO **ELSE** DO WE HAVE?
HE'S GOT TO BE SMOOTH AND DIPLOMATIC.
THAT LEAVES **YOU** OUT, MR. MAYOR.
I KNOW.
AFTER THE WAY YOU SCREAMED AT SINBAD, THEY'D BE LIKELY TO KILL YOU ON SIGHT!
I **KNOW!**
OOH, **HERE'S** SOMEONE. HE EVEN HAS THE LANGUAGE. BUT WE'LL PROBABLY HAVE TO DRAG HIM OUT OF THE BRANSTOCK AND SOBER HIM **UP** FIRST.
WHO?
YOU'RE NOT GOING TO LIKE IT.

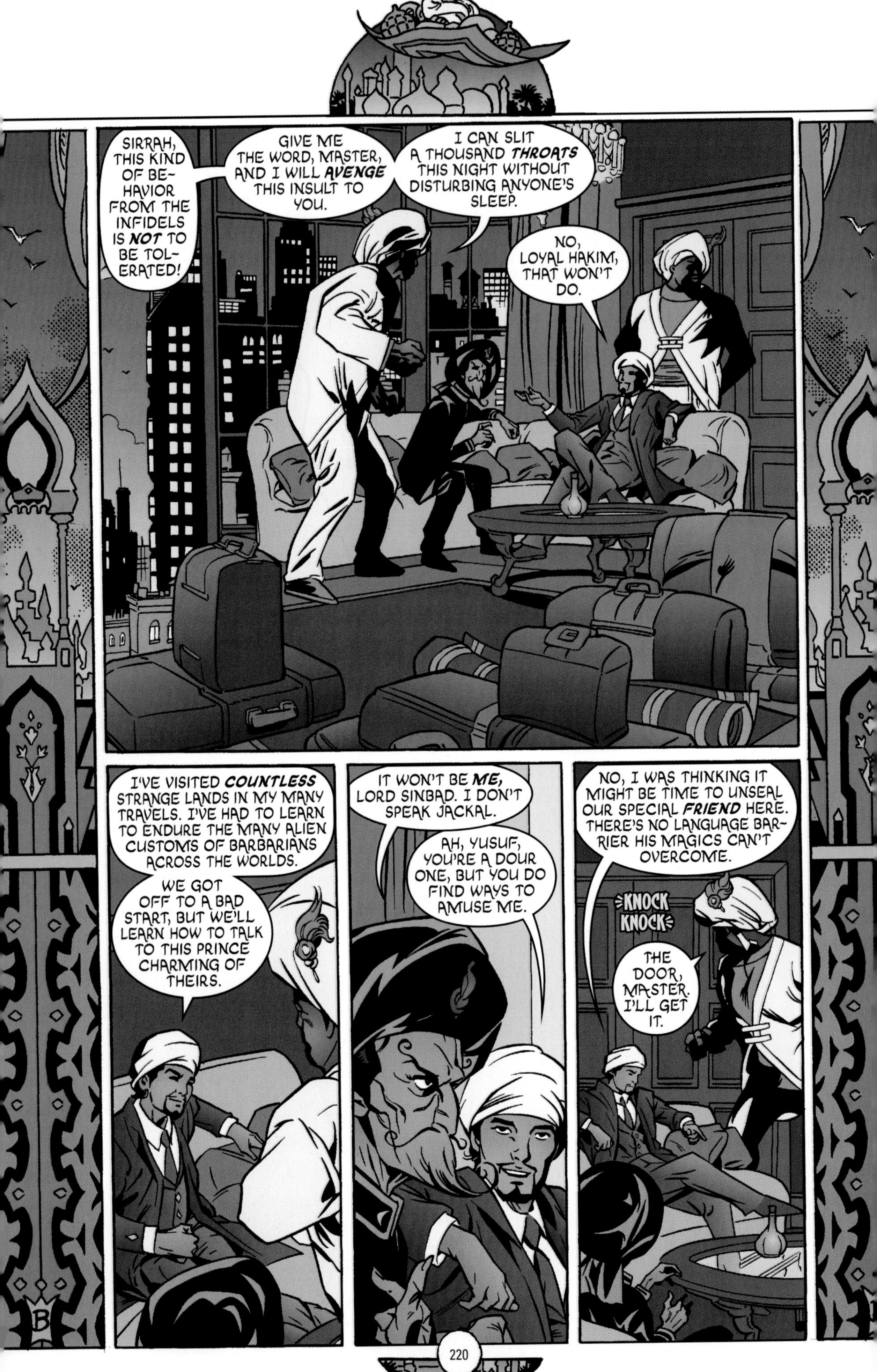

SIRRAH, THIS KIND OF BE-HAVIOR FROM THE INFIDELS IS *NOT* TO BE TOL-ERATED!
GIVE ME THE WORD, MASTER, AND I WILL *AVENGE* THIS INSULT TO YOU.
I CAN SLIT A THOUSAND *THROATS* THIS NIGHT WITHOUT DISTURBING ANYONE'S SLEEP.
NO, LOYAL HAKIM, THAT WON'T DO.
I'VE VISITED *COUNTLESS* STRANGE LANDS IN MY MANY TRAVELS. I'VE HAD TO LEARN TO ENDURE THE MANY ALIEN CUSTOMS OF BARBARIANS ACROSS THE WORLDS.
WE GOT OFF TO A BAD START, BUT WE'LL LEARN HOW TO TALK TO THIS PRINCE CHARMING OF THEIRS.
IT WON'T BE *ME,* LORD SINBAD. I DON'T SPEAK JACKAL.
AH, YUSUF, YOU'RE A DOUR ONE, BUT YOU DO FIND WAYS TO AMUSE ME.
NO, I WAS THINKING IT MIGHT BE TIME TO UNSEAL OUR SPECIAL *FRIEND* HERE. THERE'S NO LANGUAGE BAR-RIER HIS MAGICS CAN'T OVERCOME.
KNOCK KNOCK
THE DOOR, MASTER. I'LL GET IT.

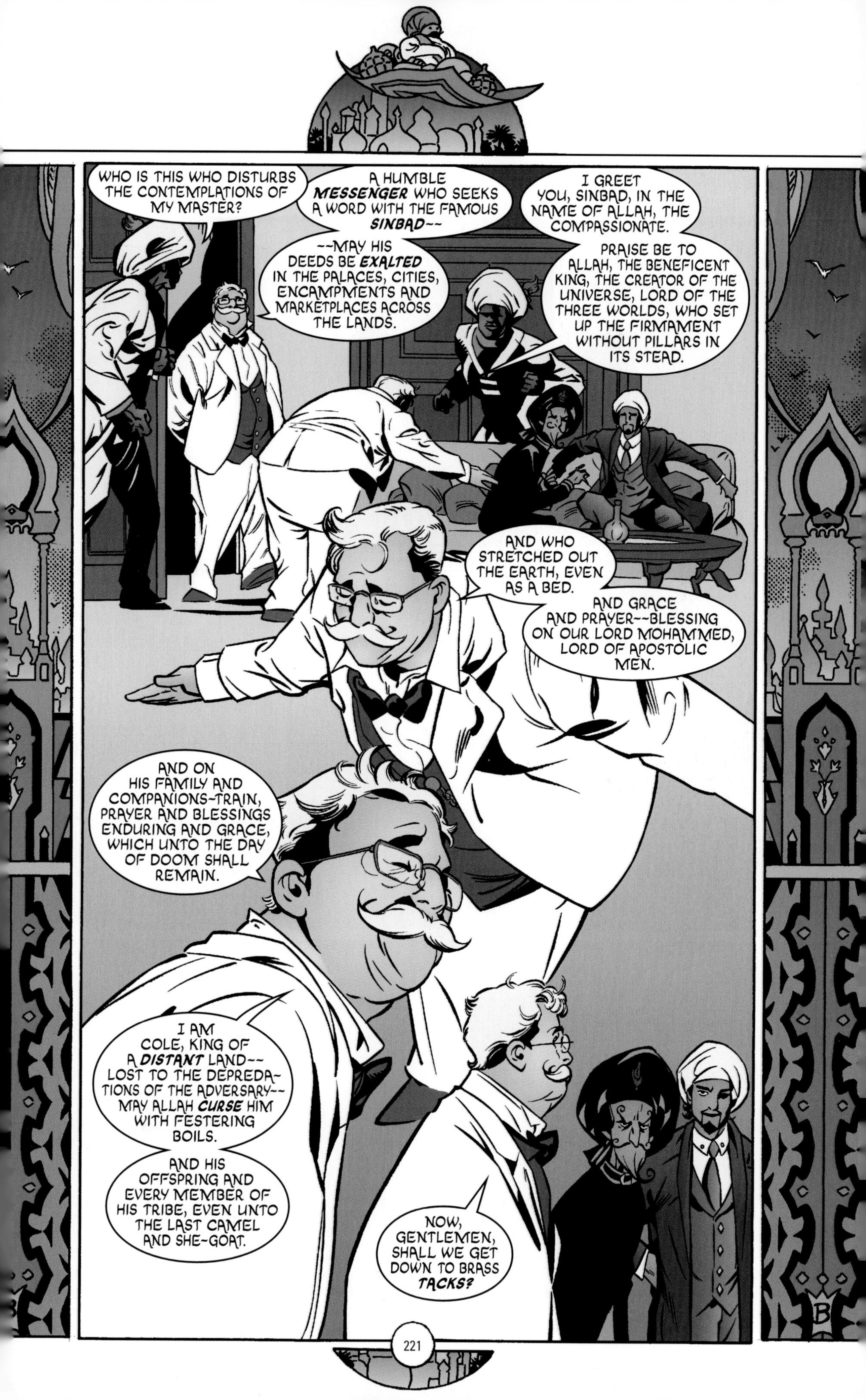
WHO IS THIS WHO DISTURBS THE CONTEMPLATIONS OF MY MASTER?
A HUMBLE MESSENGER WHO SEEKS A WORD WITH THE FAMOUS SINBAD--
--MAY HIS DEEDS BE EXALTED IN THE PALACES, CITIES, ENCAMPMENTS AND MARKETPLACES ACROSS THE LANDS.
I GREET YOU, SINBAD, IN THE NAME OF ALLAH, THE COMPASSIONATE.
PRAISE BE TO ALLAH, THE BENEFICENT KING, THE CREATOR OF THE UNIVERSE, LORD OF THE THREE WORLDS, WHO SET UP THE FIRMAMENT WITHOUT PILLARS IN ITS STEAD.
AND WHO STRETCHED OUT THE EARTH, EVEN AS A BED.
AND GRACE AND PRAYER--BLESSING ON OUR LORD MOHAMMED, LORD OF APOSTOLIC MEN.
AND ON HIS FAMILY AND COMPANIONS-TRAIN, PRAYER AND BLESSINGS ENDURING AND GRACE, WHICH UNTO THE DAY OF DOOM SHALL REMAIN.
I AM COLE, KING OF A DISTANT LAND--LOST TO THE DEPREDATIONS OF THE ADVERSARY--MAY ALLAH CURSE HIM WITH FESTERING BOILS.
AND HIS OFFSPRING AND EVERY MEMBER OF HIS TRIBE, EVEN UNTO THE LAST CAMEL AND SHE-GOAT.
NOW, GENTLEMEN, SHALL WE GET DOWN TO BRASS TACKS?

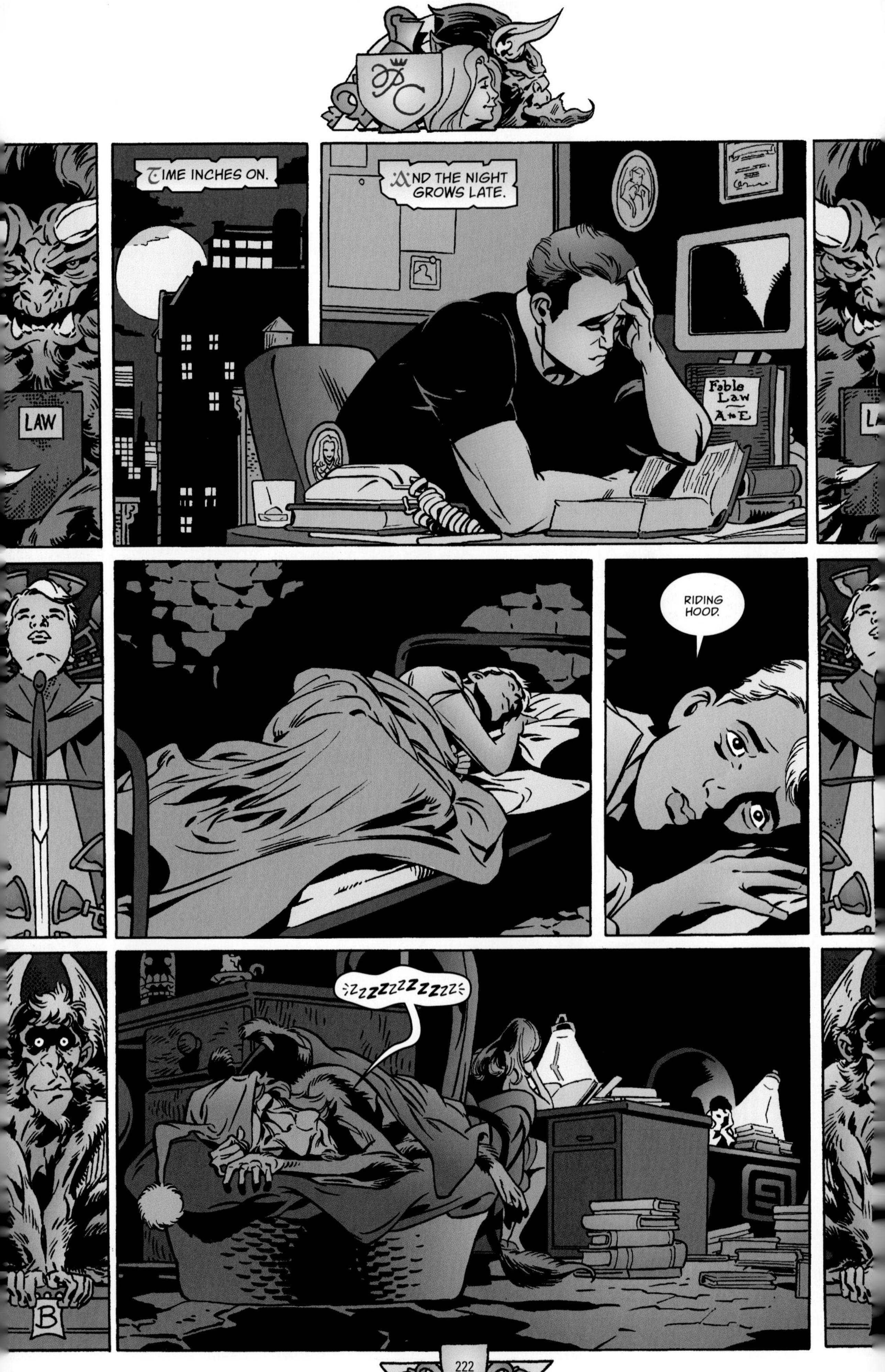
TIME INCHES ON.
AND THE NIGHT GROWS LATE.
LAW
Fable Law A to E
RIDING HOOD.
ZZZZZZZZZZZZ

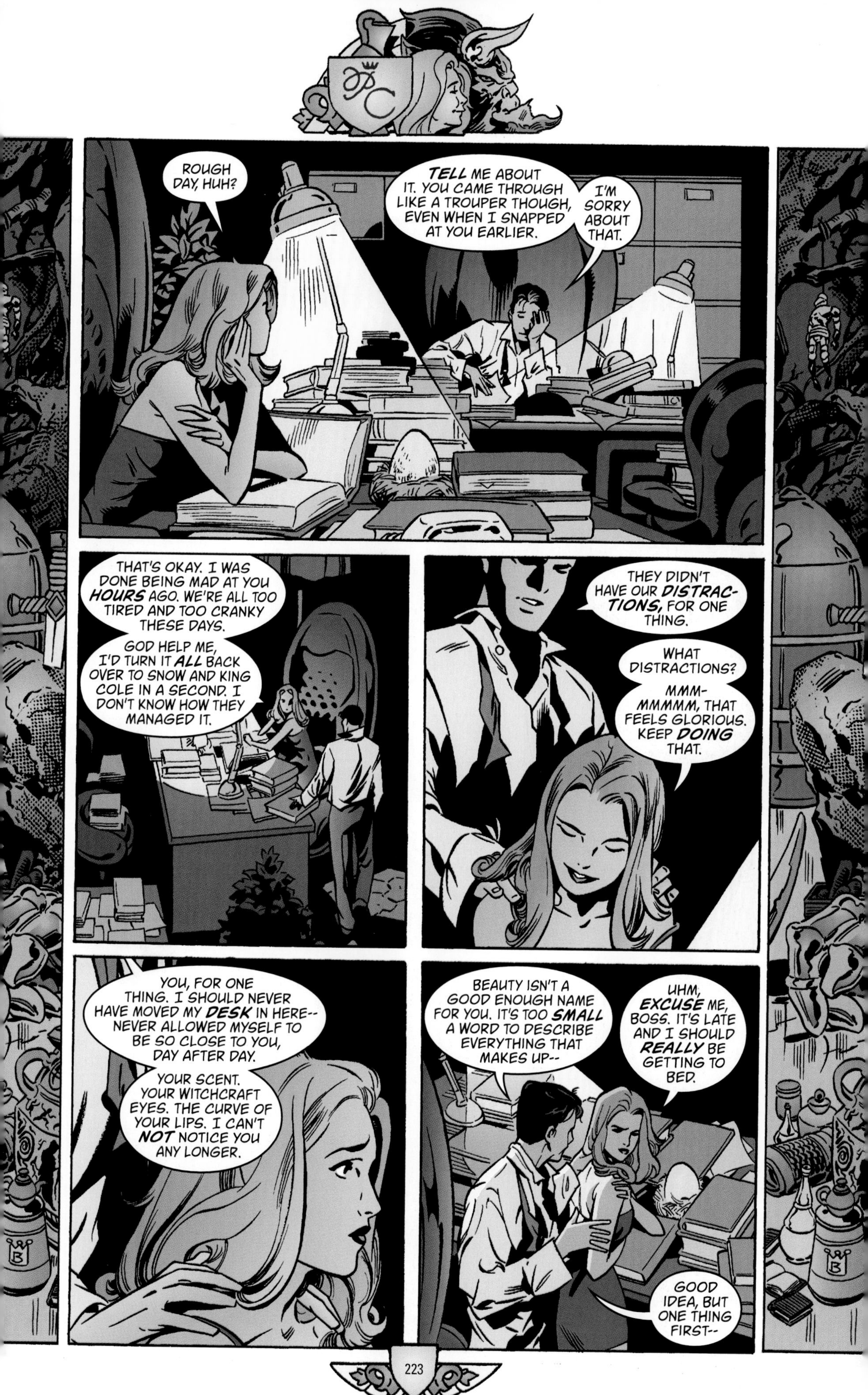
ROUGH DAY, HUH?
TELL ME ABOUT IT. YOU CAME THROUGH LIKE A TROUPER THOUGH, EVEN WHEN I SNAPPED AT YOU EARLIER.
I'M SORRY ABOUT THAT.
THAT'S OKAY. I WAS DONE BEING MAD AT YOU HOURS AGO. WE'RE ALL TOO TIRED AND TOO CRANKY THESE DAYS.
GOD HELP ME, I'D TURN IT ALL BACK OVER TO SNOW AND KING COLE IN A SECOND. I DON'T KNOW HOW THEY MANAGED IT.
THEY DIDN'T HAVE OUR DISTRACTIONS, FOR ONE THING.
WHAT DISTRACTIONS?
MMM-MMMMM, THAT FEELS GLORIOUS. KEEP DOING THAT.
YOU, FOR ONE THING. I SHOULD NEVER HAVE MOVED MY DESK IN HERE--NEVER ALLOWED MYSELF TO BE SO CLOSE TO YOU, DAY AFTER DAY.
YOUR SCENT. YOUR WITCHCRAFT EYES. THE CURVE OF YOUR LIPS. I CAN'T NOT NOTICE YOU ANY LONGER.
BEAUTY ISN'T A GOOD ENOUGH NAME FOR YOU. IT'S TOO SMALL A WORD TO DESCRIBE EVERYTHING THAT MAKES UP--
UHM, EXCUSE ME, BOSS. IT'S LATE AND I SHOULD REALLY BE GETTING TO BED.
GOOD IDEA, BUT ONE THING FIRST--

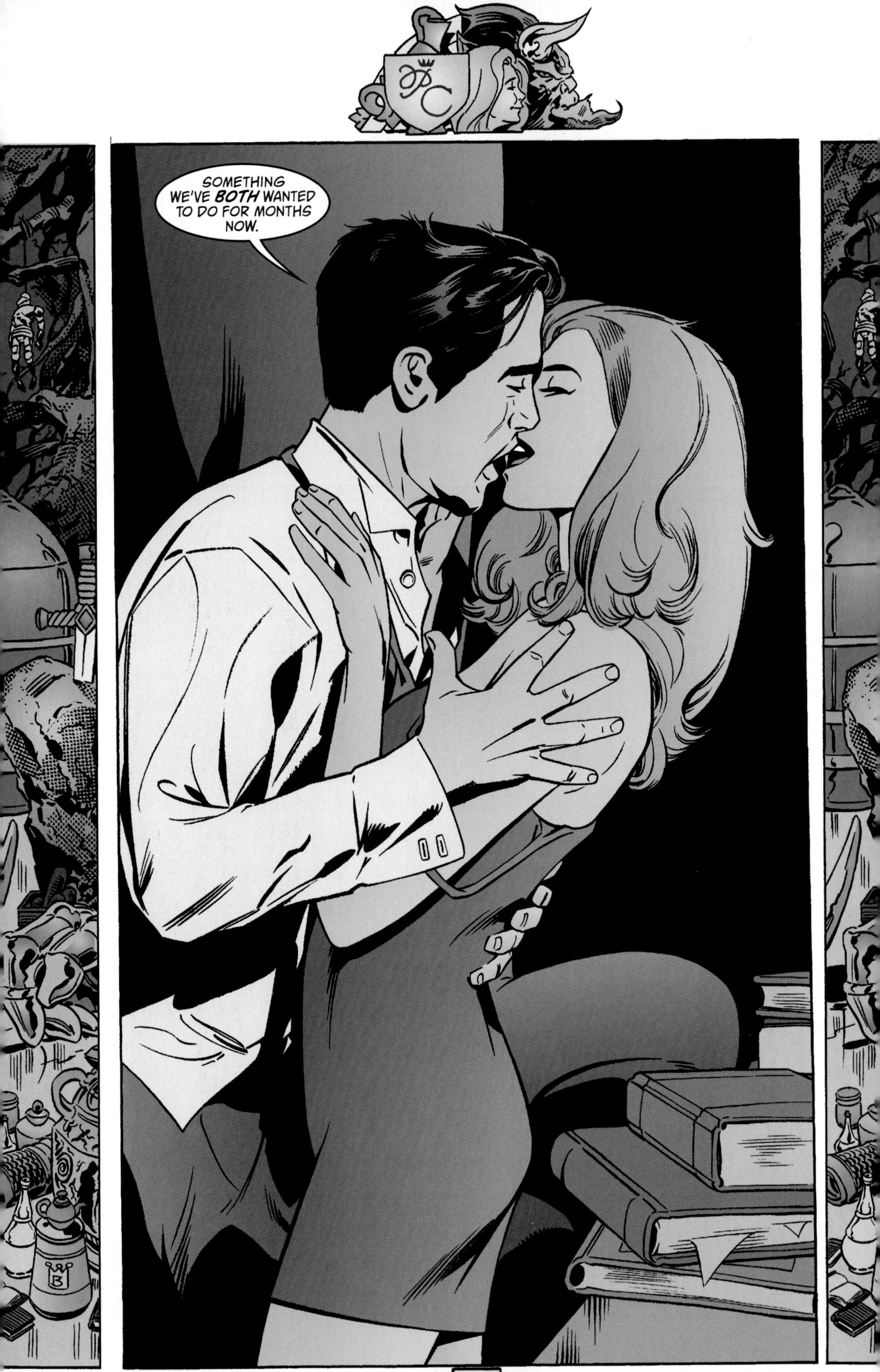
SOMETHING WE'VE **BOTH** WANTED TO DO FOR MONTHS NOW.

Next: D'jinn and Tonic, with a Twist!

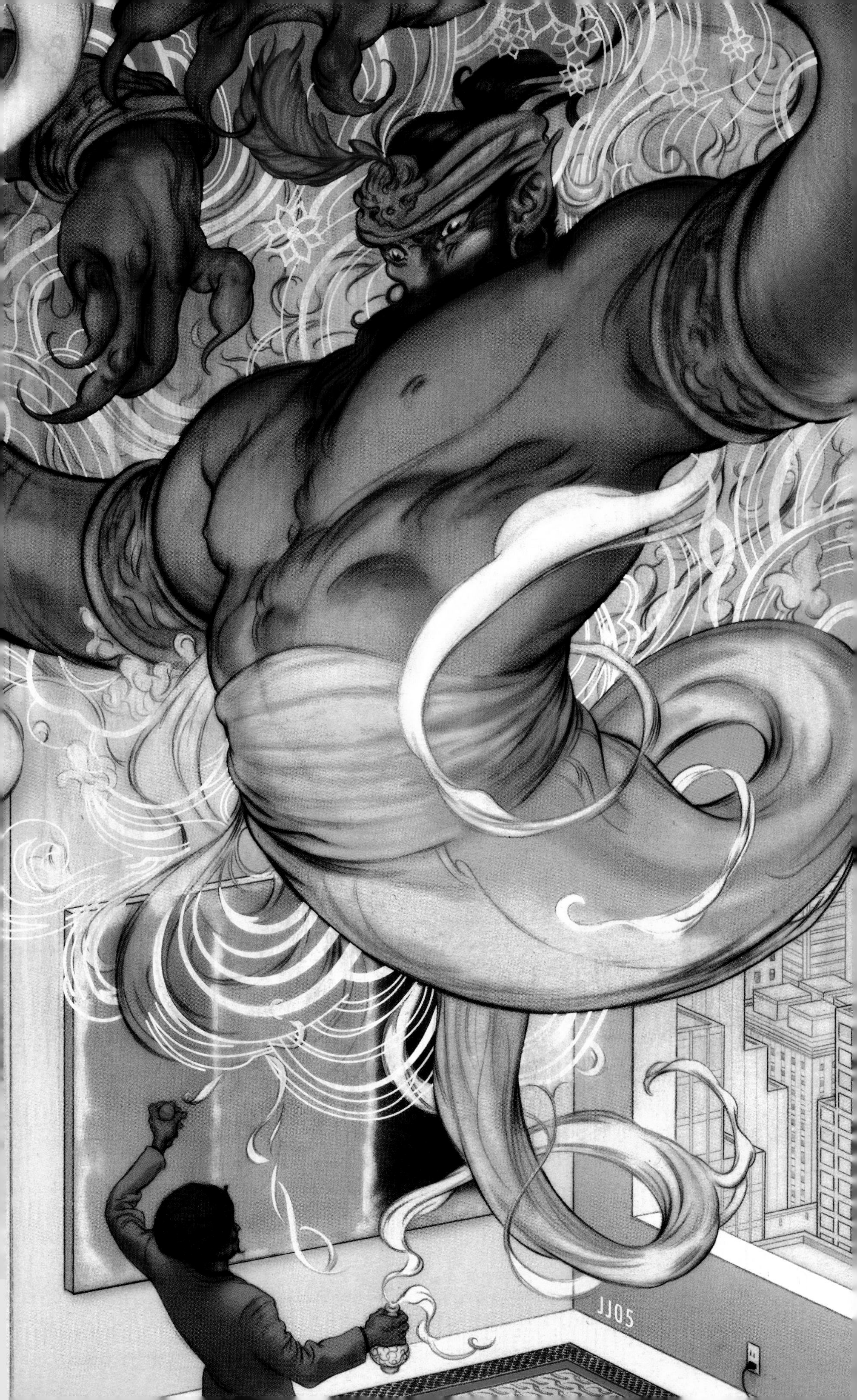
JJ05

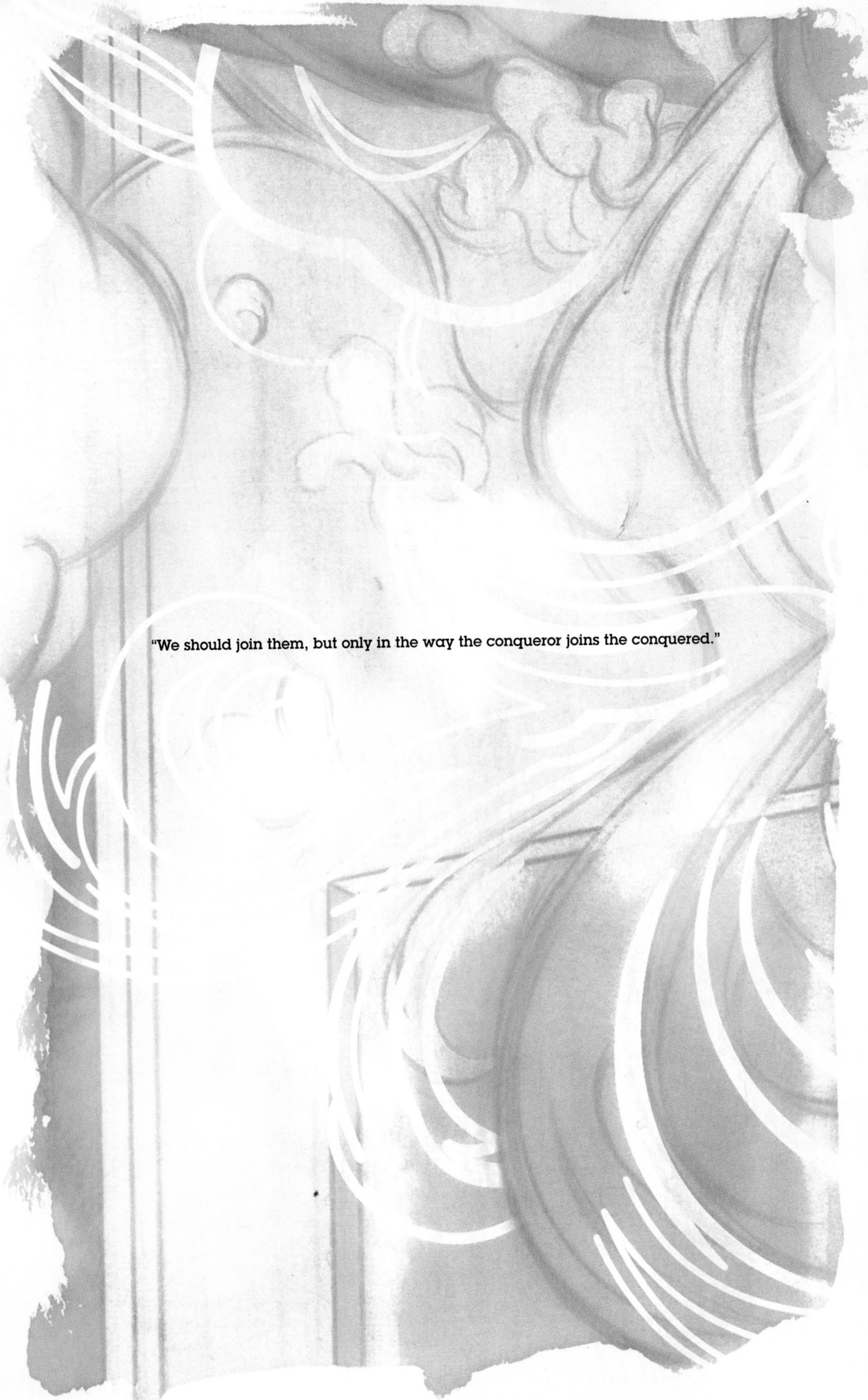
"We should join them, but only in the way the conqueror joins the conquered."

UHM...

OKAY.

THAT WAS *SOME* KISS.

ACTUALLY THAT WAS AN *EXTRAORDINARY* KISS.

I THOUGHT SO, TOO.

DJINN & TONIC WITH A TWIST

Chapter Two of Arabian Nights (and days)

BILL WILLINGHAM	MARK BUCKINGHAM	STEVE LEIALOHA	DANIEL VOZZO
WRITER-CREATOR	PENCILLER	INKER	COLORS
JAMES JEAN	TODD KLEIN	ANGELA RUFINO	SHELLY BOND
COVER ART	LETTERS	ASST. EDITOR	EDITOR

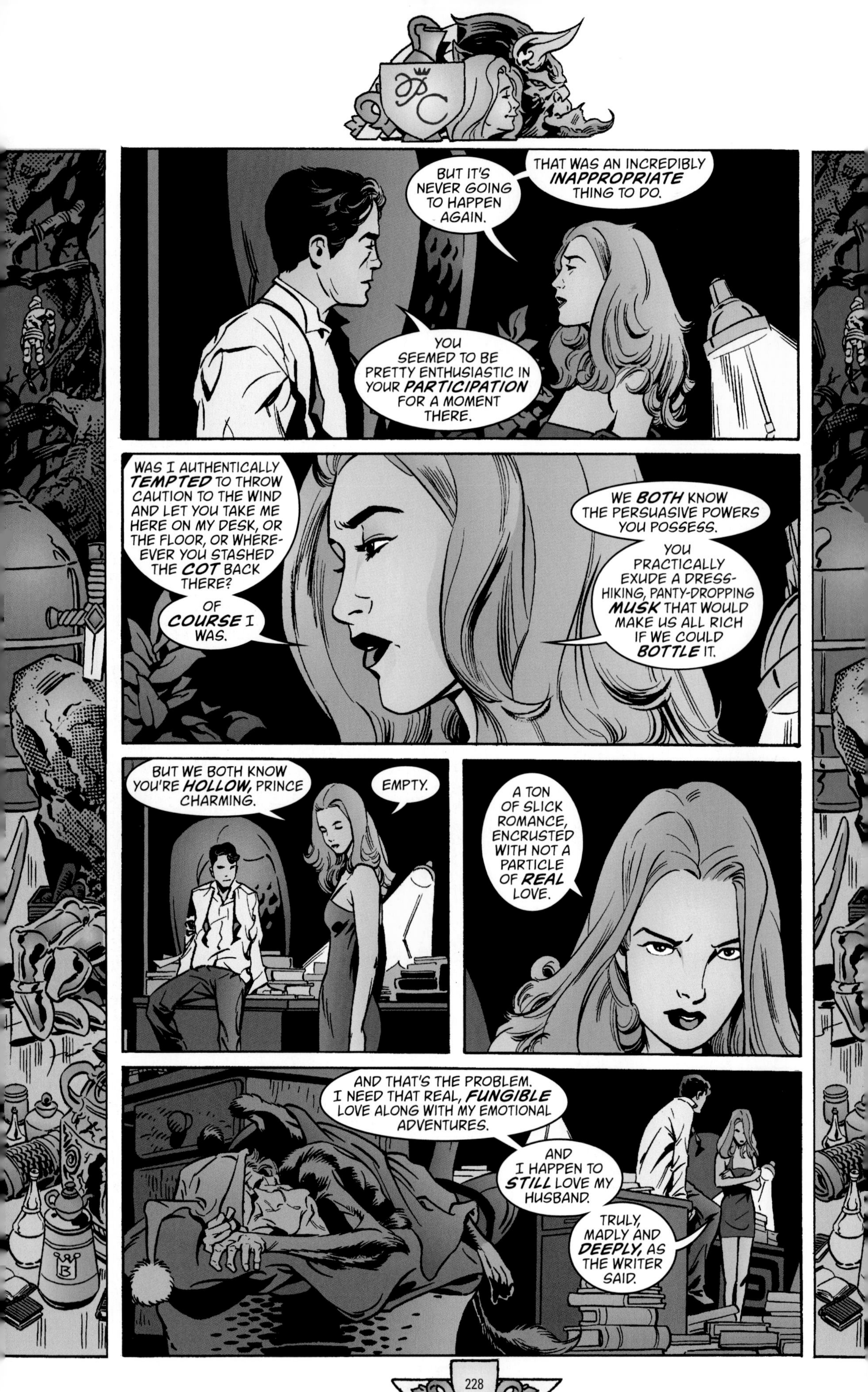

THAT WAS AN INCREDIBLY INAPPROPRIATE THING TO DO.
BUT IT'S NEVER GOING TO HAPPEN AGAIN.
YOU SEEMED TO BE PRETTY ENTHUSIASTIC IN YOUR PARTICIPATION FOR A MOMENT THERE.
WAS I AUTHENTICALLY TEMPTED TO THROW CAUTION TO THE WIND AND LET YOU TAKE ME HERE ON MY DESK, OR THE FLOOR, OR WHERE-EVER YOU STASHED THE COT BACK THERE?
OF COURSE I WAS.
WE BOTH KNOW THE PERSUASIVE POWERS YOU POSSESS.
YOU PRACTICALLY EXUDE A DRESS-HIKING, PANTY-DROPPING MUSK THAT WOULD MAKE US ALL RICH IF WE COULD BOTTLE IT.
BUT WE BOTH KNOW YOU'RE HOLLOW, PRINCE CHARMING.
EMPTY.
A TON OF SLICK ROMANCE, ENCRUSTED WITH NOT A PARTICLE OF REAL LOVE.
AND THAT'S THE PROBLEM. I NEED THAT REAL, FUNGIBLE LOVE ALONG WITH MY EMOTIONAL ADVENTURES.
AND I HAPPEN TO STILL LOVE MY HUSBAND.
TRULY, MADLY AND DEEPLY, AS THE WRITER SAID.

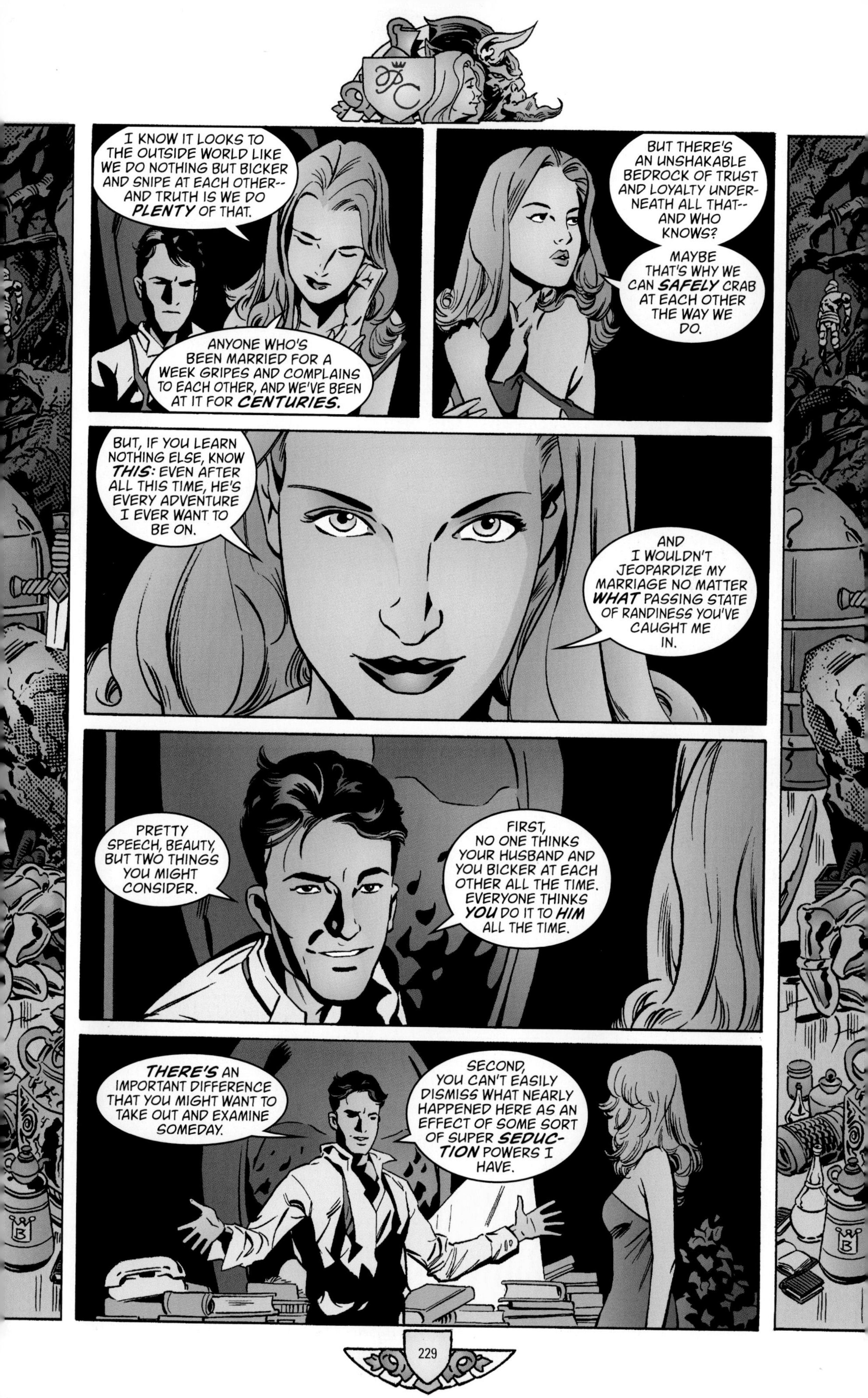
I KNOW IT LOOKS TO THE OUTSIDE WORLD LIKE WE DO NOTHING BUT BICKER AND SNIPE AT EACH OTHER-- AND TRUTH IS WE DO PLENTY OF THAT.
ANYONE WHO'S BEEN MARRIED FOR A WEEK GRIPES AND COMPLAINS TO EACH OTHER, AND WE'VE BEEN AT IT FOR CENTURIES.
BUT THERE'S AN UNSHAKABLE BEDROCK OF TRUST AND LOYALTY UNDER-NEATH ALL THAT-- AND WHO KNOWS?
MAYBE THAT'S WHY WE CAN SAFELY CRAB AT EACH OTHER THE WAY WE DO.
BUT, IF YOU LEARN NOTHING ELSE, KNOW THIS: EVEN AFTER ALL THIS TIME, HE'S EVERY ADVENTURE I EVER WANT TO BE ON.
AND I WOULDN'T JEOPARDIZE MY MARRIAGE NO MATTER WHAT PASSING STATE OF RANDINESS YOU'VE CAUGHT ME IN.
PRETTY SPEECH, BEAUTY, BUT TWO THINGS YOU MIGHT CONSIDER.
FIRST, NO ONE THINKS YOUR HUSBAND AND YOU BICKER AT EACH OTHER ALL THE TIME. EVERYONE THINKS YOU DO IT TO HIM ALL THE TIME.
SECOND, YOU CAN'T EASILY DISMISS WHAT NEARLY HAPPENED HERE AS AN EFFECT OF SOME SORT OF SUPER SEDUC-TION POWERS I HAVE.
THERE'S AN IMPORTANT DIFFERENCE THAT YOU MIGHT WANT TO TAKE OUT AND EXAMINE SOMEDAY.

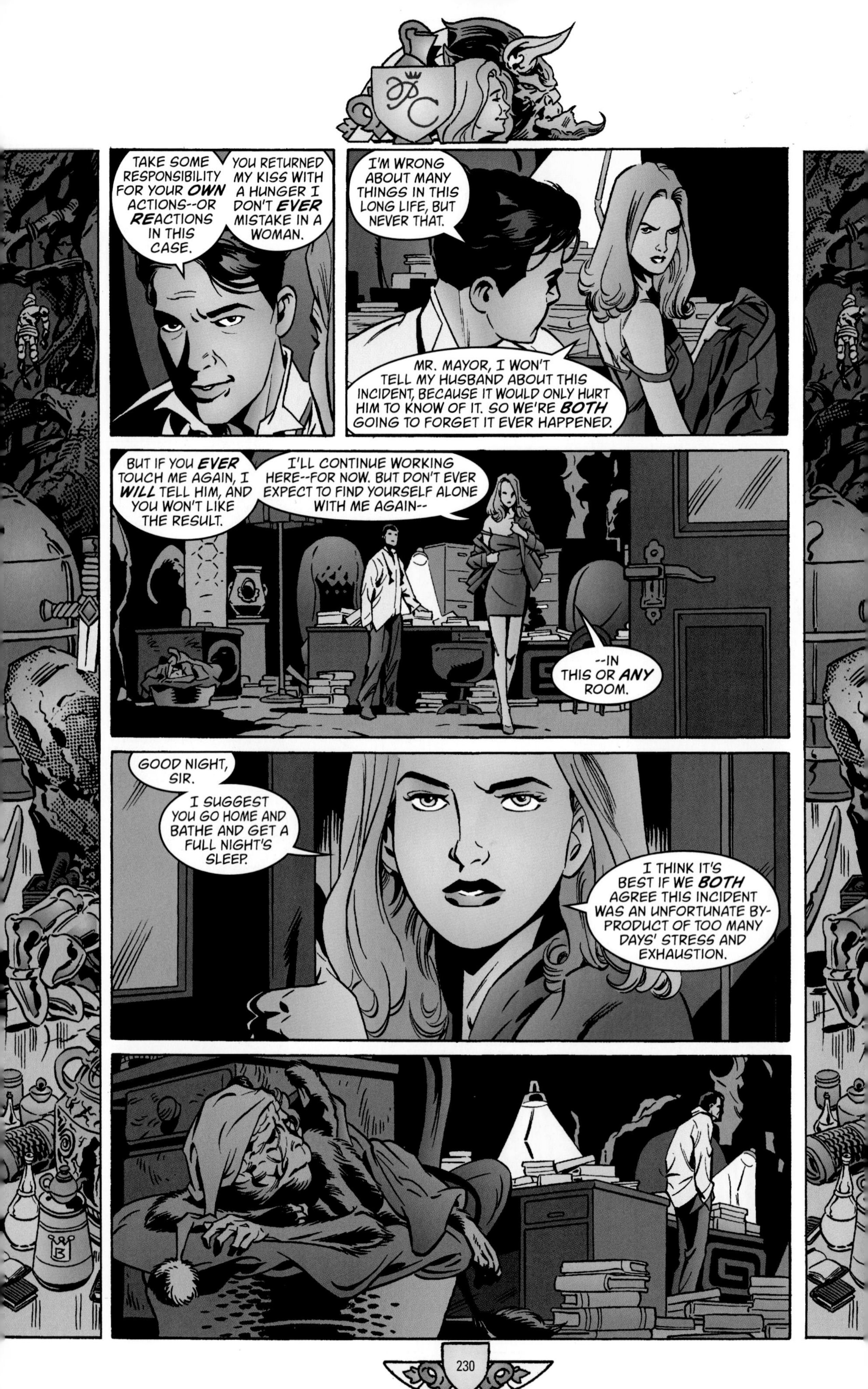
TAKE SOME RESPONSIBILITY FOR YOUR **OWN** ACTIONS--OR **RE**ACTIONS IN THIS CASE.
YOU RETURNED MY KISS WITH A HUNGER I DON'T **EVER** MISTAKE IN A WOMAN.
I'M WRONG ABOUT MANY THINGS IN THIS LONG LIFE, BUT NEVER THAT.
MR. MAYOR, I WON'T TELL MY HUSBAND ABOUT THIS INCIDENT, BECAUSE IT WOULD ONLY HURT HIM TO KNOW OF IT. SO WE'RE **BOTH** GOING TO FORGET IT EVER HAPPENED.
BUT IF YOU **EVER** TOUCH ME AGAIN, I **WILL** TELL HIM, AND YOU WON'T LIKE THE RESULT.
I'LL CONTINUE WORKING HERE--FOR NOW. BUT DON'T EVER EXPECT TO FIND YOURSELF ALONE WITH ME AGAIN--
--IN THIS OR **ANY** ROOM.
GOOD NIGHT, SIR.
I SUGGEST YOU GO HOME AND BATHE AND GET A FULL NIGHT'S SLEEP.
I THINK IT'S BEST IF WE **BOTH** AGREE THIS INCIDENT WAS AN UNFORTUNATE BY-PRODUCT OF TOO MANY DAYS' STRESS AND EXHAUSTION.

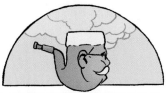

THE VERY NEXT DAY...

GOOD MORNING, GRIMBLE.

CAPITAL DAY, ISN'T IT?

SURE, IT'S PRETTY NICE, YOUR HONOR.

YOU DON'T HAVE TO ADDRESS ME BY THAT SPECIFIC *HONORIFIC*, GRIMBLE. I'M NO LONGER THE MAYOR.

KING COLE WILL DO.

YOU SEEM IN RARE GOOD SPIRITS TODAY, SIR.

THAT I *AM*, MY SOMNAMBULANT BRIDGE TROLL.

THAT I AM.

I'M ON THE WAY TO BEGIN MY SECOND NEGOTIATION SESSION WITH OUR ESTEEMED *GUESTS* FROM THE FAR LEVANT.

IF IT'S ANYTHING LIKE THE *FIRST*, ADVENTURE AND INTRIGUE AWAIT.

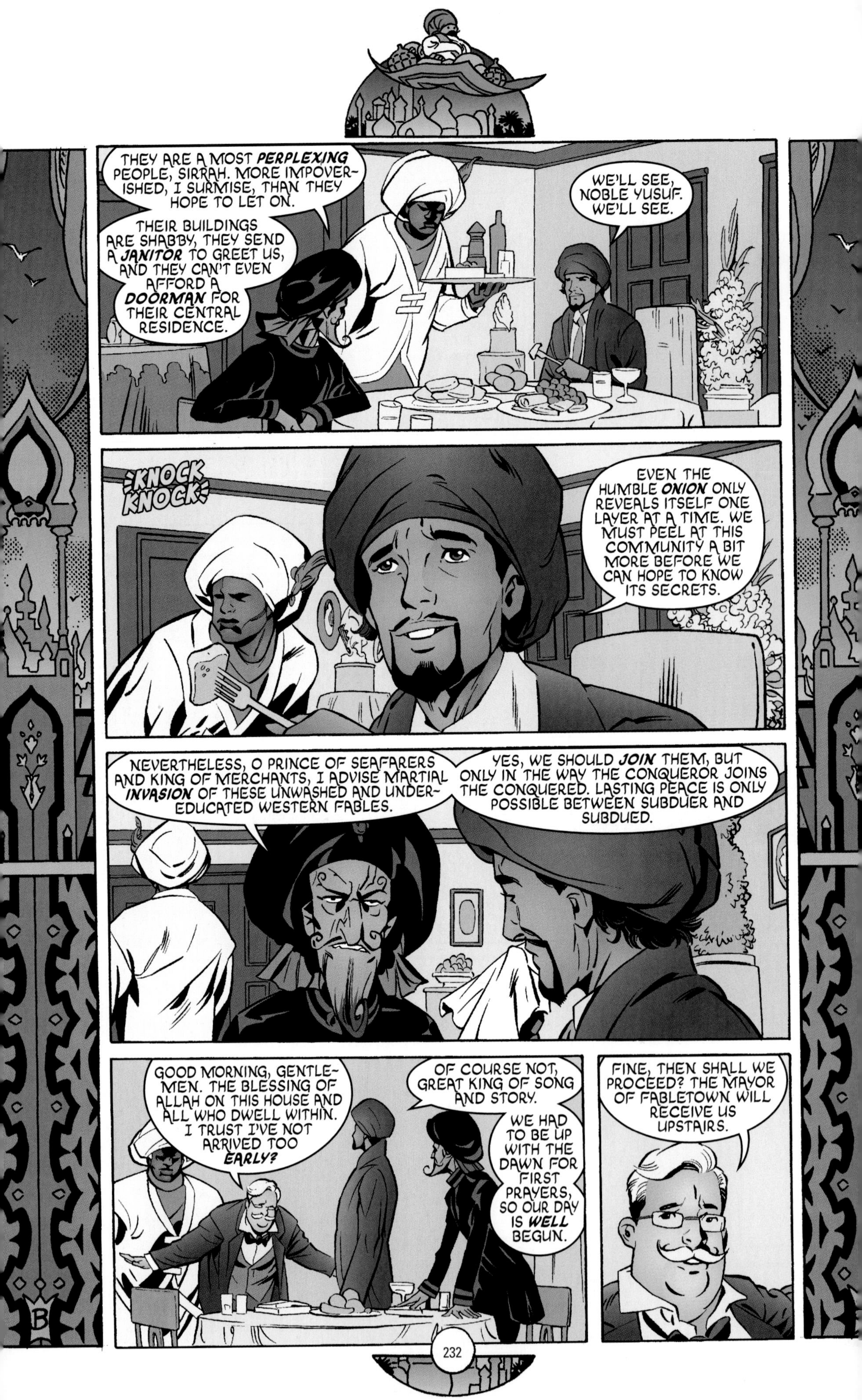

THEY ARE A MOST PERPLEXING PEOPLE, SIRRAH. MORE IMPOVER-ISHED, I SURMISE, THAN THEY HOPE TO LET ON.
THEIR BUILDINGS ARE SHABBY, THEY SEND A JANITOR TO GREET US, AND THEY CAN'T EVEN AFFORD A DOORMAN FOR THEIR CENTRAL RESIDENCE.
WE'LL SEE, NOBLE YUSUF. WE'LL SEE.
KNOCK KNOCK
EVEN THE HUMBLE ONION ONLY REVEALS ITSELF ONE LAYER AT A TIME. WE MUST PEEL AT THIS COMMUNITY A BIT MORE BEFORE WE CAN HOPE TO KNOW ITS SECRETS.
NEVERTHELESS, O PRINCE OF SEAFARERS AND KING OF MERCHANTS, I ADVISE MARTIAL INVASION OF THESE UNWASHED AND UNDER-EDUCATED WESTERN FABLES.
YES, WE SHOULD JOIN THEM, BUT ONLY IN THE WAY THE CONQUEROR JOINS THE CONQUERED. LASTING PEACE IS ONLY POSSIBLE BETWEEN SUBDUER AND SUBDUED.
GOOD MORNING, GENTLE-MEN. THE BLESSING OF ALLAH ON THIS HOUSE AND ALL WHO DWELL WITHIN. I TRUST I'VE NOT ARRIVED TOO EARLY?
OF COURSE NOT, GREAT KING OF SONG AND STORY.
WE HAD TO BE UP WITH THE DAWN FOR FIRST PRAYERS, SO OUR DAY IS WELL BEGUN.
FINE, THEN SHALL WE PROCEED? THE MAYOR OF FABLETOWN WILL RECEIVE US UPSTAIRS.

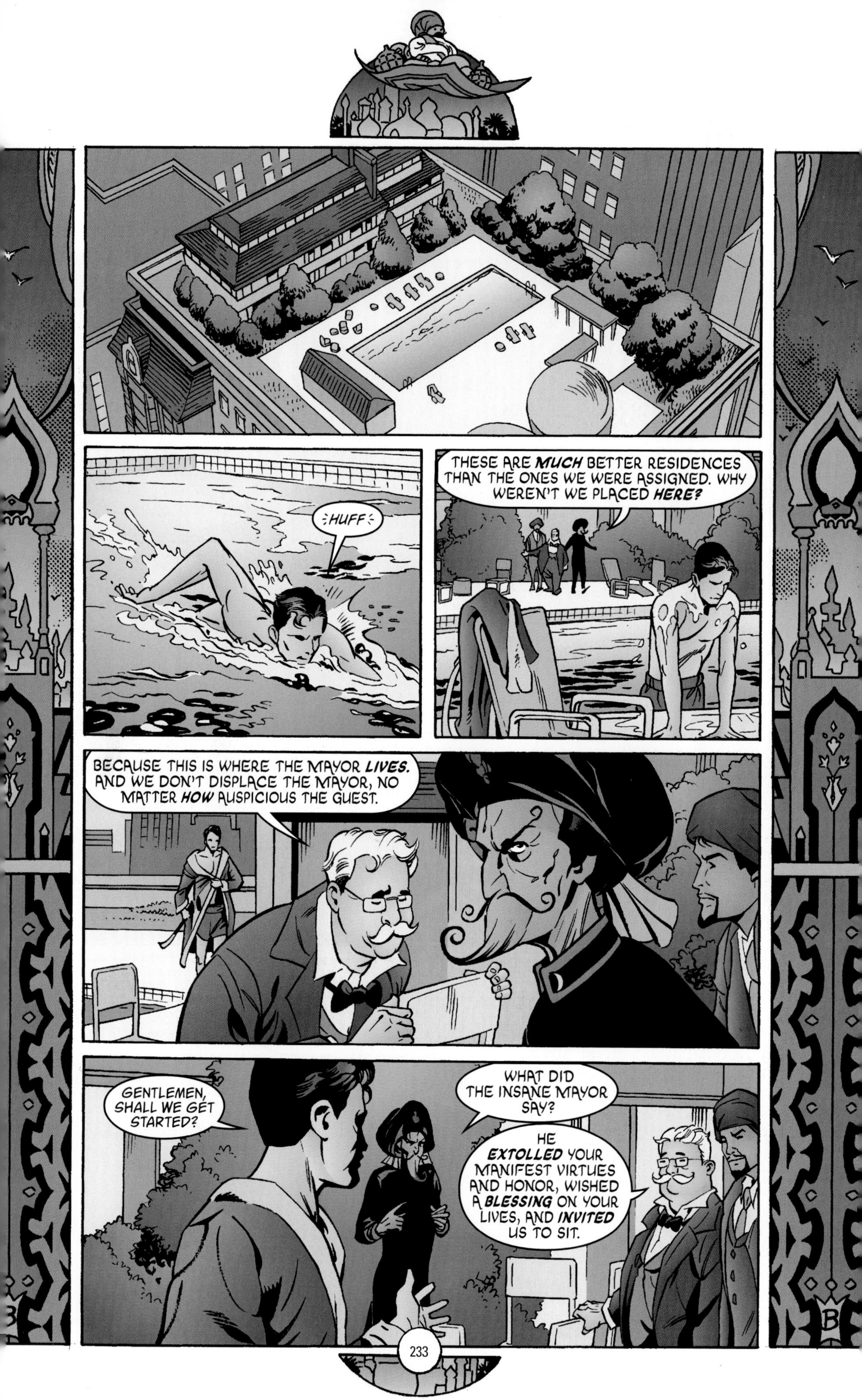
HUFF
THESE ARE MUCH BETTER RESIDENCES THAN THE ONES WE WERE ASSIGNED. WHY WEREN'T WE PLACED HERE?
BECAUSE THIS IS WHERE THE MAYOR LIVES. AND WE DON'T DISPLACE THE MAYOR, NO MATTER HOW AUSPICIOUS THE GUEST.
GENTLEMEN, SHALL WE GET STARTED?
WHAT DID THE INSANE MAYOR SAY?
HE EXTOLLED YOUR MANIFEST VIRTUES AND HONOR, WISHED A BLESSING ON YOUR LIVES, AND INVITED US TO SIT.

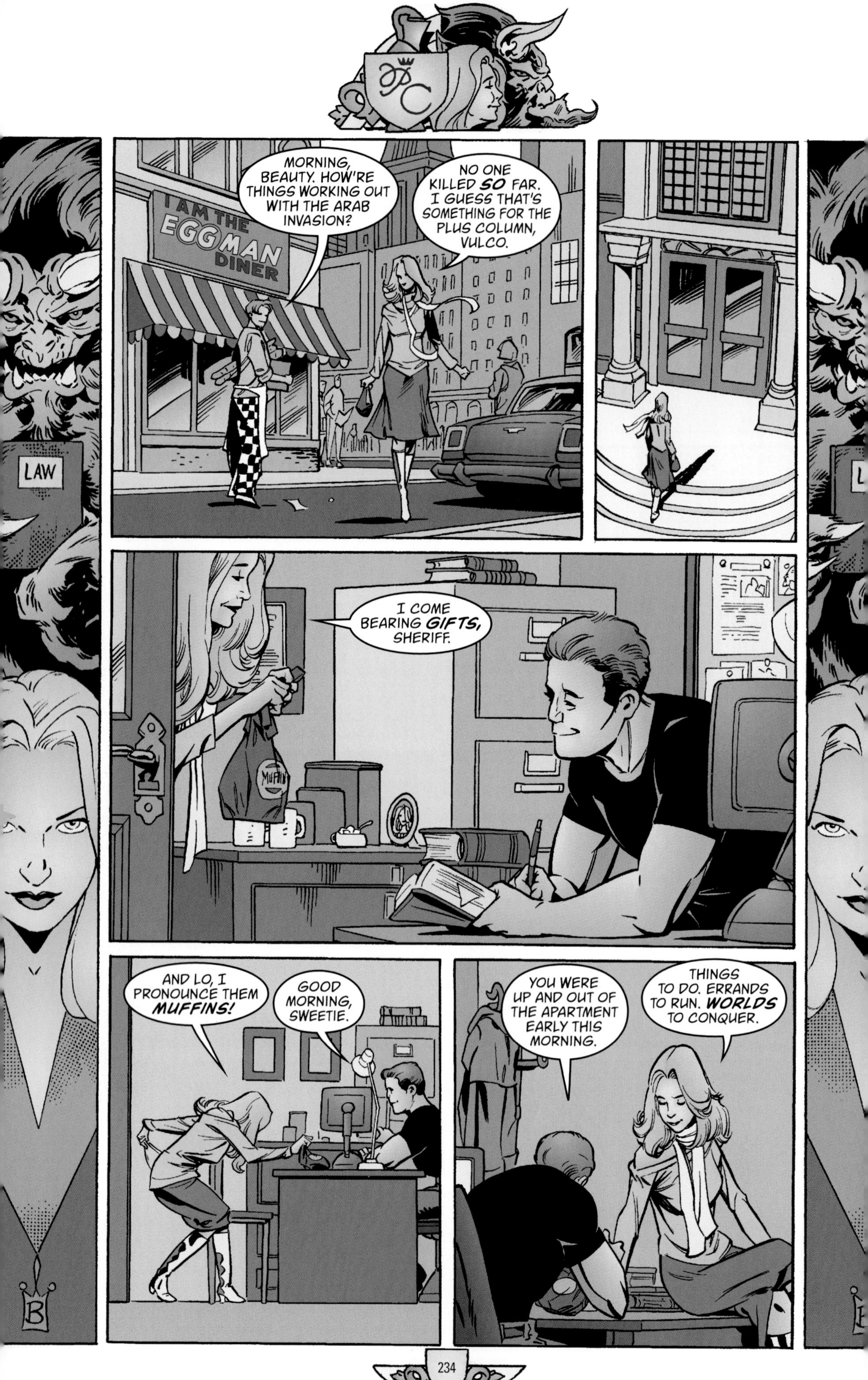

I AM THE EGGMAN DINER
MORNING, BEAUTY. HOW'RE THINGS WORKING OUT WITH THE ARAB INVASION?
NO ONE KILLED SO FAR. I GUESS THAT'S SOMETHING FOR THE PLUS COLUMN, VULCO.
LAW
I COME BEARING GIFTS, SHERIFF.
AND LO, I PRONOUNCE THEM MUFFINS!
GOOD MORNING, SWEETIE.
YOU WERE UP AND OUT OF THE APARTMENT EARLY THIS MORNING.
THINGS TO DO. ERRANDS TO RUN. WORLDS TO CONQUER.

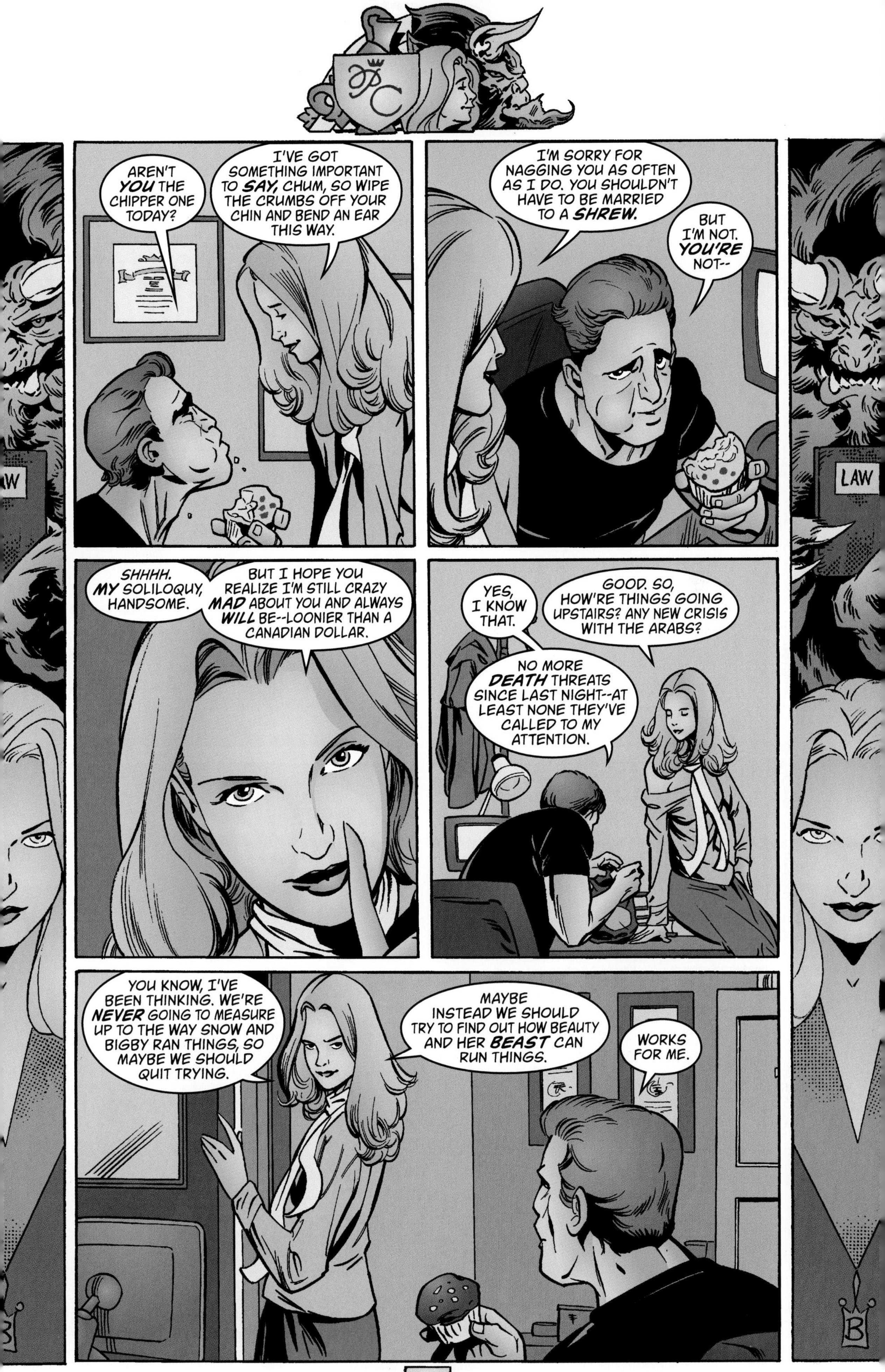
AREN'T YOU THE CHIPPER ONE TODAY?
I'VE GOT SOMETHING IMPORTANT TO SAY, CHUM, SO WIPE THE CRUMBS OFF YOUR CHIN AND BEND AN EAR THIS WAY.
I'M SORRY FOR NAGGING YOU AS OFTEN AS I DO. YOU SHOULDN'T HAVE TO BE MARRIED TO A SHREW.
BUT I'M NOT. YOU'RE NOT--
SHHHH. MY SOLILOQUY, HANDSOME.
BUT I HOPE YOU REALIZE I'M STILL CRAZY MAD ABOUT YOU AND ALWAYS WILL BE--LOONIER THAN A CANADIAN DOLLAR.
YES, I KNOW THAT.
GOOD. SO, HOW'RE THINGS GOING UPSTAIRS? ANY NEW CRISIS WITH THE ARABS?
NO MORE DEATH THREATS SINCE LAST NIGHT--AT LEAST NONE THEY'VE CALLED TO MY ATTENTION.
YOU KNOW, I'VE BEEN THINKING. WE'RE NEVER GOING TO MEASURE UP TO THE WAY SNOW AND BIGBY RAN THINGS, SO MAYBE WE SHOULD QUIT TRYING.
MAYBE INSTEAD WE SHOULD TRY TO FIND OUT HOW BEAUTY AND HER BEAST CAN RUN THINGS.
WORKS FOR ME.
LAW
LAW

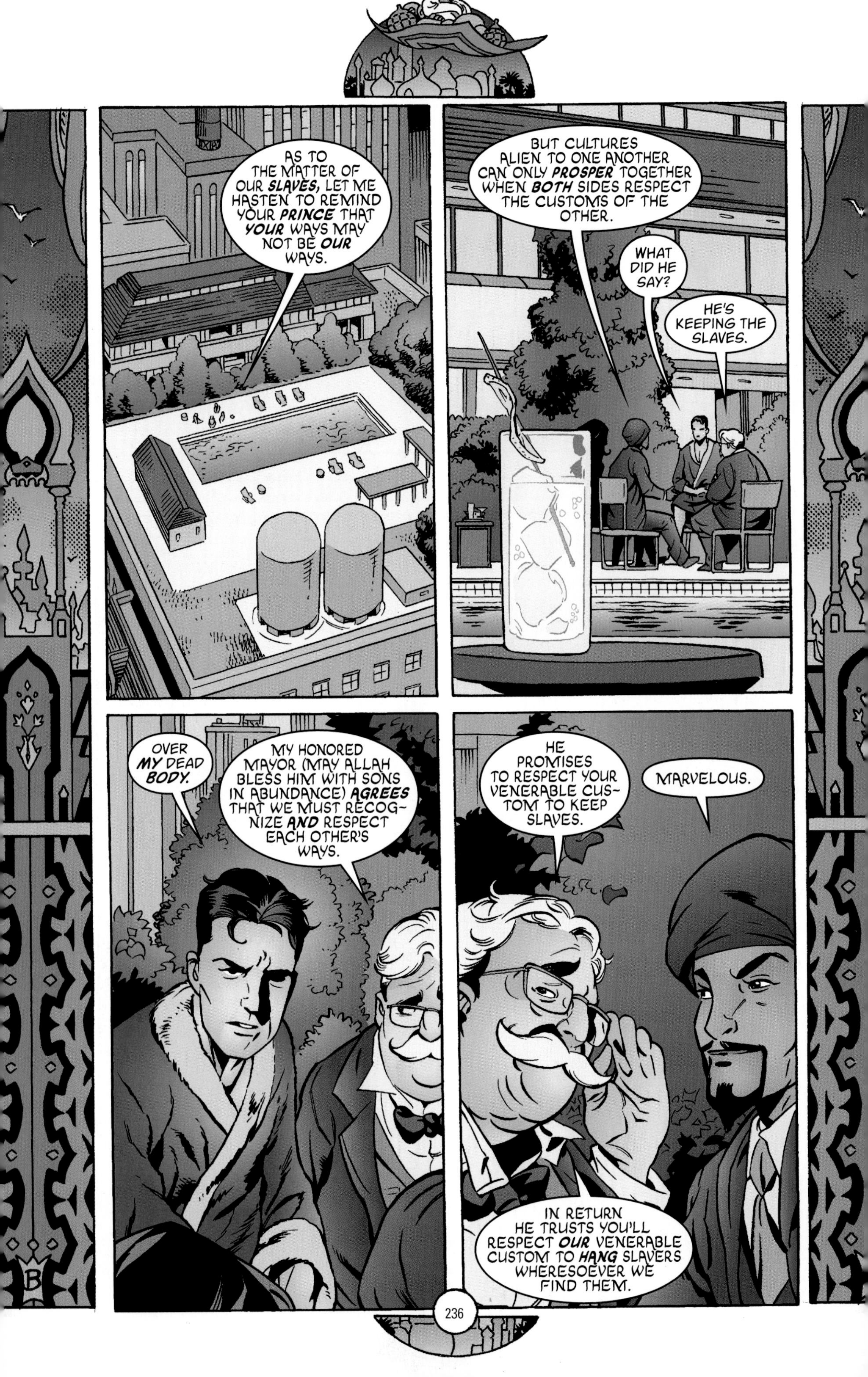
AS TO THE MATTER OF OUR SLAVES, LET ME HASTEN TO REMIND YOUR PRINCE THAT YOUR WAYS MAY NOT BE OUR WAYS.
BUT CULTURES ALIEN TO ONE ANOTHER CAN ONLY PROSPER TOGETHER WHEN BOTH SIDES RESPECT THE CUSTOMS OF THE OTHER.
WHAT DID HE SAY?
HE'S KEEPING THE SLAVES.
OVER MY DEAD BODY.
MY HONORED MAYOR (MAY ALLAH BLESS HIM WITH SONS IN ABUNDANCE) AGREES THAT WE MUST RECOG-NIZE AND RESPECT EACH OTHER'S WAYS.
HE PROMISES TO RESPECT YOUR VENERABLE CUS-TOM TO KEEP SLAVES.
MARVELOUS.
IN RETURN HE TRUSTS YOU'LL RESPECT OUR VENERABLE CUSTOM TO HANG SLAVERS WHERESOEVER WE FIND THEM.

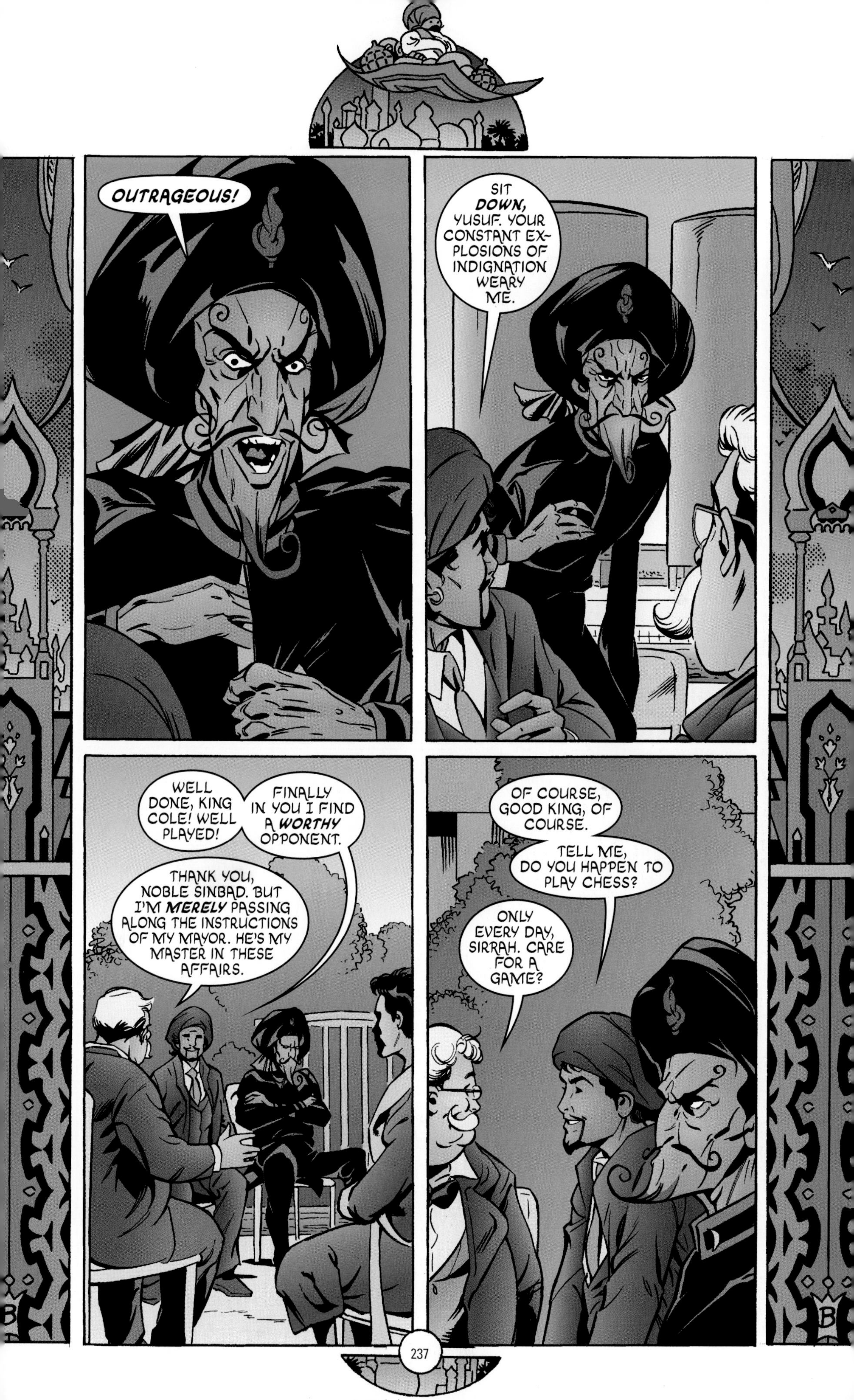
OUTRAGEOUS!
SIT DOWN, YUSUF. YOUR CONSTANT EXPLOSIONS OF INDIGNATION WEARY ME.
WELL DONE, KING COLE! WELL PLAYED!
FINALLY IN YOU I FIND A WORTHY OPPONENT.
THANK YOU, NOBLE SINBAD. BUT I'M MERELY PASSING ALONG THE INSTRUCTIONS OF MY MAYOR. HE'S MY MASTER IN THESE AFFAIRS.
OF COURSE, GOOD KING, OF COURSE.
TELL ME, DO YOU HAPPEN TO PLAY CHESS?
ONLY EVERY DAY, SIRRAH. CARE FOR A GAME?

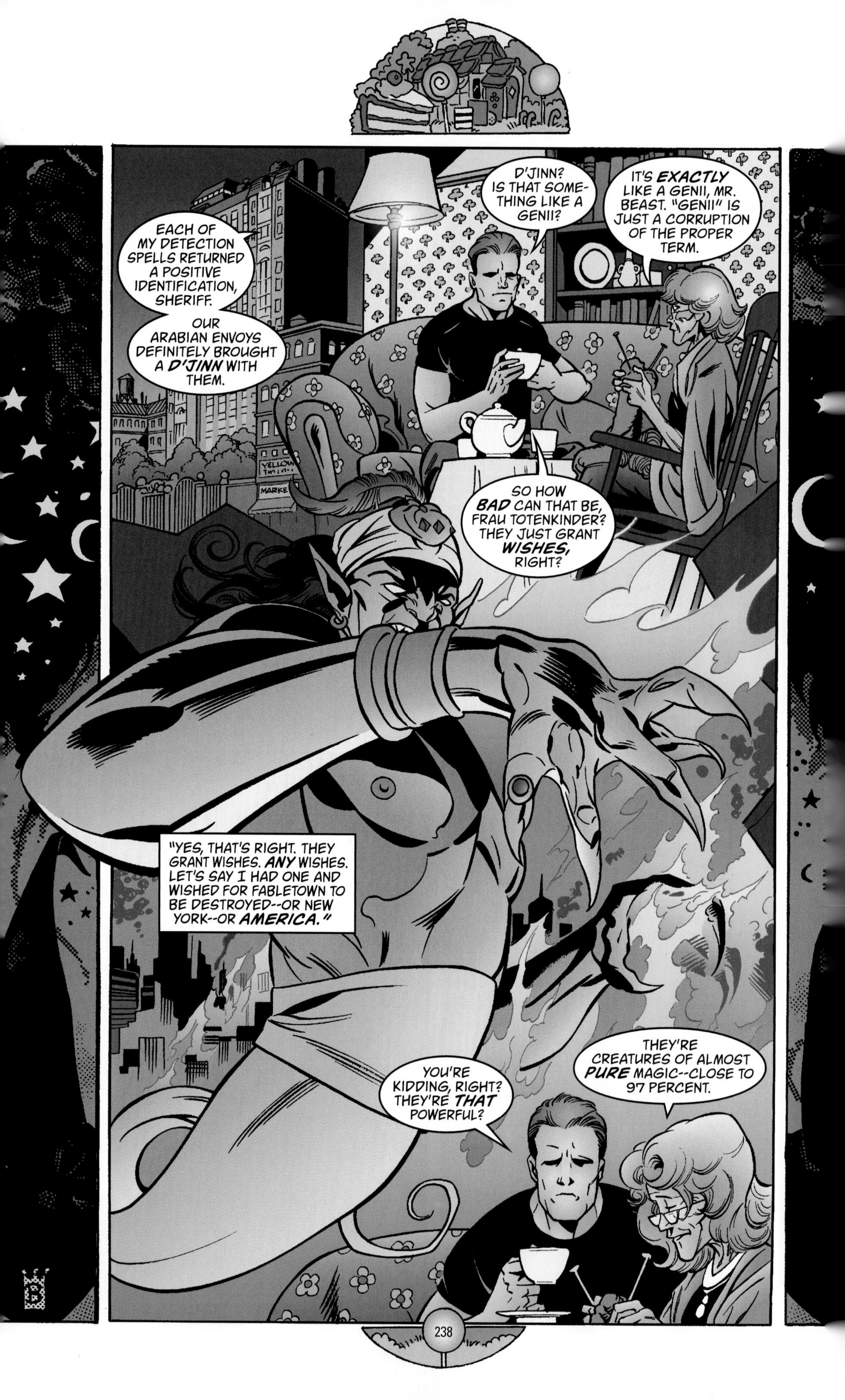

EACH OF MY DETECTION SPELLS RETURNED A POSITIVE IDENTIFICATION, SHERIFF.
OUR ARABIAN ENVOYS DEFINITELY BROUGHT A D'JINN WITH THEM.
D'JINN? IS THAT SOMETHING LIKE A GENII?
IT'S EXACTLY LIKE A GENII, MR. BEAST. "GENII" IS JUST A CORRUPTION OF THE PROPER TERM.
SO HOW BAD CAN THAT BE, FRAU TOTENKINDER? THEY JUST GRANT WISHES, RIGHT?
"YES, THAT'S RIGHT. THEY GRANT WISHES. ANY WISHES. LET'S SAY I HAD ONE AND WISHED FOR FABLETOWN TO BE DESTROYED--OR NEW YORK--OR AMERICA."
YOU'RE KIDDING, RIGHT? THEY'RE THAT POWERFUL?
THEY'RE CREATURES OF ALMOST PURE MAGIC--CLOSE TO 97 PERCENT.

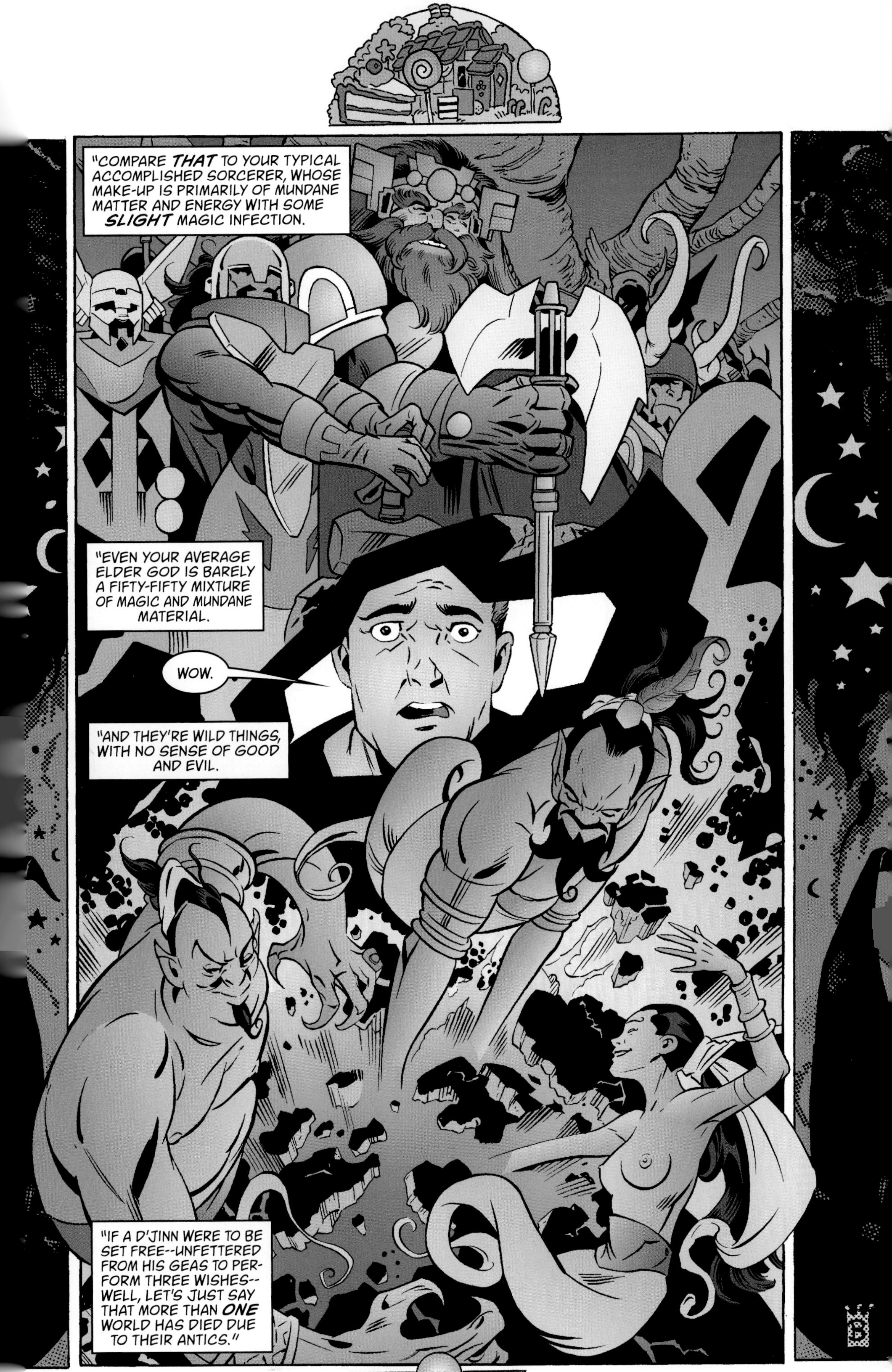
"COMPARE THAT TO YOUR TYPICAL ACCOMPLISHED SORCERER, WHOSE MAKE-UP IS PRIMARILY OF MUNDANE MATTER AND ENERGY WITH SOME SLIGHT MAGIC INFECTION.
"EVEN YOUR AVERAGE ELDER GOD IS BARELY A FIFTY-FIFTY MIXTURE OF MAGIC AND MUNDANE MATERIAL.
WOW.
"AND THEY'RE WILD THINGS, WITH NO SENSE OF GOOD AND EVIL.
"IF A D'JINN WERE TO BE SET FREE--UNFETTERED FROM HIS GEAS TO PERFORM THREE WISHES--WELL, LET'S JUST SAY THAT MORE THAN ONE WORLD HAS DIED DUE TO THEIR ANTICS."

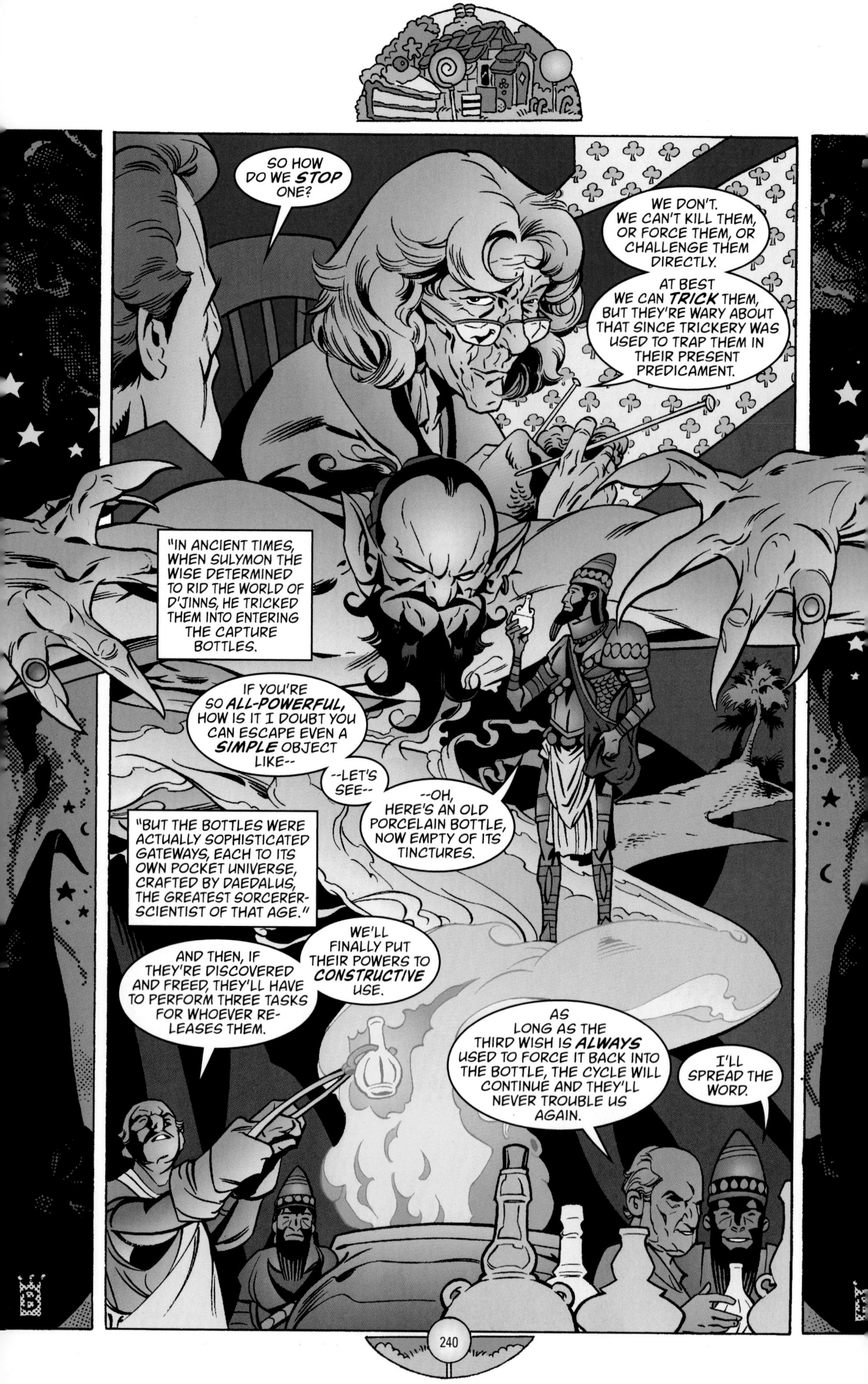
SO HOW DO WE STOP ONE?
WE DON'T. WE CAN'T KILL THEM, OR FORCE THEM, OR CHALLENGE THEM DIRECTLY.
AT BEST WE CAN TRICK THEM, BUT THEY'RE WARY ABOUT THAT SINCE TRICKERY WAS USED TO TRAP THEM IN THEIR PRESENT PREDICAMENT.
"IN ANCIENT TIMES, WHEN SULYMON THE WISE DETERMINED TO RID THE WORLD OF D'JINNS, HE TRICKED THEM INTO ENTERING THE CAPTURE BOTTLES.
IF YOU'RE SO ALL-POWERFUL, HOW IS IT I DOUBT YOU CAN ESCAPE EVEN A SIMPLE OBJECT LIKE--
--LET'S SEE--
--OH, HERE'S AN OLD PORCELAIN BOTTLE, NOW EMPTY OF ITS TINCTURES.
"BUT THE BOTTLES WERE ACTUALLY SOPHISTICATED GATEWAYS, EACH TO ITS OWN POCKET UNIVERSE, CRAFTED BY DAEDALUS, THE GREATEST SORCERER-SCIENTIST OF THAT AGE."
WE'LL FINALLY PUT THEIR POWERS TO CONSTRUCTIVE USE.
AND THEN, IF THEY'RE DISCOVERED AND FREED, THEY'LL HAVE TO PERFORM THREE TASKS FOR WHOEVER RE-LEASES THEM.
AS LONG AS THE THIRD WISH IS ALWAYS USED TO FORCE IT BACK INTO THE BOTTLE, THE CYCLE WILL CONTINUE AND THEY'LL NEVER TROUBLE US AGAIN.
I'LL SPREAD THE WORD.

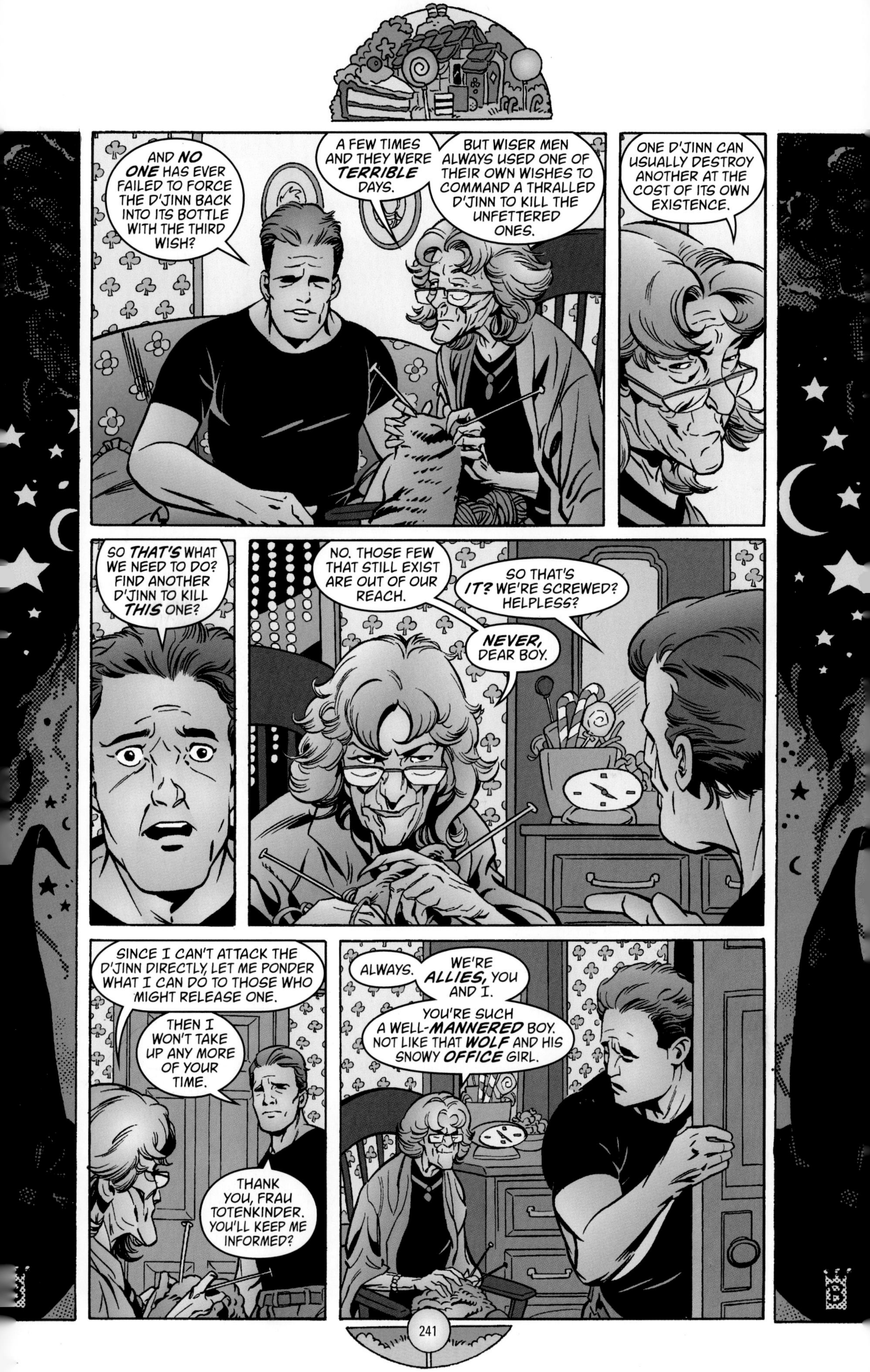
AND NO ONE HAS EVER FAILED TO FORCE THE D'JINN BACK INTO ITS BOTTLE WITH THE THIRD WISH?
A FEW TIMES AND THEY WERE TERRIBLE DAYS.
BUT WISER MEN ALWAYS USED ONE OF THEIR OWN WISHES TO COMMAND A THRALLED D'JINN TO KILL THE UNFETTERED ONES.
ONE D'JINN CAN USUALLY DESTROY ANOTHER AT THE COST OF ITS OWN EXISTENCE.
SO THAT'S WHAT WE NEED TO DO? FIND ANOTHER D'JINN TO KILL THIS ONE?
NO. THOSE FEW THAT STILL EXIST ARE OUT OF OUR REACH.
SO THAT'S IT? WE'RE SCREWED? HELPLESS?
NEVER, DEAR BOY.
SINCE I CAN'T ATTACK THE D'JINN DIRECTLY, LET ME PONDER WHAT I CAN DO TO THOSE WHO MIGHT RELEASE ONE.
THEN I WON'T TAKE UP ANY MORE OF YOUR TIME.
THANK YOU, FRAU TOTENKINDER. YOU'LL KEEP ME INFORMED?
ALWAYS.
WE'RE ALLIES, YOU AND I.
YOU'RE SUCH A WELL-MANNERED BOY. NOT LIKE THAT WOLF AND HIS SNOWY OFFICE GIRL.

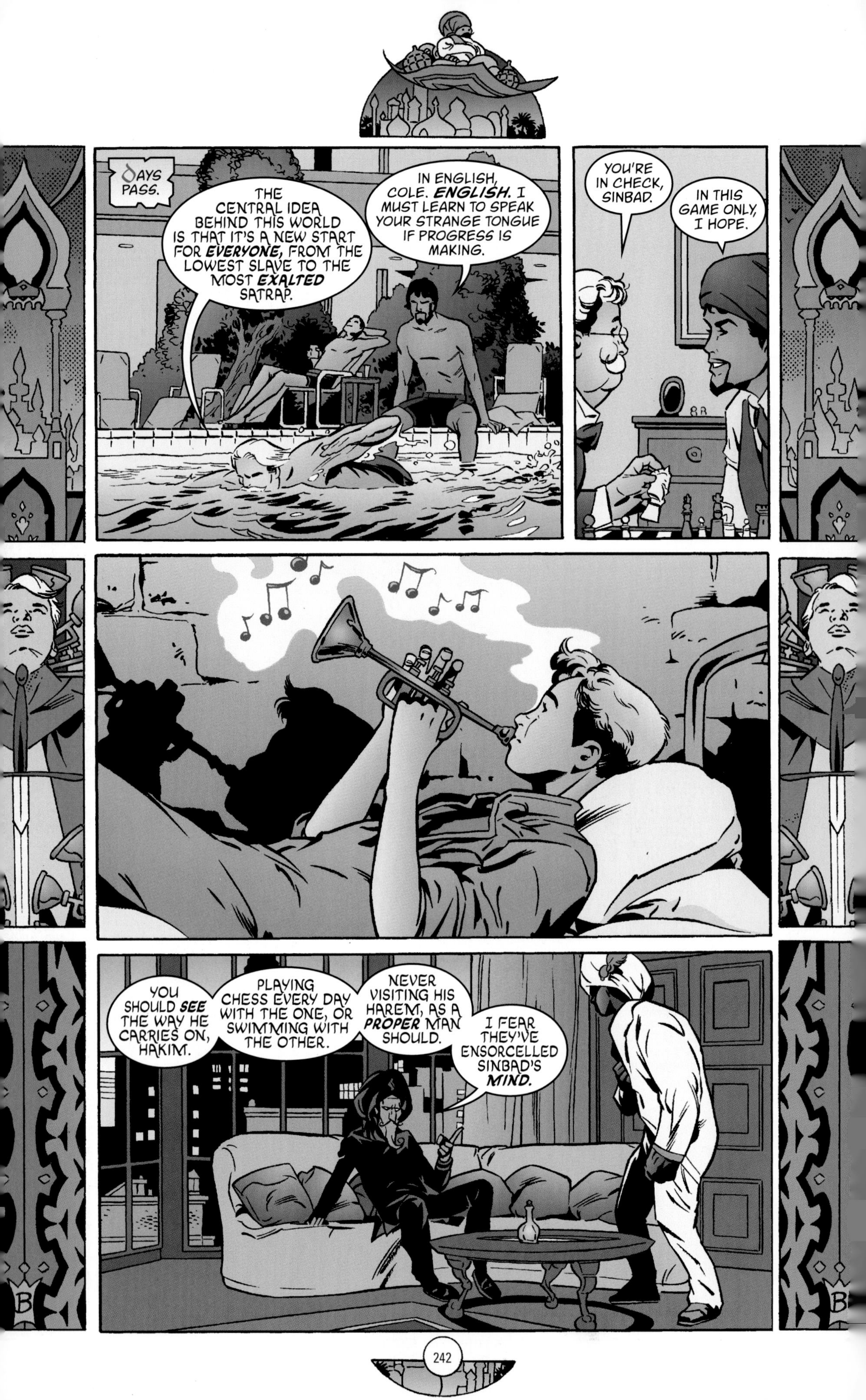
DAYS PASS.
THE CENTRAL IDEA BEHIND THIS WORLD IS THAT IT'S A NEW START FOR EVERYONE, FROM THE LOWEST SLAVE TO THE MOST EXALTED SATRAP.
IN ENGLISH, COLE. ENGLISH. I MUST LEARN TO SPEAK YOUR STRANGE TONGUE IF PROGRESS IS MAKING.
YOU'RE IN CHECK, SINBAD.
IN THIS GAME ONLY, I HOPE.
YOU SHOULD SEE THE WAY HE CARRIES ON, HAKIM.
PLAYING CHESS EVERY DAY WITH THE ONE, OR SWIMMING WITH THE OTHER.
NEVER VISITING HIS HAREM, AS A PROPER MAN SHOULD.
I FEAR THEY'VE ENSORCELLED SINBAD'S MIND.

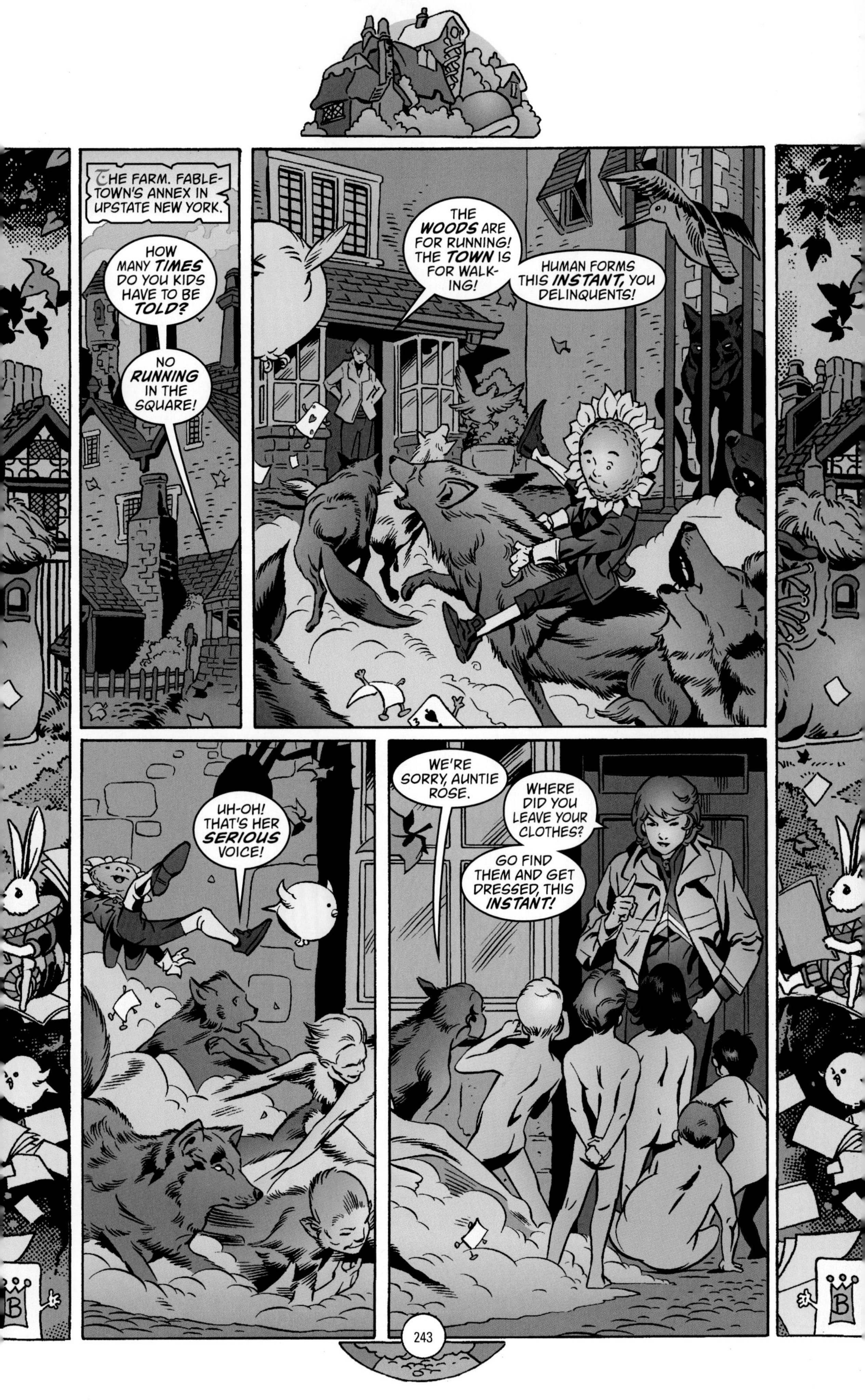
THE FARM. FABLE-TOWN'S ANNEX IN UPSTATE NEW YORK.
HOW MANY TIMES DO YOU KIDS HAVE TO BE TOLD?
NO RUNNING IN THE SQUARE!
THE WOODS ARE FOR RUNNING! THE TOWN IS FOR WALK-ING!
HUMAN FORMS THIS INSTANT, YOU DELINQUENTS!
UH-OH! THAT'S HER SERIOUS VOICE!
WE'RE SORRY, AUNTIE ROSE.
WHERE DID YOU LEAVE YOUR CLOTHES?
GO FIND THEM AND GET DRESSED, THIS INSTANT!

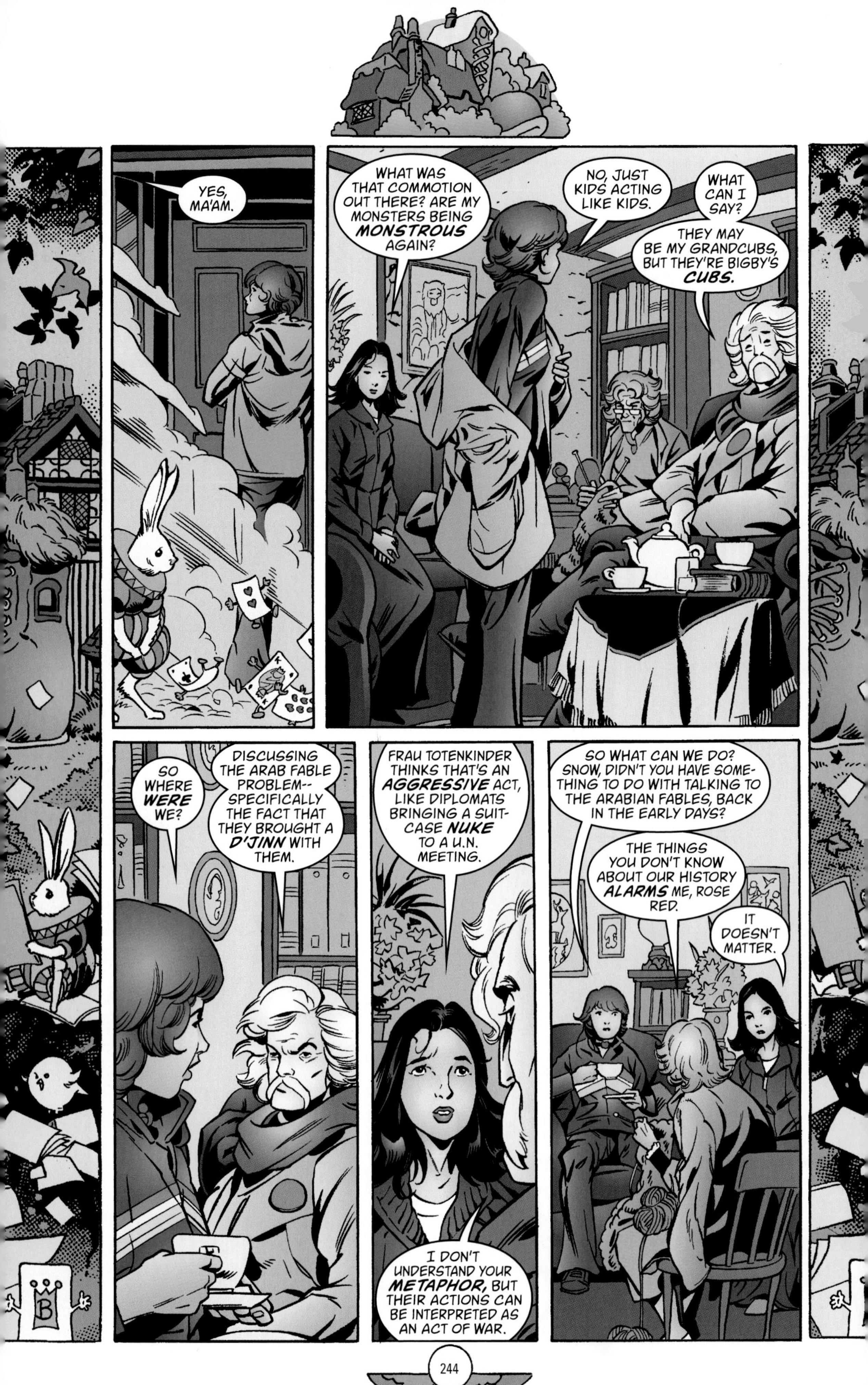
YES, MA'AM.
WHAT WAS THAT COMMOTION OUT THERE? ARE MY MONSTERS BEING MONSTROUS AGAIN?
NO, JUST KIDS ACTING LIKE KIDS.
WHAT CAN I SAY?
THEY MAY BE MY GRANDCUBS, BUT THEY'RE BIGBY'S CUBS.
SO WHERE WERE WE?
DISCUSSING THE ARAB FABLE PROBLEM-- SPECIFICALLY THE FACT THAT THEY BROUGHT A D'JINN WITH THEM.
FRAU TOTENKINDER THINKS THAT'S AN AGGRESSIVE ACT, LIKE DIPLOMATS BRINGING A SUIT-CASE NUKE TO A U.N. MEETING.
I DON'T UNDERSTAND YOUR METAPHOR, BUT THEIR ACTIONS CAN BE INTERPRETED AS AN ACT OF WAR.
SO WHAT CAN WE DO? SNOW, DIDN'T YOU HAVE SOME-THING TO DO WITH TALKING TO THE ARABIAN FABLES, BACK IN THE EARLY DAYS?
THE THINGS YOU DON'T KNOW ABOUT OUR HISTORY ALARMS ME, ROSE RED.
IT DOESN'T MATTER.

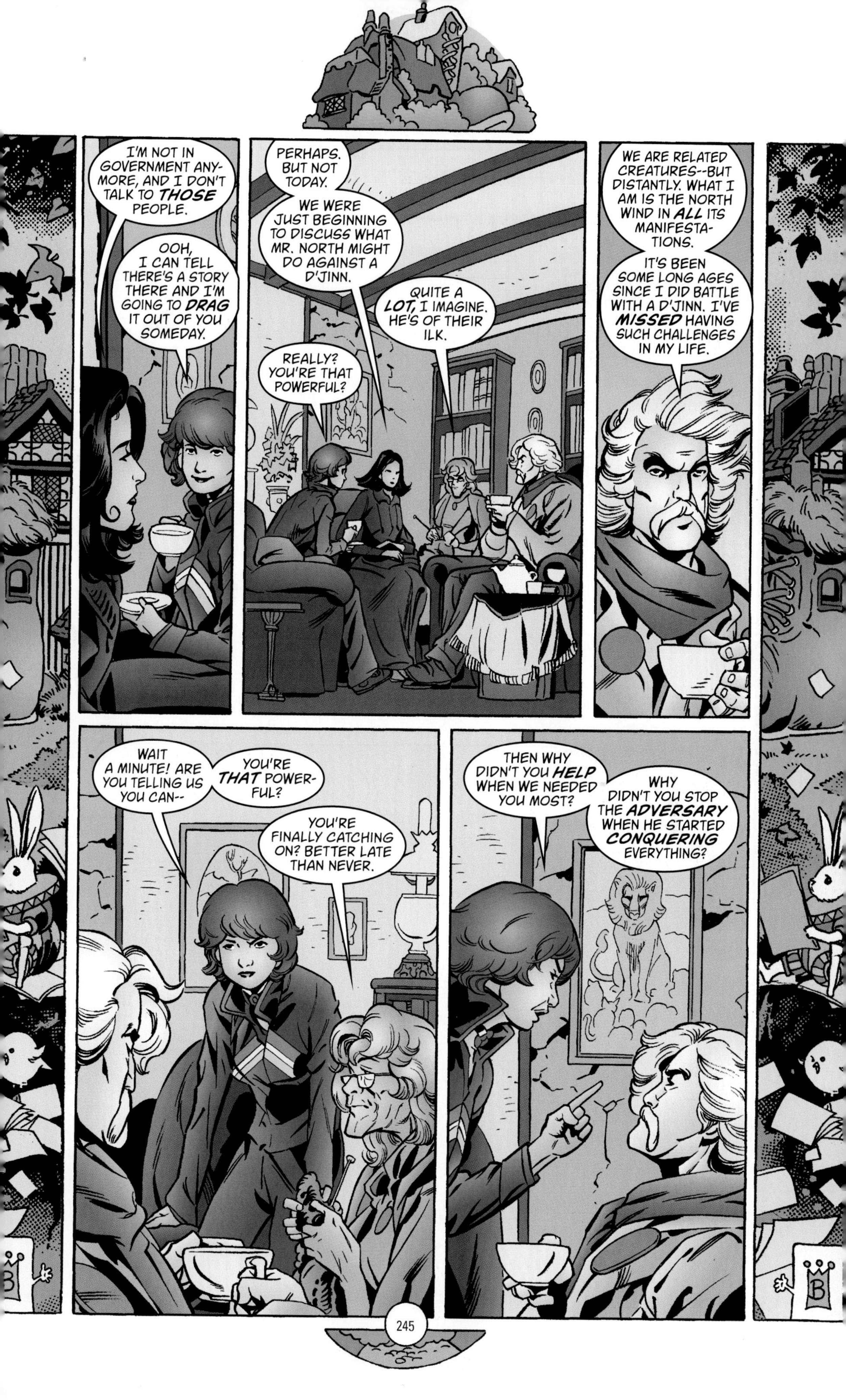

I'M NOT IN GOVERNMENT ANY-MORE, AND I DON'T TALK TO THOSE PEOPLE.
OOH, I CAN TELL THERE'S A STORY THERE AND I'M GOING TO DRAG IT OUT OF YOU SOMEDAY.
PERHAPS. BUT NOT TODAY.
WE WERE JUST BEGINNING TO DISCUSS WHAT MR. NORTH MIGHT DO AGAINST A D'JINN.
QUITE A LOT, I IMAGINE. HE'S OF THEIR ILK.
REALLY? YOU'RE THAT POWERFUL?
WE ARE RELATED CREATURES--BUT DISTANTLY. WHAT I AM IS THE NORTH WIND IN ALL ITS MANIFESTA-TIONS.
IT'S BEEN SOME LONG AGES SINCE I DID BATTLE WITH A D'JINN. I'VE MISSED HAVING SUCH CHALLENGES IN MY LIFE.
WAIT A MINUTE! ARE YOU TELLING US YOU CAN--
YOU'RE THAT POWER-FUL?
YOU'RE FINALLY CATCHING ON? BETTER LATE THAN NEVER.
THEN WHY DIDN'T YOU HELP WHEN WE NEEDED YOU MOST?
WHY DIDN'T YOU STOP THE ADVERSARY WHEN HE STARTED CONQUERING EVERYTHING?

WHY **WOULD** I? GOVERN-MENTS COME AND GO. I'VE SEEN EMPIRES RISE AND FALL AND DISAPPEAR INTO THE DUST TO BE FORGOTTEN.

I'M APART FROM SUCH CONSIDERATIONS. THE ADVERSARY'S MINIONS KNOW TO LEAVE ME ALONE, AND THAT IS ENOUGH.

BUT YOU'RE HERE NOW, **HELPING** US!

THIS IS DIFFERENT. YOU'RE **FAMILY.**

CALM DOWN, ROSE. YOU'LL BUST SOMETHING.

MR. NORTH, YOU'RE SAYING YOU'D BE WILLING TO FIGHT THIS D'JINN? YOU COULD **KILL** IT?

I'D **WELCOME** THE SPORT.

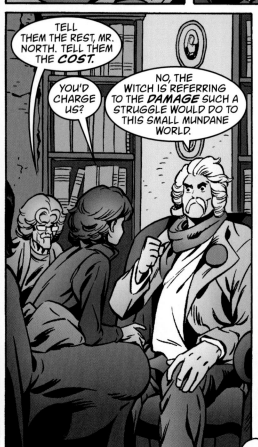

TELL THEM THE REST, MR. NORTH. TELL THEM THE **COST.**

YOU'D CHARGE US?

NO, THE WITCH IS REFERRING TO THE **DAMAGE** SUCH A STRUGGLE WOULD DO TO THIS SMALL MUNDANE WORLD.

TO THE WORLD?

YES, YOUR PEOPLE WOULD HAVE TO **MOVE** AGAIN.

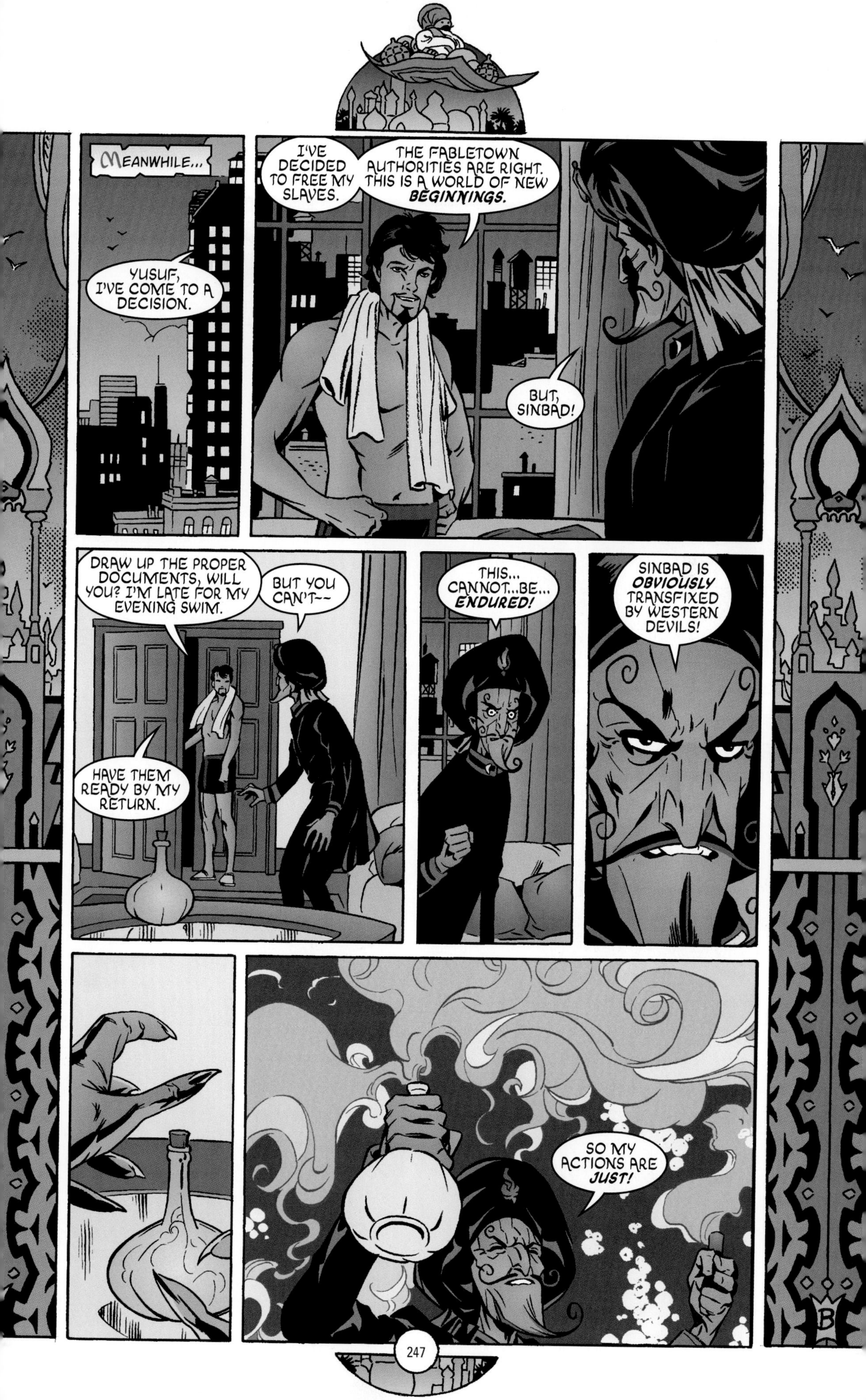
MEANWHILE...
YUSUF, I'VE COME TO A DECISION.
I'VE DECIDED TO FREE MY SLAVES.
THE FABLETOWN AUTHORITIES ARE RIGHT. THIS IS A WORLD OF NEW BEGINNINGS.
BUT, SINBAD!
DRAW UP THE PROPER DOCUMENTS, WILL YOU? I'M LATE FOR MY EVENING SWIM.
BUT YOU CAN'T--
HAVE THEM READY BY MY RETURN.
THIS... CANNOT...BE... ENDURED!
SINBAD IS OBVIOUSLY TRANSFIXED BY WESTERN DEVILS!
SO MY ACTIONS ARE JUST!

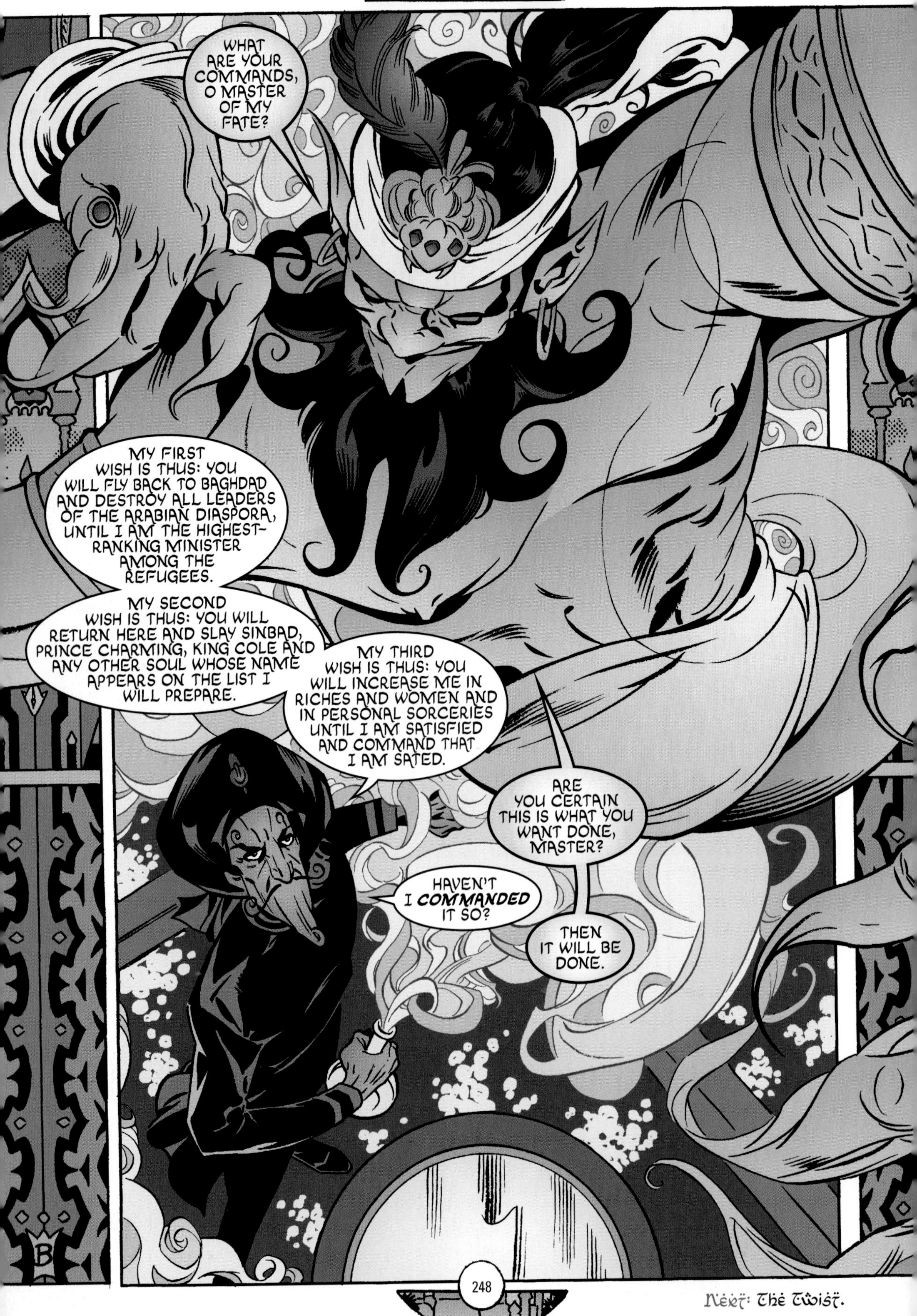
WHAT ARE YOUR COMMANDS, O MASTER OF MY FATE?
MY FIRST WISH IS THUS: YOU WILL FLY BACK TO BAGHDAD AND DESTROY ALL LEADERS OF THE ARABIAN DIASPORA, UNTIL I AM THE HIGHEST-RANKING MINISTER AMONG THE REFUGEES.
MY SECOND WISH IS THUS: YOU WILL RETURN HERE AND SLAY SINBAD, PRINCE CHARMING, KING COLE AND ANY OTHER SOUL WHOSE NAME APPEARS ON THE LIST I WILL PREPARE.
MY THIRD WISH IS THUS: YOU WILL INCREASE ME IN RICHES AND WOMEN AND IN PERSONAL SORCERIES UNTIL I AM SATISFIED AND COMMAND THAT I AM SATED.
ARE YOU CERTAIN THIS IS WHAT YOU WANT DONE, MASTER?
HAVEN'T I ***COMMANDED*** IT SO?
THEN IT WILL BE DONE.

Next: The Twist.

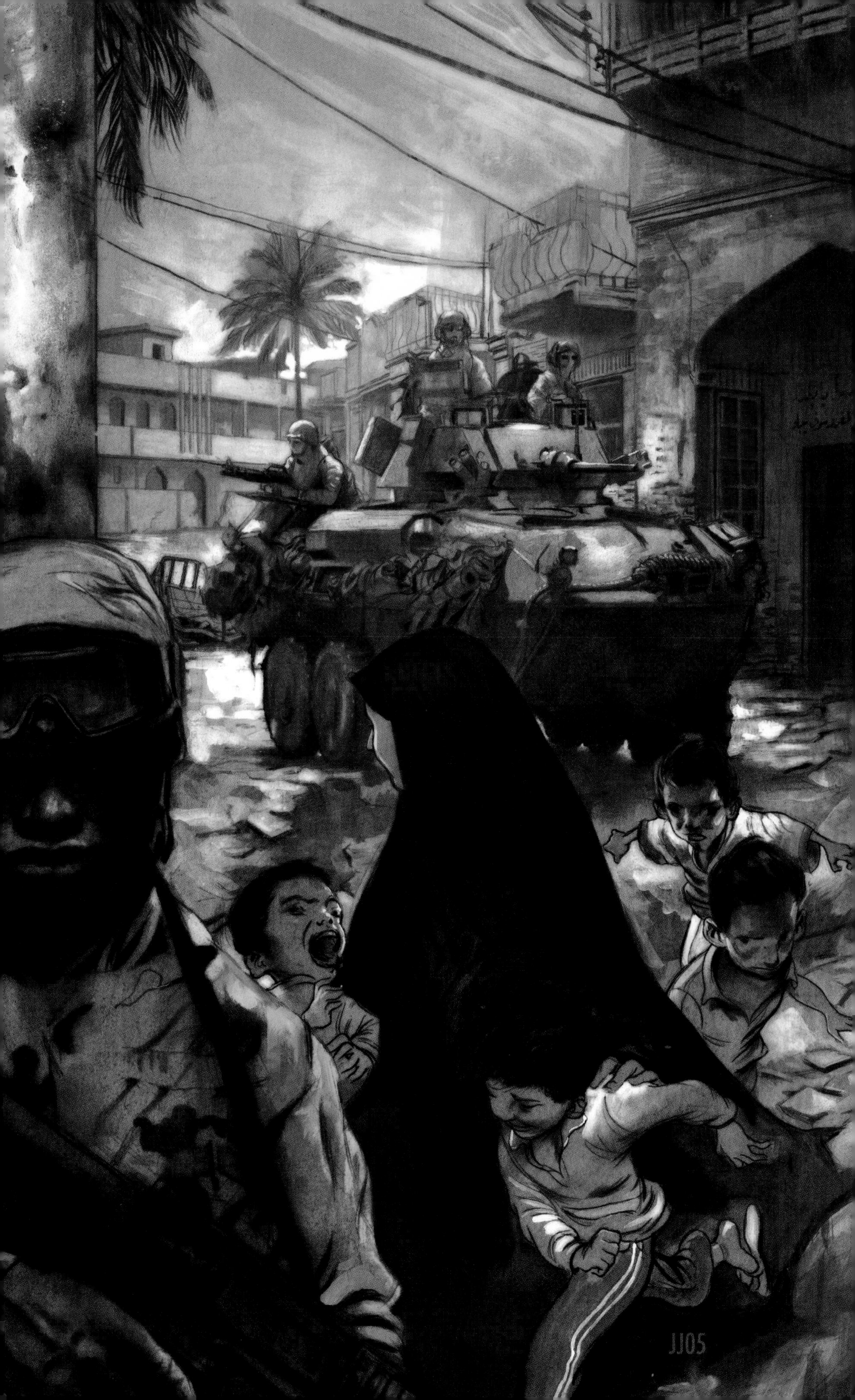
JJ05

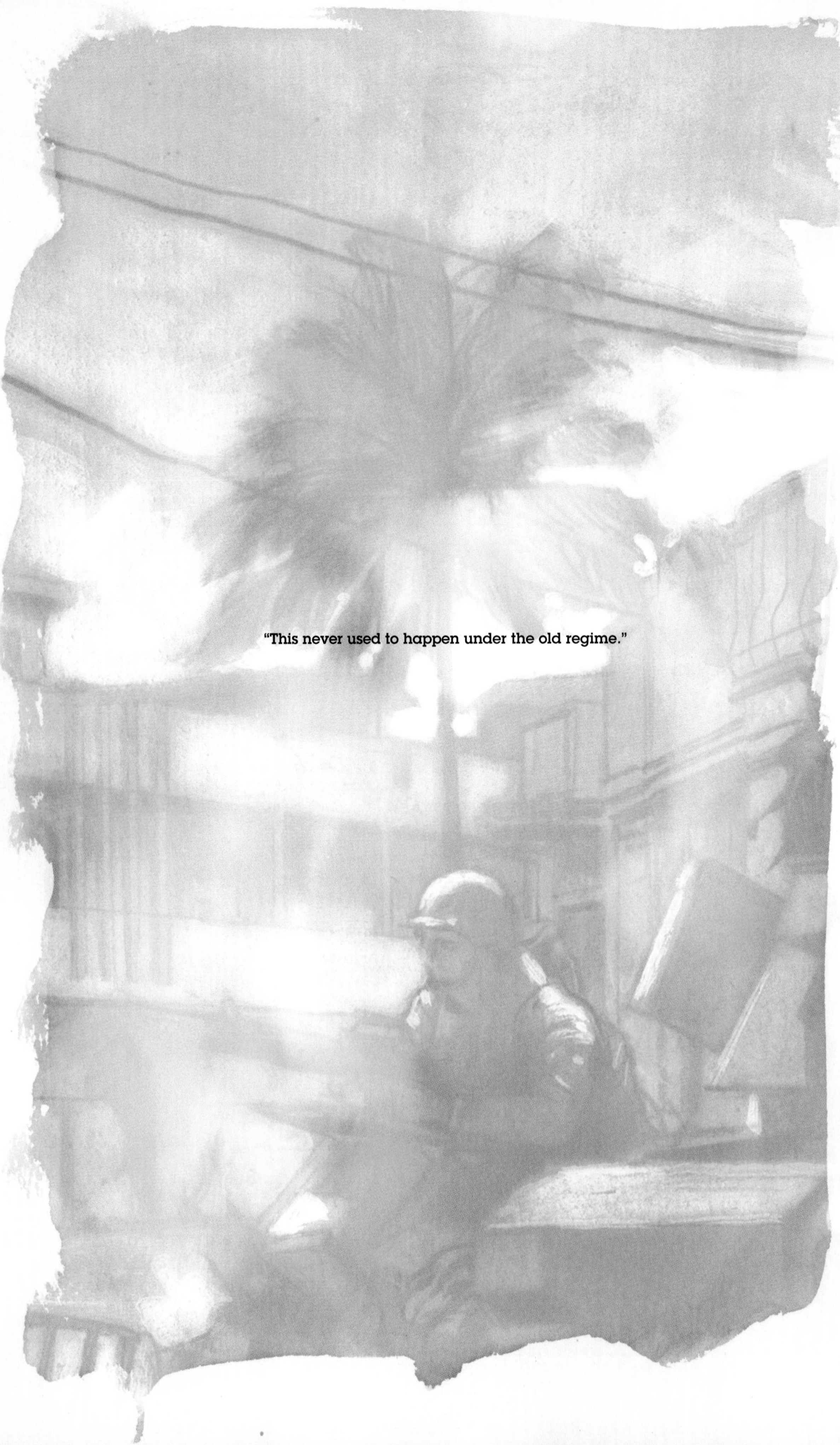
"This never used to happen under the old regime."

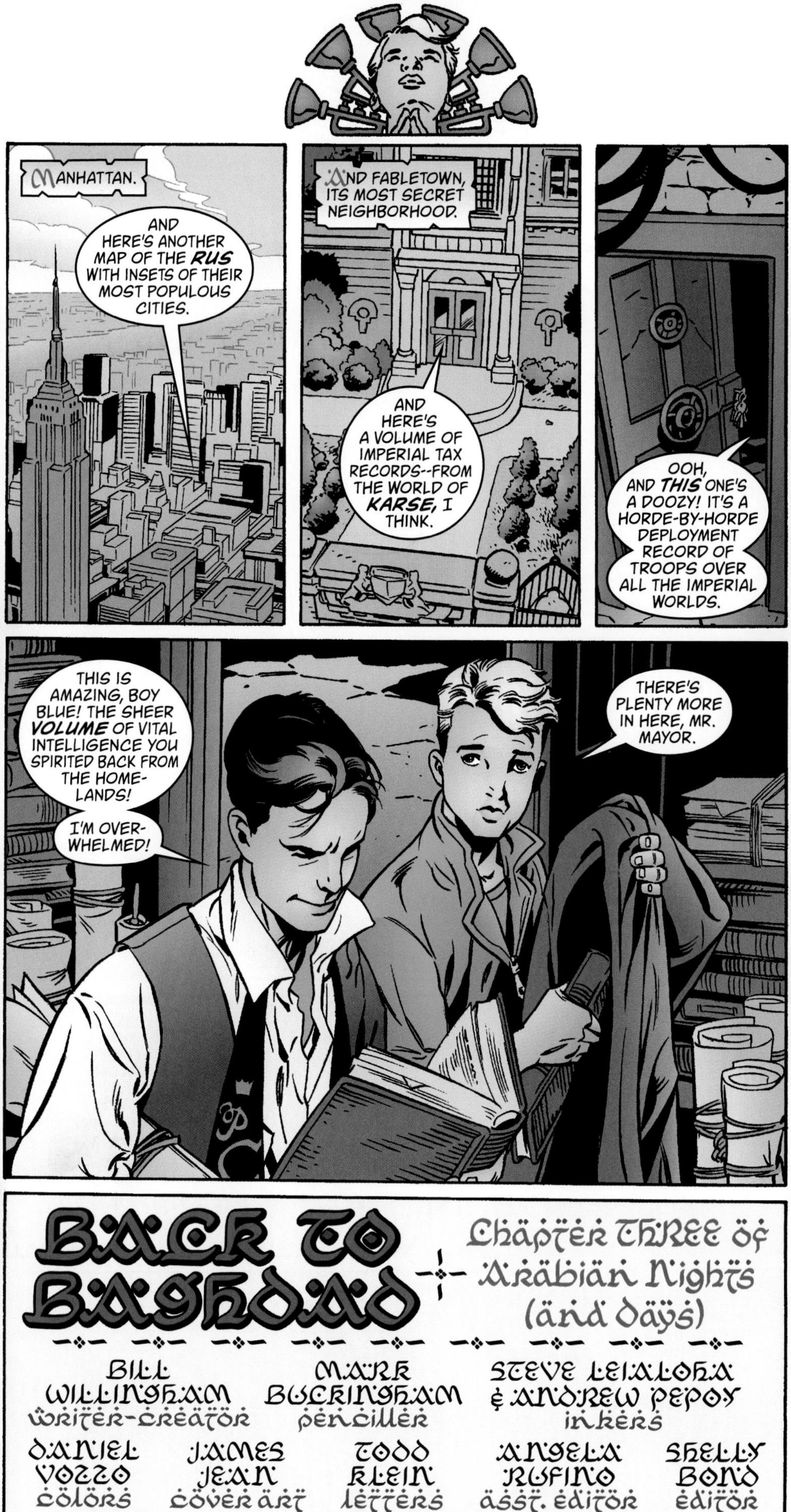

MANHATTAN.
AND HERE'S ANOTHER MAP OF THE RUS WITH INSETS OF THEIR MOST POPULOUS CITIES.
AND FABLETOWN, ITS MOST SECRET NEIGHBORHOOD.
AND HERE'S A VOLUME OF IMPERIAL TAX RECORDS--FROM THE WORLD OF KARSE, I THINK.
OOH, AND THIS ONE'S A DOOZY! IT'S A HORDE-BY-HORDE DEPLOYMENT RECORD OF TROOPS OVER ALL THE IMPERIAL WORLDS.
THIS IS AMAZING, BOY BLUE! THE SHEER VOLUME OF VITAL INTELLIGENCE YOU SPIRITED BACK FROM THE HOMELANDS!
I'M OVERWHELMED!
THERE'S PLENTY MORE IN HERE, MR. MAYOR.
BACK TO BAGHDAD
Chapter THREE of Arabian Nights (and days)
BILL WILLINGHAM writer-creator
MARK BUCKINGHAM penciller
STEVE LEIALOHA & ANDREW PEPOY inkers
DANIEL VOZZO colors
JAMES JEAN cover art
TODD KLEIN letters
ANGELA RUFINO asst. editor
SHELLY BOND editor

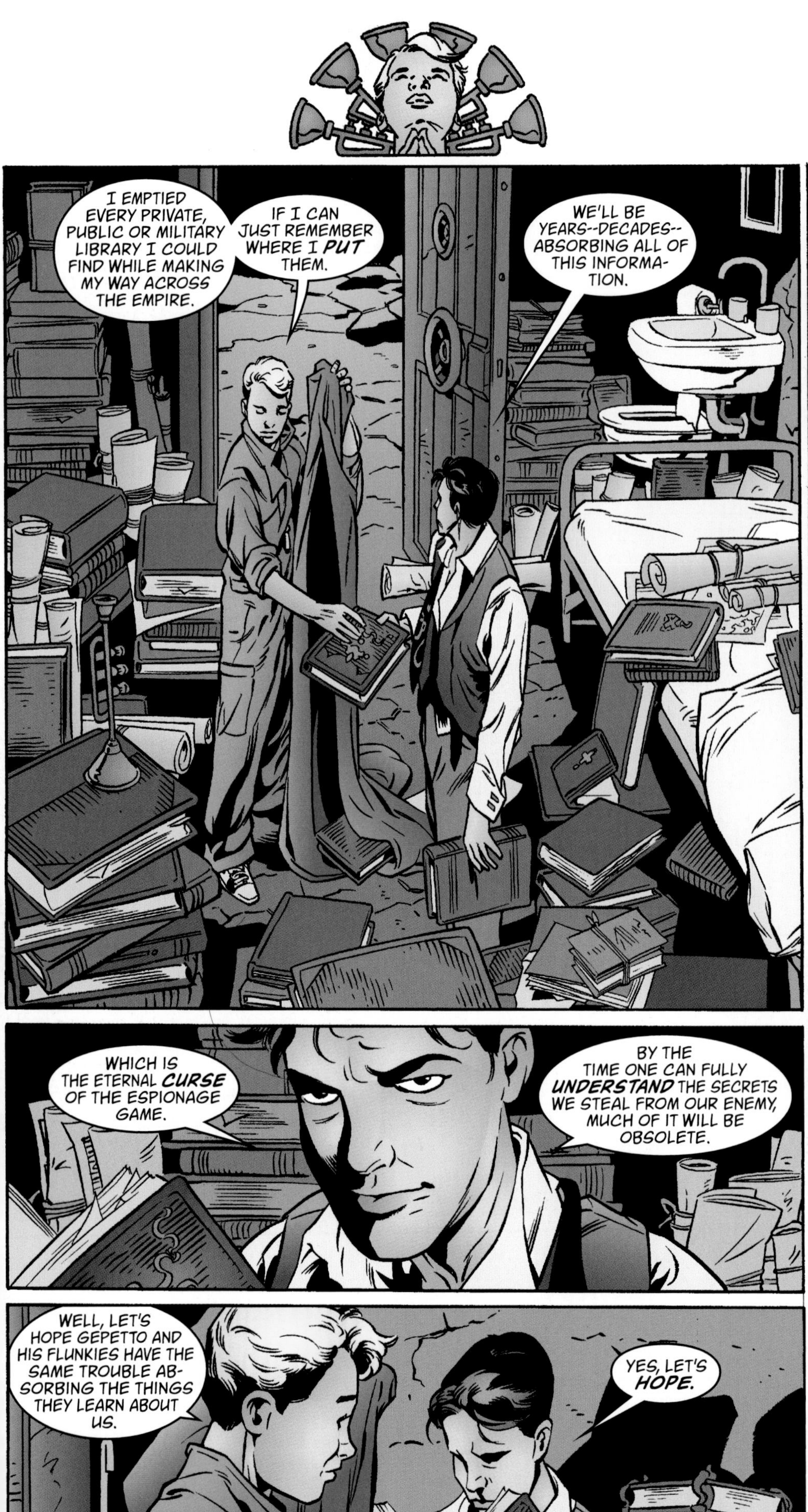

I EMPTIED EVERY PRIVATE, PUBLIC OR MILITARY LIBRARY I COULD FIND WHILE MAKING MY WAY ACROSS THE EMPIRE.
IF I CAN JUST REMEMBER WHERE I *PUT* THEM.
WE'LL BE YEARS--DECADES--ABSORBING ALL OF THIS INFORMATION.
WHICH IS THE ETERNAL ***CURSE*** OF THE ESPIONAGE GAME.
BY THE TIME ONE CAN FULLY ***UNDERSTAND*** THE SECRETS WE STEAL FROM OUR ENEMY, MUCH OF IT WILL BE OBSOLETE.
WELL, LET'S HOPE GEPETTO AND HIS FLUNKIES HAVE THE SAME TROUBLE ABSORBING THE THINGS THEY LEARN ABOUT US.
YES, LET'S ***HOPE.***

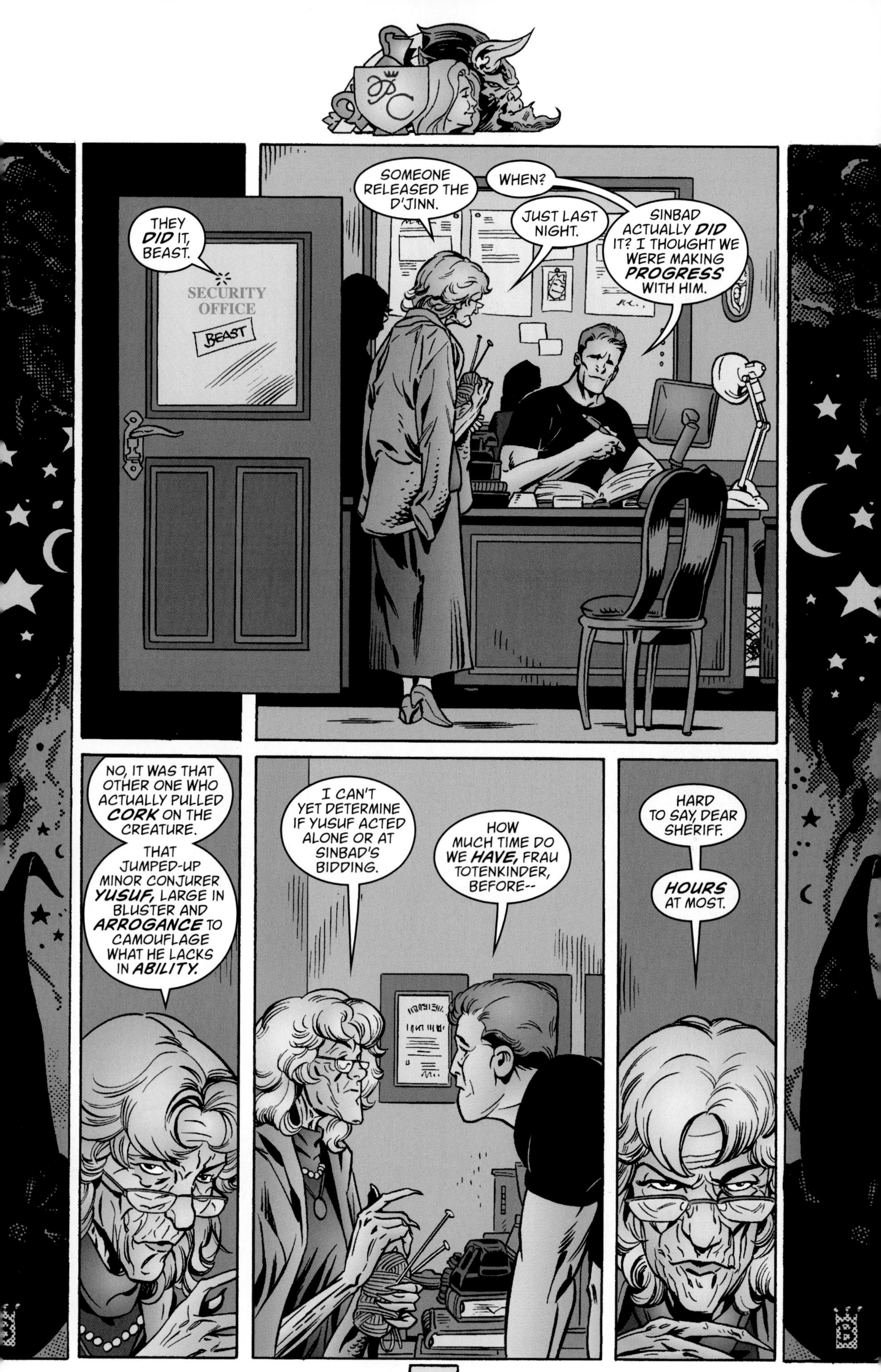

THEY DID IT, BEAST.
SECURITY OFFICE
BEAST
SOMEONE RELEASED THE D'JINN.
WHEN?
JUST LAST NIGHT.
SINBAD ACTUALLY DID IT? I THOUGHT WE WERE MAKING PROGRESS WITH HIM.
NO, IT WAS THAT OTHER ONE WHO ACTUALLY PULLED CORK ON THE CREATURE.
THAT JUMPED-UP MINOR CONJURER YUSUF, LARGE IN BLUSTER AND ARROGANCE TO CAMOUFLAGE WHAT HE LACKS IN ABILITY.
I CAN'T YET DETERMINE IF YUSUF ACTED ALONE OR AT SINBAD'S BIDDING.
HOW MUCH TIME DO WE HAVE, FRAU TOTENKINDER, BEFORE--
HARD TO SAY, DEAR SHERIFF.
HOURS AT MOST.

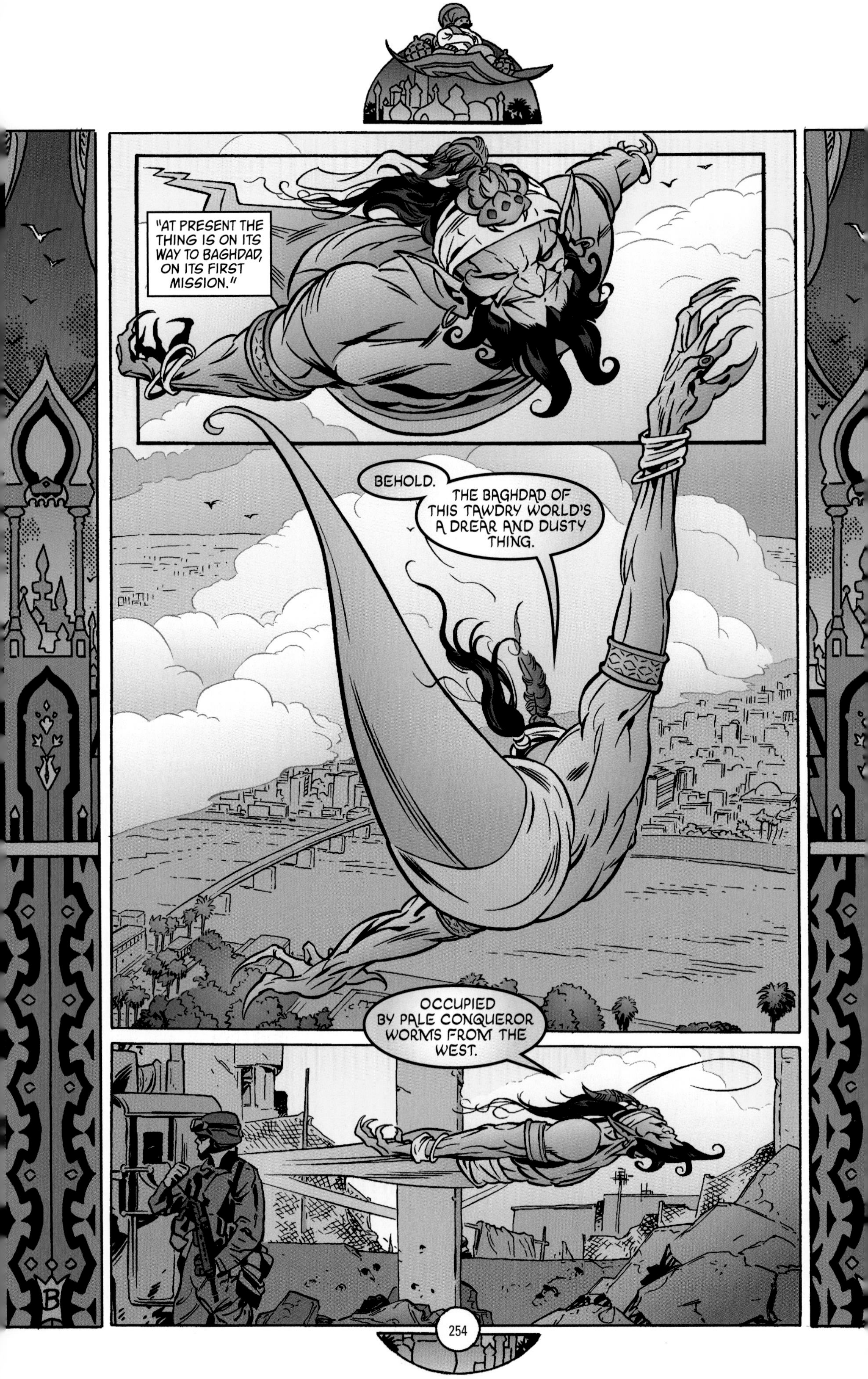
"AT PRESENT THE THING IS ON ITS WAY TO BAGHDAD, ON ITS FIRST MISSION."
BEHOLD.
THE BAGHDAD OF THIS TAWDRY WORLD'S A DREAR AND DUSTY THING.
OCCUPIED BY PALE CONQUEROR WORMS FROM THE WEST.

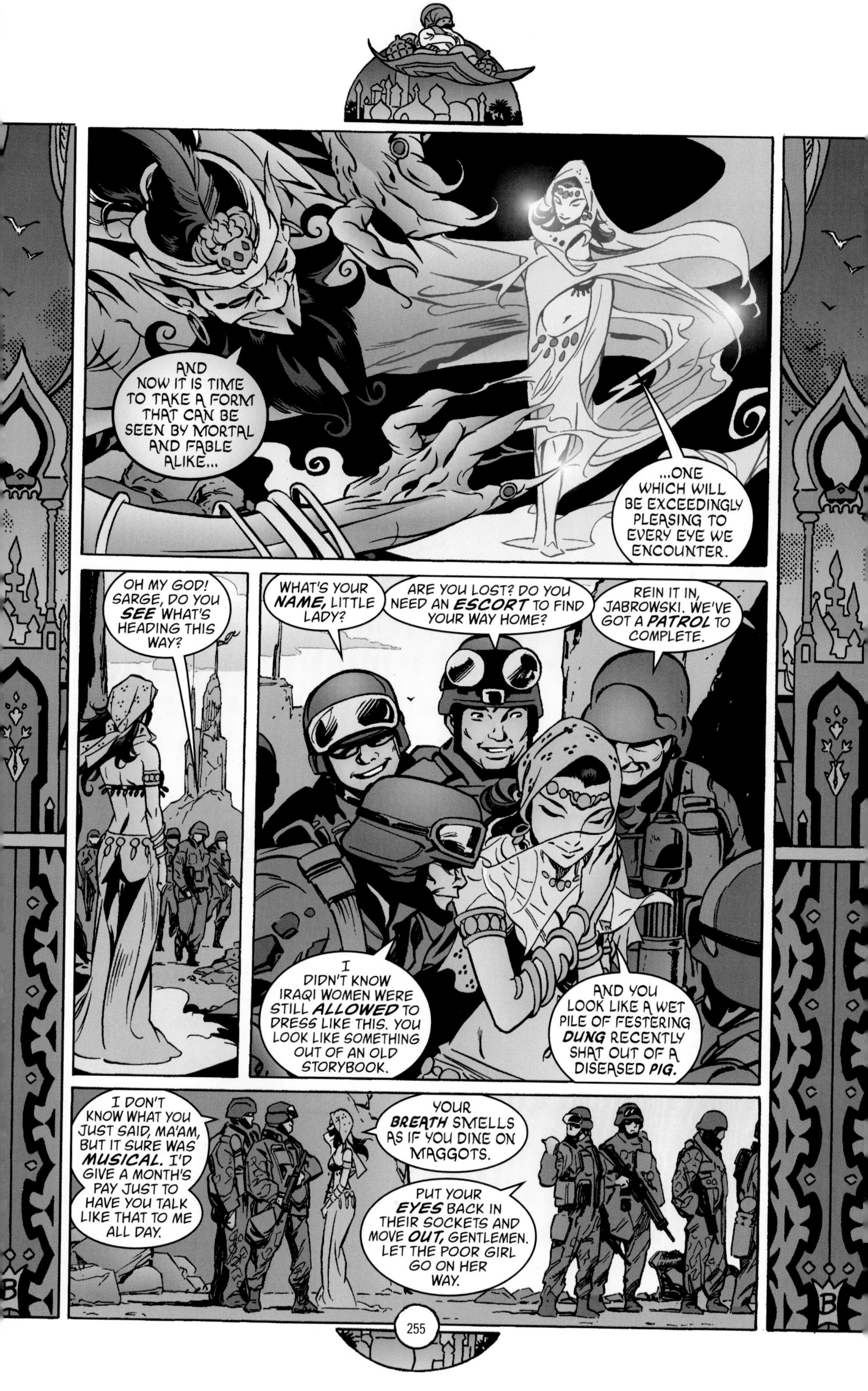
AND NOW IT IS TIME TO TAKE A FORM THAT CAN BE SEEN BY MORTAL AND FABLE ALIKE...
...ONE WHICH WILL BE EXCEEDINGLY PLEASING TO EVERY EYE WE ENCOUNTER.
OH MY GOD! SARGE, DO YOU SEE WHAT'S HEADING THIS WAY?
WHAT'S YOUR NAME, LITTLE LADY?
ARE YOU LOST? DO YOU NEED AN ESCORT TO FIND YOUR WAY HOME?
REIN IT IN, JABROWSKI. WE'VE GOT A PATROL TO COMPLETE.
I DIDN'T KNOW IRAQI WOMEN WERE STILL ALLOWED TO DRESS LIKE THIS. YOU LOOK LIKE SOMETHING OUT OF AN OLD STORYBOOK.
AND YOU LOOK LIKE A WET PILE OF FESTERING DUNG RECENTLY SHAT OUT OF A DISEASED PIG.
I DON'T KNOW WHAT YOU JUST SAID, MA'AM, BUT IT SURE WAS MUSICAL. I'D GIVE A MONTH'S PAY JUST TO HAVE YOU TALK LIKE THAT TO ME ALL DAY.
YOUR BREATH SMELLS AS IF YOU DINE ON MAGGOTS.
PUT YOUR EYES BACK IN THEIR SOCKETS AND MOVE OUT, GENTLEMEN. LET THE POOR GIRL GO ON HER WAY.

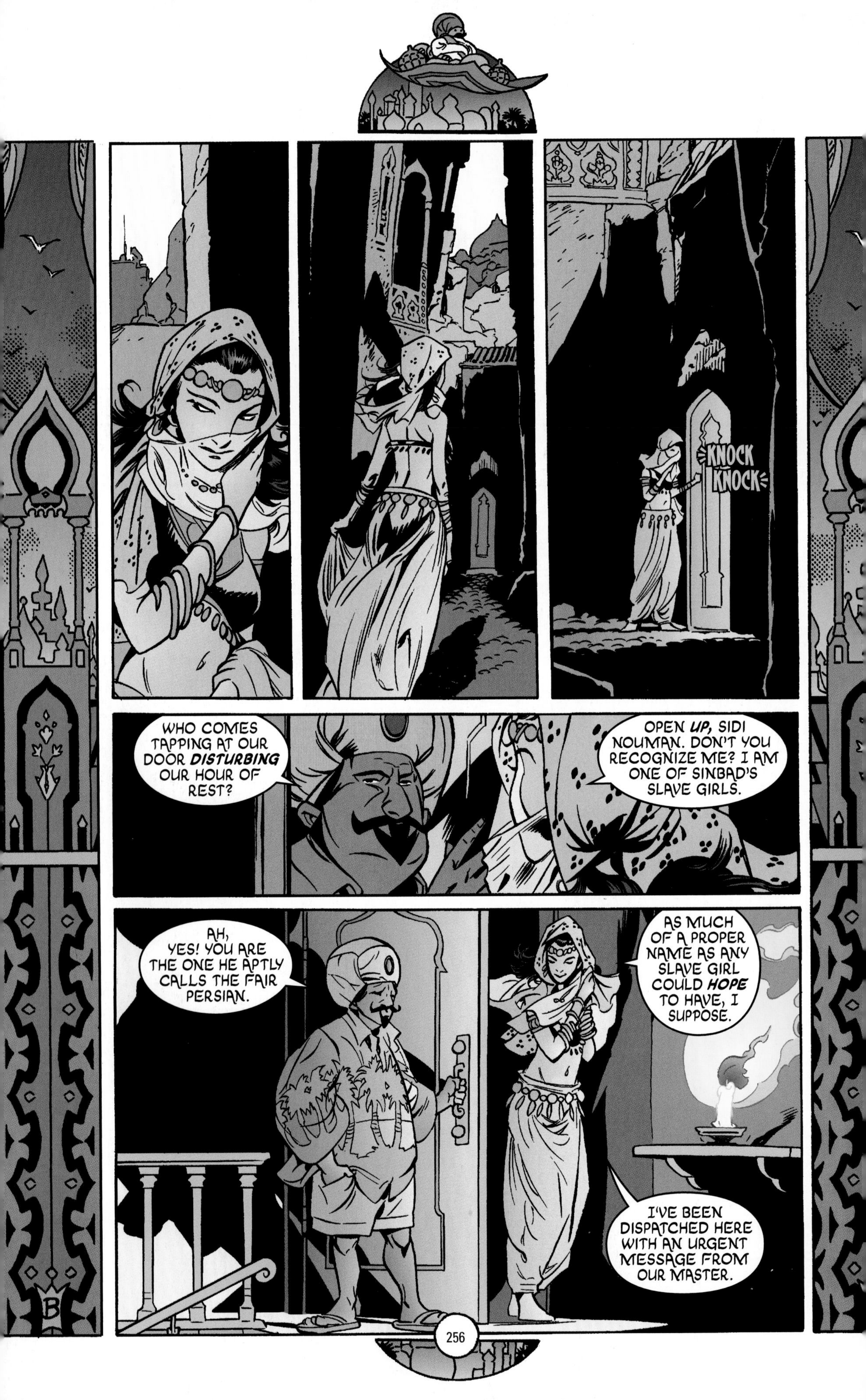
KNOCK
KNOCK
WHO COMES TAPPING AT OUR DOOR DISTURBING OUR HOUR OF REST?
OPEN UP, SIDI NOUMAN. DON'T YOU RECOGNIZE ME? I AM ONE OF SINBAD'S SLAVE GIRLS.
AH, YES! YOU ARE THE ONE HE APTLY CALLS THE FAIR PERSIAN.
AS MUCH OF A PROPER NAME AS ANY SLAVE GIRL COULD HOPE TO HAVE, I SUPPOSE.
I'VE BEEN DISPATCHED HERE WITH AN URGENT MESSAGE FROM OUR MASTER.

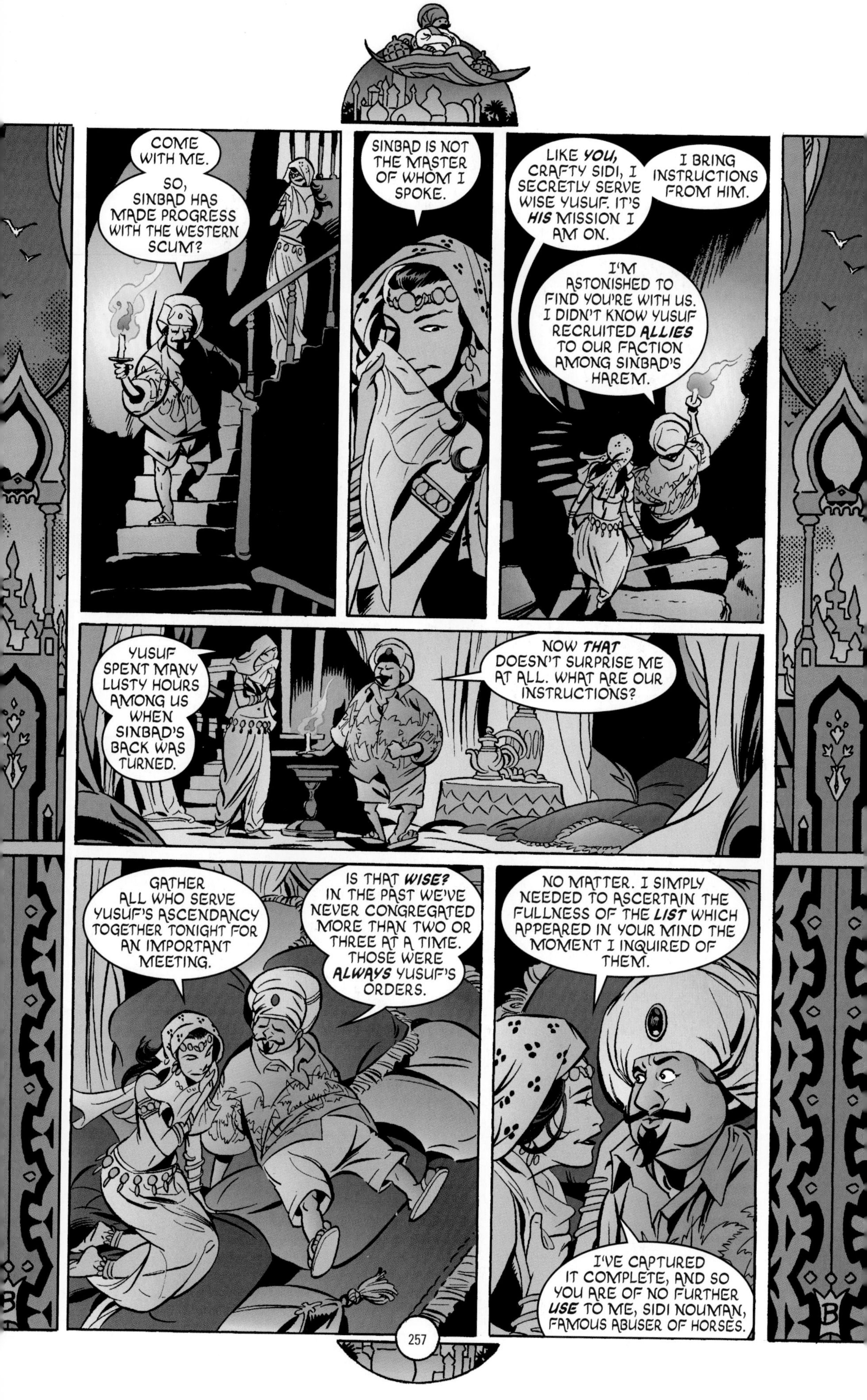

COME WITH ME.
SO, SINBAD HAS MADE PROGRESS WITH THE WESTERN SCUM?
SINBAD IS NOT THE MASTER OF WHOM I SPOKE.
LIKE YOU, CRAFTY SIDI, I SECRETLY SERVE WISE YUSUF. IT'S HIS MISSION I AM ON.
I BRING INSTRUCTIONS FROM HIM.
I'M ASTONISHED TO FIND YOU'RE WITH US. I DIDN'T KNOW YUSUF RECRUITED ALLIES TO OUR FACTION AMONG SINBAD'S HAREM.
YUSUF SPENT MANY LUSTY HOURS AMONG US WHEN SINBAD'S BACK WAS TURNED.
NOW THAT DOESN'T SURPRISE ME AT ALL. WHAT ARE OUR INSTRUCTIONS?
GATHER ALL WHO SERVE YUSUF'S ASCENDANCY TOGETHER TONIGHT FOR AN IMPORTANT MEETING.
IS THAT WISE? IN THE PAST WE'VE NEVER CONGREGATED MORE THAN TWO OR THREE AT A TIME. THOSE WERE ALWAYS YUSUF'S ORDERS.
NO MATTER. I SIMPLY NEEDED TO ASCERTAIN THE FULLNESS OF THE LIST WHICH APPEARED IN YOUR MIND THE MOMENT I INQUIRED OF THEM.
I'VE CAPTURED IT COMPLETE, AND SO YOU ARE OF NO FURTHER USE TO ME, SIDI NOUMAN, FAMOUS ABUSER OF HORSES.

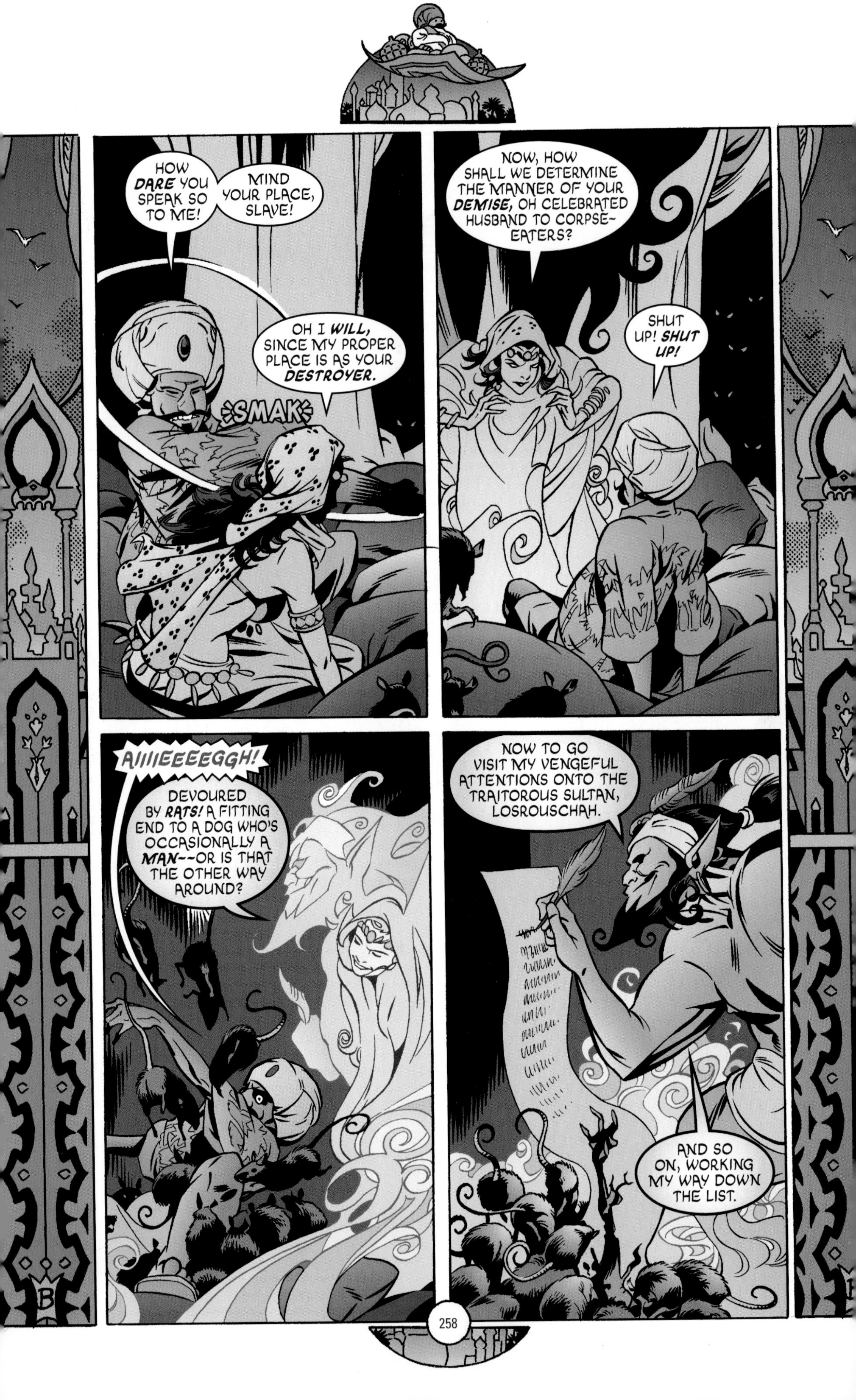
HOW DARE YOU SPEAK SO TO ME!
MIND YOUR PLACE, SLAVE!
OH I WILL, SINCE MY PROPER PLACE IS AS YOUR DESTROYER.
SMAK
NOW, HOW SHALL WE DETERMINE THE MANNER OF YOUR DEMISE, OH CELEBRATED HUSBAND TO CORPSE-EATERS?
SHUT UP! SHUT UP!
AIIIIEEEEEGGH!
DEVOURED BY RATS! A FITTING END TO A DOG WHO'S OCCASIONALLY A MAN--OR IS THAT THE OTHER WAY AROUND?
NOW TO GO VISIT MY VENGEFUL ATTENTIONS ONTO THE TRAITOROUS SULTAN, LOSROUSCHAH.
AND SO ON, WORKING MY WAY DOWN THE LIST.

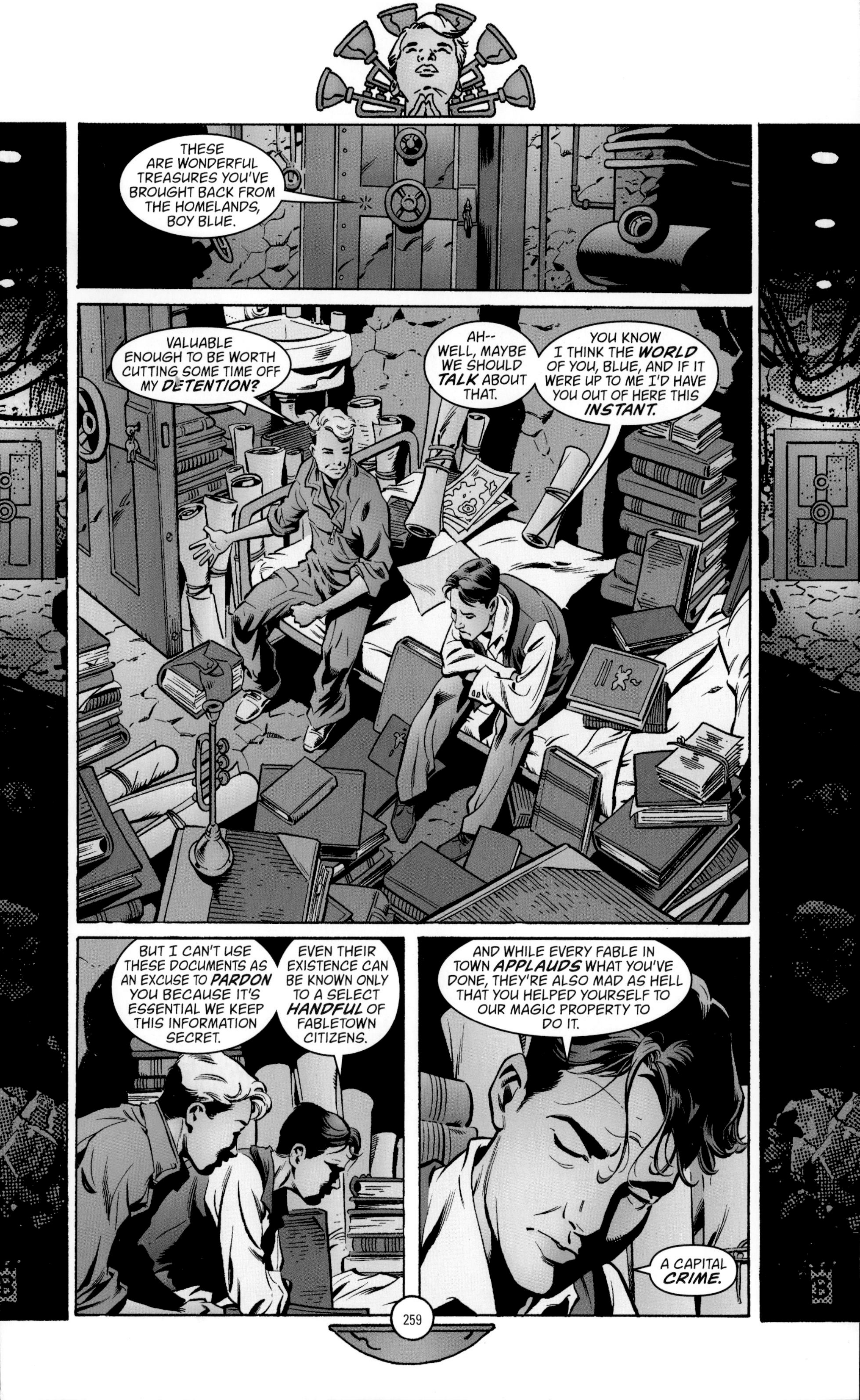
THESE ARE WONDERFUL TREASURES YOU'VE BROUGHT BACK FROM THE HOMELANDS, BOY BLUE.
VALUABLE ENOUGH TO BE WORTH CUTTING SOME TIME OFF MY DETENTION?
AH-- WELL, MAYBE WE SHOULD TALK ABOUT THAT.
YOU KNOW I THINK THE WORLD OF YOU, BLUE, AND IF IT WERE UP TO ME I'D HAVE YOU OUT OF HERE THIS INSTANT.
BUT I CAN'T USE THESE DOCUMENTS AS AN EXCUSE TO PARDON YOU BECAUSE IT'S ESSENTIAL WE KEEP THIS INFORMATION SECRET.
EVEN THEIR EXISTENCE CAN BE KNOWN ONLY TO A SELECT HANDFUL OF FABLETOWN CITIZENS.
AND WHILE EVERY FABLE IN TOWN APPLAUDS WHAT YOU'VE DONE, THEY'RE ALSO MAD AS HELL THAT YOU HELPED YOURSELF TO OUR MAGIC PROPERTY TO DO IT.
A CAPITAL CRIME.

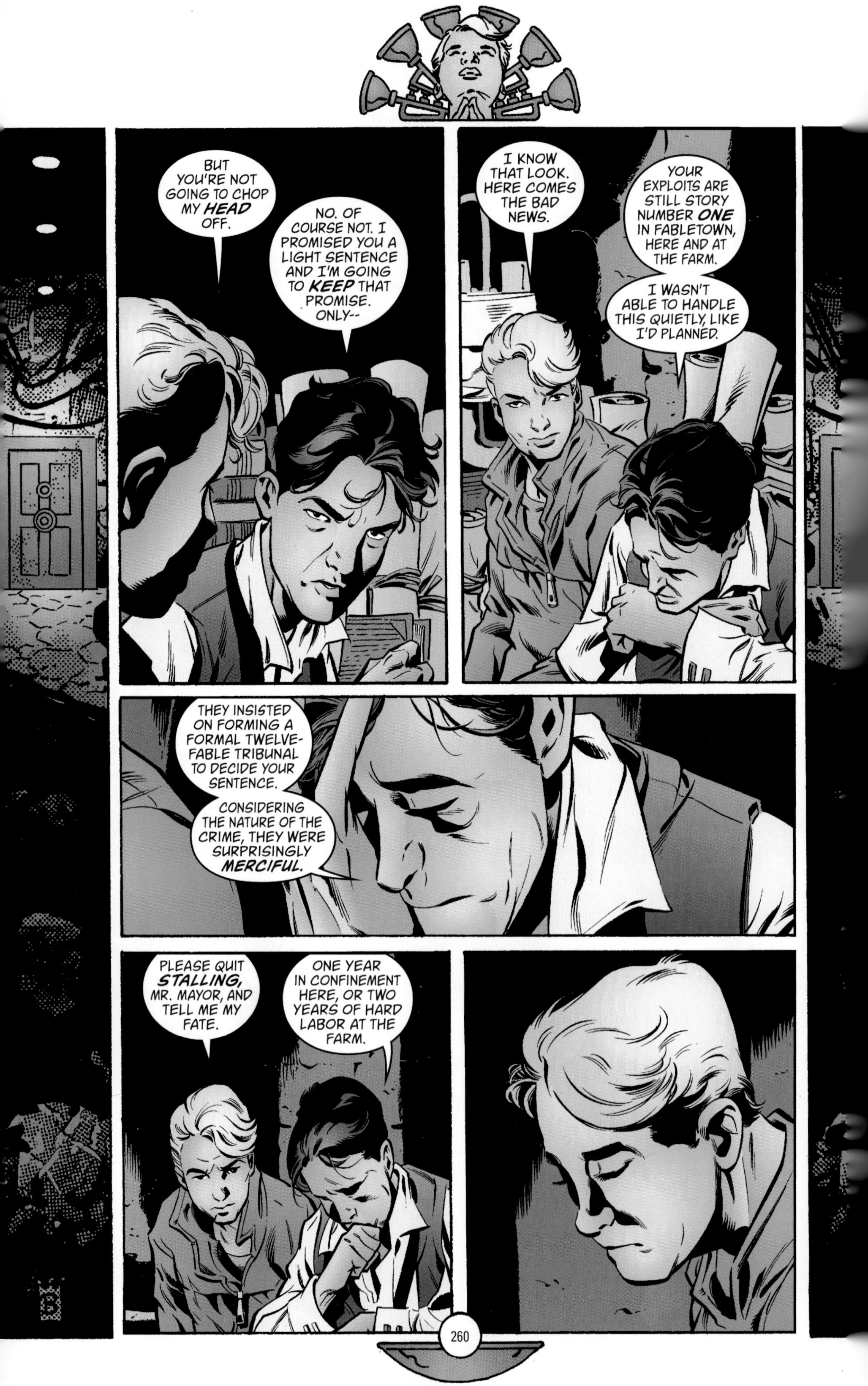

BUT YOU'RE NOT GOING TO CHOP MY HEAD OFF.
NO. OF COURSE NOT. I PROMISED YOU A LIGHT SENTENCE AND I'M GOING TO KEEP THAT PROMISE. ONLY--
I KNOW THAT LOOK. HERE COMES THE BAD NEWS.
YOUR EXPLOITS ARE STILL STORY NUMBER ONE IN FABLETOWN, HERE AND AT THE FARM.
I WASN'T ABLE TO HANDLE THIS QUIETLY, LIKE I'D PLANNED.
THEY INSISTED ON FORMING A FORMAL TWELVE-FABLE TRIBUNAL TO DECIDE YOUR SENTENCE.
CONSIDERING THE NATURE OF THE CRIME, THEY WERE SURPRISINGLY MERCIFUL.
PLEASE QUIT STALLING, MR. MAYOR, AND TELL ME MY FATE.
ONE YEAR IN CONFINEMENT HERE, OR TWO YEARS OF HARD LABOR AT THE FARM.

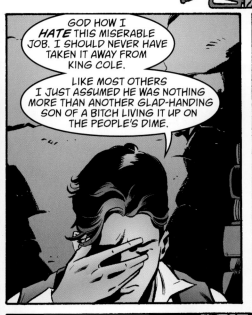

GOD HOW I *HATE* THIS MISERABLE JOB. I SHOULD NEVER HAVE TAKEN IT AWAY FROM KING COLE.

LIKE MOST OTHERS I JUST ASSUMED HE WAS NOTHING MORE THAN ANOTHER GLAD-HANDING SON OF A BITCH LIVING IT UP ON THE PEOPLE'S DIME.

TURNS OUT HE KNEW HOW TO ORGANIZE, DELEGATE, SMOOTH RUFFLED FEATHERS AND GENERALLY GET THE JOB DONE. HE WAS A *GENIUS* AT IT.

WITH ALL DUE RESPECT, PRINCE CHARMING, YOU SHOULD'VE *CONSIDERED* THAT BEFORE YOU RAN FOR OFFICE.

TYPICALLY--IF SNOW'S STORIES ABOUT YOU ARE *TRUE,* AND I BELIEVE THEY ARE--YOU SIMPLY SAW SOMETHING YOU WANTED AND CHASED AFTER IT, WITHOUT ANY MORE THOUGHT THAN THAT.

WISDOM, JUDGMENT AND DELAYED GRATIFICATION ARE *ALIEN* TO YOU.

YOU'RE ENTIRELY DEFINED BY WHAT YOU COVET.

AND NOW YOU EXPECT ME TO FEEL *SORRY* FOR YOU? NOT A CHANCE. MY COMPASSION'S RESERVED FOR THOSE YOU SCREW OVER IN THE PROCESS OF GETTING WHAT YOU WANT.

YOU WANTED TO BE MAYOR AND NOW YOU ARE. SO *PLEASE* QUIT CRYING ABOUT HOW TOUGH THE JOB IS AND *DO* IT.

YOU CAN START BY HAULING ALL OF THIS *CRAP* OUT OF MY CELL SO I CAN GET SOME *SLEEP.*

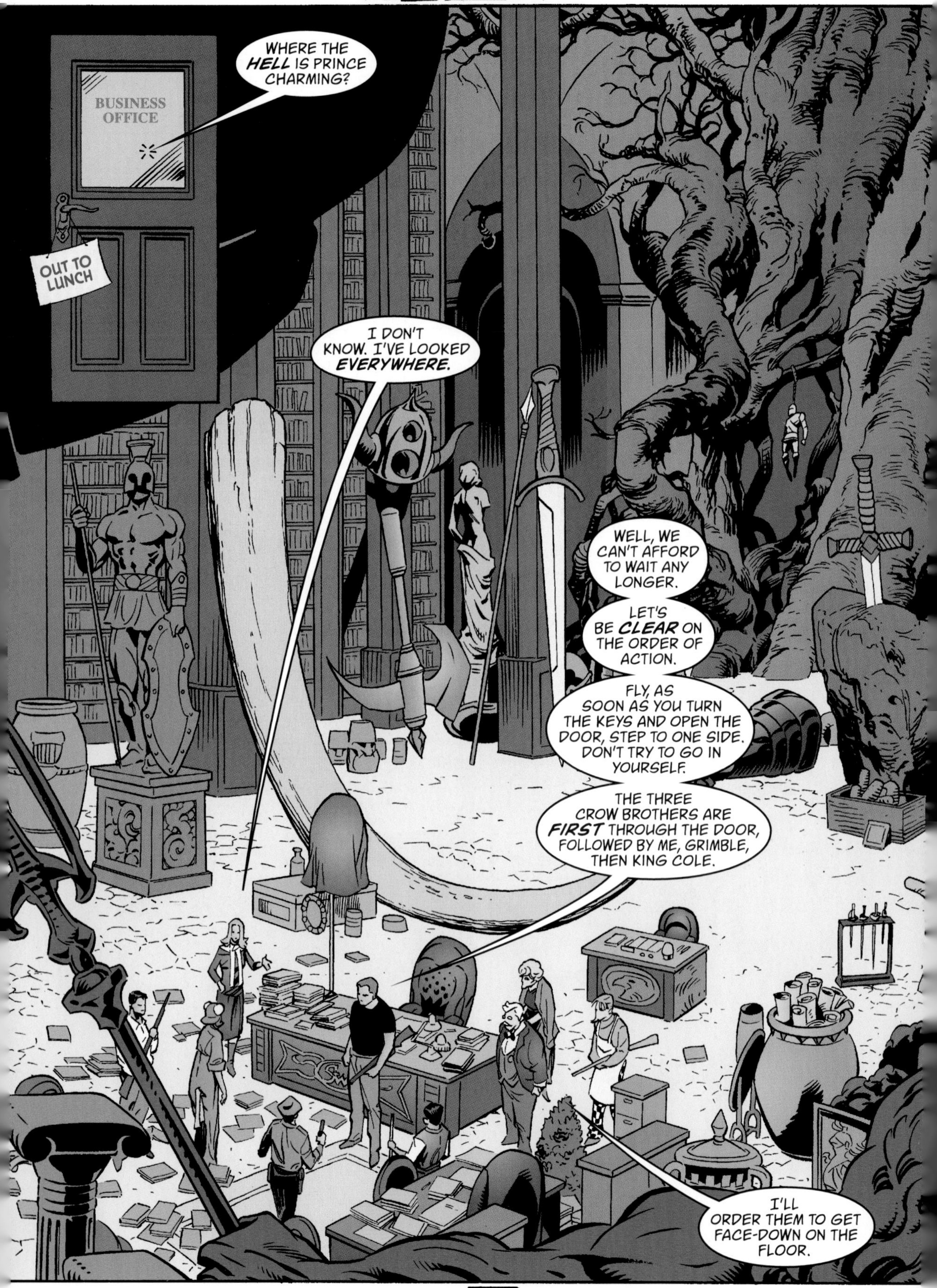
BUSINESS OFFICE
OUT TO LUNCH
WHERE THE *HELL* IS PRINCE CHARMING?
I DON'T KNOW. I'VE LOOKED *EVERYWHERE*.
WELL, WE CAN'T AFFORD TO WAIT ANY LONGER.
LET'S BE *CLEAR* ON THE ORDER OF ACTION.
FLY, AS SOON AS YOU TURN THE KEYS AND OPEN THE DOOR, STEP TO ONE SIDE. DON'T TRY TO GO IN YOURSELF.
THE THREE CROW BROTHERS ARE *FIRST* THROUGH THE DOOR, FOLLOWED BY ME, GRIMBLE, THEN KING COLE.
I'LL ORDER THEM TO GET FACE-DOWN ON THE FLOOR.

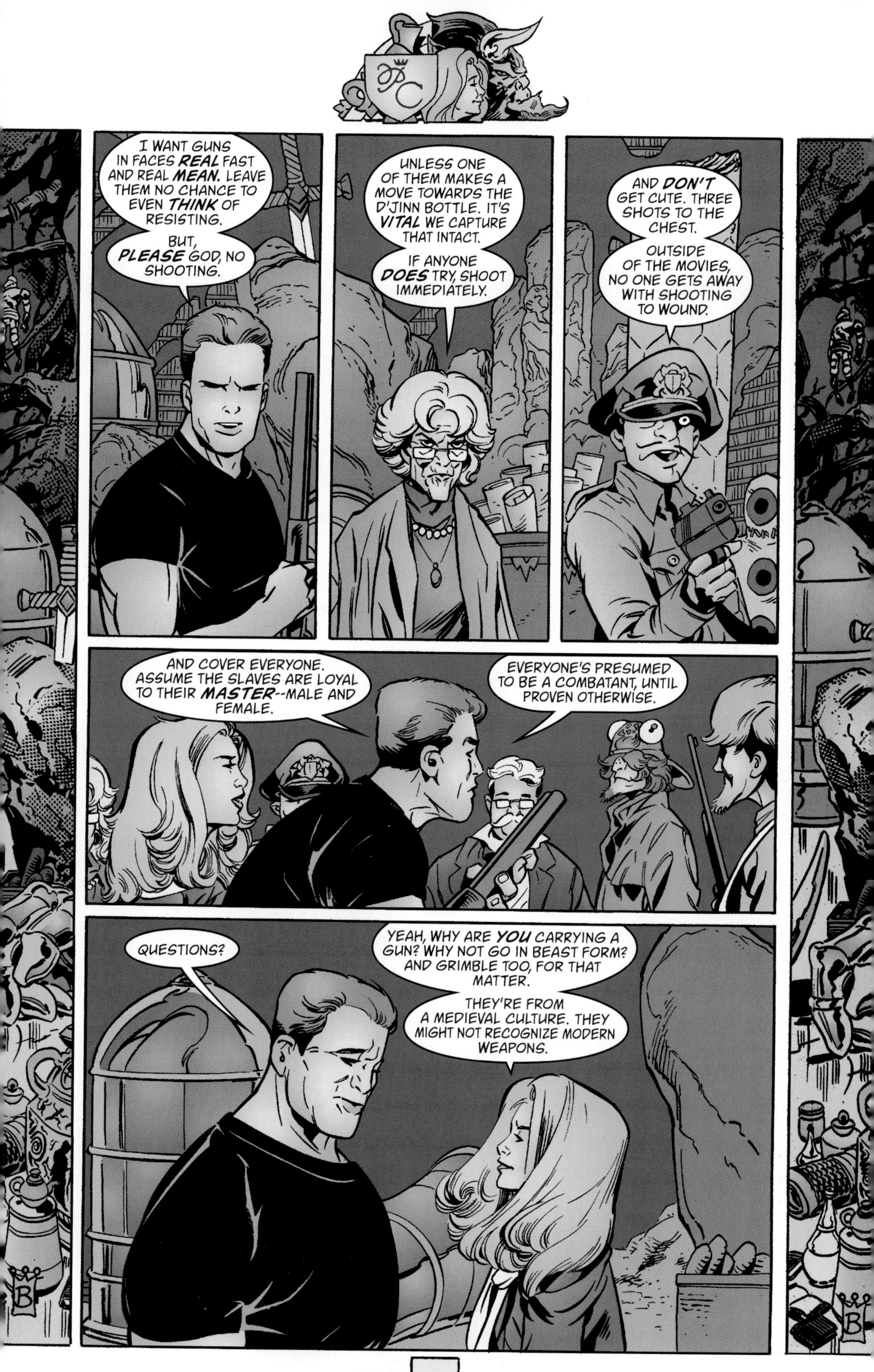
I WANT GUNS IN FACES REAL FAST AND REAL MEAN. LEAVE THEM NO CHANCE TO EVEN THINK OF RESISTING.
BUT, PLEASE GOD, NO SHOOTING.
UNLESS ONE OF THEM MAKES A MOVE TOWARDS THE D'JINN BOTTLE. IT'S VITAL WE CAPTURE THAT INTACT.
IF ANYONE DOES TRY, SHOOT IMMEDIATELY.
AND DON'T GET CUTE. THREE SHOTS TO THE CHEST.
OUTSIDE OF THE MOVIES, NO ONE GETS AWAY WITH SHOOTING TO WOUND.
AND COVER EVERYONE. ASSUME THE SLAVES ARE LOYAL TO THEIR MASTER--MALE AND FEMALE.
EVERYONE'S PRESUMED TO BE A COMBATANT, UNTIL PROVEN OTHERWISE.
QUESTIONS?
YEAH, WHY ARE YOU CARRYING A GUN? WHY NOT GO IN BEAST FORM? AND GRIMBLE TOO, FOR THAT MATTER.
THEY'RE FROM A MEDIEVAL CULTURE. THEY MIGHT NOT RECOGNIZE MODERN WEAPONS.

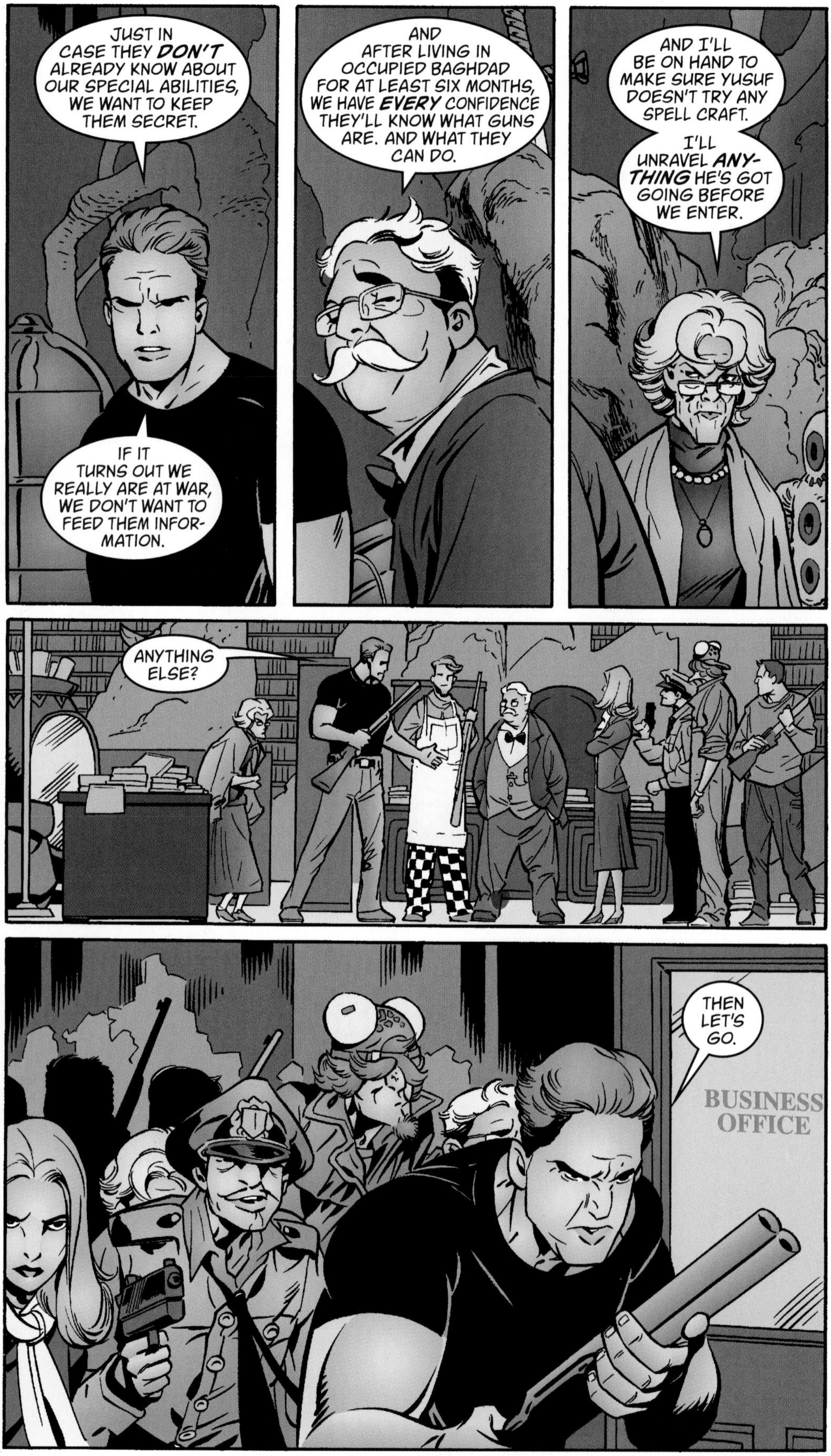

JUST IN CASE THEY DON'T ALREADY KNOW ABOUT OUR SPECIAL ABILITIES, WE WANT TO KEEP THEM SECRET.
IF IT TURNS OUT WE REALLY ARE AT WAR, WE DON'T WANT TO FEED THEM INFORMATION.
AND AFTER LIVING IN OCCUPIED BAGHDAD FOR AT LEAST SIX MONTHS, WE HAVE EVERY CONFIDENCE THEY'LL KNOW WHAT GUNS ARE. AND WHAT THEY CAN DO.
AND I'LL BE ON HAND TO MAKE SURE YUSUF DOESN'T TRY ANY SPELL CRAFT.
I'LL UNRAVEL ANYTHING HE'S GOT GOING BEFORE WE ENTER.
ANYTHING ELSE?
THEN LET'S GO.
BUSINESS OFFICE

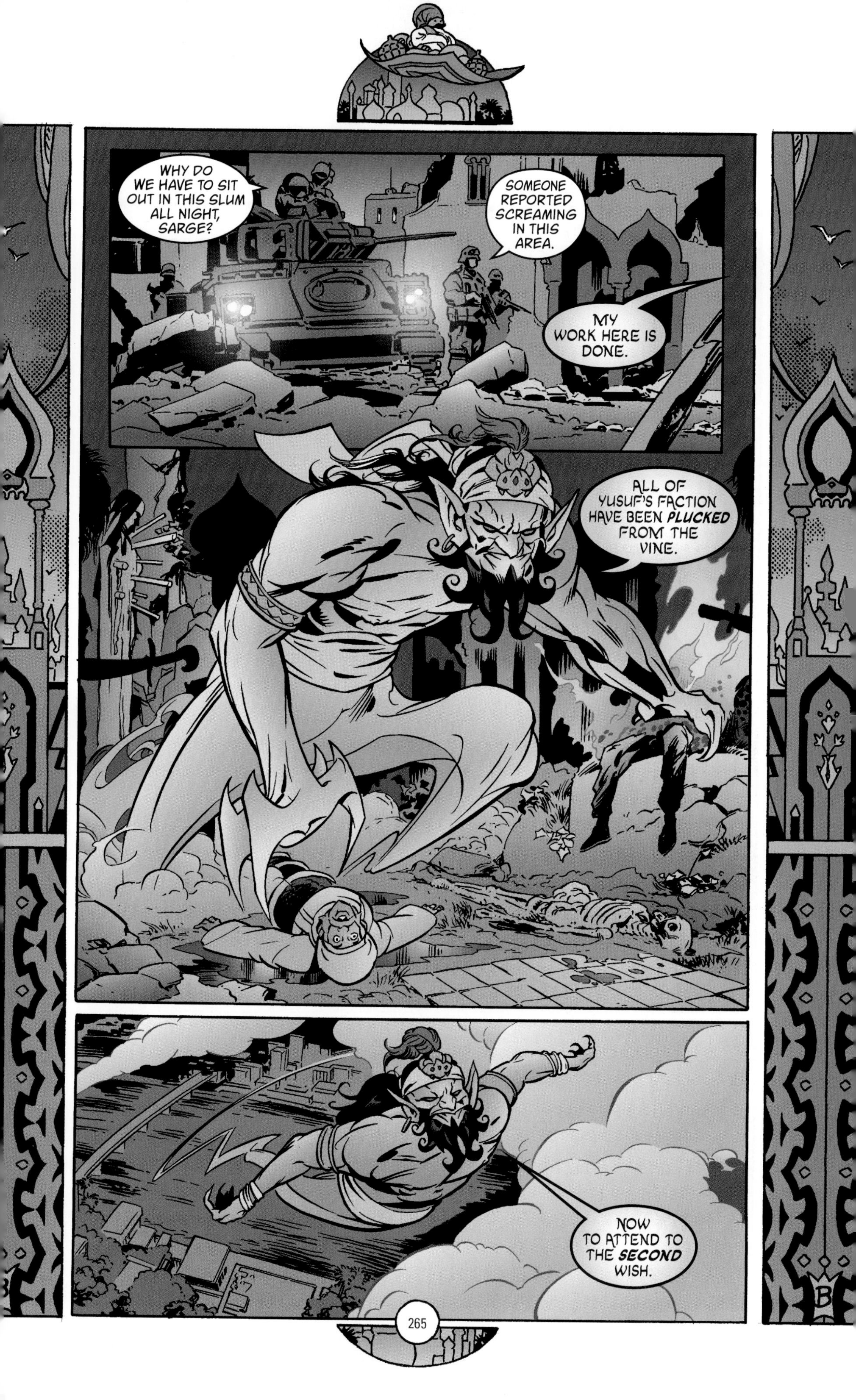
WHY DO WE HAVE TO SIT OUT IN THIS SLUM ALL NIGHT, SARGE?
SOMEONE REPORTED SCREAMING IN THIS AREA.
MY WORK HERE IS DONE.
ALL OF YUSUF'S FACTION HAVE BEEN PLUCKED FROM THE VINE.
NOW TO ATTEND TO THE SECOND WISH.

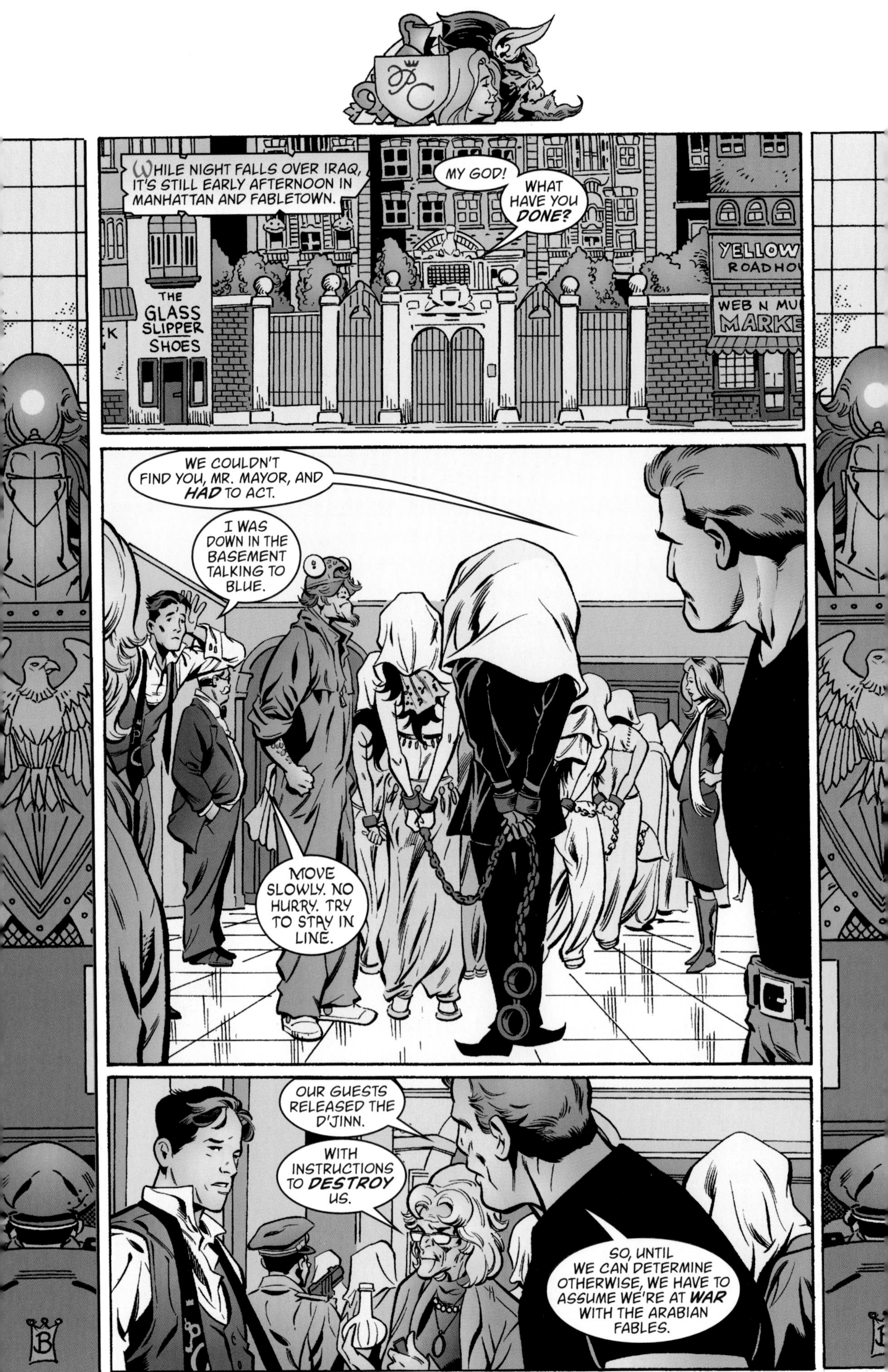
THE GLASS SLIPPER SHOES
WHILE NIGHT FALLS OVER IRAQ, IT'S STILL EARLY AFTERNOON IN MANHATTAN AND FABLETOWN.
MY GOD!
WHAT HAVE YOU DONE?
WE COULDN'T FIND YOU, MR. MAYOR, AND HAD TO ACT.
I WAS DOWN IN THE BASEMENT TALKING TO BLUE.
MOVE SLOWLY. NO HURRY. TRY TO STAY IN LINE.
OUR GUESTS RELEASED THE D'JINN.
WITH INSTRUCTIONS TO DESTROY US.
SO, UNTIL WE CAN DETERMINE OTHERWISE, WE HAVE TO ASSUME WE'RE AT WAR WITH THE ARABIAN FABLES.

BUT--

THERE'S A CHANCE YUSUF ACTED ALONE. SINBAD SEEMED GENUINELY **SURPRISED** WHEN WE BURST IN ON THEM.

LET'S HOPE THAT'S THE CASE.

BUT WHAT ARE YOU **DOING**? WHERE ARE YOU **TAKING** THEM?

SINCE BLUE'S OCCUPYING THE DETENTION CELL, WE'RE GOING TO LOCK THEM IN THE DUNGEONS IN THE BACK CORRIDORS OF THE BUSINESS OFFICE.

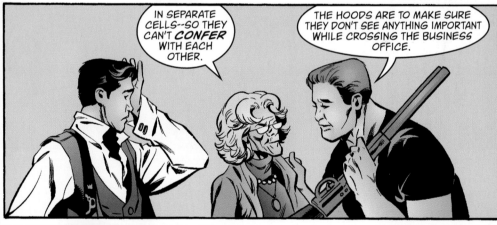

IN SEPARATE CELLS--SO THEY CAN'T **CONFER** WITH EACH OTHER.

THE HOODS ARE TO MAKE SURE THEY DON'T SEE ANYTHING IMPORTANT WHILE CROSSING THE BUSINESS OFFICE.

BUT WHAT'S THE **POINT**?

IF THE D'JINN IS ABOUT TO DESTROY US--

WELL, **YES.** MAYBE WE SHOULD RETIRE TO THE SHERIFF'S OFFICE AND DISCUSS THAT.

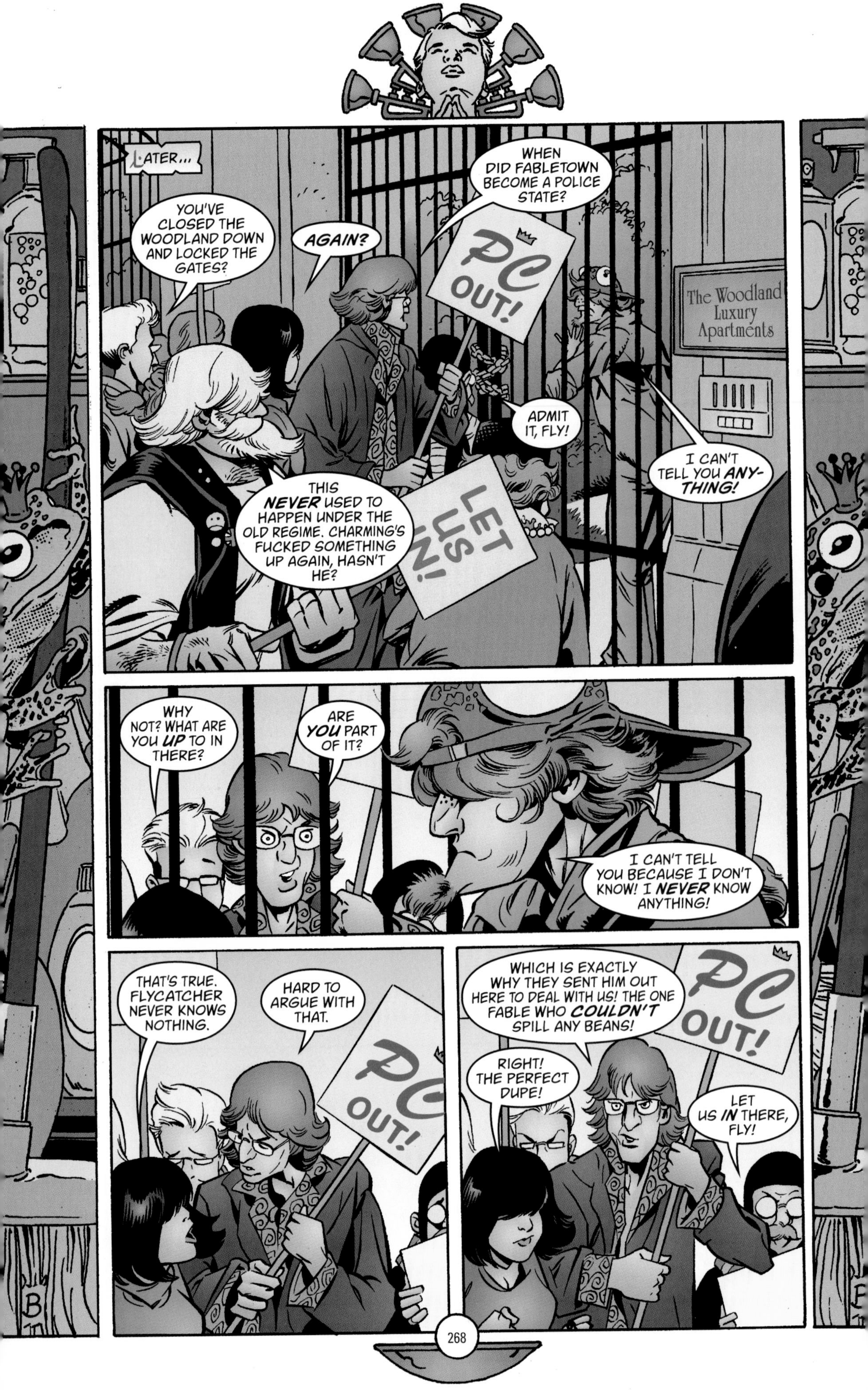
LATER...
YOU'VE CLOSED THE WOODLAND DOWN AND LOCKED THE GATES?
AGAIN?
WHEN DID FABLETOWN BECOME A POLICE STATE?
PC OUT!
The Woodland Luxury Apartments
ADMIT IT, FLY!
I CAN'T TELL YOU ANYTHING!
THIS NEVER USED TO HAPPEN UNDER THE OLD REGIME. CHARMING'S FUCKED SOMETHING UP AGAIN, HASN'T HE?
LET US IN!
WHY NOT? WHAT ARE YOU UP TO IN THERE?
ARE YOU PART OF IT?
I CAN'T TELL YOU BECAUSE I DON'T KNOW! I NEVER KNOW ANYTHING!
THAT'S TRUE. FLYCATCHER NEVER KNOWS NOTHING.
HARD TO ARGUE WITH THAT.
PC OUT!
WHICH IS EXACTLY WHY THEY SENT HIM OUT HERE TO DEAL WITH US! THE ONE FABLE WHO COULDN'T SPILL ANY BEANS!
PC OUT!
RIGHT! THE PERFECT DUPE!
LET US IN THERE, FLY!

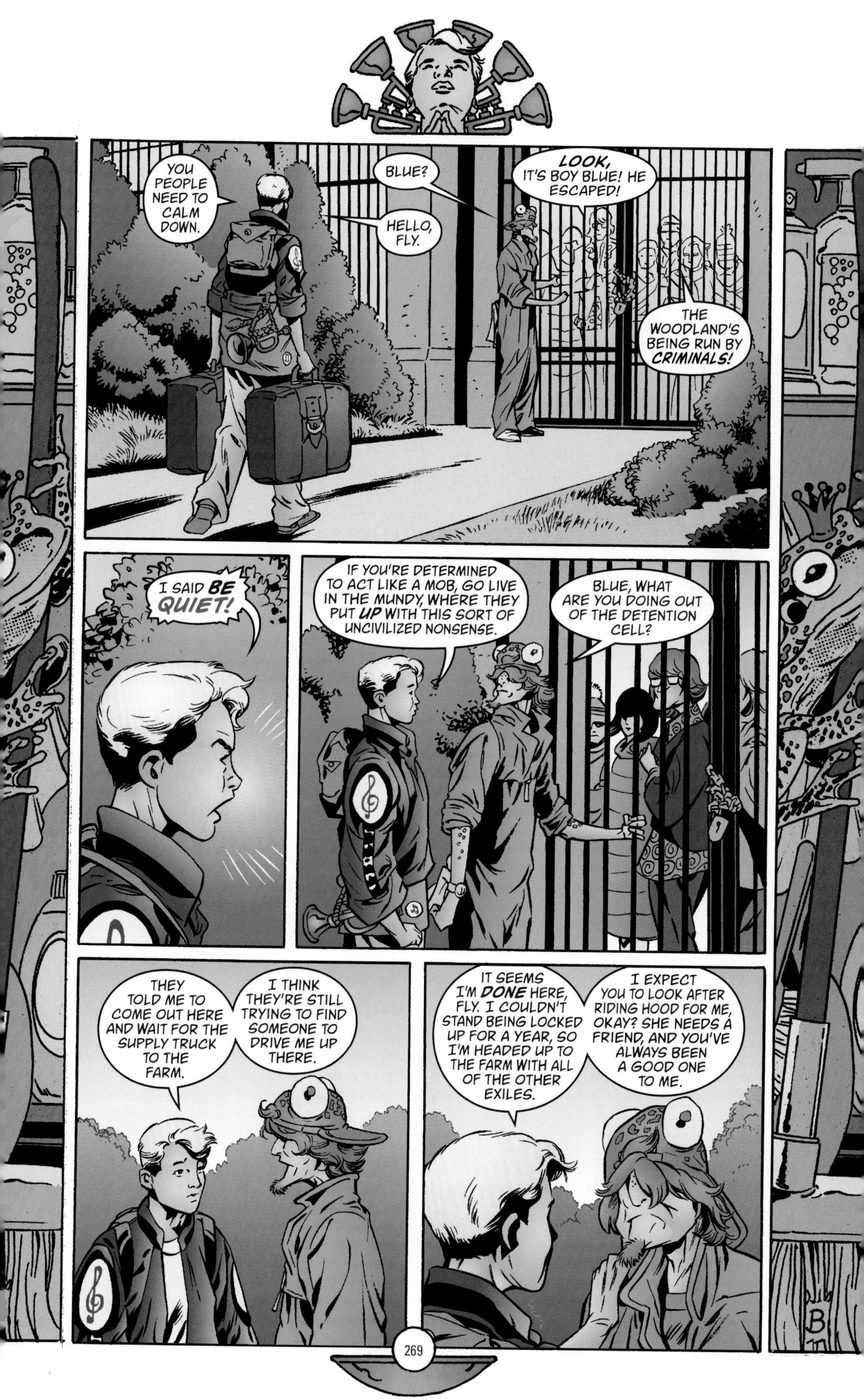

YOU PEOPLE NEED TO CALM DOWN.
BLUE?
HELLO, FLY.
LOOK, IT'S BOY BLUE! HE ESCAPED!
THE WOODLAND'S BEING RUN BY CRIMINALS!
I SAID BE QUIET!
IF YOU'RE DETERMINED TO ACT LIKE A MOB, GO LIVE IN THE MUNDY, WHERE THEY PUT UP WITH THIS SORT OF UNCIVILIZED NONSENSE.
BLUE, WHAT ARE YOU DOING OUT OF THE DETENTION CELL?
THEY TOLD ME TO COME OUT HERE AND WAIT FOR THE SUPPLY TRUCK TO THE FARM.
I THINK THEY'RE STILL TRYING TO FIND SOMEONE TO DRIVE ME UP THERE.
IT SEEMS I'M DONE HERE, FLY. I COULDN'T STAND BEING LOCKED UP FOR A YEAR, SO I'M HEADED UP TO THE FARM WITH ALL OF THE OTHER EXILES.
I EXPECT YOU TO LOOK AFTER RIDING HOOD FOR ME, OKAY? SHE NEEDS A FRIEND, AND YOU'VE ALWAYS BEEN A GOOD ONE TO ME.

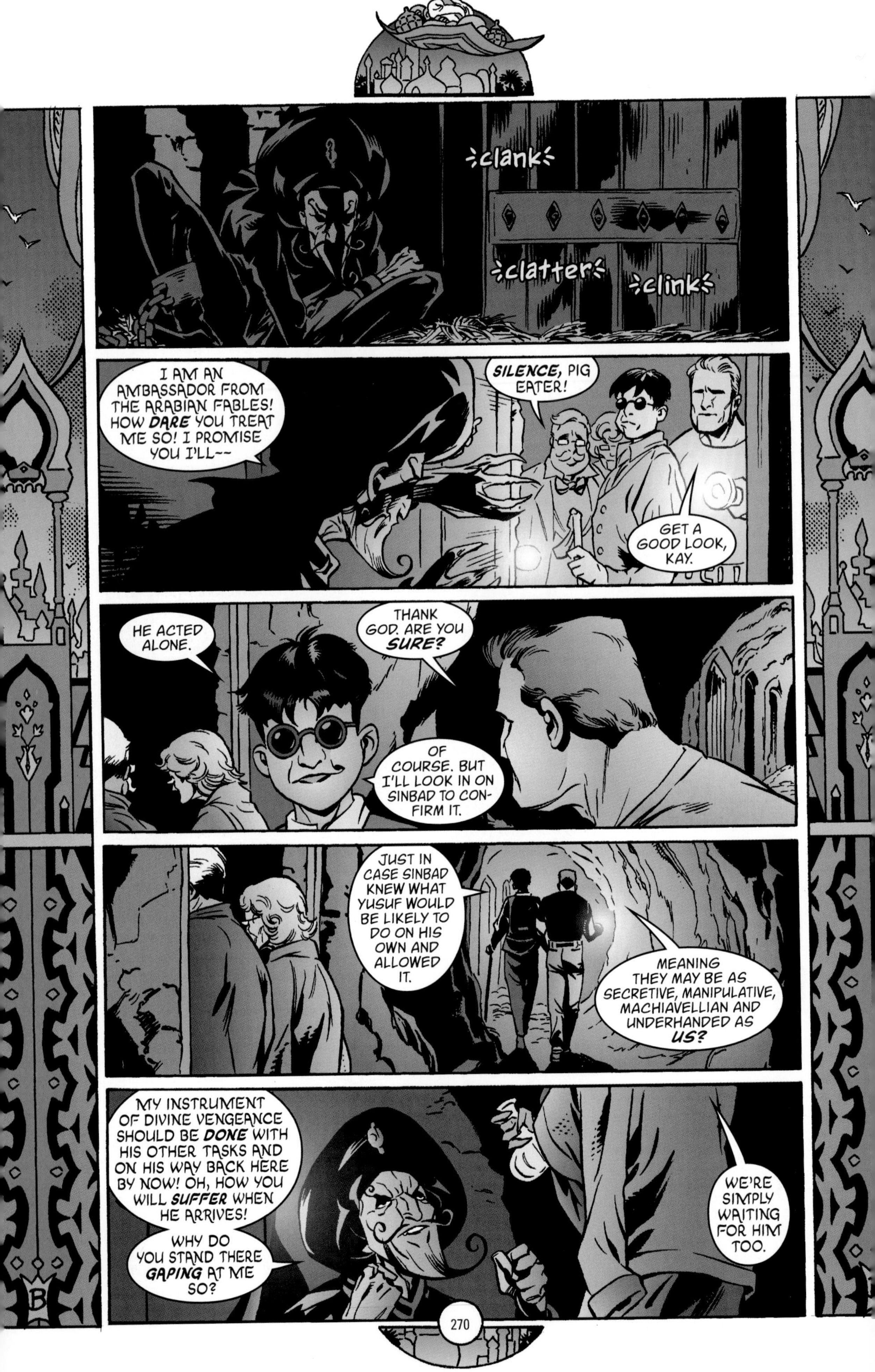

clank
clatter
clink
I AM AN AMBASSADOR FROM THE ARABIAN FABLES! HOW DARE YOU TREAT ME SO! I PROMISE YOU I'LL--
SILENCE, PIG EATER!
GET A GOOD LOOK, KAY.
HE ACTED ALONE.
THANK GOD. ARE YOU SURE?
OF COURSE. BUT I'LL LOOK IN ON SINBAD TO CONFIRM IT.
JUST IN CASE SINBAD KNEW WHAT YUSUF WOULD BE LIKELY TO DO ON HIS OWN AND ALLOWED IT.
MEANING THEY MAY BE AS SECRETIVE, MANIPULATIVE, MACHIAVELLIAN AND UNDERHANDED AS US?
MY INSTRUMENT OF DIVINE VENGEANCE SHOULD BE DONE WITH HIS OTHER TASKS AND ON HIS WAY BACK HERE BY NOW! OH, HOW YOU WILL SUFFER WHEN HE ARRIVES!
WHY DO YOU STAND THERE GAPING AT ME SO?
WE'RE SIMPLY WAITING FOR HIM TOO.

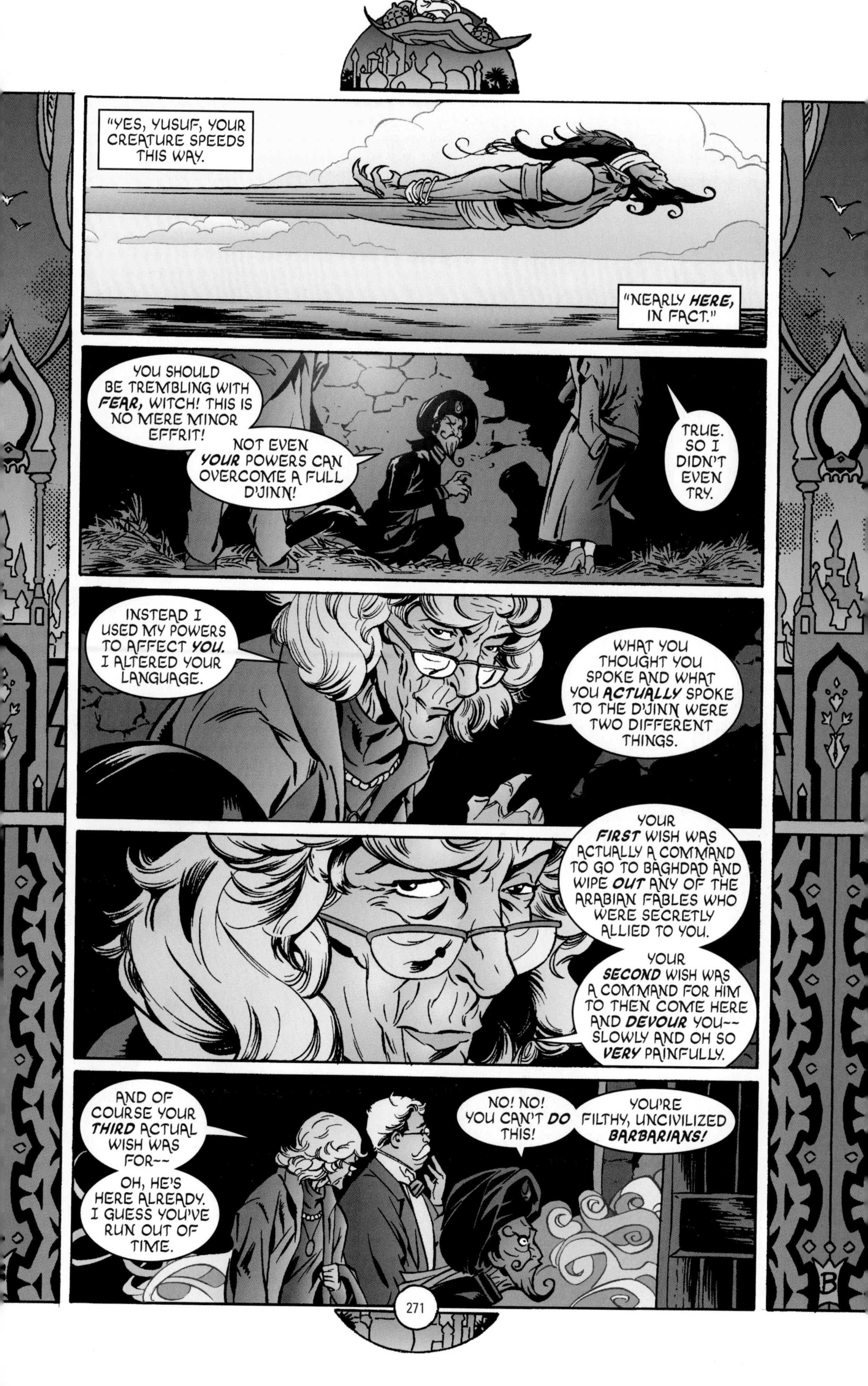
"YES, YUSUF, YOUR CREATURE SPEEDS THIS WAY.
"NEARLY HERE, IN FACT."
YOU SHOULD BE TREMBLING WITH FEAR, WITCH! THIS IS NO MERE MINOR EFFRIT!
NOT EVEN YOUR POWERS CAN OVERCOME A FULL D'JINN!
TRUE. SO I DIDN'T EVEN TRY.
INSTEAD I USED MY POWERS TO AFFECT YOU. I ALTERED YOUR LANGUAGE.
WHAT YOU THOUGHT YOU SPOKE AND WHAT YOU ACTUALLY SPOKE TO THE D'JINN WERE TWO DIFFERENT THINGS.
YOUR FIRST WISH WAS ACTUALLY A COMMAND TO GO TO BAGHDAD AND WIPE OUT ANY OF THE ARABIAN FABLES WHO WERE SECRETLY ALLIED TO YOU.
YOUR SECOND WISH WAS A COMMAND FOR HIM TO THEN COME HERE AND DEVOUR YOU-- SLOWLY AND OH SO VERY PAINFULLY.
AND OF COURSE YOUR THIRD ACTUAL WISH WAS FOR--
OH, HE'S HERE ALREADY. I GUESS YOU'VE RUN OUT OF TIME.
NO! NO! YOU CAN'T DO THIS!
YOU'RE FILTHY, UNCIVILIZED BARBARIANS!

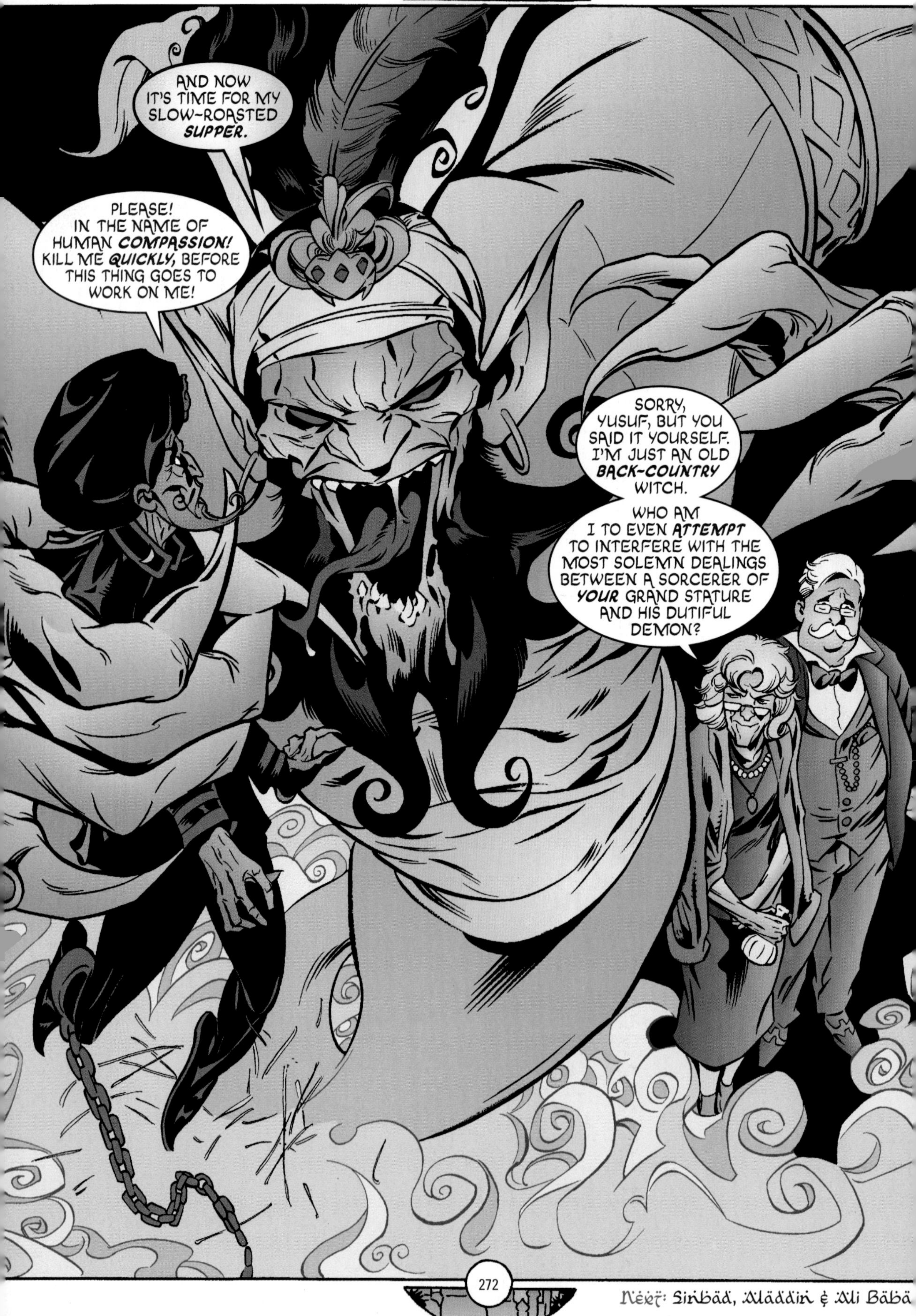
AND NOW IT'S TIME FOR MY SLOW-ROASTED SUPPER.
PLEASE! IN THE NAME OF HUMAN COMPASSION! KILL ME QUICKLY, BEFORE THIS THING GOES TO WORK ON ME!
SORRY, YUSUF, BUT YOU SAID IT YOURSELF. I'M JUST AN OLD BACK-COUNTRY WITCH.
WHO AM I TO EVEN ATTEMPT TO INTERFERE WITH THE MOST SOLEMN DEALINGS BETWEEN A SORCERER OF YOUR GRAND STATURE AND HIS DUTIFUL DEMON?

Next: Sinbäd, Aläddin & Ali Bäbä

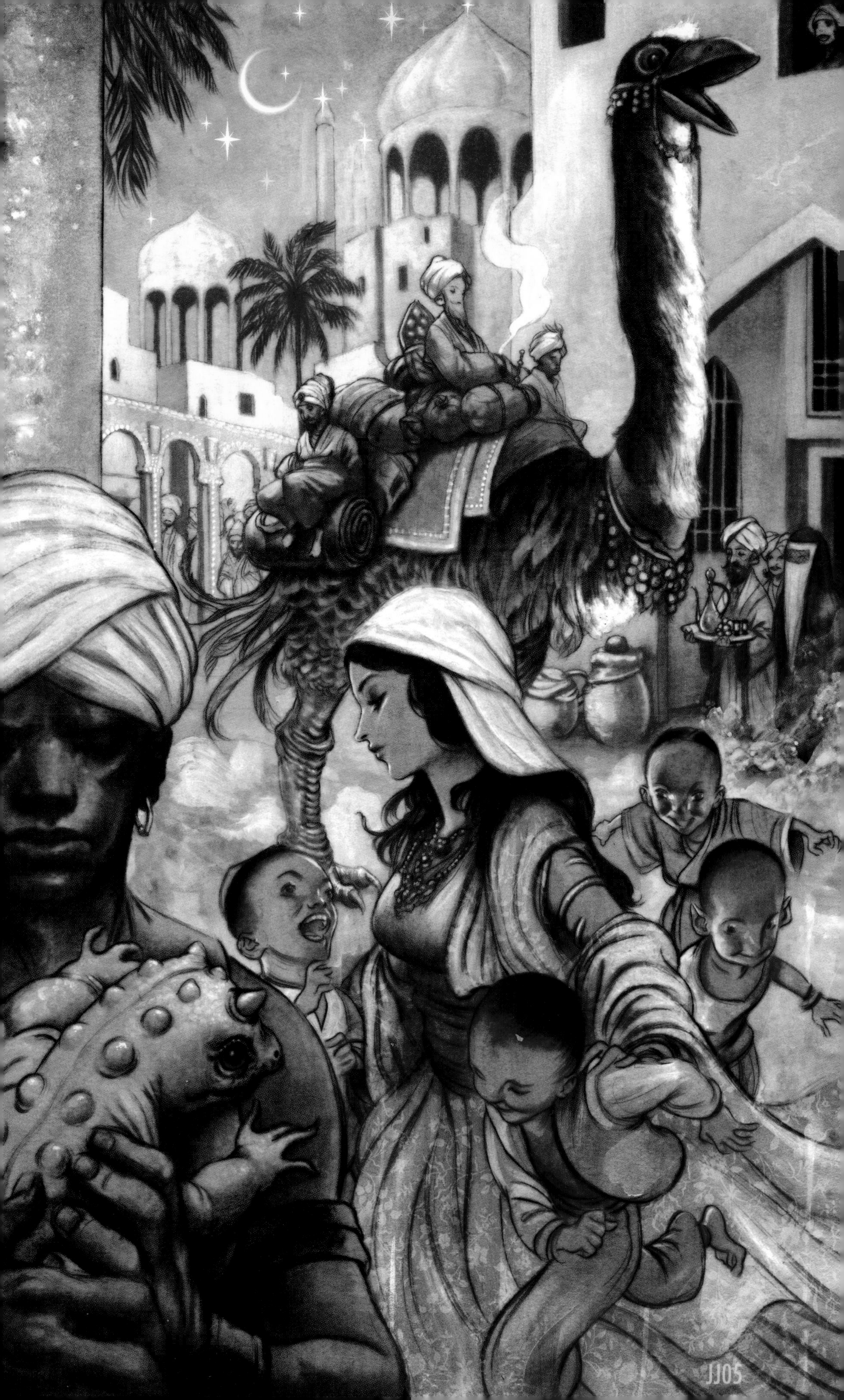
JJ05

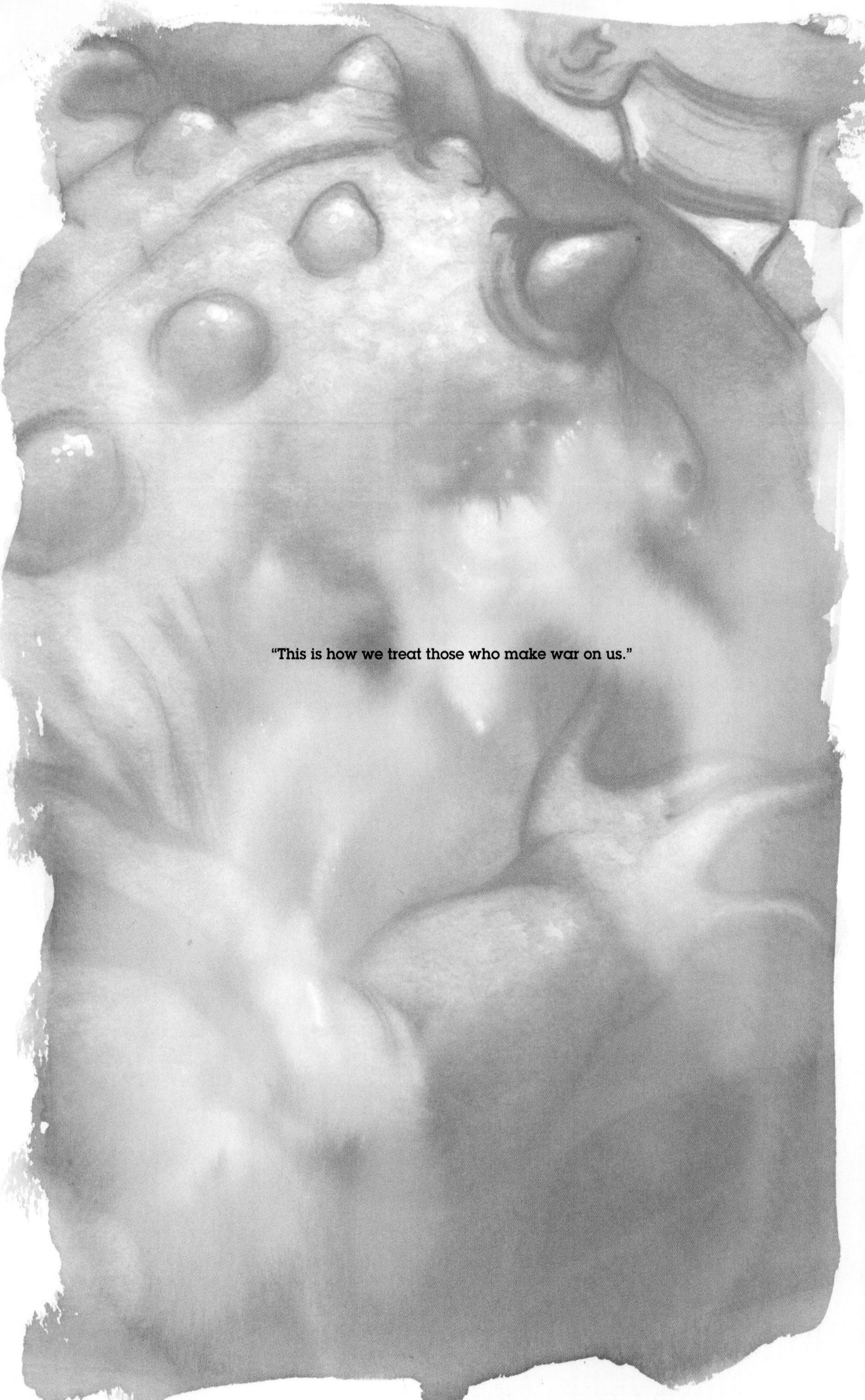

"This is how we treat those who make war on us."

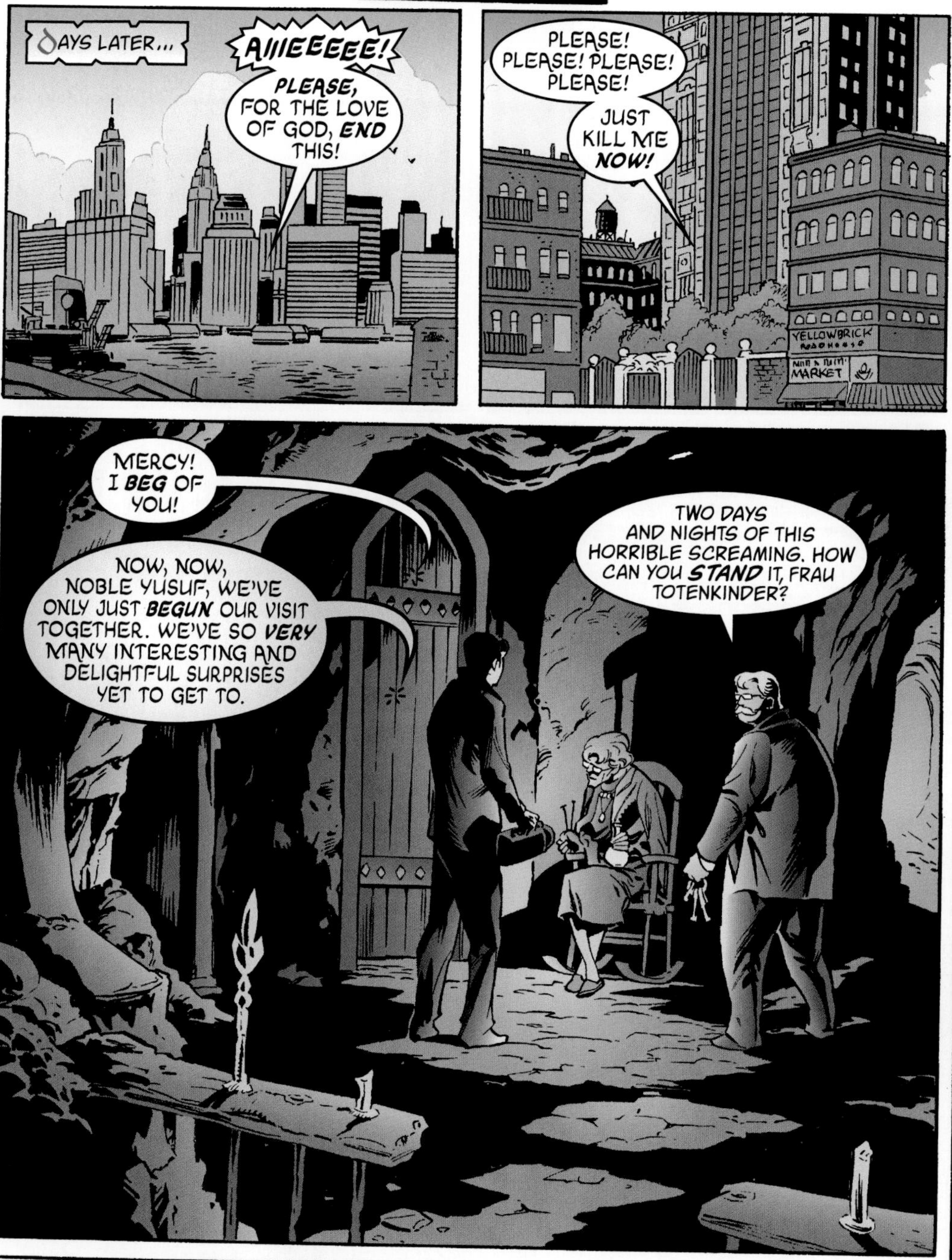

DAYS LATER...
AIIIEEEEE!
PLEASE, FOR THE LOVE OF GOD, END THIS!
PLEASE! PLEASE! PLEASE! PLEASE!
JUST KILL ME NOW!
YELLOWBRICK
MARKET
MERCY! I BEG OF YOU!
NOW, NOW, NOBLE YUSUF, WE'VE ONLY JUST BEGUN OUR VISIT TOGETHER. WE'VE SO VERY MANY INTERESTING AND DELIGHTFUL SURPRISES YET TO GET TO.
TWO DAYS AND NIGHTS OF THIS HORRIBLE SCREAMING. HOW CAN YOU STAND IT, FRAU TOTENKINDER?

ACT OF WAR

Chapter FOUR of Arabian Nights (and Days)

BILL WILLINGHAM writer-creator
MARK BUCKINGHAM penciller
STEVE LEIALOHA & ANDREW PEPOY inkers
DANIEL VOZZO colors
JAMES JEAN cover art
TODD KLEIN letters
ANGELA RUFINO asst. editor
SHELLY BOND editor

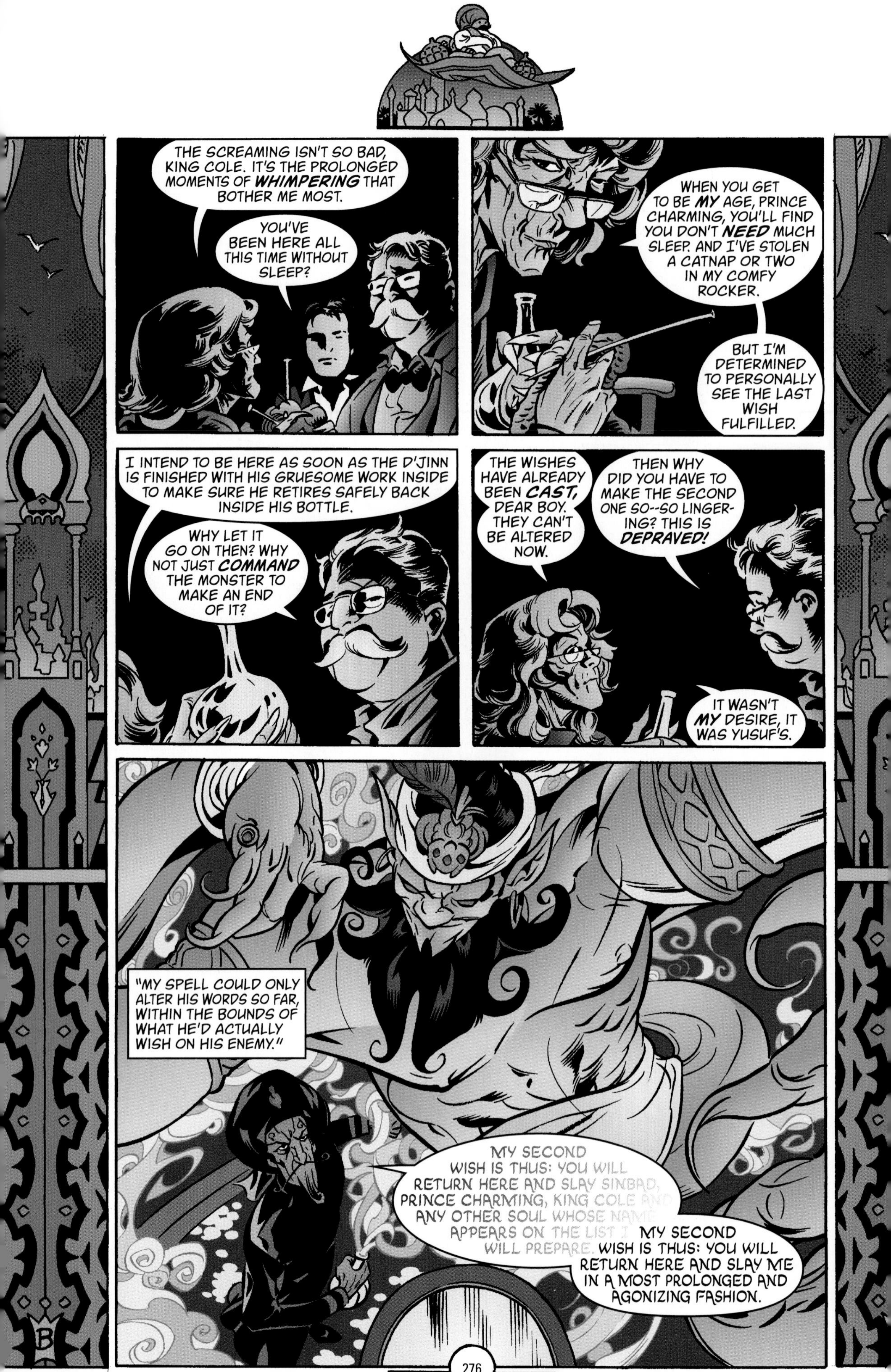
THE SCREAMING ISN'T SO BAD, KING COLE. IT'S THE PROLONGED MOMENTS OF WHIMPERING THAT BOTHER ME MOST.
YOU'VE BEEN HERE ALL THIS TIME WITHOUT SLEEP?
WHEN YOU GET TO BE MY AGE, PRINCE CHARMING, YOU'LL FIND YOU DON'T NEED MUCH SLEEP. AND I'VE STOLEN A CATNAP OR TWO IN MY COMFY ROCKER.
BUT I'M DETERMINED TO PERSONALLY SEE THE LAST WISH FULFILLED.
I INTEND TO BE HERE AS SOON AS THE D'JINN IS FINISHED WITH HIS GRUESOME WORK INSIDE TO MAKE SURE HE RETIRES SAFELY BACK INSIDE HIS BOTTLE.
WHY LET IT GO ON THEN? WHY NOT JUST COMMAND THE MONSTER TO MAKE AN END OF IT?
THE WISHES HAVE ALREADY BEEN CAST, DEAR BOY. THEY CAN'T BE ALTERED NOW.
THEN WHY DID YOU HAVE TO MAKE THE SECOND ONE SO--SO LINGER-ING? THIS IS DEPRAVED!
IT WASN'T MY DESIRE, IT WAS YUSUF'S.
"MY SPELL COULD ONLY ALTER HIS WORDS SO FAR, WITHIN THE BOUNDS OF WHAT HE'D ACTUALLY WISH ON HIS ENEMY."
MY SECOND WISH IS THUS: YOU WILL RETURN HERE AND SLAY SINBAD, PRINCE CHARMING, KING COLE AND ANY OTHER SOUL WHOSE NAME APPEARS ON THE LIST I WILL PREPARE.
MY SECOND WISH IS THUS: YOU WILL RETURN HERE AND SLAY ME IN A MOST PROLONGED AND AGONIZING FASHION.

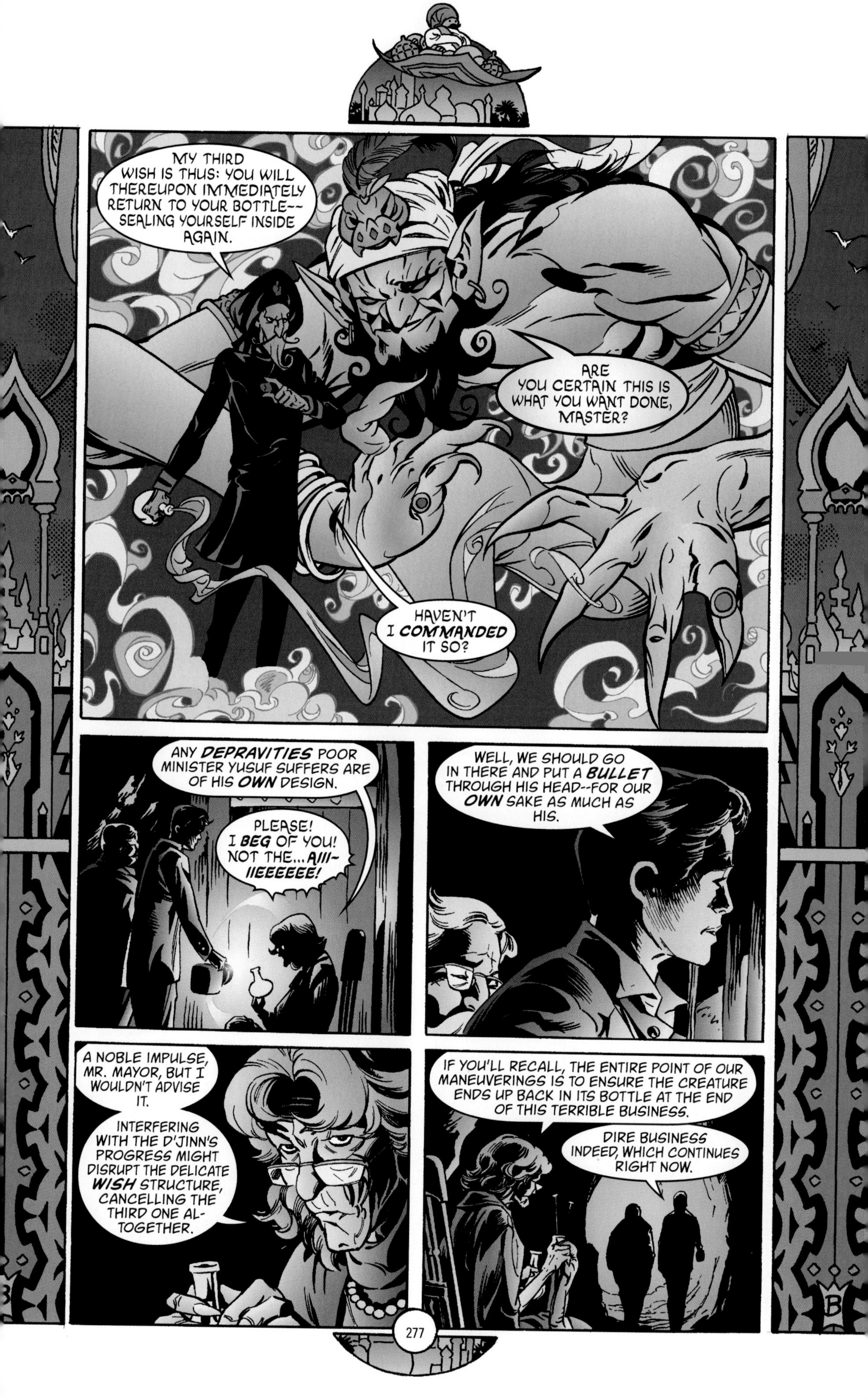
MY THIRD WISH IS THUS: YOU WILL THEREUPON IMMEDIATELY RETURN TO YOUR BOTTLE-- SEALING YOURSELF INSIDE AGAIN.
ARE YOU CERTAIN THIS IS WHAT YOU WANT DONE, MASTER?
HAVEN'T I COMMANDED IT SO?
ANY DEPRAVITIES POOR MINISTER YUSUF SUFFERS ARE OF HIS OWN DESIGN.
PLEASE! I BEG OF YOU! NOT THE...AIII-IIEEEEEE!
WELL, WE SHOULD GO IN THERE AND PUT A BULLET THROUGH HIS HEAD--FOR OUR OWN SAKE AS MUCH AS HIS.
A NOBLE IMPULSE, MR. MAYOR, BUT I WOULDN'T ADVISE IT.
INTERFERING WITH THE D'JINN'S PROGRESS MIGHT DISRUPT THE DELICATE WISH STRUCTURE, CANCELLING THE THIRD ONE AL-TOGETHER.
IF YOU'LL RECALL, THE ENTIRE POINT OF OUR MANEUVERINGS IS TO ENSURE THE CREATURE ENDS UP BACK IN ITS BOTTLE AT THE END OF THIS TERRIBLE BUSINESS.
DIRE BUSINESS INDEED, WHICH CONTINUES RIGHT NOW.

READY TO DO THIS, KING COLE?

LEAD THE WAY.

REMEMBER ALL YOUR LINES?

=CLICK-CLACK=

SINBAD?

AGHH, THAT LIGHT IS TOO *MUCH*, AFTER HOWEVER MANY DAYS IN THE DARK!

HOW LONG *HAS* IT BEEN?

TWO DAYS.

AND *THIS* IS HOW YOU TREAT THE CREDENTIALED ENVOY FROM THE ARABIAN FABLES?

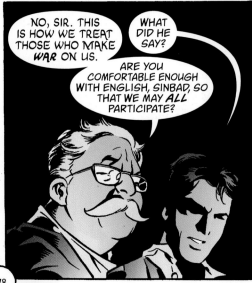

NO, SIR. THIS IS HOW WE TREAT THOSE WHO MAKE *WAR* ON US.

WHAT DID HE SAY?

ARE YOU COMFORTABLE ENOUGH WITH ENGLISH, SINBAD, SO THAT WE MAY *ALL* PARTICIPATE?

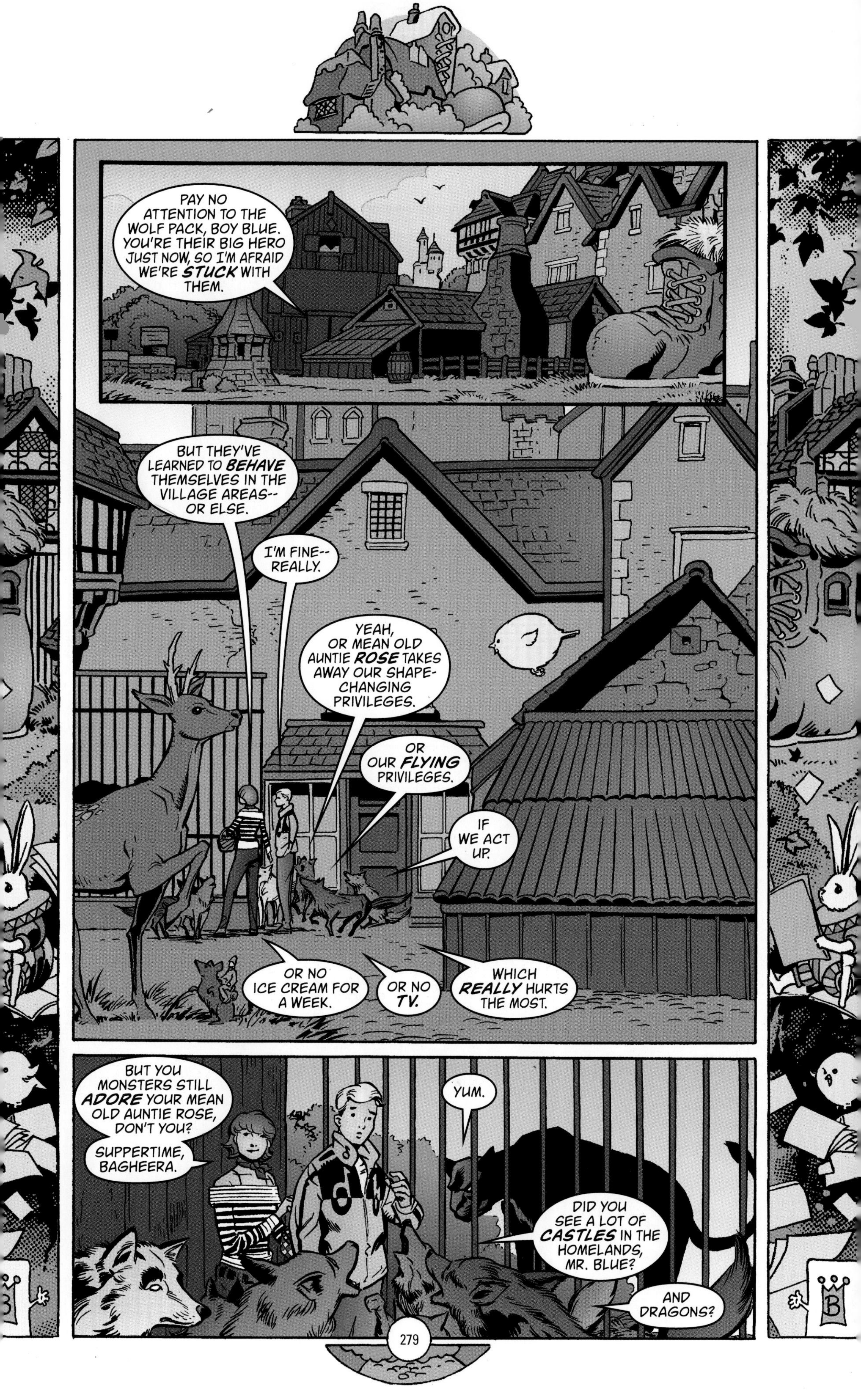

PAY NO ATTENTION TO THE WOLF PACK, BOY BLUE. YOU'RE THEIR BIG HERO JUST NOW, SO I'M AFRAID WE'RE STUCK WITH THEM.
BUT THEY'VE LEARNED TO BEHAVE THEMSELVES IN THE VILLAGE AREAS-- OR ELSE.
I'M FINE-- REALLY.
YEAH, OR MEAN OLD AUNTIE ROSE TAKES AWAY OUR SHAPE-CHANGING PRIVILEGES.
OR OUR FLYING PRIVILEGES.
IF WE ACT UP.
OR NO ICE CREAM FOR A WEEK.
OR NO TV.
WHICH REALLY HURTS THE MOST.
BUT YOU MONSTERS STILL ADORE YOUR MEAN OLD AUNTIE ROSE, DON'T YOU?
SUPPERTIME, BAGHEERA.
YUM.
DID YOU SEE A LOT OF CASTLES IN THE HOMELANDS, MR. BLUE?
AND DRAGONS?

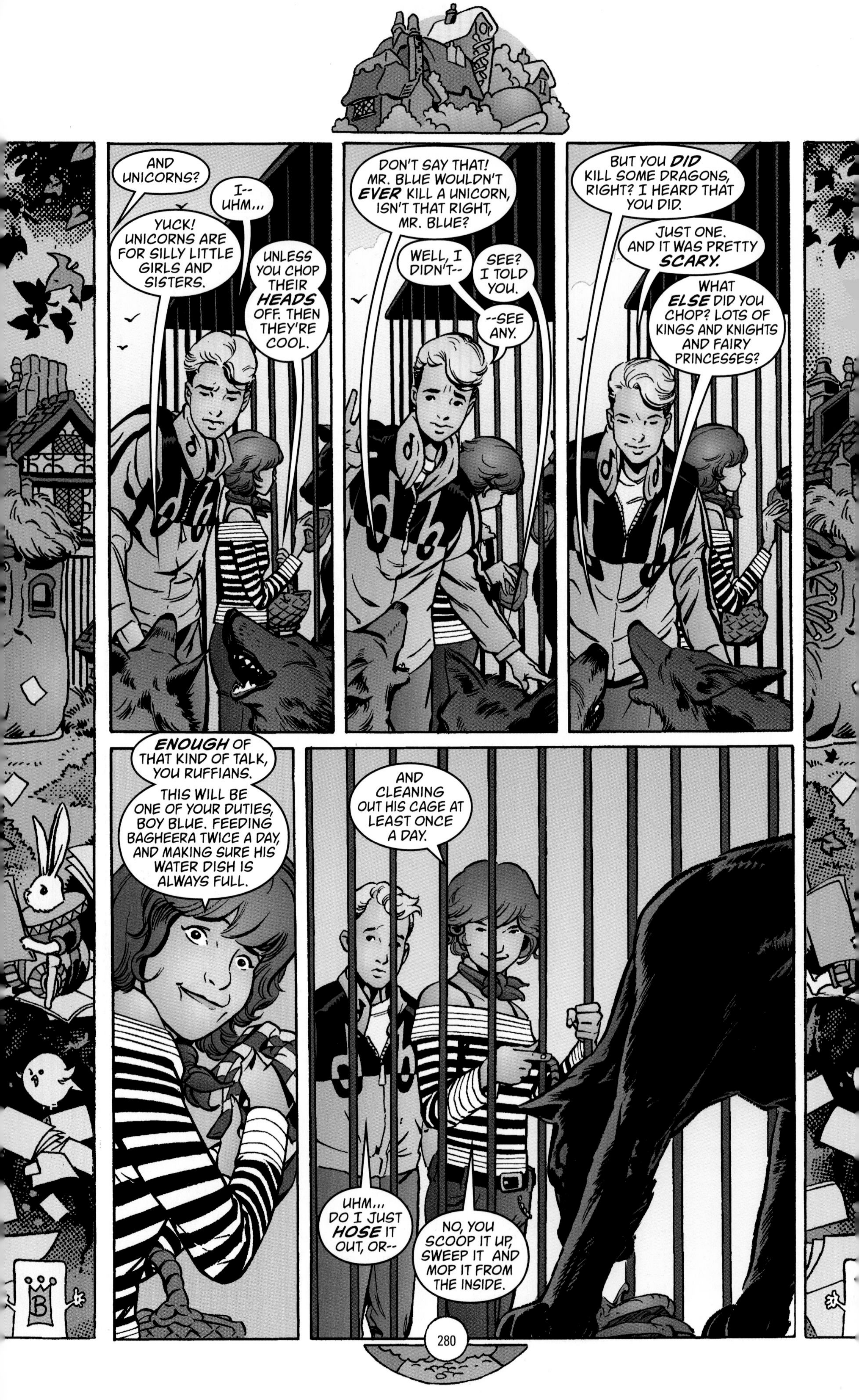
AND UNICORNS?
I-- UHM...
YUCK! UNICORNS ARE FOR SILLY LITTLE GIRLS AND SISTERS.
UNLESS YOU CHOP THEIR HEADS OFF. THEN THEY'RE COOL.
DON'T SAY THAT! MR. BLUE WOULDN'T EVER KILL A UNICORN, ISN'T THAT RIGHT, MR. BLUE?
WELL, I DIDN'T--
SEE? I TOLD YOU.
--SEE ANY.
BUT YOU DID KILL SOME DRAGONS, RIGHT? I HEARD THAT YOU DID.
JUST ONE. AND IT WAS PRETTY SCARY.
WHAT ELSE DID YOU CHOP? LOTS OF KINGS AND KNIGHTS AND FAIRY PRINCESSES?
ENOUGH OF THAT KIND OF TALK, YOU RUFFIANS.
THIS WILL BE ONE OF YOUR DUTIES, BOY BLUE. FEEDING BAGHEERA TWICE A DAY, AND MAKING SURE HIS WATER DISH IS ALWAYS FULL.
AND CLEANING OUT HIS CAGE AT LEAST ONCE A DAY.
UHM... DO I JUST HOSE IT OUT, OR--
NO, YOU SCOOP IT UP, SWEEP IT AND MOP IT FROM THE INSIDE.

DON'T WORRY. BAGHEERA WON'T **EAT** YOU.

YOU WON'T EAT BOY BLUE, **WILL** YOU, BAGHEERA?

NOT AS LONG AS THE FAT, JUICY **BEEF-STEAKS** KEEP COMING.

BREATHE, BOY BLUE. BREATHE.

BAGHEERA WAS JUST **KIDDING** YOU. **TELL** HIM YOU WERE JUST KIDDING, BAGGY.

I'M **FAIRLY** CONFIDENT I WAS JUST KIDDING.

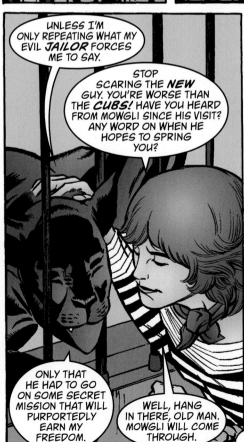

UNLESS I'M ONLY REPEATING WHAT MY EVIL **JAILOR** FORCES ME TO SAY.

STOP SCARING THE **NEW** GUY. YOU'RE WORSE THAN THE **CUBS!** HAVE YOU HEARD FROM MOWGLI SINCE HIS VISIT? ANY WORD ON WHEN HE HOPES TO SPRING YOU?

ONLY THAT HE HAD TO GO ON SOME SECRET MISSION THAT WILL PURPORTEDLY EARN MY FREEDOM.

WELL, HANG IN THERE, OLD MAN. MOWGLI WILL COME THROUGH.

OF COURSE HE WILL. MOWG WAS RAISED BY WOLVES.

WOLVES KNOW HOW TO GET THINGS DONE.

281

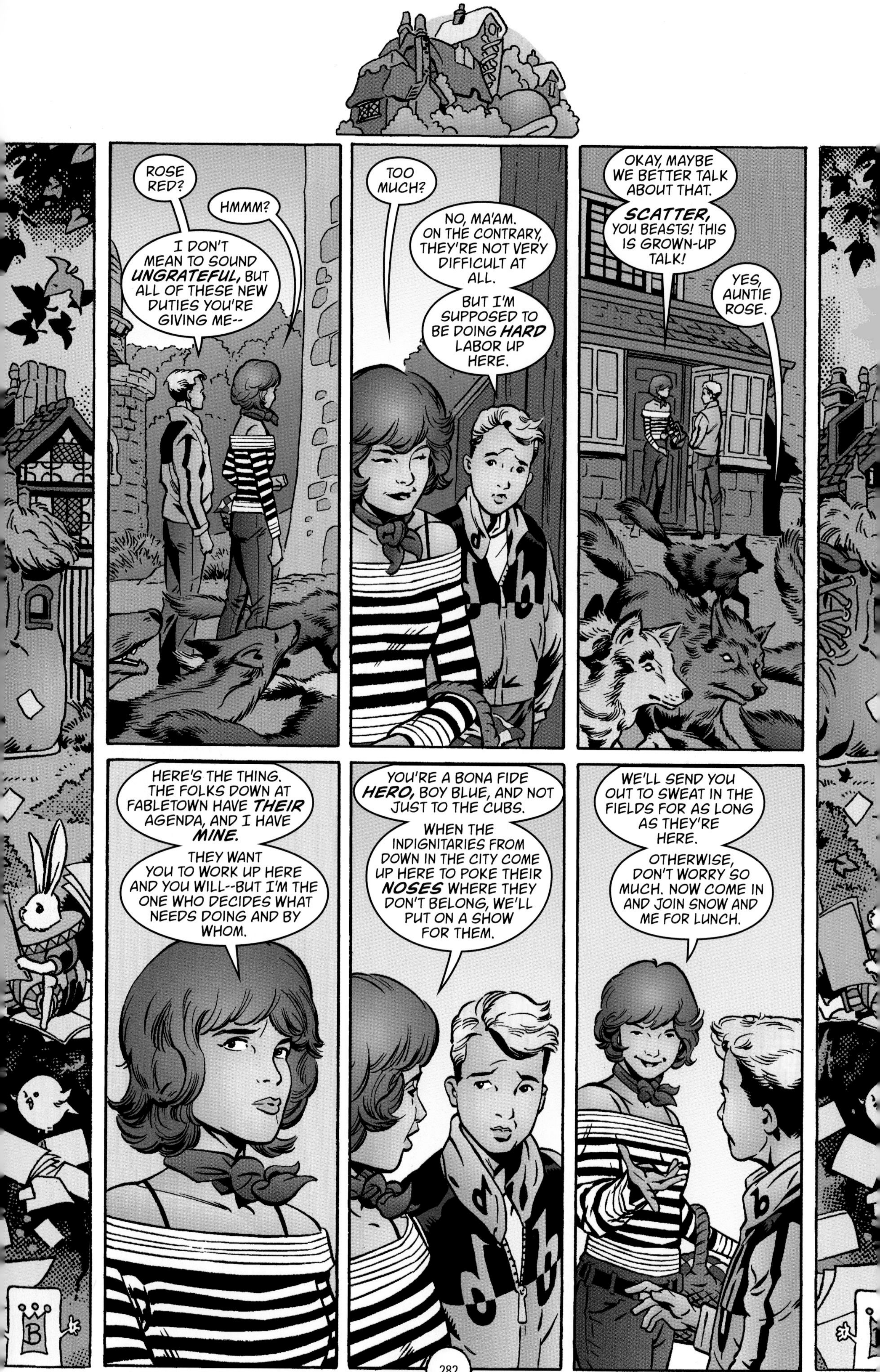

ROSE RED?
HMMM?
I DON'T MEAN TO SOUND **UNGRATEFUL,** BUT ALL OF THESE NEW DUTIES YOU'RE GIVING ME--
TOO MUCH?
NO, MA'AM. ON THE CONTRARY, THEY'RE NOT VERY DIFFICULT AT ALL.
BUT I'M SUPPOSED TO BE DOING **HARD** LABOR UP HERE.
OKAY, MAYBE WE BETTER TALK ABOUT THAT.
SCATTER, YOU BEASTS! THIS IS GROWN-UP TALK!
YES, AUNTIE ROSE.
HERE'S THE THING. THE FOLKS DOWN AT FABLETOWN HAVE **THEIR** AGENDA, AND I HAVE **MINE.**
THEY WANT YOU TO WORK UP HERE AND YOU WILL--BUT I'M THE ONE WHO DECIDES WHAT NEEDS DOING AND BY WHOM.
YOU'RE A BONA FIDE **HERO,** BOY BLUE, AND NOT JUST TO THE CUBS.
WHEN THE INDIGNITARIES FROM DOWN IN THE CITY COME UP HERE TO POKE THEIR **NOSES** WHERE THEY DON'T BELONG, WE'LL PUT ON A SHOW FOR THEM.
WE'LL SEND YOU OUT TO SWEAT IN THE FIELDS FOR AS LONG AS THEY'RE HERE.
OTHERWISE, DON'T WORRY SO MUCH. NOW COME IN AND JOIN SNOW AND ME FOR LUNCH.

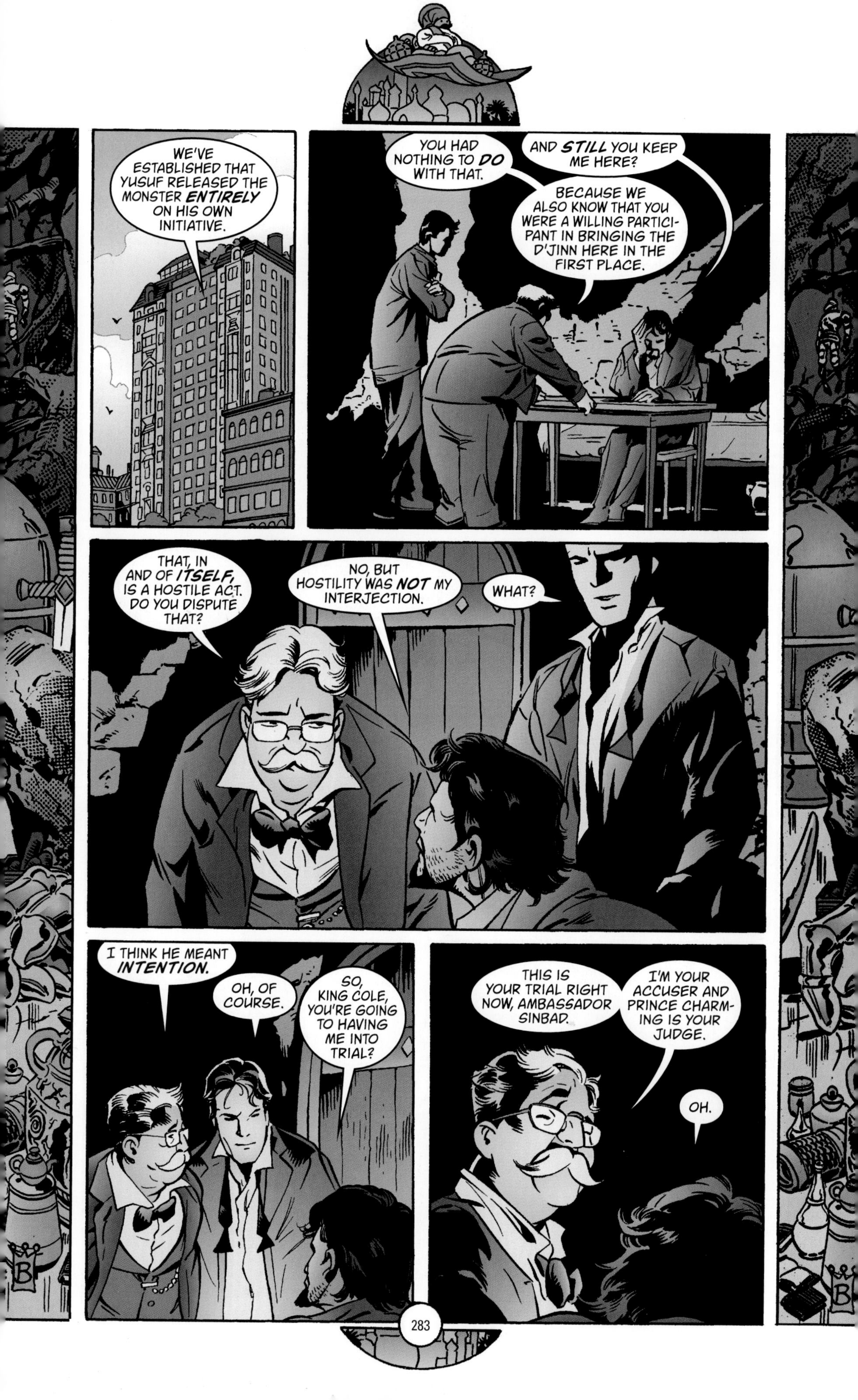

WE'VE ESTABLISHED THAT YUSUF RELEASED THE MONSTER ENTIRELY ON HIS OWN INITIATIVE.
YOU HAD NOTHING TO DO WITH THAT.
AND STILL YOU KEEP ME HERE?
BECAUSE WE ALSO KNOW THAT YOU WERE A WILLING PARTICIPANT IN BRINGING THE D'JINN HERE IN THE FIRST PLACE.
THAT, IN AND OF ITSELF, IS A HOSTILE ACT. DO YOU DISPUTE THAT?
NO, BUT HOSTILITY WAS NOT MY INTERJECTION.
WHAT?
I THINK HE MEANT INTENTION.
OH, OF COURSE.
SO, KING COLE, YOU'RE GOING TO HAVING ME INTO TRIAL?
THIS IS YOUR TRIAL RIGHT NOW, AMBASSADOR SINBAD.
I'M YOUR ACCUSER AND PRINCE CHARMING IS YOUR JUDGE.
OH.

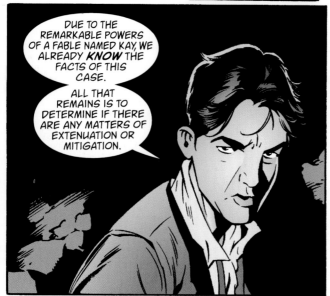

DUE TO THE REMARKABLE POWERS OF A FABLE NAMED KAY, WE ALREADY *KNOW* THE FACTS OF THIS CASE.

ALL THAT REMAINS IS TO DETERMINE IF THERE ARE ANY MATTERS OF EXTENUATION OR MITIGATION.

I DON'T UNDERSTAND.

IS THERE ANY *EXCUSE* FOR WHAT YOU DID? WHY DID YOU BRING THE D'JINN WITH YOU?

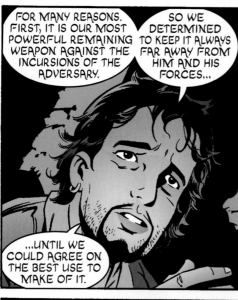

FOR MANY REASONS. FIRST, IT IS OUR MOST POWERFUL REMAINING WEAPON AGAINST THE INCURSIONS OF THE ADVERSARY.

SO WE DETERMINED TO KEEP IT ALWAYS FAR AWAY FROM HIM AND HIS FORCES...

...UNTIL WE COULD AGREE ON THE BEST USE TO MAKE OF IT.

I WAS GIVEN THE CHARGE OF KEEPING IT. SO, WHEN I WAS DISPATCHED TO COME HERE, NATURALLY THE VESSEL MUST COME WITH ME.

HEY.

BUT YOU DIDN'T KEEP IT IN A SECURE PLACE. YOU LEFT IT SITTING OUT ON YOUR TABLE, WHERE *ANY-ONE* IN YOUR HOUSE-HOLD COULD GET AT IT.

WHAT HAPPENED TO THE ENGLISH?

WELL, MY SLAVES WOULDN'T TOUCH IT BECAUSE THEY KNOW THEIR PLACE.

AND YUSUF? THOUGH HE WAS EVER THE CRANKY CONTRARIAN, I THOUGHT HE WAS ULTIMATELY *LOYAL.*

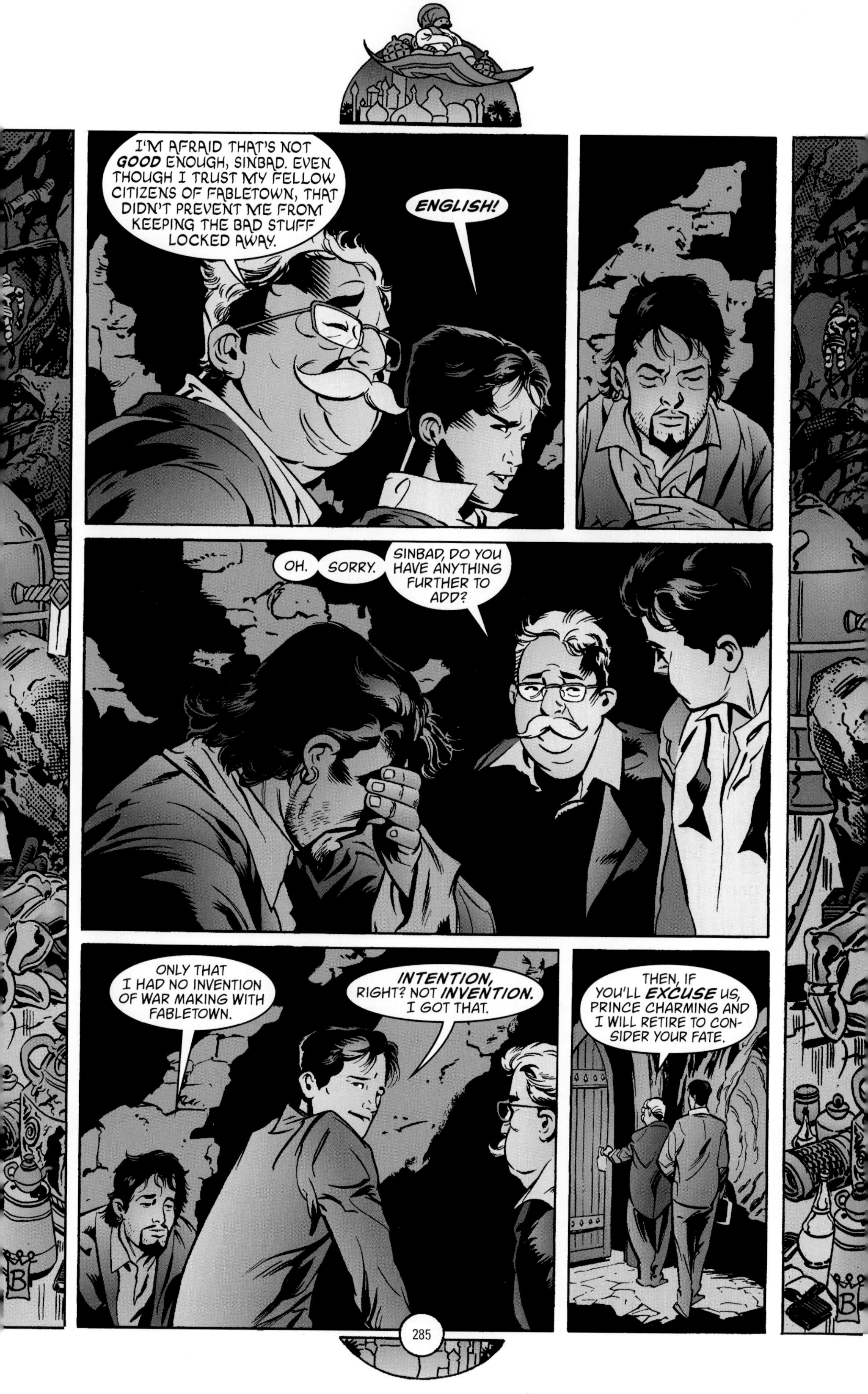
I'M AFRAID THAT'S NOT GOOD ENOUGH, SINBAD. EVEN THOUGH I TRUST MY FELLOW CITIZENS OF FABLETOWN, THAT DIDN'T PREVENT ME FROM KEEPING THE BAD STUFF LOCKED AWAY.
ENGLISH!
OH.
SORRY.
SINBAD, DO YOU HAVE ANYTHING FURTHER TO ADD?
ONLY THAT I HAD NO INVENTION OF WAR MAKING WITH FABLETOWN.
INTENTION, RIGHT? NOT INVENTION. I GOT THAT.
THEN, IF YOU'LL EXCUSE US, PRINCE CHARMING AND I WILL RETIRE TO CONSIDER YOUR FATE.

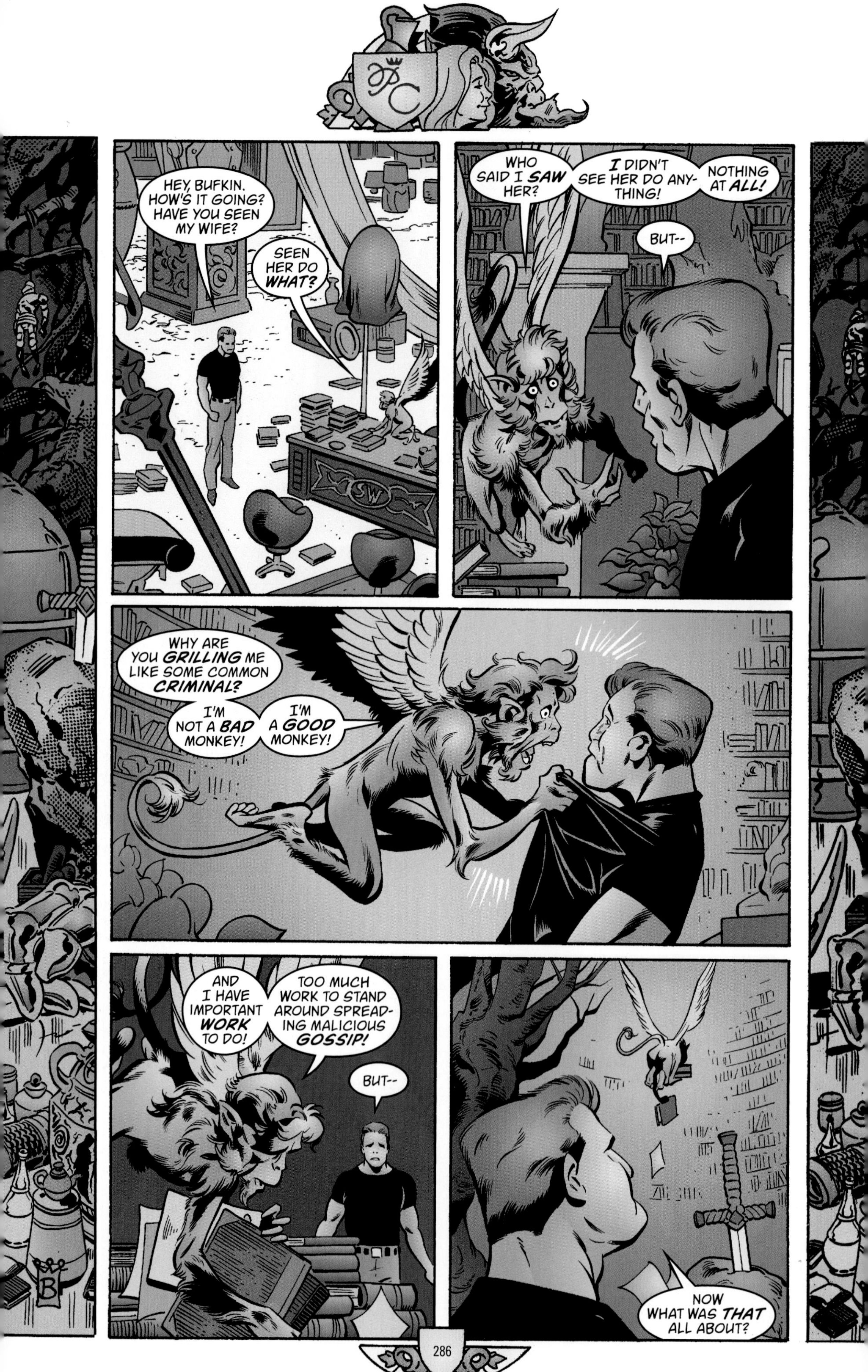

HEY, BUFKIN. HOW'S IT GOING? HAVE YOU SEEN MY WIFE?
SEEN HER DO WHAT?
WHO SAID I SAW HER?
I DIDN'T SEE HER DO ANY- THING!
NOTHING AT ALL!
BUT--
WHY ARE YOU GRILLING ME LIKE SOME COMMON CRIMINAL?
I'M NOT A BAD MONKEY!
I'M A GOOD MONKEY!
AND I HAVE IMPORTANT WORK TO DO!
TOO MUCH WORK TO STAND AROUND SPREAD- ING MALICIOUS GOSSIP!
BUT--
NOW WHAT WAS THAT ALL ABOUT?

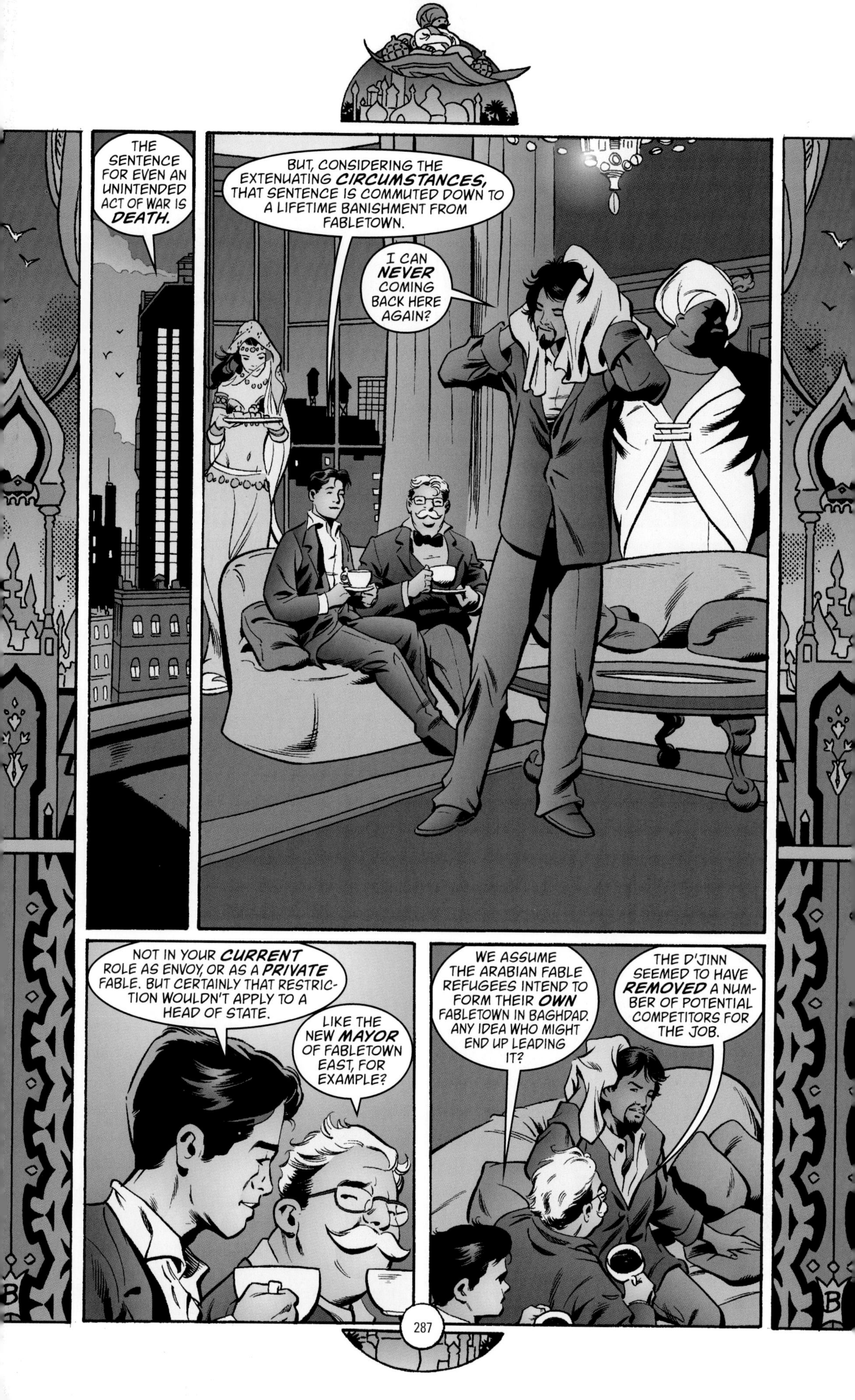
THE SENTENCE FOR EVEN AN UNINTENDED ACT OF WAR IS DEATH.
BUT, CONSIDERING THE EXTENUATING CIRCUMSTANCES, THAT SENTENCE IS COMMUTED DOWN TO A LIFETIME BANISHMENT FROM FABLETOWN.
I CAN NEVER COMING BACK HERE AGAIN?
NOT IN YOUR CURRENT ROLE AS ENVOY, OR AS A PRIVATE FABLE. BUT CERTAINLY THAT RESTRICTION WOULDN'T APPLY TO A HEAD OF STATE.
LIKE THE NEW MAYOR OF FABLETOWN EAST, FOR EXAMPLE?
WE ASSUME THE ARABIAN FABLE REFUGEES INTEND TO FORM THEIR OWN FABLETOWN IN BAGHDAD. ANY IDEA WHO MIGHT END UP LEADING IT?
THE D'JINN SEEMED TO HAVE REMOVED A NUMBER OF POTENTIAL COMPETITORS FOR THE JOB.

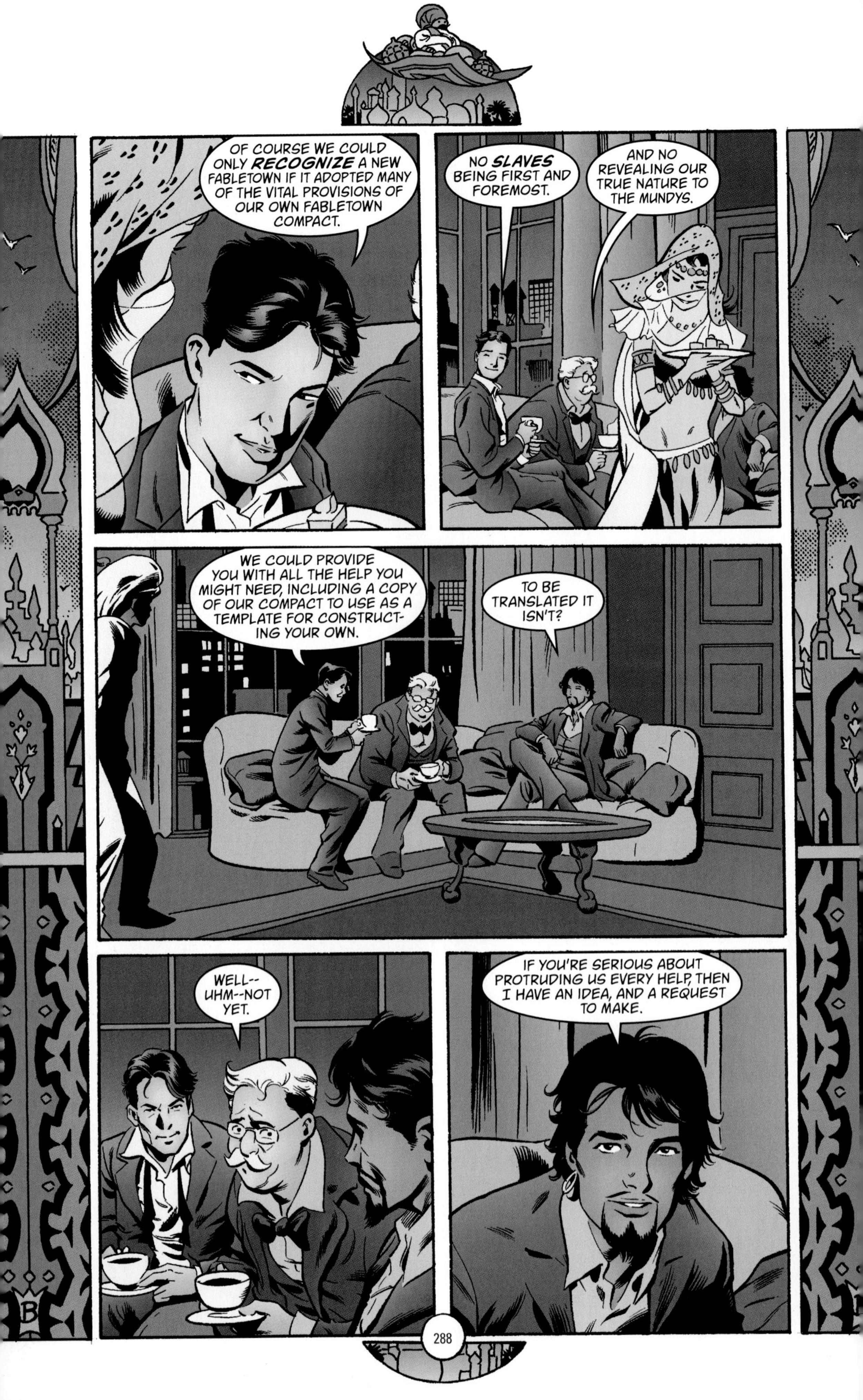

OF COURSE WE COULD ONLY RECOGNIZE A NEW FABLETOWN IF IT ADOPTED MANY OF THE VITAL PROVISIONS OF OUR OWN FABLETOWN COMPACT.
NO SLAVES BEING FIRST AND FOREMOST.
AND NO REVEALING OUR TRUE NATURE TO THE MUNDYS.
WE COULD PROVIDE YOU WITH ALL THE HELP YOU MIGHT NEED, INCLUDING A COPY OF OUR COMPACT TO USE AS A TEMPLATE FOR CONSTRUCTING YOUR OWN.
TO BE TRANSLATED IT ISN'T?
WELL--UHM--NOT YET.
IF YOU'RE SERIOUS ABOUT PROTRUDING US EVERY HELP, THEN I HAVE AN IDEA, AND A REQUEST TO MAKE.

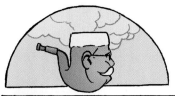

FROM THIS MOMENT ON YOU'RE NO LONGER MY *SLAVES*--OR SLAVES OF *ANYONE*, IN FACT.

AND NOW YOU EACH HAVE YOUR FIRST IMPORTANT DECISION TO MAKE. YOU CAN ACCOMPANY ME BACK TO BAGHDAD AS FREE FABLES.

OR YOU'VE ALL BEEN INVITED TO REMAIN HERE AS NEWLY EMANCIPATED CITIZENS OF FABLETOWN.

ARE YOU ALL PACKED, KING COLE?

I THINK SO. I HOPE I HAVEN'T FORGOTTEN ANYTHING IMPORTANT.

FABLETOWN WEST'S OFFICIAL AMBASSADOR TO FABLETOWN EAST. NOT *BAD*, OLD MAN.

WE'LL SURE MISS YOU AROUND HERE, THOUGH. YOU TAKE CARE OF YOUR-SELF.

ELEVEN DAYS LATER...

A CITY UNDER OCCUPATION. IT'S GOING TO BE DIFFICULT SETTING UP A NEW FABLETOWN HERE, SINBAD.

NOT AT ALL, KING COLE. OUR COMMUNITY WON'T BE ESTABLISHED IN THIS DREAR PLACE.

COME WITH ME AND SEE WHAT MARVELS AWAIT.

YOU LIVE UNDER-GROUND?

NOT QUITE. COME ALONG AND THE OTHERS WILL SEE TO OUR BAGGAGE.

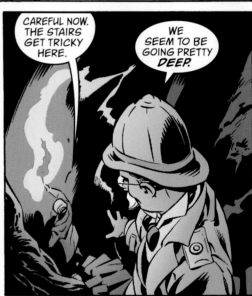

CAREFUL NOW. THE STAIRS GET TRICKY HERE.

WE SEEM TO BE GOING PRETTY *DEEP*.

AND NOW, GREAT KING, LET ME INTRODUCE YOU TO THE *TRUE* BAGHDAD.

BUT--

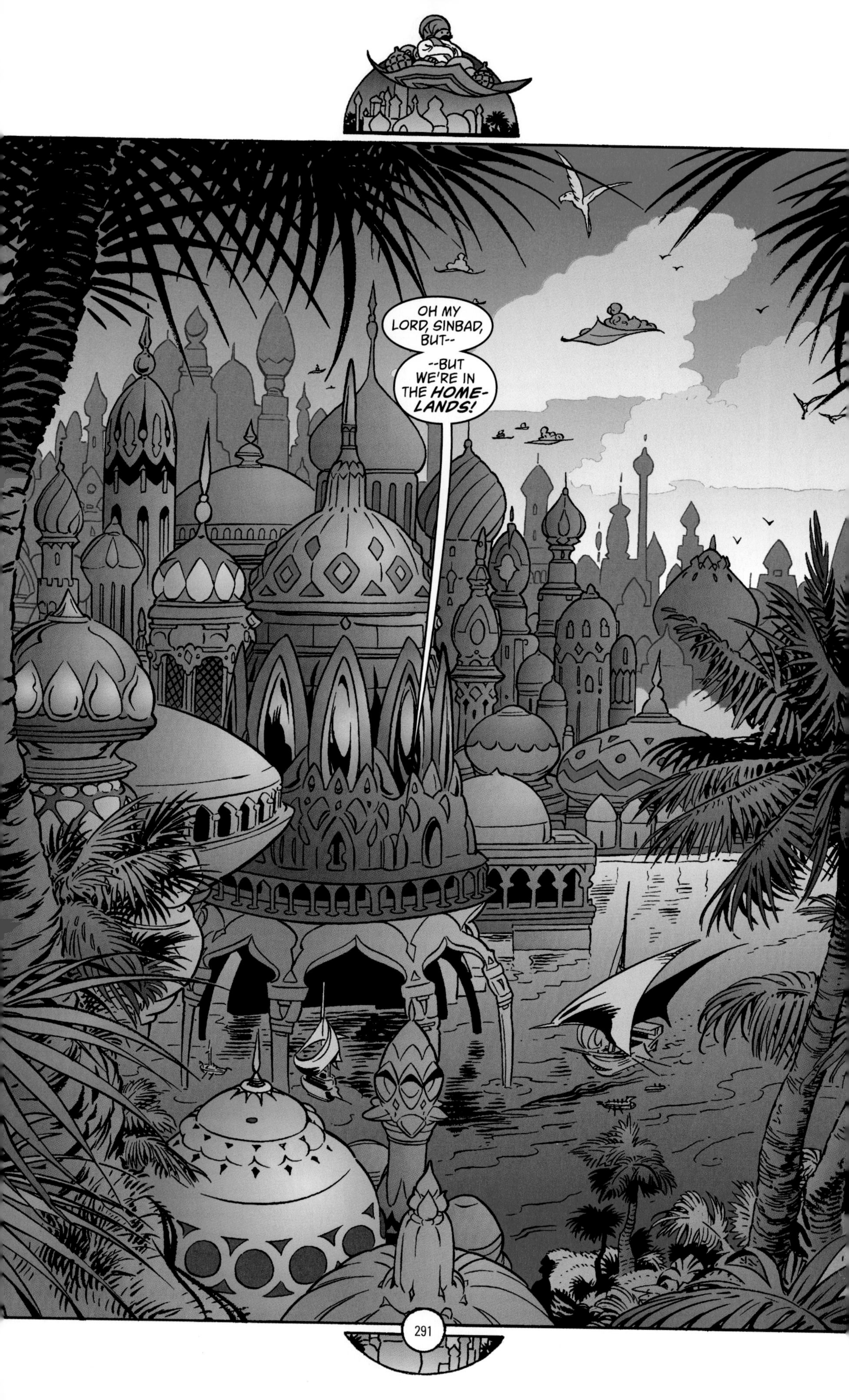
OH MY LORD, SINBAD, BUT--
--BUT WE'RE IN THE *HOME-LANDS!*

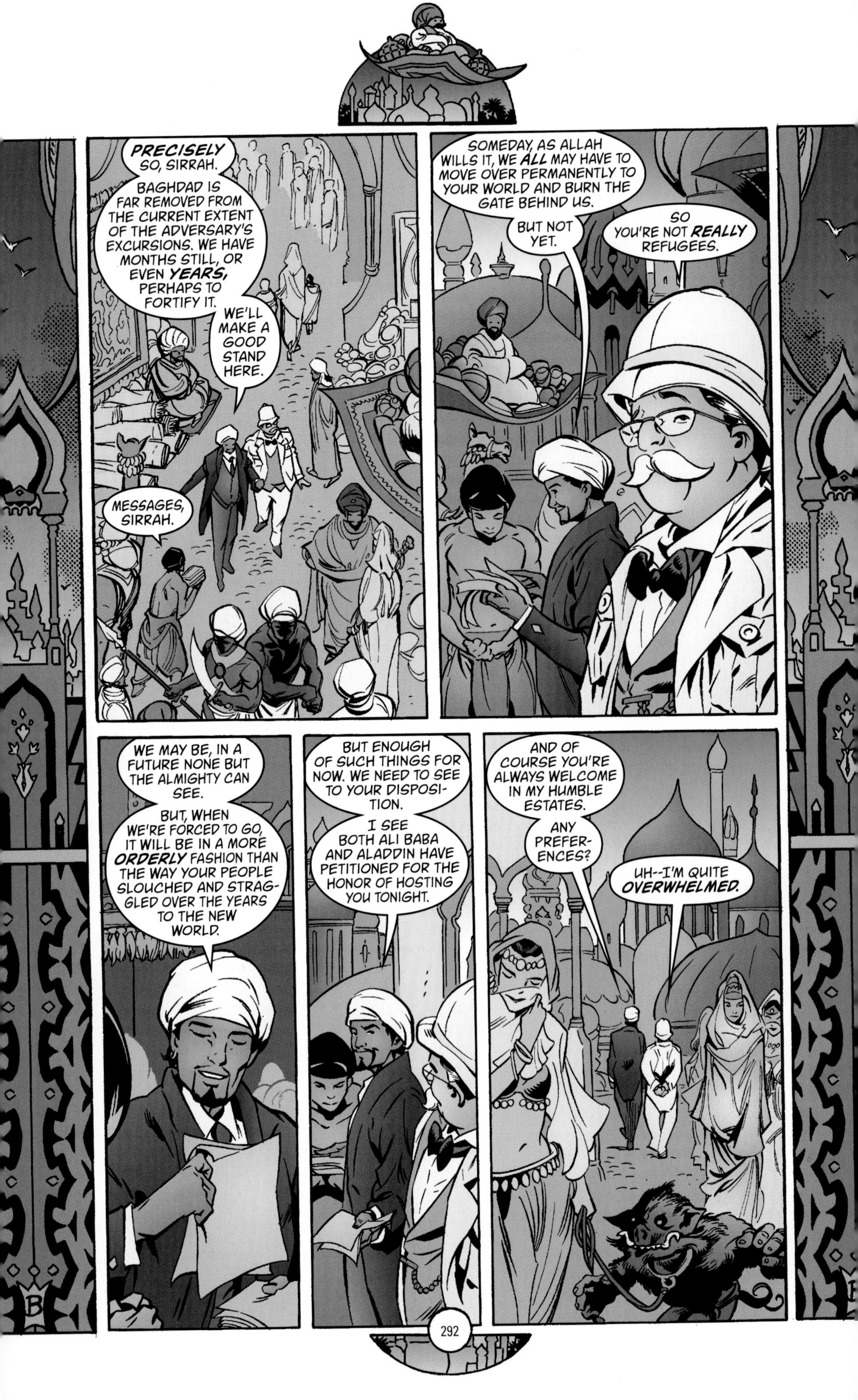
PRECISELY SO, SIRRAH.
BAGHDAD IS FAR REMOVED FROM THE CURRENT EXTENT OF THE ADVERSARY'S EXCURSIONS. WE HAVE MONTHS STILL, OR EVEN YEARS, PERHAPS TO FORTIFY IT.
WE'LL MAKE A GOOD STAND HERE.
MESSAGES, SIRRAH.
SOMEDAY, AS ALLAH WILLS IT, WE ALL MAY HAVE TO MOVE OVER PERMANENTLY TO YOUR WORLD AND BURN THE GATE BEHIND US.
BUT NOT YET.
SO YOU'RE NOT REALLY REFUGEES.
WE MAY BE, IN A FUTURE NONE BUT THE ALMIGHTY CAN SEE.
BUT, WHEN WE'RE FORCED TO GO, IT WILL BE IN A MORE ORDERLY FASHION THAN THE WAY YOUR PEOPLE SLOUCHED AND STRAGGLED OVER THE YEARS TO THE NEW WORLD.
BUT ENOUGH OF SUCH THINGS FOR NOW. WE NEED TO SEE TO YOUR DISPOSITION.
I SEE BOTH ALI BABA AND ALADDIN HAVE PETITIONED FOR THE HONOR OF HOSTING YOU TONIGHT.
AND OF COURSE YOU'RE ALWAYS WELCOME IN MY HUMBLE ESTATES.
ANY PREFERENCES?
UH--I'M QUITE OVERWHELMED.

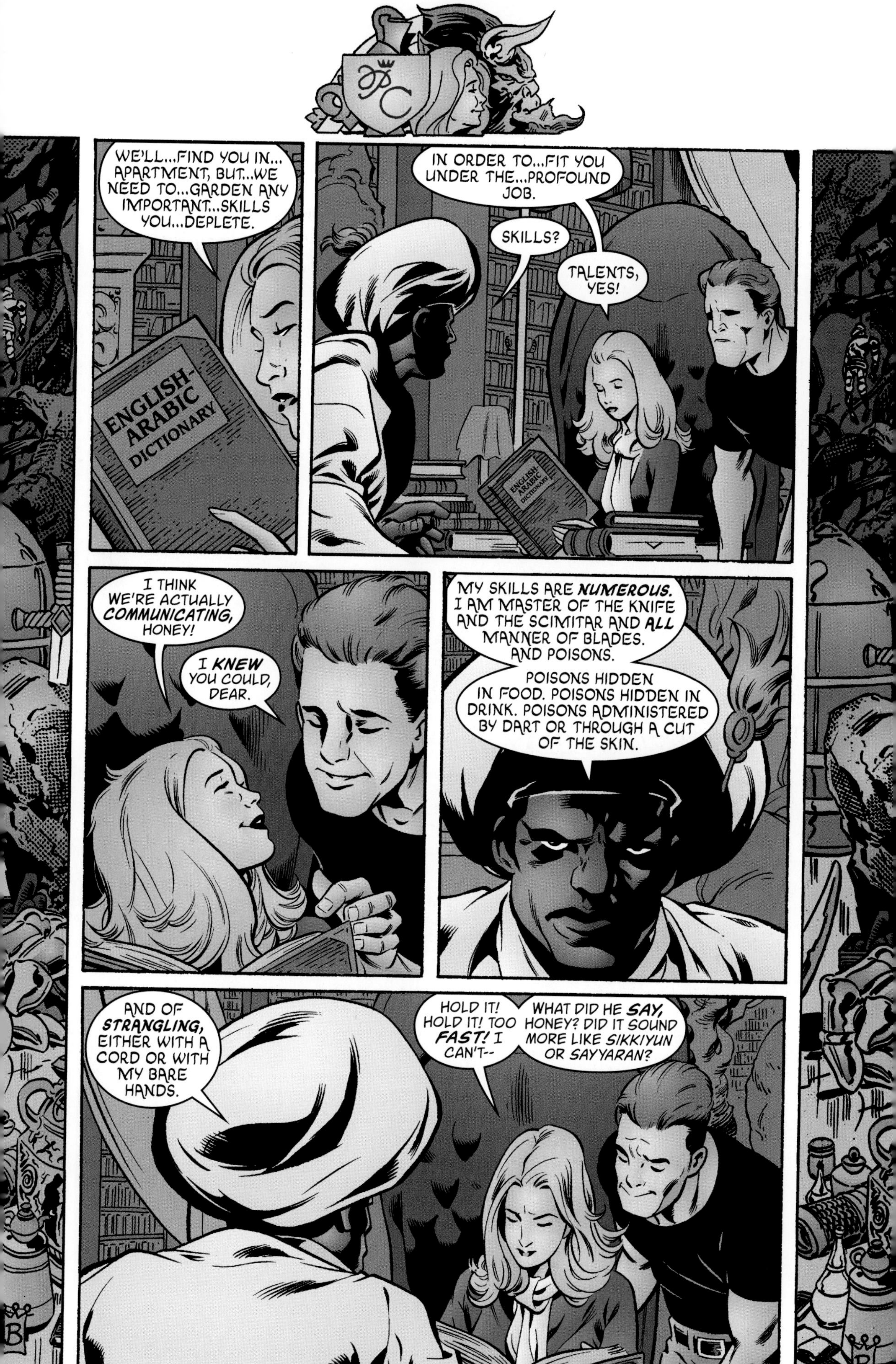
WE'LL...FIND YOU IN... APARTMENT, BUT...WE NEED TO...GARDEN ANY IMPORTANT...SKILLS YOU...DEPLETE.
ENGLISH-ARABIC DICTIONARY
IN ORDER TO...FIT YOU UNDER THE...PROFOUND JOB.
SKILLS?
TALENTS, YES!
I THINK WE'RE ACTUALLY COMMUNICATING, HONEY!
I KNEW YOU COULD, DEAR.
MY SKILLS ARE NUMEROUS. I AM MASTER OF THE KNIFE AND THE SCIMITAR AND ALL MANNER OF BLADES. AND POISONS.
POISONS HIDDEN IN FOOD. POISONS HIDDEN IN DRINK. POISONS ADMINISTERED BY DART OR THROUGH A CUT OF THE SKIN.
AND OF STRANGLING, EITHER WITH A CORD OR WITH MY BARE HANDS.
HOLD IT! HOLD IT! TOO FAST! I CAN'T--
WHAT DID HE SAY, HONEY? DID IT SOUND MORE LIKE SIKKIYUN OR SAYYARAN?

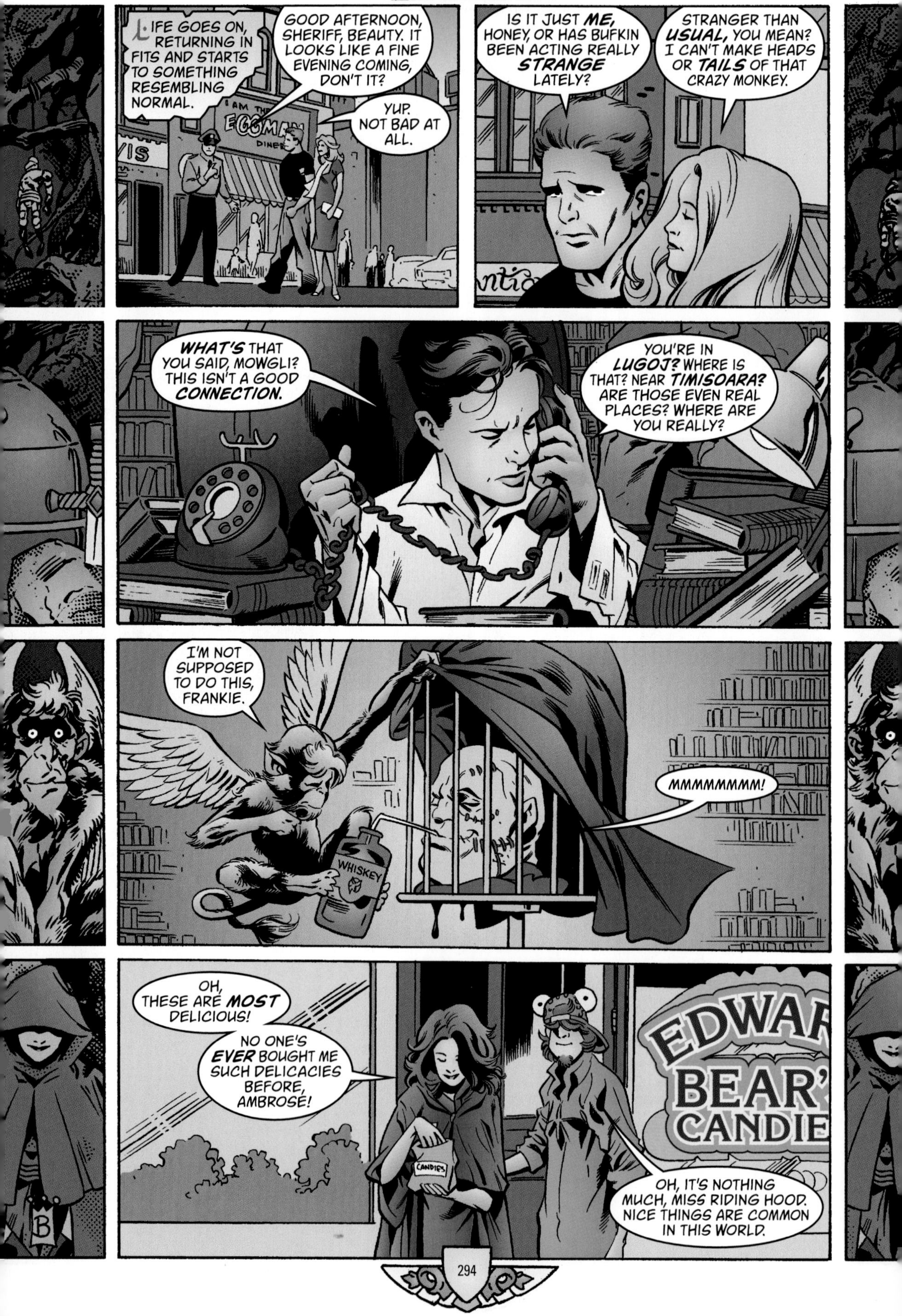
LIFE GOES ON, RETURNING IN FITS AND STARTS TO SOMETHING RESEMBLING NORMAL.
GOOD AFTERNOON, SHERIFF, BEAUTY. IT LOOKS LIKE A FINE EVENING COMING, DON'T IT?
YUP. NOT BAD AT ALL.
IS IT JUST ME, HONEY, OR HAS BUFKIN BEEN ACTING REALLY STRANGE LATELY?
STRANGER THAN USUAL, YOU MEAN? I CAN'T MAKE HEADS OR TAILS OF THAT CRAZY MONKEY.
WHAT'S THAT YOU SAID, MOWGLI? THIS ISN'T A GOOD CONNECTION.
YOU'RE IN LUGOJ? WHERE IS THAT? NEAR TIMISOARA? ARE THOSE EVEN REAL PLACES? WHERE ARE YOU REALLY?
I'M NOT SUPPOSED TO DO THIS, FRANKIE.
WHISKEY
MMMMMMMM!
OH, THESE ARE MOST DELICIOUS!
NO ONE'S EVER BOUGHT ME SUCH DELICACIES BEFORE, AMBROSE!
CANDIES
EDWAR
BEAR'
CANDIE
OH, IT'S NOTHING MUCH, MISS RIDING HOOD. NICE THINGS ARE COMMON IN THIS WORLD.

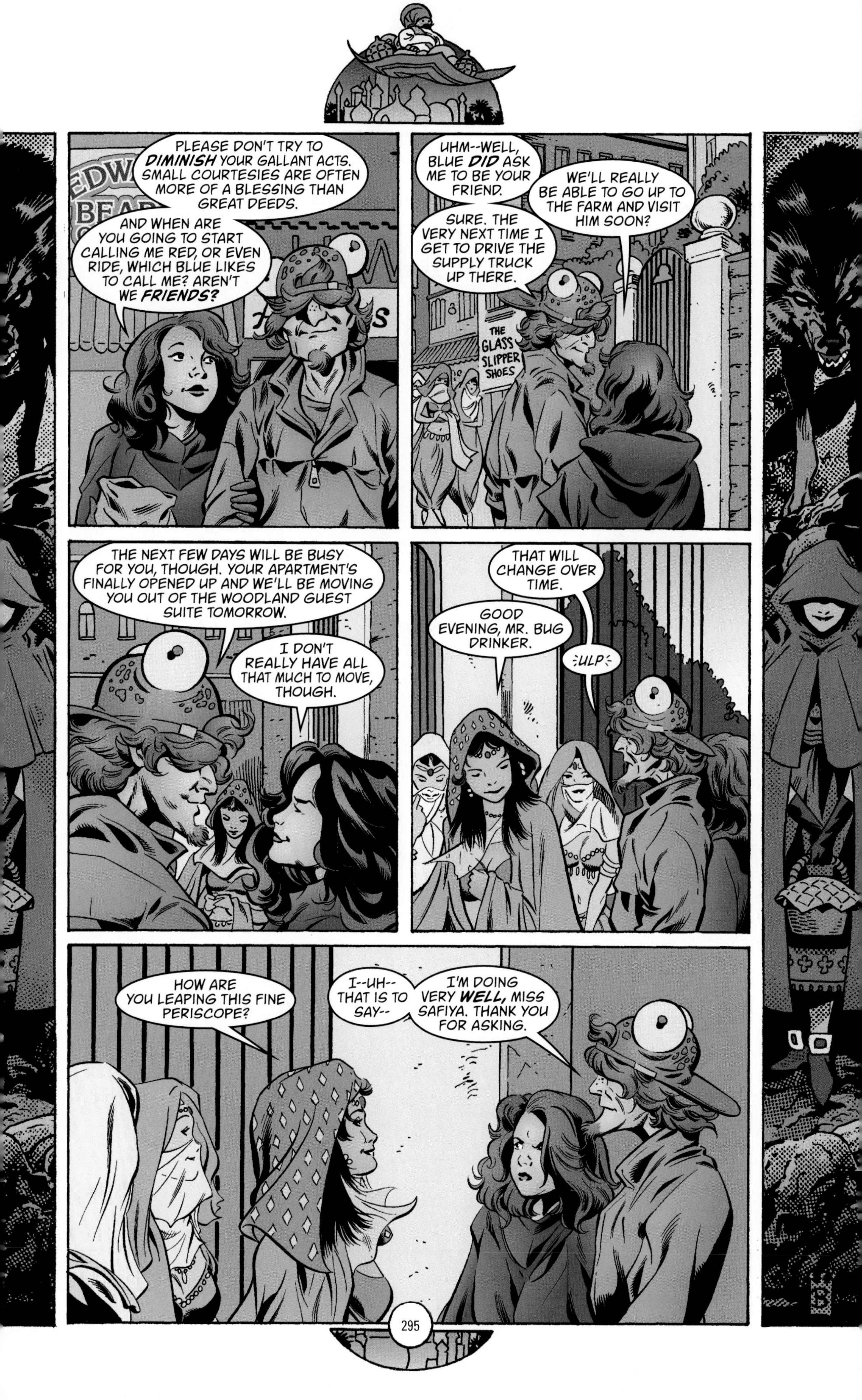
PLEASE DON'T TRY TO DIMINISH YOUR GALLANT ACTS. SMALL COURTESIES ARE OFTEN MORE OF A BLESSING THAN GREAT DEEDS.
AND WHEN ARE YOU GOING TO START CALLING ME RED, OR EVEN RIDE, WHICH BLUE LIKES TO CALL ME? AREN'T WE FRIENDS?
UHM--WELL, BLUE DID ASK ME TO BE YOUR FRIEND.
WE'LL REALLY BE ABLE TO GO UP TO THE FARM AND VISIT HIM SOON?
SURE. THE VERY NEXT TIME I GET TO DRIVE THE SUPPLY TRUCK UP THERE.
THE GLASS SLIPPER SHOES
THE NEXT FEW DAYS WILL BE BUSY FOR YOU, THOUGH. YOUR APARTMENT'S FINALLY OPENED UP AND WE'LL BE MOVING YOU OUT OF THE WOODLAND GUEST SUITE TOMORROW.
I DON'T REALLY HAVE ALL THAT MUCH TO MOVE, THOUGH.
THAT WILL CHANGE OVER TIME.
GOOD EVENING, MR. BUG DRINKER.
ULP
HOW ARE YOU LEAPING THIS FINE PERISCOPE?
I--UH-- THAT IS TO SAY--
I'M DOING VERY WELL, MISS SAFIYA. THANK YOU FOR ASKING.

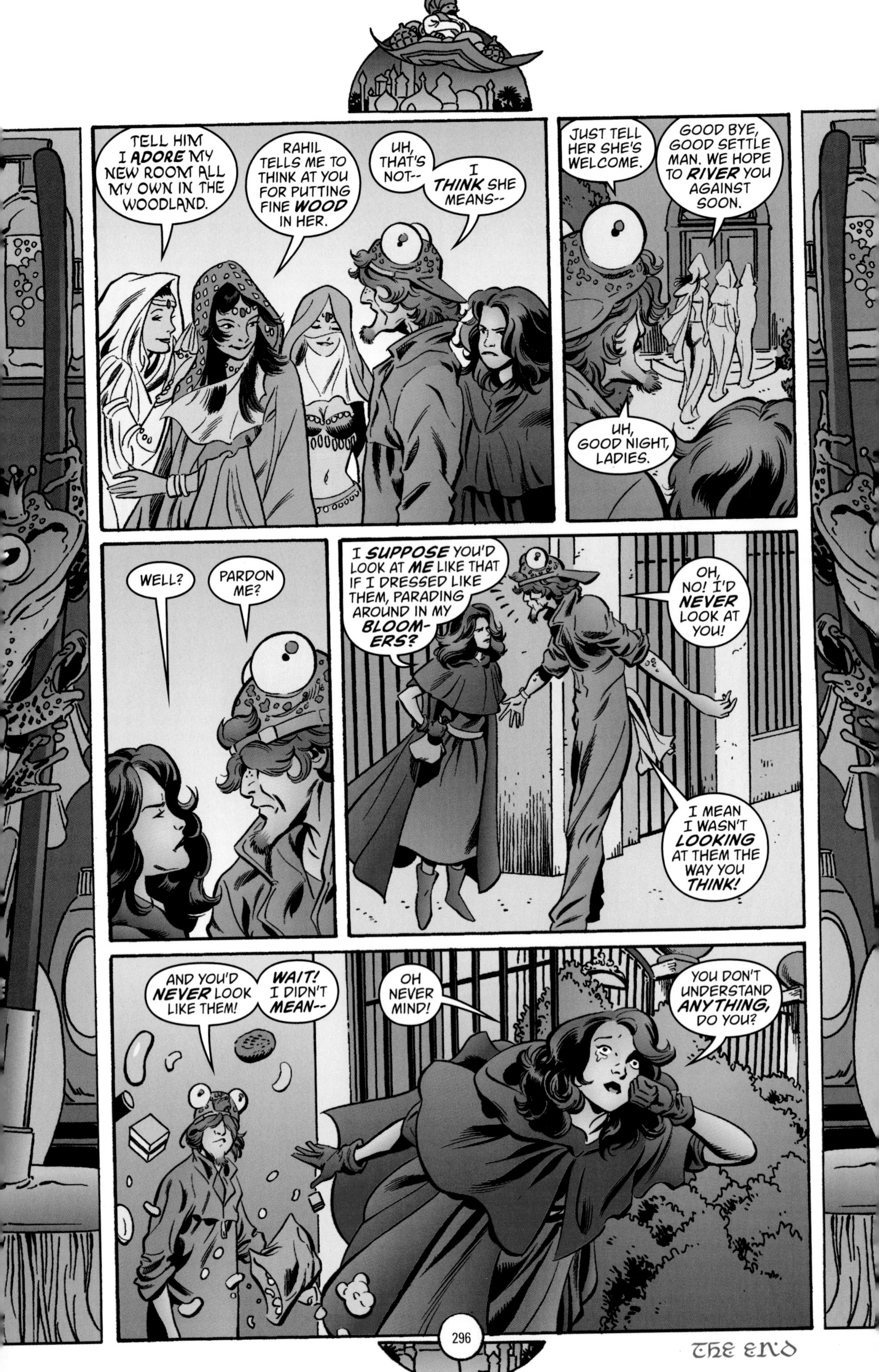
TELL HIM I ADORE MY NEW ROOM ALL MY OWN IN THE WOODLAND.
RAHIL TELLS ME TO THINK AT YOU FOR PUTTING FINE WOOD IN HER.
UH, THAT'S NOT--
I THINK SHE MEANS--
JUST TELL HER SHE'S WELCOME.
GOOD BYE, GOOD SETTLE MAN. WE HOPE TO RIVER YOU AGAINST SOON.
UH, GOOD NIGHT, LADIES.
WELL?
PARDON ME?
I SUPPOSE YOU'D LOOK AT ME LIKE THAT IF I DRESSED LIKE THEM, PARADING AROUND IN MY BLOOMERS?
OH, NO! I'D NEVER LOOK AT YOU!
I MEAN I WASN'T LOOKING AT THEM THE WAY YOU THINK!
AND YOU'D NEVER LOOK LIKE THEM!
WAIT! I DIDN'T MEAN--
OH NEVER MIND!
YOU DON'T UNDERSTAND ANYTHING, DO YOU?

THE END

Treasures from the Woodland Vaults

Character designs by Mark Buckingham

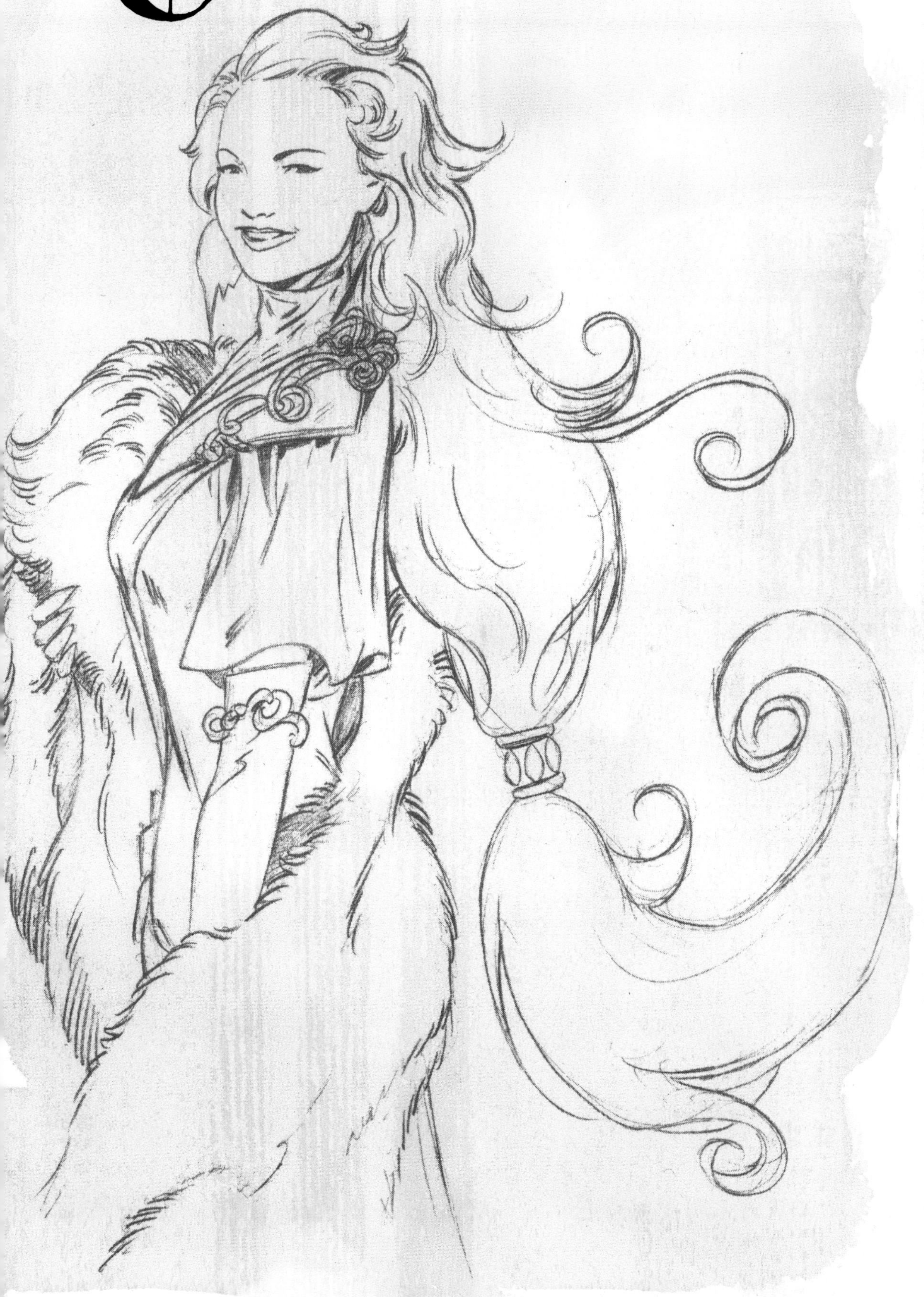

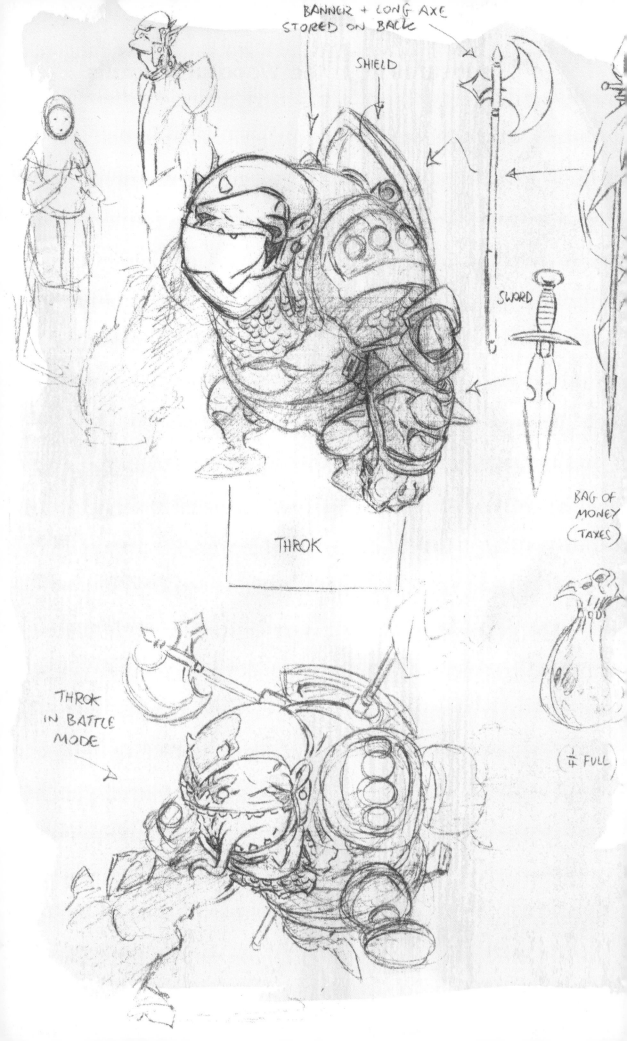

BANNER + LONG AXE
STORED ON BACK

SHIELD

SWORD

THROK

BAG OF
MONEY
(TAXES)

(¼ FULL)

THROK
IN BATTLE
MODE

FABLES - THE HOMELANDS

GOBLINS:
IMPERIAL TAX COLLECTORS

LONG-SWORD
+
MACE

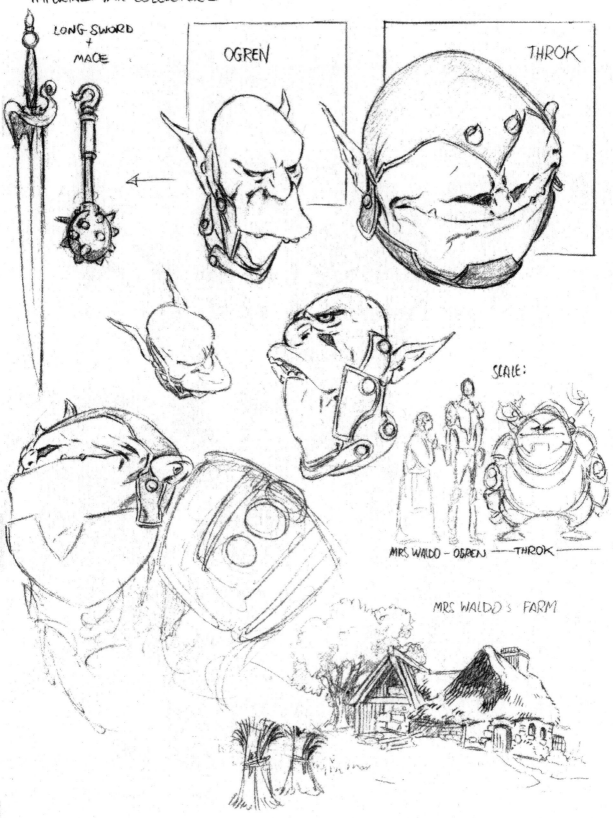

OGREN

THROK

SCALE:

MRS WALDO — OGREN — THROK

MRS WALDO'S FARM

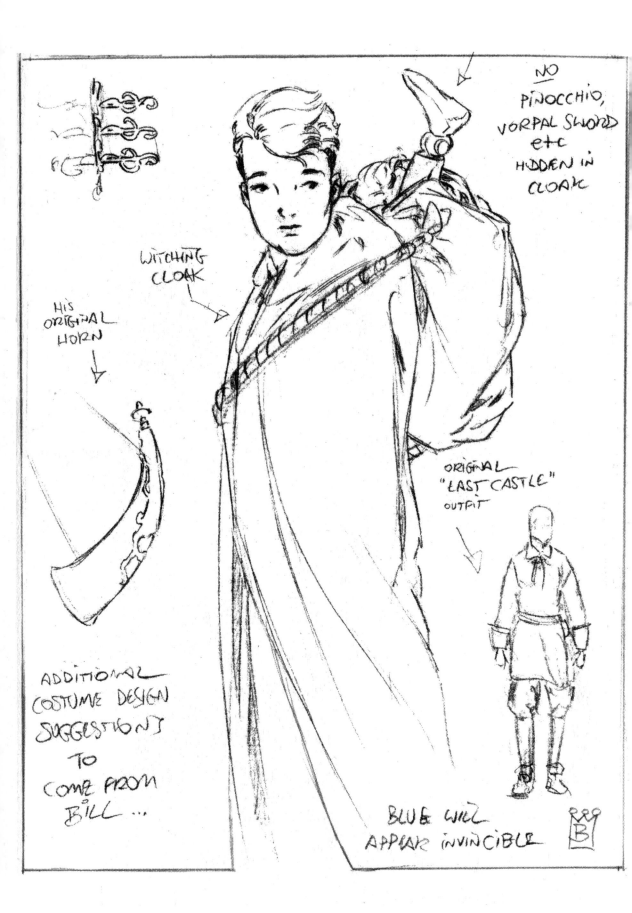

NO
PINOCCHIO,
VORPAL SWORD
etc
HIDDEN IN
CLOAK

WITCHING
CLOAK

HIS
ORIGINAL
HORN

ORIGINAL
"LAST CASTLE"
OUTFIT

ADDITIONAL
COSTUME DESIGN
SUGGESTIONS
TO
COME FROM
BILL ...

BLUE WILL
APPEAR INVINCIBLE

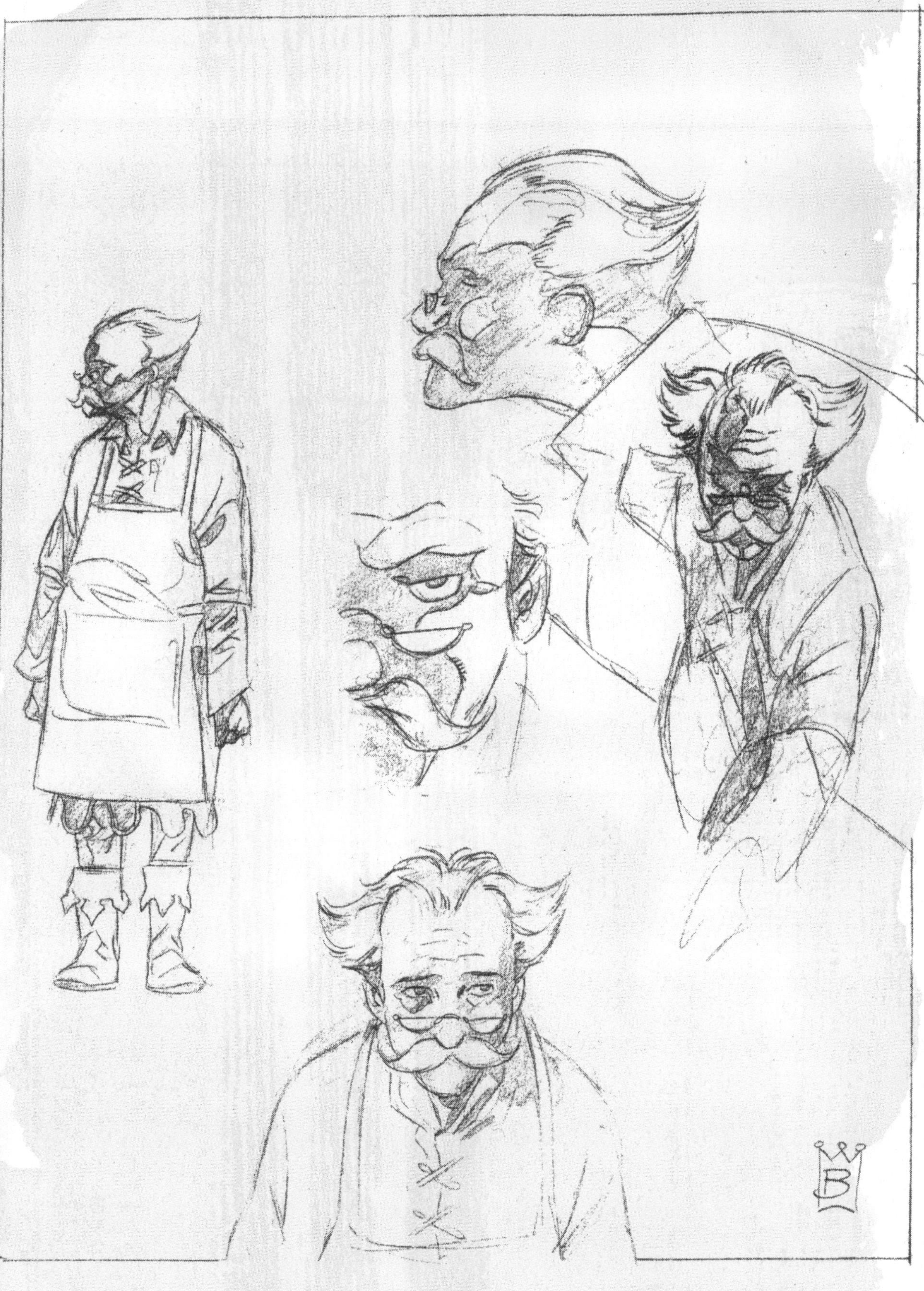

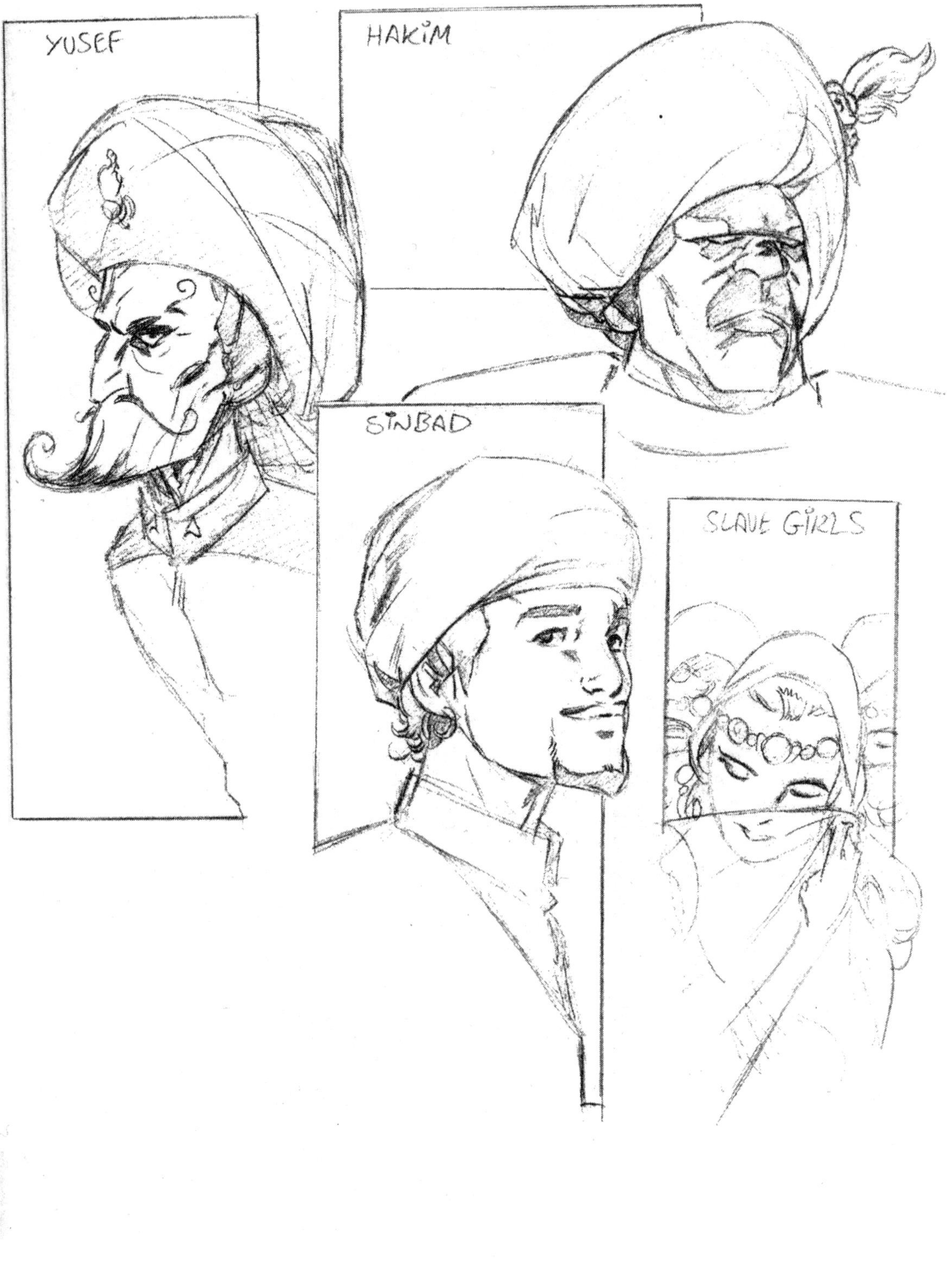
YUSEF
HAKIM
SINBAD
SLAVE GIRLS

Bill Willingham has been writing and sometimes drawing comics for more than twenty years. During that time he's had work published by nearly every publisher in the business and he's created many critically acclaimed comic book series, including *The Elementals*, *Coventry*, PROPOSITION PLAYER and FABLES. His other credits are vast and impressive but far too many to mention here. Currently, he lives in his own personal corner of the American Midwest and can be visited at clockworkstorybook.net.

Born in 1966 in the English seaside town of Clevedon, **Mark Buckingham** has worked in comics professionally since 1988. In addition to illustrating all of Neil Gaiman's run on the post-Alan Moore *Miracleman* in the early 1990s, Buckingham contributed inks to THE SANDMAN and its related miniseries DEATH: THE HIGH COST OF LIVING and DEATH: THE TIME OF YOUR LIFE as well as working on various other titles for Vertigo, DC and Marvel through the end of the decade. Since 2002 he has been the regular penciller for Bill Willingham's FABLES, which has gone on to become one of the most popular and critically acclaimed Vertigo titles of the new millennium.

A thirty-year veteran of the industry, **Steve Leialoha** has worked for nearly every major comics publisher in the course of his distinguished career. Titles featuring his artwork include DC's BATMAN, SUPERMAN and JUSTICE LEAGUE INTERNATIONAL, Vertigo's THE DREAMING, THE SANDMAN PRESENTS: PETREFAX and THE SANDMAN PRESENTS: THE DEAD BOY DETECTIVES, Marvel's *The Uncanny X-Men*, *Spider-Woman* and *Dr. Strange*, Epic's *Coyote*, Harris's *Vampirella* and many of Paradox Press's BIG BOOK volumes. Since 2002, he has inked Bill Willingham's hit Vertigo series FABLES, for which he and penciller Mark Buckingham won the 2007 Eisner Award for Best Penciller/Inker Team. Leialoha also provided pen-and-ink illustrations for Willingham's 2009 FABLES novel, *Peter & Max*.

Wielding a decidedly contemporary style and an eye for crisp detail, **David Hahn** has illustrated issues of *Spider-Man Loves Mary Jane* and *Marvel Adventures: Fantastic Four* for Marvel and BITE CLUB, FABLES, LUCIFER and FRINGE for DC, as well as the licensed title *The Batman Handbook* for Quirk Books. He was nominated for both an Eisner Award and an Ignatz Award for his creator-owned series *Private Beach*, published by Slave Labor Graphics, and he has written and drawn a second creator-owned miniseries, *All Nighter*, for Image Comics. He currently resides in Portland, Oregon, and is a founding member of Portland's Periscope Studio.

The first Filipino artist to win an Eisner Award, **Lan Medina** has applied his intricate style to a wide variety of comic book titles. After gaining prominence illustrating Vic J. Poblete's "Devil Car" feature in the 1980s Filipino horror magazine *Holiday*, Medina went on to win acclaim in North America with Image Comics' *Aria* and the Vertigo series AMERICAN CENTURY and FABLES. His other notable works include Marvel's *The Punisher*, *Foolkiller* and *Storm*, for which he earned a Glyph Comics Fan Award.

An Eisner Award winner and nominee for the Hugo and Inkwell Awards, **Andrew Pepoy** has worked for U.S., British, and French publishers and has inked thousands of pages for dozens of comics titles, including FABLES, *The Simpsons*, *The X-Men*, *Archie* and *Lanfeust*. He is also the creator, writer and artist of his own Harvey Award-nominated series, *The Adventures of Simone & Ajax*, and he has brought his knack for retro glamor with a modern twist to writing and drawing Archie Comics' *Katy Keene* and drawing the *Little Orphan Annie* newspaper strip.

Comics artist and painter **Dan Green** began his career in the early 1970s pencilling and inking for a variety of DC titles, including DARK MANSION, G.I. COMBAT and STAR SPANGLED WAR STORIES. Through the '70s, '80s and '90s his focus shifted more exclusively towards inking, and he contributed long runs on such flagship Marvel titles as *X-Men*, *Wolverine*, *Spider-Man* and *The Avengers* as well as working on JUSTICE LEAGUE OF AMERICA, SUPERGIRL and WONDER WOMAN for DC and HELLBLAZER: PAPA MIDNITE and FABLES for Vertigo. He also co-wrote and provided watercolor art for the 1986 graphic novel *Doctor Strange: Into Shamballa*, and in 2001 Bulfinch Press published a collection of works by Edgar Allan Poe entitled *The Raven and Other Poems and Tales* featuring 20 of his pencil illustrations. Green lives and works in upstate New York.

James Jean was born in Taiwan in 1979. Raised in New Jersey, he graduated from New York City's School of Visual Arts in 2001. Along with his award-winning cover art for DC Comics, Jean has produced illustrations for *Time Magazine*, *The New York Times*, *Wired*, *Rolling Stone*, *Spin*, *Playboy*, ESPN, Atlantic Records, Target, Nike, and Prada, among many others. He currently lives and works in Santa Monica.